HUNTING EVIL

Also by Guy Walters

Fiction
The Traitor
The Leader
The Occupation
The Colditz Legacy

History
The Voice of War (edited with James Owen)
Berlin Games

For more information on Guy Walters and his books,
visit his website at www.guywalters.com

HUNTING EVIL

How the Nazi War Criminals Escaped and the
Hunt to Bring Them to Justice

Guy Walters

BANTAM PRESS

LONDON • TORONTO • SYDNEY • AUCKLAND • JOHANNESBURG

TRANSWORLD PUBLISHERS
61–63 Uxbridge Road, London W5 5SA
A Random House Group Company
www.rbooks.co.uk

First published in Great Britain
in 2009 by Bantam Press
an imprint of Transworld Publishers

A CIP catalogue record for this book
is available from the British Library.

ISBNs 9780593059913 (cased)
9780593059920 (tpb)

Addresses for Random House Group Ltd companies outside the UK
can be found at: www.randomhouse.co.uk
The Random House Group Ltd Reg. No. 954009

The Random House Group Limited supports The Forest Stewardship
Council (FSC), the leading international forest-certification organization.
All our titles that are printed on Greenpeace-approved FSC-certified
paper carry the FSC logo.
Our paper procurement policy can be found at
www.rbooks.co.uk/environment

Typeset in 11/14pt Sabon by
Falcon Oast Graphic Art Ltd.
Printed and bound in Great Britain by
CPI Mackays, Chatham, ME5 8TD

2 4 6 8 10 9 7 5 3

Mixed Sources
Product group from well-managed
forests and other controlled sources
www.fsc.org Cert no. TT-COC-2139
© 1996 Forest Stewardship Council
FSC

This book is for my brother,

DOMINIC WALTERS

Mundus vult decipi

Petronius

Contents

Preface   1

1   'The air became cleaner'   7
2   'To the uttermost ends of the earth'   43
3   'The Man Who Never Forgets'   77
4   Helping the Rats   105
5   The Odessa Myth   131
6   'Peculiar travel matters'   157
7   Extremely Sensitive Individuals   207
8   In Hiding   243
9   Eichmann   267
10 Rough Justice   311
11 'This whole Nazi-hunting thing'   338
12 What Remains   373

Epilogue   409
Notes   413
Bibliography   485
Picture Acknowledgements   503
Index   505

Preface

IF BOOKS turned out exactly the way in which authors expected, writing would be an unsatisfying process indeed. When I started this project three years ago, my knowledge of the subject matter was conventional: the Nazis escaped with the help of a network called Odessa, they ended up living in vast *estancias* in Latin American jungles, and were stalked by fearless and redoubtable Nazi hunters such as Simon Wiesenthal. The subject was clearly engaging and the huge interest shown in my book proposal confirmed my belief that the topic required an account that was both compelling and historically rigorous. It was only when I started my in-depth research that I realized that so much of what I held to be true was simply not so. For a while, I wanted to change the title to *Hunting Evil (Or Not),* but I never dared suggest it to my editor for fear that he would think I had sold him a pup. Although much of what I have learned contradicts what I knew, there is no doubt that the book is the better for it, and the constant process of discovery has maintained my excitement over what has been a long haul, both temporally and topographically.

As is so common, I have found the truth to be far more satisfying than what has been served up by junk historians in print and online. I have also found the truth to be utterly scandalous, and on numerous occasions I have felt genuine anger at what I have discovered. I make no apology for the occasions at which that emotion shines through, because it was certainly new to me that the British employed a senior officer in one of the *Einsatzgruppen* as an MI6 agent. It was also disturbing to discover that Simon Wiesenthal, for so long held to be some sort of secular saint, fabricated not only his role in the Eichmann hunt, but also countless other episodes in his life. I was also annoyed by the lack of political will for hunting Nazi criminals, many of whom could have easily been brought to justice had governments allocated even comparatively meagre resources to their pursuit. Some might suggest that as well as being angry I sometimes display retrospective wisdom, but once again, I make no apology. I certainly do my best to place any decisions made within their context, but where I judge those decisions to have been in-correct, I do not shy from condemnation. One of the privileges of writing history – and surely one of its purposes – is to make such judgements. Of course, the conclusions I reach are open to question and scrutiny, but I believe they are the correct ones based on the evidence available to me. I positively encourage correspondence, and interested readers can contribute their thoughts to the forum pages on huntingevil.com, which also contains various features such as animated maps and films that are intended to complement these printed pages.

Unlike a website, a book does not of course have an almost end-less capacity, and I have had to be ruthless in my selection of material. With potentially tens of thousands of escapees to write about, it would have been impossible to capture the whole story of how the Nazis fled and how they were tracked down (or not). Instead, I have presented the stories of a handful of criminals whose experiences are representative of the many. That these individuals – who include Josef Mengele, Adolf Eichmann, Franz Stangl – are well known will I hope serve to increase the readability of what follows. The other group of characters includes the hunters, and here I had a much easier time when it came to casting. The figure of Simon Wiesenthal was unavoidable, and it is he upon whom much of my focus is trained. Some may feel that I have been overly harsh on the man, and that I have run a professional danger in seemingly allying myself with a vile host of neo-Nazis, Revisionists, Holocaust deniers, anti-Semites and other such nasty cranks. I should stress that I belong firmly outside any of these squalid camps, and it is my intention to wrestle criticism of Wiesenthal away from their clutches. As well as the hunters and hunted, I also write about the helpers, who include figures such as Juan Perón and Catholic priests such as Alois Hudal and Krunoslav Draganović. Thousands of people helped Nazis escape, but, once again, I have had to ration myself. I have nevertheless allowed myself the luxury of recounting the comic story of the British fascist and quondam camel specialist Arnold Leese, which would surely make the stuff of a comic film or play. My final group of characters is that of the 'hired': those criminals whom the Allies, including the Soviet Union, exploited as intelligence assets. Shockingly, there were many for me to choose from, and although the story of Barbie can stand on its own, I felt it important to enrich this aspect by revealing a host of other criminals who were used. I am more forgiving than some of the use of such criminals, and I have restrained myself from making naive and simplistic moral judgements, but at times it has been hard not to bang my head against the screen out of sheer frustration at the cynicism displayed by those who employed mass murderers.

I am aware that some may be disappointed at what I have omitted. Readers with more legalistic minds than mine might wish for more material on topics such as due process, statutes of limitations, legislation and trials, but I have reckoned them to be outside my remit. I have also shied away from writing about more recent cases, which, although important, involve figures who are seemingly insignificant compared to those such as Eichmann. Some of these cases – especially that of John Demjanjuk – are also ongoing, and I felt it prudent not to dwell on subjects which have not yet been resolved. Although I regret these omissions, I am not sorry to let down the lovers of conspiracy theory. There have been too many books about this topic that make the most outrageous claims – especially about 'Odessa' and the direct involvement of Pius XII in engineering escapes – and I have refrained from entertaining such claims. My rule of thumb in preparing this book was that every fact I included had to be defendable in a court of law, which was a frustratingly high, but necessary, standard to maintain. However, conspiracy theorists are not so rigorous, and as a result are able to present material that is sensational and back it up with little more than a knowing tap against the nose. Conspiracy theorists rely on an absence of documentation to 'prove' their cases, whereas I feel that the duty of the conscientious historian is to draw only on solid evidence. Naturally, I have included conjecture of my own, but this is clearly flagged as such, despite there being an enormous temptation to claim truthfulness in the interests of commercialism. Even without the more outlandish theories, there is more than enough within these pages to make the general reader as surprised as I was when I discovered the true nature of Nazi hunting and its personalities.

Some may be deterred by the vast quantity of footnotes, but I suggest that these need be consulted only by the more academic reader. Those who peruse them will notice that I am particularly indebted to a number of other researchers and writers, and I fully acknowledge the excellent work of – in alphabetical order – Tom Bower, David Cesarani, Uki Goñi, Ernst Klee, Holger M. Meding, Gerald L. Posner and John Ware, Matteo Sanfilippo, Heinz Schneppen, Matthias Schröder, Gitta Sereny and Gerald Steinacher. At times I diverge from the conclusions they reach, but all of their works are invaluable for anybody who wishes to dig further. This book, however, is far from being a mere synthesis of secondary sources, and I am also grateful to the staffs of the archives I have used in the United Kingdom and the United States.

I am also particularly grateful to my interviewees, who included both Nazi and Nazi hunter alike. Their names are listed in the bibliography, but I would particularly wish to thank Eli M. Rosenbaum, the Director of the Office of Special Investigations, who has given me a great deal of time and corresponded regularly and at length. During the course of my research, I have noticed that the world of Nazi hunting can be as political as any other, and I have no doubt that there are some who will argue that in some respects my alignment with Rosenbaum is perhaps too close. For what it is worth, I happen to think that in many respects he is right, and the evidence tends to support his claims.

I have received assistance from numerous people in a number of countries. In Argentina and Paraguay, I was fortunate to have Tim Phillips and his wife Victoria as my guides and hosts. Matt Chesterton, Harry Hastings, Oliver Balch and Lilian Ruiz were also of great help in Buenos Aires and Asunción. In the United States, George Pendle and Charlotte Taylor were kind to once more let me stay in their Manhattan apartment. In that same city, Shelley M. Lightburn graciously guided me through the tortuous process of accessing the UNWCC archives, and Justin McKenzie Smith and Sara Yearsley at the UK Mission to the UN were instrumental in helping my application go through smoothly. In the Ukraine, Professor Yuriy Rashkevych and Natalya Vovk were instrumental in establishing the nature of Simon Wiesenthal's academic record, as was Magdalena Tayerlová in Prague. In Austria, I drew on the resourcefulness of journalists Christian May and Michael Leidig, without whom I would have floundered. In Rome, the incomparable Dr Johan Ickx kindly shepherded me through the Hudal archive, which proved to be a goldmine, and my friend and former co-editor James Owen and his wife Marialuisa were kind and accommodating hosts.

In addition, I would also like to thank the following in alphabetical order for their expertise, support and in some cases linguistic ability: Simon Andreae, Tobyn Andreae, the late Bill Bemister, Peter Bennett, Michael Burleigh, Shaun Byrne at Lloyds TSB, Mike Constandy of Westmoreland Research, Debra Conway, Charles Cumming, James Delingpole, Andrew and Samantha de Mello, Marc Dierikx, Roger and Sandra Downton, Ute Harding, Lucy Hawking, Jason Hazeley and Sue Knowles, Sarah Helm, Nicholas Hodge, James Holland, Johan Ickx, Tobias Jones, Mary Kenny, Robert D. Leighninger Jr, Dan Mutadich, James Owen, Stephen Plotkin at the John F. Kennedy Presidential Library, Marta Urbańska, Belinda Venning, Richard and Venetia Venning, Dirk Verhofstadt, Martin and Angela Walters, Adrian Weale, Ed West, Julia Weston, Neil Wigan, Tory Wilks.

My editors, Simon Thorogood at Transworld and Charlie Conrad at Random House, deserve special mention for their patience and wisdom. I am extremely grateful they have allowed this project to stretch on for far longer than they – or I – had anticipated. My agents, Tif Loehnis in London and Luke Janklow in New York, are my twin pillars who have supported me now for almost a decade, and I am enormously appreciative of the efforts they have made to enable me to continue to live by the pen. Claire Dippel, Tim Glister, Kirsty Gordon, Rebecca Folland, Claire Paterson, Lucie Whitehouse and all other Janklovians are deserving of my utmost respect. Above all, Annabel, William and Alice are the ones who have given me the most. I can only hope that what follows does something to repay them for all the unhealthy number of hours their husband and father spent in his shed full of swastika-festooned books.

Guy Walters
Broad Chalke
May 2009

Chapter One

'The air became cleaner'

ON 6 MAY 1945, two middle-ranking SS officers stood on a small road bridge in the Austrian Alpine resort of Altaussee. Below them raced a clear mountain stream, and above loomed the giant pale-grey limestone of the Loser plateau. Nearby stood several wooden houses and cottages, whose *gemütlich* interiors are designed for late-night schnapps in front of fires after exhausting mountain hikes or invigorating swims in the therapeutic waters of the lake. However, neither man would have had his mind on such pleasant activities. Instead, they were discussing their options now that the American tanks were just a few miles away. As SS officers, neither relished the prospect of Allied captivity, yet both had different ideas of their next moves.

The younger man, an *SS-Sturmbannführer* – the equivalent of a major in the German army – intended to stay. A member of the Nazi party since he was sixteen, the thirty-year-old Dr Wilhelm Höttl had spent his war working for the *Sicherheitsdienst* or SD, the SS intelligence service, and had served in Vienna, Berlin and Budapest. Although his career was meteoric, he was not without his detractors. One of his superiors had described him as 'the typical troublesome

Viennese – a liar, a toady, a schemer, and a pronounced operator'.[1] Such qualities are arguably useful for intelligence work, and it was these that Höttl intended to draw on. With his experience of waging a secret war against communist cells, he reckoned that he might be of use to the Americans, and instead of treating him as a war criminal, they might even regard him as an asset.

Höttl's hopes were far from vain. Since February, he had been in contact with the American Office of Strategic Services (OSS), the forerunner to the CIA, in an attempt to broker a separate peace deal for his native Austria. The putative deal was codenamed 'Herzog', and was the formulation of Höttl's boss, SS-Obergruppenführer (General) Ernst Kaltenbrunner, himself an Austrian and the head of the Reich Security Main Office (*Reichssicherheitshauptamt* or RSHA).[2] Höttl had made several trips to Switzerland to talk to representatives of Allen Dulles, the OSS station chief in Berne, and he was keen to ingratiate himself with the Americans, offering them information about Axis military preparations for a desperate last stand in the so-called 'Alpine Redoubt', as well as about gold shipments that were to be buried deep in the Austrian mountains.[3] Unfortunately for Höttl, events overtook him, and before he could arrange a meeting between Dulles and Kaltenbrunner, an 'independent' Austria was declared in Russian-occupied Vienna on 27 April. Höttl made a final attempt to reach Switzerland at the beginning of May, but with French troops on the Austro-Swiss border, he was forced to stop when he had reached Liechtenstein and returned to seek refuge in Altaussee.[4] Unbeknown to him, the Americans were indeed making plans for his exploitation. On 21 April, Dulles reported that 'Höttl's record as [an] SD man and collaborator [of] Kaltenbrunner is of course bad, but I believe he desires to save his skin and therefore may be useful'.[5] Another OSS officer agreed, although he advised caution: 'To avoid any accusation that we are working with a Nazi reactionary,' reported Edgeworth Murray Leslie to Dulles, 'I believe that we should keep our contact with him as indirect as possible.'[6]

The other man standing on the bridge that day did not share Höttl's fluid sense of loyalty to the Nazi regime. Nine years older and one rank senior, the *SS-Obersturmbannführer* (lieutenant colonel) was far from interested in peace deals and was convinced that the fight was still worth waging. He told Höttl that his intention was to hide in the mountains with a group of trustworthy young SS men, where he felt his Alpine skills would enable him to survive for years.[7] Höttl would have had no doubt that his superior was sincere, as he had witnessed the depth of his commitment to the evils of Nazism. In fact, the two men had worked together in Hungary after the Germans had occupied that country the previous March. Höttl's job was to run SD counter-espionage operations[8] while his fellow Austrian's brief was to implement the role of the bland-sounding *Referat* IV B 4 of the RSHA in the newly occupied territory. The *Obersturmbannführer* was to do his job well and with much zeal, because by June 1944, he had managed to deport some four hundred thousand Jews to be gassed at Birkenau.[9] The older man's name was Adolf Eichmann.

As the two men stood on the bridge, Höttl may have reflected on a meeting the two men had had in Budapest one morning in late August 1944. Höttl had been relaxing in his apartment when Eichmann had entered in a markedly nervous state because of the recent coup in Romania against the pro-Axis leader Ion Antonescu. With the country about to join the Allies, Eichmann was worried that nothing could now stop a Russian advance into Hungary and Austria. 'Eichmann then swallowed several glasses of brandy,' Höttl was to recall, 'one after the other [. . .] I set a bottle of arak down with a glass, so he could help himself.'[10]

Eichmann, who Höttl noticed was unusually wearing battledress, found little solace in the brandy. Towards the end of the conversation, he stood to say farewell to Höttl, and added, 'We shall probably never see each other again.' When his subordinate asked him why, Eichmann told him that the Allies knew he was responsible for the deportation of so many Jews, and that they considered him a 'top war criminal'. Höttl then decided to question him as to the extent of the extermination programme. Höttl said:

> To my surprise, Eichmann responded to that [. . .] He said that the number of murdered Jews was a very great Reich secret . . . Eichmann told me that, according to his information, some six million Jews had perished until then; four million in extermination camps and the

remaining two million through shooting by the Operations Units and other causes such as disease.

Eichmann then indicated that Himmler thought the figure had to be higher, but he was convinced that the total of six million was correct.[11] Although Eichmann was steady on his feet, Höttl cautioned his superior against driving with a bellyful of alcohol. The warning was doubtless ignored, as by many accounts Eichmann was no stranger to the brandy bottle.[12]

Now, just over eight months later, Eichmann appeared to be in a somewhat more redoubtable mood. He told Höttl that he intended to resist, but after many years of stress and spirits, he hardly looked the figure of some mighty Nazi recrudescence. Just 5½ feet tall, the balding Eichmann was also very slight; his face was bony and his cheeks sunken. His face was afflicted by a nervous twitch, and he had an unpleasant and exaggerated laugh. Since he was constantly under the influence of alcohol, much of his courage was probably of the Dutch variety.[13] It was just as well that he was going into the mountains, because his fellow Nazis wanted to have little to do with him. Eichmann's boss, Kaltenbrunner, was also holed up in Altaussee and he saw his subordinate's presence as baleful.

'Eichmann burst in on us like a Typhoid Mary,' Höttl recalled, 'the personification of all the crimes that were now haunting Kaltenbrunner and his cohorts, the apocalyptic memento of their own sins.' According to Höttl, Kaltenbrunner told Eichmann 'to get the hell out of Altaussee, as fast as he could'.[14]

However, before he left, Eichmann had some personal business to attend to – he had to say goodbye to his family, who were renting his uncle's chalet a few hundred yards down the road at Fischerndorf 8.[15] Eichmann later recalled how in turn he took his wife Vera and three sons into his arms. 'I clung to them with a fervour that is only possible in such circumstances,' he would write. 'The smallest was only three years old. Just three – and I was seeing him for the last time. I knew that the finest gift a German father can bequeath his son is the gift of discipline. And so I beat him.'[16] Dressed in his camouflage uniform and carrying a submachine gun, Eichmann took the young Dieter between his knees and repeatedly struck him with his hand 'in a calm and considered manner'. The reason behind this brutal farewell was to impress upon the boy that he should not go near the edge of the lake, into which he had recently fallen. 'How he howled as my hand rose and fell! But, as it happened, he never fell into the water.'[17] Before he left, the man who had been responsible for the deaths of so many now presented his wife with the means of destroying herself and the children. He handed her four poison capsules and said: 'If the Russians come, you must bite them; if the Americans or the British come, then you needn't.'[18] He kept a capsule for himself too, although, according to Höttl, the fanatical Eichmann was more likely to try to shoot it out if he were cornered.[19]

The *Obersturmbannführer* now headed into the hills to join his team of 'trustworthy' SS men, who were ready for him at the Blaa-Alm, an inn-cum-hunting lodge hiding in a secluded valley 3 miles north of Altaussee.[20] However, with the American army now so close, Eichmann decided to prune his cadre, and paid off most of his men. With a small group of officers, he then made his way 2 miles northwest to the hamlet of Rettenbach-Alm. Although the party had now descended some 1,000 feet, their new spot was far more secluded.[21] It was at this point that the party realized that no matter how deeply it penetrated into the Alps, it would be far safer if it divested itself of its most toxic constituent: Eichmann himself.

Ironically, the party's misgivings were voiced by a figure whose own toxicity was strong – SS-Obersturmführer Anton Burger, the commandant of Theresienstadt concentration camp from 1943 to 1944, before which he had worked in Auschwitz.[22] 'We've been talking about the situation,' said Burger. 'We mustn't fire on the English or the Americans; the Russians aren't coming here. You're being looked for as a war criminal, not us. If you leave and appoint a different commander, then you do a great service to your comrades.'[23] It was impossible for their leader not to agree, and after a farewell schnapps, Eichmann headed north, accompanied by his adjutant, SS-Obersturmführer Rudolf Jänisch.

Despite Eichmann's fine talk to Höttl of waging his own private war, he and Jänisch must have quickly realized that scurrying around the mountains in their SS uniforms was foolhardy. As a result, the two men decided to adopt new uniforms and even new identities, and so SS-Obersturmbannführer Adolf Eichmann now became the more humble Obergefreiter (Corporal) Bart of the Luftwaffe.[24] The two men hiked through the mountains, and Eichmann would years later recall spotting an abundance of wildlife, including roe-deer, chamois, foxes and hares. He wrote:

> These wild animals I knew well from childhood days in the mountains and forests of Upper Austria. Not that I had been a good huntsman. I never found any pleasure in shooting to kill. I think the man who can look through the sights of his rifle into the eyes of a deer and then kill it is a man without a heart in his body. I thanked God that in the war I had not been made the actual instrument of killing anybody.

Such was the magnitude of Eichmann's self-delusion. He would continue to deny his role as an instrument of slaughter for the rest of his life. But for the time being he had his own pelt to save. 'But anyhow, I was the quarry now,' he acknowledged. 'The hunted animal. Unprotected by "out of season" rules.'[25]

Back in Altaussee, the remaining Nazis prepared themselves for the arrival of the Americans. Some, such as the scheming Höttl, had decided to stay, but others, like Eichmann, opted to disappear into the mountains. The most notorious of these was Ernst Kaltenbrunner, the head of the RSHA since January 1943. Established by Himmler in 1939, the RSHA combined all three of the Nazi state's police forces, which included the Gestapo, the Criminal Police, and the SD, for which Höttl worked. The role of the RSHA was to track down and arrest all enemies of the state, before handing them over to the concentration-camp system. As those enemies also included the Jews in Germany and the occupied territories, the RSHA had a definitive role in executing the 'Final Solution'.[26] Thanks to Eichmann's efforts, it was also extra-ordinarily effective.

Kaltenbrunner, then, was a major criminal, and as Eichmann's boss, arguably a greater one. Towering at 6 feet 7 inches (2.01 metres), the stocky 41-year-old even looked like a criminal, with a pockmarked face, the type of thin mouth that is usually described as cruel, and a scar that stretched from his left ear down to his mouth.

Just being in his presence made many feel uneasy. 'His small, penetrating, brown eyes were unpleasant,' wrote one Nazi, 'they looked at one fixedly, like the eyes of a viper seeking to petrify its prey . . . From the first moment [I met him] he made me feel quite sick.'[27] Despite his disturbing physical presence, Kaltenbrunner had the requisite blue-eyed blonde 24-year-old mistress with him in Altaussee.[28] Countess Gisela von Westarp had even born her lover twins, Ursula and Wolfgang, who had been delivered in a cowshed in the village on 12 March.[29]

The Kaltenbrunner-Westarp circle during that May also featured a couple called the Scheidlers. The husband, SS-Obersturmbannführer Arthur Scheidler, was Kaltenbrunner's adjutant. Born in 1911, Scheidler had been educated at business school and had worked for a rail freight firm before he joined the SS in November 1934. One of his earliest jobs was as a guard at Sachsenburg concentration camp, although his acumen with finances was soon noticed, and he became an administrator in the SD's account department in 1935. In 1939 he became an administrative aide to the infamous Reinhard Heydrich, Kaltenbrunner's predecessor as chief of the RSHA. Conscientious and diligent, Scheidler embodied the type of middle-class efficiency that the Nazi apparatus required, and despite doubts about his lack of combat experience, he started to work directly for Kaltenbrunner in November 1943.[30] Scheidler's wife was a vivacious and attractive 33-year-old brunette called Iris. A Viennese by birth, Iris had previously been married to a Dr Rudolf Praxmarer, who was a friend of Kaltenbrunner when they had studied at the University of Graz.[31] The couple separated amicably in July 1943, and Iris became Frau Scheidler the following month. As well as being the mother of two children by Praxmarer, Iris was expecting her first baby with her new husband at the end of June. She combined parenthood with working for the official Nazi photographer Heinrich Hoffmann, which gave her access to what passed for high society in Nazi Germany, including Eva Braun and Baldur von Schirach, the leader of the Hitler Youth. In short, the Scheidlers were a well-connected couple, and they were at the heart of the Kaltenbrunner clique in Altaussee, a clique made cosier by the fact that Iris's former husband was the SS Chief of Hospitals and military commander of

Altaussee.[32] And, just to make the circle that little bit tighter, Iris and
Höttl were lovers.[33] The Scheidlers lived at the Villa Hohenlohe, an
imposing house in the centre of town, and even today Iris Scheidler
is remembered. 'She was tall and very pretty,' recalled one villager,
who admitted being somewhat smitten whenever he served her at
the post office.[34]

Kaltenbrunner's house in Altaussee was the Villa Kerry, which
was situated on the outskirts of town and looked over the lake.
Before he fled, like some villain in a potboiler, Kaltenbrunner buried
his treasure in his garden. According to one estimate, he had shipped
to Altaussee 50 kilograms of gold bars, fifty cases containing gold
articles, two million US dollars, the same number of Swiss francs,
five cases of jewels, and a stamp collection worth five million gold
marks.[35] Although it is impossible to be definitive about how much
booty Kaltenbrunner had at his personal disposal, there was no
doubt he had a lot – too much to bury under his lawn. Instead, he
wanted to hide much of the treasure in a mountainside which he
would have then had dynamited, stopping not only himself getting
his hands on it, but also anybody else. It appears that Arthur
Scheidler talked his boss out of this almost childish gesture.[36]

Kaltenbrunner fled the Villa Kerry on 7 May. With him travelled
the loyal Scheidler, two SS men, and two hunters, Fritz Moser and
Sebastian Raudaschl, who acted as guides. Their destination was a
small hunting lodge near Wildensee Alm, a good five-hour hike up
to the Loser plateau, where the snow lay up to 20 to 30 feet thick.
The party reached the hut late that night, and had to shovel the
snow from the entrance. Eventually, they stumbled into the hut, and
collapsed on to some hard straw mattresses while the huntsmen
made tea. Like Eichmann, Kaltenbrunner and Scheidler had adopted
new identities, with Kaltenbrunner now posing as a senior military
doctor called Dr Josef Unterwogen, while Scheidler acted as his
colleague. The party could now do little more than sit and listen to
their leader speculating about whether the Americans would want
to employ him in a fight against the Soviets.[37] To keep their spirits
up, the group did have some creature comforts, in the form of
champagne, French bonbons and American tax-free cigarettes.

Kaltenbrunner's hoped-for collaborators arrived in Altaussee on
9 May, the day after VE Day. Far from securing the village with

overwhelming force, the Americans deployed just five soldiers, one tank and one jeep, all under the command of Major Ralph Pearson of the 80th Infantry Division of Patton's Third Army.[38] Not far behind them were two members of the US 80th Counterintelligence Corps (CIC): Captain Robert E. Matteson and his interpreter Sydney Bruskin. Matteson was a political-science teacher and a Harvard MA, and his job was to hunt down and arrest ranking Nazis, and to collate as much intelligence as possible. In Altaussee he would have some rich pickings. Among those he arrested were General Erich Alt of the Luftwaffe; Walter Riedel, the construction chief of the V-2 rocket programme at Peenemünde; Gunther Altenburg, the German Minister Plenipotentiary to Greece; William Knothe, General Counsel of the Foreign Office; and Dr Bailent Homan, a minister in the Hungarian puppet government installed by the Nazis. Matteson also paid a visit to the Villa Kerry, and there he found Wilhelm Waneck, the chief of the RSHA's intelligence section for southeastern Europe; Werner Göttsch, an SD official; and an expectant Wilhelm Höttl. All were arrested and sent off for interrogation.[39]

But Matteson did not have the man he really wanted: Kaltenbrunner. For the next two days, he questioned members of the Kaltenbrunner clique, but no information was forthcoming. In fact, Matteson found that Gisela von Westarp and Iris Scheidler were themselves anxious to discover what had happened to their men. Finally, on the morning of 11 May, Matteson got his break. Kaltenbrunner and his team had been spotted in their hut by an Altaussee forest ranger who was a member of the Austrian resistance movement. Matteson quickly assembled his team, which consisted of four Austrian guides, all of whom had served in the Wehrmacht. However, a nervous Major Pearson insisted that Matteson take along a squad of American GIs, much to the CIC man's reluctance.

'I was afraid their presence might bring on a pitched battle,' Matteson recalled, 'leaving either a dead or an escaped Kaltenbrunner, and my arguments achieved at least the compromise agreement that I would have the authority to use the infantry squad in any manner I saw fit.' Matteson ordered the squad to stick well to the rear, although the GIs themselves were deeply uncomfortable at being led by men who had been their enemy just three days before. 'They wanted it made clear that if they made a single false step, the guides would be dead ducks. After coming through the war alive, they didn't want to get killed with peace and home in sight.' Before the team left that night, Matteson visited Westarp and Scheidler. Despite her condition, Iris insisted that she came along, claiming that if her husband and Kaltenbrunner saw her in the search party, they would be unlikely to start shooting. Perhaps ignorant of the logistics of helping a 34-week-pregnant woman up a snow-covered mountain in the middle of the night, Matteson agreed, but Iris soon thought better of the idea, and decided not to come. However, Matteson did secure assistance of a more practical nature from Westarp – a letter from her to her lover, urging him to accompany Matteson into the safe custody of the American forces, rather than allow himself to be captured by the Russians, who would probably kill him on sight.

Matteson's motley crew departed at midnight, their leader sporting a pair of lederhosen, an Alpine jacket and hat, and spiked shoes. The plan was for an unarmed Matteson to pose as an innocent passerby when they approached the hut in the early morning. Considering the potential ruthlessness of a man like Kaltenbrunner, there can be no doubting the American's bravery. However, he had to get to the hut first, and progress was slow. 'There were unexpected obstacles,' Matteson would write. 'Trees swept down by snowslides lay across the path, and the footbridge over the Stammern stream had been carried away by the spring floods.' Matters were not helped by the GIs, who were laden with weaponry and lacked spiked mountaineering shoes. Three of them were injured in falls as they wound their way up the narrow trail, and had to be left behind. Nevertheless, by five o'clock in the morning, just as dawn was breaking, Kaltenbrunner's lair came into view. The hut lay at the end of an exposed down-slope, just below the crest of a ridge. Matteson now had two options: should he and his team skirt the ridge, using the overhanging crags as cover, or should they just proceed directly down the slope in full view of the hut? The team was tired, and skirting the ridge would be exhausting work. Wary of his men's condition, Matteson plumped for the latter.

As they approached, it looked as though the hut was deserted. The ranger's information had either been wrong or out of date. When the team got within 300 yards, Matteson left his guides and the GIs behind a small ridge and advanced alone. 'The shutters were tightly closed,' Matteson recalled. 'No smoke was coming from the chimney; no fresh foot-tracks were visible in the snow.' He soon reached the door and knocked on it – there was no response. He then tried the door, but it was bolted. Just as he was about to give up, Matteson heard a noise coming from the room to his left. He rattled the shutter on the window, determined to get some response. Eventually, the window opened, and a bleary-faced man asked, 'What do you want?' The man was not Kaltenbrunner, but Matteson asked if he could come in, as he was cold. The man refused. The American then thrust Gisela von Westarp's letter forward, which the man read carefully before telling Matteson that he had no idea to whom the letter was referring, and that he himself was just a passerby.

Just then, the man noticed something over Matteson's shoulder. Matteson turned, and saw the four guides advancing down the slope with their rifles. He turned back to see the man making for a revolver next to the bed. 'I retreated to the protection of the cabin's west side,' said Matteson, 'and he slammed the shutter shut. The guides, alarmed, brought the eight infantry boys down in a half-circle around the front of the cabin.' The man opened the front door and stepped on to the porch, but as soon as he saw the advancing troops, he darted back inside, bolting the door behind him. Matteson called out for the occupants to come out and surrender. There was no reply. 'For ten minutes we kept repeating the call, but with no results. Not wishing to start shooting, we went on to the porch and began to knock down the door.'

This had the desired effect, and shortly four men emerged from the hut, their hands above their heads. Although Kaltenbrunner was immediately recognizable, he denied his identity, as did Scheidler. The other two men admitted they were SS guards, and claimed that they had nothing to do with Kaltenbrunner. Inside the hut, Matteson found Kaltenbrunner's identity disc in the ash in the fireplace, but still the giant pockmarked-face Austrian claimed to be Dr Unterwogen. By eleven thirty that morning, the party had arrived back at Altaussee. News travels quickly in rural communities, and the Salzkammergut that May was no exception, because the group was met by a large crowd on the main street. As Matteson took his charges into custody, Iris and Gisela leaped from the crowd and kissed and hugged their men. As Matteson wryly observed, 'Kaltenbrunner and Scheidler now had to drop their masks.'[40]

It is not known whether Vera Eichmann was among the crowd that Saturday morning. Had she been, she might have wondered whether her husband was going to be the next Nazi to be brought down the mountain.

In the small Bavarian village of Autenried some 220 miles northwest of Altaussee, the wife of another Nazi war criminal was reflecting on the whereabouts of her husband. Just a few days before, on 3 May, Irene Mengele had been listening to the radio when she heard Allied reports outlining the crimes for which her husband had been responsible while serving in Auschwitz.[41] The crimes that SS-Hauptsturmführer (Captain) Dr Josef Mengele had committed were so horrific that Irene must have struggled to believe them. Like many Germans, she probably suspected that the reports were nothing more than victors' propaganda. Even when the Germans were presented with actual photographs of piles of corpses from concentration camps such as Dachau, many dismissed the images as pictures of the victims of the Allied raid on Dresden.[42] But the reports were true, and they were based on the stories of those who had actually survived Mengele. Numerous testimonies gathered by the Allies revealed that a hitherto obscure doctor was actually a sadist of the highest order, and a sadist who inflicted the utmost savageries in the name of science. As one report was to put it years later, Mengele 'became synonymous with the evil of Auschwitz, the site on which more people were murdered than any other in recorded human history'.[43]

One of these testimonies was given by Katherine Neiger, a 23-year-old Czechoslovak Jew who had survived both Auschwitz and Belsen. Arrested with her parents and her two sisters on 23 October 1941, she and her family were initially sent to a ghetto in Poland before being transferred to Auschwitz. During the same week that Irene Mengele was listening to her radio and on the same day that Höttl and Eichmann were bidding an uneasy farewell on the bridge in Altaussee, Neiger told her story to Major P. Ingress Bell, a British officer serving on the staff of the Judge Advocate General.

At AUSCHWITZ Concentration camp there was a Doctor named MENGELE. When my draft arrived at the camp we were made to parade in front of him. He sorted out the fit ones and all others, old people, sick people, pregnant women, and every child were sent to the gas chamber. The rest after having their hair shaved and being washed were examined naked and further selections were made for the gas chamber. From then on similar examination took place every few days. Any person with visible signs of illness, disease or anything else was sent straight to the gas chamber.[44]

Neiger's father, mother and baby sister were among those who were gassed. She and her remaining sister were transferred to Belsen in August 1944 and survived typhus, malnutrition and physical abuse. But it was Mengele who decided her initial fate, and what Neiger witnessed has now become an enduring image of the Holocaust: that of the darkly handsome young doctor in his white laboratory coat, selecting those who were to live and those who were to be gassed. According to another survivor, Mengele performed his role with a calm demeanour. 'He had a gentle manner,' remembered Arminio Wachsberger, a Jew from Rome, 'and a quiet poise that almost always lay between the edges of smugness and the height of charm. He whistled a Wagnerian aria as he signalled right or left for prisoners.'[45] Some even spoke of Mengele as a dangerously glamorous figure. One female inmate thought that he had 'star quality' and that he was a 'very charismatic man'.[46] Certainly, the 33-year-old cut a *bella figura* at the selections, with his tight-fitting SS uniform, medals, white gloves, and highly polished boots and cane.[47]

But Mengele was not always so serpentine sleek. He had a vicious temper that would be vented with the mildest provocation. One Auschwitz inmate, Ruth Guttmann, once witnessed one of the doctor's vicious outbursts.

. . . on one occasion I saw DOCTOR MENGELE, who was the Chief Doctor, seize and beat with a stick an elderly woman who had been cutting wood. I do not know the reason for the beating nor do I know what effect it had on the victim, but using a stick he struck the woman very hard some ten or a dozen times, starting on the lower part of the back and finishing with one or two particularly vicious blows on the side of the neck, which might obviously do considerable physical harm.[48]

However, such punishments were comparatively mild compared to what the doctor practised in his laboratory. Mengele's Ph.D. thesis had been an examination of differences between the lower jaw structures of four racial groups, and he had always maintained a keen interest in racial anthropology.[49] In Auschwitz, Mengele was able to pursue his studies unmolested by niceties such as patient welfare, or indeed patient survival. His subjects, especially young twins, were experimented on as if they were little more than rats. Surgery was performed without anaesthesia, healthy limbs were amputated, diseases injected, wounds infected.[50] The supposed medical value of this barbarity was an effort to improve 'racial hygiene', and Mengele had no shortage of material. As a result, he was able to exterminate his subjects just in order to dissect them and to analyse the results of his experiments. One Jewish doctor, Miklós Nyiszli, forced by Mengele to act as an assistant, recalled how Mengele would calmly set about his work.

> In the work room next to the dissecting room, fourteen Gypsy twins were waiting and crying bitterly. Dr Mengele didn't say a single word to us, and prepared a 10cc and 5cc syringe. From a box he took Evipal [a fast-acting barbiturate] and from another box he took chloroform, which was in 20cc glass containers, and put these on the operating table. After that the first twin was brought in . . . a fourteen-year-old girl. Dr Mengele ordered me to undress the girl and put her head on the dissecting table. Then he injected the Evipal into her right arm intravenously. After the child had fallen asleep, he felt for the left ventricle of the heart and injected 10cc of chloroform. After one little twitch, the child was dead, whereupon Dr Mengele had her taken into the corpse chamber. In this manner all fourteen twins were killed during the night.[51]

So where was this man during that week in May 1945, this child-murderer who had a wife and one-year-old son of his own? He was 250 miles away, in a town called Saaz in the Sudetenland, the

German-occupied part of Czechoslovakia.[52] Although he was still calling himself Josef Mengele, he was now wearing the uniform of an army officer, and not that of the SS. He had fled Auschwitz on the night of 17 January, taking with him his notes on his experiments, no doubt believing that his inhumanity would actually benefit mankind.[53] Like many, Mengele headed west away from the Russian advance, and within ten days he was at Gross Rosen concentration camp, where he remained for three weeks. But the Russian advance was relentless, and Mengele soon joined a retreating German army unit, with whom he stayed for two months.[54] On 2 May, the unit arrived at Saaz, where Mengele had the fortune to run into a friend from his pre-war days, Dr Otto-Hans Kahler, who was working for a field hospital.[55]

Dr Kahler found his old friend severely depressed and talking openly about committing suicide. That day, Hitler's death was announced on the radio and, according to Kahler, 'Mengele made quite a fuss, refusing to believe the report that Hitler was dead.'[56] Mengele also admitted that he had performed selections in Auschwitz, a revelation that did not stop Kahler seeking and receiving his commander's permission for his friend to join them.[57] For the next few days, a nervous Mengele stayed with the unit, during which time he formed some sort of relationship with a nurse, to whom he entrusted his precious notes. Mengele knew that if he were captured and the notes examined, he would be sentenced to death.

On 8 May, the day of the German surrender, Mengele's unit was encamped in the Erzegebirge Mountains in Saxony, some 20 miles northwest of Saaz. The area, which had been invaded by neither the Russians nor the Americans, constituted an unoccupied no man's land, although it was notionally under American control. Mengele was one of fifteen thousand troops trapped in this limbo. In the confusion, he had also lost his protector, Dr Kahler, and he now found that his adopted comrades were suspicious of his real identity. Their suspicions were inflamed by the fact that a nervous Mengele had little talent for remaining under cover. At the roll-call each day, he would use a different name. 'He evidently couldn't remember what name he had given the day before,' recalled Colonel Fritz Ulmann, 'so he must have used four or five additional names. He was secretive and I knew he had to be SS.'[58]

It was hardly surprising that Mengele was so edgy, as he knew it would be only a matter of time before he was captured. 'As long as we had food the only thing that worried us was when the area would fall,' Mengele remembered. 'Finally, as the food was becoming more and more scarce, and the rumours that the Russians would occupy the area increased, we decided to take action.'[59] In the middle of June, the unit decided to make a break for Bavaria, as it was safely within the American Zone of Occupation. 'With several vehicles and a sanitation unit we formed a column,' said Mengele, 'and with some deception we succeeded in passing through the Americans. We bypassed their subsequent roadblocks and reached Bavarian territory.'[60] Now that he was deep within the American zone, it would not be long before Mengele and the unit were interned. Indeed, on or around 15 June, Mengele was taken to Schauenstein POW camp 75 miles north of Nuremberg, where he was reunited with his friend Dr Kahler. His captors had no inkling what a big fish they held, especially as the fish told them he was called 'Josef Memling'.[61] It would not be the last alias that the 'Angel of Death' was to use.

Back in Altaussee, the Americans were still arresting the plethora of Nazis who had taken refuge in that small Alpine village. Among them was a tall, well-built 37-year-old Austrian *SS-Hauptsturmführer* called Franz Stangl, who had been hiding in the house of a police officer with whom Stangl and his family had sometimes spent their holidays.[62] Stangl never knew how the Americans had discovered him, although he strongly suspected his host, who maintained that the betrayal must have been the fault of one of his juniors. Stangl was taken to the prison at Bad Ischl, some 15 miles by a road that circumnavigated where Eichmann was hiding. When he was interrogated, the softly spoken and well-mannered[63] Stangl revealed that he was indeed an SS officer, and that he had spent his war conducting anti-partisan activities in Italy and Yugoslavia. He may also have told the Americans about his role as the special supply officer for the *Einsatz Poll*, a huge project for fortifying the Istrian peninsula between Italy and Yugoslavia which involved some five hundred thousand workers. 'I was responsible for getting everything,' Stangl said, 'shoes, clothes, food . . . Everybody, army and SS, had to help me. I carried a paper signed by the General stating that "Hauptsturmführer Stangl is authorized to act in uniform or civvies and all services are requested to give him every assistance in the execution of his command." ' Stangl recalled how he even had a man with him whose only job was to cart trunks full of cash which would be used to secure items such as petrol and fabric on the black market.[64]

What the polite Stangl never told his captors was what he had been doing between August 1942 and August 1943. It was hardly surprising, as there are few men who would willingly admit that they have been responsible for the deaths of eight hundred thousand people.[65] But that was what Stangl had done, in a clearing in a wood some 60 miles northeast of Warsaw, near a village called Treblinka.[66] Established in June or July 1942, Treblinka was one of four extermination centres set up under Himmler's secret Operation Reinhard to massacre Poland's 2,284,000 Jews. Unlike Auschwitz, the Reinhard camps were not primarily labour camps, and their sole purpose was to slaughter those who were crammed into the ghettos of cities such as Warsaw, Lublin, Kraków and Lvov. Until Operation Reinhard, the killings had largely been carried out by *Einsatzgruppen*, roving groups of alcohol-fuelled SS men who simply shot any Jews they found. Although the *Einsatzgruppen* had killed some half a million, their methods were considered both inefficient and psychologically damaging to the murderers themselves. Camps such as Treblinka represented a means of streamlining the answer to the 'Jewish Problem', and they introduced a frightening new form of killing: that of industrial-scale murder.

Like any other 'factory', Treblinka required its bosses, foremen and labour force. In most societies, finding the men – and women – willing to work in such places would be difficult, if not impossible, but in Nazi Germany, there already existed a qualified cadre of those who had overseen a previous murder programme: *Aktion T-4*. Named after the villa at Tiergartenstrasse 4 in Berlin, *Aktion T-4* was formulated in the summer of 1939 as a programme for killing Germany's incurable psychiatric cases, and in doing so creating more bed space for future military casualties.[67] Run by Philipp Bouhler and Dr Karl Brandt, *Aktion T-4* was personally sanctioned by Hitler to expand 'the authority of physicians, to be designated by name, to the end that patients considered incurable according to the best human judgement of their state of health, can be granted a mercy death'.[68] Over the next two years, 70,273 were murdered, either by poison gas or lethal injection, in 'euthanasia' centres such as Schloss Hartheim, near Linz, some 120 miles west of Vienna.[69]

Supervising the killings at this ominous castle was Franz Stangl, who was appointed in November 1940. A career policeman in his native Austria since 1931, Stangl had risen rapidly through the ranks. He was a loyal Nazi even when the party was illegal in Austria, and the *Anschluss* in 1938 further helped Stangl's progress. When he was approached for the *T-4* job by Kriminalrath Werner, Stangl claimed to have had some misgivings. 'I . . . I was speechless,' he recalled. 'And then I finally said I didn't really feel that I was suited for this assignment [. . .] He said he understood well that that would be my first reaction but that I had to remember that my being asked to take this job showed proof of their exceptional trust in me.'[70] Werner explained that Stangl wouldn't be doing the killings himself, as they would be carried out by doctors, but that he was to be responsible for providing security and ensuring that the killings were carried out 'by the book', or, as Werner put it in a classic example of Nazi euphemism, 'to ascertain that the protective regulations regarding the eligibility of patients would be adhered to'. Werner continued to reassure Stangl by telling him that a pending disciplinary action would be dropped, and that such killings were already carried out legally in America and Russia. The *Kriminalrath* added that the programme was for the best for the population as a whole, as it would not only promote 'racial hygiene' but also save the Reich money. (By the end of the programme, graphs had been produced showing how much the murder of the 70,273 would save by 1951: some 885,439,800 Reichsmarks.)[71] Stangl agreed, and his decision would set him down a path that would lead to his becoming one of the most notorious murderers in history. Unlike his fellow Austrian Adolf Eichmann, Stangl was not motivated by ideological anti-Semitism, but rather by a sense that he should follow orders. No fanatic, Stangl always maintained that he was merely a policeman doing his job. If anybody embodied the banality of evil, it was Stangl.

At Hartheim, Stangl claimed that he still felt uneasy about his new posting, 'for a long time. After the first two or three days I told Reichleitner [a friend and colleague] that I didn't think I could stand it,' Stangl said. 'By then I'd heard that the police official who'd had the job before me had been relieved upon his request because he had stomach trouble. I too couldn't eat – you know, one just couldn't.'[72] However, like a dutiful policeman, Stangl continued with his work, and even found reassurance from a mother superior and a priest, who once bemoaned to Stangl that a severely crippled sixteen-year-old boy was not accepted by the programme. 'How could they refuse to deliver him from this terrible life?' the nun asked. 'Who was I then,' reasoned Stangl, 'to doubt what was being done?'[73]

It was this mindset displayed by Stangl and other supervisors of the *T-4* programme that earned them their places on Operation Reinhard. And such was the level of slaughter at Treblinka that it did not take long for Stangl to dehumanize the 'cargo'[74] that his factory processed. 'I rarely saw them as individuals,' he said. 'It was always a huge mass. I sometimes stood on the wall and saw them in the tube . . . they were naked, packed together, running, being driven with whips . . .'[75] The other way to deal with his job was simply to get drunk, Stangl's favourite medicine being a large glass of brandy taken at bedtime.

No amount of alcohol could drown the horror that was Treblinka. For the inmates, many of whom spent no more than a matter of minutes in the camp before they were gassed, the scenes were infernal. One survivor, Yankel Wiernik, wrote:

Only on arriving did the horrible truth dawn on us. The camp yard was littered with corpses, some still in their clothes and some naked. Their faces distorted with fright and awe, black and swollen, the eyes wide open, with protruding tongues, skulls crushed, bodies mangled. And blood everywhere, the blood of our children, of our brothers and sisters, our fathers and mothers.[76]

Another witness, a Polish railwayman, Franciszek Zabecki, saw examples of the utmost brutality:

One mother threw a small child wrapped in a pillow from the wagon, shouting: 'Take it, that's some money to look after it.' In no time an

SS man ran up, unwrapped the pillow, seized the child by its feet and smashed its head against a wheel of the wagon. This took place in full view of the mother, who was howling with pain.[77]

Stangl was to 'improve' matters, by ensuring that his 'cargo' had no inkling of its fate. His victims soon found themselves arriving at a dummy railway station complete with phoney timetables and flowers. After they were unloaded, the Jews were immediately separated by gender and had their valuables confiscated. The women and children were then sent to the left, and the men to the right. The women were herded into a barracks where they had to strip naked before being driven down a path flanked by barbed wire – the 'tube' over which Stangl stood. 'This path led through a small grove to the building that housed the gas chamber,' wrote Abraham Jacob Krzepicki, who escaped from Treblinka in September 1942. 'Only a few minutes later we could hear their terrible screams, but we could not see anything, because the trees of the grove blocked our view.'[78] The male cargo was dealt with in a similar fashion. Stangl took some pride in the efficiency of his factory. 'This was the system,' he said. 'It worked. And, because it worked, it was irreversible.'[79]

It was not a pride that Stangl shared with his captors in Bad Ischl in May 1945. Neither was it a pride he shared with his three daughters or his wife Theresa, who managed to visit him in prison, where he was held not by the Americans but by his fellow country-men. 'We couldn't talk much,' Theresa Stangl recalled, 'but at least he was alive. The prison where he was, was awful. I never saw it, but he told me – it was a real cage.'[80] In July, Stangl was transferred to Glasenbach POW camp 5 miles south of Salzburg, where he was just one of twenty thousand prisoners.[81] Conditions were not much better than they were at Bad Ischl, and Stangl had to sleep on the floor without any blankets. 'It was pretty rough,' said Stangl, 'for a long time.'[82]

The more sharp-eyed prisoners at Glasenbach may have spotted a small building perched on a mountain ridge some 10 miles south. Had they seen it, many would have known it to be the 'Eagle's Nest', a chalet built 1,834 metres up the Kehlstein mountain as an official fiftieth birthday present for Adolf Hitler. The Führer himself rarely visited the 'Kehlsteinhaus', and preferred to remain in his famous Berghof complex further down the slopes. The man who commissioned the chalet was Martin Bormann, who during the course of the war had become one of the most powerful men in the Third Reich.

Born in 1900, Bormann had served late in the First World War as a cannoneer, and had felt betrayed when Germany capitulated. He returned from the front to take up work as an estate manager, but like many disillusioned former soldiers, Bormann joined a hard-right *Freikorps* unit, which promised to 'help liberate Germany from the traitors who had stabbed her in the back'. Although Bormann had never seen combat during the war, he seemed determined to prove that he was a man of action, and in 1923 he took part in the murder of Walter Kadow, a German communist and primary-school teacher, who was accused of betraying the anti-French activities of a *Freikorps* member in the Ruhr. Bormann's accomplice in the murder was Rudolf Höss, who would later find infamy as the commandant of Auschwitz. In March 1924, the two men were tried and convicted, and Bormann received a lenient one-year prison sentence in Leipzig. After he was released, Bormann joined the Nazi Party, in which his aptitude for bureaucracy enabled him to flourish. He became the party's business manager in Thuringia by 1928, and in the following year his marriage to Gerda Buch was witnessed by Hitler himself, who also agreed to be godfather to the couple's first child.

Bormann's career within the party accelerated after the Nazis came to power in January 1933. That July, he was appointed chief of staff to the deputy leader of the party, Rudolf Hess. In October he was made a *Reichsleiter*, an immensely senior post, and in November he became a member of the Reichstag. However, Bormann's big break came when Rudolf Hess undertook his mysterious flight to Scotland in May 1941. Hess, who was deputy leader of the Nazi Party and one of Hitler's most long-standing and evangelical supporters, found himself sidelined by the Führer as the war continued. Desperate to win back his master's favour, Hess flew to Scotland seemingly in order to persuade George VI to broker a peace treaty between Britain and Germany. Since he was taken into custody almost as soon as he had landed by parachute, Hess's mission was widely regarded by Nazi and Briton alike as the act of a madman. Within two days of Hess's disappearance, Hitler abolished the role of deputy leader, and appointed Bormann as the Head of the Party Chancellery. This post not only gave Bormann direct access to Hitler, but also made him the gatekeeper through which most had to pass in order to see the Führer. Bormann benefited so greatly from Hess's flight that some within the party speculated that Bormann had driven the deputy leader to make his madcap venture.[83] Whatever the truth, the 'Brown Eminence' proved himself masterful at the political infighting and intrigues that so beset the Nazi Party. As Hitler's health and grip on reality waned, Bormann's power waxed to such an extent that he was often regarded as the de facto leader of Germany.[84]

Bormann's physical presence possessed a pugnacity that intimidated many of his rivals. Short and stocky, he was the antithesis of the so-called Aryan model to which the Nazi state would have its members aspire. 'His head was always pushed forward a little and cocked slightly to one side,' one senior Nazi recalled, 'and he had the face and shifty eyes of a boxer advancing on his opponent. His fingers were short, thick and squarish and covered with black hair.'[85] Bormann also possessed a pugilist's quick mind, and was able to compress a wealth of complicated information into a form that Hitler could easily digest. Like those of the stock Machiavellian civil servant, Bormann's reports for his Führer would contain implicit solutions, which Hitler could then adopt while passing them off as his own. Bormann's power frustrated many other Nazis, but it seemed there was little they could do. 'The Führer has become so accustomed to Bormann that it's very difficult indeed to lessen his influence,' bemoaned Himmler. 'I hope I can succeed in out-manoeuvring him without having to get rid of him. He's been responsible for a lot of the Führer's misguided decisions.'[86]

But Bormann was more than just the 'Brown Eminence', the anonymous bureaucrat who played with the Nazi machine. Such an image belies the fact that he too had the blood of millions on his hands. On 9 October 1942, Bormann signed a decree insisting that 'the permanent elimination of the Jews from the territories of Greater Germany can no longer be carried out by emigration but by the use of ruthless force in the special camps of the East'.[87] He was equally brutal about the Slavs, whom he saw simply as a source of slave labour. 'In so far as we do not need them, they may die,' he wrote in a memorandum in August 1942. 'Slav fertility is not desirable.'[88] As Albert Speer was to observe, 'even among so many ruthless men, he stood out by his brutality and coarseness.' Furthermore, Speer added that 'he had no culture, which might have put some restraints on him.'[89]

Bormann might have lacked sophistication, but he made up for it with an abundance of financial savvy. It was Bormann who ensured that Hitler received a royalty every time his face was used on a postage stamp. Naturally, this earned millions of Reichsmarks. Bormann also established the 'Adolf Hitler Endowment Fund of German Industry' which 'encouraged' business leaders who had benefited from the economic boom to make 'voluntary' contributions to the Führer. Although other party leaders had had the same idea, Bormann passed a decree giving him the monopoly on such activity. In order to allay any complaints, a portion of the donations was given to senior figures such as Gauleiters and Reichsleiters, who appreciated Bormann's generosity, and further swelled the power of the Head of the Party Chancellery.[90]

Bormann would also draw heavily on his financial acumen as the tide of war turned against Germany. At the end of 1943, he is reputed to have established an organization called *Hacke* ('Pickaxe') which was so secret that even neither Hitler nor Himmler knew about it. The purpose of *Hacke* was to prepare for what Bormann saw as Germany's inevitable defeat, and to accumulate as much wealth as possible for a future Nazi resurgence. Bases of Nazi wealth were apparently established in Spain, Portugal, Argentina, Japan and Italy, and by 1944, *Hacke* was said to control some five hundred million dollars, much of which was gleaned from concentration-camp victims. According to Bormann's plan, knowledge of *Hacke* was restricted to just thirty-five senior Nazis, among them the head of the Gestapo, Heinrich Müller; Albert Förster, the Gauleiter of Danzig; and, quite possibly, Ernst Kaltenbrunner.[91] However, plans for *Hacke* were said to have backfired spectacularly, as the Russian intelligence service, the NKVD, got wind of the operation. In a sting led by General Viktor Abakumov, members of *Hacke* were blackmailed into working for the Soviets on the threat of being denounced to Himmler and Hitler.[92] The 'Brown Eminence' himself may have been one of them. Some senior Nazis, such as Walter Schellenberg, believed that Bormann might even have been a willing collaborator with Stalin. 'In 1945,' wrote Schellenberg, 'with a very clear idea of the general situation, as well as of the dangers of his own position, [Bormann] was one of those who made a determined attempt to move over into the eastern camp.'[93] Other Nazis in the intelligence field also believed that Bormann worked for the Soviets. At one point during the war, Major General Reinhard Gehlen and Admiral Wilhelm Canaris met to discuss the leak of sensitive information going via the Soviet 'Rote Kapelle' spy ring. The men agreed that the ultimate source had to be Bormann.[94] There was much similar speculation about Bormann's loyalties towards the end of the war, and numerous 'proofs' have since emerged testifying to Bormann's duplicity.[95] However, there is simply no known evidence supporting this, and neither is there much to support the existence of the clandestine Hacke, barring a report of unknown evaluation given to the CIA in the early 1960s whose authorship is still redacted.[96]

But Hacke or no Hacke, Bormann, like many Nazis, was certainly making preparations for the post-war period. On 10 August 1944, a group of German industrialists convened at the Hôtel Maison Rouge in Strasbourg[97] at Bormann's behest to discuss the future of German industry after a defeat. Although Bormann did not attend the meeting, senior figures from firms such as Krupp, Messerschmitt and Volkswagen were told by one of his representatives that the export of capital from Nazi Germany was now permitted, and that industrialists should 'export as much of their capital as possible, capital meaning money, bonds, patents, scientists, and administrators'.[98] In the vernacular, this meant get as much of your money out as you can, and get it out quick. The business leaders were also advised on a more sensitive issue. Bormann's representative told the gathering that 'after the defeat of Germany, the Nazi party recognizes that certain of its best known leaders will be condemned as war criminals. However, in cooperation with the industrialists, it is arranging to place its less conspicuous but most important members with various German factories as technical experts or members of its research and designing offices.'[99]

After the meeting, the industrialists did as they were advised, and set up hundreds of companies around the world: 58 in Portugal, 35 in Turkey, 98 in Argentina, 214 in Switzerland, 112 in Spain and 233 elsewhere.[100] However, such movements of capital did not go unnoticed. On 13 February 1945, Brigadier W. W. T. Torr, the British military attaché in Madrid, wrote to MI3, the British War Office military intelligence section that gathered information on Europe, the Baltics, Scandinavia and the USSR,[101] warning of 'German preparations for post-war activities in Spain':

> It has become increasingly obvious that the Germans, realising that defeat was inevitable, would do all they could to prepare some disguised organisation in Spain, so that whatever happened to their official representation and known commercial interests, as a result of the Allied peace terms, they would still have in being some secret means of fostering their interests, maintaining contacts and generally preparing for the day when they could once more come into the open as a commercial and military power. [. . .] Through one of my best sources, I have lately been able to discover some details of the two groups who are engaged on precisely the kind of work outlined above.[102]

By 17 April, the British calculated that 'the total of German assets recently transferred to Spain amounts to approximately 800,000,000 pesetas'.[103] It is not clear whether Martin Bormann was directly responsible for all this activity, but whatever he was up to, he was certainly not telling Himmler. After his capture, Arthur Scheidler told his interrogators that in late April, Kaltenbrunner had received a telegram from Himmler that read: 'You have been given missions by Bormann. What are they?'[104] The 'missions' in question may well have been connected with the fact that Bormann had dispatched one of his aides, Dr Helmuth von Hummel, to Salzburg with five million dollars' worth of old gold coins to finance a last-stand fight against the Allies.[105]

In the final days in Hitler's bunker the bigwigs were still playing politics but one figure had outwitted them all: Bormann. His position was dramatically revealed in a battle of wills with Hermann Göring. On the afternoon of 23 April, a telegram from Göring in

Berchtesgaden arrived. The *Reichsmarschall* enquired whether Hitler, as he was now trapped in his bunker, was effectively incapacitated as Führer. If this was the case, then Göring said that he would assume power by 10 p.m. under the edict of 29 June 1941 that named him as Hitler's successor.[106] Bormann presented the telegram to Hitler, telling him that Göring was mounting a coup, but Hitler seemed relatively unperturbed, and sent Göring a telegram to say that he was not to make any independent move.[107] A second telegram arrived from Göring at six o'clock, which was directed to Joachim von Ribbentrop, summoning him to Berchtesgaden as soon as the 10 p.m. deadline had passed. Bormann passed this message to Hitler too, insisting that this was proof of Göring's treachery. Hitler then began one of his all-too-frequent rages, which was witnessed by Albert Speer. 'Hitler was unusually excited about the contents of the telegram,' Speer recalled, 'and said quite plainly what he thought about Göring. He said that he had known for some time that Göring had failed, that he was corrupt, and that he was a drug addict.'[108]

Bormann now seized his moment to liquidate the man who stood between him and the highest office. He told Hitler that Göring should be shot, but Hitler disagreed. However, Hitler did agree that Göring should be removed from all his positions, and have his right of succession revoked. Bormann drafted the telegram, which Hitler authorized, and it was then sent. However, Bormann also dispatched another telegram, ordering the SS to arrest Göring and his advisers for high treason. 'You will answer for this with your lives,' the telegram stated. Just after midnight, the orders were carried out, and the following morning it was announced that Göring had resigned because of ill health. Once more, Bormann had proved himself to be the supreme manipulator.[109]

Nevertheless, the man was not a machine, and he too started to splinter under the pressure in the bunker. Like many, Bormann took refuge in alcohol, and often drowned his worries with Generals Krebs and Burgdorf on the bunker's upper floor.[110] He yearned for his wife Gerda and their nine children, who were staying hundreds of miles south in the Obersalzburg. A few weeks before, he had written what would be his last letter to Gerda, in which he urged her to 'keep well and strong and brave', and told her that she was 'the best mother I could possibly have wished for my children'. Perhaps mindful of such sentimentality, Bormann also adopted a defiantly Wagnerian tone. 'And if we are destined, like the old Nibelungs, to perish in King Attila's hall, then we'll go to death proudly and with our heads high!'[111]

But unlike Hitler, who poisoned and shot himself on 30 April, and Goebbels, who killed himself on the evening of 1 May, Bormann had no intention of dying. He had watched Hitler's body being engulfed in dirty petrolly flames and had even witnessed his will, but he wished for no such fate for himself. Even after Hitler's death, he continued to plot, and he was desperate to get to Plön in northern Germany in order to personally inform the new president of Germany, Grand Admiral Karl Dönitz, that Hitler had died. Travelling the 200 miles to Plön would be no easy task, but Bormann was determined that he had to be at the new centre of power. The *Führerbunker* was becoming a collection of frightened secretaries and drunken soon-to-be suicides. Bormann himself was well aware of the difficulties, as he had sent a telegram to his wife saying, 'Everything is lost. I will never get out of here. Take care of the children.'[112]

Bormann decided to leave the bunker on the night of 1 May. Although he was nominally in command of a ragtag party of escapees, there was little discipline among those gathered.[113] The plan was to separate into groups, and for each to make its way north along the underground railway to Friedrichstrasse Station. There, the escapees would surface and attempt to cross the river Spree at the Wiedendammer Bridge, sneak through the Russian lines, and head to freedom of sorts to the northwest. Dressed in the uniform of an SS general, Bormann left the bunker in the third group with Werner Naumann, the newly appointed head of what was left of the propaganda ministry, and Hans Baur, Hitler's pilot.[114] The scene in the dark U-Bahn looked apocalyptic, with dead and wounded lying about, surrounded by heaps of war junk such as ammunition cases, uniforms and gas masks. It was a grim, stinking chaos, and it was a chaos for which Bormann, as one of the leaders of a violent and gangsterish regime, was partly responsible.

In the confusion underground, the groups became separated. The escapees made their way through the dark mostly as individuals, and by the time they emerged into the ruins above the Friedrichstrasse Station, they were exposed to the risk of gunfire and Russian shells.

Bormann dashed the few hundred feet north along the Friedrichstrasse to the Wiedendammer Bridge, where he found an anti-tank barrier blocking his way. He retreated to the Admiral's Palace near the south of the bridge, where a new group soon assembled, consisting of himself, Naumann, Hitler's personal physician Ludwig Stumpfegger, the Hitler Youth leader Artur Axmann, Hitler's driver Erich Kempka, and a few others.[115] It was now around three in the morning of 2 May, and the group was pinned down. However, salvation soon appeared in the form of half a dozen tanks and some armoured cars, which were ordered to break through the barrier and thereby enable the Nazis to flee. Naumann perched on the top of one of the tanks, with Bormann and Stumpfegger immediately behind him.[116] The tank managed to get past the barrier and reached the junction with Ziegelstrasse north of the bridge, but there Bormann's luck started to run out. A round from a *Panzerfaust* hit the tank, blowing it apart. 'I saw a short flash of lightning,' recalled Erich Kempka, 'and flew to the ground where I remained lying unconsciously. My last impression was that Dr Naumann, Bormann and Dr Stumpfegger fell together and remained lying.'[117]

Miraculously, the three men appeared to have escaped serious injury, and when they came to, they retreated back to the north bank of the Spree. From there, they and a few others hurried northwest along the overground railway line to the Lehrter Station, a distance of some three-quarters of a mile. Here, Stumpfegger and Bormann decided to leave the group and went east along the Invalidenstrasse. The rest of the group decided to head west, and many managed to escape. However, Artur Axmann ran into a Russian patrol, and he turned round to follow Bormann and Stumpfegger. Within a few minutes, Axmann caught up with the two men, but they were no longer alive. Their bodies lay face up in the moonlight behind a railway bridge, and, according to Axmann, with no visible signs of injury. Because of the Russian artillery, the one-armed Axmann had no time to examine the bodies, but he assumed that they had been shot in the back.[118]

Axmann was to spend the next seven months in hiding as 'Eric Siewert' before his capture in December. It is unlikely that during that time he would have had access to the *New York Times*, but had he opened the copy dated two days after his escape, he would have been surprised to see that the man he had seen lying dead was probably now in Prague.[119] Just over a month later, on 11 June, Axmann may have heard of a report broadcast on Prague radio that announced that Bormann had now been captured and was to be tried.[120] He would have believed neither that, nor a similar announcement made on Soviet-controlled Berlin radio that same evening.[121] He also would have raised an eyebrow at the claim made by the anti-Nazi journalist Heinrich Lienau, who said that he had shared a compartment with Bormann on a slow train from Lüneburg to Flensburg early that same month.[122] On 2 August, American war crimes investigators announced that they had evidence that Bormann was in fact alive, and might be in the hands of the Russians.[123] The British suspected the same, and Bormann's name appeared on a list drafted by a Foreign Office official of war criminals who were possibly being held by the Soviets.[124] At the end of August, the Russians accused the British and Americans of holding Bormann, which the British vigorously denied.[125] In early September, it was rumoured that Bormann had in fact escaped in May on a 90-foot 'mahogany luxury yacht' from Glückstadt near Hamburg with no less a shipmate than Hitler.[126] By the time Axmann was captured, there had been several more sightings of Bormann, culminating – at least for that year – on New Year's Eve, when the Czechs declared that Bormann had been arrested by the British. The British responded by saying that they had arrested a Neumünster farmer called Marius who looked like Bormann, and that was probably where the confusion lay.[127] However, the unfortunate Marius was not Bormann, but like the man on the slow train to Flensburg, he would be one of many 'Martin Bormanns' who would be spotted all over the world for the next five decades.

Bormann would not be the only senior Nazi whose whereabouts became the subject of continual speculation. One of the most significant would be SS-Gruppenführer Heinrich Müller, the chief of the Gestapo since 1939. Last seen in Hitler's bunker on 1 May, the 44-year-old was, like Bormann, suspected by Nazis such as Schellenberg of having shifted his loyalties. In his memoirs, Schellenberg recounted how he and Müller once shared a late drink

after a conference in the spring of 1943, in which Müller openly
expressed his admiration for the Soviets. 'National Socialism is
nothing more than a sort of dung on this spiritual desert,' Müller
told him. 'In contrast to this, one sees in Russia a unified and really
uncompromising spiritual and biological force is developing.'[128]
Such talk Schellenberg found surprising, as Müller had been
vigorous in his fight against the Soviets, and had managed to turn
many members of the *Rote Kapelle* into sending disinformation
back to their Soviet masters.[129] But Schellenberg, by his own
admission, stood 'on a footing of open enmity' with Müller,[130] and
it is not inconceivable that Schellenberg saw his memoirs as an
opportunity to besmirch his former rival. Other Nazis, such as
Kaltenbrunner and Müller's subordinate Heinz Pannwitz, regarded
the notion that Müller was a Soviet agent as 'absolutely absurd'.[131]

Wherever Müller's loyalties lay, it is likely that he took them to
his grave in May 1945. However, it is unclear how he died, as the
three witnesses who saw his corpse saw it in three different places.
One of them was Fritz Leopold, a Berlin mortuary official, who
declared that the Gestapo chief's body was found in the RSHA headquarters and moved to a cemetery in the western sector of Berlin.
This was deemed the official version, and Müller's family placed a
headstone at this site. The second version was related by Müller's
subordinate Heinz Pannwitz, who had been captured by the
Russians. During his interrogations he was informed, 'Your chief is
dead.' Müller's body, the Soviets claimed, had been found in a sub-
way near the Reich Chancellery with a bullet through its head. The
third version was told by Walter Lüders, who had been part of a
burial party in the summer of 1945. Lüders claimed that the team
had found a body dressed in the uniform of an *SS-Gruppenführer* in
the garden of the Chancellery. The corpse had a wound in the back,
and in the uniform Lüders had found Müller's identity papers. The
body was then buried in a mass grave in the old Jewish cemetery in
the Soviet sector of Berlin.[132] Of these three accounts, the most
plausible is that of Lüders. Several witnesses said that Müller had
decided to stay at the Chancellery, and was adamant that he would not
try to escape with one of Bormann's teams. 'We know the Russian
methods exactly,' Müller told Hitler's pilot Hans Baur. 'I haven't the
faintest intention of . . . being taken prisoner by the Russians.'

Another claimed that Müller told him, 'the regime has fallen and . . . I fall also.'[133] For an 'inconspicuous little man',[134] Müller was to be spotted a remarkable number of times over the coming decades. He would be a man of many parts – a tourist guide in Brazil, the owner of a hardware shop in the same country, a Panamanian, a Soviet agent, a Czech agent and even an Albanian police official.[135]

Even if Müller did not change sides, there were plenty of Gestapo officers who did. The most notorious was a man who sent the following telegram at eight ten in the evening of 6 April 1944 from Lyon to the Paris branch of Department IVB of the RSHA – the Office of Jewish Affairs.

Lyon No. 5,269 4/6/44 8:10pm – FI
To the BdS – Dept IV B – Paris
Re: Jewish children's home in Izieu, Ain
Previous: None
This morning the Jewish children's home 'Colonie Enfant' in Izieu, Ain, was cleaned out. In total 41 children aged 3 to 13 were apprehended. In addition the arrest of the entire Jewish staff, 10 strong, including 5 women, was carried out. Neither cash nor other valuables could be secured. Transport to Drancy to follow on 4/7/44.
The commanding officer of the Sipo-SD Lyon
Dept IVB 61/43[136]

That night, the children – there were in fact forty-four of them – were incarcerated in Fort Montluc in Lyon, where they were interrogated. The following day, which was Good Friday, they were dispatched in manacles on a regular passenger train to go to Drancy transit camp near Paris. There, they joined several hundred other French Jews, all of whom were nervously anticipating where they would be sent next. Most of the children did not have to wait long, because one week later thirty-four of them were put on a train heading east. On the evening of 15 April, it arrived at its destination: Auschwitz. All were gassed that night. The remaining ten children followed on later convoys. They too were all gassed.[137]

The man who signed the telegram was SS-Obersturmführer (First Lieutenant) Klaus Barbie, who since 11 November 1942 had been a Gestapo officer in Lyon.[138] During his time in France's third-largest city, Barbie earned a reputation for extreme brutality in his fight against the Resistance. One of his victims was Maurice Bondet, who had been arrested in July 1943. 'He beat me without hesitation,' Bondet recalled, 'and encouraged others to do the same. When I was unconscious, he pushed me into the freezing bath, then the cosh again, and [had] acid injected into my bladder. He really enjoyed other people's sufferings . . .'[139] Another Resistance member, Mario Blandon, was also tortured by Barbie. 'The worst he did to me was pushing three-inch needles through my rib cage into my lungs,' said Blandon. 'I often collapsed and he threw me into the corridor to recover. I feigned unconsciousness and saw him inflict even worse tortures on others.'[140] Blandon saw women stripped and beaten, one of whom was clutching her three-year-old child. Another was 'forced to submit' to Barbie's sheepdog. Blandon saw Barbie kill as well, and recalled how the Gestapo officer laughed when he once shot a prisoner in the back of the head, causing the man's head to split apart and his body to flip down the stairs 'like a rabbit'.

Barbie was not averse to torturing children. Simone Lagrange was thirteen when she and her parents were arrested on 6 June 1944 for the 'crime' of being Jewish. Betrayed by their concierge's daughter-in-law, the Lagrange family was questioned by Barbie, who was stroking a cat. 'I innocently assumed he couldn't be cruel,' Simone thought. 'He had a rather . . . friendly smile. He stopped and looked my father up and down. He looked at my mother and said she was pretty. Then he turned to my mother and said, "Your little girl is pretty! Is she your only child?" My mother said, "No, I have two younger ones."' Barbie then asked where they were, but Madame Lagrange genuinely did not know, as they had been evacuated to the countryside because Lyon was being regularly bombed. Naturally, Barbie did not believe her, and he once more turned his attention to the young Simone. She too denied knowing the whereabouts of her siblings. 'He instantly dropped his "nice cop" routine,' Simone remembered. 'He put the cat down, came back to me, ripped off my hairnet, wound my hair around his hand and pulled hard. My father started. The SS guard put a pistol to his stomach which forced my father back.' Barbie kept repeating his question, and each time Simone did not reply, he would knock her down and then pull her up by the hair. 'I can't recall if I screamed,' said Simone, 'I only remember the force of the blows. I remember this rather calm man suddenly starting to scream for no reason. I was afraid.'[141]

Simone had good reason to be. Barbie sent the family to Auschwitz, where Simone's mother was gassed. She and her father survived the camp, and towards the end of the war, Simone found herself in a forced march of prisoners heading away from the Russian advance. At one point she spotted her father, whom she had not seen for a year, and asked a guard if they could meet. The guard agreed, but just before the two managed to embrace, the guard forced Monsieur Lagrange to kneel, and then shot him in the head. 'It was not Barbie who put bullets in our heads,' Simone said, 'but it was he who sent us into that hell.'[142]

Barbie would also organize mass killings. On the morning of 20 August 1944, 120 prisoners were assembled in the courtyard of Fort Montluc. They were then tied, and bundled into two buses that drove them 6 miles south to a disused building overlooking the town of Saint-Genis-Laval. The prisoners were taken to the first floor of the building, where they were each shot in the neck. A French collaborator called Max Payot witnessed the massacre. 'At this point the prisoners were forced to climb on top of the heap formed by the mass of bodies of their companions,' he remembered. 'Blood ran in torrents through the ceiling and I could distinctly hear the victims falling as they were executed.'[143] As the heap grew higher, the executioners would have to climb up it to finish off those they had inexpertly shot. After they had finished, the Germans set light to the corpses. While the flames burned, the executioners found a woman who had been accidentally spared. 'She stood up at the window and beseeched mercy,' said Payot. 'They responded with a hail of bullets in her direction . . . her face set in a horrible vision. The temperature rising, her face melted like wax.' After the killings, the Gestapo toasted their success with champagne, before dynamiting the building. The explosion littered gardens in Saint-Genis-Laval with human bones.[144] When the Resistance heard of the massacre, they shot some eighty German soldiers they were holding.[145]

Barbie's biggest coup against the Resistance was his arrest of Jean Moulin, one of the most senior members of the *Armée Secrète*. A former prefect of the Eure-et-Loir *département*, Moulin had been removed from his post by the Vichy government for refusing to dismiss left-wing town mayors. In 1941, he joined the Resistance, and soon became one of its leading figures, with orders from General de Gaulle to unify its discrete groups such as *Combat*, *Libération* and *Franc-Tireur*.[116] On 21 June 1943, Moulin convened a meeting of nine Resistance leaders to discuss the recent arrest in Paris of General Charles Delestraint, the leader of the *Armée Secrète*. The group met on the second floor of the house of Dr Frédéric Dugoujon in the centre of Caluire, a northern suburb of Lyon. The meeting was scheduled to start at 2.00 p.m., although Moulin did not arrive until 2.45 p.m. As Dugoujon's receptionist assumed he was a patient, she asked Moulin to sit in the waiting-room on the ground floor. A few minutes later, one of the Resistance men upstairs, Henri Aubry, spotted something disturbing through the window. 'Suddenly, the garden gate squeaked on its hinges,' Aubry recalled, 'and I saw a lot of leather-jacketed men swarm through it. I just had time to stand up and say, "We're cooked . . . the bastards . . . the Gestapo!" '[147] Within seconds, the Germans burst into the room, led by Barbie carrying a machine-pistol. 'He leapt at me,' Aubry said. 'In a few seconds, I had been slapped, my head banged against the wall, and my wrists handcuffed behind my back.'[148]

The group were shoved downstairs to find that Moulin was also being held. However, Moulin protested his innocence, and said that he was merely a patient called 'Jean Martel'. Nevertheless, Barbie took him along with the others to be interrogated at the École de Santé, where Moulin received the full force of Barbie's almost quotidian violence. One prisoner was shocked at the condition in which Moulin soon found himself. 'He had lost consciousness,' said Christian Pineau, 'his eyes were hollowed as if they were buried in his head. He had an ugly bluish wound on his temple. A low moan escaped from his swollen lips.'[149] Dr Dugoujon remembered seeing Moulin being dragged by two guards as he was unable to walk.[150] However, Moulin managed to maintain his spirit, and at one point, after he was asked by Barbie to draw a diagram of the Resistance networks, Moulin instead drew a grotesque caricature of his torturer.[151] Nevertheless, Moulin or one of his comrades cracked, and when Barbie established the size of fish he was holding, he took his catch to Paris.[152] There, Barbie presented an almost comatose Moulin to Karl Bömelburg, the head of the Gestapo in France, who was far from pleased at the state of the prisoner, who was incapable of speaking, let alone divulging any information. 'I hope he will pull through,' Bömelburg told his subordinate. Moulin survived for another fourteen days, after which he was put on a stretcher on a train to Germany. However, on 8 July, somewhere around Metz, the 44-year-old Moulin perished. It is still unclear whether he committed suicide or died from his wounds, but Barbie is felt by many in France to be ultimately responsible for the death of a hero whose ashes are now interred at the Panthéon.

Barbie left Lyon towards the end of August 1944 as the American forces advanced on the city. He headed north towards Dijon, but he returned to Lyon a few days later in order 'to clean up the mess' he had left behind – by which he meant those such as collaborators who might be able to testify to his crimes. Twenty or so were killed, some of whom Barbie dispatched personally. During his brief murderous return, Barbie was shot in the foot, although he managed to limp out of the city before the Americans arrived on 3 September.[153] The following month, Barbie was recommended for promotion to *Hauptsturmführer* (captain) for his 'pursuit of crime and his consistent work in defeating Resistance organisations'.[154] He received his promotion while he was recuperating in hospital, from which he was to emerge in February 1945.

Canny enough to realize that Germany had lost the war, Barbie was in no mood for a fight. He made his way to Berlin, where he was ordered to join the SD at Düsseldorf. When he reached Düsseldorf, he found that the SD had moved to Essen, and when he arrived in Essen, he discovered that the SD there had been wound up. On 1 April, Barbie attached himself to a regular army unit, but he and the troops soon realized that their position in Wuppertal was hopeless. Barbie, who was never the type of SS man to fight to the last drop of blood, especially his own, decided that self-protection was his best policy. 'So I buried my gun,' Barbie recalled. 'The four youngsters I was with and myself changed our clothes, got some false papers from the police headquarters, and headed off through the forests and pastures towards the Sauerland. It was very hard. From one day to the next, I'd become a beggar.'[155] Riding on a stolen bicycle, Barbie initially managed to escape the attention of the Americans, but his luck soon left him. Around the time of the

German surrender on 8 May, Barbie was arrested near
Hohenlimburg a few miles south of Dortmund. Arrested not for any
crime, but simply because he was of military age, Barbie now faced
being on the receiving end of an interrogation. His experience in the
Gestapo had taught him well, and he managed to secure his release
by convincing his questioner – a former concentration-camp inmate
– that he was an ordinary soldier on his way home, because, like
Eichmann, Mengele, Stangl, Bormann and so many other Nazi
criminals, Barbie was a family man.[156] He had married Regine
Willms on 25 April 1940, five days after he had been made an SS
officer, and the couple had had a daughter, Ute, at the end of the
following June.

Just as with his fellow criminals, the war had unleashed in Barbie
an uncompromising sadism that might have stayed hidden had there
not been a Gestapo to join and a Resistance to combat. Josef
Mengele might have risen to the level of a chair at a quiet university
and been remembered for some mildly groundbreaking, but ultimately flawed, genetic research. Franz Stangl might have continued
his career in the Austrian police force, and would probably have
done quite well, although he would never have made the top. Adolf
Eichmann might have made a reasonable salesman or a diligent
office administrator. As for Barbie, it was said that he might have
become a priest.[157] Had he been devoted to God as intensely as he
was to Nazism, he would have made a good one, as he also had
charm and leadership qualities. As the Resistance leader Raymond
Aubrac once said of his torturer, 'he looked like an ordinary man'.[158]
The one thing that unites all these 'ordinary men' is that they were able
to undergo a process that has been termed 'doubling', in which the
personality moulds itself into an evil environment, and allows evil and
perpetrating evil to become part of the self.[159] Others might state that
these men were merely moral cowards, but the extent of their brutality
suggests a greater flaw than cowardice. Whatever the reason, such discussions were not in abundance in May 1945. Psychoanalysis could
wait until after the men had been captured, but before then, there was
the small matter of hunting them down. As we shall see, what
happened to Barbie, Mengele, Stangl and Eichmann after the war was
just as startling as what took place during it.

Chapter Two

'To the uttermost ends of the earth'

THE QUESTION of how to deal with war criminals had been discussed even when the war was at its height. At the end of October 1943, the same month in which the British and the Americans doggedly fought their way up through southern Italy and the Russians were slowly advancing through central Ukraine, the foreign ministers of the United States, Great Britain and the Soviet Union signed the Moscow Declaration. The full text was published at the beginning of November, and anybody longing for the day when the Nazis were brought to justice would have been cheered by its contents. The Allies promised to 'pursue them [the criminals] to the uttermost ends of the earth and will deliver them to the accusers in order that justice may be done'.[1] Although the words were fine, the declaration contained little that was practical, and merely seemed to establish a moral high ground from which the Allies could continue to wage the war.[2] There was no mention of – or indeed agreement about – how the criminals would be pursued, nor how exactly they would be tried. This lack of concord was revealed at a dinner near the end of November at the Tehran Conference, during which Stalin half jokingly stated that at least fifty thousand of the

German commanding staff should be 'physically liquidated'. Roosevelt humoured Stalin by appearing to agree, and said in jest that the figure should be around 49,000. Churchill was incensed at this exchange, and took exception to the 'cold blooded execution of soldiers who fought for their country'. He added that the criminals should stand trial at the places where the crimes took place, and that executions for political purposes were objectionable. While he thundered, Stalin further enraged the British Prime Minister by saying that Churchill must have had a secret liking for the Germans.[3]

Churchill's desire to hold trials was not without its detractors. One was his own Foreign Secretary, Sir Anthony Eden, who had been reluctant to sign the Moscow Declaration. 'I am far from happy about all this war crimes business,' he wrote to his officials three weeks before the signing. '[. . .] Broadly I am anxious not to get into the position of breathing fire and slaughter against war criminals and promising condign punishment and a year or two hence have to find pretexts for doing nothing.'[4] Eden's reluctance may have been born from the poor administration of justice after the First World War, after which the Germans refused to hand over some nine hundred criminals wanted by the Allies. The victorious powers could do little but reach a farcical compromise in which German courts were allowed to bring cases against German war criminals. The cases were heard in Leipzig from 1921 to 1922, and, unsurprisingly, just a handful were convicted. To add further mockery to the Allies, most managed to 'escape' from prison within a few months.[5]

Nevertheless, there were some who were determined to establish a system by which the Nazis could be brought to justice. Among them was Viscount Simon, the British Lord Chancellor, who in August 1942 proposed a 'United Nations Commission on War Crimes' that would seek to work out the legal processes by which they might be brought to justice. The name of course had nothing to do with the United Nations itself, as that body would not come into existence until October 1945, but instead referred to the 'United Nations' coined by Roosevelt in his 'Declaration of the United Nations' in January 1942, in which the representatives of twenty-six nations pledged to continue their fight against the Axis.[6] Viscount Simon was keen for the Commission to have teeth, and to investigate and to name the wanted men. 'We can all discuss these fine points about the right Court until the crack of doom,' he told the House of Lords, 'but, unless the criminal tribunal has got those two conditions satisfied, it cannot exercise its powers.'[7] The American response to the proposed body was lukewarm, and the State Department took several weeks to reply to Simon. Although the Americans agreed to establish what would now be called the 'United Nations War Crimes Commission' (UNWCC), Roosevelt amended the text of the announcement to indicate that only the '*ringleaders* responsible for the organised murder of thousands' would be punished. Simon's version had included the perpetrators, but Roosevelt was seemingly fearful of the practicalities of searching for tens of thousands of criminals.[8]

If the Americans were lukewarm about the UNWCC, then the Soviets were positively hostile. The Russian attitude was not helped by the fact that its embassy in London only received news of the establishment of the Commission four days before the official announcement was made on 7 October 1942. This caused an irate denunciation in *Pravda*, which accused the British of seeking to make peace with Germany, and for already harbouring Nazi 'gangsters', by whom they meant Rudolf Hess.[9] For the next twelve months, the British lobbied hard to ensure the Russians joined the UNWCC, but as soon as it looked as if Stalin might relent, he would deliberately find another block over which negotiations would stumble. Stalin did not like the inclusion of the British Dominions; Stalin wanted the Baltic States to be included; Stalin wanted the incarcerated Rudolf Hess tried immediately – and so on. By the time the UNWCC had held its first meeting on 19 October 1943 – one year after it had been announced – the Soviets informed the Commission that it was quite satisfied with its own machinery, which was 'already functioning for collecting evidence of war crimes in the Soviet Union against Soviet citizens'.[10] The Russians were never to join the UNWCC, which left it severely weakened.

One of the other principal faults of the Commission was that it too quickly became a talking-shop for lawyers and bureaucrats. Reading the minutes of the UNWCC is a stultifying experience; the lack of dynamism is all too evident, perhaps because the best minds were engaged on more pressing matters. This particular issue was diplomatically expressed in a report sent from the US embassy in London to Washington. 'The Foreign Office believes that while the question of war crimes is hardly one directly connected with the prosecution of war,' wrote Freeman Matthews on 4 March 1943, 'those whose time and thought would be devoted to its study are probably precisely those who are not fully occupied with the war effort.'[11] Sub-committees were established, and interminable discussions about legal and bureaucratic processes ensued. Frustrations with the red tape were expressed in meetings, especially by the Czech representative, Colonel Dr Bohuslav Ecer, for whom the issue of war crimes was not some piece of nebulous legalese but a life-and-death matter affecting his fellow countrymen on a daily basis. During the ninth meeting of the UNWCC on 15 February 1944, Ecer urged the Commission 'to prevent the repetition of the great mistake of 1919' in which the Allies had failed to 'establish their own judicial and executive machinery in order to arrest and try the criminals'.[12] Ecer's plain speaking did not win him many friends, and he was described by an American member of the UNWCC as 'wild, unbalanced and indiscreet'.[13] Ecer was not the only member who found progress slow. At the UNWCC's thirteenth meeting on 21 March 1944, the French representative pulled no punches. 'After five months of existence, barely sixty cases have been transmitted,' declared Professor André Gros, 'most of which were incomplete and were placed in Class C [the least severe category of crime]. This number is horribly out of proportion with the real facts of German atrocities in Europe [. . .] When at the time of the armistice the Governments call for our list, our failure will be manifest.'[14] Professor Gros's words would prove to be prophetic. In the words of Eric Colban, the Norwegian representative, the UNWCC became 'a kind of legal faculty', which deviated from the very urgent and practical work that was required.[15]

Worse still, the Commission's mandate meant that it could not concern itself with the biggest crime of all: the Holocaust. In July 1944, British representatives of the World Jewish Congress (WJC) approached Sir Cecil Hurst, the UNWCC's chairman, asking the Commission to undertake a 'comprehensive investigation of and report on the war crimes perpetrated by Germany, her allies and satellites upon the Jewish community in Europe'. Although the WJC acknowledged that evidence submitted by individual governments would be enough to bring the perpetrators to justice, it maintained that only a thorough report by a body such as the UNWCC would be able to reveal the 'full knowledge . . . of the enormity of these crimes', the size of which was certainly not appreciated at the time. The members of the Commission were cool to the idea, as such a report was felt to be a 'big affair and would probably be expensive'. Instead, there was some talk 'of considering the matter further', adopting a 'resolution', and 'having the proposal referred to a committee for consideration' – all prima facie examples of bureaucratic fudge. Finally, it was agreed that Hurst should have another meeting with the WJC.[16] Hurst reported back on 8 August, informing the Commission that he had told the WJC that the 'help that the Commission could give them was limited to what could be done within the scope of its primary function, which was the investigation of individual cases of war crimes, and did not embrace crimes against the Jews committed on Axis territory'. He advised the WJC to hand over any evidence to the individual national offices of the UNWCC, who could then use the material as they saw fit. The WJC's Alexander Easterman advised Hurst that the WJC had collected a 'considerable quantity of material' that would only be useful to the UNWCC as a whole, but Hurst gave no promise that the UNWCC could use this material, 'but there might be ways in which it would be possible and desirable'.[17] In essence, the WJC went back empty-handed, and the UNWCC would never fully investigate the Holocaust as a crime in itself.

The Commission's failures began to be noticed by the press, much to the annoyance of Hurst, who had constantly complained of leaks coming from the Commission. This, he said, was 'leading people to suppose that the Commission is an incompetent body, incapable of agreeing anything, and that its members are becoming more and more dissatisfied'. But they were dissatisfied.[18] On 22 August 1944, the Dutch representative, Dr J. M. de Moor, urged the Commission to 'prepare dossiers against Hitler and other arch-criminals, since the National Offices were apparently not prepared to do so'. Hurst agreed, and set 10 November as a date by which the first definitive list of criminals should be published.[19] At last, it seemed as though something was being done, but the UNWCC would earn worldwide opprobrium on 30 August when, just five days after the liberation of Paris, Hurst chaired the Commission's first press conference. Hurst was asked whether Hitler appeared on the UNWCC roster. This completely floored Hurst, who no doubt wished that he had set a somewhat tighter deadline for his 'definitive list'. After much pre-varication, he eventually admitted that Hitler was not on the list. It got worse. The chairman was then asked the extent of the list, and Hurst acknowledged that it was 'not a very long one', and that in fact it was 'meagre'. The following day, the UNWCC was mocked in the press, although had the reporters known that the putative list was just 184 names long, fourteen of whom were responsible for the 'war crime' of destroying a statue, then the pillorying would have been greater still.[20]

Nevertheless, the disastrous press conference spurred the UNWCC into action of sorts. Further rattled by reports in September that censured the Commission for not investigating crimes against the Jews, one of the members suggested that the crimes should be considered as war crimes, and therefore could fall within the remit of the UNWCC.[21] A decision was finally taken on 7 November, and Professor D. W. Brogan agreed to compile a report on the crimes[22] – until he fell ill in January and had to abandon the report on the advice of his doctor.[23] However, there was some success with the list itself, and on 22 November, Committee I of the UNWCC presented the list to the Commission,[24] which published it the following month.[25] But the publication had little impact, and the press maintained its hostility to what it saw as a toothless and clawless creature of bureaucracy. Ecer argued that the cause of the press 'misrepresentation' was the 'exaggerated secrecy maintained by the Commission about its work', which was partly true.[26] At the UNWCC's thirty-seventh meeting in October, much discussion was spent on whether the Commission should allow the *Picture Post* magazine permission to photograph the committee room. 'It was agreed that the Chairman should inform the Lord Chancellor that it was hoped that the request would not be granted,' read the minutes.[27] Had the relatives of the 1,689 Jews gassed the day before at Birkenau been able to witness this meeting,[28] they surely would have believed that the UNWCC was little more than the very blackest of jokes.

It was hardly surprising that officials in Whitehall and Washington also regarded the Commission as little more than a joke. The Foreign Office wished for it to be closed down, with one mandarin noting that it was a 'great bore and probably a great mistake'.[29] By the beginning of 1945, the UNWCC was effectively marginalized, and became an embarrassing weekly reminder of the ineffectiveness of Allied war crimes policy. Its members continued to talk, but much of the talk was about procedure, or, worse still, about subjects that it should have been examining nearly two years before. On 7 February 1945, the Commission discussed the problem of suspected war criminals disguising themselves, and measures to deal with it. Typically, there was no resolution. 'It was decided that the whole subject should stand over till the following Wednesday,' the minutes recorded, 'and a drafting committee was appointed.'[30]

Ironically, that same day, the very question of war criminals' disguises was raised in the chamber of the House of Lords by Lord Vansittart, the government's Chief Diplomatic Adviser and former Permanent Under-Secretary at the Foreign Office. Vansittart startled the House when he declared, 'I personally have the names of certain, as I think, very sinister Germans who have been getting out lately with false passports, and I happen to know not only the names on those passports, but the identity of the creatures that they conceal.' Vansittart also said that he knew the names 'of a good few of the worst of the Gestapo butchers and torturers in Norway', and he warned the House that unless action was taken soon, 'they will be slipping across the border into Sweden and will be lost to us'.[31] Vansittart's words rankled with those who had promised to deal with the war criminals. Two days later, Viscount Simon, the Lord Chancellor, wrote to the Foreign Office demanding that it was Vansittart's duty to share his information. Simon was irked by his old friend's statement, and observed that Vansittart 'makes speeches . . . which are . . . attracting much attention, and naturally his zeal in tracking down the guilty tends to be contrasted with the supposed indifference of the Government machine'.[32] But at least 'Van' was showing zeal. He responded to the Foreign Office on 17 February and listed several names of those who had 'cover against the rainy day that is now upon them'. The names of the Gestapo agents he gave were Fehlis, Fehmer, Hoehler, Bernhard and Lipicki. In

addition, he listed two German army officers – Major General
Hans Steudmann and Colonel Walther Osterkamp – both of whom
he claimed had escaped to Argentina under false names. Vansittart's
letter was passed to Simon, complete with a withering observation
made by Richard Law, the Minister of State: 'I must say this information strikes us as rather thin basis for the allegations Vansittart
made in his speech.'[33]

By the following month, the information regarding Steudmann
and Osterkamp was found to be untrue, but not all of it was
incorrect.[34] 'Fehlis', for example, was none other than SS-
Oberführer (Senior Colonel) Heinrich Fehlis, the head of the
Gestapo in Norway. Within two months of Vansittart's speech,
Fehlis had indeed adopted a new identity – that of a German Alpine
Corps lieutenant called 'Gerstheuer' – and with seventy men he bar-
ricaded himself inside a military base near Porsgrunn, about 100
miles south of Oslo. He refused to surrender, and on 11 May, just
three days after the end of the war in Europe, he unbeknowingly
mimicked Hitler by taking poison and then shooting himself.[35]

Vansittart was not unique in warning of the likelihood of war
criminals slipping across borders. In August 1944, just one month
after D-Day, Colonel H. G. Sheen of the intelligence staff of the
Supreme Headquarters of the Allied Expeditionary Force (SHAEF)
warned his superiors that wanted Nazis were likely to escape by air
to countries such as Switzerland, Sweden, Spain, Portugal, Turkey,
and Argentina. Sheen recommended that air patrols should be
mounted to thwart such attempts, which 'should . . . where possible
be in operation before the surrender of Germany'.[36] Sheen also
suggested that naval patrols should be made of the Baltic Sea, as it
was 'most likely' that escapers would attempt to travel by small boat
over to Sweden.[37] Sheen was advised that 'full consideration' would
be given to his suggestions, but he was informed that it would be
impossible to patrol the Baltic until after any surrender.[38] Sheen
found himself reiterating his points the following March, when he
insisted that Germany needed to be 'contained' in order to thwart
any escape attempts.[39] Unfortunately, although attempts were made
to closely control air travel, those responsible for implementing it
were often found to be wanting. From 1 January 1945 to 18 March
of the same year, thirty-five cases of 'irregular and unauthorized

travel between Northwest Europe and the United Kingdom alone' were detected, many of which were the result of the 'laxity' of ground staff and air crews. Although there was no suggestion that Nazis had escaped to the United Kingdom on Allied aircraft, this somewhat shoddy approach to security suggested that a slack approach to security was endemic.[40]

Although Vansittart was coy about his sources, there was one body being established that could have supplied both Vansittart and the Foreign Office with many thousands of names. Formally opened in Paris in March 1945, the Central Registry of War Criminals and Security Suspects (CROWCASS) had been conceived by the Americans the previous autumn, although it was run by a British lieutenant colonel called William Palfrey. Intended to be the largest database of criminals ever assembled, CROWCASS adopted a punched-card index based on the Hollerith system, which was supposed to streamline the process by which information could be sorted and accessed. The raw material would consist of 'located reports' sent in by all countries, as well as detention reports and POW reports sent in by the camps. From these, CROWCASS would produce located lists and detained lists, and would be able to respond to queries about individuals. Colonel Palfrey was given a team of four hundred French women to operate the system. In theory, all looked good.[41]

But as ever with such immense and technically ground-breaking projects, CROWCASS stumbled over its own ambition. Its implementation would have been difficult enough in peacetime, but in the spring of 1945, war was still raging. The problems were myriad. It didn't help that it took Palfrey three months to obtain three floors of an American-requisitioned building on the rue des Mathurins in the 8th district of Paris.[42] Palfrey's temper would hardly have been improved by the knowledge that the building had lain empty since 8 November the previous year.[43] The colonel's next headache was that of the Hollerith machines, which required twenty thousand dollars' worth of special electric cabling which took a long time to install.[44] By the time they were set up, they had to be coaxed to work, and they frequently broke down.[45] Then there was the problem of securing the vast quantities of paper required to issue the CROWCASS lists, without which the Registry might as well have packed up. And, even if there had been enough paper and the machines had worked, it wasn't until the end of the summer that the detention reports started arriving. The camps which provided them were slow to get established, and they suffered from a severe shortage of photographic equipment to produce the mugshots.[46] On top of these issues, which were problematic enough, CROWCASS was constantly under threat from the French, who wished to requisition the upper two floors occupied by the Registry.[47] Had they succeeded, then CROWCASS would have ceased altogether, as the three floors it had were hopelessly overcrowded, and when the machines were running, some of the staff had to stand outside.[48]

Nevertheless, CROWCASS did manage to produce its first list in May, which was a combination of names gleaned from the UNWCC and the Supreme Headquarters of the Allied Expeditionary Force (SHAEF), which had drawn up its own blacklist. By the time it appeared, the list was already out of date, and was regarded as 'misleading and unreliable'. Palfrey attempted to get a second list out in June, but he was thwarted by the lack of a suitable printer in Paris. The list had to be sent to London, and it was not promised to be back until September. When it did arrive, Palfrey regarded it as useless.[49] Predictably, much of the information on its hundred thousand names was simply incorrect. The list also took weeks to distribute all over the occupied zones, and by the time it reached the various detention and POW camps, its irrelevance had increased. Furthermore, when it arrived, few would have known exactly what CROWCASS was. Even the active Dr Ecer of the UNWCC had never heard of CROWCASS.[50]

At the cost of some thirty thousand dollars per month, the Allies were getting neither value for money nor their hands on many war criminals.[51] By October 1945, CROWCASS needed to process thirty thousand cards every day, but in fact it was managing only five thousand to seven thousand.[52] As K. E. Savill of the British War Office wrote to Brigadier Richard Wilberforce the following May, CROWCASS took 'a long time to produce rather meagre results at a comparatively high cost'. The information that emerged from CROWCASS was a 'trickle', and Savill was not certain that the results 'justify the costs against the taxpayer'.[53] For Palfrey, the ineffectiveness of CROWCASS was a heavy blow. In July 1945, he had told members of the UNWCC that unless the war criminals were found, 'he considered that the war had been fought in vain'. In his view, the hunt was 'as great a task of that of winning the war'.[54] The colonel's views were clearly in a minority. As well as hunting Nazis, there were other urgent tasks faced by the victors, such as caring for displaced persons, maintaining law and order and attempting to rebuild an infrastructure that had been ruined by six years of war.

By the end of 1945, Palfrey had become the victim of military politics. Regarded as inept, he was the subject of a slandering campaign by his American subordinates.[55] It is hard to see how even the most brilliant administrator could have handled CROWCASS, but Palfrey became a useful scapegoat and was soon removed from his post. The headquarters of the US Forces European Theater (USFET), which had replaced SHAEF in July, saw CROWCASS as an expensive millstone, which was funded largely by American money and supplied with American equipment.[56]

On 15 May 1946, CROWCASS was shut down in Paris and moved to Berlin, where it arrived on 25 June, now under the wing of the Allied Control Council.[57] The move did little to improve its efficacy and matters got steadily worse. On 20 July, Lieutenant Colonel R. F. 'Freddie' Luck, the acting director of CROWCASS, wrote to Lieutenant Colonel Arthur Harris complaining that he had acquired a backlog of three to four months' work. Hampered by a lack of staff, Luck even had to act as a mail clerk, sifting through 'heaps of bumph'.[58] At the time, CROWCASS consisted of one part-time acting director (Luck), one part-time administrative director, one major, one captain, three drivers and one storeman.[59] These eight men represented the entire central hub of the Allied war crimes investigations. 'Heaven knows when we shall get caught up again,' Luck wrote. 'Sorry for such a depressing letter but I really am somewhat depressed by it all.' Three days later, Luck wrote to Harris again, this time indicating that it was an 'SOS'. A key officer had just left, and Luck was desperately worried whether he could hold CROWCASS together. 'I'm sunk by the looks of it,' he wrote, 'and unless I can get BAOR [British Army of the Rhine] + USFET to send officers now, it will be Christmas before they'll have Crowcass functioning again.'[60] Eventually, Luck got his way, but help came in dribs and drabs – a few enlisted men here, a few there. It was also agreed that two hundred carefully screened Germans could work for CROWCASS, but they took a long time to arrive. As Lieutenant Colonel Harris was to observe, 'the Allied Control Council appear to have made a complete mess of CROWCASS'.[61] The mess would continue for months. In January 1947, the Registry found that it was unable to publish its Consolidated Wanted List of some eighty thousand names which was due in March. An officer called Lewis cabled the War Office in London explaining the reason – CROWCASS was suffering a shortage of typewriter ribbons. 'Urgently require twenty-five 12 millimetre black ribbons. If can supply dispatch fastest means.'[62]

Despite the administrative failures that afflicted both CROWCASS and UNWCC, perhaps neither could have been prepared for the sheer volume of criminality that confronted the Allies as they entered Germany. As one war crimes investigator described it, an 'overwhelming tidal wave . . . flowed into our offices, almost inundating us'. That wave consisted of 'evidence upon evidence upon evidence of the grossest criminality which our minds had yet experienced . . . which weighed upon us day . . . and night'.[63] For the British, the grossest criminality was to be found in Belsen concentration camp, which they entered on 15 April 1945. What the battle-hardened soldiers found shocked them profoundly. The camp was littered with thousands of corpses, and among these remains picked the living skeletons. 'The inmates had lost all self-respect,' reported an army review, 'were degraded morally to the level of beasts. Their clothes were in rags, teeming with lice, and both inside and outside the huts was an almost continuous carpet of dead bodies, human excreta, rags and filth.'[64] One British journalist, Tom Pocock, recalled how Belsen was 'heavy with death', and how he would walk past 'piles of shoes and human hair and drifts of bone-dust and fragments'.[65] Another journalist, Alan Moorehead, watched a bulldozer shoving corpses into burial pits. 'There was a curious pearly colour about the piled-up bodies,' he wrote, 'and they were small like the bodies of children.'[66] Despite the considerable medical aid the British directed at Belsen, around three hundred former inmates perished each day. In total, some fifty thousand died at the camp.

It was shocking scenes such as these that made the British realize that the UNWCC and CROWCASS would not be capable of bringing to justice those who were responsible. Nine days after the discovery of Belsen, approval was given for the formation of two British 'War Crimes Investigation Teams' (WCITs), which were required 'owing to the numbers of war criminals now being uncovered'.[67] The teams' task was to elicit and record evidence required for the Judge Advocate General's office (JAG), which would be bringing the cases against the accused. Each team was to consist of six officers who would act as 'detectives or a recce party', and they would be supported by two staff sergeants and three drivers. Each team would be equipped with one four-seater car and one 15-hundredweight truck, as well as all the necessary photographic equipment.[68] In addition, a 'War Crimes Investigation Team Specialist Pool' was also drawn up, which would consist of a pathologist, two photographers and two NCOs.

But as with all the initial attempts at Nazi hunting, the establishment of the War Crimes Investigation Teams came too late, and in too small a measure. The officer commanding No. 1 WCIT, Lieutenant Colonel L. J. Genn of the Royal Artillery, did not make it to Belsen until 18 May, where he found some 'scratch teams' investigating. Genn went to the camp on his own, and he had little idea when his actual team would arrive to back him up. Three days later, he wrote to Brigadier H. Scott-Barrett, the Deputy Judge Advocate General (DJAG), expressing his frustrations.

I now find myself, with the help of your backing from 21 A.G. [the British 21st Army Group], able to get a little of the help that is needed and hope to get more with due expenditure of time and effort. As I told you, though, I am very far from complete as to personnel and the work, which in any case could only proceed at slightly better than its somewhat pedestrian speed up to now, will be very little accelerated with Smallwood withdrawn. I will, of course, do my best, but I feel it only right to say that I cannot feel any confidence in producing the right answer, since . . . not only have many of the horses gone, but I doubt if I have available the necessary strength to shut the stable door on those that remain.[69]

Genn sent a copy of the letter to Major Harris at the Rear HQ of the 21st Army Group, who fully acknowledged what Genn was up against, but stated that he had problems of his own, 'not least being the unheralded arrival of 17 Frenchmen', which could hardly have compared to the nature of Genn's work in Belsen. It was Genn, after all, who had the harrowing task of interviewing women such as Ruth Guttmann, who had survived both Belsen and Auschwitz, and had witnessed the deeds of men like Mengele.[70] Harris ended the letter saying that he hoped that Genn had been joined by a Corporal Petheren. 'Getting him to you was more difficult than moving an Army!' he wrote.[71] If moving an NCO was like moving an army, then assembling the WCITs was an even greater challenge. By 3 June, the two teams had only half their complement of officers, and the Specialist Pool could only boast its pathologist. Both Investigation Teams were having to borrow interpreters and short-hand clerks from other units, and No. 2 WCIT, which was investigating at Sandbostel, had recruited a member of a French searcher team 'as a makeshift'. The situation was now so parlous that one British colonel warned that 'we shall not be able to meet our responsibilities for War Crimes investigation'.[72]

The British situation was not unique. The French war crimes teams were similarly disorganized, not least because six separate agencies all had their own units. 'It seems that there is no co-ordinated head to these departments,' observed Lieutenant Colonel Brian Franks, the commander of the 2nd SAS Regiment, 'and a complete lack of co-operation between them.' Franks also noted that the French were uncooperative with the British, not because of any chauvinism, but simply because they lacked the 'machinery'.[73] Some of the French methods of investigation also lacked finesse, and on several occasions, French officers used violence to extract information from their prisoners. The No. 2 French WCIT, stationed in the Hamburg suburb of Hochkamp, was accused of often resorting to brutality. In one instance, a prisoner was attacked and bitten by an Alsatian and a Boxer, which were then held near to him while he was forced to sign a confession written in French, a language he did not understand. The French officer responsible for this interrogation was a Lieutenant Schneider, who was the purveyor of numerous cruelties. During one such session, a prisoner was beaten up and forced to stand against a wall with his hands in the air. Empty tins were thrown at his head, and when he was unable to keep his hands up, his arms and his hands were clubbed with a stick. The questioning by Schneider and two sub-lieutenants followed, during which the prisoner was repeatedly punched in the face. When he was asked to sign a 'confession', he declined, which resulted in further blows.

Compared to some of Schneider's victims, however, the man got off lightly. In the course of another 'interrogation', the Frenchman and his juniors severely beat a prisoner in the stomach, causing the man to collapse. At this point, the dogs were set on him and he was ordered to 'confess'. The prisoner refused, which earned him the reward of having his head smashed several times against the edge of a door. Understandably, the prisoner gave up and signed the piece of paper that was thrust in front of him.[74]

The French at least had a war crimes team, which was more than could be said for the Poles in the British Zone of Occupation, where there were approximately five hundred thousand Polish displaced persons and former prisoners of war in the autumn of 1945.[75] Many of these were witnesses to Nazi war crimes, but without a dedicated Polish war crimes team there was no chance of gathering any evidence from them. The effort to put together a Polish team was led by Major Tadeusz Kaczorowski of the Polish War Crimes Liaison Office. In August 1945, he approached his senior officers asking whether he could form such a unit, but he was rebuffed. 'I do not see any reason for building up the inquiry teams for war crimes in the British occupied zone,' wrote Colonel Krupski of the Polish General Staff. 'Consequently I order you stop any action of building up the inquiry organization ... because such an activity goes beyond the authorization given to you.'[76] Kaczorowski, who was a judge in his civilian life, appealed to the British War Office, who successfully persuaded Krupski to change his mind.[77]

However, the level of British assistance did not go much further. Kaczorowski asked the British if they could help to establish a team, whose members were to consist of Polish lawyers drawn from the

ranks of the former POWs. The British were reluctant, and by the
end of October 1945 they conceded only that Kaczorowski could
form an informal unit of some ten lawyers and supporting NCOs,
although there would be little or no provision for uniforms or pay.
It was emphasized to Kaczorowski that his group was not to be
referred to as a 'War Crimes Investigation Team', and they must not
pass themselves off as any sort of official unit.[78] This lack of status
hampered Kaczorowski's group immensely, whose members were
divided between Hanover, Brunswick, Paderborn and Lübeck. Every
piece of equipment, no matter how small, had to be begged for.
Permission to get even a second typewriter had to be approved by a
British brigadier.[79] But Kaczorowski's biggest problem was a lack of
transport. Initially promised some four vehicles, he received none,
which meant that the Polish investigators had no choice but to take
to their feet. 'They have to walk sometimes for considerable
distances,' wrote Kaczorowski in January 1946, 'which takes a lot
of time and often deprives them of their meals.'[80] Whatever meals
the Poles did have, they certainly didn't get them from the British, as
canteen passes had been refused the previous October.[81] To some
British officers, such a situation was intolerable, and in February
1946, Brigadier G. S. Hatton demanded that the group receive four
captured enemy vehicles that had been earmarked for them some
months previously.[82] Hatton also commented that the Polish
government in Warsaw was of little help, and had sat on the problem for at least two months.

It would have come as little comfort to the Poles to hear that they
were not the only WCIT that was suffering from post-war shortages.
On 6 November 1945, the 1st Canadian War Crimes Investigation
Unit signalled the Royal Canadian Air Force in London requesting
two important pieces of *matériel*:

A26 (.) RESTRICTED (.) request you ship airmail urgently two
copies CASSELLS GERMAN ENGLISH Dictionary fifth edition feb
45 printed in UK [. . .][83]

The reply came back two days later:

A26 UNABLE TO PROCURE COPIES OF CASSEL GERMAN

ENGLISH DICTIONARY. DICTIONARY BEING REPRINTED. EXPECTED TO BE READY EARLY 1946.[84]

It took until 16 November for the Canadian unit to respond, the frustration clear beneath the capital letters of the telegram:

UNDERSTAN FROM G/C SHORE CASSEL'S GERMAN/ENGLISH DICTIONARIES LIKELY PROCURABLE AT FOYLES CHARING CROSS ROAD LONDON (:) REQUEST YOU TRY THROUGH THEM IF NOT AVAILABLE BEST SUBSTITUTE RECOMMENDED BY THEM BE SUPPLIED SOON AS POSSIBLE.[85]

On 19 November, London was delighted to inform the unit that:

ONE SECOND HAND COPY CASSELL'S GERMAN ENGLISH DICTIONARY BEING FORWARDED BY AIR THIS DATE. REGRET UNABLE TO PROCURE SECOND COPY OR SUBSITUTE.[86]

It was not just dictionaries that were in short supply but other more vital kit. Towards the end of June 1945, the pathologist attached to the British WCIT Specialist Pool, Major William Davidson, reported that he was lacking photographic equipment, a typewriter, stationery and maps. He was also short of the manpower required to help him unearth the bodies of the victims. 'Making arrangements to get labour often consumes a whole day,' he reported on 20 September, 'and even after they start, their work is inefficient and on more than one occasion I have not been able to start the actual examination before the afternoon, which leaves too little time prior to the failing of the light for photographic purposes.'[87]

Davidson may have had hundreds of bodies to exhume, but the Investigation Teams had to find the tens of thousands of men and women who were responsible for the pathologist's raw material. The task facing this handful of officers was immense, especially as just tracking down a single criminal could take weeks. On 23 November 1945, Captain H. H. Alexander of the British No. 1 WCIT was ordered to leave Belsen and hunt down and arrest Gustav Simon, the Mosel Gauleiter who had also been the chief of the civil administration in Luxembourg. Owing to bad weather, Alexander was not able to depart until almost a week later, and he eventually reached Simon's home in Koblenz on 1 December. There, the local police told Alexander that the *Frankfurter Zeitung* newspaper had reported Simon's arrest by the Americans, which Alexander soon established to be incorrect. Nevertheless, the police supplied Alexander with the details of Simon's ex-wife's parents, and he visited them in Hermeskeil, some 100 miles southwest of Koblenz. The British captain had no luck, as the couple informed him they had not heard from their former son-in-law for a few years, and neither had they heard from their daughter since May. They did reveal that Simon's parents lived in Friedewald, and on 4 December, Alexander drove the 200 miles northeast via Frankfurt to interrogate them. Once again, Alexander was met with denial, although in a nearby village he finally found a man who told him that Simon had left Friedewald on 27 March 1945. The man did not know where Simon was heading, but he could tell Alexander that Simon's two nieces and his son lived in Marburg.

Once again, Alexander took to the road, and drove 60 miles west to Marburg, where he interrogated one of the nieces, who told him that Simon's son was living in Dassel, some 100 miles north. In Dassel, Alexander spoke to the local *Burgermeister*, who informed him that they had found some papers belonging to the son in a nearby wood, and that the son had possibly lived with a couple in the village called the Ludwigs. Alexander visited the couple at Wilhelmstrasse 89, who admitted that they had indeed looked after the young man, but they assumed he was an evacuee and knew nothing about his family. Alexander was suspicious, and interrogated the Ludwigs' daughter, who admitted that they knew exactly who the 'evacuee' was, as her sister had in fact been Gustav Simon's housekeeper. Alexander, by now convinced that the nieces held the key to the mystery, returned to Marburg and arrested them, and after interrogation in prison, they revealed that the son in fact lived with some relations in Plettenberg, 70 miles northwest of Marburg. Alexander drove there the following day, and searched the house. The relations eventually confessed that the son was actually living nearby, and when Alexander visited this new address, he found and arrested the younger Simon.

The son was not forthcoming about his father's whereabouts, but the relations certainly were. They told Alexander that Simon had visited Plettenberg on a few occasions, and he used either the name 'Volter' or Höfler' and was working as a nurseryman in the British zone. Alexander checked the registers of two local hotels, where he found that both a 'Heinrich Woffler' and a 'Hans Woffler' had stayed during the previous three months. The man calling himself 'Hans Woffler' gave his address as Schusterstrasse 1 in Einbeck, just north of Dassel. On 9 December, Alexander interrogated the son, who eventually confirmed that his father was indeed a gardener. Alexander now drove to Einbeck, where he made inquiries at the police station about 'Woffler', but no record could be found. However, at the house on Schusterstrasse, Alexander found that a man called 'Hans Woffler' appeared on a list of those who were living there. The captain showed a photograph of Simon to the householder, who said the picture was of 'Woffler', and that he worked in a nursery near Paderborn. On 10 December, Alexander drove the 60 miles west to Paderborn, and found 'Woffler's' address at the *Burgermeister*'s office. That night, he drove just 8 miles, to the village of Upsprunge, where he found Simon staying at the house of one Frau Berhorst. Alexander made his arrest, and incarcerated Simon at the local prison, where he left strict instructions that the former Gauleiter was not to be handed over to anybody apart from Alexander. The following morning, the captain drove 120 miles back to Belsen. He would have been exhausted. In total, he had covered some 2,500 miles on treacherous winter roads that had been ruined by war and neglect. The case had taken him three weeks, and he had interrogated at least a dozen individuals, and numerous policemen and civil servants. Simon, it should be remembered, was just one case, and its complexity was typical.[88] Unfortunately, the Nazi was to escape justice: he hanged himself on 21 December 1945, shortly before he was to be handed over to Luxembourg.

The slow rate at which the British were discovering Nazi criminals soon came to the notice of the British Prime Minister. On 21 November 1945, Clement Attlee sent a minute to Jack Lawson, the Secretary of State for War, expressing concern at 'the delays which have occurred in dealing with these matters'. Attlee insisted that the 'persons on whom rests responsibility for the investigation of War Crimes . . . should be officers with drive and energy and that the high priority to be accorded to War Crimes matters should be fully understood'.[89] Attlee's minute was shown by Lawson to General Sir Ronald Adam, the Adjutant General, who then passed on its contents to Field Marshal Montgomery, who was command-ing the British Army of the Rhine (BAOR); Lieutenant General Sir W. D. Morgan, the commander of the Central Mediterranean Forces; and Major General Graham, the commander in Norway. 'I feel that the obstacles to the trials have now been removed and that there need be no further delay,' Adam wrote.[90]

Adam was right. There was no need for delay, but delay there remained, because the WCITs were to stay hopelessly small and thus overworked. In November, Lieutenant Colonel Ian Neilson was appointed to run the teams, and he was surprised at how little he had under his command. 'It was just a piece of paper at that stage,' he recalled. 'There was no place to work. There was no staff.' Although Neilson was soon able to requisition vehicles, drivers and pathologists, he constantly felt undermanned and underequipped:

> If the War Crimes Unit had started in the early spring of 1945, I think we would have caught a lot more chaps – and witnesses' memories would have been a lot better than they were. Generally speaking, the whole thing was on a shoestring, and all too often one felt, 'Why on earth are we doing this?' It was all too little, too late.

In addition, lists of suspects drawn up by CROWCASS appeared to have never reached the British teams. 'I'd never heard of CROWCASS,' said Neilson. 'That's a pity. It sounds like it might have been very helpful.'[91]

Despite the shortages, the British army had the ability to mount a vast Nazi-hunting effort if it so wished, but as we shall see, despite Attlee's demands, there was a lack of wider political will to force the army to act on a larger scale. However, there were individual officers who thought this was scandalous, and one of them, Captain Yurka Galitzine, drew up, at the end of October 1945, a proposal to dramatically improve the situation. Galitzine's solution was radical, and he insisted that the matter should be treated as 'an *OPERATION OF WAR*'. First, he called for CROWCASS to be strengthened and sped up, and for more personnel and accommodation to be made available immediately. Secondly, he advocated the formation of an Emergency 'Man Hunting' Scheme, which would comprise a hundred investigators, fully equipped with transport, armed, 'and under bold and enterprising direction'. These investigators would be split into field groups, which would be able to communicate with each other and their base in London. 'The unit,' Galitzine wrote, '*must* have the same backing of the Cabinet in matters of priority as SOE during the war.' Galitzine also advocated that the unit should be allowed to travel by air, and that its members should have the full power of arrest.[92] The proposals in Galitzine's document were never acted upon. The document was passed from a colonel in the War Office to a colonel at the BAOR, but there is no evidence to suggest it went further or higher.[93]

Of all the Allied War Crimes Investigation Teams, those of the Americans seemed to be the most organized. When Lieutenant Colonel Brian Franks of the SAS was commenting on the faults of the French units, he also noted that one of the American teams he had encountered was a 'highly efficient organization'. Led by a Colonel Chaves, it included two pathologists, a professional interrogator, two lawyers, shorthand typists and photographers. Franks was surprised to find that this team was working purely on the war crimes committed against five American airmen at Gaggenau. Chaves too expressed surprise, when he discovered that one British officer was investigating twenty-seven cases simultaneously.[94]

Many of the American war crimes investigations were carried out by the Counterintelligence Corps (CIC). Originally established in August 1917 as the Corps of Intelligence Police, the fifty-strong unit ran counter-espionage operations in northern France towards the end of the First World War. Between the wars it underwent various mutations, and after the attack on Pearl Harbor it was renamed the CIC and authorized to recruit 1,026 non-commissioned officers. This was rapidly swelled to 4,431, with a provision for 543 officers. The men selected for the CIC were often expected to have some

form of legal experience, although as the war went on this require-
ment was waived, and recruits were merely expected to have an
adequate education, be of 'good character' and loyal to the flag.
This drew in recruits from all walks of life, many of whom were
lured by the word 'intelligence', which suggested a war of cloaks and
daggers rather than bombs and guns.[95]

The CIC was not a haven for shirkers, however. Six of its units
came ashore in Normandy on D-Day, and counter-espionage work
is not without its dangers. Detachments such as the 430th CIC were
tasked with the 'detection of treason, sedition, disaffection and
subversive activity and the detection and prevention of espionage
and sabotage', which meant that they dealt with desperate men who
could – and would – kill to maintain their freedom.[96] After the
invasion, the principal role of the CIC detachments was to screen
displaced persons, and to determine whether they were enemy
agents or war criminals masquerading as civilians. By the time the
Allies had entered Germany, the CIC's role was to arrest Nazis and
other Germans who represented a threat to the Allied forces. In
addition to 'normal' counter-espionage work, the CIC had to secure
Nazi Party buildings in order to safeguard the documents they
contained. As VE Day approached, the CIC often found itself
arresting war criminals, and this became a de facto duty for the
detachments, a task which became increasingly significant after
the German surrender.[97]

The British may have been envious of the resources the American
Nazi-hunting units had at their disposal, but they were a little sniffy
about their methods. 'They were very gung-ho,' recalled John Hodge,
a captain in the British War Crimes Team; 'they all had pistols and
went "Come on, let's go get him!" '[98] Hodge's observation is confirmed by Ben Ferencz, who was part of the War Crimes Branch of
the JAG Division attached to the US Third Army. Ferencz, who was
a corporal, would investigate cases in which US airmen had been
murdered after they had been shot down. 'I'd drive to where it
happened,' he said, 'and detain the Burgermeister or the most senior
guy, and get some witnesses together. I'd then line them up against a
wall and threaten to shoot them unless they wrote down exactly
what happened. I wasn't going to shoot, but they didn't know that,
because I damn well made them know that I was going to blow their

heads off. Anyway, they'd soon start scribbling!' Ferencz would then locate the bodies and photograph them, before informing the families of the victims.[99]

Ben Ferencz acknowledged that the efforts to hunt Nazis could have started sooner, 'but we had this little war on our hands'. Despite being better equipped than the other Allied investigation teams, Ferencz found that the American personnel were often lacking, largely because the war crimes units were seen as backwaters. 'I was joined by five drunken colonels,' said Ferencz, 'who were so shellshocked that there was nowhere else for them to go. No one paid any attention to the war crimes work. They all wanted to get the hell out of there as soon as possible.'[100] John Hodge said that the Americans 'weren't all that good really.' Hodge recalled an American called Becker, 'who was quite old, and all he wanted to do was to go back home to America.'[101] The Americans appeared equally unimpressed with the British, who, said Ferencz, 'were not that much interested' in war crimes work. Interested or not, the teams were certainly kept busy. 'We worked hard,' recalled Captain Brian Bone of the British team, 'and we played hard, and we drank hard.' Bone said that he and his fellow officers were kept so busy that 'we weren't aware of the big fish – quite honestly, we had enough on our hands just with the small fry.'[102]

Ironically, the Allies were to catch some of the big fish, but they threw them back, believing them to be small fry. In Schauenstein camp, 'Josef Memling', the name Josef Mengele had now adopted, was thankful that he did not have his blood group tattooed on his left upper arm. Since such marks were carried by most SS men, they became an easy method for the Allies to identify those who had joined the ranks of the supposed Nazi élite. Luckily for him, Mengele had refused a tattoo, saying it was medically superfluous.[103] Although he was unlikely to be identified, Mengele grew increasingly anxious. 'The Americans then took us from one camp to another,' he recalled, 'in which the very small rations became even smaller, and our hopelessness grew.'[104] At the end of July 1945, Mengele and his friend Dr Kahler were moved to Helmbrechts camp, some 100 miles north of Nuremberg. It was here that Mengele had another piece of luck – he was released after just one week. Without an SS tattoo, and with a convincing identity as an army doctor, the Americans had no reason to suspect that the 34-year-old was not just another German officer who wanted to go home. Even if Mengele had used his real name, then it is likely he would have still been released. The absence of any CROWCASS list in the camp would have made the name 'Mengele' no more significant than 'Memling'.[105] Besides, Mengele was not the only German being released from Helmbrechts. That July, some two thousand were discharged from the camp. The Allies were simply unable to cope with the millions they had captured, and to avoid starving their prisoners, hundreds of thousands had to be set free.

Had CROWCASS been better organized, then Mengele would not have been released. His name did appear on the July list, but that was at a printer back in England.[106] 'Mengele' was number 240 on the UNWCC's list published in May, but that had barely been circulated.[107] Along with Eichmann and Müller, Mengele also appeared on a blacklist of German police and SS compiled by MI14, but that list was not publicized.[108] However, there was even some doubt whether 'Mengele' was in fact his real name. In June, the UNWCC research department hazarded that Mengele was in fact called 'Margde',[109] whereas the British suspected he might in fact be 'Peter Mendelei'.[110] Even by December 1945, the British were guessing that Mengele was in his mid-forties, and that he was possibly from East Frisia, which meant that they were out by a decade and roughly 500 miles.[111] By May the following year, Mengele's 'correct' name was 'Rennau', and in May 1947, it was suspected to be 'Scapesius'.[112]

After he had been released, Mengele made for Donauwörth near his hometown of Günzburg in Bavaria. Stuffed inside his army uniform were two sets of discharge papers – one in the name of Fritz Hollmann, and the other in his real name. The former set was a modified version of the papers of Colonel Fritz Ulmann, who had been working for the camp administration and in whom Mengele had confided.[113] On the way to Donauwörth, Mengele met a farmer who was walking two bicycles. Both men were going in the same direction and so, out of mutual convenience, the two cycled to Donauwörth together. Mengele was fearful of being stopped by an American patrol while in possession of two sets of papers, so he hid the Mengele set inside the handlebars of his bicycle. When he returned the bicycle to the farmer, he forgot to retrieve the papers, and so he had no choice but to live as 'Hollmann'.[114]

In Donauwörth, Mengele visited the home of his old schoolfriend, Dr Albert Miller, whose wife Ottilie answered the door. 'I saw a soldier standing in front of me,' she recalled. 'He said, "Good day, my name is Mengele." Later, my husband came home and we had dinner. I remembered him saying, "Don't believe everything you hear about me. It's not true." '[115] It is hard to establish how Mengele might have known what was being said about him. If he had access to a radio, then perhaps he would have heard a broadcast mentioning his name, but radios – along with newspapers – were in short supply in the camps. Mengele would have known that what he had done would look wrong in the eyes of others, and he was already trying to convince his old friends that the Allies were Goebbels-like in the deceitfulness of their propaganda. Convinced or not, the Millers decided to help their visitor by promising to inform Mengele's family that he was safe. However, for reasons that are unclear, Mengele did not stay with his old schoolfriend. Miller himself was taken into custody by the Americans for his wartime role in the Nazi Party and Mengele claims in his unpublished autobiography that this arrest happened while he hid in the Millers' back room. After the Americans had departed, Mengele writes that he escaped into the night.[116] Although Miller certainly was arrested, Mengele's account seems fanciful, as the troops would have conducted a search of the house for any evidence.

What happened to Mengele during the summer of 1945 is unclear. According to his own account, he made his way into the Russian zone to retrieve the research notes he had left with the nurse. Although he had told the Millers this was his intention, the journey would have been immensely hazardous.[117] 'It was a crazy undertaking to cross the guarded border,' Mengele wrote. 'It seems an incredible journey.'[118] A more credible account places Mengele living rough in a wood outside his hometown of Günzburg, where his family provided him with food.[119] Whatever the truth, by the end of September, Mengele had appeared at the Munich home of a pharmacist friend, who sheltered him for the best part of a month. Once again, the 'Angel of Death' defended his wartime actions. 'I

don't have anything to hide,' he told his friend. 'Terrible things
happened at Auschwitz, and I did my best to help. One could not do
everything. There were terrible disasters there. I could only save so
many. I never killed anyone or hurt anyone.'[120] Notwithstanding the
obvious lie that he was not responsible for any deaths, Mengele's
statement, if correctly reported, is a supreme example of that of a
man whose moral sphere had grown dangerously small. Mengele
felt that his role in the selections was saving lives rather than ending
them. There is a hideous logic to Mengele's mindset, but only if such
reasoning is contained within a morally corrupt system. Mengele, after
all, could have refused to participate in such a system. Nobody forced
him to work at Auschwitz. Instead, he embraced it. And, once he had
done that, he was capable of defining his morality only within the context of that environment. To men such as Mengele and Eichmann, that
system was all. No wonder, then, that Mengele in fact thought he had
done his duty as a good doctor. After Nazism had collapsed, such men
were left with the options of admitting their criminality, or continuing
to behave as if the system were extant and claiming innocence. 'I can
prove I am innocent of what they could say against me,' Mengele told
his Munich friend. 'I am building the facts for my defence. I want to
turn myself in and be cleared at a trial.'[121]

The pharmacist thought that a bad idea. 'You will never get a fair
trial,' he told Mengele. 'If you turn yourself in, you will either be
shot on the spot or you will get a trial and then be hanged.'[122] The
pharmacist put Mengele in touch with a man called 'Wieland', who
arranged for the fugitive to get a job as a farmhand in the village of
Mangolding, about 45 miles southeast of Munich. The farm was
owned by Georg and Maria Fischer, who were told that their new
employee, 'Herr Hollmann', had just returned from the Soviet zone
after an unsuccessful attempt to find his wife. The Fischers were
suspicious as to his true identity, but they kept quiet. 'He was only
looking for a place to hide after the war,' recalled Georg Fischer's
brother, Alois. 'He must have been a Nazi, and we thought he must
have been top brass.'[123] 'Hollmann' worked hard for his ten marks
per week, and although he was mostly reserved, he could be good
company, even dressing up as Santa Claus on St Nicholas's Day.
Mengele found the work physically tough and stultifying, and he
privately attempted to apply scientific rigour to the process of

growing potatoes. 'The frequency of the various sizes followed the binomial distribution according to the Gauss Diagram,' he later wrote, having claimed to improve the Fischers' yield of consumable potatoes.[124]

Agricultural work was also to feature in Adolf Eichmann's life on the run, but in May 1945, the only occupation of 'Obergefreiter Bart' of the Luftwaffe was to avoid being arrested. After leaving the Blaa-Alm, Eichmann and Jänisch headed northwest into Germany, sleeping out in the open or in barns. 'The danger of capture was very present,' Eichmann recalled, 'for the Allied patrols were operating everywhere.'[125] After a few days, the two men were indeed captured, but, according to Eichmann, 'it was just a question of, as it were, walking out the front door'.[126] Eichmann now made his way to Salzburg, the location of his honeymoon ten years before. The romantic nature of the city made Eichmann feel wistful, and as he sat next to the castle on top of the hill, he ruminated about his actions during the war. Like Mengele, Eichmann's morality was still contained within a system that no longer existed externally, but certainly remained present within the minds of its more fanatical adherents.

> Had I turned into a soulless person, a wicked man, a murderer? I went on plying my conscience with questions. Had I done anything in the war but my duty and my obligations? Had I done anything but remain loyal to my oath and obedient to my orders? And my conscience answered me reassuringly. No, nothing else. Had I killed defenceless people, or ordered them to be killed? No, no, no. What in the devil's name did they want of me? I took my orders and did my duty.[127]

Eichmann's words reveal a less sophisticated manner of thinking than that of Mengele, who rarely excused his deeds on the grounds of 'obeying orders'. Eichmann's defence was time-stained and, for someone who had shipped millions to their deaths, bathetic.

It was in Salzburg that Eichmann claimed to have received help – as had Mengele – from a nurse. With an increasing number of American roadblocks, the city had quickly become more of a prison than a hideout for the fugitive. Resolving that he had to adopt 'the cunning of a fox', Eichmann approached an attractive young woman who was wearing the uniform of a Red Cross nurse. 'I'm an SS-Obersturmbannführer,' he informed her. 'Will you help me get out of this town?' The nurse willingly agreed, and took Eichmann – complete with a phoney limp – past an American control point. Eichmann's next challenge was to cross into Bavaria, and at the border post, he joined a fake funeral cortège that he reckoned was stuffed full of disguised former SS men. However, Eichmann's luck was finally to run out. Shortly after he had entered Germany, he was picked up by an American patrol.[128]

'Obergefreiter Bart' did not last long in American captivity, because an inspection of the Luftwaffe corporal's left arm revealed the letter 'A' tattooed near his armpit. Eichmann had attempted to eradicate his SS blood group brand by burning it with cigarettes, a painful process that had failed. Although there was no chance of denying his SS membership, Eichmann certainly did not admit his real identity. Instead, he now became SS-Untersturmführer (Lieutenant) Otto Eckmann of the 22nd Waffen-SS Cavalry Division, the surname chosen because of its similarity to his own. Had someone recognized him and addressed him as 'Eichmann', he could claim to any inquisitive captor that he had misheard.[129] Upon his capture, Eichmann recalled how the American troops purloined his fountain pen and wristwatch, which they exchanged for two jars of beer and two dozen eggs which he and three fellow captives ate raw in the shade of an American tank. Such halcyon moments were not typical, and while Eichmann was incarcerated in a makeshift camp, his mood darkened. 'Germany is destroyed, Germany is destroyed,' he would repeat to himself. 'Oh God, do not abandon the Reich. Let me die, but help the Reich.'[130] Eichmann's wish for the regime to be everlasting was not the product of loyalty, but more the pleadings of a man who realized that his life only made sense if the Reich were still in existence. As with all fanatical Nazis, it was not so much a belief that the Nazi system was superior, but the sub-conscious desire to reinstate a machine in which he had a slot. There were very few places – if any – outside Nazism for men who had become like Eichmann. As he himself was to admit: 'You see, one becomes completely accustomed to obedience and discipline and to voluntary subordination. We Germans at that time had made such a virtue of discipline and obedience that we felt lost and undecided without orders.'[131]

'Otto Eckmann' was soon moved to Weiden camp, 60 miles east of Nuremberg, where he was incarcerated until August 1945. He was then transferred to a larger camp at Oberdachstetten, 30 miles west of Nuremberg. Eichmann remembers being treated 'very correctly' by the Americans, and the prisoners even received a tobacco ration.[132] But Eichmann knew that he could not remain hidden indefinitely, and that his cover story would not withstand repeated interrogation. Because the 22nd Waffen-SS Cavalry Division had been formed and had served in Hungary, Eichmann would have been able to provide some convincing background colour to his identity, but 'sooner or later the truth would catch up on me' he acknowledged.[133] He also worried that he would be spotted by one of the *Judenkommissionen*, which were parties of Jewish camp survivors who travelled from camp to camp identifying criminals. Eichmann considered taking poison as the ultimate means of escape, but he had lost his capsule, and neither was the camp's pharmacist able to assist.[134]

Eichmann was finally forced to act by what happened in a courtroom just 30 miles away from his camp. Just before lunch on 14 December 1945, an American prosecutor, Major William Walsh, was addressing the court at the International Military Tribunal at Nuremberg. Walsh was identifying what he called the 'ultimate objective of the Nazi party and the Nazi-controlled State' – the extermination of the Jews. He told the court that four million Jews had been killed in the camps, and a further two million by units such as the *Einsatzgruppen*. His evidence was an affidavit made on 26 November by Wilhelm Höttl, who had been attempting to ingratiate himself with the CIC by telling them all he knew.[135] Walsh said that Höttl's information had come from Adolf Eichmann, and was revealed to Höttl at the meeting that had taken place in Höttl's Budapest apartment during the summer of 1944.[136] Eichmann's name and significance barely resonated with the court, but it would certainly do so the following month.

On 3 January 1946, another former Nazi told the world the full extent of Eichmann's criminality. The testimony was given by Dieter

Wisliceny, an *SS-Hauptsturmführer* who had worked with Eichmann in carrying out the 'Final Solution'. Questioned by Lieutenant Colonel Smith Brookhart, Wisliceny recalled a meeting that had taken place in the summer of 1942 with Eichmann in Berlin. Wisliceny was inquiring as to the fate of 52,000 Slovakian Jews who had been sent to Poland as 'workers'. At that point, Wisliceny claimed to have no inkling of what their real fate might have been, and he begged Eichmann to allow a delegation from Slovakia to check on their fellow countrymen. Eichmann informed him that permission for such a visit could not be granted, for the simple reason that most of the Jews in question were no longer alive. Wisliceny asked Eichmann who had issued such an order, where-upon Eichmann took a file from a safe and extracted a document with a red border, which meant that it was for immediate action. The document, which was signed by Himmler, said that Hitler had ordered 'the final solution of the Jewish question'.[137] Lieutenant Colonel Brookhart then asked what was meant by the term 'final solution'. Wisliceny's reply was emphatic: '[Eichmann] said that the planned biological annihilation of the Jewish race in the Eastern Territories was disguised by the concept and wording "final solu-tion" [. . .] It was perfectly clear to me that this order spelled death to millions of people.'[138]

In his affidavit to the tribunal, Wisliceny observed that the order from Himmler 'gave Eichmann authority to kill millions of people'.[139] It was an order that Eichmann of course obeyed, and Wisliceny related his final meeting with Eichmann in February 1945, in which he showed a horrific pride in what he had achieved. 'I laugh when I jump into the grave,' Eichmann said, 'because of the feeling that I have killed 5,000,000 Jews. That gives me great satis-faction and gratification.'[140]

Within days, Eichmann heard about Wisliceny's testimony via the POW grapevine.[141] He approached some former SS officers in the camp and told them his real identity. Despite the monstrousness of his crimes, his comrades agreed to help him, and soon Eichmann had been issued with forged papers and civilian clothing. Clearly, an escape network of sorts had been established,[142] but Eichmann was once again to claim that it was a nurse who helped him. 'This nurse I met was beautiful, brown-eyed and with a heart of gold,' he recalled.[143] Over the course of a few meetings held with the camp's barbed wire as their only intermediary, the nurse supplied Eichmann with everything he required, right down to a hunter's hat complete with a goat's beard. She also supplied information. 'We spent hours in close conversation at the wire,' Eichmann said. 'But we were not whispering sweet nothings. This patriotic German angel was telling me the lie of the land, the distances and the difficulties I would have in my escape.'[144]

Although the nurses who supposedly helped both Eichmann and Mengele may have been fictional, and invented to cover the identity of their actual assistants, women certainly did help Nazis on the run. At the end of the war, one CIC source reported that some German women had established 'a courier network to Nazis hiding out from the occupational authorities', and that these women were conveying messages, supplying food, and even carrying arms. The same source felt that the Americans' 'chivalrous official attitude towards many women' was allowing this courier network to flourish.[145] This attitude may have been bolstered by the arrival of warm weather, and, according to one US intelligence report, the resulting 'appearance of Germany's female population in colourful spring dresses'. The report continued with the tactfully worded assumption that the 'German populace, long schooled to covert practices, doubtless find many willing soldiers'.[146] The spirit of these reports was indeed correct, as women would be at the very heart of the Nazi escape networks.

Eichmann made his escape on the night of 5 February 1946. He picked his way through the wire, and emerged as 'Otto Henninger' from Prien in Bavaria. 'For a moment, I stood outside and felt as helpless as a little child,' he recalled. 'I was on my own. I had no orders. But then I knew I had to move. And move fast.'[147] Eichmann's first destination was his new 'home town' 200 miles south. There, he met Nelly Krawietz, the sister of an SS sergeant who had been in the Oberdachstetten camp. He stayed there for some six weeks, not knowing that just under 5 miles away in Mangolding, 'Fritz Hollmann' was labouring on the Fischers' farm. By the middle of March, Eichmann had begun to grow wary of the increasing number of American patrols, and he and Krawietz travelled the length of the country to Hamburg, where they parted.

Eichmann then made his way 20 miles southwest to Eversen, where he was employed as a forester by the brother of a fellow SS officer who was incarcerated in Oberdachstetten.[148] Unlike Mengele, Eichmann took a certain masculine pride in his new role as an agricultural worker. 'Soon the hands that had always worked with a pen took on the rough and calloused look of the bark of the very trees I was hewing,' he wrote. 'My physique grew hard and strong . . . and in my simple communion with nature I found a quiet, happy contemplation. My soul and my conscience were cleansed.'[149] For the next three years, this supposedly happy soul enjoyed his time as a forester, but he admitted, 'I was still a mole, living in the underground, pretending to be someone I was not.'[150]

While Eichmann chopped wood, the world began to hear more about him. On 15 April 1946, the former commandant of Auschwitz, Rudolf Höss, was called as a witness at Nuremberg in an attempt to prove Ernst Kaltenbrunner's lack of involvement in the Final Solution. Questioned by Kaltenbrunner's lawyer, Kurt Kauffmann, Höss admitted that it was Eichmann who was responsible for marshalling millions of Jews towards the gas chambers. Höss also recalled meeting Himmler in the summer of 1941 to receive his order to start his genocidal operations at Auschwitz, but it was Eichmann who was Himmler's Lord High Executioner. 'He came to Auschwitz to discuss details with me on the carrying out of the given order,' said Höss. 'As the Reichsführer [Himmler] had told me during our discussion, he had instructed Eichmann to discuss the carrying out of the order with me and I was to receive all further instructions from him.'[151] Höss was to testify that Eichmann repeatedly visited Auschwitz, and that he was 'intimately acquainted with the proceedings'.[152] Indeed, it was Eichmann who helped Höss site the gas chambers, and it was Eichmann who promised to find a suitable gas that was in ready supply.[153] And it was Eichmann, the man now with a clean conscience, who helped assemble a collection of skeletons for Dr August Hirt at the Anatomical Institute in Strasbourg. Eichmann provided the logistical apparatus by which 109 Jews, 2 Poles and 4 'Asiatics' were transported in the summer of 1943 from Auschwitz to the camp at Natzweiler, where they were gassed. This collection was then sent to Strasbourg, where it was studied and 'defleshed'. As the Allies approached the city, the skeletons were dissolved in acid, an arrangement, according to one of Hirt's assistants, that was 'for the best in view of the whole situation'.[154]

With the growing realization that Eichmann was a major criminal, the Allies started to search for him. On 21 October 1946, the CIC received an important lead via an intermediary from the wife of the former Hitler Youth leader Baldur von Schirach: Eichmann was living in the Oberbayern district of Bavaria. She also revealed the location of Eichmann's wife, Vera.[155] On 26 November, a CIC agent interrogated her at Fischerndorf 8 in Altaussee. Frau Eichmann, who was now living under her maiden name, Liebl, said that she and her husband had been divorced since March 1945, which was a lie. She claimed that he had told her he was returning to Prague, which was also untrue. But Vera Eichmann had one more fabrication to impart. Her husband, she said, had been shot by the Czechs in November 1945. She had gathered this from Eichmann's sister, but unfortunately she did not know where she now lived. The CIC had another source, however, whose information conflicted with that of Frau Eichmann. This informant told the Americans that Eichmann had stayed in the mountains until November, at which point he decided to pass himself off as a Jew, and hid in various Jewish camps until he emigrated to Palestine. There, Eichmann was reputed to have come into contact with the Grand Mufti of Jerusalem, Haj Muhammed Amin al-Husseini, who was a notorious Nazi sympathizer. Eichmann, according to the source, was now in Egypt under the protection of King Farouk.[156] The idea that Eichmann may have been sheltering in the Middle East was not so absurd. In June 1944, Eichmann told a Zionist called Rudolf Kasztner that the Grand Mufti was his 'best friend'. Dieter Wisliceny had told Kasztner around the same time that the Grand Mufti had played a 'fatal part' in the German decision to exterminate the Jews. Eichmann and the Grand Mufti, then, had a lot in common. Kasztner reported these conversations to the Americans in January 1946, so when the CIC heard that Eichmann was in Egypt or Palestine, it would not have seemed unfeasible.[157]

Nevertheless, the CIC did not give up, and in January 1947, they interrogated Eichmann's parents and his brother, Friedrich. The latter believed that Eichmann had shot himself, as he had always promised to do if Germany lost the war. The parents claimed not to have a clue, which was probably true.[158] However, the CIC had another source who had more of an idea: Wilhelm Höttl. On the same day that he made his affidavit to the International Military Tribunal in November 1945, Höttl had also provided the Americans with a lead concerning a mistress of Eichmann. The woman had owned a small manufacturing plant near Linz, which she had sold to the state at some point between 1942 and 1944. Höttl advised the CIC to go through the records of the Trade Chamber in Linz, where they should easily be able to establish her name. It was Höttl's hunch that Eichmann would stay with his mistress, and not his wife, 'with whom he entertained no intimate relationship'.[159] The CIC appeared to reconsider Höttl's information in January 1947, but it is unclear as to what extent they followed it up. Even if they had, such a search would not have been fruitful, as Eichmann was chopping wood hundreds of miles north of Linz.

By February, many believed that Eichmann was in fact dead. Although his name appeared on List 7, published that month, of the key Nazi personnel wanted by the UNWCC, a note added next to it read: 'Believed to have committed suicide US CIC Source'.[160] The British thought the same, probably based on information received from the Americans. On 6 February, Major Denis Comper of the British War Crimes Group wrote to the officer in charge of the Legal Section of the Group informing him that an 'exhaustive search' had been carried out for Eichmann, and that the only clue was that 'he may have committed suicide'. 'Apart from that,' Comper wrote, 'there is absolutely no trace of this man [. . .] Unless instructions are received to the contrary this case will be considered closed by this unit.'[161] As there is no surviving evidence to indicate that the British hunted Eichmann, Comper's reference to an 'exhaustive search' must be to that carried out by the CIC. For the time being, Eichmann had succeeded.

Chapter Three

'The Man Who Never Forgets'

IT WAS not just the Americans who were hunting Eichmann. The informant who had told the CIC that Eichmann was with the Grand Mufti might have been a 37-year-old Galician Jew who had recently been liberated from Mauthausen.[1] The man's name was Simon Wiesenthal and, since the early 1960s, that name has become synonymous with Nazi hunting. Nominated four times for the Nobel Peace Prize,[2] the recipient of a British knighthood, the United States' Presidential Medal of Freedom, the French Légion d'honneur and at least fifty-three other distinctions, Wiesenthal's standing is that of a secular saint. Often credited with some 1,100 Nazi 'scalps', Wiesenthal is remembered above all for his efforts to track down Eichmann. He was regarded as the Nazi hunter par excellence, and Wiesenthal's name towers above all others who worked – and continue to work – in seeking these most evil men and women.

However, Wiesenthal's reputation is built on sand. He was a liar, and a bad one at that. From the end of the war to the end of his life in 2005, he would lie repeatedly about his supposed hunt for Eichmann as well as his other Nazi-hunting exploits. Wiesenthal would also concoct outrageous stories about his war years and make false claims about his academic career. Indeed, there are so many inconsistencies between his three main memoirs, and between those memoirs and contemporaneous documents, that it is impossible to establish a reliable narrative from them alone. These accounts are also strewn with numerous inaccuracies, which make it hard to reconcile the unreliable figure that emerges with that of the brilliant sleuth. In addition, Wiesenthal's scant regard for the truth makes it possible to doubt *everything* he ever wrote or said. Nevertheless, his figure is a complex and important one, and for the story of Nazi hunting to be told properly, a thorough examination of his life story must be conducted. His motives for telling so many untruths also need to be ascertained. If there was a motive for his duplicity, it may well have been rooted in good intentions.

Wiesenthal claimed that he started to hunt for Eichmann within a few weeks of leaving Mauthausen. Although Eichmann's name meant little or nothing to him during the war, he later claimed that the name soon meant a great deal. The first occasion was in June 1945, when he was visited by a Captain Choter-Ischai at the offices of the OSS in Linz. The captain, who had served in the Jewish Brigade of the British army, told his fellow Jew that Eichmann had been born in Palestine, and that he should look up the name. 'I went through the lists and found the name Eichmann,' Wiesenthal later claimed. 'He was said to have been active in Austria, Czechoslovakia, France, Greece and Hungary.'[3] Wiesenthal was provided with more details in Vienna the following month when he visited the offices of the Jewish Agency for Palestine. There, he found a file which stated that Eichmann was allegedly born in Sarona, the 'German Templar colony in Palestine', and that he was able to speak German, Hebrew and Yiddish. It listed his rank as an *SS-Obersturmbannführer*, and said that he was a 'High Official of Gestapo HQ, Department for Jewish Affairs'.[4] Some of this in- formation was incorrect. Eichmann had some knowledge of Yiddish, but of Hebrew he had very little.[5] Nor was he born in Palestine, but in Solingen, 20 miles east of Düsseldorf in the Rhineland.

Back in Linz, Wiesenthal recalled how even his landlady, Frau Sturm, added a piece of startling information when she saw Eichmann's name in one of his files. 'Eichmann!' she exclaimed.

'That must be the SS-General Eichmann who commanded the Jews. Do you know that his parents live in our street, at No. 32, just two houses away?'[6] According to her tenant, two members of the OSS questioned Eichmann's parents the following day, who said that they believed their son to be in Prague. Their denials were so emphatic that Wiesenthal was not sure whether the 'Eichmann' in the Jewish Agency's files was the same as the one who was reputed to live in Linz.[7]

On 1 August 1945, Wiesenthal claimed that one of his voluntary helpers, 'Max', contacted him to say that Eichmann was hiding at Fischerndorf 8 in Altaussee.[8] 'Strictly speaking,' he would write in 1989, 'I need only have taken a Jeep and two soldiers, and Eichmann would have found himself under arrest.'[9] It is puzzling that he should have made such a claim four decades later, not least because in his book *The Murderers Among Us,* published in 1967, Wiesenthal correctly established that Eichmann was nowhere near Altaussee in August 1945.[10] Furthermore, if he really did believe that Eichmann was in Altaussee, why did he not take the 'Jeep and two soldiers' and cover himself in glory? Instead, Wiesenthal writes that he informed the CIC in Bad Aussee, which in turn instructed the Austrian police to make the arrest, which again seems startling.[11] The war had only been over for three months, and at that time the CIC was not minded to entrust the Austrians with the arrest of a major criminal such as Eichmann. The Austrian police supposedly visited the wrong address – Fischerndorf 38 rather than Fischerndorf 8 – where they luckily found Eichmann's former escape partner SS-Obersturmführer Anton Burger, whom they arrested.[12] Wiesenthal told the CIC that they had raided the wrong address, and soon a CIC agent visited number 8, where he found Eichmann's wife, who told the American that she had divorced Eichmann, and that she had not seen him since she left Prague in March 1945.[13] Wiesenthal, his suspicions aroused, travelled to Altaussee, where he questioned the owner of the Parkhotel, Frau Maria Pucher, who told him that Eichmann had stayed there with his wife at the beginning of May, and had stolen one of her husband's civilian suits.[14] However, as Wiesenthal himself admitted in 1967, he 'wasn't much of an investigator in those days', and curiously he did not himself discuss Frau Pucher's testimony with Eichmann's wife while he was in Altaussee.[15] Instead, he left it to the CIC, who found Frau Eichmann was sticking to her story. But by 1989, the then eighty-year-old Wiesenthal would give the impression that he had indeed visited Frau Eichmann with the CIC. 'We confronted Frau Eichmann-Liebl with that statement,' he wrote, 'but she stuck to hers: she hadn't seen her husband since her divorce in Prague.'[16] However, it is unlikely that the CIC would have brought him along, as Wiesenthal did not work for the CIC at that time.[17]

But there are greater problems with Wiesenthal's story. As we know, the Americans did not visit Eichmann's wife in August 1945. In fact, the CIC in Oberösterreich did not start investigating Eichmann until October 1946.[18] Their attention was brought to the house at Fischerndorf 8 through an intermediary of Frau von Schirach that same month, and this intermediary could not have been Wiesenthal, because he says, quite specifically, that he received his information from his helper called 'Max' on 1 August 1945, and he passed it on immediately.[19] Another of Wiesenthal's claims is also incorrect. Although Anton Burger was indeed arrested by the Austrian police, his arrest was not on the instructions of the CIC, and it had nothing to do with any putative search by Wiesenthal for Eichmann. Burger was arrested simply because he had been spotted by a local huntsman behaving suspiciously with a box near a hut.[20] However, the most damaging attack on Wiesenthal's story comes from Tuviah Friedman, a fellow Nazi hunter with whom he worked in Linz, who stated that in 1945 neither of them had heard the name 'Eichmann', and 'nor did we know about the decisive part he played in the "Final Solution of the Jewish Problem in Europe"'. In fact, Wiesenthal's colleague claims that they only heard about Eichmann in 1946.[21] If this is the case, then everything that Wiesenthal claims about his hunt for Eichmann in 1945 and in early 1946 is a lie.

Unless this testimony and the dates and information on all the CIC documents are incorrect, the kindest explanation is that Wiesenthal's memory has let him down over the years. However, throughout his long life, the one attribute that many ascribed to him was his astonishing memory. '[He] possesses what is usually called a photographic memory,' wrote a friend of many decades. 'He is a man who cannot forget.'[22] In 1961, when Wiesenthal was inter-viewed for the Yad Vashem archive by the Israeli journalist Haim

Maas about his war years, Maas noted that his interviewee had a 'phenomenal memory for names and circumstances, even dates'.[23] If Wiesenthal's memory was not at fault, then why did he make so many errors? There can only be one explanation. He was attempting to falsely establish that he was always on Eichmann's trail. In claiming that he had knowledge of Eichmann immediately after the war, Wiesenthal was able to claim credit for the actions of others, and by doing so he could weave his way into the heart of the story. However, Wiesenthal would fabricate many more stories concerning his 'hunt' for not only Eichmann, but also men such as Mengele. Wiesenthal also appears to have invented episodes about his life before his liberation from Mauthausen.

What we do know is that Simon Wiesenthal was born on 31 December 1908 in his parents' bedroom in Buczacz in Galicia. Now in the Ukraine and called Buchach, the town was then part of the Austro-Hungarian Empire.[24] The Wiesenthals were Jewish, and Simon's father, Asher, had fled the pogroms in Russia in 1905.[25] Buczacz made a good place to settle, as six thousand of its ten thousand inhabitants were Jewish, while the remainder were Poles and Ukrainians. Despite forming the majority, the Jews lacked both political and financial security. Although they did not live in a ghetto, they were gathered in the centre, while the more prosperous Poles and Ukrainians lived on the periphery.[26] Asher Wiesenthal made a good living trading in commodities such as sugar, and the family enjoyed a certain level of affluence. Two years later, another boy, Hillel, was born, and Wiesenthal displayed the jealousy typical of an elder sibling. 'I felt that my mother was devoting herself exclusively to my little brother,' he recalled.[27] However, a few years later, the family would be torn apart in the way common to so many millions – Asher Wiesenthal was killed in 1915 while serving on the Eastern Front.[28]

In order to escape the marauding Cossacks, the family moved to Vienna, where they settled on the Bäuerlegasse in the Jewish quarter. They returned to Buczacz two years later, where they were safe for a while. After the Armistice, Buczacz changed hands frequently, but for children such as Wiesenthal, the only sign that the town was under a new regime was the changing portrait behind their teacher's desk.[29] However, in 1920, the eleven-year-old Wiesenthal was to

suffer his first anti-Semitic assault.[30] During a brief occupation of
the town during the Kiev Offensive, in which the Poles and the
Ukrainians drove the Soviets east, forces loyal to the Ukrainian
leader Simon Petliura demanded that the Jews of Buczacz supply
them with a vast amount of alcohol. 'I can still see it as vividly as if
it happened yesterday,' Wiesenthal told a biographer years later.
'One day they demanded 100 litres of Schnapps to be delivered
before nightfall.'[31] If the Jews did not comply, then the town would
be burned down. The Jews managed it, but they had to endure the
drunken Ukrainians stalking their streets. 'We were virtual prisoners
in our houses,' said Wiesenthal. Unable to get out to buy food,
Wiesenthal's mother asked their neighbour across the street if she
could have some yeast to bake some bread.[32] Afraid to venture out
herself, she decided that it would be safer to send a child over the
road. Wiesenthal dashed across and fetched the yeast, but on his
return, a Ukrainian on a horse appeared. Drawing his sabre, he
charged straight at the young boy, and stabbed Wiesenthal's right
thigh down to the bone. The soldier rode off, leaving the eleven-
year-old bleeding in the street. People screamed from all around, and
Wiesenthal was soon carried back into his house. A doctor was
called, who evaded the attentions of the Ukrainians by clambering
through cellars and gardens to get to his patient. The wound was
stitched and dressed, but the scar, according to Wiesenthal, would
always remain. 'As I grew bigger,' he told one biographer, 'the scar
also grew bigger.'[33] Wiesenthal regarded his scar as part of a long
line of evidence that proved that he was protected 'from violent
death by an unseen power that wanted him kept alive for a
purpose'.[34]

Three years later, in 1923, Wiesenthal entered the Humanistic
Gymnasium in Buczacz, where he met his future wife, Cyla Müller,
who was a distant relative of Sigmund Freud.[35] That year also
marked a tragedy in Wiesenthal's life, as his brother Hillel broke his
back after a fall; the young boy died later the same year. In 1926,
Wiesenthal's mother remarried and moved with her new husband to
Dolina in the foothills of the Carpathian Mountains.[36] However,
Wiesenthal decided that he would rather continue at the
Gymnasium, and during the term time he stayed with Cyla and her
parents, and visited his mother during the holidays. In 1927,

Wiesenthal failed his *Matura*, which meant that he was unable to pass out of school. According to Cyla, her boyfriend failed not because he was incapable, but more because he liked playing truant in order to concentrate on his drawing.[37] Wiesenthal did pass the following year, when he was nineteen. This enabled him to go to university, where his drawing skills made architecture a natural course of study. Wiesenthal's first choice was the Technical University at Lviv, which was only 80 miles away. However, the university, which was then under Polish rule, allowed only a limited number of places for Jews, and Wiesenthal was denied a place.

Wiesenthal instead enrolled at the Czech Technical University in Prague in 1928. 'It was a new world for me,' Wiesenthal recalled. 'There were more than 30,000 foreign students.'[38] For a young Jew from a relative backwater, the city was a liberating experience. He found his métier as a raconteur, and he even appeared under the footlights as a stand-up comedian.[39] Throughout the rest of his life, Wiesenthal's skill as a storyteller would stand him in good stead. In fact, his background was ideal for any aspiring fabulist. Like many from Galicia, Wiesenthal would have spent his childhood immersed in the Polish literary genre of *gaweda szlachecka* – 'noblemen's chat' – in which increasingly tall stories would be told over the dinner table. Jews, with many trades and professions closed to them, were also apt to magnify their own experiences in order to appear more successful. Wiesenthal would have been further influenced by the otherworldliness of the mystical Hasidic tales, which originated and flourished in eastern Europe. In a place such as Buczacz in the 1920s, truth was therefore a relatively elastic concept, and Wiesenthal's later accounts of his achievements can partly be seen as products of this attitude.

Despite – or perhaps because of – his success on the stage, Wiesenthal's studies went less well. Although he matriculated on 21 February 1929, Wiesenthal never completed his architecture degree. He passed his first state examination on 15 February 1932, and then he left that same year.[40] Most biographies – including that on the Simon Wiesenthal Center's website – state that Wiesenthal did graduate from the Czech Technical University.[41] At this point, the nature of Wiesenthal's further education grows distinctly murky. According to some biographies – all of which were published during their subject's lifetime – Wiesenthal was eventually allowed to enter Lviv Technical University in either 1934 or 1935, from where in 1939, seven years after he left Prague, he gained his Polish diploma as an architectural engineer.[42] However, the Lviv State Archives have no record of Simon Wiesenthal having studied at Lviv Technical University.[43] The archives have records for other students, but not for Wiesenthal. Nevertheless, Wiesenthal was to claim fraudulently throughout his life that he did have a diploma – his letterheads proudly display it – but there were some who had their justified doubts. Tuviah Friedman recalled how when he first met Wiesenthal, 'he presented himself as a chartered engineer whose diploma was lost in the concentration camps'. Wiesenthal told his comrade that he had studied in Prague, but Friedman 'never understood why he couldn't get a copy of his diploma from Prague'.[44] And, even if Friedman's memory is at fault concerning Prague, it is hard to understand why Wiesenthal could not get a copy of his diploma from Lviv. Curiously, in one of his earlier memoirs, *The Murderers Among Us*, there is no mention of Wiesenthal having attended any form of educational establishment in Lviv.[45] His supposed studies at the Technical University in that city are only mentioned in later accounts.[46]

If Simon Wiesenthal was not studying in Lviv from the mid-1930s until the war, what was he doing? Without a diploma, he could not have been a practising architect, a fact which is further supported by the absence of his name in the definitive pre-war *Katalog Architektów i Budowniczych* (Catalogue of Architects and Builders).[47] A curriculum vitae Wiesenthal completed after the war states that he worked as a supervisor in a table factory in Lviv until December 1939, on a wage of eight hundred zlotys.[48] On 9 September 1936, he married Cyla in a rabbi's house in Lviv. Three years later, on 22 September 1939, Lviv surrendered to the Russians. According to Wiesenthal, he and his family only managed to escape the Soviet anti-Jewish measures by bribing an NKVD commissar to give them regular passports, rather than the so-called Paragraph II passports which were issued to Jews. This enabled him to stay in Lviv until the Nazi invasion of June 1941, although he was reduced to working as a mechanic in a factory making bedsprings.[49] However, an Israeli intelligence report on Wiesenthal tells a different story. It states that Wiesenthal was sent to a labour camp, after which he was 'put to work as an engineer in a pen factory in Odessa'.[50] When this was put to Wiesenthal by his biographer Hella Pick in the early 1990s, he maintained that it was 'pure invention'. The only link he had with Odessa was that his boss in Lviv had sent him there on several occasions to help draw up plans for a new factory. However, the curriculum vitae clearly shows that Wiesenthal *was* in Odessa from December 1939 to April 1940, where he worked for the Soviets as an 'architect' on a wage of 1,500 roubles. He then returned to Lviv, where he appeared to continue similar work on the same salary until the end of June 1941 – the time of the Nazi invasion. Wiesenthal even told the CIC a similar story in May 1948, when he revealed that between 1939 and 1941 he worked as a Soviet senior engineer in Odessa and Lviv.[51] Wiesenthal told Pick that the CIC interrogation was 'an almost unrecognizable distortion of the facts'.[52] If this was so, then why did he enter similar facts on his curriculum vitae? To another biographer, Wiesenthal would admit that he had indeed spent time in Odessa, where he apprenticed as a 'building engineer' for twenty-one months, but it was from 1934 to 1935.[53] This claim clearly contradicts what Wiesenthal told at least two biographers and the CIC, as well as his own curriculum vitae. The ultimate confirmation of Wiesenthal's duplicity comes from his own words in his 1961 memoir, *Ich Jagte Eichmann*, in which he clearly states that he had been in Odessa in 1940 and 1941. Perhaps mindful of this contradiction, in his 1967 memoir, *The Murderers Among Us*, he merely states that he had been there 'before the war'.[54] Therefore there can be little doubt that Wiesenthal, far from being a victim of the Soviet invasion, in fact benefited from it. His salary nearly doubled, and his professional status was enhanced. Later, Wiesenthal would claim a deep 'aversion to Communism',[55] but from 1939 to 1941, he was happy to keep any aversion quiet in order to take the Soviet shilling.

When Lviv fell to the Nazis, Wiesenthal claimed that he and a Jewish friend called Gross were arrested by a Ukrainian auxiliary policeman at 4 p.m. on Sunday 6 July 1941. In at least three of his autobiographies, Wiesenthal is very specific about this time and date – in fact, it is one of the few dates that remain constant in his ever-shifting life story. Frogmarched to Brigidki prison, Wiesenthal was put in a line of some forty other Jews in a courtyard. Then the Ukrainians started shooting each man in the neck, working their way down the line towards Wiesenthal. However, Wiesenthal was literally saved by the bell – in this instance a peal of church bells signifying evening Mass. Incredibly, the Ukrainians halted their execution in order to go to worship. Wiesenthal, along with some twenty other survivors, was then led to the cells, where he claims he fell asleep. He was woken a few hours later by a Ukrainian former work colleague called Bodnar, who was now serving as an auxiliary policeman. Bodnar had decided he wanted to save Wiesenthal and Gross from the continuation of the massacre, and so he told his comrades that the two men were in fact 'Russian spies', which would mean that they would have to be questioned. Although they would be brutally treated, they would have a greater chance of survival. Unsurprisingly, Wiesenthal and his friend agreed, and, as Bodnar predicted, the two Jews were indeed badly beaten and Wiesenthal lost two front teeth. Bodnar managed to stop his fellow Ukrainians from killing the men, and he deposited them in the Ukrainian commissar's office in the early morning. As the commissar was not yet at work, Wiesenthal and Gross decided to clean his office, and when he arrived, the delighted commissar told them to go home.[56] According to Wiesenthal's 1989 memoir, *Justice Not Vengeance*, Bodnar helped only Wiesenthal, and instead of taking Wiesenthal to the commissar's office, he took him straight back home.[57]

Although this seems more plausible, the story in either form does raise questions concerning the possibility that a suspected spy would manage to get away quite so easily. Certainly, the Ukrainians carried out a brutal series of pogroms in Lviv in early July 1941, and it is not unlikely that Wiesenthal was the near victim of such a rampage.[58] Wiesenthal's specificity about the date and time is notable, however, because whenever Wiesenthal is so specific, he is usually lying. In fact, according to *his own* testimony that he gave to the American War Crimes Branch after the war, he was actually arrested on 13 July 1941, and he managed to escape 'through a bribe'.[59] There is *no mention* of his being helped by a sympathetic Ukrainian, or posing as a Russian spy. That Wiesenthal brought the date forward to 6 July is also significant, as there had been a pause in the pogroms in Lviv in the middle of that month, and they were not to start again until 25 July.[60] By placing his arrest at the beginning of July 1941, his story would fit in with the timing of the Ukrainian pogroms. The story of his sensational escape – one of the most famous of Simon Wiesenthal's war, and one that has helped to establish the notion of his divine mission – is in all likelihood a complete fabrication.[61]

From June until November 1941, Wiesenthal's curriculum vitae merely states that he was 'without work'. During this time, he and his wife Cyla were moved into the ghetto in Lviv, having been expelled from their flat by an SS man in order to house a Polish prostitute.[62] Although the ghetto was squalid, it represented a limited type of freedom, which came to an end when the couple were dispatched to Janowska, a concentration camp just outside Lviv. Wiesenthal was made to work in the Eastern Railway Repair Works (the OAW), where he had to paint over Soviet insignia on railway engines with swastikas and new inscriptions. Cyla had a job polishing brass and nickel and, for a while, conditions were bearable. Wiesenthal was soon promoted to draughtsman, although he worried about his and Cyla's eventual fate. Although Cyla was Jewish, she was blonde, and Wiesenthal reckoned that she had a chance of surviving if she escaped and adopted the identity of a non-Jewish Pole. Wiesenthal approached members of a Polish underground cell in the OAW, and he cut a deal with them to supply all the details of the Lviv railway junction in return for providing his wife with false papers. After a false start, Cyla eventually made it to Warsaw, where she worked in a radio factory and would survive the war.[63]

It was at the OAW where Wiesenthal worked for the man who he would claim to be his saviour. Adolf Kohlrautz was the Senior Inspector at the works, and Wiesenthal discovered that despite being German, he was secretly anti-Nazi. According to Wiesenthal, he and Kohlrautz built up such a rapport that he even allowed Wiesenthal to keep two pistols that he had received from the Polish underground movement.[64] On 20 April 1943, Kohlrautz's friendship with Wiesenthal was tested to its very limits, as, once again, Wiesenthal was apparently selected for a mass execution. The call for this massacre was a grim celebration of Hitler's fifty-fourth birthday, and the SS at Janowska picked a number of Jewish intelligentsia who would be sacrificed.[65] When the SS were seemingly unable to find enough intellectuals among the several thousand Jews in the main body of the camp, Wiesenthal recalled how he and two others were taken from the OAW despite the protestations of Kohlrautz, who said that he needed the men.[66] Wiesenthal was driven 2 miles by truck to the camp, where he joined his fellow Jews. Silently, they walked towards a huge sandpit which was 6 feet deep and 1,500 feet long. A few dead bodies were visible in the pit.[67] The Jews were forced to undress and were then herded in a single row down a barbed-wire corridor known as 'The Hose' up to the edge of the pit. An SS man called Kauzer proceeded to shoot each Jew, allowing the bodies to fall into the sandpit. There was no doubt that Wiesenthal was about to die. However, a whistle interrupted the sound of the gunshots, and with it came the shout of 'Wiesenthal!' An SS man called Koller ran forward, and told Wiesenthal to follow him. 'I staggered like a drunk,' Wiesenthal said. 'Koller slapped my face twice and brought me back to earth. I was walking back through the hose, naked. Behind me, the sounds of shooting resumed, but they were over long before I had reached the camp.'[68] Wiesenthal was deposited back at the OAW, where he found a beaming Kohlrautz, who had appealed to the camp commander that it was essential that Wiesenthal was kept alive. He convinced him that Wiesenthal was needed to paint a poster that would feature a swastika, and the words 'We Thank Our Führer'. 'I'm glad it wasn't too late, Wiesenthal,' Kohlrautz said. 'Come to think of it, it isn't only the Führer's birthday. It's yours too.'[69]

Yet again, Wiesenthal had seemingly cheated death in a miraculous fashion. We only have Wiesenthal's word for this story, as, according to Wiesenthal, Kohlrautz was killed in the battle for Berlin on 19 April 1945. (He told a biographer that Kohlrautz was killed on the Russian front in 1944.)[70] In an affidavit Wiesenthal made in August 1954 about his wartime persecutions, he neglects to include this story – which would surely be regarded as a major per- secution – although he does mention the comparatively trivial offence of being hit several times, by, among others, a man called 'Georg Gross' of Eberswalde near Berlin.[71] (It can only be assumed that this is a different 'Gross' from the man with whom Wiesenthal would sometimes say he had been arrested in July 1941.) Wiesenthal even mentions Kohlrautz in the same document, but does not record the German's life-saving intervention. Neither does he record Kohlrautz's action in the testimony he gave to the Americans in May 1945, and merely states that he is a 'potentially useful source of further information', although he does acknowledge that Kohlrautz and a man called Werner Schmidt 'were of great assistance in preventing many cruelties'.[72] At the very least, in both these documents, Wiesenthal is ungrateful to Kohlrautz for saving his life. It is of course equally possible that the event is simply another fabrication.

On 2 October 1943, Wiesenthal escaped from the camp. Kohlrautz warned him that the camp and its prisoners were shortly to be liquidated, and the German issued passes to Wiesenthal and his friend Arthur Scheiman, a former circus director, to visit a stationery shop in town. Accompanied by a Ukrainian guard who Wiesenthal describes as being 'stupid-looking', the two men managed to slip out the back of the shop while the Ukrainian waited outside. From this point until the middle of 1944, there are so many versions of what happened to Wiesenthal that it is impossible to establish a reliable train of events. According to his August 1954 affidavit, Wiesenthal says that he hid in a friends' barn outside Lviv until January 1944 when the Gestapo captured him and took him back to Lviv. There, he was tortured until he slit his wrists, and then 'although it was somewhat unusual', he was sent to the prison's infirmary from where he was released back to a supposedly renascent Lviv Labour Camp in March. Wiesenthal claims he was evacuated along with the rest of the camp's inmates in July. This account also tallies with an application Wiesenthal made in 1955 for reparations.[73]

However, in *The Murderers Among Us*, Wiesenthal claims that he was not arrested until 13 June 1944 – some six months after the version on the affidavit. He and a friend were found by two Polish policemen and an SS man hiding under the floorboards of a friend's ground-floor flat. When they were searched, the SS man found Wiesenthal's diary, as well as a list of SS guards that Wiesenthal had compiled during his time at Janowska. Miraculously, Wiesenthal's pistol was not found, although it was later discovered at the police station by one of the Polish detectives. Once again, there was another stroke of luck – the detective decided to keep it to sell on the black market.[74] Despite his incriminating list of SS personnel, Wiesenthal was not taken to the Gestapo, but was transferred to Janowska camp, which he claims had been re-established after all other accounts state that it had been liquidated in November 1943.[75] In *Justice Not Vengeance*, published in 1989, the story is similar, although the arrest is made in April 1944 and not June.[76] Both accounts claim that the Gestapo only came for Wiesenthal two days later, and as he was being transferred to the Gestapo headquarters, he slashed his wrists with a small razor blade and passed out, losing 2,000 grams of blood.[77] There was another miracle. Instead of being left to die for being a spy, Wiesenthal was taken to the Gestapo prison hospital where he was nursed back to health in order that he could be interrogated. However, in both these accounts, Wiesenthal was never interrogated, and the following month, he was taken down to the courtyard to join a group of Jews for 'deportation'. 'I looked at the others the way some people on an aeroplane look at their fellow travellers,' Wiesenthal said. 'If there should be a crash, they are thinking, these will be my companions in death.'[78] Yet again, there was a miracle, this time in the form of an explosion on the nearby Sapieha Street, where an aircraft had been shot down. Smoke filled the Gestapo headquarters, and Wiesenthal and his fellow Jews were quickly evacuated to Janowska camp.

What neither *Justice Not Vengeance* nor *The Murderers Among Us* mention is Wiesenthal's supposed career as an officer in the partisans, whom he claimed in a post-war affidavit to have joined after his escape from Janowska in October 1943.[79] In his CIC interrogation in May 1948, Wiesenthal told his questioner that he joined a group that was operating in the Tarnopol area east of Lviv. The group belonged to the *Armija Ludowa* (AL), the pro-Soviet Polish partisans, and according to Wiesenthal he was immediately made a lieutenant 'on the basis of my intellect'.[80] He was soon promoted to major, and he claimed to have been instrumental in 'building bunkers and fortification lines'. 'We had fabulous bunker constructions,' he told the CIC. 'My rank was not so much as a strategic expert as a technical expert.' By February, Wiesenthal and his group were surrounded, and he changed out of his AL uniform into Polish civilian clothes before going into hiding. During his CIC interrogation, Wiesenthal said that he was eventually captured in June, although he would later claim that not only was he holding documents concerning SS guards, but that he also had maps of partisan emplacements that he had drawn up to help the Russian army. 'I had to do something useful with my time,' he said.[81] It seems extraordinary that Wiesenthal would not have destroyed such documents if he feared capture by the Germans, although he would claim that they were coded in such a way that only he could understand them.[82] Presumably they were not coded to the extent that the Germans could not tell what they were, because as Wiesenthal himself admitted, 'I owe it specially to these circumstances that I was not killed right away . . . for these records seemed to be very valuable partisan documents.'[83]

Wiesenthal's account of his time in the partisans raises yet more questions. Although the AL was not anti-Semitic, it is extremely surprising that it willingly made a Jew an officer. Notwithstanding Wiesenthal's Jewishness, it is unlikely that any partisan movement would swiftly embrace a complete stranger, let alone make him an officer. It is also curious that Wiesenthal was able to join the AL after escaping from Janowska in the autumn of 1943, as the AL was not formed until January 1944. Wiesenthal may have joined the *Armija Krajowa* (AK), which was formed in 1942, but he was most specific in his CIC interrogation that he joined the AL. It is also possible that he joined the forerunner to the AL, the *Gwardia Ludowa* (GL), but by the autumn of 1943, partisan operations around Lviv were being run by Soviet partisans. Wiesenthal's referral to wearing a uniform is also suspect, as partisan groups were not uniformed forces. It is also unlikely that whichever partisan group Wiesenthal claimed to have joined would have had such a 'fabulous' series of bunker constructions that required Wiesenthal's special technical skills. The partisans relied on mobility to stay out of German clutches, and any fortifications that they did build were little more than dug-outs. Wiesenthal's maps of the partisan emplacements are also problematic. The AL had plenty of liaison men with the Russians, and there was no discernible need for Wiesenthal to produce such sketches. It is also unfeasible that his fellow partisans would have allowed him to produce such potentially compromising material, in which case Wiesenthal would have had to have made it secretly. Again, not only is this unlikely, but also it would have been extremely risky for Wiesenthal. Had he been caught by his fellow partisans, they would have assumed that he was a spy. If Wiesenthal really did join the partisans, and he really did make such sketches, then for whom was he making them?

In his account of his war years for Yad Vashem, he tells yet another story. In this instance, Wiesenthal does not claim to join the AL, but instead a more motley band. According to one biographer, 'there were a few Jews, a Polish priest and several other Poles, some French and Belgian prisoners of war who had escaped, and a sprinkling of Russians and Ukrainians.'[84] This hardly sounds like a body which could have built 'fabulous bunker constructions' and neither does it sound like a body which would have had a formal system of promotion that would have enabled Wiesenthal to climb from lieutenant to major. The only formalized partisan group that Wiesenthal talks about in this account is the AK, who he says helped to hide him despite the fact that he was a Jew.

With at least four wildly different accounts of Wiesenthal's activities between October 1943 and the middle of 1944, serious questions must be raised. Some, such as the former Austrian Chancellor Bruno Kreisky, repeatedly accused Wiesenthal in the 1970s and the 1980s of being a collaborator with the Gestapo. Kreisky's claims were supported by unsubstantiated evidence provided by the Polish and Soviet governments, and when Wiesenthal took Kreisky to court, Wiesenthal won. Two affidavits made by former members of the German army also indicate that Wiesenthal was a collaborator, but such claims must be treated with caution.[85] Smearing Wiesenthal is a popular pastime for anti-Semites, Holocaust deniers, so-called 'Revisionists' and other such cranks. But the multiplicity of conflicting stories demands that such questions must be raised by researchers who have no agenda.

Whatever the truth, Wiesenthal appeared to be back in Lviv in the middle of 1944. The camp commandant at Janowska was SS-Hauptsturmführer Friedrich Warzok, who apparently welcomed Wiesenthal as 'the lost son who has come back'.[86] Rather than having Wiesenthal shot, Warzok decided to spare his life, as well as those of the thirty-three other Jews who remained in the camp. According to Wiesenthal, Warzok kept them alive in order to keep himself in his job. Without a camp to run, Warzok would have been sent to the front.[87] On 19 July 1944, Warzok took his protective shield of Jews to the railway station, from where they were put on a train heading west. After travelling just 60 miles, the party got off at Przemyśl, and Warzok told them that they were going to pose as 'non-German forced labourers' for the *Organisation Todt*. He then revealed that they were in fact going to head to Slovakia, where they would hide in a wood until the war was over. He ordered the Jews to remove their yellow star badges, and to avoid any talk of what had happened at Janowska. 'We 34 Jews became the life insurance for almost 200 SS men,' Wiesenthal recalled. 'We were all going to be a happy family.'[88] This incredible odyssey would end at the beginning of September, when Warzok's senior officer established what he was doing. Most of the Jews in Warzok's party were executed, but, once again, Wiesenthal miraculously survived, and he soon found himself in Plaszów concentration camp, where he was put to work digging the bodies out of mass graves and burning them.[89] Presumably, this must have been the most gruesome of jobs, but Wiesenthal makes no mention of it in *The Murderers Among Us* and *Justice Not Vengeance*. This scene is memorably captured in the 1993 film *Schindler's List*. It is perhaps just a coincidence that Wiesenthal only revealed his role in unearthing and burning the corpses after that film had come out.

In November, Wiesenthal was moved 200 miles northwest to Gross-Rosen near Wrocław, where he had the more agreeable task of peeling potatoes. It was at Gross-Rosen where he was to hear that his wife had in all likelihood died during the Warsaw Uprising when the AK had tried to liberate Warsaw. Her street had been destroyed by the Germans, and Wiesenthal's informant told him that 'Topiel Street is one large mass grave.'[90] Despite this heart-wrenching news, the miracles would not desert Simon Wiesenthal. Forced to work barefoot in the quarry for failing to correctly acknowledge an SS man, he soon learned that the team of a hundred prisoners assigned to the *kommando* shrank by one each day. After a few days, Wiesenthal felt sure that his turn was about to come. 'My executioner was behind me,' he recalled, 'poised to smash my head with a rock. I turned around, and the man, surprised, dropped his stone. It crushed my toe. I screamed.'[91] Wiesenthal's quick reactions and yell apparently saved his life, because there was some form of

industrial inspection at Gross-Rosen that day – Wiesenthal thought
it may have been by the Red Cross – and so he was stretchered away
to the first-aid station. One of his fellow prisoners, who was a
doctor, diagnosed that an amputation was required, and his toe was
cut off without anaesthesia while two men held him still. The
following day, Wiesenthal said that he developed a fever and he was
in agony. 'The doctor came back,' he remembered, 'and saw that I
had a septic blister on the sole of my foot. So they cut it open and
the gangrene spurted all over the room.'[92] Yet again, one of
Wiesenthal's 'miracles' is open to doubt. First, the story – and it is a
dramatic one – appears in no other memoir or statement. Secondly,
if the Red Cross really were inspecting Gross-Rosen that day, then
the SS would have temporarily halted any executions. As it was,
Kaltenbrunner only allowed the Red Cross access to certain camps
in March 1945, and Wiesenthal was to leave Gross-Rosen in
January or February of that year. Even if the 'inspection' were
carried out by some other body, it is hard to ascertain what body it
might have been which would have stopped an SS man finishing
Wiesenthal off. Thirdly, the medical consequences seem entirely
implausible.

With either nine toes or ten, Wiesenthal managed to walk 170
miles west to Chemnitz when Gross-Rosen was evacuated. 'Each
day we covered around twenty miles,' he recalled. 'We slept in the
snow, and during a march that lasted four to five days all we had by
way of sustenance was one kilo of bread each.'[93] Although
Wiesenthal's figures must be out, walking on a gangrenous foot with
a recently amputated toe would have been hellish. Instead of a shoe,
Wiesenthal had only the sleeve of an old coat which was wrapped
around his foot with some wire. For a walking stick he had a
broomstick. Of the six thousand prisoners who marched out, only
4,800 arrived in Chemnitz.[94] With his infected foot, Wiesenthal was
lucky to be one of those who made it. At Chemnitz, the prisoners
were put on trains, and they were taken briefly to Buchenwald
before being sent by train on to Mauthausen camp, about 13 miles
southeast of Linz in Austria.

Wiesenthal arrived at the camp on the frozen night of 7 February
1945. In *The Murderers Among Us*, he tells how he and a fellow
prisoner, Prince Radziwill, linked arms to march the 4 miles uphill

to the camp. However, the effort was too great, and the two men collapsed into the snow. An SS man fired a shot between them, but as the two men did not get up, they were left for dead. At this point, Wiesenthal said that he and Radziwill passed out in the sub-zero temperature. Just before dawn, the camp authorities sent out lorries to collect those who had died on the march, and the bodies of Wiesenthal and Radziwill were so frozen that they were assumed to have perished. Thrown on to a pile of corpses, the two were transported to the crematorium, where it was realized by the prisoners assigned to the *kommando* that Wiesenthal and Radziwill were not dead. The two men were given a cold shower to thaw them out, and Wiesenthal was then taken to Block VI – the 'death block'.[95] In his account to Yad Vashem, Wiesenthal mentioned that the infection from his foot had now turned blue-green, and that it had spread right up to his knee.[96]

Wiesenthal lay in the block for three months until the end of the war. Too weak to get out of bed, he claimed he survived – incredibly – on 200 calories a day, along with the occasional piece of bread or sausage smuggled to him by a friendly Pole called Eduard Staniszewski, whom Wiesenthal had known in Poznań.[97] Staniszewski also brought Wiesenthal pencils and paper, which the 'architect' used to design a fabulous coffee-house that Staniszewski was going to open after the war.[98] In another account, Wiesenthal recalled how Staniszewski was in fact the emissary of the *kapos* – the inmates who acted as guards – and Wiesenthal drew birthday pictures for them in exchange for the extra nutrition. The same account also records how Wiesenthal drew pictures and made collages of the horrors of Mauthausen, although quite how he was able to get around the camp to observe such horrors in his weakened state and with his infected leg is unclear.[99] Many of the pictures were collected to form a book called *KZ Mauthausen: Pictures and Words*, which Wiesenthal published in 1946. Some have suggested that the images were largely the product of Wiesenthal's active imagination. One image is certainly the result of plagiarism. Wiesenthal's drawing, which is dated 1945, shows the result of an execution by firing squad carried out at Mauthausen. Tied to three stakes are the bodies of three inmates who have just been shot. Behind them is an agricultural fence, beyond which rages some sort of inferno.

However, the three figures are identical to those in a selection of photographs in the June 1945 issue of *Life* magazine, which shows three German soldiers shot by an American firing squad during the Battle of the Bulge. There can be no doubt that Wiesenthal copied the photographs of the German soldiers and passed the drawing off as a scene that took place in Mauthausen. When it was put to Wiesenthal many years later that this is what he had done, he merely told his biographer that it was 'all part of the character assassinations orchestrated against him from certain quarters in the United States'.[100] According to the same biographer, the pictures of Mauthausen were 'virtually the last time that he exercised those gifts' of draughtsmanship, which she puts down to a form of self-denial, the same quality that he displayed when he refused to return to architecture.[101] As we now know, Wiesenthal could not 'return' to that field, as he had never qualified as an architect. His refusal to draw also suggests the possibility that he was in fact no draughtsman, and that the pictures were not even his. Those with an aptitude for drawing rarely give it up.

Mauthausen was liberated on 5 May 1945. Despite weighing just 100 pounds, Wiesenthal struggled outside to greet the American tanks. 'I don't know how I managed to get up and walk,' he recalled.[102] Wiesenthal's ability to walk is indeed surprising, so it must be assumed that his severely infected leg had recovered during the previous three months. If it had done so, then it would have to have been cured by either amputation or antibiotics. We know the former did not take place, and the latter was emphatically not a common cause of treatment for ailing Jews in Nazi concentration camps. Once again, it appears as though another miracle had taken place. 'I do not remember how I managed to get from my room to the courtyard,' Wiesenthal wrote in *The Murderers Among Us*. 'I was hardly able to walk. I was wearing my faded, striped uniform with the yellow "J" in a yellow and red double triangle.'[103] (Wiesenthal's badge indicates that he was a Jewish political prisoner, although it is not known for what political offence he was incarcerated in addition to his Jewishness.) Wiesenthal collapsed before he reached the tank, and an American soldier lifted him up and took him back to his bunk, where he was nursed back to health.

A few days later, Wiesenthal was assaulted by a Polish former prisoner. 'As I shuffled along a dark corridor,' Wiesenthal recalled, 'a man jumped at me and knocked me down.'[104] Wiesenthal was knocked unconscious, and when he revived, two friends informed him that his assailant was a Polish 'trusty', and they speculated that Wiesenthal had been attacked because the Pole was angry that Wiesenthal was still alive. The Pole was forced to apologize, and Wiesenthal put the incident behind him. However, by the late 1980s, Wiesenthal had dramatically changed the story. The trusty was no longer without a name, and was now called Kazimierz Rusinek, who was in charge of issuing passes. In the new version of the story, Wiesenthal had visited Rusinek's office just two days after the liberation in order to get a pass to leave the camp for a few hours. (He had clearly recovered swiftly.) Instead of giving him a piece of paper, Rusinek beat him and threw him out into the courtyard, referring to Wiesenthal as a 'damned *Muselman*', which was the term used for prisoners who were so weak that they would shortly be murdered. As in the first story, Rusinek was to make an apology, which Wiesenthal accepted.[105] Rusinek would later become Deputy Minister of Culture and Art under the Communist regime in Poland, and he was one of those in the late 1970s who accused Wiesenthal of being a collaborator. It is surely no coincidence that Wiesenthal ascribed this assault to Rusinek, who died in 1984, in order to defame him. Nevertheless, Wiesenthal's story is extremely unconvincing. Why would a Pole – no matter how antiSemitic – hit a Jew simply for being a *Muselman*? It is more likely that Wiesenthal was beaten up because he was suspected of being a collaborator.

The rapidity of Wiesenthal's recovery is so astonishing that it is doubtful whether Wiesenthal was as ill as he claimed. Just twenty days after the liberation, he wrote to the US camp commander asking whether he could be involved in assisting 'the US authorities investigating war crimes'. Claiming to have been in thirteen concentration camps – he had in fact been in no more than six – Wiesenthal supplied a list of ninety-one names of those who he felt were responsible for 'incalculable sufferings'. Among them were Warzok; the SS commander in Galicia, SS-Gruppenführer Fritz Katzmann; Amon Göth, the commandant of Plaszów; as well as numerous SS guards and members of the Gestapo.[106] According to most accounts,

Wiesenthal asked if he could join the American war crimes investigators, and they refused, telling him he was not well enough. After he had gained some weight, he returned, and he was assigned to a Captain Tarracusio, with whom Wiesenthal claimed to have captured his first 'scalp', a snivelling SS guard called Schmidt. 'There were many others in the weeks that followed,' Wiesenthal later wrote. 'You didn't have to go far. You almost stumbled over them.'[107]

In his post-war curriculum vitae, Wiesenthal does not mention his work for the Americans, and instead lists his only occupation as the vice-chairman of the Jewish Central Committee for the US zone, based in Linz. His income was one thousand schillings.[108] The task of the Committee was to draw up lists of survivors which other survivors could consult in their hunt for their relatives. People would fight over the lists as they desperately searched, their efforts all too often without reward. Much of Wiesenthal's work took place in the Bindermichel displaced persons' camp just outside Linz,[109] and for at least a year after the war, Wiesenthal's other task was to lobby hard for his fellow Jews; he even became president of the Paris-based International Concentration Camp Organization. He also forged contacts with the Jewish Brichah organization, which smuggled Jews out of Europe to Palestine.[110] It was a member of Brichah, Asher Ben-Nathan, who had provided Wiesenthal with the file on Eichmann during his visit to Vienna in 1946.

It was not until February 1947 that Wiesenthal would form the organization that would make him famous – the Jewish Historical Documentation Centre in Linz.[111] Based at Goethestrasse 63 in Linz, the Centre was funded by Aaron Silberschein, a former Polish MP who had become a businessman in Geneva.[112] The aim of the Centre was to collate as much information on the Final Solution, with a view to securing the indictments of war criminals. Wiesenthal claimed to have started the body because of an anti-Semitic remark made by an American officer, which made him realize that the Allies would never hunt down the Nazis to the extent that was required. Sadly, Wiesenthal was to be proved right. 'It was our – the survivors' – obligation to carry on with the work on our own,' he said.[113] Wiesenthal was the first to admit that the Documentation Centre was an amateur affair, and that it lacked money and detective expertise. However, what it did have was enthusiasm, and Wiesenthal and his band of thirty volunteers travelled around the displaced persons' camps, collecting evidence on the atrocities from former concentration-camp inmates. In all, Wiesenthal's team compiled 3,289 questionnaires, which is a far more impressive feat than anything the Allies had achieved.[114]

It was only now that Wiesenthal was involved in the search for Eichmann, although his accounts of it must be treated with caution. In both *Justice Not Vengeance* and *The Murderers Among Us*, Wiesenthal allows himself to take much of the credit for securing a vital piece of the Eichmann jigsaw: a photograph. In fact, the idea for obtaining a likeness of Eichmann was that of Asher Ben-Nathan, who had visited Dieter Wisliceny in prison. There, Eichmann's lieutenant told him that he did not know the whereabouts of his former boss, but he could tell Ben-Nathan that Eichmann's driver, who was in prison in Vienna, knew the address of Eichmann's mistress. Ben-Nathan interrogated the driver, who revealed that the mistress was called Maria Mistelbach and lived in Urfahr, the district in which Linz lay.[115] Ben-Nathan instructed one of his 'field-workers', Manus Diamant, to befriend Frau Mistelbach in the hope that she might have a photograph. Posing as a former Dutch SS man, Diamant introduced himself to Mistelbach, and the two soon became lovers. 'It was hard,' Diamant recalled. 'I always carried a camera and said my hobby was photography.'[116] The ruse was to work, but it was six months before Mistelbach eventually showed her lover her photograph album. As the couple turned its pages, Mistelbach pointed to a photograph and said, 'That's my Adolf.' Diamant made a copy without Mistelbach's knowledge, and Ben-Nathan circulated further copies around various groups, including that of Wiesenthal.[117] However, in *The Murderers Among Us*, Wiesenthal claims that Diamant 'jubilantly brought it [the photo-graph] back to me, was relieved of his assignment, and returned to a more normal life'.[118] This suggests that Diamant in some way reported to Wiesenthal, which was not the truth. 'Wiesenthal had nothing to do with the discovery of the photograph,' Diamant would later insist.[119]

In late 1947, Wiesenthal performed what he regarded as his greatest service in the hunt for Eichmann. Through an American contact, Wiesenthal had heard that Eichmann's wife had applied to the district court in Bad Ischl for a death certificate for her divorced husband. 'I was too shocked to speak,' said Wiesenthal. 'Once Adolf Eichmann was officially declared dead, his name would automatically disappear off all the "Wanted" lists.'[120] The judge had told the contact that Eichmann's death had been witnessed in Prague on 30 April 1945 by one Karl Lukas, who Wiesenthal soon discovered was married to the sister of Eichmann's wife. Wiesenthal told his contact as much, and the judge correctly dismissed the application.[121] Thanks to Wiesenthal's intervention, Eichmann was kept officially alive, although the Americans and the British of course had called off their searches earlier that year. In *The Murderers Among Us*, Wiesenthal would write that this was his 'most important contribution in the search for Eichmann'. Unfortunately, as we shall see, this so-called contribution was just one more of Simon Wiesenthal's many lies.

There were other Jews who were hunting Nazis in far more effective fashion than either Wiesenthal or the Allies. Among them was Tuviah Friedman, who helped to establish a Documentation Centre in Vienna in 1946. A survivor of the ghetto in Radom in Poland, Friedman fled from the Szkolna Street camp before its inmates were dispatched to Auschwitz in July 1944. Until the first Soviet troops entered Poland, he and a friend hid in the woods, subsisting on a diet of raw potatoes. At one point, Friedman was captured by the Germans, but he managed to kill his sleeping guard and escape. 'I gripped the bayonet that was in the soldier's belt,' he wrote, 'and gently slipped it from its sheath. Sick with fear, I raised it and plunged the bayonet into his neck. I was nauseated by the sensation of ripping his flesh.'[122] When the Soviets arrived, the 22-year-old Friedman joined a group of Polish militia in Radom. Tasked with restoring order and curbing the excesses of partisan groups, the militia also had to hunt down Germans, Poles and Ukrainians who had committed war crimes against the Poles. 'With burning enthusiasm, I embarked on this last chore,' Friedman wrote.[123] For weeks, he helped to round up scores of criminals, and he was soon posted to Danzig, where he continued Nazi hunting. He and his team interrogated hundreds of suspected criminals, and

Friedman, most of whose family had been murdered in Treblinka, was not shy of using physical coercion to get to the truth. One middle-aged German, who swore he had been a schoolmaster, but had in fact been a brutal concentration-camp guard, felt Friedman's wrath. 'His answers incensed me, and I struck him severely until I drew blood,' Friedman wrote.[124] Despite being warned to curb his temper, Friedman was unable to control himself. 'I became more brutal in my dealings with the German prisoners,' he admitted. Nevertheless, he was able to justify his actions, because he felt that the beatings produced results quickly.[125] Friedman's ruthless efficiency meant that he would have been made an officer, but the idea of cosying up to the Communist Party did not appeal. Instead, like so many other Jews, he decided to head to a new life in Palestine.

Friedman reached Vienna on 4 April 1946. There, he was contacted by Asher Ben-Nathan, who persuaded him to delay his emigration in order to establish a Jewish Historical Documentation Centre in Vienna. With a monthly budget of two hundred dollars, Friedman and his staff of eight not only hunted Nazis but also worked for the *Haganah*, the secret Jewish paramilitary organization that was assisting the exodus to Palestine. Over the next two years, Friedman claimed that his team discovered some 250 Nazi criminals, most of whom were arrested.[126] Like Wiesenthal, Friedman would later claim that he spent much of this time obsessing about Eichmann. However, Friedman was clearly frustrated by due process and the slowness at which justice was dispensed. He came up with a radical and violent solution. 'We thought that if one of the dozens of camps in which top Nazis were being held turned out to be in Austria,' he recalled, 'we would gather together a very special group of volunteers and blow up the camp.'[127] Friedman's plan to commit mass murder never came to fruition, not because of any moral qualms, but rather because there was a risk to the Allied soldiers and civilian volunteers, as well as the possibility that the negotiations for the establishment of a Jewish state would be affected.[128]

However, there were Jews who did murder their former oppressors. Many came from the ranks of the Jewish Brigade, which had been formed in 1944 as part of the British army. Some five thousand strong, the 'brigaders' saw action in April 1945 in the final part of the Italian campaign, and after the war they were stationed in Tarvisio, near where the borders of Austria, Yugoslavia and Italy met. The Brigade's job was to guard the border, which was no easy task. 'We had a lot of fun and games,' recalled Alfred Levy, who was a private in the Brigade, 'as the Yugoslavs used to move the border posts in the middle of the night. They also used to loot Austria, especially Klagenfurt, from where they took whole trainloads.'[129] While those such as Levy guarded the border, there were others who used their time to wreak vengeance on the Germans. 'There were rumours going about the Brigade that there were three to four men on the hunt,' said Morris Harris, a signaller. 'We thought it was a good idea, and I think our officers turned a blind eye. There was a high spirit to find Germans and kill them, both before VE Day and after.'[130] That spirit was motivated by very personal reasons. 'Some of those seeking vengeance had families who had died in the camps,' said Gideon Fiegel, a private. 'We were a pretty hardened lot. We might have taken the view that some of the victims had what was coming to them, and we were most probably not all that sympathetic.'[131]

Fiegel claimed that the killings were carried out 'very efficiently', partly because the avengers knew how to speak German and were thus able to get around easily. They also relied upon other talents to track down their prey. Cyril Pundick, a 26-year-old dispatch rider with the Brigade, was one of those who went on such hunting expeditions in the mountains around Tarvisio. Pundick recalled:

> I used to go with a fellow called Bobby Ackerfield. He was a boxer. The other chap was called Hans Wald. However, we didn't go looking for them, because we knew where they were. This Bobby Ackerfield found out from the women where they were. I didn't know his technique, but he was amazingly good looking and he spoke pretty good Italian.

Both Wald and Ackerfield had lost their families in the camps, and when they found a German, they hauled him out of his house and interrogated him for little more than fifteen minutes. 'Ackerfield knew right away whether they were a Nazi or not,' said Pundick.

While the interrogation took place, Pundick stood outside the house making sure that their victims' Italian girlfriends did not interfere. If the German had been a member of the regular army, he was spared, but if he had served in the SS, he would be shot. The three men would then return by foot to their camp, where they would keep quiet about their night's work. 'Nobody knew anything,' said Pundick.[132]

Sometimes the Nazis would be dispatched even more swiftly. One of the teams used a covered truck on their nocturnal hunts, the floor of which was covered with mattresses. 'To get in at the back,' said one Jewish avenger, 'you had to put a foot on the bumper, part the tarpaulin and thrust your head in first. The moment the German's head appeared inside, one of us seized him by the throat and jerked him forward, falling back on the mattress as he did so.' This would cause the victim to perform an involuntary somersault, and, as he was still being grasped around the neck, his neck would break. If it did not, then the man would be strangled. This technique was once used while the victim's wife stood right next to the truck. 'If he had been able to utter a word or a cry,' said the team member, 'his wife would have started to scream and that might have had serious consequences for us.' Instead, the woman watched the truck drive away, unaware that her husband was dead by the time the driver had let in the clutch.[133] It is impossible to estimate accurately how many suspected Nazis were killed by such actions. Cyril Pundick said that he went on four or five such 'outings' in the few months he was stationed around Tarvisio. As they were certainly not nightly affairs, and conducted by a minority of the Brigade, the number killed cannot total more than five hundred.

One Jewish group from Lublin in Poland, which called itself *Nakam*, the Hebrew for 'vengeance', formulated a plan that, had it succeeded, would have overshadowed anything committed by the Jewish Brigade or mooted by Tuviah Friedman.[134] The group's target was the US internment camp at Nuremberg-Langwasser, which held 36,000 former members of the Gestapo and SS, all of whom the group intended to kill. At the beginning of 1946, members of *Nakam* installed themselves in civilian jobs in the camp, and it was soon established that the best way to carry out the mass murder was to poison the internees' bread. On the morning of Saturday

13 April, the plan was put into effect. Three of the Jews hid inside the bakery in Nuremberg, and as soon as night fell, they started to coat the loaves with arsenic. However, a storm was raging outside, and the group's activities were curtailed by some nightwatchmen who had heard a window being smashed in the gale. Nevertheless, some two thousand loaves were poisoned. As each loaf was shared by five to six men, the number of fatalities was expected to run into thousands.[135] On Monday morning, the bread was delivered, and throughout the day, around 1,900 prisoners fell sick with acute stomach pains.[136] The total rose to 2,238, and just over two hundred were hospitalized, but none were to die.[137] According to one account, the reason for the prisoners' relative good fortune was that the arsenic had been diluted by one of the *Nakam* team, who was secretly working for the Jewish leadership in Palestine, which had no desire to be implicated in an act of mass murder.[138] Other accounts would claim covered-up death tolls of between two hundred and a thousand, but these are unlikely, and besides, would have been impossible to have kept hidden.[139] The most plausible explanation is that the arsenic was simply ingested in insufficient quantity by each of the intended victims. Nearly 2 ounces of pure arsenic are required to kill the average man, and the amount of arsenic coating the crust of each slice of bread would have been considerably less than that. Despite an extensive search, the members of *Nakam* got away, and some eventually ended up in Palestine. Ironically, they would use similar escape routes to those used by the very men they wanted to kill.

Chapter Four

Helping the Rats

ON 4 JUNE 1943, a group of army officers led by Colonel Arturo Rawson mounted a *coup d'état* in Argentina. With ten thousand troops under his command, Rawson marched into Buenos Aires and overthrew the government of the country's twenty-fifth president, Ramón Castillo. Rawson installed himself as Argentina's twenty-sixth president, a position that he held for precisely three days. His choice of cabinet members infuriated the officers who had backed him, and on 7 June, Pedro Pablo Ramírez was sworn in as the twenty-seventh president. Ramírez fared somewhat better and lasted until 25 February 1944, when he was replaced by his deputy, Edelmiro Julián Farrell. Despite serving just eight months, Ramírez would leave an important legacy: he maintained Argentina's links with Nazi Germany. Such links would prove of immense consequence to men such as Eichmann and Mengele, as Argentina would prove to be uniquely hospitable not only to fugitives of their ilk, but also to the capital and expertise that the Nazis would bring. The relationship between the two countries throughout the war may have outwardly wavered, but they remained firm, if clandestine, friends.

In Gibraltar on 14 October 1943, the British arrested a short, plump 52-year-old German-Argentine who would partly reveal the nature of that relationship.[1] Travelling with his wife on the SS *Monte Albertia* from Bilbao to Buenos Aires, Ernesto Hoppe was on a secret mission for his employer, the German intelligence service the Abwehr. On 10 October, MI6 had been informed that Hoppe's task was to 'assure the safekeeping in Argentina of the fortunes of high Nazi leaders who are planning to flee to Argentina after the fall of Hitlerism in Germany'.[2] Hoppe arrived in Britain ten days later, and on 29 October he was transferred to Camp 020 interrogation centre on the edge of Ham Common in Surrey. Hoppe was reluctant to talk, and while he was receiving hospital treatment for cancer in December, he even managed to escape. His object was to contact the Argentine embassy, which had steadfastly refused to assist him. 'Through an extraordinary chain of circumstances,' wrote Colonel Robin 'Tin Eye' Stephens, the commander of Camp 020, 'this grotesque figure, hatless, in hospital blue, with overlong trousers turned up to his knees, without money and speaking scarcely any English, succeeded in getting a call through to the Argentine embassy.'[3] The clergyman who had allowed the escapee the use of his phone grew suspicious, and Hoppe was arrested after two and a half hours on the run. Hoppe was returned to Camp 020, where he soon began to talk. He revealed that his mission was to receive a U-Boat that was to land 110 miles southwest of Buenos Aires during the Carnival towards the end of February. The submarine would unload around forty cases, each of which would be marked with an 'A', a 'B' or a 'C'. Those marked with an 'A' were to be taken to a bank, while those with a 'B' would also bear the word '*Vorsicht*' – 'With Care' – and were to be deposited with two Nazi brothers outside Buenos Aires. The cases marked 'C' contained documents, and these were to be sent to a certain Herr Baumgarten in Buenos Aires. Hoppe speculated that cases 'A' and 'B', in addition to cash, would contain bonds, gold and jewellery, all of which would be worth not less than ten million Reichsmarks.

If the Argentinians were able to wash their hands of Hoppe, they would not be able to do so with Osmar Hellmuth, whom the British arrested in Trinidad on 30 October 1943. The 34-year-old Hellmuth was en route from Buenos Aires to Berlin, where he was due to meet

Hitler, Himmler and other Nazi leaders to reassure them that if Argentina were to cut its diplomatic ties with Germany, it would not reflect the real sentiments of the Argentine government.[4] Another part of Hellmuth's mission was to request that the Germans release the Argentinian tanker *Buenos Aires*, which was moored at Gothenberg, and load it with arms. The boat was then to sail as an Argentinian man-of-war, and thus be exempt from any Allied searches. However, the Argentinians could not have chosen a worse man for the job. The Allies had known him to be a spy since 1942, when he was identified in a book called *The Nazi Underground in South America* by Hugo Fernández Artucio.[5] Even though the Argentinians must have known this, they had hoped that issuing Hellmuth with a diplomatic passport would ensure that he would travel unmolested; by arresting him, the British flouted diplomatic convention. Hoppe's interrogation at Camp 020 further revealed his inadequacies as a linkman between Nazi Germany and Ramírez. 'Until September 1943,' Colonel Stephens wrote in his report, 'Hellmuth was an obscure insurance agent in Buenos Aires. He was, however, a social upstart and he had intrigued for years with the Nazis, in whom he saw a chance of personal aggrandizement.'[6] Hellmuth lacked Hoppe's obstinacy, and within a week he told all to his interrogators. As a result of his confession, the Allies were able to exert more pressure on Argentina to break off its diplomatic relations with Germany, which it did in January 1944.

Hellmuth also revealed some of the tradecraft of his mission. When he received his orders in the President's Casa Rosada in September 1943, he was given one half of a signed card. When Hellmuth reached Madrid, he was to present his half to a contact at the Argentinian embassy who would produce the other half. Hellmuth would then be entrusted with the complete dossier concerning the arms deal, and flown to Berlin in a plane provided by Himmler.[7] Hellmuth said that the man who supplied him with the card was a Colonel Juan Domingo Perón. At some point during his questioning, Hellmuth's MI6 interrogators showed him a press cutting from an issue of *Time* magazine dated 20 December 1943. The cutting featured a picture of a sober-suited President Ramírez, who cut an insubstantial figure next to the burly form of Perón, who was wearing a crisp white uniform. The caption identified Perón as

the Under-Secretary of War, Secretary of Labour and Welfare, head
of the 'Colonels' Clique' that had brought Ramírez to power, and
the 'actual boss of Argentina'. When Hellmuth was asked whether
Time magazine was correct in attributing such influence to Perón, he
said that he did not know.[8]

Time magazine was right: Perón was indeed the 'power behind
the Presidential throne', and it is he, more than any other figure,
who helped the Nazis to escape. Born in 1895, Perón was a career
army officer who had spent two years in Italy between 1939 and
1941 as the Argentinian military attaché in Rome. As well as establishing contacts with Mussolini's regime, Perón was reputed to have
forged links with the German intelligence services. Walter
Schellenberg maintained that when Perón returned to Argentina, he
met SS-Hauptsturmführer Siegfried Becker, who was head of the SD
in Argentina. Perón, said Schellenberg, had a 'world view similar to
ours'.[9] After much infighting within the 'Colonels' Clique', Perón
eventually became the twenty-ninth president of Argentina on 4
June 1946, and he would remain in office until September 1955.

Throughout his time in government, Perón made no secret of the
fact that he wished to encourage German emigration to Argentina.
In 1944, when he was Secretary of Labour, Perón told a group of
British diplomats that he wanted to import large numbers of
German scientists and technicians after the war to boost Argentinian
industrialization.[10] Such a desire would not have unduly surprised
the British, as they had already identified Argentina as being the
most likely place for the Nazis to hide. 'It is the only neutral country
in which spies or undesirable aliens wanted by the police can safely
and comfortably disappear,' an MI5 report stated. 'There are unique
opportunities of concealing people, illicit wireless stations and
money on *estancias* in the interior.'[11] Lord Halifax, the British
ambassador to Washington, suspected that the Germans in
Argentina would 'wax fat and arrogant, as is their wont', and that
the 'shallow and shiftless sort of Argentine' would soon 'find the
German jackboot on his neck'.[12] Halifax was perhaps being unfair,
as the Germans had been migrating to Latin America for nearly a
century. Of all the immigrants, the Germans were the best received,
owing to what one Argentinian president described in 1860 as 'their
proverbial honesty, their tireless devotion to work, and their pacific

character'.[13] Life for the settlers was tough, and the savagery of the Latin American climate meant that farms often failed. Like many such expatriate groups, the Germans usually married within their own communities, but intermarriage was permitted so long as the non-German wife maintained a Germanic household.[14] By the 1930s, the German community in Argentina could boast a population of some 250,000.[15] In Buenos Aires, the community was especially strong, and there were at least 160 *Vereine*, which were clubs or associations dedicated to recreational and cultural pursuits, such as beer-drinking, sports and literary appreciation.[16]

One 'pursuit' that came to the community in the 1930s was Nazism, which appealed to the same sort of German that it appealed to in Europe: the downtrodden victim of the global slump. In Buenos Aires, crowds gathered daily outside the offices of the German Welfare Society (DWG), which not only included unemployed blue-collar workers, but also laid off white-collar employees with wives and children. 'The army of the unemployed has grown to shocking proportions,' the DWG reported in 1931. 'Day by day the troop of unemployed camping out [in the offices] grows.'[17] The Argentine *Landesgruppe* (Country Group) of the Nazi Party was formed in 1931 with just fifty-nine members, but by the time the Nazis came to power, thousands were attending Nazi rallies at the Teatro Colón in Buenos Aires.[18] Many of the *Vereine* were taken over by Nazis or absorbed into the Nazi framework. The German Riding Club, for example, became the headquarters for the mounted SS.[19] However, by no means all Germans in Argentina became Nazis, and many from the managerial classes only joined in order to protect their business interests. And, just as in Nazi Germany itself, the spread of Nazism in Argentina sowed suspicion among the German community. Those who had relatives back in the Fatherland were especially mindful of toeing the Nazi line, in case they were considered 'un-German'.[20]

When Argentina declared war on Germany in March 1945, the world knew where Argentina's real sympathies lay. Pressured by the US State Department, the Argentine government seized around 250 German-owned businesses, and expelled some sixty 'spies and undesirables'. Most were to return by the middle of 1948, and many of the businesses were restored to their owners.[21] Despite this seeming compliance, the secret links were never stronger, and the preparations to move Nazi capital and personnel to Argentina continued in earnest. According to one observer, it appeared that Germans had started to arrive in Buenos Aires in the middle of 1944. In March 1945, the British authorities intercepted a letter dated 14 January of that year, sent by a Canadian expatriate to a friend in Scotland.

> You ask if there is a luxury palace waiting for Adolf out here? Certainly if he comes over in a submarine with a cargo of hard cash! During the last half year you see a new type of Boche sailing around the streets of B.A. They look like ranker officers or picked NCOs with that 'HERREN-VOLK' gloss in their eye to show that they are used to power and bullying. I think they are 'pensioned' Gestapo officers whose names figure in the Allied War-Criminals lists.[22]

On 10 March 1945, a 34-year-old blond, blue-eyed *SS-Hauptsturmführer* called Carlos Fuldner flew into Madrid from Berlin.[23] Born in Buenos Aires in 1910, Fuldner's family had left Argentina in 1922 and returned to Germany, although the young Fuldner would retain dual nationality. In 1932, he joined the SS, and he became a *Hauptsturmführer* just two years later. However, Fuldner was no model of rectitude, and having abandoned a pregnant wife, he proceeded to swindle a Munich businessman, a shipping company and even the SS. By the autumn of 1935, he had decided to flee Germany and head to Argentina. On 17 October, he boarded the SS *Antonio Delfino* at Lisbon, although the SS had not given up on him. As the ship neared Brazil, a German liner bound for Bremerhaven drew up alongside, and Fuldner was forced to go back to Germany. He was arrested by the Gestapo, imprisoned and thrown out of the SS. In 1937, he was cleared of the fraud charges, but his slate was not clean enough to rejoin the SS. Between then and 1945, Fuldner's movements are a mystery, but it seems that he worked in Spain, and perhaps fought for the Spanish Blue Division on the Russian front. Whatever he had done, it was clearly enough to impress the SS, because he had been reinstated as a *Hauptsturmführer* by the time he arrived in Madrid that March.[24]

Fuldner's mission in Madrid was highly secret. He brought with him a vast amount of cash, as well as a collection of art that he hoped to sell. All this would finance his mission, which, he told the German embassy, was 'to keep up relations between Spain and Germany after the war'.[25] In all likelihood, and judging by his later activities, Fuldner's 'mission statement' was nothing less than a euphemism for an escape organization that would run war criminals between Europe and Argentina via Spain. During his time in Spain, he established a network of contacts that would prove immensely useful over the coming years. Nevertheless, his presence did not go unnoticed by the Allies, who constantly impressed on the Spanish the need to throw him out. As a result, Fuldner led a peripatetic life until he eventually fled 'home' to Argentina in 1947. It was there that Fuldner would be embraced by Juan Perón, who realized that Fuldner was just the man he needed to bring about his long-wished-for immigration of German 'technicians', many of whom would be wanted war criminals.[26]

In order to realize his dream, Perón assembled a group of some of the most unsavoury characters in the southern hemisphere. Many were fugitives from Europe themselves, which scarcely seemed to concern Perón, despite the fact that Argentina had agreed in September 1945 not to 'grant refuge to those guilty and responsible of war crimes'.[27] Among them was Pierre Daye, a Belgian writer who had led the parliamentary wing of the pro-Axis Rexist Party before the outbreak of war. An adventurer with a taste both for the high life and the seedy, the 55-year-old Daye had met Hitler at least twice, and had even received a blessing from Pius XII. In March 1944, sensing that the war would not go the way he wished, Daye fled to Spain, where he spent the next three years propping up bars in expensive hotels and assisting former comrades who had found themselves in Spanish refugee camps. Daye was sentenced to death *in absentia* by a court in Brussels in December 1946, which made his presence in Spain too troublesome for Franco's regime, and so in May 1947 he flew to Argentina.[28] In July, Buenos Aires would welcome another collaborator who would join Perón's team. During the war, René Lagrou had been the leader of the Flemish SS from 1940 to 1941, and he had organized the action against the Jewish community in Antwerp. A former lawyer, Lagrou was captured by the Allies in France, but he escaped to Spain. When he arrived in

Argentina, he used the name 'Reinaldo von Groede', and, working with Fuldner and Daye, he would play a vital role in issuing landing permits to war criminals.[29] In early December 1947, Perón gathered his team for two days of meetings at the Casa Rosada. It included Fuldner, Daye, Lagrou, and also Rodolfo Freude, Perón's spy chief. Daye was impressed by the meeting and his fellow participants, many of whom had been condemned to death back in Europe. 'The President knew it,' Daye wrote in his memoirs, 'and I admire his independence of opinion and the courage with which he received us in the national official palace.'[30] Perón's opinions certainly were 'independent'. He considered the Nuremberg trials a 'disgrace' and an 'unfortunate lesson for the future of humanity'. 'Now we realize that they [the Allies] deserved to lose the war,' he would say years later.[31]

As a result of the meeting, Fuldner was dispatched back to Europe that same month to set up the escape network in earnest.[32] Shuttling between the 'Argentine Emigration Centre' at Marktgasse 49 in Berne and the 'Delegation for Argentine Immigration in Europe' in Genoa, Fuldner would mastermind the escapes of hundreds of 'technicians' to Argentina. However, the former *SS-Hauptsturmführer* could not work in Berne without the assistance of the Swiss, who were willing to allow their country to be used as a 'transit country' for many of the fleeing Nazis.[33] Fuldner also had the cooperation of the Swiss police, whose chief, Heinrich Rothmund, had been responsible for closing the Swiss borders to Jews fleeing from the camps.[34] In Genoa, Fuldner would also receive help, although not principally from the police. Those to whom Fuldner would be most indebted were members of the Catholic Church, for it was they who supplied him with his human cargo.

In June 1948, Heinrich Rothmund visited Rome to participate in a series of Swiss–Italian immigration talks. While he was there, he received a letter from Fuldner, in which Perón's agent wrote that he was sorry not to be in Rome, because it would have been 'wonderful to . . . consider some questions that concern your fatherland and my home country'.[35] However, Fuldner was able to arrange a meeting between Rothmund and his chief supplier of war criminals, the Croatian Monsignor Krunoslav Draganović, who had 'rendered great services to my country, providing passages to South

America for hundreds of people'.[36] Although Fuldner described those who had benefited from Draganović's services as 'refugees', most of them had displayed a depth of turpitude during the war that made them not qualified to be labelled as such. Draganović was unfit to wear the robes of a cleric, but that same costume enabled him to hide the guilty. Like Fuldner and Perón, the 44-year-old Draganović would be one of the prime movers in helping the war criminals to escape.

During the war, Draganović had been a supporter of the Ustasha, the Croatian nationalist movement that took control of the 'independent' state of Croatia after the Axis powers had invaded in April 1941. Led by their *Poglavnik*, Ante Pavelić, the Ustashi formed one of the most murderous regimes that flourished during the war. During his four years in power, Pavelić presided over a policy of genocide whose implementation was far more barbaric than anything seen in the Nazi-run death camps. Jews, Serbs, Gypsies and political opponents were murdered by or with hammers, knives, guns, iron bars, whips, fire, gas, starvation, suffocation, trampling, freezing, hanging, hoes, belts, axes, grenades and hatchets. In Jasenovac concentration camp, 60 miles southeast of Zagreb, some 85,000 to 100,000 were dispatched using such methods.[37] Children were not spared the gruesome executions. Babies and infants were tied into sacks and then thrown into a ditch which was filled with the corpses of their mothers.[38] They were also killed with iron hammers and thrown into ovens at the tile factory. On occasion, they would be buried half alive in ditches, and the earth would continue to rise and fall as they struggled in their death throes.[39] Sometimes, the eyes of the victims would be gouged out and used as trophies. Curzio Malaparte, an Italian journalist who met Pavelić during the war, recorded how his eye was drawn to a basket on the desk of the *Poglavnik*. 'The lid was raised and the basket seemed to be filled with mussels or shelled oysters,' wrote Malaparte. 'Ante Pavelić removed the lid from the basket and revealed the mussels, that slimy and jelly-like mass, and he said smiling, with that tired good-natured smile of his, "It is a present from my loyal ustashis. Forty pounds of human eyes." '[40]

Such was the nature of the company that Draganović kept. Although his hands were not bloodied by such crimes, he supported those who were, and even served as a chaplain at Jasenovac, where he would have had full knowledge of the crimes committed there.[41] Draganović also played a key role in the 'Bureau of Colonization' which forced Serbs to convert to Catholicism, as well as stealing their property and giving it to Croatians.[42] In the words of one US intelligence officer, Draganović thought that 'the ideas espoused by this arch-nationalist organization, half logical, half lunatic are basically sound concepts.'[43] In August 1943, as a delegate of the Croatian Red Cross, he came to Rome, where he worked to assist Yugoslav internees. According to one report, Draganović refused to help any Serbians, and only assisted his fellow Croatians.[44] Draganović was also given a more delicate task while he was in Rome. He was entrusted not only with the archives of the Croatian Legation, but also with the valuables smuggled by the Ustashi.[45] He left the city at the end of the year, but he returned in January to continue his relief work. Some accounts have stated that during this period Draganović was establishing contacts throughout the Vatican in order to help the Ustashi escape after the war. This is not unlikely, but the suggestion that Draganović was in consultation concerning his plans with Pius XII is groundless.[46]

Although the role of the Pope during the war is too vast a topic to be discussed here, there can be little doubt that Pius XII was more sympathetic to regimes that wished to maintain the Church than those that wished to destroy it. The Pope had granted Pavelić an audience in May 1941, which caused much bad feeling in British diplomatic circles.[47] The Pontiff, however, believed Pavelić to be a 'much maligned man and not guilty of murder', a belief that he could not have sincerely maintained as the persecutions in Croatia – and the reports of them – became widespread.[48] Nevertheless, in October 1942, the British heard that the Pope was due to receive Pavelić again, which rekindled the British animus. On 3 October, D'Arcy Osborne, the British envoy to the Vatican, met Giovanni Montini, the Under-Secretary of State, and told him that as Pavelić was responsible for the murder of some six hundred thousand Serbs, another audience 'would arouse bitter criticism'. Montini told Osborne that he knew nothing about the visit, but that as it was the Pope's practice not to discriminate, he probably would meet Pavelić. 'I suggested that I should have thought the line would be drawn at a man whose hands were dripping with the blood of thousands of innocent victims,' Osborne wrote to the Foreign Office.[49] Sir Orme Sargent replied a few days later: 'I approve your language.'[50] Osborne's words appeared to have an effect, because Pius XII did not meet Pavelić that October. However, on the afternoon of 2 September 1943, he did hold an audience for 110 Croatian military policemen who were in Italy for training. Some of these men were reputed to have served in Jasenovac. Although the Pope may not have been aware of the murderous nature of some of those he met, the fact that he received such a large group of Ustashi is indicative that he was walking a dangerous diplomatic line. Each of the military policemen received a gift and a papal blessing, in which the Croatian press rejoiced.[51]

At the end of the war, Draganović was in an ideal position to help his beloved Ustashi. Initially, his task was to travel around internment camps in northern Italy and Austria checking on the fate of the Ustashi members who had been captured.[52] At some point, he was entrusted with 45 kilograms of gold, which had largely been stolen from the Jewish and Serbian victims of the Croatian regime.[53] However, in January 1946, a former general in the Croatian army and Pavelić's son-in-law, Vilko Pesnikar, relieved Draganović of the treasure at gunpoint, and used the riches to establish a 'transport society' of his own, which soon failed.[54] The theft did little to discourage Draganović from going about his 'relief work', and soon San Girolamo, the Croatian monastery at 132 Via Tomacelli in Rome, became the central focus for all covert Ustasha activity. There, on the mezzanine floor, Draganović founded the 'Committee of Croatian Refugees in Rome', which was nothing less than a front for his people-smuggling activity.[55] The monastery was also a home for fugitive Ustashi, and, as a result, the security was tight. In early 1947, the CIC managed to place an agent inside the monastery to confirm the presence of the wanted men, but it soon became too dangerous for the spy to stay in place. Nevertheless, he was able to reveal the exhaustiveness of Draganović's precautions.

> In order to enter this Monastery one must submit to a personal search for weapons and identification documents, must answer questions as to where he is from, who he is, whom he knows, what his purpose is in the visit, and how he heard about the fact that there were Croats

in the Monastery. All doors from one room to another are locked and
those that are not have an armed guard in front of them and a password is necessary to go from one room to another. The whole area is
guarded by armed Ustashi youths in civilian clothes and the Ustashi
salute is exchanged continually.[56]

The agent also reported the names of some of the senior Ustashi who
either lived in the monastery or who visited regularly. They included
not only Pesnikar, who had clearly had some sort of rapprochement
with Draganović, but also the former Deputy Minister of Foreign
Affairs, the former Minister of the State Treasury, the former
Education Minister, the former Commander-in-Chief of the Ustasha
Air Force and the former Transport Minister. 'These Croats travel
back and forth from the Vatican several times a week in a car with
a chauffeur whose license plate bears the two initials CD, "Corpo
Diplomatico",' reported the agent.[57]

Such activity led the CIC's Special Agent, Robert Clayton Mudd,
to deduce that Draganović's activities 'links him up with the plan of
the Vatican to shield these ex-Ustashi nationalists until such time as
they are able to procure for them the proper documents to enable
them to go to South America'. Furthermore, according to Mudd, the
Vatican was 'endeavoring to infiltrate them into South America in
any way possible to counteract the spread of the Red doctrine'.[58]
Could Mudd have been right in asserting that the Vatican was
directly involved? The British appeared to agree. In December 1947,
a British diplomat wrote to J. V. Perowne at the Foreign Office,
telling him that the Vatican 'has permitted the encouragement, both
overt and covert, of the Ustashi [. . .] There is surely all the difference between shelter to, let us say, a dissident Slovene priest, and
giving positive aid to a creature like Pavelic.'[59] (Like the CIC, the
British had also penetrated San Girolamo, but they were alarmed to
discover that Draganović and the Ustashi were being tipped off
regarding any moves against them by other British intelligence
officers.[60] Draganović was also said to be close to a British colonel
called Findlay, who was the Director of the Displaced Persons and
Repatriation section of the occupation force in Italy, as well as his
assistant, a Major Simcock.)[61] Many years later, a British intelligence
officer would claim that Draganović had the backing of the highest

level of the Vatican. He asserted that Pius XII 'knew everything about Father Draganović's activities, otherwise he would never have stayed in his position'.[62] Whatever the truth of these allegations, there can be no doubt that elements within the Vatican supported Draganović. What is still unknown, and may always be so, is the involvement of the Pope himself. As the Vatican's archives from this period remain closed, the vacuum of knowledge has unfortunately been filled with speculation, much of which cannot be substantiated. If the Pope did indeed have a relationship with the venal Draganović, then, as we shall see later, he would not have been the only figure who did so who should not have done.

Draganović's most important charge was Pavelić himself, who had fled Croatia on 7 May 1945.[63] According to US intelligence reports, he took with him around eighty million dollars, most of which were in the form of gold coins.[64] Pavelić's retinue consisted of three trucks of soldiers and a truckload of NCOs. It set out from the *Poglavnik*'s villa near Zagreb on the afternoon of 6 May, and it journeyed 50 miles north to Rogaška Slatina. The following morning, Pavelić made his way 20 miles north to Maribor, which is about 10 miles south of the Austrian border, where the dictator changed his name to 'Ramírez' and his clothes to civvies. The column then headed for Judenburg, some 90 miles northwest, although its progress was stymied by some Russian tanks. 'When we heard this,' recalled one of the Ustashi bodyguards, 'we jumped from the trucks and ran towards the nearby hill. The *Poglavnik* also got out of his car. He tried to stop us and pleaded with us to stay with him. However, as most of us had never been in combat and were terrified of the Russian tanks, we continued to run.' Pavelić was soon left with a mere handful of NCOs and some officers.[65] It is unclear what happened next. According to his daughter, the former dictator was put up by a sympathetic Austrian on a 'peasant estate' in the Alps somewhere near St Gilgen, 30 miles northwest of Altaussee in the American Zone of Occupation. Pavelić shared a house with an Italian maid. 'He spent his time in the woods,' his daughter recalled, 'picking mushrooms and catching fish. He even sent us some of these and we in turn sent him some of the bread rations we had received.'[66] If Pavelić had indeed made it to the American zone, then he would have had to have crossed the British zone to have got there.

Pavelić's relationship with the British has been the subject of much conspiracy theory, some of which may be true. Certainly, the Russians, the Yugoslavs and the Americans believed either that Pavelić had cut some kind of deal with the British to secure his freedom or that they were secretly holding him prisoner. In July 1945, the Yugoslav ambassador in London, Dr Ljubo Leontić, informed the Foreign Office that Pavelić had been imprisoned 'by the troops of Field Marshal Alexander, and . . . is now in the part of Austria under the control of the British Army'.[67] The Yugoslavs reiterated their claim the following month, and added that Pavelić was being held by the British in Klagenfurt.[68] The British maintained that they did not hold Pavelić, and that he was rumoured to be in the American zone in the Salzburg area, which tallies with what Pavelić's daughter would later recall.[69] In October, the Foreign Office again wrote to the Yugoslavs, stressing that 'every effort is being made to discover the present whereabouts of Dr Pavelic'.[70] The Yugoslavs refused to believe the British, and on 14 December 1945, they publicly claimed that the British 'maintain they do not know the residences of [Field Marshal] Nedich and Pavelitch, although our own authorities indicate exactly in which town and street these criminals are living freely.' The Yugoslavs added that the Foreign Office had broken a 'verbal promise' to return the two men.[71] This had to be untrue, as even if the British were holding Pavelić, they would not have told the Yugoslavs as such. All they had promised was that Pavelić would be handed over if he were found. For the next year, this game of diplomatic tennis would continue between the two countries. Tito was suspicious that the British were harbouring Pavelić in order to use him to overthrow the new Communist regime in Yugoslavia, whereas the British, mindful of the shortcomings in the Balkan judicial process, refused to hand over suspects to the Yugoslavs unless there were prima facie cases against them. Even Stalin weighed in, accusing Churchill, in the aftermath of his famous 'Iron Curtain' speech in early March 1946, of wanting Pavelić to be reinstalled in Yugoslavia. 'Churchill wants to assure us that these gentlemen from Fascist circles will establish and guarantee complete democracy,' said the Soviet leader.[72] The British, meanwhile, claimed that they had searched everywhere that the Yugoslavs had asked them to, and they had had no joy.[73]

The Americans were also convinced that the British had sheltered Pavelić. In October 1946, a CIC report confidently stated that 'there can no longer be any doubt that the British aided the escape of Dr Ante Pavelich'. The report claimed that in the spring of 1945 the British were about to hand over Pavelić and some 1,500 Ustashi to Tito's men, but at the last minute the former *Poglavnik* was taken away in the night by a British jeep. 'Reasons for the action are not known, but Pavelich was indubitably spirited away by the British themselves.'[74] Unfortunately, this report provides no evidence for this bold assertion, and its reliability must also be questioned, as it refers to Draganović as 'Marjanovich'. But there were other reports made by the Americans, all of which suggest that Pavelić bribed the British in return for his freedom, and throughout the summer of 1945 he was hidden by British intelligence in Klagenfurt.[75] Around this time, a British Lieutenant Colonel Johnson was reputed to have made off with two truckloads of Ustasha treasure, accompanied by a number of priests and heading for an undisclosed location in Italy. Another US report states that the British impounded 150 million Swiss francs owned by the Ustashi at the Austro-Swiss border, and allowed the remainder, some two hundred million Swiss francs, to proceed to the Vatican.[76]

All such reports must be treated with caution. Post-war Austria and Italy were awash with agents, many of whom were peddling highly suspect intelligence. CIC agents themselves could also be remarkably unprofessional in the way they gathered their 'product'. Richard West, a member of the British Intelligence Corps in Trieste in 1949, recalled meeting a CIC agent who would have been dismissed had his superiors known how he was operating. 'He had got hold of some Albanian newspapers,' said West, 'and gave them to an Albanian to get translated, and he translated all this absolute drivel. He passed it off as though he had a man in Tirana. It made me realize how ridiculous most intelligence services are.'[77] Of course, by no means all intelligence was worthless, but until the British intelligence files on Pavelić are released, which is unlikely, it is hard to be definitive, and it would be a mistake to adopt a tone of knowing cynicism as a replacement for actual knowledge. However, as we shall see, the British, like the Americans, would employ war criminals in their nascent fight against Communism, but such agents

were not of the stature of a former head of state, or quite so blood-
stained as Pavelić. Nevertheless, he would have made a remarkable
intelligence asset, and it is possible that the British may have traded
the contents of Pavelić's brain for his freedom. As we shall also discover, the British were quite happy to lie to their Allies (and indeed
their own politicians and diplomats) concerning the employment of
war criminals, so denials made by bodies such as the Foreign Office
cannot be trusted.

Pavelić's ability to remain undetected in the British zone does raise
suspicion, but then it also appears, according to his daughter, that
he lived in the American zone, where he was seemingly unmolested.
In fact, the Americans knew the whereabouts of Pavelić's daughter,
as she claims she and her family had to report to them regularly. If
the Americans had wished to discover where Pavelić was hiding,
they could have simply followed his daughter on her numerous visits
to him in the woods near St Gilgen. The fact that they did not do so
suggests that they probably already knew his location and they were
leaving him alone.[78] American involvement with Pavelić was widely
suspected. In Trieste in 1949, Richard West encountered a man who
he thought to be a Yugoslav agent. 'He came up to me and said that
he had a very interesting piece of information,' West said. 'He gave
me an address in Rome for Ante Pavelić. I got very excited by this and
I rushed to the chief of my section. He tore up my memo and said,
"It's no use trying to get Pavelić, the Yanks are backing him." '[79]

It is also conceivable that Pavelić's supposed association with the
Allies was nothing more than Russian and Yugoslavian disinformation and propaganda, which often accused the British and the
Americans of being complicit with Fascists in an attempt to sully the
name of Western democracy and thereby promote Communism. If
the Yugoslavs were so certain as to Pavelić's whereabouts, as they
had claimed in December 1945, then why did they not assassinate
him? They were certainly not averse to conducting such operations.
On 10 November 1945, three Yugoslav agents gained admittance to
the Judenburg displaced persons' camp and slit the throats of Dr
Sekula Drljević and his wife. Drljević had been the figurehead of the
pro-Axis Montenegrin puppet state, and was a friend of Pavelić.[80]
The Yugoslavs could have even hunted Pavelić more openly, because
in May 1946, the State Department registered no objection to

the Yugoslavs searching for Pavelić in the US zone in Austria.[81] The Yugoslavs also had a mission in the British zone, and although it was only allowed to hunt non-Yugoslavs, it is feasible that it could have searched for Pavelić without telling the British.[82]

In the spring of 1946, Pavelić had made his way to Rome disguised as a Catholic priest and calling himself 'Don Pedro Gonner'.[83] It is not clear exactly where the former dictator lived. Some reports placed Pavelić in Castel Gandolfo, the Pope's summer residence, but this seems far-fetched.[84] At some point, Pavelić hid under Draganović's wing at San Girolamo, but then he also was reported to have hidden at numerous other Catholic institutions, including the Monastery of St Sabina, the Catholic college on Via Giacomo Belli, and even inside the Vatican itself.[85] This last location raised the eyebrows of a senior official in the US State Department. 'While I am aware of, and appreciate, the Vatican's humanitarian attitude towards criminals who may have shown any indication of repentance,' the official wrote to American diplomats in Rome, 'it seems to me that Pavelic's peculiarly unsavory record would make it difficult for the Church to afford him protection.' The diplomats shared such doubts. 'Pavelić, like Kilroy, seems to be everywhere,' they reported. 'Or so the reports of dozens of sleuths would indicate.'[86] Nevertheless, the sleuths were adamant that Pavelić's presence in Rome had the Pope's blessing. In August 1947, CIC agent William Gowen reported that Pavelić was 'receiving the protection of the Vatican'. Gowen supported his claim by stating that the Vatican felt that extraditing Pavelić would only 'weaken the forces fighting against atheism and Communism in its fight against the Church'. Pavelić might have been a monster, the thinking went, but he was less of one than Tito, who was backed by the greatest monster of all: Stalin.[87]

What the American diplomats ignored were the Vatican's known sympathies for the Ustasha. In August 1945, the Holy See requested the British not to hand over six hundred Ustashi to Yugoslavia. The British did not reply, and the Vatican repeated its request, this time in the name of the Pope himself. Once again, the British refused, saying that they would not protect war criminals. In another instance, the Yugoslavs asked the Allies to extradite five Ustashi who were hiding in the Vatican's Oriental Institute. The British told the Vatican that the fugitives were not 'Thomas à Beckets', and that by sheltering them, the Vatican was violating the United Nations' order that required criminals to be sent back to the territories in which they had committed their crimes. Unsurprisingly, the Vatican did not comply. In April 1947, the Vatican asked the Allies to release fifteen Nazi collaborators from prison, saying that they were 'humanitarians'. The Foreign Office was disgusted by the Vatican's position, and told D'Arcy Osborne in a set of 'icy instructions' to inform the Holy See that these 'humanitarians' had given 'their support and approval to [the Ustasha] regime which flouted humanitarian principles and which condoned atrocities unsurpassed in any period of human history'.[88]

By the summer of 1947, the British and the Americans knew exactly where Pavelić lived, and they even knew the security arrangements that had been implemented at the building in the Trastevere district.

> [Pavelić] is living on Church property under the protection of the Vatican, at Via Giacoma Venezian [sic] No. 17-C, second floor. On entering the building you go along a long and dark corridor. At the end of the corridor there are two stairs, one to the left and one to the right. You must take the right. On the right the rooms are numbered 1, 2, 3 etc. If you knock once or twice at door No. 3 an unimportant person will come out. But if you knock three times at door No. 3, door No 2 will open. It leads to the room where Pavelic lives, together with the famous Bulgarian terrorist Vancia Mikoiloff [sic] and two other persons. About twelve other men live in the building. They are all Ustasha and make up Pavelic's bodyguard. When Pavelic goes out he uses a car with a Vatican (SCV) plate.[89]

Plans were soon laid to arrest Pavelić, but because he was seemingly being protected by the Vatican, such an action could only take place when the criminal was away from its precincts. Such an action would have been 'an extremely tricky operation', warned an American general, 'requiring elaborate co-ordination between US, British and Italian authorities and the maintenance of absolute secrecy'.[90] Nevertheless, on 7 July 1947, the CIC's Chief of Operations in Rome passed on an order from the Assistant Chief of Staff of the US forces in the Mediterranean theatre, who 'desires that Subject [Pavelić] be taken into custody on sight'. The order must have caused a panic, because seven days later a handwritten note was added at the bottom of the document: 'New instructions: "Hands Off".'[91] As a result, Pavelić was never arrested.

This new order would appear to be proof that the Allies were sheltering a figure whose genocidal past was as repellent as Hitler's. Although it is unlikely that Pavelić was being used as an agent himself, he was still a potent figurehead for the remnants of the Ustasha, some of whom were being employed by the British and the Americans in the intelligence war against Tito. Had Pavelić been handed over to Tito, then those Ustasha agents may have been less willing to serve their new masters.[92] This argument was put forward by both Allies at a meeting between Lieutenant George F. Blunda of the US Army's Intelligence Division and two MI6 officers at the British embassy in Rome on 11 August 1947. One of the MI6 officers, Wing Commander Derck Verschoyle, a former literary editor of The Spectator, told Blunda that the Americans should arrest Pavelić without British involvement. Blunda declined, and said that such an arrest 'would not [be] to our best interests as a number of Croats have been used as informers . . . [and they] are known to be loyal to Pavelic's anti-Communist activities and Catholic fanaticism'.[93] As a result, the Allies passed the buck to the Italians, who it was decided would make the actual arrest while being monitored by the British and the Americans. However, the arrest never happened, because Verschoyle claimed that he had been unable to lure Pavelić off Vatican territory. Another possible reason was that Pavelić had had a major medical operation in September, which had been life-threatening.[94] In addition, Pavelić's arrest would reveal the complicity of elements of the Vatican in hiding him. As Agent Gowen was to write, 'Pavelić's contacts are so high and his present position is so compromising to the Vatican, that any extradition of [Pavelić] would deal a staggering blow to the Roman Catholic Church.'[95]

Pavelić may not have been a sleeping dog, but he was certainly allowed to lie. The following year, he was even able to leave his Vatican kennel. On 11 October 1948, a heavily bearded and bespectacled Hungarian widower called 'Pal Aranyos' carrying a

Red Cross passport numbered 74369 boarded the Italian SS *Sestriere* at Genoa. He arrived in Buenos Aires on 6 November, and was whisked off the boat by Perón's agents.[96] However, Pavelić was one of the few Croats who made his way to the southern hemisphere without the assistance of Krunoslav Draganović. The priest, Pavelić felt correctly, was just too close to the British and the Americans.[97] How the *Poglavnik* did escape has, up until now, always been something of a mystery, and it has been suggested that he was aided by another Catholic priest, or he simply made his own arrangements.[98] However, Pavelić was possibly helped by another network, which will we turn to later.

Draganović was not the only Catholic priest in Rome smuggling war criminals. An equally important figure was that of Bishop Alois 'Luigi' Hudal, the rector of an Austro-German church and seminary, the Santa Maria dell'Anima on the Via della Pace, two blocks east of the Piazza Navona. Sometimes working in association with Draganović, Hudal would help to rescue scores of Nazi war criminals, including two of the most notorious: Franz Stangl and Adolf Eichmann. Hudal would later claim that his mission as a priest was to help anybody who sought his assistance, be they Nazi, Communist or Jew, but the truth is that Hudal's charity extended mostly to the former.[99] In fact, Hudal's sympathies had lain with Hitler's regime for many years, and in 1936, he had even written a book called *The Foundations of National Socialism*, in which he had attempted to construct a bridge between Christianity and Nazism. Hudal sent a copy of the book to Hitler, which he had inscribed, 'To the Architect of German Greatness'.[100] The book was not a complete apologia for Nazism, and at its conclusion, Hudal argued that when 'National Socialism coincides with a new philosophy of life which is exalted to the level of a dogma, [. . .] in such a case to remain silent and to wait would equal an approval and at the same time a denial of the Faith.' For Hudal, true leadership could only come from the Church, and in the book's closing paragraph, he declared that Nazism could never be fully accepted by the Church. 'The words of the Apostle prevail: "One shall obey God more than man" and also that other phrase in Rome, which has so often been voiced against numerous heresies throughout the centuries, *"Non possumus!"* '[101]

As a result of this position, the book was banned in Germany, and after the *Anschluss*, in Austria.[102]

Despite his apparent misgivings about Nazism, Hudal would end up keeping company with some of the leading figures of the Far Right in Europe and the Americas. During the war, he was reputed to drive around Rome with a Greater Germany flag on his car, and he was even said to own a Golden Nazi Party Badge.[103] Those who met him remembered Hudal as 'a man of very small stature and he was always trying to "big note" himself'.[104] Another recalled how his 'lively dark eyes looked good-natured under his bushy eyebrows, and his slightly forward lips optimistically suggest openness and honesty'.[105] Born in 1885, the Austrian Hudal had been ordained in 1908, and in 1911, he joined the Santa Maria dell'Anima. During the First World War, he served as a chaplain in the German army, and returned to his hometown of Graz to take up a professorship. In 1923, he was appointed rector of the Santa Maria dell'Anima and he would remain in Rome for the rest of his life. In 1932, Hudal was disappointed not to be made Archbishop of Vienna. According to one bishop, Hudal was passed over by the Austrian government because he was too 'nationalistic'.[106] Nevertheless, Hudal would have been gratified the following year when he was ordained as a titular bishop by the Cardinal Protector of the Anima, Eugenio Pacelli, who would become Pope Pius XII in 1939.

In the spring of 1943, Hudal is reputed to have met SS-Obersturmbannführer Walter Rauff, who had pioneered the use of gas vans to kill Jews as an alternative to shooting, in order to lessen the 'considerable burden' on those pulling the triggers.[107] According to an account given by Alfred Jarschel, a former Hitler Youth leader, Rauff was putting out feelers in Rome and the Vatican in order to establish a potential escape network.[108] However, Jarschel's story is highly dubious, as it appears in his 1969 book *Fleeing Nuremberg*, which he published under the name Werner Brockdorff. This book is a curious combination of accurate history and outright fabrication, the former helping to give credence to the latter. Rivalling many of the absurd claims made by Simon Wiesenthal, Jarschel's book is a source of a great number of the myths concerned with fugitive Nazis. It is theoretically possible that Hudal could have met Rauff when he was posted to Italy, and it is also possible that the two men may have spoken about escape routes, but there is simply no evidence.

Nevertheless, throughout the war, Hudal was to earn a reputation for being if not pro-Nazi, then at least embarrassingly sympathetic. At the outbreak of war in 1939, Pius XII removed his patronage from the Anima, and at Christmas, a reply to Hudal's Christmas greetings to the Pope was cynically addressed to the 'Aryan College' rather than to the 'Santa Maria dell'Anima'. Hudal would also find that when he led German and Austrian pilgrims into parts of the Vatican that would normally be open to a priest of his seniority, his way would be blocked by the Swiss Guard.[109] Hudal's politics were so well known that when the Allies entered the city in June 1944, the Anima was searched. An OSS report from around that time reported Hudal to be 'a renegade in the full sense of the word, he belongs to the worst category of priests who dabble in politics, being unscrupulous [and] without character'.[110]

If Pius XII had any misgivings about Hudal, then they appeared to have dwindled after the liberation of Rome. Hudal was asked to head up 'Assistenza Austriaca', which was part of the Pope's Pontifical Commission of Assistance that helped refugees.[111] To aid him in his work, Hudal was issued with a pass to tour the internment camps in order to give 'normal religious assistance to catholic internees'.[112] For Hudal, this was a literal godsend, as it enabled him to establish his escape network. 'I thank God that He [allowed me] to visit and comfort many victims in their prisons and concentration camps,' he wrote years later, 'and [to help] them escape with false identity papers.' Hudal's motivation was a belief that the war had been little more than the 'rivalry of economic complexes', which had been dressed up and sold to the masses with 'catchwords like democracy, race, religious liberty and Christianity'. Because of this, Hudal claimed to feel 'duty bound after 1945 to devote my whole charitable work mainly to former National Socialists and Fascists, especially to so-called "war criminals".'[113] Of course, at the time, Hudal would never have been so brazen, and so he made sure that he courted the Allies, and presented himself as the dutiful Catholic priest. An OSS report noted that the Austrian group was 'almost pathetically anxious to do everything to please the Allies [. . .] They eagerly clutch at any hint of Allied interest in them however lowly the quarter from which it comes.'[114] As a result of such cravenness, the OSS regarded them as a 'small group of idiots', but warned that they posed a threat if they associated with former members of the German armed forces.

Hudal was no idiot, and he did indeed forge contacts with the German military. His chief assistant in his 'refugee' work was a Captain Reinhard Kops, who had served in the Abwehr and had been incarcerated by the British in Hamburg. In 1947, after a year of captivity, he escaped, and assuming the name of 'Hans Mahler', he fled to Rome. Like many refugees, Kops found sustenance at the papal mess hall, which was open to all in need. There, Kops was delighted to find many Germans in a similar situation, all of whom were from the 'best homes'. He was soon put in touch with Hudal, who secured him employment in the library of the Salvatorian Order near St Peter's Square. That Christmas, Hudal gathered Kops and some two hundred of his 'refugees' for a celebration, and told them, 'You can rest assured the police will not find you here, it is not the first time people have lived in the catacombs of Rome.' Kops was in fact Hudal's linkman between his operation and the Delegation for Argentine Immigration in Europe (DAIE) in Genoa. Kops's contact at the Delegation was a former Italian officer called Franz Ruffinengo, who also assisted Draganović in getting his men to Argentina. 'I clutched in Rome the hand Franz extended to me from Genoa,' Kops would write later. At some point, Kops even lived in Genoa, where he shared a flat with some Croat and German refugees who were sheltered by one of Draganović's agents.[115]

It was Ruffinengo who taught Kops how to run the escape route. After Assistenza Austriaca – which acted as a kind of pseudo-consulate – had provided a 'refugee' with an identity card signed by Hudal, the fugitive would then apply for a Red Cross passport, which would often be issued without too many questions being asked. As the Red Cross was severely overstretched, there was no hope that its personnel could check the identity of applicants. Furthermore, the signature of a bishop carried much weight, and although suspicions about Hudal were widespread in the intelligence community, they were hardly the talk of town. The escapee would then make his way to Genoa, where he would be assisted by a combination of Kops, Ruffinengo, a Draganović agent, the DAIE, as well as the offices of the 'National Committee for Emigration to Argentina', which was supported by another senior Catholic, Archbishop Giuseppe Siri.[116] After the appropriate documentation was secured, the fugitive would be placed on a boat bound, more often than not, for Buenos Aires. Sometimes Hudal would pay Draganović for his services, because, in the words of a CIC report, Draganović would show 'no interest in business which did not concern Ustashi and Nazis, and which did not yield him a particular financial benefit'. The Croat priest, it was said, received 'large compensation' from Hudal.[117]

It is still unclear from where Hudal received all his funds. Assistenza Austriaca received some limited donations from the Vatican, but this would not have been sufficient to have paid for the passage of the thousands of refugees that Hudal wished to send to South America.[118] Money was also sent from the American 'War Relief Services – National Catholic Welfare Conference', which sent a cheque drawn on the Bank of Rome for just under thirty thousand lire.[119] However, as a passage to Buenos Aires could cost around a hundred thousand lire, such a donation was nugatory. Many fugitives had to raise their own money, and as – in the words of Kops – some of them came from 'the best homes', this would not have been a great problem. Hudal's operation was not awash with cash, and even if the Vatican turned a blind eye towards it, there is no evidence that it gave any more to Hudal's Assistenza Austriaca than it did to any of the twenty other regional offices of the Pontifical Commission of Assistance. In order to realize his grand scheme, Hudal decided to turn to the man at the other end of his 'ratline': Juan Perón. In August 1948, the bishop wrote to the President in a somewhat oleaginous tone:

In my capacity as Director of the Department for Assistance for Refugees from Austria and from the former Danubian Monarchy, I have, over the course of the last three years, experienced such strong disappointment over the impossibility of the immigration of these victims that my conscience as a Bishop and patriot urges me to put to Your Excellency's extraordinary goodwill the devout proposal to willingly and generously grant, just this once, the special quota of 5000 visas including the same number of 3rd Class ship passages for

Austrian and German refugees who have suffered particularly badly as a consequence of the post-war period and who come recommended by their own Bishops. Such a quota could be split 3000 : 2000 between the Germans and the Austrians.

We have such first-rate, hard-working, qualified and suitable people in every aspect, but according to the unfortunate rules of the IRO [International Refugee Organisation] no Austrians or Germans can be accepted if, for example, they have served in the Army even as the lowliest of soldiers. Where, in the history of humanity, did military service ever constitute a moral crime, closing all doors to a peaceful and honest future?

Whilst many people, often with dubious documents, continue to leave Europe at the expense of the IRO, our poor officers and soldiers are refused despite the unquestioned fact that without their sacrifices the Europe we see today would already be Bolshevik and certainly every conference or discussion about the building of the West would be rendered superfluous.

So many times I have read newspaper articles about the generosity and far-sighted policies of the Argentines and especially about the noble sentiments of Your Excellence – facts which enter the names of Argentina and of Your Excellence into the immortal pages of Christianity and humanity.

This also gives me the courage to make an appeal to your worthy character, an appeal inspired by the principles of charity towards my poor compatriots following continuous personal contact with the poverty in these post-war times.

I ask you therefore to consider with goodwill my devoted proposal whose fruition would be a real light and hope for many families in Germany and Austria during these dark and uncertain times.[120]

Notwithstanding Hudal's hypocrisy concerning 'dubious documents', which was second to none, it is clear that he was desperate to change a regular trickle of refugees into a flood. Hudal sent the letter via his friend Dr Walter Schilling in Buenos Aires, who passed it on to Vicente Santos, a correspondent on the *Hispano-America* newspaper.[121] This circuitous route from Hudal to Perón suggests that the operation was not running as effectively as some have painted it. The President did not reply until 11 November, and even then, there was not much to give Hudal hope. The response came from Juan Duarte, who was Eva Perón's brother and Perón's private secretary, and he merely informed the bishop that the letter had been passed on to the Immigration Ministry, 'in order that it may be considered'.[122] However, it appears that Hudal's request may have fallen on stony ground. Perón had granted five thousand visas to refugees from Italy the year before, and to have granted another five thousand may have attracted unwanted attention from the Americans and the British.[123]

As it was, Carlos Fuldner had returned to Buenos Aires that September, which was indicative that Perón was winding down the whole operation.[124] Reinhard Kops also arrived in Buenos Aires that month, although he had found it hard to raise sufficient money and paperwork, another sign that Perón was slowly closing the door.[125] Initially, Kops, who now called himself 'Juan Maler', found that Argentina hardly contained the milk and honey that he might have wished for. He was employed in a metalwork factory earning one peso and sixty cents per hour, and he rented a room for eighty pesos per month.[126] However, he soon found work on the magazine *Der Weg* (*The Way*), an unashamedly far-right publication that was read by those who still did not regard Nazism as a dirty word. Kops was to correspond regularly with Hudal, and on 22 April 1949, he told his former protector that it was 'complete chaos at the local immigration authorities'. 'Is it not possible,' he asked Hudal, 'for the Vatican (Croatians?) to deal with this unendurable situation?' Kops claimed that half of the authorities sat behind closed doors, and the 'decent' refugees had no chance of pleading their cases, whereas the 'wanglers' had once again found 'new channels'.[127] For the time being, the glory days of the 'Roman way' seemed to be over, but as we shall see, Hudal had enabled some of the worst criminals of the war to escape and forge new lives on the other side of the world. Fuldner's Argentine Emigration Centre in Marktgasse in Berne was closed down in the spring of 1949, which doubtless added to the chaos in Buenos Aires. However, the work of Hudal and Draganović was far from over.

Chapter Five

The Odessa Myth

ITALY and the Vatican were not the only countries accommodating fugitive Nazis and their collaborators. In Spain, a network as effective as that run by Draganović and Hudal – if not more so – managed to help thousands of war criminals from 1944 onwards. Once again, this network was masterminded by a Catholic priest, one José La Boos, who had connections with Reinhard Kops in Genoa, as well as numerous German financiers who kept their money in Franco's Spain.[1] Boos's network is far less notorious than its Italian equivalent, partly because its refugees were not as 'stellar' as those who went through Rome, and also because it did not appear to have the indirect blessing of the Vatican. Nevertheless, the 'Iberian Way' is of great importance, because its machinations gave rise to the story of the ODESSA network, whose existence has been debated for decades. The Spanish network is also remarkable because of the identity of the person who ran it, who was not some shadowy former SS-Colonel but in fact a rather thickset naturalized Spanish spinster in her mid-forties called Clarita Stauffer.

In late February 1948, the Chief European Reporter of the *Daily Express*, Sefton Delmer, found himself at the Madrid offices of the

'Social Assistance Organization' of the Spanish Falange party at 14 Galileo Street.[2] Delmer, who had been educated in Germany, had served in the British Political Warfare Executive during the war, and was responsible for black propaganda broadcasts to Germany. Throughout late 1944 and early 1945, Delmer's phoney German radio stations started to 'reveal' that many senior Nazis had already fled to Argentina. These stories were intended to convince the German population that their leaders were deserting them, but Delmer's broadcasts were so seemingly authentic that they actually fooled both the Soviets and the Americans. The former even embellished them, and soon reports that appeared in communist newspapers were picked up by newspapers in Britain and the United States, giving rise to a 'validation loop' concerning fleeing Nazis and a 'Fourth Reich' in Argentina. One such story that appeared in the Russian publication *Red Fleet* in March 1945 claimed that twenty thousand former Gestapo men had already fled to Spain, which was a preposterous exaggeration.[3] For a while, the American State Department remained convinced. 'There has been so much smoke on this subject we feel there must be some fire,' wrote Edward Stettinius, the Secretary of State, to the US embassy in Montevideo in December 1944. 'All our information indicates that Nazis are working on a major plan to smuggle picked individuals, funds, formulae, etc., out of Germany to certain countries, including Argentina.'[4] However, the Americans were unable to confirm any of the stories, and after several months of investigations, they discovered that the information had originated from 'Radio Atlantic', which was located near London. In April 1945, the American embassy in London enquired whether the Foreign Office knew anything about the broadcasts, and the British were forced to admit that they had been the source of the disinformation all along.[5] But Delmer's broadcasts, although fakes, would prove to be prophetic, because behind the doors of 14 Galileo Street lived and worked the head of an escape network similar to the one he had dreamed up over three years before.

Delmer, posing as a German, was let in to the building by a young fair-haired German, who warned him that the lady of the house was ill, and that she would probably not be able to see him. Instead, he was ushered into her secretary's office, which was festooned with lists of those who had escaped into Spain over the Pyrenees. 'Fräulein Stauffer is ill,' explained the secretary, an elderly man who went by the name of Herr Vost, 'because she works so terribly hard. She's always on the go, travelling around, seeing people, getting the men out of the Spanish prisons and out of the internment camps, getting them jobs and getting them out of the country.' Vost told Delmer that the organization was currently looking after more than eight hundred men. At this point, the reporter revealed where he was from, which unsurprisingly caused Vost 'a bit of a shock'. However, he finally allowed Delmer to meet his boss, and Delmer was led through a dark 'German-looking' dining room into a bedroom which featured a black oak crucifix, under which lay the ailing Clarita Stauffer.

'Her face, with its fanatical blue eyes, auburn hair parted in the middle, heavyish, energetic chin, is of the kind I always find impossible to age,' Delmer wrote. The 44-year-old Stauffer explained that she was suffering from pleurisy, but the constantly ringing telephone next to her bed was no respecter of her illness. Delmer was right when he suggested that Stauffer's chin was energetic. Stauffer was not only an excellent swimmer and an accomplished pianist, but also a champion skier. In February 1938, she became the first woman to compete in the 'The Flying Kilometer of St. Moritz', and she reached 65.59 miles per hour down slopes of 35 degrees, although she fell before the end of the race. 'Her father, Conrad Stauffer, had married a Loewe, and had moved to Madrid in 1889 to establish and run the Mahou beer factory. Clarita was educated in Germany, although she moved back to Spain just before the Civil War in 1936.[7] During the conflict, Stauffer became an active member of the Falange, and joined its *Sección Femenina*, which was headed by Pilar Primo de Rivera, the sister of José Antonio Primo de Rivera, who led the Falange until his execution by the Popular Front government in November 1936. Stauffer's energy saw her elevated to the position of head of the press and propaganda department of the *Sección Femenina*, and she also did some work for the *Auxilio de Invierno* (Winter Relief Fund), which was modelled on the Nazis' *Winterhilfe*. In 1940, Stauffer produced a book about the *Sección Femenina*, in which her black-clad form can be seen working at her desk underneath portraits of Pilar and José Antonio Primo de

Rivera, as well those of Franco and Hitler. In the book, she wrote
about the injustices meted out to women in Russia, and blamed
the cost of nurseries in that country on communist Jews.[8] In the
summer of 1943, Stauffer accompanied Pilar Primo de Rivera on a
trip to Germany, where they met many leading Nazis, such as
Goebbels, Artur Axmann, Baldur von Schirach, and General
Wilhelm von Faupel, who had worked as military adviser in
Argentina in the 1920s, and had spent time in Spain assisting Franco
during the Civil War.[9] Faupel was seen by some as 'the real master
of Spain', and by 1943 he was liaising with the Spanish to allow the
Iberian peninsula to become a post-war Nazi refuge.[10] Although
Faupel was widely believed to have committed suicide in May 1945,
it was rumoured that he had actually fled to Spain, where he was
finding work for German soldiers and officers.[11] After their meeting,
Faupel and Stauffer were reputed to have maintained regular
contact, and there can be little doubt that the general provided
Stauffer with much useful information that would enable her to run
her network.[12]

    Stauffer was not coy about her activities in front of Delmer. She
told him that the Spanish authorities were fully aware of her work,
and they even helped to weed out any communists among the
refugees. Stauffer revealed that although many of the fugitives
wanted to return to Germany, some wished to emigrate to Buenos
Aires, and for these, Stauffer collaborated with a network run by a
widow called Cissy von Schiller, who had lived in Spain and since
1947 had been based in Buenos Aires. Schiller was the aunt of a
Luftwaffe lieutenant colonel, Ernst Abro Kleyenstueber, who during
the war had been based at the German embassy in Madrid, and had
established a network of Nazi agents which went by the name
'Ogre'.[13] Stauffer's clients would often come by air from Rome, or
by boat from Genoa to Barcelona, which certainly meant that she
had connections with agents of Hudal and Draganović such as
Ruffinengo and Kops. Stauffer's lack of discretion may appear
surprising, but she had many reasons to feel secure. Her Spanish
citizenship meant that the Allies could not request her extradition as
an 'obnoxious German'. Her closeness to Pilar Primo de Rivera also
helped, as well as her cosy relationship with the authorities. Her
fourth piece of armour was provided by the wealthy Germans and

former Nazis who infested the Spanish capital, and Stauffer would use their connections and their capital to carry out what she saw as her patriotic duty.[14]

Stauffer was right to feel safe. When Delmer's article appeared, the British MP Tom Driberg raised the matter in the House of Commons, although Christopher Mayhew, the Under-Secretary of State at the Foreign Office, ducked the question by merely discussing the recent thwarting of an escape attempt through Denmark. In private, the Foreign Office felt that the matter could not be raised with other governments merely 'on the strength of a newspaper article'. The British embassy in Madrid did acknowledge that the article was 'substantially correct', but it could not act on it. As one official wrote, 'Our status for objecting to the entry of Germans into Spain is not very strong.'[15]

In truth, the British knew all about Stauffer's activities, but there was nothing they could – or would – do to stop them. In June 1947, the Madrid embassy identified Stauffer's group as having the making of a 'widespread and well-protected Nazi resistance movement'. Stauffer was described as a 'fanatical Nazi', who was believed to be in touch 'with the most notorious Germans now hiding from repatriation'. However, the intelligence suggested that the real masters of the organization were the former Nazis themselves, and that a 'policy of indoctrination and propaganda will be initiated as soon as the organization feels itself sufficiently well-based and widespread'.[16]

Stauffer's group was not the only such 'Nazi cell'. The embassy's report also mentioned a group with a somewhat literal name of 'Death or Spain', which aimed at the immigration of fanatical young Nazis into Spain from Germany. Another organization went by the name of '88', the two numbers standing for 'H', the eighth letter of alphabet. The Hs stood for 'Heil Hitler', and the group, which was based in Barcelona, formed a link between Spain and various neo-Nazi groups throughout Europe.[17] 88 was probably the same group as Edelweiss-88, which would leave cryptic messages in the Spanish press. In the *Gaceta del Norte* in Bilbao on 4 April 1946, an American agent spotted the following message on the announcements page: 'Edelweiss-88, ONE peseta. For such a big letter one peseta is not enough. Useless to send long letters to me. I do not have time to read them.'[18] Edelweiss-88, like 'Death or Spain', never amounted to much, and was affected by infighting among its thuggish ranks. In May 1946, three of its members, one of whom was a priest, kidnapped one of their comrades because they suspected he had been hoarding cash. He was roughed up, and then taken to a house in Santander where some form of electrical apparatus awaited him. It was only thanks to the intervention of a female member that the victim was not electrocuted. He was eventually released, but only when he had parted with eight thousand pesetas.[19]

In February 1948, the Americans discovered another network, although it had no name. Based in Cartagena in southern Spain, it was run by one Heinrich Stotzel, who worked as a technician in the naval shipyard. The job was a cover for his real line of work, which was smuggling fugitives into Spain via Mallorca.[20] That same month, the 'Committee of Charity and Aid for Refugees' was identified as helping to smuggle Nazis, and, like Stauffer's organization, it was headed by a Catholic priest: a Father Juan Guim from Seville.[21] Although the Allies knew much about these organizations, they did little to break them up. 'I do not know whether there is any more that we can do to expel more Germans from Spain,' wrote one Foreign Office official in November 1947, 'but I have a feeling that they have now got so well bedded down with the aid of Franco, it is improbable that we shall be able to do much more.'[22]

What Delmer didn't see at 14 Galileo Street that day in February 1948 – perhaps because Stauffer was ill – was the amount of kit that Stauffer had at her disposal to issue to her 'clients'. Her nephew, Enrique Mahou, would recall years later how the 'living-room, the dining-room and all the rooms of the house were filled with dozens of pairs of boots, shirts, jackets, trousers, socks and gloves for the soldiers who came fleeing from France.'[23] Mahou remembered his aunt as being a 'special person, generous, and willing to help', which she indeed was. The only problem was that those who benefited from her nature were fugitive Nazi war criminals. Stauffer's busiest time had been during the previous two years, when she was assisting the Nazis who had been interned in the camp at Miranda de Ebro, 50 miles south of Bilbao in northeastern Spain. Among the imprisoned were men who were reported 'to have the faces of torturers formerly employed in German concentration camps'. Several had been in the SS, and some wanted to set up a neo-Nazi unit.[24] Stauffer worked as hard as she could to secure their release. Largely funded by Johannes Bernhardt of the huge German–Spanish trading conglomerate SOFINDUS, Stauffer drove around in an official car of the *Auxilio Social* (Social Assistance), and was aided by one Marianne Witte, a former secretary with the Gestapo. Stauffer managed to free many prisoners by informing the authorities that her organization would pay for their care, as well as providing the guarantors the authorities required to assume responsibility for the former prisoners. Stauffer then found accommodation for the fugitives, whom she housed with the *Auxilio Social*, as well as at a convent. The energetic Stauffer also ran a boarding house near Oviedo, which was for the female members of the German diplomatic corps and the Nazi Party. For those who wished to emigrate, Stauffer's service would 'facilitate' their departure, and it was reported that she had a 'very close collaboration' with one Piñella at the appropriate ministry.[25] Stauffer also welcomed those who arrived in Barcelona from Italy, and for these newcomers she served as a vital link between them and the Argentine consul in that city.[26] It was hardly surprising that by the end of 1947, Stauffer was out of pocket. At a meeting of the escape organization convened by Hans Brandau, a former SS man and assistant to Himmler, Stauffer was voted a reimbursement of five thousand pesetas, although some of those present, who included some 'very well dressed German officers', objected to such use of funds.[27]

A few months after her meeting with Sefton Delmer, Clarita Stauffer's organization was reputed to have carried out one of its biggest coups: the flight of Ante Pavelić. The evidence for this was given to the CIA in May or June 1952 by a Hungarian refugee, who had been 'a prominent editor and journalist' in his home country. At the time, the Agency was unable to evaluate the reliability of the Hungarian's information, but today much of it can be shown to be correct.[28] Although the refugee's report was chiefly concerned with former Nazis who were being used by the Soviets as intelligence assets in the Balkans and the Near East, it did reveal the existence of two 'transportation groups' established by the Nazis to 'transport personnel, money and the like'. One of them was called 'Insap', which was based in Munich, and organized by an SS major called Pabbara, who helped Muslim former members of the SS escape to Syria and Lebanon.[29] The other group, the Hungarian claimed, was called 'Odessa', and it was organized by one 'Clara Stauffler', with centres in Rome and Madrid. According to the report: 'The Odessa group transported Dr Ante Pavelic from Italy under the name of Aranyos, Pal, and passport 74,369 issued by the Red Cross in Rome on 5 July 1948. The groups also transported personnel to Syria, Egypt, Pakistan and other Near East Countries.'

What gives the report credibility is the correct cover name used by Pavelić, as well as his passport number. In 1952, it would have been nearly impossible for the CIA to have verified the information, because Pavelić's passport would have been hidden in a cabinet somewhere in the Dirección Nacional de Migraciones in Buenos Aires, where it would be unearthed in the late 1990s.[30] The report also mentioned some other familiar names: 'One of the group's leading agents is former SS 1st Lt. Arthur Scheidler who lives somewhere in Germany. His wife, Iris Scheidler, is also an agent and lives in Altassee [sic] [. . .] Von Hammel, personal adjutant to Martin Borman, who was recently arrested in Austria, also belonged to this group.' Although Scheidler was of course an SS lieutenant colonel, and the names of Bormann and von Hummel were spelled wrong, the Hungarian's allegation must still be taken seriously because of the accuracy of the references to Pavelić. Hummel, along with some five million dollars' worth of gold coins, had been captured in Salzburg in Austria, although the capture had been in 1946 and not 'recently'.[31] In addition, the Hungarian mentioned that the group featured an arms dealer called 'Franz Roetsel', who used the name 'Habib Said'. Again, this tallies with information apparently given to Simon Wiesenthal at the time of the Nuremberg Tribunal. Wiesenthal claims to have been approached by a former Abwehr officer who told him all about the mysterious ODESSA, which stood for *Organisation der ehemaligen SS-Angehörigen* (the Organization of Former SS Members), and that one of its key agents was a 'Haddad Said', who Wiesenthal later discovered to be an SS officer called 'Franz Röstel'.[32]

Was there an Odessa, and did it indeed feature Clarita Stauffer, the Scheidlers, Röstel, as well as numerous other agents, possibly including Hudal and Draganović? Of course, partly owing to Frederick Forsyth's book *The Odessa File*, with its confident assertion that the organization exists, the Odessa is commonly regarded as a historical truth.[33] Forsyth's research was largely based on material given to him by Simon Wiesenthal, who had introduced a wide audience to the organization in his books *Ich Jagte Eichmann* in 1961 and *The Murderers Among Us* in 1967. According to Wiesenthal, the Odessa was a vast and sinister network of former Nazis, who smuggled each other, arms and treasure around the world with a fiendish degree of secrecy. In other, later accounts, the Odessa is described as an umbrella group which helped Nazis in various ways, of which escaping was just one. The escape network arm of Odessa is sometimes referred to as '*Die Spinne*' (The Spider).[34] More sensational versions place the Odessa at the heart of every modern evil, and claim that it is responsible for insinuating a clandestine version of the Fourth Reich into the fabric of Western society.[35] Indeed, so widespread is the belief in the Odessa that history professors at reputable universities believe in it.[36] And, as we shall see later, the term has gained so much currency that even neo-Nazis who try to kill people claim that they are from the Odessa.

The truth about the Nazi escape organizations, beneath the mushroom clouds of smoke, is that they were similar to an old-boy network, or perhaps even the loose web of terrorist cells and groups that are today placed under the name of al-Qaeda.[37] After the war, there were countless organizations that assisted escaping Nazis, and some of these groups had names – such as '*Konsul*', '*Scharnhorst*', '*Sechsgestirn*', '*Leibwache*', '*Lustige Brüder*' – and some did not.[38] Instead of one big fire under the smoke, there were instead many small ones, the combination of their multiple and toxic emissions suggestive of a single large inferno. Assistance would also be provided on an ad hoc basis, sometimes by an individual or a handful of individuals rather than by a coordinated group. In May 1945, the British Second Army reported that a *Burgermeister* had issued one thousand false military government travel permits to wanted persons.[39] In July, three Catholic priests were arrested for helping to run an illegal mail service for SS and civilian internees.[40] The following month, it was discovered that some German doctors were helping SS men to remove their blood-group tattoos, and were furnishing them with false medical reports to ensure their immediate release.⁴¹ Of course, the notion that a supposedly highly secret society of cunning former SS men would give itself the name 'The Organization of Former SS Members' is in itself open to disbelief. If the word 'Odessa' must be used today, then it might be used as an umbrella term to refer to all the secret 'transportation societies' that looked after fugitive Nazis.

However, as we have seen, the records do show that there was something called 'Odessa'. Far from being the globalized tentacled monster of popular imagination, it appeared to start as little more than a watchword, and would become a term loosely ascribed to the group that took fugitives from Germany and Austria down to Rome and Genoa, and from there to Spain and Argentina. One of the earliest recorded mentions of 'Odessa' is in a CIC memo dated 3 July 1946, in which an underground organization at an SS internment camp in Auerbach was identified. It was not called 'Odessa', but the word was employed as a codeword in order to gain 'special food privileges and special food consideration' from the Red Cross in Augsburg. The term also had currency further afield, in towns such as Kempten, Rosenheim, Mannheim and Berchtesgaden, where it was applied to small cells of unrepentant SS members in order to provide them with a feeling of solidarity. As these groups lacked any form of organization and leadership, the CIC was not overly troubled.⁴² However, in November, the Czechs informed the Americans that they had caught wind of an organization called 'ODESSA' that was operating in the British Zone of Occupation, and that it had held its first meeting in Hamburg in September.⁴³ The following January, the CIC sent an agent into the internment camp at Dachau, who reported that there was an escape organization operating there under the name of 'ODESSA' and organized by SS-Obersturmbannführer Otto Skorzeny, who was himself a prisoner. 'This is being done with the help of the Polish guards,' the agent reported, '[who] are helping the men that receive orders from Skorzeny to escape.'⁴⁴ The informant disclosed that the organization was 'worldwide' and that it provided Portuguese papers for those who wished to travel to Argentina. For those who decided to stay in

Germany, the group would provide employment and documentation.[45] However, neither the Americans nor the British were able to verify any of the informant's claims. 'Key personalities have been closely watched,' the CIC reported, 'but none of their activities have extended beyond the establishment of contact with former SS personnel in their locale.' The CIC also felt that Skorzeny's name was simply being used for 'backing and prestige'.[46] One of the most important figures in the network was identified as being an SS-Obersturmbannführer Ruhl, who had escaped from Dachau and was not only assisting escapes, but also trying to procure money and arms.[47] On 6 January 1947, Ruhl was arrested, and the CIC noted with some satisfaction that as a result 'the organization has deteriorated'.[48]

The name of Otto Skorzeny has often been linked with the Odessa, and like the Odessa, it has been the subject of much mythologizing and speculation. This is hardly surprising, as the huge scar-faced Austrian enjoyed a legendary reputation throughout the war which would endure until his death in 1975. Skorzeny's greatest coup had been his rescue of Mussolini in July 1943, which had earned him the Knight's Cross and the epithet of 'Hitler's Favourite Commando'. The mission was the stuff of a boy's war comic, featuring a perilous glider-borne raid on a mountain top and a hair-raising flight in a tiny Fieseler Stork into which the substantial frames of Mussolini and Skorzeny were crammed. In October 1944, Skorzeny was responsible for another *coup de main*, when he led the kidnapping of the son of Admiral Miklós Horthy, the Hungarian Regent. Hitler had learned that Horthy had been secretly negotiating to surrender to the Soviets, which would have isolated a million German troops. Skorzeny's mission was successful, and Horthy was forced to abdicate, which allowed the installation of a pro-German government and Hungary's continued membership of the Axis. Later that year, Skorzeny was to play a significant role in the Battle of the Bulge, during which he dispatched several troops disguised as American soldiers behind enemy lines in order to spread both confusion and the rumour that Skorzeny was planning to assassinate Eisenhower. This boosted Skorzeny's already considerable notoriety, and his celebrity was enhanced by the appearance of 'Wanted' posters bearing his photograph.[49] Towards the end of the war,

Skorzeny reluctantly assisted the Nazis' poorly led guerrilla movement, the *Werwolf*, which was conceived to act as a 'stay-behind'
movement in the territories that the Allies had occupied. Skorzeny is
often credited as being a luminary in *Werwolf*, whereas he in fact
saw it as a drain on the *matériel* he required for his own SS 'Ranger'
unit. Himmler had even offered the leadership of *Werwolf* to
Skorzeny, but he had declined, telling the Reichsführer that he had
too little time to spare.[50] Towards the end of the war, Skorzeny made
his way to the Austrian Alps to assist in preparations for the 'Alpine
Redoubt', but he eventually surrendered himself to the Americans
on 15 May 1945 at Radstadt, 30 miles southwest of Altaussee.[51]

Despite his heroics, many Nazis regarded the self-publicizing
Skorzeny with scepticism, and even hatred. One Abwehr officer
described him as 'megalomaniac' and said that he often 'drew up the
most fantastic projects', which were unfeasible.[52] It was also felt by
some that Skorzeny had received undue credit for the Mussolini
operation, and that he had exaggerated his role during a radio
broadcast two days after the event.[53] In addition, the collapsing
Third Reich was littered with rumours that Skorzeny had secured
for himself vast quantities of treasure. Skorzeny later claimed that he
had been approached towards the end of the war by a group of
German bankers, who asked him to fly some $14 million worth
of gold to Argentina. Skorzeny declined, because he felt that his
future was with Germany, and that it was his destiny one day to be
President of Germany.[54] Such hubris was typical of Skorzeny, who
by many accounts was both politically naive and not particularly
intelligent.[55] One American even described him as 'child-like in
many ways'.[56] His CIC interrogator regarded him as 'politically
short-sighted to the point of naivity [*sic*]', and even SS-
Sturmbannführer Karl Radl, Skorzeny's adjutant, regarded his boss
as being gullible, overly enthusiastic, and a poor leader with a bad
eye for detail.[57]

This then, was the figure many claim to have led the Odessa, or
its supposed escape subsidiary, *Die Spinne*. It is hard to conceive
how a man like Skorzeny could have operated such a vast, sophisticated and clandestine network: he would have been hopelessly ill
qualified for such a task. His CIA file reveals a man very different
from that portrayed in his own memoirs or the plethora of flattering

biographies.[58] Instead, it shows a character who is desperate to find a role after his glory years during the war. Big schemes such as organizing a pan-European army perished as soon as they were hatched, and he courted intelligence agencies around the world with the gauche eagerness of a teenage suitor. After his acquittal by an American military tribunal in September 1947, and his escape from internment in July 1948, Skorzeny would eventually end up in Madrid, where he was reputed to have had access to a vast fortune and been at the very heart of the Odessa network, or *Die Spinne*. Those who knew him at this time dispute such a portrait. 'I would definitely think this not to be the case,' said Jere Whittington, who as a young captain was attached to the office of the American attaché in Madrid. In early 1951, Whittington had befriended Skorzeny and his mistress Ilse, the niece of the former Reich Minister of Economics Hjalmar Schacht, and, with whisky supplied by the CIA, he often entertained the couple at his apartment. 'They were living "on economy",' Whittington recalled, 'and they were embarrassed that they were never able to reciprocate my hospitality.' The couple were so straitened that they enlisted the American to help them find a Christmas tree. 'I had the only station wagon in Madrid,' said Whittington, 'and Skorzeny asked me if I could drive him and friend out to one of the forests outside the city. His friend turned out to be the former German ambassador to Argentina, and together, we cut down three trees.'[59] The notion of Skorzeny's wealth has always been a key indicator of his involvement with the Odessa, but the testimony of those such as Whittington suggests that Skorzeny was anything but rich. Naturally, Skorzeny could have posed as a pauper, yet such cunning does not sit easily on his shoulders, and when Skorzeny was to come into money later in life, he certainly did not hide it.

But the rumours that Skorzeny was involved with *Die Spinne* would persist. In October 1950, *Reynolds News* claimed that he was the head of the European arm of the organization, and that he was assisted by Hartmann Lauterbacher, the former Gauleiter of South Hanover-Brunswick and a senior figure in the Hitler Youth. According to the report, *Die Spinne* was smuggling wanted Nazis via Rome to a 'not-so-secret headquarters' near Buenos Aires on the River Plate. The article then listed some of those who had now

appeared in Argentina, among them being Kurt Tank, the designer
of the Focke-Wulf 190 fighter. Although Tank was indeed in
Argentina, as we shall see his escape had nothing to do with
Skorzeny or *Die Spinne*. The article's accuracy was further com
promised by a photograph of 'eight former Luftwaffe pilots' shown
posing at the supposedly secret base, which also featured a long line
of jet fighters 'in which they are trained to keep abreast of air
developments'. The conjunction of the photograph and the headline
that read 'Under a grim name the Nazis are building a new war
machine' gave the impression that *Die Spinne* was helping to
assemble a neo-Nazi arsenal in South America. However, the eight
pilots featured were all in fact Argentinian, and the fighters were
Gloster Meteors supplied by the British. The Argentines were quite
open about where the picture was taken, which was the Naval Air
Base Comandante Espora 400 miles southwest of Buenos Aires.[60]
Skorzeny's connection with Rome had also been reported in the
Christlicher Nachrichtendienst (Christian News Service) earlier that
year, in which it was claimed that both he and Lauterbacher were
being accommodated by Hudal at the Santa Maria dell'Anima. The
bishop vigorously denied this, and claimed that he had never had
contact with either man.[61] Hudal's denials were almost certainly
true, because on 16 October that year – the day after the report in
Reynolds News – Skorzeny wrote to Hudal asking him to forward a
letter to a friend called Leo Schulz who was due to visit the bishop
on 21 October. Skorzeny began his letter by asking Hudal to forgive
him for troubling him 'as an unknown', and disguised his identity by
simply signing himself as 'Rolf', which was part of his cover name,
Rolf O. S. Steinbauer.[62] (It is a testamant to Skorzeny's ego and
inability to maintain proper secrecy that he used his actual initials in
the middle of his false identity.) If Skorzeny was the kingpin of *Die
Spinne*, then he would have certainly been known to Hudal.
Unfortunately for Skorzeny, Hudal never passed on the letter to
Schulz, and today it remains at the archive of the Santa Maria
dell'Anima. In the letter, Skorzeny writes of his regret that he could
not come to Rome, 'because a flight to Rome and back is still a considerable amount', which is further testimony that Skorzeny was not
a rich man, and hardly the mastermind of a vast and powerful network of former Nazis, if indeed such a network even existed. The

letter does show that Skorzeny had links with Germany, because towards the end he writes, 'I heard from Alfred that the work in Hamburg went especially well, and I assume you played a considerable part in it. I thank you heartily for it . . .'[63]

The absurdity of *Die Spinne* was successfully captured by a former British SOE agent in the 28 June 1951 issue of the British magazine *The Listener*. Stanley Moss, who with Patrick Leigh Fermor had abducted a German general off Crete in April 1944, professed that he suffered from the 'generally recognized British weakness for exploring the case histories of our defeated enemies'.[64] As a result, Moss was researching the story of Mussolini's 'Hundred Days' from his fall from power to his execution. Naturally, the story of his rescue by Skorzeny would feature heavily, and so, when 'Hitler's Favourite Commando' was spotted enjoying a Pernod on the Champs Elysées on the afternoon of 13 February 1950, Moss immediately set off for Paris to interview him. Accompanied by a friend called Captain Michael Luke, Moss arrived in the French capital only to find that the newspapers had picked up on his 'hunt for Scarface'. The publicity attracted the attention of a 'small, dark-haired man' calling himself Captain Jaques Kaminski, who said that he had worked for *Die Spinne* in Italy, but had fallen out with the organization over money. Kaminski claimed not only that Skorzeny was the European head of *Die Spinne*, but also that Martin Bormann, no less, masterminded the global organization from Argentina. Bormann's name usually serves as a vital indicator that whatever intelligence being imparted is highly dubious, and this occasion would prove to be no exception, as Kaminski was to lead the two Britons on a *chasse pour une oie sauvage*. Shortly afterwards, Kaminski introduced them to another purported agent from *Die Spinne*, who happened to be in Paris over from Argentina. Codenamed 'Alfredo', the agent met them at a café at eleven o'clock one morning, and he seemed like something out of a cheap thriller – Latin in appearance, and 'very smartly dressed in a chalk-stripe suit, Panama hat, and correspondent shoes'. To complete the *film noir* image, under the table sat a Boxer dog. Alfredo then told them that he too had fallen out with *Die Spinne* over finances, but he was able to confirm that Skorzeny and Bormann were its two heads, and that the escape network ran under the cover of a 'South American import–export firm'. *Die Spinne* had recently arranged for the flight of two Luftwaffe aces, as well as a 'well-known scientist' who had worked for Focke-Wulf. Moss was needlessly coy in his report about the identities of the firm and the personalities. Their names were starting to be mentioned in newspapers, and at the time of Alfredo's 'revelation', the presence of Kurt Tank and of the aces Hans-Ulrich Rudel and Adolf Galland in the southern hemisphere was known by many. The firm to which 'Alfredo' referred would have been CAPRI, which was established by Carlos Fuldner in Buenos Aires as a company for which his human cargo could work. This too was well known, to the extent that the German community in Argentina jokingly dubbed it the '*Compañia Alemana Para Recién Immigrados*' (German Company for Recent Immigrants).[65] Therefore, whatever the mysterious 'Alfredo' told Moss and Luke was hardly proof of access to some inside knowledge, or indeed evidence of the existence of *Die Spinne*. Moss and Luke promised to follow up a promising lead in Zurich that Alfredo had supplied, but before they left they consulted a former comrade who now worked for British intelligence in Paris. Their friend told them that Kaminski was in fact a Soviet agent, and even though he may have penetrated *Die Spinne*, what he had said had come straight off a script supplied by Moscow.[66] Moss and Luke would meet Kaminski several more times, but it became apparent that their contact was peddling little more than disinformation and was implicating Skorzeny in activities for which he bore no responsibility. 'Like Skorzeny himself,' Moss wrote, 'we realized that we were being used as communist pawns.' The result of such disinformation is that history becomes almost ineradicably tainted, and there is a danger of relying on intelligence reports as accurate conveyers of truth.

The likelihood that the existence of *Die Spinne*, and Skorzeny's involvement with it, was at least a Soviet exaggeration – and quite possibly a complete fabrication – is furthered by an examination of the *Brown Book*, a piece of East German propaganda published in 1966, in which it was claimed that Skorzeny ran *Die Spinne* from his home in Denia on the Costa Blanca in southern Spain. 'The founding of the Nazi secret organization the "Spider" is his work,' the book reported, 'which not only had at its disposal substantial resources from the pool of looted riches of the SS, but also enjoys the support of leading German trusts.'⁶⁷ Although Skorzeny did indeed own a small hotel in Denia, no evidence was ever unearthed that showed that he ran an escape network from it.⁶⁸

Why would the Russians wish to frame Skorzeny? The answer is simple. Skorzeny was indeed helping Nazis, but he was doing so openly, and in the full view of the West German government. The Soviets and their satellites saw this laissez-faire attitude as nothing less than an unmerited rehabilitation of war criminals, an accusation that certainly had merit, as the *Brown Book*, for example, is not a complete work of fiction. The clubbable and charming Skorzeny spent his years after the war consorting with every significant Nazi and fellow Fascist traveller on the planet, earning himself a notoriety that made him an easy target for Soviet propaganda and intelligence chicanery. On 10 January 1953, a German calling himself 'Gunther Buhn' turned up at the US embassy in Madrid and told the Americans that Skorzeny was the head of a 'pro-Russian faction of a secret Spanish society comprised of former SS members'. In addition, he supplied the Americans with 'evidence' that Skorzeny was depositing vast sums of money into his wife's account every month, the implication being that he was financed by Moscow. Buhn implored the Americans to break into Skorzeny's office, and even gave them a sketch of the 'code system used for papers to be found in his safe'. However, the Americans were quickly able to establish that the information Buhn supplied was largely bunkum, and the approach made by Buhn had all the hallmarks of a Soviet disinformation operation.⁶⁹ But Buhn did not give up, and on 27 February, he appeared at the American consulate in Marseille under the name of 'Kluf'. This time, he had a much better story to tell, and he now spoke of a new neo-Nazi organization called 'HIASS', which aimed to infiltrate pro-Soviet former SS officers into West Germany in order to 'work for a "New Germany" under the protection of Soviet Russia'. Kluf also drew what he claimed to be the symbol of HIASS – a convoluted squiggle – although he was not sure what words the letters HIASS actually stood for. He blended his fantasy with some real intelligence in order to add some degree of plausibility, but once again, the Americans found 'Kluf' unconvincing, and it is probable that the 'intelligence' that he was offering was another attempt at Soviet bloc disinformation. If that is not the case, then it is hard to establish how the supposedly penniless Kluf/Buhn was able to finance his gallivanting around southern Europe.[70]

Just as the work of Sefton Delmer had gone through a 'validation loop' that saw the Allies chasing their own tails, the story of Skorzeny's relationship with *Die Spinne* and the Odessa went through a similar process. It is a story that does contain some small truths, but they have been distorted and magnified out of all recognition by a mixture of intelligence operatives, journalists and a willing audience. It is likely that Skorzeny did help some Nazis to escape at some point, and may have acted as point of contact between a few escapers and their helpers, but the notion that the Austrian masterminded some secret society is fanciful, not least because nearly every move he made was monitored by the Americans, and in all likelihood, several other nations. The fact that Buhn's information was so easily dismissed was owing to the intensity of surveillance under which men such as Skorzeny unwittingly operated. For example, when Buhn told the Americans about Skorzeny's safe, Robert Bieck, the acting Air Attaché at the embassy, was able to provide the CIA with exact details of the safe.[71] In short, if Skorzeny was running an escape network, the Americans would have known about it.

Throughout the mid-1940s, the Allied intelligence services would receive a few more reports about 'Odessa', but they suggested that the organization was little more than a catch-all term used by former Nazis who wished to continue the fight. Furthermore, the nature of the Odessa seemed to change depending on who was being interrogated. In December 1947, the CIC in Donauwörth questioned a former SS officer called Robert Markworth who had been arrested for attempted bribery. Markworth claimed that he was on a secret mission for the Odessa, the role of which was to infiltrate the Russian military government and had nothing to do with escaping.[72] Earlier that year, the Americans had been told by an informant that the way to contact the organization was simply to mingle with the crowds around a selection of mainline railway stations until 'one was accosted by someone with the word ODESSA'. The informant, whom the Americans did not know and who had simply volunteered his information, tried his luck in Hanover, where he met a 'Herbert Ringel', who claimed that the aim of the Odessa was 'the planning of an eventual revolution'. Information throughout the group was spread by a network of contacts, none of whom knew the name of the next person in the chain. The method of identification was the presence of 'three small spots in the shape of a triangle at the base of the thumb and forefinger of the right hand'. 'Ringel' also showed the informant his Odessa *Ausweis*, which featured the supposed Odessa symbol on its cover: two crossed arrows laid over the letters 'ODSSA'. The Americans graded the informant as 'F3', which indicated that his unreliability could not be judged, and that his information was possibly true.[73] In fact, what he had reported was highly likely to have been yet more disinformation, and an amateur attempt at that. The notion that the Odessa would issue its members with identity documents was absurd, and the presence of the three spots equally so. It also seems implausible that a member of the Odessa would offer such secrets to a stranger at Hanover railway station. The same year, yet another organization calling itself 'ODESSA' was discovered in Rosenheim by the CIC, although it seemed to consist of little more than a dozen men, some of whom had previously been imprisoned for theft and possession of arms. The CIC reported that it had penetrated the group, and it noted how the word 'Odessa' was used as a kind of code. The leader of the group, Hans Schuchert, was described as a 'fanatical SS soldier who always greets his friends with "Heil Odessa".' At a dance at the Gasthaus Plestkeller in Ziegelberg just outside Rosenheim,[74] Schuchert requested a number for SS members. 'Now comes a dance for Odessa,' he said. 'That means for the SS.' Although some of the guests were shocked, nobody – including some policemen present – registered any complaint.[75]

By the early 1950s, reports of the Odessa and *Die Spinne* had died down, and if the organization ever did exist, then it fizzled out like all the other neo-Nazi cells with their grand ideas. Many Nazis, including Skorzeny, publicly helped their former comrades by donating time and money to organizations such as '*Bruderschaft*' and HIAG (Mutual Help Association of Former Waffen-SS Members), the full German name of which – *Hilfsgemeinschaft auf Gegenseitigkeit der Angehörigen der ehemaligen Waffen-SS* – sounded similar to the full name of Odessa. Such organizations were tolerated by the West Germans and the Allies, but like all groups that featured former Nazis, they were thoroughly penetrated by the intelligence services.[76] And when a group became too ambitious and threatened to subvert the Federal Republic's budding democracy, it was wound up. The most sensational example of this was the arrest by the British of the 'Naumann Circle' on the night of 14–15 January 1953. Headed by Werner Naumann, the former Reich propaganda minister and fellow escapee of Martin Bormann from the *Führerbunker*, the group aimed at nothing less than a re-establishment of a Nazi state. 'Let us form a conspiracy of several hundred men,' said Naumann in a speech made in Düsseldorf on 2 November 1952, 'and we will be a force which, behind the scenes at first, but in full publicity one day will obtain the realisation of its ideals.'[77] Naumann's papers revealed that he was at the hub of a vast network of Nazis such as Skorzeny, Rudel, Axmann and Lauterbacher, as well as foreign sympathizers such as Sir Oswald Mosley and his wife Diana, and Eberhard Fritsch, the publisher of *Der Weg* in Buenos Aires for whom Hudal's helper Reinhard Kops worked. In addition, Naumann appeared to have established a network of SS agents who reported to him.[78] If the Odessa existed in any form, then Naumann and those in his circle – who were Nazi 'aristocrats' to a man – would have been those who ran it. However, in the six lorryloads of confidential material confiscated from Naumann, there are no mentions of any escape organizations, or of the Odessa, or *Die Spinne*.[79]

Intriguingly, Naumann's diary entry for 21 August 1950 recounts a meeting with Artur Axmann, the former Hitler Youth leader, and another survivor of the flight from the *Führerbunker*. During the conversation over afternoon coffee, Axmann told Naumann that he was 'attracted by Skorzeny's plan' and that he wanted 'to help him'.[80] On the surface, this looks as though it might be a glimpse of something like the Odessa, but it is more likely to refer to Skorzeny's plan to raise a 200,000-strong cadre of men that could be moved to Spain in the event of a war with the Soviets. Skorzeny had been in Germany that same month attempting to drum up support for what would be yet another of his overly ambitious plans.[81] By the spring of 1952, the plan had apparently mutated into a desire to smuggle former members of the SD, the Abwehr and SS officers 'experienced in special raids' into Spain via Switzerland.[82] Later that year, the CIA was informed by a 'reliable Luftwaffe veteran' that Skorzeny was in cahoots with Naumann in trying to establish an 'underground organisation of Nazi-minded individuals with the immediate objective of preventing German integration with the Western Powers and with the ultimate objective of reestablishing an authoritarian German state'.[83] The arrest of the Naumann Circle would clearly have dealt a blow to Skorzeny's scheming, and there is no evidence that Skorzeny was even partially successful in realizing his dream. Until his death in 1975, Skorzeny would be linked with all manner of affairs – from supplying arms to the Egyptian president Gamal Abdel Nasser to being a lover of Evita Perón – some of which are probably true.[84]

But what of the report given to the CIA in mid-1952 by the Hungarian refugee that featured Clarita Stauffer and the Scheidlers working for 'Odessa'? Stauffer certainly helped Nazis escape, but once again, there is no record that her organization 'traded' under such a name or that of *Die Spinne*. The Scheidlers, however, represent a far greyer area. After he was arrested by Captain Matteson in May 1945, Arthur Scheidler was interned, and while he languished, the sexually generous Iris began an affair with an American colonel. In early 1947, the lovestruck officer allowed Iris to visit her husband in order to seek his permission for a divorce. While the couple discussed their marriage, Arthur Scheidler revealed to his wife that some of the gold that he and Kaltenbrunner had hidden had gone missing.[85] How he was able to establish this from behind bars is unclear, but from then on, Iris no longer sought a separation, the attraction to her husband perhaps rekindled by his potential access to vast riches. Rumours that the Scheidlers were in possession of hidden treasure began to spread throughout the Salzkammergut, and in the middle of 1947, Iris was questioned by the Bad Aussee police. Although she denied any knowledge of the whereabouts of the booty, she did agree that she would 'cooperate in finding out the hidden assets of gold and foreign exchange'. Iris also passed on rumours concerning the existence of a cache reputedly buried outside the gates of Ebensee concentration camp, a sub-camp of Mauthausen, as well as the news that 'a considerable quantity of gold' had been found 15 miles north of Altaussee in the cellar of a house in Altmünster, which was inhabited by a Frau Koplin.[86] If Iris ever got her hands on any gold, she kept it well hidden, because there is simply no evidence to suggest that she was wealthy. Gossip spreads swiftly in rural areas, and no doubt Iris's reputation as a scarlet woman was easily augmented by equally juicy tales of an attic full of gold. Every time Iris bought a round of drinks, the locals would whisper that it was funded by a stash of loot.[87] Iris did have a secret, however, that had nothing to do with gold or the Odessa: she was an informer for the CIC. Until she left Altaussee in the late 1940s, Iris fed the Americans information concerning various Nazi personalities.[88] During this period, she was also said to have continued some form of relationship with Wilhelm Höttl after he had been released from Klessheim in December 1947.[89] It is unclear whether the two became lovers once more, but Iris certainly became part of the nascent networks Höttl had been asked to run by the Americans.[90] However, the friendship would deteriorate, and according to one 1952 report, the 'two families have been on the "outs" for about two years.'[91]

In the late 1940s, Iris moved to Salzburg, where she opened a clothing concession within the OH Hotel, but continued to offer intelligence to the CIC. With Arthur still interned, Iris soon became the lover of an employee of the hotel called Heinz Grimms. The brother of her new boyfriend was a communist journalist called Willie Grimms, who, despite his political inclinations, gave information to the CIC through Iris. Her affair with Heinz would end upon his imprisonment for black-market activities, and when her husband was released in 1948, Iris would appear 'anxious' whenever Grimms came up in conversation. In 1950, she opened a boutique called 'Wiener Modelle' at Franz Josef Kai 9 in Salzburg, and from the same address Arthur worked as a salesman for a tool and motor-parts firm. Nevertheless, Iris kept up her intelligence work, although seemingly not just on behalf of the Americans. In late 1951, the CIC were informed that Iris's shop acted as the meeting-point for various suspected agents of the notoriously brutal Hungarian Secret Police, the AVH (Államvédelmi Hatóság). One of Iris's Hungarian associates was alleged to be Istvan Serenyi, a former journalist who had been imprisoned by the Communists and then released to spy in Austria. However, Serenyi was said to have turned his back on the East, and instead joined a secret group of former members of the fascist Arrow Cross party. From December 1951 to January 1952, the CIC tapped the Scheidlers' phone and opened their mail, but they found no evidence that Iris was linked to Serenyi, and all they could confirm was that she did indeed sell clothes, and Arthur was involved in selling and importing car parts.[92]

It is possible that the Hungarian journalist who gave information to the CIC about 'Odessa' in mid-1952 was Istvan Serenyi. Even if the CIC intercepts did not reveal a link between the Scheidlers and the Hungarians, in a small city such as Salzburg intelligence tittle-tattle would have been epidemic. A figure such as Serenyi may have got to hear about the Scheidlers on the intelligence grapevine, which is no more reliable a source of information than a knitting circle. Whispers of 'Odessa' would have abounded, just as would whispers of any other putative secret society. But Serenyi or not, reliable or not, the Hungarian journalist certainly knew something that very few in Europe would have known in 1952: Ante Pavelić's fake name 'Pal Aranyos' and his Red Cross passport number, 74369.

Another person interested in the Scheidlers was Simon Wiesenthal. On 3 April 1952, Wiesenthal wrote a long letter to the journalist Ottmar Katz concerning Nazi gold and how Kaltenbrunner's treasure was supposedly used to finance Nazi escape routes. In the letter, a poor copy of which is housed at the National Archives in Washington, DC, Wiesenthal appears to demonstrate that Arthur Scheidler had a key role in transporting the loot. Wiesenthal also told Katz about various secret Nazi societies, such as *Scharnhorst*, *Sechsgestirn*, *Edelweiss*, *Spinne* and PAX. Wiesenthal also writes about 'Odessa', which, he informs Katz, is an escape organization that transported fugitives to Bishop Hudal in Rome, and from where they headed to Madrid and South America.[93] Interestingly, Wiesenthal makes no further claims for the Odessa, unlike those he would make in his 1967 memoir, *The Murderers Among Us*. In that version, Wiesenthal claims that he was told about the organization during the Nuremberg trial by a former senior Abwehr officer whom he calls 'Hans'. The mysterious 'Hans' relates the activities of the Odessa in great detail, and he provides names, places, routes and the identities of some of those who had escaped, who included Martin Bormann and Adolf Eichmann.[94] The picture that Wiesenthal claimed to have drawn in 1946 is therefore a very different and much larger version than the one he painted six years later for Ottmar Katz. Why is this? It is possible that Wiesenthal was withholding information from Katz, but this is unlikely, as the letter is both long and crammed with information about other discoveries. The more likely explanation for this discrepancy is that Wiesenthal in the 1960s was wishing to portray himself as having been wiser than others, whereas the sum total of what he really knew about the supposed 'Odessa' in the early 1950s is what he told Katz. Wiesenthal would also write that as he 'found out more about the operations of ODESSA, I realised why the Allied intelligence services knew nothing about it'. As we have seen, those services knew plenty about 'Odessa', and such a statement is typical of Wiesenthal's self-inflation.

'Hans' was not a cover name – he was a pure invention. Wiesenthal's source for his intelligence on the Odessa was not a friendly Abwehr officer but a former SD man who had been running highly dubious networks for the Americans until they had sacked him in September 1949. The intelligence he gathered had been evaluated as poor, and the CIC regarded him as dishonest.[95] There was also an ongoing suspicion that the man would peddle intelligence to the highest bidder, no matter on what side of the Iron Curtain the money came from. On 16 January 1950, the CIC in Upper Austria learned that Wiesenthal, who it described as the 'recognised leader of the Jewish DP's in Upper Austria' and the 'chief Austrian Agent of the Israeli Intelligence Bureau', had recruited Wilhelm Höttl. Even the CIC acknowledged that Höttl was a dangerous war criminal, who had been exonerated only because he had turned state's witness at Nuremberg.[96] According to the CIC source, Höttl

... furnished at least one lengthy (100 page) report to date, of which Source is aware. The report deals with the whereabouts and present activities in Austria of former prominent NSDAP members, all details known to HOETTL on the VdU and the SPIDER organization. Source evaluated the content material of the report as grossly exaggerated.[97]

The CIC graded the source's information as being 'probably true' as 'similar data has been circulating in Jewish circles in Linz for the past several weeks, though always of the rumor category'. However, the information was confirmed by a field office source, who was described as being 'fairly reliable'. The source's information was correct, because in September 1959, when Wiesenthal wrote to the Israeli ambassador concerning Adolf Eichmann, he cited Höttl as a source.[98] In 2008, Höttl's daughter said that her father had 'always told me that Wiesenthal used SS men as his sources', which makes his employment of an SS man such as Höttl perfectly likely.[99]

Furthermore, far from being an escape network, *Die Spinne*, or 'SPIDER', was in fact the name of the underground organization of the VdU – the *Verband der Unabhängigen* (the Federation of Independents) – a right-wing Austrian political party that would be absorbed into the Freedom Party in 1956.[100] The aims of *Die Spinne* were to restore the *Anschluss* with Germany and to make good what the Nazis had lost.[101] Predictably, the man who ran this secret organization was Höttl himself,[102] and it would appear that the former SD man was happy even to provide information on his own network to Wiesenthal, although it is safe to assume that much of what he supplied would have been of little or no worth.

There can also be little doubt that much of what Wiesenthal told Katz in his letter was yet more bunkum fed to him by Höttl. It is instructive that the letter to Katz should end up in Höttl's file at the US National Archives. As a result, it is extremely difficult to trust anything that the gullible Wiesenthal would later present to the world concerning 'Odessa' and how the Nazis escaped. Even Nazis such as Reinhold Kops, who wrote a set of candid memoirs in 1987, denied the existence of the 'so-called Odessa organization'.[103] Alfred Jarschel, whose fanciful *Fleeing Nuremberg* is full of the most outrageous stories about Nazi escapes – including the 'flight' of Martin Bormann – was withering about the 'Odessa' story, and saw it as little more than a line Wiesenthal would peddle to journalists.[104] One of those to whom Wiesenthal told his story was Antony Terry of the *Sunday Times* in London, who, in July 1967, wrote an article describing how the Odessa functioned, and claimed its greatest scoop had been the rescue of Martin Bormann.[105] If Terry's editor had known that the ultimate source of much of the piece was a duplicitous former SD man, then he might have put the article on the spike. Or probably not. After all, it was a great story. The rest, thanks to Frederick Forsyth, was pure fiction.

Chapter Six

'Peculiar travel matters'

WHILE MARTIN Bormann's remains rotted beneath the rubble-strewn streets of Berlin, the International Military Tribunal tried him *in absentia*. Found guilty on Counts Three and Four of the prosecution's charges – War Crimes and Crimes against Humanity – Bormann was sentenced to death in October 1946.[1] In the middle of the night after the sentence was announced, several people in the Styrian region of Austria heard a speaker on the radio claiming that he was the 'Guardian of National Socialism Bormann', and he called on the population to remain quiet until instructions were given for a general uprising. He closed the speech with the words '*Heil Deutschland!*'[2] As no body had been found, rumours that the 'Brown Eminence' had made good his escape flourished for the next few decades. Bormann's character made him the perfect conduit for the conspiracy theorists' claims – he was, after all, a secretive and powerful figure, and a post-war life spent in the shadows manipulating a vast and clandestine network suited the image. Sightings of Martin Bormann were as ubiquitous as those of Elvis Presley decades later, and in some instances, no less comedic. Bormann was a monk in Rome.[3] Bormann was a forester in the Kassel area.[4]

Bormann was leading the *Edelweiss Piraten* in the Tölzer Mountains.[5] Bormann had landed in Argentina by submarine.[6] Bormann was living in a small village in Salamanca in Spain.[7] Bormann was in Egypt.[8] Bormann was a hunter in the Tyrol called 'Carlo'.[9] Bormann was working for the Soviets.[10] Bormann was suffering from gastritis in a hotel in Córdoba in central Argentina.[11] Bormann was seen on a bus in São Paulo.[12] Bormann frequented the Ali Baba nightclub in Asunción, Paraguay, with Josef Mengele.[13] Bormann was a priest in Brazil.[14] Bormann was in fact none of these people, because in 1995, the *News of the World* could exclusively reveal that Bormann had really lived out his days as one Peter Broderick-Hartley in Reigate in Surrey.[15] Although hindsight fosters the temptation to deride such sightings, the lack of a corpse meant that they were inevitable. The frequency was doubtless intensified by the fact that there are a lot of stout, balding, white, middle-aged men in the world.

How then was Bormann supposed to have escaped? There are numerous versions, all of which feed off each other. According to Simon Wiesenthal's 1967 memoir, *The Murderers Among Us*, in the autumn of 1945 Bormann and an unnamed woman were smuggled by an Austrian Red Cross worker from Flensburg near the German–Danish border down to the Alpine village of Nauders, which lies just 2 miles from where the Austrian, Italian and Swiss borders meet. The Red Cross worker, who had no inkling of the couple's identity, but was handsomely rewarded with jewellery, then escorted Bormann to a monastery in the Italian Tyrol. At the gate of the monastery, Bormann turned to his guide and told him who he was, and added, 'You've done something terrific. If you don't talk about it, you'll get some money every month as long as you live.' Despite rubbishing other stories about Bormann, Wiesenthal writes that he found this particular account 'contained many credible elements'. It may have done, but Wiesenthal was surely too eager to accept a story that he acknowledged was second-hand. It also seems completely absurd that Bormann, having successfully kept his anonymity for the entire length of Germany, should run the risk of revealing his real name to a man he barely knew.[16]

In 1968, the Israeli journalist Michael Bar-Zohar described Bormann's supposed odyssey in his book *The Avengers*.[17] In this

version, Bormann made his way south from Flensburg before crossing into Italy at the Brenner Pass, possibly assisted by a
Nauders-based guide called Rudolf Blass, who was reputed to have
also helped Heinrich 'Gestapo' Müller. The escape was supposedly
managed by an organization called *Die Schleue* (the 'Lock-gates'),
which hid Bormann in the Italian Tyrol in order for him to be near
his cancer-stricken wife who was living in Merano. However, one
day Bormann was recognized by the widow of a Jewish doctor that
his family had employed in the 1930s, and he was forced to take
refuge in a monastery near Lake Garda. From there, Bormann travelled to Rome, before taking a 'coasting vessel' from Genoa to
Spain, where he remained until the end of 1947. He then took a boat
to Buenos Aires, armed with a tourist-class ticket 'like any ordinary
passenger'. In his account, Bar-Zohar, like Wiesenthal, makes sure
that he dismisses other versions of Bormann's escape, yet at the same
time he offers no evidence for his own account. Another similarity
to Wiesenthal's version is the use of what appears to be credible
detail – Blass, for example, is a common name in the cemetery in
Nauders[18] – but again the story falters because it is entirely without
foundation.

The most sensational account of Bormann's 'escape' appeared in
Ladislas Farago's 1974 book *Aftermath*. Farago, who actually
claimed to have met Bormann on his sickbed in a convent in the
Andes in 1973, added much flesh to the bones of the previous two
stories. The mountain guide was now called 'Hanno Bernhard', and
Bormann crossed the Alps at the Resia Pass, although he did find
refuge at a monastery before he descended to the vicinity of Merano
to be near his ailing wife. After Gerda Bormann had died on 22
March 1946, her husband adopted the identity of a priest called
'Luigi Bogliolo', and he lived in Bolzano for two years before being
spotted by the doctor's wife.[19] Although Farago acknowledged that
he was uncertain about what happened to Bormann next, he
suggested that the fugitive travelled to Rome and joined the Hudal
network. However, Farago was able to confidently pick up the trail
at Bormann's arrival in Buenos Aires on 17 May 1948 on the
Giovanni C out of Genoa, where he claimed that he was met by
Perón's security chief, Ludwig Freude. Bormann was disguised as a
Jesuit priest called 'Juan Gómez', an alias that was soon superseded

by the surprising choice of 'Eliezer Goldstein', under which Bormann was issued Identity Certificate No. 073,909 by the Apostolic Nunciature in Buenos Aires. This then enabled him to be granted a police identity certificate (numbered 1,361,642), and on 12 October 1948, 'Señor Bormann' received his all-important 'blue stamp', which enabled him to remain in the country indefinitely. 'I have the paper recording these facts,' Farago wrote, 'an authentic copy of the document still on file at the Immigration Office. A reproduction of the original can be found in the Document section.'[20] Unfortunately for Farago, he had been duped. The documents that he had were in fact forgeries, and had been sold to him by corrupt Argentinian spies and policemen.[21] Such are the perils of paying for information.[22]

Of course, in the late 1940s, the Allies were not sure that Bormann was dead, so he was hunted like any other Nazi criminal. Naturally, units like the CIC had little to go on except for rumour and the testimonies made by members of Bormann's retinue, many of whom had as much inkling as to the fate of their employer as the investigators. In April 1945, two officers of the US Military Intelligence Service Center drove to northern Italy to follow a lead that indicated Bormann was with his wife in Italy. When they eventually found a house where Frau Bormann may have lived, it was empty, and the locals reported that 'no strange German has ever visited the Bormann house'.[23] In early 1946, the Americans launched Operation Baker, in which they dispatched an agent into the Kassel area in order to find Bormann. The agent's cover was that of a Nazi hoping to establish a resistance network around Frankfurt, and naturally he wanted to liaise with Bormann. The CIC suspected that Bormann's chauffeur, SS-Oberscharführer Alfred Leibrandt, was in touch with his old boss, who was masquerading as a forestry worker and living in the home of a real forester called Köster, whose house was stuffed with money, jewellery and provisions. The mission was doomed to fail, but the USFET intelligence officers continued to collate as much information on Bormann as they could.[24] Crucially, they spoke to Bormann's dentist, SS-Oberführer Hugo Blaschke, who remembered his former patient's teeth in great detail, as he had last treated them in March 1945.[25] The report made by Blaschke would prove to be vitally important – and controversial – a few decades later.

The Americans would follow many leads concerning Bormann, and despite their lack of success, they did not agree with the British, who thought that the man was dead. In February 1946, Major Hugh Trevor-Roper of MI5 produced a report which confirmed Bormann's death. It was Trevor-Roper who had famously investigated Hitler's last days, and after his initial report he was unclear as to whether Bormann had died. 'Evidence was obtained concerning Bormann's fate,' wrote Trevor-Roper, 'but this evidence did not seem sufficiently consistent or conclusive to justify an official statement.' However, Trevor-Roper soon found an additional witness who had seen Bormann lying dead, and as this testimony tallied with his other sources, he believed it to be correct.[26] The Americans were not convinced. 'USFET are not in favour of publishing Major TREVOR ROPER's statement on the Death of Bormann,' read one memorandum. 'They consider that if BORMANN turns out to be alive confidence will be shaken not only in our account of the death of BORMANN but in the death of HITLER as well.'[27] This was a sensible objection, because at the time, although it seemed clear to most reasonable people that Hitler had died, the Russians were claiming that Hitler was alive and being protected by the West.[28] There was no shortage of stories that the Führer was alive. In July 1945, news reports in Moscow claimed that Hitler and Eva Braun were in Argentina.[29] In October, the British Legation in Copenhagen received a call from a Danish woman whose friend had dreamed that Hitler was a monk in a monastery in Algeciras.[30] The dream was taken seriously enough to be passed on to the Foreign Office in London. Two months later, in Madrid, the American Strategic Services Unit was informed that Hitler had in fact escaped to the Balearic Islands.[31] Although Hitler's corpse was not quite as globe-trotting as that of Bormann, it certainly got around.

Of all the searches made for Bormann, the one which would have seemed at the time to have had some promise was that carried out in Argentina and Uruguay by Special Agent Francis E. Crosby of the FBI in July and August 1948. Crosby had been dispatched by J. Edgar Hoover on the direct orders of President Truman, who had requested 'a preliminary investigation of a report from one John Griffiths, that Martin Bormann, Adolph Hitler's deputy fuehrer, is in the River Plate area of Latin America'.[32] Griffiths was an American businessman based in Montevideo, although he also worked in the Cultural Department of the American embassy in Buenos Aires. In May 1948, he travelled to Washington at his own expense to inform Justice Robert H. Jackson – the chief counsel of the American prosecution team at Nuremberg – that he had heard from one Juan Serrino, an employee of the port authorities in Buenos Aires, that a German called 'Don Martin' was living on an *estancia* in Paraguay. Apparently, the mysterious 'Don Martin' had been 'one of the most important members of the Nazi leadership in Germany', and in July 1947, Serrino had even met 'Don Martin' at a lunch in Fray Bentos in Uruguay. When Serrino approached Griffiths with this inform- ation, he was shown a photograph of Bormann, whom he instantly identified as being 'Don Martin'. When Jackson heard Griffiths's story, he went straight to Truman, who showed only mild interest and refused to sanction an FBI investigation. Nevertheless, Jackson persisted, and on 16 June 1948, he sent a memorandum to the President arguing that it would be dangerous to neglect an investi- gation of the lead. 'First, it is possible that Bormann is there,' Jackson wrote. 'Second, even if he is not, publicity might be given to the fact that this information was laid before United States officials who did nothing and therefore are charged to be, in effect, protect- ing him.' Jackson warned that such a claim would have propaganda value to the Russians.[33] On 21 June, Truman authorized the investigation.

Although Crosby was an experienced agent, he was ill qualified to conduct such a task. He spoke little Spanish, and he knew little of the machinations of the German communities in Argentina and Uruguay. However, such shortcomings mattered little, because when he arrived in the region at the beginning of July, he was to be un- convinced by what he learned from Griffiths and Serrino. The former, Crosby reported, 'seems to have a detective complex in exaggerated form. It apparently never occurs to Griffiths that among all the allegations and reports he had received and in turn furnished, there was not one single specific fact which could be verified independently.'[34] As for Serrino, Crosby was just as scathing: 'In the one interview I had with him, the informant talked in very general terms, and furnished no fact susceptible of independent verification.'[35] Before he considered hunting for

Bormann, Crosby consulted the intermediary of Serrino and Griffiths, a journalist called Julio Genovés García, who was reputed to have his own information about 'Don Martin'. Once again, Crosby was unimpressed. 'This individual [. . .] is apparently a rabid anti-Peronista who inspires Griffiths' complete confidence,' he stated in his report. Crosby concluded that the whole affair was nothing more than a disinformation plot to smear Perón. He returned to Washington at the end of August, and on 8 September, Hoover wrote to Jackson informing him that 'it does not appear [. . .] that any facts were furnished which could serve as a basis for further investigation.'[36]

The one place where Bormann did come to life was in the cinema. In December 1948, filmgoers were treated to *Rogues' Regiment* starring Dick Powell as Whit Corbett, an intelligence officer tasked with tracking down 'Martin Bruner', played by Stephen McNally. During the opening sequence of the film, the Americans are said to 'have scoured every corner of the Earth for this man, but so far without success'. Corbett's hunt takes him to Saigon, where Bruner has inveigled himself into the ranks of the French Foreign Legion. After several adventures, Corbett and justice triumph over the dastardly Bruner, and the last shot shows a hangman's noose looming over the Nazi.[37] The film was written by Robert Buckner, a journalist and author who spent several months researching his subject. In an interview designed to whip up some pre-release controversy, Buckner claimed that Bormann's wife and children knew that their husband and father did not die in Berlin, and that only Bormann knew for certain whether Hitler was alive or dead.[38] Although some were inclined to believe such claims, fewer found Buckner's film convincing. 'If credibility is by-passed more than once,' commented one critic, 'it is all done briskly and with good will.'[39] Another described it as 'cockeyed fiction', but raised the valid point that it was no more so than the 'insanity' of the mess in which Berlin was still mired.[40] Nevertheless, films such as *Rogues' Regiment* concerning hidden Nazis were popular, and they almost became a genre in themselves, a genre that would reach its apotheosis in the 1970s with films such as *The Boys from Brazil* and *Marathon Man*.

*   *   *

While cinemagoers and some Allied units were concerning themselves with Nazis who did not exist, actual Nazis were making their escapes. Among them was Franz Stangl, the former commandant of Treblinka, who had been incarcerated at Glasenbach camp since July 1945. Initially, Stangl had had to 'suffer' the deprivation of having no bunk or blankets, but gradually, conditions had improved for the twenty thousand prisoners. In May 1946, the inmates were allowed to construct their own makeshift beds, and in the winter, 'we built sort of wooden chests in which we slept,' Stangl recalled.[41] By the spring of 1947, Stangl and his fellow prisoners were being permitted to make a stove, and with the provision of proper bunks and blankets, as well as parcels from home, life was quite tolerable. Stangl's wife Theresa delivered her husband a food parcel every week, although she was not allowed to see him. Another of those who visited Glasenbach during this time was Simon Wiesenthal, who regarded the place as being almost luxurious. 'The internees were well fed and sunburnt,' he wrote, 'and they led a pleasant life. They had amusing company from another part of the camp, where the wives of high-ranking Nazis and some former women concentration camp guards were interned.'[42] In the late summer of 1947, Stangl's relatively idyllic existence came to end when the Austrians, who had been investigating the Euthanasia Programme at Schloss Hartheim, requested that Stangl should be handed over for trial. As a result, he was moved to a regular prison in Linz.

While Stangl awaited his trial, he was moved to an open prison. Despite the fact that the Austrians knew him to be the police superintendent of an institution that had killed many hundreds, if not thousands, he was clearly felt not to be the type who would escape. Had the Austrians known about his role in exterminating nearly a million people at Treblinka, they might have secured him better, but instead he enjoyed surprising freedoms, and even his wife was allowed to visit him. 'In this prison many prisoners [. . .] had single rooms and they allowed us to be alone for as long as we liked,' she remembered. 'It really was "open" – we could go for walks and everything. He could have walked out of there any time he chose.'[43] But for several months, Stangl made no attempt to walk out. According to Theresa Stangl, her husband felt that he should stay and face justice, a decision based more on a sense of duty than any desire for moral reckoning. His wife implored him to leave, especially when she learned that a driver at Schloss Hartheim had received a four-year prison sentence. 'That's when I went to Paul,' she said, referring to her husband by one of his middle names, 'and told him that it couldn't go on like this. "If this driver gets four years," I said to him, "what will you get, having been police superintendent of that place?" '[44]

Stangl soon heeded his wife's advice and he made his preparations to escape. With a fellow prisoner, Hans Steiner, Stangl assembled a basic escape kit consisting of little more than a rucksack filled with tinned food. Theresa gave him around five hundred Austrian schillings, a watch, a ring and a necklace. He was also equipped with the identity card written in four languages that was issued to all Austrians at the end of the war. Although as a prisoner Stangl did not have one of his own, he was given one by a fellow prisoner who had been arrested sometime after the war. Stangl simply replaced the man's picture with his own.[45] And then, on 30 May 1948, Stangl and Steiner did simply walk out.

The first stage of their journey was to make their way 130 miles south to Graz, but in order to save money, they walked rather than took the train. In Graz, Stangl sold the jewellery, and also had the good fortune to encounter an old comrade from his Operation Reinhard days. One day, while he and Steiner were walking past a building site, a man ran out and yelled, 'Herr Hauptsturmführer!' The man was Gustav Wagner, the former deputy commandant of Sobibor. Compared to Stangl, Wagner was almost small fry, responsible as he was for the deaths of some two hundred thousand. Wagner told them that he was penniless, and asked where they were going. When Stangl told him, he begged to join them, and Stangl agreed.[46]

Stangl knew exactly where to go: the Santa Maria dell'Anima. 'Originally, we had intended to ask my wife's former employer, the Duca di Corsini, to help us,' said Stangl. 'But then I heard of a Bishop Hulda at the Vatican in Rome who was helping Catholic SS officers.'[47] Stangl of course meant 'Hudal', and despite this error made some two decades later, there can be no doubt that the bishop and his 'relief work' was well known throughout the German POW

community. The three men now made their way some 250 miles
west to Merano in the Italian Tyrol, which was a popular port of call
for fleeing Nazis, as well as being the home town of a cousin of
Theresa Stangl. The journey involved crossing the Alps, during
which Stangl's experience as a mountaineer was invaluable. 'It was
very difficult for the two others,' said Theresa Stangl, 'but [. . .] he
managed to get them across.'[48] Eventually, the three men reached
Merano, where Steiner and Wagner hid in some woods while Stangl
went into the centre of the town to find his wife's cousin.
Unfortunately for Stangl, the cousin was not in evidence, and after
taking a rest in a church, he was arrested by the *carabinieri*. 'I think
[it was] just because I was walking in the street,' Stangl recalled.
'And I suppose I look foreign.'[49] After a walk of a few hundred miles
and an Alpine crossing, he would have also looked a mess. Merano
is a smart tourist town, and Stangl's state of dishevelment would
have marked him out more than his Austro-Germanic features.
However, Stangl was able to persuade his captors that he was no
fugitive, and after producing a sob story that he needed to support
his wife and family, the generous *carabinieri* released the former
commandant of Treblinka.

During the summer of 1948, Stangl and Wagner arrived in Rome.
Along the way, Steiner had returned to Austria to give himself up to
the Americans, an option not open to his two travelling companions
who had the blood of over a million people on their hands.[50] When
the two men arrived in the Italian capital, they had little idea of how
they might contact Hudal. Fortunately for Stangl, he met a former
comrade on a bridge over the Tiber, who asked him, 'Are you on
your way to see Hudal?' Stangl admitted that he was, but that he did
not know how to find him. The friend told him, but advised Stangl
that he should visit the following day. Stangl ignored his friend's
advice, and he and Wagner arrived at the Santa Maria dell'Anima
within half an hour. They soon met Hudal. 'The Bishop came into
the room where I was waiting,' he recalled, 'and he held out both his
hands and said, "You must be Franz Stangl. I was expecting
you." '[51] Much has been made of Hudal's apparent anticipation of
Stangl's visit, and it has been suggested that it is evidence that the
Odessa was involved. However, two other possibilities are more
likely. First, Stangl's comrade could have already told Hudal that

Stangl would be with him, or secondly, Hudal was advised by a priest somewhere else in Italy that Stangl and Wagner were on their way. As we shall see shortly, there were a number of Catholic priests who supplied Hudal with escapees.

After their arrival, Hudal made his guests write down brief resumés of their careers, which can still be found in the archives of Bishop Hudal in the Santa Maria dell'Anima. Dated 20 August 1948, the documents are handwritten and signed by the two mass murderers in their own names. Such was the level of trust that Stangl and Wagner placed in the bishop that they even supplied their dates and places of birth. If Hudal had wanted to screen these particular 'guests' for criminality, then he could have easily done so. Nevertheless, in his resumé, Stangl does omit his service in *Aktion T-4* and Operation Reinhard, which he probably suspected would have tested Hudal's charity to breaking point. Instead, Stangl presented a bland portrait of a career policeman, in which he was a captain in the *Schutzpolizei* (Municipal Police), although he admits that his other rank as an *SS-Hauptsturmführer* caused his internment by the Americans. Wagner's resumé is no less anodyne, and he too merely offers up a picture of a regular policeman. There is no mention of Sobibor, or indeed of any work outside Germany.[52]

Hudal then provided accommodation and some money for the two men, and told them to wait until their papers were ready. Despite Hudal's assistance, Stangl's mood lowered. 'Paul wrote to me from Rome sounding very depressed,' Theresa Stangl recalled.[53] There was little for the two men to do, except to spend their days not attracting the attention of the *carabinieri*. Stangl did, however, volunteer to do some masonry work for some nuns, which earned him extra food. But the wait was not long, because within a fortnight, Hudal had issued them with two Red Cross passports. 'They'd reversed my name by mistake,' said Stangl; 'it was made out to Paul F. Stangl. I pointed it out to the bishop. I said, "They made a mistake, this is incorrect. My name is Franz D. Paul Stangl."' Hudal merely patted Stangl's shoulder and said, 'Let's let sleeping dogs lie – never mind.'[54] Hudal also supplied Stangl with an exit visa to Syria and his passage, and had even arranged a job in a textile mill. The latter was especially thoughtful of Hudal, as Stangl had written on his resumé that he had worked in textiles before becoming a policeman. Wagner was also provided with a new life in the Middle East.

Stangl left for Damascus in September.[55] Compared to other criminals who had benefited from Hudal's assistance, he had been processed very swiftly. This suggests that Hudal was aware of Stangl's real wartime activities, and that he was keen to ferret him out of the country as soon as possible. However, if Hudal really had known about Stangl and Treblinka, then it is more likely he would have issued him with a passport bearing a false name. In addition, around the time of Stangl's arrival in Rome, Hudal was having problems with transporting his charges to South America, and it may be that the Syrian option simply offered a more efficient alternative. It would appear that Stangl had no problems travelling to the Middle East, and he settled down quickly, making friends with fellow fugitives. Life was frugal, as he was saving money in order to pay for his family to join him, but according to his letters back to Theresa in Austria, he was 'relaxed, calm, liberated'.[56]

In May 1949, Stangl sent his wife tickets for Damascus. His wife then applied for an exit visa for the family, which she had little problem in obtaining. At first, the Austrian authorities were concerned that the children might be sold into slavery, but they were reassured when Theresa produced letters from Stangl in Damascus. 'There was no secret whatever about our leaving,' Frau Stangl claimed; 'everybody knew we were going to join Paul in Damascus.' The packing cases were even painted with Stangl's name and address, and when the police asked her why she was leaving her hometown of Wels, she told them it was in order 'to join my husband who escaped'. Theresa's brazen admission is even enshrined on the official documentation, which features the words 'Mann geflüchtet' ('husband escaped').[57] The family arrived in Damascus later that month after an uneventful journey. They found a husband and father who seemed much more at ease with himself – the 'happy and sweet man he had been years before all the horror'.[58] For the time being, the future for the Stangls seemed rosy. That rosiness would not last for long.

What is extraordinary about Stangl's flight is its relative ease. Much of it was revealed to the journalist Gitta Sereny in the early 1970s, and its revelations caused some to question whether Stangl and his wife had been altogether truthful with their interviewer. 'I'm afraid she led you by the nose,' Sereny was told by Simon Wiesenthal, who scoffed at the idea that Stangl merely walked to freedom. 'What nonsense,' Wiesenthal commented. 'How could he have, without papers, passport – what about the frontier? It's all lies; he obviously had papers provided for him by Odessa.'[59] Wiesenthal makes this claim in his 1967 memoir, *The Murderers Among Us*, but he offers no proof.[60] He also states that Frau Stangl left Austria for an 'unknown destination' on 6 May 1949, and travelled to Switzerland, where she picked up her Syrian visas. Again, this is nonsense, as Frau Stangl was quite open where she was heading, and she received her visas while she was still in Austria. Had Wiesenthal simply checked the paperwork at the local police station, he would have found out exactly where she was heading, and who she was going to see. Perhaps he did, but, as was his custom, Wiesenthal was simply presenting his readers with a manufactured mystery that only he could solve, and thereby placing himself at the heart of the hunt. In his 1989 memoir, *Justice Not Vengeance*, he churlishly did not acknowledge any of Sereny's findings, despite the fact that they had been revealed in 1974. Instead, he merely repeats his canard that Stangl had escaped with 'Odessa's help'.[61] There is not one mention of 'Odessa', or any such organization, in Hudal's archives, either in connection with Stangl or anybody else. Naturally, the archives may have been filleted, but this too is unlikely, as the resumés of Stangl and Wagner would have certainly been excised.

Neither are they the only Nazis who still feature in the records. On 15 February 1948, Johann Corradini, the Catholic priest in the village of Vipiteno, 30 miles northeast of Merano, wote to Bishop Hudal requesting that he help the Pape family. Corradini told Hudal that he knew the family 'very well', and they had been living for three years in his parish, and that Alice Pape and her two sons, Georg and Ingo, were members of the Catholic Church. However, there was a slight problem with the father, Otto Pape, who was not a Roman Catholic. Corradini informed Hudal that Herr Pape had given him an assurance that he would convert, but so far he had not had the opportunity to do so.[62] One reason why Pape may not have embraced Rome was that 'Otto Pape' was not his real name, which was in fact Erich Priebke.

Although he was not a major war criminal like Stangl, Priebke's crimes were still vile. As a thirty-year-old Gestapo *Hauptsturmführer* in Rome, Priebke had taken part in the notorious massacre in the Ardeatine Caves on 24 March 1944 in which 335 prisoners were murdered as a reprisal for the killing of thirty-three German policemen by a partisan bomb in the Via Rasella the day before. The attack was so shocking that when Hitler heard about it at his 'Wolf's Lair' headquarters in East Prussia he demanded that the German revenge should 'make the world tremble'. After initially desiring that a whole quarter of Rome should be destroyed, he stipulated that thirty Italians should be killed for every dead German.[63] By the time the order had made its way south, the ratio had been altered to 10:1, and the man in charge of its implementation was the Chief of the SD in Rome, SS-Obersturmbannführer Herbert Kappler. The victims were to be drawn from those among the prison population who had already been condemned to death, but in the whole of the city, there were only three men who fitted that category. As a result, the net had to be spread wider to include those 'worthy of death'.[64] 'The whole of that night we searched the records,' Priebke recalled, 'and could not find a sufficient number of persons to make up the number required for execution.'[65] Another search was made, this time encompassing those who had committed 'outrages' against German troops, or had been found in possession of firearms or explosives, or who had been leaders of 'underground movements'. Eventually, the right number was found, and at ten o'clock the following morning Kappler called his officers together.

> [He] told us that the Commander of the Police Regiment, whose men had been killed, declined to carry out the execution, and that the men from the Headquarters at Via Tasso were to be the executioners. He said that this thing was a horrible thing to do and to show the men that they had the backing of the officers, all the officers were to fire a shot at the beginning and a further shot at the end.[66]

At midday, the SS men set out to perform their horrific task, and when they arrived at the cave complex, they found their victims ready for the slaughter, their hands tied behind their backs. The man who had brought them there was Priebke, and while the shootings took place, it was Priebke who checked the victims off his list, a grim inverted roll call.[67] The prisoners went into the cave in groups of five, and were shot in the back of the head by the same number of SS men. Often, the shots were fired at such close range that the victims' skulls exploded.[68] As the bodies mounted, subsequent victims were made to climb up the bleeding pile, before they too were added to it. As well as attending to his list, Priebke played a more direct part, and shot a man in the second or third party that went in, as well as another towards the end of the day.[69] Not all the SS men were quite so willing. Herbert Kappler recalled how he discovered that one of his officers, an SS-Hauptsturmführer Wetjen, had not fired a shot. 'I spoke to him in a comradely manner,' Kappler said, 'and went into the cave with him to fire another shot at his side and at the same time as he.'[70] Nevertheless, taking part in the killings did not seem compulsory. When it came to the turn of 37-year-old SS-Untersturmführer (Second Lieutenant) Günter Amonn to take a shot, he found that he could not do it. He recalled:

I raised my sub-machine gun but I was too afraid to fire. The other four Germans fired one shot each into the back of the necks of the other four prisoners who fell forward. Upon seeing the state in which I was in, another German pushed me out of the way and shot the prisoner who I had been detailed to shoot.

Crucially, it appears that Amonn was not punished for his refusal, which meant that those such as Priebke could not plead that they had no choice. Amonn could have been lying about his non-participation, but he was not listed by Kappler as one of those who took part. At the end of the day, the cave was dynamited, and the SS returned to their mess at the Villa Massino. 'The reprisal has been carried out,' Kappler announced. 'I know that it has been very hard for some of you but in cases like this the lens of war must be applied. The best thing for you all to do is to get drunk.'[71]

Priebke was arrested in Bolzano by the Americans on 13 May 1945. He remembered:

My wife was with me and there was a knock on the door. An American soldier said, 'In half an hour come down with one suitcase and one blanket.' They let my wife and children stay but I was sent off in a big truck. As we went along, some Italians shouted '*Tedeschi!*' at us, and made throat-slitting gestures.[72]

Priebke spent the next twenty months in a variety of POW camps, including Camp Afragola outside Naples, where he was finally questioned about the massacre on 28 August 1946. Priebke admitted his role in full, even including the two murders he carried out.[73] 'I had nothing to deny in my interrogation,' he said. 'Nobody felt guilty, because reprisals were permitted to all armies in this time.'[74] It is curious that the British took so long to question Priebke, as the widow of one of his victims wrote to the Allied Commission in January 1946 demanding justice be done.[75] Later that year, Priebke was transferred to the POW camp near Rimini. One of his companions was SS-Obersturmbannführer Walter Rauff, the inventor of the mobile gas vans and the alleged helper of Bishop Hudal. Rauff had managed to smuggle a pair of wirecutters into the camp, although he was not to need them. 'On Christmas Eve, there came a wagon that projected a film in colour to the camp,' Priebke recalled. 'The film finished just before midnight. An officer brought me the wirecutters and said, "Regards from the Colonel." And it turned out that the Colonel, who was a small man, hid under the lorry as it drove out!'[76]

Priebke's turn was to come a week later, on New Year's Eve. The former Gestapo officer had made his plans carefully, and had identified that the best place to escape from the camp was from the latrines in the Cossack area of the compound. During the celebrations, Priebke and four others brought a bottle of wine to the Cossacks to give the impression they were doing nothing more suspicious than seeing in the New Year with their former allies. However, Priebke was wearing his escape outfit, which consisted of some overalls given to him by some Ustashi in Camp Afragola, and an English officer's overcoat – 'very good it was'. He also wore gloves and had on him his 'nécessaire' – a washbag.

At 2 o'clock in the morning, the Russians said it was time to go. They had their *pissoire* outside, near the road. There was a big searchlight on the road, and we had to cut the wire quite near the lookout guard.

It was very cold and we had to put something against the ground. One of my men, an *Unteroffizier*, had already made three escape attempts, so he said, 'Well Captain, I'm the man who knows how to cut the wire!' He was back very quickly, and then I led the way. It was dark, and when I was near the lookout I heard footsteps, and they were changing the guard. I went on. I got to the hole in the barbed wire, and I saw that it was only big enough for a cat or something, not for me! So I had to leave the nice overcoat. I put the necessarium near my head and crossed the road. Of course, the guard could have fired at any time. It was very dangerous. At last I came to the other side. Near the road there was a little water, and I had to lie in it. I then had to have an excrement, which I had to do very quickly! Then the other men came through and we went to Rimini, which was about an hour away.[77]

Predictably, the first place the fugitives made for was the residence of the Bishop of Rimini, Luigi Santa. Unfortunately for Priebke's team, the bishop was out, and they were directed to a convent. 'They opened it up,' said Priebke, 'and put us in a room. There was nothing to eat, but at last they brought something up. It was not much and it was not very good.' The following day, the escapees decided to part ways. Priebke was given enough money by his companions to take the train, and he made his way north to his family in Vipiteno. At Bologna, he changed trains, and then he travelled until the stop before Vipiteno, where he alighted, fearing a reception committee at his final destination. Instead of making for his wife's house, Priebke went to the house of the local priest, where he found a housekeeper who was delighted to see him. The priest let him stay for two weeks, and allowed Priebke's wife, Alice, to visit him. After the fortnight, Priebke was reunited with his family, although he told his two sons that he was in fact their 'Uncle Karl'. The elder boy, Georg, who was six and a half, saw through the deception.

Priebke and his family stayed in Vipiteno until October 1948. During this period, many of his fellow perpetrators of the Ardeatine massacre were tried and convicted. Herbert Kappler was sentenced to life, although his junior officers received lesser sentences. The Allies were not satisfied that all the murderers had been brought to justice, and on 26 September 1947, the British War Crimes Group in South East Europe distributed a list of six SS officers wanted in connection with the case. Three of the men had never been caught, whereas the others, who included Priebke, had all managed to escape. Curiously, the British thought Priebke had made his getaway in August 1946, but Priebke is adamant that he fled the Rimini camp at the end of that year.[78] The British were in luck, because on 21 October, the Chief of the American War Crimes Branch in Austria informed them that Priebke was living in Vipiteno. When the British received this information, it was annotated with the words 'Looks possible. In workbook for arrest 31 Oct 47.'[79] It seemed as if Priebke's luck was finally about to run out.

However, the quarry caught wind of the British operation. 'One day there was a word going round that the English were making a big search to find all the Germans,' he recalled. 'So I stayed in a little village high up in the mountains, and I went there for four months.' Once again, it was the Church that helped him, and it would continue to do so, for it was in the following February that Father Corradini wrote to Hudal. It is unclear whether Hudal responded to the priest's request, but another priest would shortly come to their aid. Around this time, Alice turned to Father Pobitzer at the Franciscan monastery in Bolzano for assistance. Pobitzer explained that the family's best opportunity was to obtain some form of British identity document, or to be issued with Red Cross passports. Pobitzer reassured Alice that he would help them by contacting the Rome headquarters of the Red Cross.[80] It is highly likely that Pobitzer soon wrote to Hudal, because the archives at the Santa Maria dell'Anima contain a brief outline of Priebke and his family, which shows that they could be contacted via Father Pobitzer. However, just as in the letter sent by Corradini, the surname 'Pape' is used.[81] Priebke claimed that the name was not his choice, although whoever chose it was presumably seeking to boost Priebke's Catholic credentials in a somewhat hamfisted – or ironic – fashion. The identity of the family was also obscured by the false declaration that Alice, Georg and Ingo had all been born in Riga.

Priebke also enlisted the help of a Fascist called Alfredo Beccherini whom he had met in Brescia in April 1945. Beccherini had fled to Argentina, and he had written to Priebke in Vipiteno saying that he could secure the necessary visas for the family. 'I gave him all my personal dates, for my wife, my children, myself, when we born, where we were born,' Priebke said. 'He said OK. Then at last a paper came to enter Argentina. To my big surprise it was not in the name "Priebke", but "Pape". And all my family were born in Riga.' Priebke then went to Father Pobitzer, and told him that he was concerned about the change of name. Pobitzer told him not to worry, and that it was probably a decision made by the Argentinians, who may not have wanted to advertise their assisting a fugitive. If Priebke wanted to change the documentation, it would take three to four months. The papers, which were numbered 211712/48, stayed as 'Pape'.[82] The documents at the Santa Maria dell'Anima do not support Priebke's words. Thanks to the existence of the letter from Corradini, it is clear that the use of the name 'Pape' and Riga as the birthplace of his wife and children had been going on for months. The decision to adopt an alias was more likely to have been made by Priebke than by the Argentinian officials in Carlos Fuldner's DAIE offices in Genoa. In Rome, other preparations were being made for the Priebke family. On 26 July 1947, the Pontifical Commission of Assistance issued 'Otto Pape' a Vatican identity document numbered PCA 9538/99. This then enabled Hudal to obtain a Red Cross passport in the same name.

By early September, the family was nearly ready to depart to the southern hemisphere. However, Priebke had one more important task in Vipiteno: he had to become a Roman Catholic. On 13 September 1948, he was baptized by Father Corradini.[83] Equipped with a new religion, Priebke then travelled to Rome to acquire a new identity. It was Father Pobitzer who had told him exactly where to go. 'I went to see Bishop Hudal,' Priebke said. 'He was a very gentle man. When I told him who I was, he said, "Oh, it's a special pleasure for me to help you. I am pleased to help those who in the past I have opposed."'[84] Hudal handed Priebke a blank Red Cross passport.[85] 'Hudal gave me nothing which was written,' he later claimed.[86] The meeting was brief, and Priebke returned to Vipiteno to fetch his wife and children. In mid-October, the 'Pape' family headed to Rome, where Red Cross passports were issued to Alice and the boys. The next step was Genoa, from where they were to embark for Buenos Aires. Once again, Priebke's luck was holding.

It was in Genoa where near disaster struck. When Priebke

presented his papers to the Argentine official, he was informed that the Argentine government had stopped just two days before accepting refugees who had been born behind the Iron Curtain. The use of Riga as a birthplace for his wife and children had spectacularly backfired. However, help was at hand in the form of 'Didi', a friend of Priebke who happened to work in Genoa as a director of the shipping company ITALMAR. It was 'Didi' who pulled the necessary strings, but unfortunately, the 'Pape' family had lost their initial berth. This problem was sorted out by Monsignor Karlo Petranović, who acted as Draganović's agent at the port. Petranović had ten places reserved for Croats in the third-class cabins of the *San Giorgio*, and he offered four of them to Priebke for ten thousand lire in addition to the costs of the tickets themselves. The purchase left Priebke penniless, but he had no choice.[87] The ship steamed out of Genoa on 23 October. Priebke recalled:

> While the crew slipped the moorings and our friends became very small shapes, strong feelings crowded my soul. When I was working in the 1920s on the Ligurian coast, I met a farmer who had lived in the hills above Rapallo and spent all day carrying vegetables to a restaurant. He told me that in a few days he would have a party to celebrate his move to Valparaíso. 'Where?' I asked. 'In Chile, on the Pacific Ocean.' The idea that a man should end up a few days later forever on the other side of the world left me appalled. Today it touched me.[88]

Unlike the men he had shot in the Ardeatine Caves, at least Erich Priebke had a future.

The Argentinian entry papers issued to 'Otto Pape' were numbered 211712/48. The subsequent documents, numbered 211713/48, were given to one 'Helmut Gregor', which was a cover name for a man who was spending his days grading potatoes in Bavaria.[89] From 1945 to 1948, Josef Mengele toiled on the farm in Mangolding, and he seldom ventured very far from it. The highlight of his week was a trip to the small town of Riedering, where he would see a fellow doctor called 'Wieland' who had arranged his employment. The visits lifted Mengele's morale, and he even gave bunches of wild flowers to Wieland's wife.[90] The mysterious Wieland, who has never been traced, played a key role during this period of Mengele's life, because it was Wieland who visited Mengele's family in Günzburg to tell them that Josef was alive. Unlike many of the Nazi fugitives, Mengele came from a wealthy family, which had made its fortune selling farm machinery. In early 1946, Mengele met his brother Karl Jr next to an autobahn about 6 miles away from the farm.[91] Karl was accompanied by Hans Sedlmeier, who was the sales manager of the family firm and a trusted servant of the Mengele family, as well as being a childhood friend of Josef. Over the coming years, Sedlmeier's loyalty would be severely tested, but it would never falter.

As it appeared that Karl and Sedlmeier had not been followed, Mengele's family judged it sufficiently safe for Irene Mengele to see her husband. During the summer, she left their son Rolf with Mengele's parents, and she saw Mengele on the shores of the Simssee lake, which was less than a mile from Mangolding. During the summer, the area was busy with holidaymakers, and the couple were able to mingle among the crowds after they had checked that Irene was not being followed.[92] As Mengele grew more confident that he was not in danger, he was sufficiently emboldened to travel the 80 miles to Autenried to see his wife and son. For this comparatively long and hazardous journey, Mengele would use the 'Fritz Hollmann' identity papers, which caused a ruction between him and Wieland, who insisted that their use unnecessarily jeopardized Colonel Fritz Ulmann, from whom Mengele had obtained and then modified the documents. The reprimand caused Mengele to lose his temper, and he ripped up the documents in front of Wieland. 'There, are you satisfied?' he shouted. 'I don't need them!'[93] Mengele must have regretted his impetuosity, because the lack of papers isolated him still further, and effectively stymied his conjugal excursions. Perhaps that was just as well, because it was becoming clear to both husband and wife that their marriage was over. Many of the visits had turned into marital rows, in which a jealous Mengele forbade Irene from enjoying male company, no matter how innocently. 'Father was insanely jealous,' Rolf, Mengele's son, recalled. 'During their short meetings in the forest, he made scenes that embittered her.'[94] In a quasi-autobiographical account Mengele wrote during this period, in which he referred to himself in the third person, he declared that 'with the passing of the Third Reich it was also the end of his marriage – it had simply ceased to exist, as had so many others . . . One had to clear away and build anew.'[95]

The combination of his disintegrating marriage, the boring farm work and his deteriorating relationship with Wieland made Mengele realize that his position was unsustainable. His fragile mood was further damaged by knowledge gleaned from a Rosenheim newspaper that Rudolf Höss, the former commandant of Auschwitz, had named Mengele during the course of the Nuremberg Tribunal in April 1946.[96] In his 'autobiography', Mengele devoted much space to justifying his actions, but he now knew that to attempt to do so at an Allied tribunal would be to risk a trip to the gallows. Only one option was available, and that was to emigrate to Argentina.

In the spring of 1948, Mengele began to make his preparations. Although there is no evidence, it is likely that a combination of Wieland, his family and Sedlmeier put him in touch with elements of Carlos Fuldner's escape network. In April, the commune of Termeno, just south of Bolzano, issued 'Helmut Gregor' with Carta d'Identità No. 114.[97] This document was probably sent to the DAIE office in Genoa, and it was from there that landing permit 211713/48 was issued.[98] As soon as Mengele had heard that his papers were ready, in the first week of August 1948 he left the Fischers and their farm without bidding them farewell. 'We always thought that he only wanted to hide,' recalled Alois Fischer, 'and that someday he would disappear. And that's what did happen – suddenly he disappeared.'[99] Mengele took his suit and money, and he headed towards Günzburg in order to be near his family, who had doubtless financed the procuring of his identity. For the next eight to nine months, it is unclear exactly where Mengele lived, but some accounts place him in a forest outside the town.[100] During this time, he tried to resurrect his marriage, and attempted to persuade Irene to come to Argentina with Rolf when he had settled down. Irene declined, not least because she had already met the man who was to be her second husband.

With little to keep him in Germany, 'Helmut Gregor' left in the middle of April 1949. The first leg of his voyage was a train ride to Innsbruck, during which he was questioned by two Austrian customs officials. From Innsbruck, Mengele headed south to the village of Steinach am Brenner, which lies at the northern end of the Brenner Pass that connects Austria with Italy. He arrived on 17 April, which was Easter Sunday, and he stayed the night in an inn. The following morning, Mengele rose early in order to meet the guide who would take him across the pass. However, the guide had lost his border pass, and therefore could not take Mengele over to the Italian town of Brenner. Instead, Mengele had to go it alone.[101] The challenge was not as great as it might seem. The walk from Steinach to Brenner takes little more than two hours, and although there are some steep sections, they would have posed no problems for a fit 38-year-old man who had worked on a farm for four years.[102] In his 'autobiography', Mengele recalls that the walk took him only one hour, which meant that his route could not have been difficult. As Mengele crossed during a full moon, he was able to see edelweiss and the bottom of the pass itself.[103] His only companions would have been the Alpine cattle, their bells gently tolling as dawn rose.

At 5.45 a.m., Mengele caught the first train to Vipiteno, where he stayed for a month at the Golden Cross Inn. During his sojourn, he was helped by at least three different characters, who provided him with documentation and travel guidance. One of these figures was called 'Erwin', and it was he who gave Mengele a suitcase that is reputed to have contained some of his specimens from Auschwitz. As Erwin also gave him money and news from home, it is likely that he was in fact Hans Sedlmeier, who was so loyally doing the bidding of the Mengele family. Erwin then told Mengele that his route was to take him to Milan via Bolzano, and then on to Genoa. Mengele did as he was told, and he arrived in Genoa on 20 May 1949. There, he was met by 'Kurt', who bought 'Helmut Gregor' a passage on the *North King*, which was due to leave in five days' time. Kurt's contacts were very good, and he shuttled Mengele around the various offices in Genoa with much efficiency. 'His actions and mannerisms suited his small round body,' Mengele observed. 'There was an industriousness in his walk as well as his speech.'[104] Kurt ensured that Mengele obtained a Red Cross passport, a medical certificate and an Argentinian entry visa.

However, it was the application for the final document, an Italian exit visa, that nearly proved catastrophic for Mengele. Instructed by Kurt to slip a twenty-thousand-lire note into his documents, Mengele was startled to find that the bribe earned him a trip to a prison cell. Unfortunately, the normal official was on holiday, and his replacement was not as corruptible.[105] Mengele spent a few anxious days in his cell, where his company consisted of a crippled street musician and a morphine-addicted doctor, both of whom he regarded with the type of contempt he had displayed for 'inferior' human beings in Auschwitz.

Yet fortune was to favour the 'Angel of Death', because Mengele was soon released. Kurt had come to his aid, as had the normal Italian official, who had returned from his leave. 'Suddenly they discovered their mistake,' Mengele wrote in his third-person auto-biography, 'and the policeman is unusually friendly and asks Andreas [Mengele] if he is a Jew and some more questions.'[106] Mengele's ticket on the *North King* was upgraded as an apology, and on 25 May, Mengele stood on the ship's deck as he watched the Genoese shoreline retreat. 'Waves, all is waves,' he pondered. After the ship had left Italian territorial waters, he went down to his cabin to sleep.[107]

Just like Franz Stangl, neither Erich Priebke nor Josef Mengele escaped with the assistance of an organization called 'Odessa'. Priebke insisted that the organization was a myth. 'I always say that Odessa is the invention of an Englishman,' he said, referring to Frederick Forsyth. 'I would have been lucky if somebody had helped me, but there was no Odessa.' Priebke cited the lack of financial assistance he received as evidence that the group did not exist. The organization to whom he owed the greatest debt was the Catholic Church. 'I was born a Protestant but changed to Catholic because the Catholics did many good things for my wife and me,' he admitted.[108] At times, Mengele's escape seems so well arranged that only something like Odessa could have put it together, but a more reasonable explanation is that the deep pockets of the Mengele family were able to secure the level of assistance that Nazis of more financially modest means were unable to enjoy. Nevertheless, the experiences of both men reveal a network of sorts, albeit one that was ad hoc and subject to foul-ups. The motives of the personalities involved were varied, although the two most powerful drivers were misdirected Christian charity and money. A sympathy for Nazism was common to all, but to a man like 'Kurt', who was clearly little more than the worst sort of tout, money would have counted above all else. For a figure like Hudal, the desire to assist his fellow Catholics – and, better still, to convert Protestants – would have been his primary concern.

Despite this lack of evidence, Simon Wiesenthal was adamant that Mengele had indeed fled under the protection of the Odessa. However, his account of Mengele's flight is so inaccurate that it would be imprudent to accept Wiesenthal's insistence that the Odessa existed. In *The Murderers Among Us*, Wiesenthal bullishly stated that he was 'able to trace Mengele's movements quite exactly'. Wiesenthal's confidence was misplaced, because nearly the whole of his version is incorrect. According to his version, the former Auschwitz 'doctor' lived unmolested in Günzburg for 'five pleasant years' where 'no one bothered him', even though 'many people knew that he'd worked in one of those camps.' Furthermore, Wiesenthal claimed that it was only in 1950 that his name began to be mentioned in trials. Wiesenthal stated authoritatively that Mengele escaped with the aid of 'powerful friends in the ODESSA organization' in 1951, and that he made his way into Italy via the Reschen Pass. From there, he went to Spain, and he ended up in Buenos Aires in 1952.[109] All of these facts are incorrect, which might have been forgivable in 1967, but Wiesenthal was to reiterate them in *Justice Not Vengeance* in 1989, by which time a tremendous amount of reliable material had come to light that baldly contradicted his claims.

Wiesenthal was also partially wrong about the escape of Adolf Eichmann. In both his memoirs, he writes that Eichmann was interned at the camp at Cham, whereas he was actually some 120 miles west at Oberdachstetten. From there, Eichmann escaped to northern Germany, which was correct, but Wiesenthal then placed him with his uncle in Solingen, north of Cologne, which was untrue. After 'things became too hot for Eichmann', Wiesenthal wrote, the mass murderer went south to the Aussee region, 'where he felt safer than he did anywhere else'. This was also untrue, and, in addition, groundless. It is not until Eichmann's movements in the summer of 1950 that Wiesenthal's accuracy improved, when he wrote that

Eichmann made his escape via Rome and Genoa, albeit with the help of the Odessa.[110] Again, what is striking about Wiesenthal's version is that he made no attempt to correct it when new and reliable evidence became available. He had stuck so long and so resolutely to the Odessa fable that it was impossible for him to revise his opinion without losing the credibility he didn't deserve.

While Eichmann was supposedly in Solingen, he was still in fact working as a forester in Eversen near Hamburg. Although 'Otto Henninger' enjoyed the work, the shadowy nature of his existence gnawed at him. 'I was still a mole,' he recalled, 'living in the underground, pretending to be someone I was not. I could not even read anything beyond children's stories without attracting suspicion on to me from the simple folk amongst whom I lived.'[111] In 1948, his employer went bust, and Eichmann was out of work.[112] Salvation came in the form of an old booklet entitled *The Healthy Hen and You* which had been published by the Nazi Farmers' Organization. Like Heinrich Himmler before him, Eichmann decided his future was in chicken farming. He rented a small patch of land off his landlady and bought some timber from the forest reserve to make his coops. 'By carefully following the instructions of this fine little Nazi book, I became a successful chicken farmer,' Eichmann wrote. 'That is the secret of success, you see. You MUST obey instructions – exactly.' By his own account, Eichmann's business went well, and he even sold his produce to British soldiers. 'At first I was nervous to meet them, but no one was suspicious of the quiet little egg-farmer.'[113]

For a while, all seemed well, but Eichmann yearned for his wife and family, who were still living in Altaussee. Although he reckoned that he could live as 'Otto Henninger' indefinitely, he wanted to find his own personal final solution. His relatively idyllic existence was also tarnished by the constant – and unfounded – concern that the Allies were closing in. He became particularly wary of a customer who had started to buy an unusually large number of eggs, whom he suspected of spying on him. In early 1950, Eichmann decided to act, and he made discreet inquiries about how it might be possible to arrange 'peculiar travel matters'. Soon, he was visited by a former SS officer from Hamburg, who, in return for three hundred marks,

Above: Adolf Eichmann as a *Scharführer* in the SD in the late 1930s.

Below: Josef Mengele (*second from left*) relaxing with fellow SS officers in Auschwitz in July 1944.

Above: Franz Stangl, the commandant of the Treblinka extermination camp, where some 800,000 were murdered.

Left: Martin Bormann, the head of the Party Chancellery and Hitler's 'Brown Eminence'.

Above: Ante Pavelić, the head of the wartime Croatian puppet state, salutes a crowd in Rome with fellow dictator Benito Mussolini in May 1941.

Right: A famous Latvian aviator, Herberts Cukurs would also earn a reputation as the 'Hangman of Riga' during the liquidation of the ghetto.

Above: Klaus Barbie, the 'Butcher of Lyon', was recruited by American – and possibly British – intelligence after the war.

As head of the RSHA, Ernst Kaltenbrunner was a notable early scalp for the Nazi hunters in the American Counterintelligence Corps.

Left: Former SD officer Heinz Felfe spied for the British and West Germans after the war, although his loyalties lay further east.

Right: As a senior officer in *Einsatzgruppe B*, Dr Friedrich Buchardt was the most murderous of the Nazis known to have been employed by MI6.

Left: Despite being responsible for the execution of many SOE agents, Horst Kopkow was eagerly recruited by the British, who even faked his death.

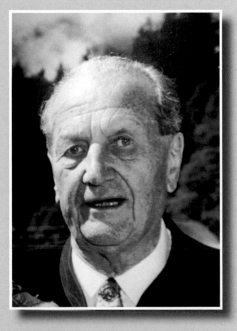

Above: Exploited by nearly every intelligence agency after the war, former SD officer Wilhelm Höttl also supplied highly dubious information to Simon Wiesenthal.

Left: Viktors Arājs, the head of the brutal *Sonderkommando Arājs* in Latvia, turned down a British offer to spy behind the Iron Curtain.

Above: Monsignor Krunoslav Draganović with several of his 'clients' at the Genoa quayside.

Right: As head of the Austrian–German seminary in Rome, Bishop Alois 'Luigi' Hudal was well placed to help many Nazis as they fled to South America and the Middle East.

Clarita Stauffer (*seated*) was an active member of the Spanish Falange, and after the war masterminded the escape of hundreds of Nazi criminals from internment camps. Note the portraits in her office.

The involvement of the SS commando officer Otto Skorzeny in masterminding Nazi escape networks has long been alleged, but bears little evidence.

It was chiefly owing to the Argentine dictator Juan Perón that thousands of Nazis were able to escape to South America.

Above: SS-Hauptsturmführer Carlos Fuldner was instrumental in establishing Perón's escape network in Europe.

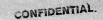

...und Freiheit (Honor
...has its seat in Ham

A specialist on camel medicine and Britain's first elected fascist, Arnold Leese tried to establish a British network to help Nazis escape.

Signs of ODESSA? The symbol of the rumoured secret escape organization, and *(inset)* the squiggle that reportedly represented HIASS, another neo-Nazi network. Such reports were largely the product of Soviet disinformation.

Above: Members of the British War Crimes Investigation Unit in the mess at Bad Oeynhausen in late 1945. Captain Brian Bone is on the far left.

Left: The British War Crimes Team, Christmas 1945. Captain Cartmell is seated far right. Next to him is Major Alan Nightingale.

Left: Lieutenant Colonel Ian Neilson was appointed commanding officer of the British War Crimes Team in November 1945. 'It was all too little, too late,' he recalled.

Right: Simon Wiesenthal in 1947 addressing Displaced Persons in Linz.

Left: Sir Robert Vansittart (*left*) and Viscount Simon. Their demands for a robust approach to Nazi hunting would go unsatisfied.

Right: Lieutenant Colonel Gerald Draper (*left*) and Group Captain Tony Somerhough of the British War Crimes team.

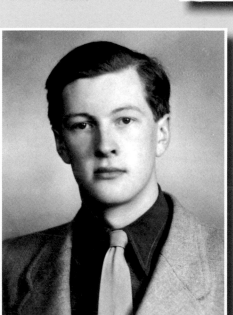

Captain John Hodge was shot in the back of the leg while arresting an SS man in May 1946. Hodge recovered; the suspect was hanged.

A former colleague of Simon Wiesenthal, Tuviah Friedman was to pour scorn on Wiesenthal's achievements. Both, however, would exaggerate their involvement in the hunt for Adolf Eichmann.

Escape routes and hiding places: Josef Mengele and Adolf Eichmann found the walk over the Brenner Pass (*left*) an easy one. Both men took less than two hours to get over the border.

Eichmann's first refuge was the Blaa-Alm hunting lodge three miles north of Altaussee. It was here that the criminal paid off his men.

17 Via Giacomo Venezian in Rome, where Ante Pavelić lived on the second floor. Although the British and the Americans knew his whereabouts, they were never to arrest the former dictator.

Fischerndorf 8 in Altaussee, where Eichmann's family lived from the end of the war until they joined him in Argentina in mid-1952.

supplied Eichmann with precise instructions on how to travel down the 'Submarine Route' to South America. 'Every detail, every stopping place, every contact was related to me,' Eichmann recalled. 'I had what I needed. My orders.'[114] Unfortunately, the name of the SS officer is not known, but it is tempting to speculate whether he was the 'Alfred' Otto Skorzeny referred to in the letter he had written in October 1950 to Leo Schulz, the Alfred whose 'work in Hamburg' had just gone very well. Alfred could also be Erich Priebke's mysterious Argentinian 'Alfredo Beccherini', or the dandyish 'Alfredo' in Stanley Moss's Paris escapade, who had just come over from Argentina. However, until more evidence is produced, these connections must remain as pure speculation. What is clear is that Eichmann paid a lot of money for the information. In 1950, 300 marks were worth approximately $1,260. At the time of writing, that is equivalent to around $15,000, or £10,000. Eichmann claimed that he had saved 2,500 marks from his egg business – something like $100,000 or £75,000 today. As that is a considerable sum for a humble egg farmer to have saved in less than two years, Eichmann must have sold a lot of eggs or had access to other funds. Of course, Eichmann may have recalled the figures incorrectly, and there is plenty of variance with the computations of spending power across decades and currencies, but it is apparent that the fugitive was not living on the breadline.[115]

Like Stangl, Priebke and Mengele before him, Eichmann headed south. He left Eversen in late April 1950, dressed in the collar and tie of a 'gentleman traveller', and still using the 'Otto Henninger' alias.[116] On his way, he was sheltered by various convents and monasteries, including that of the St Raphael Community in Bavaria, which was a particularly ironic choice. During the Nazi years, Eichmann's own department of the SD had kept a watch on the St Raphaelverein for assisting Jews who had converted to Catholicism. Those whom Eichmann had once persecuted were now helping him, which is perhaps a testament to the blindfolds that some priests wore when they extended their charity.[117] Eichmann's first challenge was crossing the border from Austria into Germany. However, at a Bavarian market town, he suffered his first mishap. The forester who was supposed to escort him across the border had broken his leg, and Eichmann had to wait for a week at an inn in a frontier village until a replacement could be found. 'I felt very con-spicuous,' he recalled, 'for it was only the beginning of May and there were not yet many tourists to mingle with.'[118] Eichmann was further alarmed by the ubiquity of the green-uniformed Border Police, who visited the hostelry frequently. Despite sporting a Tyrolean outfit and a goatee beard, Eichmann felt increasingly visible underneath his disguise.

After a week, a hunter was found who would take Eichmann over the border for fifty marks. The two men spent the night of the cross-ing in a mountain hut, and when they awoke, the guide noticed a Border Policeman approaching. 'Here comes a Green One,' the hunter warned Eichmann. 'He just wants a cup of coffee. Lie down on the shelf in the cupboard until he is gone.' Eichmann did so, and spent what felt like hours crammed into the small space, suppress-ing a strong need to cough. The policeman soon left, having unwittingly revealed the routes of that morning's border patrols, which enabled Eichmann and the hunter to descend into Kufstein in Austria without being troubled. After a celebratory glass of schnapps, Eichmann took a taxi 50 miles southwest to Innsbruck, which lay in the French zone of Austria, and where he had been given a choice of two contacts.

The first, a former *SS-Untersturmführer* (second lieutenant) who owned a repair shop, took a dislike to Eichmann. 'They send every damned vagabond to me,' he snapped. 'Find your own way. See that French lieutenant over there? If you don't clear off at once, I'll see you get arrested.'[119] Eichmann scarpered, and walked over to his second contact, one 'Frau Huber', who lived in a brewery. Unfortunately, the building had also become the headquarters of the French Security Police, and Eichmann mistakenly entered their part of the building rather than that of Frau Huber. He found himself face to face with a French officer, to whom Eichmann guiltily blurted out too much information, telling the officer that he was from Linz and looking for Frau Huber, and that she was a relative of his uncle, and he needed a bed for the night. Nevertheless, the Frenchman was not suspicious and merely directed Eichmann next door. When he eventually met Frau Huber, she gave him some schnapps and sent him on his way to a 'mountain inn near the Brenner Pass', which would almost certainly have been in Steinach am Brenner. 'The Submarine Route was working exactly according to plan,' Eichmann later wrote, which was perhaps a generous assessment.[120] Had Eichmann been a Jew attempting to flee to Palestine, he may have had an easier time of it, especially in Innsbruck, where the French gave 'every assistance' to escaping Jews, and even provided them with *lasciapassari* to cross the frontier into Italy.[121]

Eichmann was led over the Brenner Pass by an innkeeper, although his suitcase was taken by a 'splendid pedalling priest' along the road. On the other side of the pass, Eichmann celebrated with a glass of South Tyrolean red wine before being taken by taxi to Merano. It was here that the fugitive finally received his identity papers in the name of 'Riccardo Klement', a pseudonym he would keep for many years. As with Mengele, the ID certificate, numbered 131, had been issued in the middle of 1948 in the commune of Termeno. Some have suggested that this proves that Eichmann wanted to leave Europe around this time, but this conflicts with Eichmann's own testimony, which is reasonably candid about his cover names and methods of escape. There would have been no reason for Eichmann to have dropped his 'Henninger' alias, and to have replaced it with the papers of 'Klement', whose birthplace of Bolzano would have looked unusual in Germany, would have been unnecessarily risky.[122] Furthermore, Eichmann had no reason to lie about when he received his documentation in the name of Klement, and neither did he need to fabricate the point at which he reached his decision to leave his hens. It is possible that the ID papers issued at Termeno were 'off the peg', and merely needed the addition of a photograph and a date of birth in order to give the impression that they were bespoke.[123] Eichmann also claims that in Merano he was issued with his Argentinian landing permit, which was numbered 231489/48.

According to his memoir, Eichmann's last stop in Europe was in Genoa. Simon Wiesenthal claimed that Eichmann travelled through Rome, and although this is not an unreasonable supposition, it makes little sense logistically. A meeting between Eichmann and Hudal is darkly appealing, but it is unlikely and there is no evidence for it. The fugitive was getting all the help he needed outside Rome, and to have made a spurious trip down to the Italian capital would have been entertaining yet more risk. In Genoa on 1 June 1950, Eichmann received his Red Cross passport, which stated that his profession was a 'tecnico', which in a gruesome way he had been. The photograph shows a tight-lipped balding 'Klement' wearing round spectacles, a sober bow tie, a plain white shirt and a sports jacket. On his top lip he sports an unimpressive moustache. He looks very much like a mildly despised, but forgettable, deputy headmaster.[124] The passport was signed by another helpful priest, a Franciscan father called Edoardo Dömöter, who at one time Hudal had directly supplied with travel documents.[125] During the fortnight he had to wait for his boat to sail to Buenos Aires, Eichmann was 'kept safely out of the sight of prying eyes' by an old monk called 'Pater Franciscus', who is likely to have been Dömöter. 'We became firm friends,' Eichmann wrote, 'playing many a game of chess and drinking many a glass of Chianti.' On 16 June, the day before he was about to sail, Dömöter invited Eichmann to Mass, despite the fact that the fugitive had formally left the Church in 1937. 'It can do no harm,' Dömöter said. Eichmann slapped the priest on the back and called him 'my good old Pharisee'. He went to Mass and received Dömöter's blessing. As far as Eichmann was concerned, it was the least he could do. 'It was odd how throughout my escape journey I was helped by Catholic priests,' he later wrote. 'They did so without question. In their eyes, I was just another human being on the road.'[126]

The following day, Eichmann left Europe on the *Giovanni C.* As they sailed, Eichmann was photographed on deck between two fellow passengers. He wore the same clothes as he had done for the passport photograph, except he was wearing a hat and the suggestion of a smile. 'I felt like a hunted animal who had at last shaken off his pursuers,' he recalled. 'I felt a surge of freedom. But I felt a sadness too. And in my pocket to remind me of my sadness I carried a handful of soil which I had gathered up from my German Fatherland on my journey across the mountains.'[127]

The so-called 'Vatican' and 'Iberian' routes were not the only ways which the Nazis fled from Europe. In the middle of 1946, the Swedish and Danish authorities became aware of an escape network that was transporting wanted men from Denmark to Sweden, from where they would travel to Argentina.[128] The network was financed by a German businessman called Friedrich Schlottmann, and run by a gutsy German-Argentine in his early twenties called Carlos Werner Eduardo Schulz. During the network's early days, Schulz posed as the representative of the Evangelical Church in La Plata in Argentina, and persuaded the Norwegians to hand over any Nazis festering in their cells for emigration to Argentina. The Argentine consulate in Stockholm was only too happy to assist the young Schulz, and it provided the necessary documentation for the men to enter Argentina. Schulz supplied fake Red Cross passports, which were often so amateur they did not even feature the holder's photograph.[129]

In 1947, the Argentinians realized that this new 'Nordic route' had great potential, and they called on the services of a former Danish SS officer called Günther Toepke to smuggle wanted Nazis, as well as scientists and technicians, from Germany to Sweden via Denmark. For several months, the work of *Dienstgruppe Dänemark* (Service Group Denmark) flowed smoothly, with Toepke feeding Schulz with plenty of good scalps for Perón. Among them was Kurt Tank, the designer of the Focke-Wulf 190, who escaped in the latter stages of 1947. Travelling with Tank was an Austrian atomic scientist of dubious worth called Ronald Richter, who, as we shall see, would establish Perón's ill-fated nuclear-energy project.[130] Other notables included SS-Hauptsturmführer Kurt Gross, a luminary of Nazi espionage activity in Spain and South America during the war, and Carl Vaernet, a Danish SS doctor who claimed that he had discovered a 'cure' for homosexuality. Often labelled the 'Danish Mengele', Vaernet had experimented on human guinea pigs by castrating them and implanting artificial sexual organs.[131]

For a few months, the Swedes appeared to tolerate the increasing number of Nazis who sailed into their country and then flew out on commercial airliners bound for Switzerland and ultimately Buenos Aires. However, during April or May, they arrested two members of the network: Richard Krügher, a former Luftwaffe pilot, and Sixten Haage, a Swedish student. Although the Swedes had tried to maintain secrecy about the arrests, they were soon publicized, and caused some members of the network to go to ground. The police admitted that they were 'now on the trail of a strong international Nazi underground league that helped more Nazis than Sweden ever dreamed about'. In June, the two men were brought to trial and convicted, although the nature of their sentences was kept restricted. Naturally, all this secrecy only caused much speculation among the press corps, with one newspaper hinting that one of the league's clients was none other than Martin Bormann.[132] The group soon began to unravel. On 17 November 1947, Schulz was arrested in Stockholm, and during his trial he admitted the complicity of members of the Argentine consulate. Shortly afterwards, the two men in question and the consul were politely asked to leave the country, while Schulz was deported. His arrest did not deter him, and for the next few years he based himself in Spain, where he was alleged to have helped Carlos Fuldner's network.[133] In the early 1950s, he would appear in Buenos Aires as a director of the Argentine–German company CAPRI.[134]

In February 1948, the British embassy in Copenhagen informed the Foreign Office that Toepke's network was little more than a 'rather crudely executed plot'.[135] If Toepke's efforts were crude, they looked positively sophisticated when compared to those made by a seventy-year-old retired veterinarian in Britain in the second half of 1946. In June that year, two Dutch former SS men escaped from the prisoner-of-war camp at Kempton Park racecourse in Surrey, 15 miles southwest of central London. Herman Meijer and Hendrich Tiecken had been held in the camp since the previous August, and by the following spring, they had decided they had had enough. Wearing British army battledress, the two men cut their way through the perimeter barbed wire just before midnight on 12 June, and walked some 13 miles southwest to Woking, from where they took a bus 6 miles south to Guildford. At around noon, they knocked on the door of 20 Pewley Hill, which was answered by a burly man sporting a moustache and a dimpled chin. 'Can I see Mr Leese?' Meijer asked. The man looked them up and down. 'I happen to be Mr Leese,' he replied. Meijer then asked if he and Tiecken could come in, and Leese brought them into the drawing room.[136]

The two Dutchmen had certainly chosen a man who shared – or perhaps exceeded – their political sympathies. Born in Lancashire in northern England in 1878, Leese had been a specialist on the treatment of camels, and enjoyed the rare distinction of having a camel parasite named in his honour: *Thelazia leesei*.[137] After serving in the Royal Army Veterinary Corps during the First World War, Leese returned to England, where he established a successful veterinary practice and published the seminal *A Treatise on the One-Humped Camel in Health and in Disease* in 1928.[138] As well as even-toed ungulates, Leese's other obsession was with Jews, and his vicious anti-Semitism led him to embrace fascism after the war. In 1924, Leese claimed the dubious honour of being the first constitutionally elected fascist in England by securing a seat on the council in Stamford. However, the virulent Leese soon found his fellow members of the British Fascist Party rather too 'kosher' for his liking, and in 1928 he founded the Imperial Fascist League, which he led from 1932 to 1940. In September 1936, Leese was sentenced to six months' imprisonment for 'effecting a public nuisance' with his publication of a newspaper accusing the Jews of ritual murder. The sentence did nothing to lessen the extremity of his views, and in September 1938, during the Munich Crisis, he wrote to Adolf Hitler offering his services. 'It is almost inconceivable that there should be war over this affair,' Leese wrote. 'The world is not yet quite made. The Jew cannot control the spirit, and no one is interested in the Czechs except the Jew and his touts.'[139] For much of the war, Leese was incarcerated under Defence Regulation 18B, although he was released because of ill health in 1943. Sickness did not diminish his anti-Semitism and his book *The Jewish War of Survival* contained, according to one MI5 officer, 'some of the most pernicious anti-Jewish propaganda which has come our way'.[140] Including such views as:

> The Jews will also win the next round unless those of us who possess intelligence and character will use both and realize as Disraeli wrote — ALL IS RACE, and seek to eliminate from our civilization and culture the Jewish influence which has caused the great bloody schisms between the western peoples of kindred race and spirit.[141]

The book also contained the suggestion that Charles Lindbergh's son, who had been kidnapped in March 1932, was the victim of a Jewish ritual slaughter for that year's Purim feast day. It was thanks to the public expression of views such as this that the Security Service closely monitored Leese's activities, both intercepting his mail and on occasion tapping his telephone line.

Meijer and Tiecken had therefore chosen a rather unsuitable person to assist them in their flight. Nevertheless, Leese was keen to help, although he did not wish his wife or housekeeper to find out. He let the escapers stay for one night, and the following morning, after bringing the men breakfast, he supplied them with details of the Argentine embassy in London. He also gave them an address of a business called Nu-Era Household Products in Dalston Junction in the East End of London where the two men would find more suitable sanctuary. Leese told them that when they arrived, they should ask for a Mr Alfred Cooper, but if he were not there they should go to 57 Fellows Street to see a Mr McCarthy.[142] At both addresses, Leese advised them to use the password: 'We have been sent by a man who likes cats very much.' (Leese did indeed like cats, especially his own cat, Nandy, to whom he ascribed a sixth sense. In 1940, Leese had noticed how Nandy had become particularly affectionate two days before his arrest and internment.[143] Unbeknown to his master, it would not be long until the cat was to display his 'radar-like' quality once more.) Leese also gave the fugitives five pounds, and late on the morning of 15 June, the two men took a Green Line bus from Guildford to Marble Arch. Instead of first making for the premises of Nu-Era, Meijer and Tiecken walked to Fellows Street, where the door was opened by a woman who they would later know to be Mrs McCarthy. Meijer informed her that they had been sent by their new felinophile friend, whereupon the woman understandably looked perplexed and closed the door on them. At Nu-Era, the escapers had better luck, and they were soon taken under the wing of one Ray Alford, who sheltered them at his house at 62 Ufton Road in Hackney.

The house was accustomed to having unfamiliar guests, as Alford admitted that he had let it be used as a hideout for deserters during the war, and that both he and Alfred Cooper were deserters. Meijer and Tiecken were to stay at Ufton Road until early September, and they spent their time reading and studying. The only highlight of their stay was Meijer's visit to the Argentine ambassador's house in Belgrave Square one afternoon at the end of July. Unfortunately for

Meijer, the ambassador was either out or would not see him, but he was advised that he could meet him at nine thirty the following morning at the embassy itself in Wilton Crescent. Meijer made the appointment, although he was interviewed by a man he described as a 'counsellor'. 'Upon reaching an interview room I put my cards on the table,' Meijer recalled, 'and told him everything about Tiecken and myself [. . .] I told him about our plan to go to the Argentine and asked him if he could supply the necessary papers for that purpose.'[144] The diplomat refused to help, although he was friendly, and promised not to say anything to the British. The deflated Meijer returned to the East End and broke the bad news to his companion.

At around midnight on 7 September, there was a knock on the door of number 62. The door was answered by Ray Alford's father while Ray waited with the two fugitives. After a few seconds he turned to them and hissed, 'Get out! Police!' The three men bolted out of the back door and ran to the end of the garden, where they scaled a low wall on to the roof of a workshop. They lay there for a short time while the police searched the house and garden, before jumping off and vaulting over a fence into the next street. They quickly made their way to 57 Fellows Street, where they were now put up by the McCarthy family. Three days later, Leese was informed of the close shave in a letter from one of his associates, Anthony Gittens. The letter, which was intercepted by MI5, was written in a highly penetrable code, which no doubt caused few problems for the cryptographers at the Security Service.

Bodger & Bodger had 4 interesting visitors name of Percy yesterday evening. They called a bit late when everybody had gone to bed wh. was a bit of an embarassment. However old pa Loftus Bodger came down and showed them the usual hospitality but like all ill-bred people they seemed keen on staying [. . .] Young Bodger and his cousins who are always shy in company decided to go for a walk and give the dog a chance to test the lamp posts by moonlight. After dislodging every slate and dustbin lid for miles around and awaking the ruddy neighbourhood, doggy got his fill of lamposts [sic] and fearing the Percy family might still be guzzling the household Tea, decided to spend the night with the O'Carthy's.[145]

*

Meijer and Tiecken stayed at number 57 until the middle of October. During this time, Leese began to solicit donations from his political allies. On 18 September, he wrote to a friend asking if she could help 'towards the same business as the Argentine affair', as the expenses were 'heavy & continue'.[146] One benefactor was the Duke of Bedford, who was a well-known 'fellow traveller', although Leese was careful not to tell His Grace what the money was being used for.[147] Another contributor was the elderly Lady Claire Annesley, who was a friend of the Duke and Unity Mitford.[148] While Leese plotted, MI5 was listening in. At the end of September, they learned about his nascent escape network and the two POWs. During one conversation Leese said that the only reason he was in a hurry to get the two men out of England was because he feared 'Jewish vengeance'. Furthermore, the escape route was in its 'infancy', although he had much 'bigger schemes in mind'.[149] Leese's schemes certainly were big. In October, MI5 established that his long-term goal was to establish 'machinery for passing fugitive Nazis from Germany via this country to Spain and South America, and to link up with Nazi nuclei which are thought to be forming abroad'.[150] Leese's vaulting ambition o'erleaped itself. The extent of his 'Odessa' was little more than two frustrated Dutchmen holed up in a house in the East End, a severe shortage of funds, and an anxious McCarthy family, who were keen to see the backs of their 'guests'. The fact that MI5 knew all about what was going on guaranteed that Leese's plans would be doomed.

On 15 October, Meijer and Tiecken were taken by McCarthy on the train to Worthing, 50 miles south of London on the Sussex coast, where they were delivered to their new home, which was the loft of 107 Littlehampton Road. Their hosts, a Mr and Mrs Edmunds, ran a boarding kennel from the address, and they soon grew fond of their new 'pets'. On 25 October, they wrote to Leese in the highly decipherable code so beloved of this very British 'Odessa'. 'The cousins are v. well,' wrote Gwyn Edmunds, 'and full of life. We grow v. fond of them.'[151] While the Dutchmen settled into their new abode, Leese busied himself trying to arrange their passage out of the country. During the latter half of November, he wrote to the Edmundses, advising them that a certain Captain Batt in Hamble in Hampshire might be able to help the fugitives. According to Leese,

Batt, having served in Palestine, 'knew the Jewish question'. Frederick Edmunds drove Meijer over to Hamble, where they met Captain Batt, who told them that a friend was soon to be taking a motor trawler to Peru, and that Meijer could be taken on as a steward. As there was no guaranteed place for Tiecken, Meijer declined. Batt then suggested that he could take them to Ireland in April, when his own boat was ready to put to sea again. Meijer left the invitation open. At the beginning of December, Leese visited number 107 for the day, and he, Edmunds, Meijer and Tiecken discussed how an escape network might be established. 'This talk was of a general nature,' Meijer later related, 'and no specific plans were laid.'[152]

Even if the group had made any plans, they would not have had a chance to put them into action, because by then MI5 had heard enough. At eight o'clock on the morning of 15 December, two plain-clothed policemen entered the loft while Meijer and Tiecken were getting dressed and arrested the fugitives. The Edmundses were also arrested, as were the McCarthys, the Alfords, Anthony Gittens and Arnold Leese himself. Of these, seven were brought to trial, and the jury had little trouble in finding them guilty. Two days before he received his sentence, Leese recalled how his cat, Nandy, once again displayed the unusual affection that had last been manifested before his internment in 1940. 'He followed me about all over the house and garden,' Leese wrote, 'and it was so marked that [. . .] my wife became convinced that I was in for a stiff term of imprisonment.' Nandy was right. Each of the defendants received twelve months in gaol. Leese was sent to Pentonville, where, because of his previous stretch, he was treated like 'an old lag'. On 17 November 1947, he was released, claiming he was in 'a poor state', which was probably true.[153] Nevertheless, Leese was to live another nine years, during which time he never relented in his attacks on the Jews. Upon his death in 1956, he bequeathed his house in Holland Park in west London to the British Nazi Colin Jordan, who renamed it Arnold Leese House and used it as the headquarters of the White Defence League. Even after his death, Leese's work was to continue, but any chances of a British 'Odessa' died with him.

The one British figure who might have made a better job of such a network would have been Sir Oswald Mosley. Like Leese, Sir

Oswald and his wife Diana, Lady Mosley, had been interned for the best part of the war, but, despite their incarceration and the post-war revelation of Nazi atrocities, their devotion to fascism remained undimmed. During 1947 and 1948, Mosley slowly founded the Union Movement (UM), a political party that aimed to marry fascism with the concept of European union. Many meetings were deliberately held near internment camps, and German POWs were able to attend under the guise of offering German lessons to UM members. As one observer noted, the prisoners 'would be de-Nazified in the daytime and listen to these fascist meetings in the evening'.[154] Mosley was still a potent figure for those on the Far Right, and even recordings of his voice would be enough to raise the roof. At a garden party meeting of the fascist British League in Essex on 27 September 1947, Mosley's 1934 speech at the Albert Hall was played to those present, who included twelve German POWs. No typical garden party, the event also featured a rendition of the 'Horst Wessel Lied', and speeches in German that culminated in 'Heil Hitler!'[155]

Unlike Leese, Mosley was careful to keep within the bounds of the law. When two fugitive German POWs stopped by his house near Ramsbury in Wiltshire in late 1946, he fed them, but then called the police.[156] When Leese heard about this, he was furious, and wanted to publicize the fact in order to discredit Mosley in the eyes of Mosley's more fanatical supporters.[157] Even if Mosley and his followers secretly approved of Leese's efforts, they were politically astute enough to realize that such actions did not reflect well on British fascists in general – as if the fascists had any sort of reputation worth upholding. 'This kind of thing has always been a curse to our movement,' said Charlie Watts, a senior figure in Mosley's hierarchy, 'because people link it up with us and you can't blame them for that when so many of our people do the same kind of thing.'[158] This statement would suggest that scores of people were harbouring fugitive POWs in Britain, and it may well have been true, as it was not only fascists who were sympathetic to the plight of the prisoners. In 1947, Norman and Evelyn Cox, a Quaker couple who lived near the POW camp at Billingshurst in Sussex, twice gave shelter to fugitive Germans, and even lent them bicycles to get to Southampton. Like many, the Coxes thought the young men deserved to go back home. After all, the reasoning went, the war had ended two years ago.[159] It was also not unknown for young women to help Germans escape, for reasons that are obvious. In January 1947, Franz Oprzondek, a 26-year-old former member of the *Afrikakorps*, was charged with 'conduct prejudicial to good order and discipline' for consorting with a Mrs Oshe Thompson, who had hidden him for seventeen days in her caravan in Worcestershire the previous December. 'Franz is not a Nazi,' Mrs Thompson said outside the camp where Oprzondek was being court-martialled. 'He has been a prisoner of war for five years – naturally I was sorry for him.'[160]

As soon as the law allowed, the Mosleys made a great play of employing POWs as labourers on their farm. Mosley found himself particularly in concord with those who had been in the SS, 'who were passionately European and supported my advanced European ideas'.[161] These warm feelings were mutual, and in October 1947, one of Mosley's German quondam labourers called Peter Keller wrote to Mosley not only to thank him for a parcel of clothing Sir Oswald and Lady Mosley had sent, but also for 'the frank way in which you spoke to me . . . it seemed . . . as if a voice from our home country had spoken to us, and we were deeply moved'.[162] The Mosleys also ensured that the Germans who worked for them received creature comforts – especially cigarettes, which were still in short supply.[163] Like Gwyn Edmunds, it also appeared that the Mosleys grew fond of their charges. On 17 January 1947, the following telephone conversation took place between Sir Oswald and his wife, Diana, who had enquired as to how the POWs' work was coming along.

Lady Mosley:	Is it all looking much tidier?
Sir Oswald:	Yes it is. They are amazing workers of course – wonderful workers.
Lady Mosley:	Are they sweet?
Sir Oswald:	Awfully nice, yes.
Lady Mosley:	Yes I'm sure.
Sir Oswald:	Charming.[164]

It was Lady Mosley herself who established an organization that had the trappings of a Nazi support network. In December 1948, she founded the Bond of Brotherhood, which was an aid programme designed for UM members to send food and clothing to needy Germans. Appeals were made regularly in the party's magazine, *Union*, and assistance was offered from many quarters, even from as far away as South Africa.[165] The scheme was so well publicized in Far Right circles that even Bishop Hudal in Rome heard about it. In late January 1949, Dr Walter Schilling in Buenos Aires wrote to the bishop asking him to send a 'few lines' to Mosley, and saying that he had often mentioned Hudal to Sir Oswald. It is not known whether Schilling revealed to Mosley the full extent of Hudal's work, but Schilling did tell Hudal that Lady Mosley 'has recently put herself at the head of a relief organisation for Germany'. Hudal would have doubtless approved. Schilling then supplied Hudal with Mosley's cover address, which was care of a Miss E. Price, 31 Talgarth Mansions, London W14.[166] The Bond of Brotherhood was, according to the pages of *Union*, a 'very considerable success', and in July 1949, the magazine claimed that 'hundreds of our German colleagues and their families are reaping the benefits of the kindness of those Britons . . . who have made great voluntary sacrifices to join Lady Mosley in the work she has undertaken.'[167] Such claims must be treated with caution, but there is no doubt that Lady Mosley did her utmost to help the German people, or at least certain sections of them, for those for whom she felt the most sympathy were fellow adherents of her *Weltanschauung*.

Throughout the late 1940s and the 1950s, the Mosleys travelled extensively around the world cementing links between UM and fascists on the Continent, and the recent opening of British Security Service files on the couple reveals that their love of fascism was undimmed.[168] The Mosleys' aim was to create a global fascist 'collective', and it was a project on which they spent a vast amount of money and time. Fascist Spain was a favourite destination, which they visited in July 1949 and May 1950. During one of these visits, the Mosleys even met Franco's Foreign Minister.[169] In November 1950, Mosley travelled to Buenos Aires, where he met many leading exiles of the European fascist community, including Kops's employer Eberhard Fritsch, the publisher of *Der Weg*; Ferdinand Durcansky, the Foreign Minister in the pro-Axis wartime puppet government installed in Slovakia; and Hudal's friend and correspondent, Walter

Schilling. It was perhaps no coincidence that Mosley stayed at the Hotel Lancaster, which was diagonally opposite the offices of CAPRI.[170] On 2 June 1951, Mosley was in Basle, Switzerland, where he met not only members of the SS help organization *Bruderschaft*, but also Werner Naumann, whose underground activities Mosley agreed to help finance.[171] On 25 October 1952, the two men met again at a lunch in Paris, where, according to Naumann, they discussed 'publishing ventures'.[172]

It was after this meeting that an exchange of coded letters took place between Mosley, Naumann and none other than Otto Skorzeny, concerning a transaction they labelled 'cement'. On 31 October, Mosley wrote to Naumann from the Hôtel Continental in Paris, advising him that he had a good friend who could help with 'cement'.[173] Three weeks later, Naumann received a letter from Skorzeny in Madrid.

> Ilse also told me that you can make good offers in Cement. I can see here a definite possibility for the Canary Isles. Please be good enough to send me here by return a detailed quotation for all possible kinds available. If you can possibly quote 'CIF Canaries' all the better. In any case it would be interesting to know the present rates in force if, as I assume, you want to quote from Rotterdam or Antwerp.[174]

On 13 December, Skorzeny wrote again to Naumann, stating that he was glad that Naumann had shown 'an appreciation of the fact' that Skorzeny had obtained 'an offer from competitors', which he had been forced to do because his 'agent in the Canary Islands' explained that Naumann's offer had been too high. Skorzeny cautioned Naumann that even if Naumann's offer were accepted, they should be mindful of the costs of 'freight rates to Brazil'.[175]

On Boxing Day, Mosley wrote to Naumann expressing gratitude for his help and 'comradeship'. He then mentioned 'R', who was in fact the highly decorated Luftwaffe pilot Hans-Ulrich Rudel, whose memoirs Mosley would publish in English.

> I received today the message about R. As things stand I cannot travel there before 20.1.53. Also my first business friend is returning from

America just at that time; most important. Can you please obtain from R the address of Dr von Groede in Brazil for my second business friend whom you met recently. I will then write an introduction to van G (*Cement*).[176]

Owing to Naumann's arrest the following month, these discussions about 'cement' would be put to a halt. Nevertheless, the letters offer a tantalizing glimpse of a project that involved Britain's most notorious fascist, a former Nazi minister who wanted to dismantle German democracy, a celebrated SS colonel connected with numerous neo-Nazi activities, and Dr von Groede, whose real name was René Lagrou, a key member of Perón and Fuldner's Nazi escape network and an agent of the Argentine secret service.[177]

Unfortunately, without any more evidence, it is impossible to be sure what 'cement' refers to. The men may well have been referring to actual cement – Skorzeny's passport after all claimed that he was a dealer in the material.[178] If the project somehow involved importing cement into the Canary Islands, then it was certainly a good business to attempt to break into. In 1947, the islands imported 8,344 tons of cement from Britain. In 1948, that figure had more than quadrupled to 36,459 tons.[179] However, the involvement of René Lagrou would suggest that the project had little to do with building materials. Another explanation is that 'cement' may refer to illegal currency movements, an economic instrument of which Mosley was something of a master. However, the same set of correspondence refers to such practices somewhat openly, and distinctly from 'cement'. Whatever the word did refer to, what makes the correspondence especially intriguing is the mention of Lagrou. Although it is highly unlikely that Mosley and Naumann were arranging the transportation of Nazi war criminals, they were certainly hatching some sort of plan with a man who had done so. It is possible to interpret the documents as preparations for an escape, but their ambiguity makes many other alternatives equally likely.

While those such as Eichmann, Mengele and Stangl were hiding and escaping, the organizations that were tasked with hunting them were suffering from a shortage of manpower and *matériel*, administrative indecision and a lack of political will. The British army's War Crimes Investigation Unit (WCIU) was particularly badly affected by this noxious cocktail. On 24 April 1946, the WCIU's commanding officer, Lieutenant Colonel Alan Nightingale, reported that 'the shortage of officers in this Unit is now even more acute than when the Unit was first formed.' Nightingale complained to the Deputy Judge Advocate General (DJAG) that although his team was supposed to have twenty-seven investigating officers, it had only fourteen, of whom two were being demobilized the following month. The search team – later to be known as 'Haystack' – was similarly undermanned, and instead of its full complement of four- teen officers, it had only nine, of whom three were going back to Britain by 16 June. At the level of other ranks, the situation was even more parlous. Instead of the twenty sergeants allocated to it, Haystack had a mere five. Nightingale pleaded for the backing of 'as high an authority as possible' to remedy the situation, but his appeal went unheard.[180]

In Austria, the British Element of the Allied Commission (ACA) was having comparable problems. Two days after Nightingale wrote his letter, Major General Winterton was complaining in a similar vein to the Control Office for Germany and Austria in London. Winterton's concern was that the ACA lacked the manpower to investigate atrocities, a responsibility it had been given in February 1946. 'Approximately one hundred cases of alleged atrocities have been partially investigated,' Winterton wrote, 'but they are not nearly ready for trial.' Winterton anticipated that once the Austrians became aware that the ACA was investigating such crimes, further reports would snowball in, all of which would have to be examined. Winterton gave the example of the trial of the perpetrators of the Eisenerz Death March in April 1945, on which a British lieutenant colonel had been working for three months, and which had also occupied the time of a large part of the staff of the ACA's Legal Division and the Field Security Section. 'Mass graves have been found all along the route,' Winterton stated, 'each one of which is capable of producing an investigation and trial comparable with that of Eisenerz.' As it was not his place to decide how to proceed, Winterton posed the following to his superiors in London: 'The question to be decided is whether the difficulty of providing the additional manpower required by the Commission outweighs the duty to maintain law and order, and to bring those guilty of these crimes to justice, and legitimate criticisms on failure to carry out this duty.' Winterton requested that he be furnished with an answer as soon as possible, as it was 'not possible to carry out the commitments involved'.[181]

Over the next four years, that question would never be answered explicitly, although the lack of manpower in organizations such as the WCIU and the ACA allows the obvious inference to be drawn: logistical difficulties did indeed outweigh the desire to bring justice. The resulting overstretch meant that British war crimes officers were absurdly overworked, which had predictable consequences. On 14 May 1946, Major Peter Davies, the British War Crimes Liaison Officer in the French zone of Germany, informed Group Captain Tony Somerhough of the Judge Advocate General's office that one of his officers, Captain Charles Kaiser, had covered 11,000 miles in three months, and had 'never managed to complete everything that he was required to do'. Kaiser's health suffered to the extent that he was 'in a very nervous state when he was withdrawn, due to over-work'. Davies added that the lack of an extra officer had brought his work to a 'stand-still'.[182] Had fugitives such as Adolf Eichmann been aware of this situation they might have decided they had no need to go to Argentina.

Despite the frequent pleas for more manpower, the War Establishment Committee of the BAOR decided on 29 May to cut the WCIU by twelve officers and forty-eight other ranks. To add further insult, Lieutenant Colonel Nightingale was given the impression that he had 'got off lightly'. Lieutenant Colonel J. Leicester-Warren of the office of the Judge Advocate General (JAG) was incensed, as he had believed that the cut was going to be far less deep, and he appealed to the BAOR to reconsider.

> [. . .] It is felt that a much higher principle is at stake. It is absolutely essential that the fullest possible support should be given to those engaged on the detection of war crimes so long as this remains a military commitment and it is of paramount importance that further cuts in personnel should be prevented. [. . .] It does not seem to be appreciated in certain branches of this Headquarters that the War

Crimes Investigation Unit is engaged on priority work or that it is a highly specialized unit [. . .] It is hoped, therefore, that this matter will be taken up by you on the highest possible level so that this Headquarters may be informed that the detection of war crimes is still a first priority in this theatre, and irresponsible elements prevented from sabotaging our efforts and thereby making it very difficult for us to achieve the targets which have been set for us on a Cabinet level.[183]

The cuts went through, and, once again, the consequences did not require a soothsayer. In August, Major Harry Cartmell reported that cases were being held up by two to three months because the WCIU now had only one pathologist, whose workload was 'intolerable'.[184] What those such as Cartmell and Leicester-Warren could not have known was that at the most senior level of government there was little appetite for Nazi hunting. In November 1946, the Cabinet itself took the decision in principle to discontinue war crimes trials, which was felt to be a reflection of the public mood to 'wipe the slate clean'. According to Sir Hartley Shawcross, the Attorney-General and the chief British prosecutor at Nuremberg, no less a figure than Winston Churchill was worried about the 'possible crimes the Allied powers had committed'. To continue pursuing Axis criminals might only cause attention to be drawn to those crimes committed by the hunters themselves.[185]

Nevertheless, the war crimes teams were not immediately swept away, but were instead subject to administrative changes. In January 1947, the WCIU was repackaged with various other bodies into the War Crimes Group (North West Europe), although a separate Group in South East Europe (WCG SEE) would not be established until June. However, the creation of the new Group was held up because of all things, a lack of radiators. At the beginning of March 1947, Group Captain Somerhough requested that suitable heating should be installed at the offices of the Group's Legal and Executive sections at 3 Luisenstrasse in Bad Oeynhausen. 'Please treat this matter as one of utmost urgency,' Somerhough pleaded, 'as the whole amalgamation of War Crimes Group (North West Europe) is held up until such time as this house is fit for occupation.'[186] By the end of the month, the building was still not ready. 'On inspection it has been found that the lighting is completely unsuitable for office work,' Somerhough reported, once again insisting that the matter be treated as urgent.[187] Another problem was the question of transportation, which was a problem that affected the whole of the BAOR. In July, the Group reported that it was short of fifteen drivers, and in August, the War Crimes Group (South East Europe) had so few vehicles that its investigators and searchers 'were standing idle'.[188] The Group in South East Europe, which was based in Klagenfurt in Austria, was further hampered by a shortage of interpreters and investigators, although Brigadier Henry Shapcott, the DJAG, thought that the Group had more than enough manpower. In November 1947, Shapcott informed the Group's commanding officer, Lieutenant Colonel P. J. Heycock, that he considered 'your existing members very adequate', and furthermore, that 'you have too many for the work you have outlined to me as outstanding'. The Group's reply was made through clenched teeth, as Heycock's deputy politely informed the brigadier of the immense practical difficulties it faced.

> I am sure that you appreciate that our geographical position is by no means a satisfactory one. The scene of the crime is invariably several hundred miles to the South of us, whilst the criminal is several hundred miles to the North. In addition, our cases concern crimes committed by a German Army in Italy. This Army was constantly moving and had little contact and no common language with the civil population. Consequently the evidence as to who the perpetrator of a crime is, is always very slender. The best that the people on the spot can usually say, is that the criminal was a German soldier. As there were seven hundred and fifty thousand German soldiers in Italy, the tracing of the individual is always a lengthy business.[189]

The fine words of the Moscow Declaration in October 1943 stating that the Allies would chase the criminals 'to the uttermost ends of the earth' had never seemed so hollow.

The War Crimes Groups' investigation efforts were further weakened by the quality of their personnel, many of whom lacked backgrounds in either legal or detective work. In September 1947, Lieutenant Colonel Gerald Draper, the officer commanding the

Legal Section of the War Crimes Group in North West Europe, complained that the 'standard of investigation is deteriorating'. Draper
listed a whole gamut of shortcomings, which included evidence
being recorded inaccurately, a lack of coordination with the
pathologist, affidavits prepared in 'an idle manner', useless labelling
of exhibits, and depositions presented in a non-chronogical order.[190]
Such problems seemed mild compared to some of the highly
unlegalistic behaviour exhibited by some British soldiers. In August
1946, Hildegard Knoedler, a former guard at the Draeger Works
concentration camp, found herself on the receiving end of an
unusual punishment meted out by one Sergeant Dow of the Field
Security Section in Hamburg. After questioning her, Dow informed
Knoedler that she was in a lot of trouble, but instead of sending her
to prison, he told her he would in fact administer some *Körperstrafe*.
He then made her undress completely, laid her across his knee and
beat her with his hand and a riding whip. After he had finished,
Dow made her get dressed and told her to report for the same treatment the following week. When Knoedler did so, she begged for it
to stop, but he insisted that the punishment would continue every
week for the next five weeks. Dow's superiors soon heard of these
fetishistic beatings, and Dow was posted elsewhere.[191] Lieutenant
Colonel Draper would also not have liked the methods adopted by
Captain Brian Bone of the Haystack search section after he had
arrested a *Burgermeister* who was suspected of shooting the injured
RAF crew of a downed Halifax bomber.

> I started the questioning and it became clear to us that this man was
> going to be a difficult nut to crack despite the very precise evidence
> against him. He started by being arrogant and denying his role in the
> murders, but he started to crumble when I drew my Mauser, cocked
> it loudly and pointed it at him. I told him I would have no hesitation
> in shooting him if he did not start telling the truth. He started
> quivering with fright but soon got hold of himself and refused to
> speak until one of the NCOs quietly walked past him. Suddenly he
> was on the floor behind the upturned chair completely dazed as to
> how he had got there. I didn't see what had happened as I was writing
> on a pad on my knees and the NCO answered me by saying that the
> stupid bugger must have tripped![192]

Other members of the Group found that the threat of violence was equally effective. Captain Charles Kaiser would visit suspects 'with a large black dog', or he would make them stand in the corner for hours.[193] However, a 'softly-softly' approach could also be effective. One of the Group's NCOs, Lance Bombardier Greville Janner, recalled how he was instructed to make arrests.

> When you catch someone, do not say to him: 'You are a vile killer. Your time has come. Say goodbye to your family because you will never see them again.' No. Resist the temptation. Instead, smile and say: 'So sorry to trouble you, but we've been asked to take you to somewhere nearby, for a few questions. You'll probably be home tonight, but perhaps you'd like to pack a few clothes, just in case you're away for a night or two.' Then get the person into the car and, with renewed apologies, put on the handcuffs. 'So sorry, it's just a matter of routine. They'll be off in a few minutes when we reach our destination. We'll be there in time for lunch . . .'[194]

Janner was also told that the best time to make an arrest was at night, when the suspects would be caught dozily off guard. However, not all night-time captures went smoothly. On the evening of 11 May 1946, Major Peter Davies, Captain John Hodge and Sergeant John Robbins went to arrest a former SS man called Heinrich Hornetz at his house near the town of Fulda, some 60 miles northeast of Frankfurt. In order to enter the house, Davies smashed a bedroom window, and soon Hornetz was in handcuffs. During the course of the arrest, Hornetz's wife ran out of the house shouting: '*Englischer Schweinehund!*', and within moments, five gunmen had surrounded the building. The British tried to leave through the front door, but they were fired upon, and in the confusion Hornetz escaped. Major Davies ran and recaptured him, but while the four men made their way to the car, the nineteen-year-old Hodge was shot in the back of the leg at a range of 3 yards. When they arrived at the vehicle, they found that its distributor had been smashed and water poured in the petrol tank. The party then ran through the village until they came to the house of the *Burgermeister*, who refused to let them in. With the gunmen still chasing them, they dashed into the woods, but Davies warned his pursuers that if they approached, Hornetz would be shot through the head. This threat caused the gunmen to hold back, and eventually Davies, Hodge, Robbins and Hornetz arrived at the next village after a trek of 5 miles, where Hodge's wound was dressed by American troops.[195] The 37-year-old Hornetz was tried for the crimes he had committed on the staff at Neue Bremme concentration camp, and was executed on 30 July.[196]

Despite all the impedimenta that beset them, most of the individuals in the War Crimes Groups did their best. However, it became increasingly apparent that hunting down and trying and convicting the many thousands of war criminals was an impossible task. In the spring of 1947, the British launched Operation Fleacomb, which was designed to sift through the 4,261 suspects awaiting trial and to release those for whom there was insufficient evidence of criminality as well as those whose crimes were considered relatively trivial. 'It is a stock taking operation on a vast scale,' Somerhough wrote, 'at which we propose to examine the goods and offer a great many of them at bargain prices.'[197] By the end of June, some 2,100 'goods' had been released, which Somerhough regarded as a 'complete success'.[198] That number crept up to 2,502 by August, which left the British holding 1,759 suspects, of whom 1,133 were wanted by other Allied nations.[199] By the end of 1947, further releases, trials and extraditions resulted in the British holding just 612 male war crimes suspects, and within six months, a mere 146.[200] The British were not alone among the Allies in carrying out similar 'stock taking' exercises. Colonel Clio E. Straight, the head of the American War Crimes Group, recalled how 'headquarters was always ordering me to "Hurry up",' which resulted in him cutting the number of atrocities to be investigated from 3,603 to 793. Thousands of suspects were also released from the American camp at Dachau. 'There was no method,' said Straight, 'no discussion about handing cases or bodies over to the Germans. We just plain turned them loose.' It mattered little that Straight's files contained evidence of some 2,500 criminals who were never to be hunted.[201]

On 13 March 1948, Somerhough brought together three of his officers to discuss the 'future rundown of the Group'. Lieutenant Colonel Nightingale told the meeting that the Field Investigation Section had only around forty suspects to trace, which seemed to be

an extraordinarily small number.[202] Over the next five months, the
Group was wound down, and in August 1948, it was disbanded. For
those such as Greville Janner, who had risen to the rank of sergeant,
the end came as a shock. 'I was really upset,' he recalled. 'We still
had ten thousand people on our books. These were criminals, murderers, concentration camp guards – and they disbanded it because
they wanted to concentrate on the Russians. It was just filthy politics.'[203]

Janner was right. The appetite for hunting Nazis was simply not
there. As Colonel Straight said, 'to carry on and try thousands
would have been expensive', and in the late 1940s and early 1950s
there was an enormous political will to move on from the war and
to confront what was seen as the new enemy: the Soviet Union.[204]
But to wage the Cold War required warriors who knew the new
enemy and had already fought against it. This meant that some of
those the Allies were hunting would soon become their new helpers,
even if they were the worst sort of Nazi criminal. Filthy politics
would have to triumph over any higher principle.

Chapter Seven

Extremely Sensitive Individuals

'MY TRAVELS never seemed to end. I had no job, and had to keep constantly on the move.' So spoke Klaus Barbie of his months immediately following the war.[1] Like many Nazis in his situation, Barbie turned to agricultural work as a means of supporting himself, but such work was sporadic and hardly suited the former SD man's mercurial penchant for making a dishonest living. He gravitated towards Hamburg, the bombed-out city that played host to many a wheeler and dealer, but he did not stay for long, and by October 1945 he had rejoined his family 200 miles south in Bursfelde, where he worked the black market in nearby Kassel with two former SS officers.[2] His activities soon attracted the attention of the Americans, and he was given a fourteen-day prison sentence for an unknown misdemeanour.[3] Fortunately for Barbie, whose name appeared on the UNWCC's 1944 list as 'Barbier', he was not identified as the 'Butcher of Lyon', because either his captors did not have a list, or Barbie was using the false name of 'Becker', or, most likely, a combination of both.[4] After his release, Barbie continued to forge alliances with former Nazis. On 19 October 1945, he met two men called Naumann and Kurt Barkhausen in Ödelsheim, and the three agreed that they should maintain contact with as many 'old comrades' as possible.

By the end of the year, Barbie had moved to Marburg, 80 miles southwest of Bursfelde, where he lived in the house once inhabited by the Brothers Grimm.[5] While his family moved back to Trier, Barbie posed as a student, although his real studies involved working out scams that could not only keep him solvent, but also help finance and expand a resistance movement called the *Organisation für den Deutschen Sozialismus* (Organization for German Socialism), led by a former Luftwaffe lieutenant colonel called Winter. Barbie was one of the prime movers in the group, the grand aim of which was to be accepted by the Allies as the real power in Germany in the event of war with Russia. The ODS dovetailed with a similar group called the *Organisation Süddeutschland* (Southern Germany Organization), which had been shepherding Nazis into Switzerland under the stewardship of Major General Kurt Ellersieck, who was also a member of the ODS. During the course of 1946, Barbie used his experience as an SD officer to help build up the ODS into a reputedly formidable organization which claimed to have a network of contacts throughout Europe and possibly within the Soviet Union. What Barbie and his comrades did not know – or pretended not to know – was that the group had been penetrated by a former German intelligence officer called Emil Hoffman who reported to the British.[6] The CIC also had an informant within the group, who was posing as a Swiss Nazi. As the year wore on, both the Americans and the British had assembled a good picture of the organization, which the British had codenamed 'Football Match', and had identified the real name of the mysterious 'Becker'.[7]

What the group needed above all was money, and in April 1946, Barbie met Naumann and Barkhausen at the house of one Fridolin Becker in Kassel to discuss their parlous financial situation. Barbie suggested a remedy that would be risky, but would certainly improve matters. He had heard that a Baroness von Forster had recently been released from custody for dealing in foodstuffs on the black market, but her main activity was buying up jewellery in order to safeguard herself against any currency devaluation. Apparently, she had already converted a 'considerable part' of her fortune into gems, and Barbie suggested that the family should be given 'an opportunity of serving their fatherland'. Naumann and Barkhausen knew exactly what that meant, and the three men started to plan a raid.[8]

At quarter to ten on the evening of 19 April, Baroness von Forster answered the door of her home in Parkstrasse in Kassel. She was surprised to find three policemen standing there, one of whom told her that she had been denounced for dealing in gemstones on the black market. The baroness denied this, but the three men entered her flat and began to make a perfunctory search. The senior policeman asked to see her jewellery, and among it he found some precious stones wrapped up in a piece of paper. He used this as a pretext to confiscate the entire collection, and then informed the baroness that she would need to come down to the police station. When they reached the bottom of the stairs, the policeman told the baroness to return to her flat to fetch her identity papers. When she did so, the three men disappeared. Barbie, who had played the part of the senior policeman, estimated their haul to be worth some fifty thousand to a hundred thousand marks.[9]

Throughout 1946, Barbie operated within the seedy world of Nazis and conmen. As well as selling off the jewellery, Barbie's other source of income appeared to be dealing in forged ration cards and identity forms, and those other black-market staples, cigarettes and coffee. Barbie continued his activities for the ODS, and in the autumn of 1946 he attended important meetings of senior members in Dortmund and Hamburg.[10] His role within the group was procuring money, radio equipment and printing presses, and at one point, Barbie claimed that he had learned how to forge some three hundred different documents.[11] For the time being, the Allies were playing a waiting game with the group, as they wished to gather more intelligence before making any arrests. However, Barbie narrowly avoided being captured in Marburg in August 1946, when a German woman who was riding in a jeep pointed out Barbie to her American driver. The vehicle drew up alongside him, and Barbie was ordered into it. 'I knew they were taking me to prison,' he recalled. 'Marburg has very narrow streets, and when we reached the post office, we had to slow down to let a tram pass. I then thought, "It's now or never!"'[12] To a gasp from the pedestrians, Barbie jumped out and ran down an alley. The American driver crashed into a tree, but recovered his composure quickly enough to take a shot at Barbie. A bullet grazed his finger, but Barbie was able to scramble over a wall. He hid in the house of a woman who would subsequently tell the American search party that she had seen their quarry run past and jump over a hedge.

In Hamburg on 12 November Barbie would get into a worse scrape. That evening, he and two fellow ODS members were on a tram when Barbie noticed that a car with British police markings was following them. Barbie and his associates alighted from the tram at the railway station, and as they made their way to their train, they were grabbed by members of the British Field Security Section. 'Well, my friend,' said the British captain, 'we are not the Americans. You are not going to run away from us!' Barbie would later claim that he was taken into an office and then beaten up, an act of savagery which would cause him to be anti-British for the rest of his life. Although it is not known whether Barbie talked, there was scarcely a need to make him, because the British had found his notebook. Inside it was a record of his activities and, crucially, the names and addresses of scores of contacts. It was a bad mistake for a former Gestapo officer to have made. For two days the men languished in their cells in a converted coal cellar. However, on the evening of the 14th, Barbie managed to break his cell's lock with a piece of scrap iron, and the three men crept past their guard, who was engrossed in playing his flute. Barbie made it back to Kassel, where, on 11 December, he was present for the birth of his second child, Klaus-Jörg.[13]

In early February 1947, the British and the Americans decided to break up not only the ODS but various other resistance organizations they had been monitoring for the past several months, which included one with the ominous-sounding name 'Organization for Bacteriological Warfare Research'. On the night of the 22nd–23rd of that month, Operation Selection Board was mounted, during which ninety-six members of these groups were arrested.[14] One of the most important targets was Barbie himself, whose notebook proved invaluable for tracking down the suspects. However, that night, Barbie was staying not at his usual address in Marburg, but instead at the home of his friend Fridolin Becker in Kassel. As Becker too was a target, the CIC paid his home a visit in the small hours.

During the raid, Barbie had just enough time to hide in the bathroom and then jump out of a window at the rear of the building. He made his escape through the garden and into the night.[15] Once again, Barbie was on his own.

The former 'Butcher of Lyon' appeared to live a charmed life. However, there is evidence to suggest that Barbie's constant wriggling from the clutches of the Allies had more to do with underhand dealings than good fortune. The first indication that Barbie may have been making 'arrangements' with his would-be captors lies in the nature of his relationship with Emil Hoffmann. The information gathered from those arrested during Selection Board reveals that Barbie knew exactly where Hoffmann's real loyalties lay: with the British. 'Without doubt, Barbi has known for several months,' stated an American Top Secret intelligence report in May 1947. 'It is believed that Barbi made use of Hoffmann and by cooperating with the British he hoped to be saved from being delivered to the French.'[16] A British report from the same month almost confirms the Americans' belief.

It is quite clear from later reports received from HOFFMANN that BARBI @ BECKER knew that HOFFMANN was in touch with us and it was apparent that BARBI was trying to sell us, through HOFFMANN, the idea of using him against the Russians. Furthermore, it seemed that both HOFFMANN and BARBI attributed their escape from the SELECTION BOARD arrests . . .

Frustratingly, the document is redacted at this point. It is not unlikely that the two men felt that they had been allowed to escape by the British, and the fact that the document is cut would support this.

As it happened, Barbie had nothing to escape from, as he was never even targeted by Selection Board. The very next paragraph of the document states: 'Furthermore, whereas BARBI had been omitted from the SELECTION BOARD target list on general agreement with 16 (HAMBURG) Intelligence Office, HQ Intelligence Division and CIC, HQ EUCOM . . .'[17] This sentence is crucial, as it clearly shows that Barbie was protected by at least three Allied intelligence agencies. There can be no doubt that Barbie was already working in some capacity for both Allies, and they were keen to protect him, despite their awareness of the monstrosity of his crimes. A CIA report made in 1974 shows that Barbie was certainly working for the CIC in 1946 as 'a valuable source'.[18] Barbie's arrest in Hamburg the previous November had in fact been an error, as a British Top Secret report revealed in December 1946. 'Early in November Col. BECKER or BARBI, Dr. WILKENNING and another were inadvertently arrested. They escaped within 24 hours but not before a mass of addresses and useful documents had been taken from them.'[19] It is possible that the three men were allowed to escape, although this cannot be proved. Some time later, Barbie would tell the Americans that his arrest in Hamburg made him lose 'all interest in the British, and all faith in their promises'.[20] It is not known what promises – if any – the British made to Barbie, but it is feasible that they would have guaranteed his freedom in return for information.

However, soon after Operation Selection Board, the British decided that they did want to arrest Barbie.[21] Unfortunately, they had no clue as to where the former Gestapo man had gone to ground, and as a result, Emil Hoffmann was arrested and interrogated. Hoffmann told the British that Barbie would be in Munich in mid- to late May, and could be found in either the Humpelmayer restaurant or the Roxy restaurant between noon and two o'clock every day from the 15th to the 21st.[22] Hoffmann warned the British that Barbie would be a hard man to catch. 'Before B goes into a public house he takes precautions,' he wrote on 6 May from his cell in the British military prison in Nenndorf. 'It is by no means certain that if the police locate him in a public house they will catch him. He avoids capture freely in spite of all dispositions.' Hoffmann also indicated that Barbie and his wife, whom he described as 'capable, clever and adaptable, working with him one hundred per cent', might be in the mountains in Reichenhall, Berchtesgaden or Garmisch.[23]

Barbie was in none of these places, and even if the British had arrested Barbie and asked him to work for them, they would have found that the Americans had got there first. On 28 March 1947, one month after the Selection Board arrests, Barbie was standing at Memmingen railway station when he spotted a familiar face. It belonged to Kurt Merk, a former Abwehr officer from Dijon who had collaborated with Barbie during the war, penetrating French resistance networks.[24] Merk was now working for the CIC in the Munich area, and running a network of agents for CIC officer Robert S. Taylor. Merk immediately recognized the value that Barbie might bring to his organization, and he hired him with the approval of Taylor and Taylor's chief, Lieutenant Colonel Dale Garvey, who stipulated that Barbie should 'break off any connections he may have with illegal SS elements and Selection Board personalities'.[25] Barbie was obviously keen to impress his new employers, as Taylor regarded him as 'an honest man, both intellectually and personally, absolutely without nerves or fear'.[26] Even when Barbie started in his new line of work for the CIC, other elements of the CIC were still looking to arrest him. In April and May, the CIC searched for Barbie in Stuttgart and Marburg, and it was not until the end of May that the Corps' headquarters realized that their men were chasing a man who had effectively become one of their own. Taylor clarified matters for his superiors and requested that his new source should 'be allowed to retain his freedom as long as he works for this agent'. He added that Barbie's 'value as an informant infinitely outweighs any use he may have in prison'.[27] The lack of response from CIC headquarters was taken as de facto approval, and Barbie would soon go on to become an essential part of Merk's network, which was codenamed 'Büro Petersen'.

Taylor's employment of a criminal such as Barbie did not necessarily go against CIC guidelines. In May 1947, the CIC issued a directive explaining that although it was desirable to use agents whose ideals were similar to those of the United States, this did not exclude using 'an informant of the "stab-your-neighbour" type if it seems that there is definite value to be obtained thereby. It is realized that all types of characters must be used in order to obtain adequate coverage.'[28] In fact, the CIC had no policy of forbidding the use of former Nazis, and as a result, there was nothing wrong – in the eyes of the CIC – with Taylor and Garvey employing a man like Barbie.[29] Even if this entailed a certain moral queasiness, it was felt that the intelligence war against the Communists could not be won with a clean fight. As we shall see, the Americans were not the only nation using Nazi criminals as intelligence assets, and not to have done so would have put them at a disadvantage. The CIC's position was the time-honoured one of 'my enemy's enemy is my friend', combined with the consequentialist attitude of ends justifying means. In the war against the Soviets, head boys with spotless records did not necessarily make the best operatives.

Throughout 1947, the CIC was delighted with Barbie's work. Taylor's replacement, Special Agent Camille S. Hajdu, reported that Barbie had been furnishing 'this organization with extremely good material'. Merk's new agent was so impressive that he was soon made his deputy, and took over the part of the network that investigated French intelligence activities in the American and French zones of Germany. So, once again, Barbie was working against the French – all that had changed was his master. 'In this capacity,' Hajdu reported, 'subject has so far demonstrated exceedingly impressive results.'[30]

Despite his 'good work', there were elements within the CIC who wished to question Barbie about his knowledge of former SS men and membership of the ODS. In October, the operations officer at CIC headquarters ordered Garvey to have Barbie arrested and brought to the Intelligence Centre at the European Command (EUCOM) near Frankfurt for a 'detailed interrogation'. Hajdu and Garvey protested, because such a move would severely weaken Merk's network, but their protests were ignored. After a few weeks of increasingly tetchy memoranda, Barbie was arrested on 11 December.

Barbie's interrogators barely concerned themselves with his wartime activities. Instead, the focus of their questioning was directed towards their informant's contacts with former SS men and post-war Nazi networks. Barbie was held for five months, and although he admitted that he had been in Lyon, he was un-surprisingly unforthcoming about his activities there, and did not admit his Gestapo membership. His interrogators could have given him a harder time – Barbie was listed as being a Gestapo officer and wanted by the French for murder in the CROWCASS list – but the Americans simply did not want to know. By May, they were ready to let him resume his work. The CIC acknowledged that Barbie did fall under the automatic arrest category, but it had no wish to imprison him, as 'his knowledge as to the mission of CIC, its agents, funds, etc. is too great'. If Barbie were to have escaped, then he could have handed all his information over to another intelligence service. It was a risk the CIC was not minded to take, and on 10 May 1948, Barbie was ordered back to Memmingen.[31]

However, before he went, he had to face one more interrogation – from the French. During the previous autumn, Louis Bibes, a French counter-intelligence agent operating in Germany, had heard rumours that Barbie was working for the Americans. After many weeks of negotiations, the CIC finally allowed Bibes to see him. On 14 May, the Frenchman interviewed Barbie in an old office block in Höchst near Frankfurt. Accompanied by a CIC officer, Barbie came across as a 'thin and extremely nervous man', who denied his real identity. 'I told him we had incontestable proof that he was Barbie,' Bibes recalled, 'but he continued to deny it.' This line of questioning did not impress the CIC officer, who ended the session after only ten minutes. However, Bibes was able to question Barbie again on 16 July in Munich, where he found a far more composed individual, who now admitted that he was Barbie. 'A tough cookie,' Bibes commented to the CIC man.[32] The chief line of questioning concerned the mystery of who had betrayed Jean Moulin to the Gestapo. The French suspected René Hardy, whom they would put on trial, but much to their frustration Barbie told them nothing. 'They were ready to tear him apart,' recalled John Willms, a CIC officer. 'I'd say the guy was taunting the French. He felt so secure, he could give them smart answers.'[33] Barbie had clearly received strong guarantees from the CIC that he would not be handed over to the French. The CIC had to keep its word, as it knew that if it gained a reputation for double-crossing its informants, such sources of information would soon dry up.[34]

In June, the Merk network was assigned a new CIC officer called Erhard Dabringhaus, whose family had emigrated from Germany to the United States in 1930 because of his father's disgust at Nazism. Dabringhaus found Barbie arrogant and condescending, his attitude a product of his sense of inviolable security. 'The whole situation seemed to me to be very unprofessional,' Dabringhaus later wrote. 'I was given the impression that I was there as a mere errand boy for Barbie and his friends . . . He was apparently calling all the shots.'[35] Barbie and Merk were also becoming greedy, and despite receiving some $1,700 per month, they claimed that they needed as much as $2,500 – some $35,000 in 2007. 'Dabringhaus, you've got to impress upon your supervisors that I need more money,' Barbie told him, 'especially real dollars, to operate efficiently. I really do believe I'm worth more money than I'm getting. I can barely take care of my sub-sources.'[36] Even at $1,700 per month, the Americans were not getting good value. Dabringhaus once caught Barbie dictating a newspaper report to a secretary and attempting to pass it off as his own intelligence. When Dabringhaus remonstrated with him, Barbie complained that the CIC was applying too much pressure to get good information.[37] In truth, the Merk–Barbie network was getting flabby, with informants and sub-sources scattered all over Eastern Europe, whose 'product' was often dubious. The network was further hampered by having three separate roles, all of which were overly ambitious. As well as spying on the Soviets, the group had to produce counter-intelligence against the French, as well as monitoring the activities of the Communist Party in Bavaria.[38] At this time, Barbie's supposed biggest coup was the revelation that the Czechs were mining uranium, which indicated a Soviet atomic-weapons project. Dabringhaus was delighted, but as it was later discovered that the Czechs had mined uranium before the war, the intelligence was perhaps not that explosive.[39] By October, CIC headquarters was tiring of the network and wanted to drop it, but a three-month stay of execution was negotiated. Barbie and Merk worked hard to justify their place on the CIC payroll, but finally, in April 1949, the *Büro Petersen* was disbanded.[40] However, one man from the network was kept on as an informer: Barbie.

While Barbie continued to provide information on Bavarian communists, the French intensified their demands that the 'Butcher of Lyon' should face justice. On 14 May 1949, a newspaper in Paris ran a report headlined: 'Arrest Barbie our Torturer!' The article revealed that Barbie was working as a 'peaceable businessman in Munich', and that two French resistance organizations had written to the US ambassador in Paris demanding that he be handed over.[41] The CIC headquarters directed Barbie's handlers to drop Barbie 'administratively', but to maintain the relationship.[42] Captain Eugene Kolb of the CIC in Augsburg, which was running Barbie, reacted negatively, and said that although Barbie had admitted to having used 'duress during interrogations', he had never tortured anybody. Kolb also bullishly pointed out that if the French authorities really did believe Barbie was a war criminal, 'it is almost certain that SUBJECT [i.e. Barbie] would have been extradited by now'. Furthermore, Kolb regarded Barbie as 'the most reliable informant this headquarters has', and he was in no mind to give him up.[43] Kolb's position – if he genuinely did believe Barbie's assertions – was not unreasonable. The French had not applied for extradition, and handing over seemingly good agents simply because of hearsay reports in Parisian newspapers was no way to run an intelligence organization in the new cold and dirty war. Although Kolb did not state it, there was always the danger that if Barbie were handed over to the French, he would simply tell the French all he knew about American operations. CIC headquarters clearly accepted the thrust of Kolb's argument, because for the next six months, until January 1950, no mention was made of Barbie in any of the correspondence between CIC headquarters and CIC in Augsburg.

France was not to make a formal request for Barbie to be handed over until 7 November 1949, when its embassy in Washington, DC delivered a formal note to the State Department insisting that 'this war criminal be arrested and placed before French justice'. The Americans fudged, and told the French that they needed to apply to the US High Commissioner in Germany (HICOG) via the French High Commissioner in Baden-Baden.[44] However, the French were not about to give up, especially as the trial of René Hardy was about to open, which was predicted to bring Barbie into the spotlight. On 2 March 1950, France made another formal request through the offices of the two nations' High Commissions. Amazingly, HICOG claimed never to have heard of Barbie, and that 'the inference of the several communications from the French authorities that Barbie is being granted refuge in the US zone is unjustified and un-warranted'.[45] Even if HICOG were being sincere, it would have been straightforward to have established whether there was any con-nection with Barbie simply by consulting the EUCOM and its Intelligence Centre. As it did not do this, and yet informed the French that efforts to trace Barbie had 'proved unsuccessful', the very best assessment that can be attributed to HICOG's actions is that it was incompetent.[46] At the worst, HICOG was taking part in a conspiratorial cover-up, but the documents do not support this. The most reasonable explanation is that the Americans were being disingenuous and buying time, a tactic they had adopted ever since the French had shown an interest in Barbie.

In April, proceedings against René Hardy opened, and the name of Barbie hung over the trial. Hardy's lawyer referred to Barbie as a man 'who had taken pleasure in torturing French patriots', and the judge labelled him 'a sinister torturer and war criminal'.[47] The French senate and the press echoed such sentiments, and by the beginning of May, HICOG was privately acknowledging that its refutation of the French claim that the Americans were sheltering Barbie was 'accurate insofar as any official information is available to this headquarters'.[48] These were the words of an amateur weasel, and they only emphasize the likelihood that plenty of unofficial information was on hand. Despite growing pressure, the Americans still did little, and soon even their embassy in Paris was complaining. 'We are anxious that it be understood in HICOG that the matter continues to be embarrassing to us,' wrote Woodruff Wallner of the embassy to HICOG in June. 'The problem is what to do about the apparently widespread belief that Barbier [*sic*] was not only employed by us in the past but continues to be employed by us at present, and that we are blocking his extradition.'[49]

As 1950 wore on, it became clear to HICOG, EUCOM and the CIC that a decision had to be reached. While his employers deliberated, Barbie was accommodated at a CIC safe house in Augsburg with his family, and he continued with his intelligence work. Despite the guarantees that he had been given by the CIC, Barbie grew increasingly worried that the French might kidnap him, which was a distinct possibility. Barbie's new CIC handler, Herbert Bechtold, noticed a marked change in Barbie and his family. 'They were entirely at our mercy,' he recalled. 'Barbie resented it deeply that he was not a master of his destiny. He was anxious, insecure, depressed. He felt he had no future to look forward to.'[50]

At the end of the year, a way out for Barbie and the CIC presented itself. In December, Lieutenant John Hobbins of the Augsburg CIC visited the offices of the CIC in Salzburg. There, he discovered that his colleagues had been running an operation since 1947 that could possibly solve the problem of what to do with Barbie and his family.

'The 430th CIC Detachment has been operating what they term a "Ratline" evacuation system to Central and South America without serious repercussions during these past three years,' Hobbins reported. This 'Ratline', which was employed to get CIC informants out of Europe, was supervised by CIC agent George Neagoy, who told Hobbins that he would help the Augsburg CIC get their man out. In his report, Hobbins also told his superiors about the mechanics of the Ratline, including its cost, which was a thousand dollars per adult, although 'VIP treatment' was available at $1,400. The route ran from Germany, through Austria and into Italy, where it culminated in Genoa. The one thing Hobbins was not told was the identity of the man who operated the Ratline. Hobbins might not have heard of him, but a Nazi such as Klaus Barbie may have done, because that man was none other than Father Krunoslav Draganović.

Much has been written about the Ratline and the CIC's use of Draganović. Today, the term 'ratline' is often ascribed to all the escape routes the Nazis employed to flee Europe. This is misleading, as it was not used contemporaneously, and also suggests that the routes were clearly defined, which, as we have seen, they were not. In the 1940s and the 1950s, the term was actually applied to any of the routes that the Americans used to get their informants away from danger. One CIC group, for example, operated a ratline that ran from Hungary into Austria, and had nothing to do with Draganović.[51] Furthermore, the Ratline operated by the CIC in Salzburg was not a method by which the Americans were cynically helping scores of Nazis to escape, but a covert way in which defectors and informants who had supplied useful information to the United States could be assisted. Those who travelled down the Ratline were not Nazi war criminals, but people who the CIC felt were genuinely deserving, in the words of one of the Ratline's founders, of 'a reward for services'.[52] As the formal route of offering US citizenship would have involved bureaucrats in the State Department and the Immigration and Naturalization Service asking too many awkward questions, the Ratline was a covert and yet reliable way to help those who had helped them. Despite the use of a criminal such as Draganović, the motives for establishing the Ratline were in fact born out of decency and a desire not to gain a reputation for maltreating defectors and informants. The CIC was

simply one of Draganović's clients, and to the CIC officers at the
time, paying a man like Draganović made much practical sense. Jim
Milano, the CIC officer who established the Ratline, later claimed to
be fully aware of such issues. 'Anyone we help is to be a bona fide
defector from the Soviets,' he recalled saying. 'No Nazis, no SS, no
SD, no nothing like that, no war profiteers or war criminals. I don't
like the idea that we may be subsidizing this Draganovic's other
operations [. . .] but at least we can limit our dealings to strictly our
own business.'[53] Of course, it is easy to doubt Milano's words, but
there is no evidence that indicates that the Ratline established by the
430th CIC in Salzburg was used to transport Nazis – with one
notable exception.

On or around 25 January 1951, EUCOM gave the approval for
Barbie and his family to use the Ratline to get to Bolivia.[54] From
then until March, various US agencies started assembling a new
identity in the name of 'Klaus Altmann', a name which was probably designated by Draganović. The CIC supplied the United States'
Combined Travel Board with bogus information about 'Altmann'
that ensured that Barbie was issued with a temporary travel document numbered 0121454 in lieu of a passport. The Board also
provided an Austrian transit visa and a Trieste military entry permit.
In Munich, the Italian consulate issued the 'Altmanns' a travel visa
to pass through Italy on their way down to Genoa. By the end of
February, all was ready, and on 9 March, George Neagoy and
another CIC agent escorted the 'Butcher of Lyon' and his family
from Augsburg to Salzburg.[55] After two nights in the Austrian city,
the family departed by train to Trieste. On the Austrian–Italian
border, Barbie claimed a customs official spotted something wrong
with his papers. 'Look,' Barbie pleaded, 'I've got two children.' The
customs official replied, 'Get going, and I don't want to see you
again.' Barbie assured him that he wouldn't.[56] The family arrived in
Genoa on 12 March, and was accommodated by Draganović at the
Hotel Nazionale.[57] The priest then escorted Barbie around Genoa
securing the next round of paperwork, which included an immigrant
visa to Bolivia, a travel permit from the Red Cross and an
Argentinian transit visa. When Barbie asked Draganović why he was
helping him, the Croatian replied, 'We've got to keep a sort of
reserve on which we can draw in the future.'[58] Eleven days later, on

23 March, Klaus Barbie and his family embarked on the Italian boat *Corrientes*, bound for Buenos Aires. On 3 April, the CIC in Augsburg congratulated everybody for the 'extremely efficient manner' in which the 'final disposal of an extremely sensitive individual' was dealt with. 'This case is considered closed,' the report stated, with some relief.[59] In just under thirty-two years, it would be reopened with spectacular results, but for the time being, the 'Butcher of Lyon' was safe.

Klaus Barbie was not the only Nazi war criminal to be employed by the United States in its intelligence war against Communism. And, as we shall see, neither was the United States the only country using those of the Barbie ilk. In fact, not employing Nazis was the exception rather than the rule, and any country that remonstrated another for doing so was almost certainly being hypocritical. The British, the French and the Russians all exploited characters who they should have incarcerated, but at the time the exigencies of the Cold War demanded that niceties such as 'justice' were put to one side. Today, it is easy to be moralistic about such activity, but this is to ignore the reality of espionage work and the scale of the perceived risk that the Allies faced from the Soviets. It matters not one iota whether that perception was subsequently shown to be inaccurate, because such *a posteriori* evidence was not available to men such as Kolb and Dabringhaus. As many Nazi criminals such as Barbie had access to information behind the Iron Curtain, it was reasonable to side with the position that demanded that dirty deals had to be done in the cause of the greater goods of democracy and liberalism. It is also irrelevant whether the intelligence gained from these agents ended up being worthless, because that could not possibly have been established prior to their exploitation.

Certainly, there were some within the intelligence community who felt that old-fashioned spies would be useless in the Cold War. One of them was Commander Wilfred 'Biffy' Dunderdale of MI6, who in 1939 had smuggled an intact German Enigma machine captured by the Poles into London 'in a heavily escorted diplomatic bag'.[60] In August 1945, Dunderdale held several meetings with the OSS in France, in which he expressed his conviction that it would 'not be possible to produce any regular and reliable flow of intelligence on Russia by agent penetration'. Dunderdale held to the view that the best way to produce results was through the development and application of technology, and in many ways, he was to be proved right.[61] The French also had little faith in agents, and told the OSS that they estimated no less than 95 per cent of their agents operating in the Russian zone of Germany, Russian-occupied territory and even the French zone of Germany were double agents. The French suspected that this high proportion would apply to other countries' intelligence services. 'In the light of this conviction,' reported Philip Horton of the OSS Mission to France, 'they are pinning almost all their hopes for intelligence on Russia on the technical services and the intercept system.'[62] The American intelligence agencies were less cynical about human intelligence, with the result that numerous former Nazis, criminal or not, had to be exploited in order to have any chance of gathering valuable information. Groups such as the SHAEF Counter Intelligence War Room (SCI) were so keen to exploit former Nazis that they soon found themselves running foul of the US Military Government guidelines. As early as August 1945, Captain Eric W. Timm of the SCI in Munich complained to his superiors that 'the proscribed list of persons has now grown so large that no former member of the Nazi party or Army officer, to say nothing of GIS [German Intelligence Services] personnel, can be hired'.[63]

One Nazi employed by the United States, almost as soon as he was arrested in May 1945, was Wilhelm Höttl. Even in August, there was talk about the 'Höttl exploitation' in the SCI, but with too many rumours suggesting that Höttl was utterly untrustworthy, the Americans decided not to use him.[64] Instead, Höttl was confined in an internment camp, where he was employed as an 'indigenous interrogator'. This meant that he had the opportunity to learn an enormous amount about SS and SD operations from his fellow prisoners, knowledge that he would put to good use over the coming years.[65] In October 1947, he was transferred from the camp to Salzburg, where he awaited trial before the Austrian People's Court in Vienna. However, through the mediation of Iris Scheidler, the wily Höttl managed to convince the head of the local CIC that he would be of some use, and so he was released on the condition that he would keep the Americans informed of his activities.[66] Höttl set to work establishing his private intelligence network, and by the autumn of 1948, he persuaded the CIC to sponsor two networks codenamed 'Mount Vernon' and 'Montgomery'.[67] The former aimed at penetrating Höttl's old stomping ground, Hungary, while the latter sought to gather intelligence from the Soviet zone of Austria. As an Austrian intelligence officer who had worked in Hungary, on the surface Höttl seemed the ideal figure for such a role, but in fact he was no such thing. The 'intelligence' gathered by Höttl was extremely poor, and largely fabricated by him or rehashed from journalistic sources. In addition, he embezzled funds which were meant for operational purposes and, worse still, the Americans strongly suspected that his loyalties lay elsewhere. 'Investigation and surveillance had established that HOETTL was in contact with Soviet intelligence,' stated one CIC report, 'and the suspicion was very strong that HOETTL was acting as a double agent under Soviet control.'[68]

In August 1949, the CIC dropped Höttl and his groups, which were costing $2,600 per month. 'Hoettl is considered an excellent intelligence man,' wrote Jim Milano, 'but an extremely dangerous one.'[69] Understandably, Höttl reacted badly to being dropped quite so swiftly. 'During the 10 months of our activity we rendered you 618 reports from line Montgomery and 1600 reports from line Mount Vernon,' he informed Milano. 'As to the quality of reports you will admit, that I, as a former leading functionary of the German secret service, was able to form a somewhat correct judgement.'[70] Höttl's arrogance was boundless but, in truth, he was little more than a bullshitter par excellence, who was able – for a time – to convince the less experienced American intelligence officers of the value of his work. The regular turnover of CIC staff meant that those such as Barbie and Höttl could get away with spinning many a yarn, but the Americans soon got wise. Those who didn't included Simon Wiesenthal, who, as we have seen, employed Höttl as a source; it is thanks to that relationship that our knowledge of the post-war Nazi escape networks has been so perverted. The link between the two men would also be responsible for the perversion of another element of the story, which we will come to later.

If the CIC had a few qualms about hiring former Nazis, then

Höttl had none whatsoever. An important figure in the Montgomery network was Károly Ney, a Hungarian of German descent who had served in the Hungarian army until 1943. Under the stewardship of Höttl, Ney had joined the SS, and in October 1944, he established the *SS-Regimentsgruppe Ney*, which was tasked with the 'liquidation of Jews, defeatists, saboteurs, and others inside Hungary'.[71] Ney had also supported the overthrow of Admiral Horthy, which had been so daringly executed by another of Ney's sponsors, Otto Skorzeny.[72] On 1 March 1945, Ney's regiment captured eight downed US airmen, and after it had handed three over to the Germans, the remainder were executed near the town of Súr, about 50 miles west of Budapest. In 1946, Ney and five members of his unit were put on trial and Ney was sentenced to death. However, in August, his sentence was commuted to life imprisonment, and during the following year he was released in order to form the *Keleti Arcvonal Bajtársi Szövetség* (KABSz – Alliance of Eastern Front Veterans) with the alleged backing of the CIC, the Vatican and Franco. The aim of the KABSz was to raise an underground anti-Soviet resistance group in Hungary, and, according to one report, he received 275,000 Austrian schillings from 'US intelligence authorities for his preliminary work'. Based in Salzburg, Ney set up a 'Partisan Training Centre' 50 miles east in Gmunden, where his associates were supposedly in contact with the CIC.[73] It is more than likely that Ney did enjoy the backing – or at least the blind eye – of the Americans, as an operation of such a scale could not have been mounted without their knowledge.

In 1948, Höttl hired Ney to be the operations officer for the Montgomery network, for which he was paid seven thousand schillings per month. In addition, the CIC provided food for ten men, which suggests that the Americans continued to support Ney's partisan group.[74] However, Ney and Höttl did not get along, with Höttl accusing the Hungarian of having a *Führercomplex*, which was probably accurate.[75] There was also a strong suspicion that Ney was working for French intelligence, a suspicion that was all but confirmed by the fact that Ney had twice met General Pierre Koenig, the French military governor in Germany,[76] and that he also possessed a French passport that enabled him to enter Italy.[77] In January 1949, Ney asked Höttl to give him twenty thousand schillings in order to visit Franco in Spain, but Höttl refused. As a result, Ney was sacked from Montgomery for 'operational incompetence', and moved into the French zone of Austria, a further indication that he was employed by France.[78] Although the two men would never work together again, Höttl kept himself aware of Ney's activities. In March 1949, he noted how the Hungarian had been ordered by the French to 'clarify' the connections of former Nazis with the Vatican as they emigrated to the Arab states, Spain and South America.[79]

If this is correct, then it emphatically reveals that the French were not only investigating the Nazi escape networks, but they had also employed a Nazi criminal who was as murderous as Klaus Barbie. The French must have been aware of this double standard, and it is perhaps for this reason that they did not lobby for Barbie's release as aggressively as they might, fearing that the Americans would reveal their employment of Nazis, for Ney was not the first the French had employed. In March 1946, the OSS reported that the French intelligence service BDOC was setting free former Gestapo officers in order to exploit them. The American source for this information was graded as being 'well-tried and reliable . . . with good contacts in France and Germany'.[80]

Barbie, Höttl and Ney comprised a small minority of the Nazi war criminals that American agencies such as the CIC were to hire after the war. Others included Robert Jan Verbelen, a member of the Flemish SS who was responsible for the deaths of at least 101 people in terrorist actions in wartime Belgium. As the leader of the *Veiligheidskorps* (Security Corps), Verbelen personally carried out some of these assassinations, which even included hand-grenade attacks on cafés and bars. His actions earned him the German War Meritorious Cross and promotion to *Hauptsturmführer* and, after the war, a death sentence from a Belgian court which tried him *in absentia*. Nevertheless, in 1946, Verbelen was employed by the CIC in Austria to help execute Project Newton, which was an operation to penetrate the Austrian Communist Party. Unsurprisingly, Verbelen's sources included numerous Nazi criminals, and by the end of 1950, the operation was dropped, although Verbelen would continue as a source until the mid-1950s.[81] Verbelen was granted

Austrian citizenship in 1959, but six years later, he was tried for war crimes. Sensationally, he was acquitted, and Verbelen would remain a free man until his death in 1990.

It is clear that working for the Allies was often as effective a means of escape for Nazi war criminals as clandestine emigration to South America. In one way, it was superior, as the criminals were often free to remain in their home country and benefit from the protection of the intelligence service for which they had worked. One Nazi who would enjoy such treatment was Horst Kopkow, a former *Hauptsturmführer* in the Gestapo, who was arrested in a village on the Baltic coast by the British on 29 May 1945. Almost as soon as they detained him, the British knew they had quite a catch, as Kopkow's wartime role had been to capture enemy spies and saboteurs, which naturally included British SOE agents. As the head of *Referat* IV A 2 in Kaltenbrunner's RSHA, it was Kopkow's office that ensured such agents were brutally interrogated and then 'disappeared' to concentration camps such as Buchenwald and Ravensbrück. It has been estimated that Kopkow was responsible for the deaths of around three hundred Allied agents, who included the celebrated Violette Szabo and Noor Inayat Khan. Another victim was MI6 agent Major Frank Chamier, who had parachuted into Germany but had been captured almost immediately and taken to Sachsenhausen and Ravensbrück, where he died.[82] As well as organizing such executions, Kopkow had an intimate knowledge of the RSHA's counter-intelligence operations against both the British and the Russians. In Holland, the Gestapo enjoyed considerable success against the SOE with Operation North Pole, in which it had played back radio transmissions to London with false information. The devastating effect of this was the capture of fifty-four British agents, of whom forty-seven were executed through the auspices of Kopkow.[83] Against the Soviet-backed Red Orchestra spy network, Kopkow was similarly effective. He personally arrested many of the group's leading members, including Harro Schulze-Boysen, who was a first lieutenant on the Luftwaffe's Leadership Staff. It was Kopkow who sanctioned the torture of men such as Schulze-Boysen, who was executed at Plötzensee Prison in Berlin in December 1942.[84]

Kopkow was canny enough to give his captors what they wanted.

'Kopkow realised fully his situation,' his interrogators reported, 'and knows it is hardly possible for him to hide much or cover up his activities. [. . .] His attitude is that his only chance for a milder judgement is to tell as much as possible. He also declares he is fully prepared to make any declaration of loyalty required.'[85] This last sentence certainly gives the impression that Kopkow was either offering his services, or accepting an offer. Whatever the case, Kopkow certainly talked. The British even supplied him with his former secretary, Fräulein Bertha Rose, and instead of a traditional question-and-answer format, the interrogation involved little more than the British officers listening to Kopkow dictate to Fräulein Rose. 'He was allowed more or less complete freedom,' the report stated, 'and was seldom interrupted.'[86] Kopkow only seemed to stray from the truth when it came to the case of Major Chamier, who he claimed had died in an air raid in Berlin. The intelligence officers appeared to believe this, perhaps because they were inwardly jubilant at the riches that Kopkow was handing them. The former Gestapo man even told them about Russian plots against Britain, for which Kopkow had 'radio proof' – evidence gathered by radio intercepts.[87] At one point, the information was of such good value that one interrogator wondered whether Kopkow was 'deliberately trying to throw suspicion between the English and the Russians or is he genuinely telling matter of facts [sic]'.[88]

While British intelligence officers questioned Kopkow, British war crimes investigators were trying to find him. Among them was Vera Atkins, the SOE leader who had briefed many of the agents whose executions Kopkow had processed. Attached to the office of the Judge Advocate General, throughout 1946 Atkins found the name 'Kopkow' cropping up with increasing frequency. By the summer, she had ascertained the extent of Kopkow's criminality, and before she departed for London in August, she issued an urgent request to the Haystack section of the British War Crimes Group in North West Europe.

Kopkow is wanted in connection with deaths of British agents in Nazi concentration camps, particularly Natzweiler and Dachau. All reports and documents of captured agents were sent to Kopkow. And he ordered their removal to concentration camps and liquidation. If

arrested please advise VMA [Vera May Atkins] in the UK. He was
last known at the Reichssicherheitshauptamt [RSHA] Amt IV.[89]

In September, Atkins was shocked to discover from one of the war
crimes suspects she was interrogating that Kopkow was in British
hands. She told Haystack that Kopkow was probably at the MI5
camp in the British Zone of Occupation at Bad Nenndorf. If
Haystack did indeed make any inquiries, then it is likely they would
have been politely brushed off.

As it was, Kopkow's capture by the British was not especially
secret. In October 1945, the Counter Intelligence Bureau of the
BAOR issued one of its fortnightly news sheets, in which it was
stated that information 'from KOPKOW and other officers' was
helping the British to build up a 'detailed picture of the Amt IV
division', which was the division to which Kopkow's *Referat* had
belonged. The news sheet, although it was graded 'Secret' – and not
'Top Secret' as many documents were – had a fairly wide
distribution.[90] The British Military *Arrestanstalt* had even reported
the amount of money Kopkow had on his person when he was
apprehended – 3,108 Reichsmarks – in a cable to the Control
Commission for Germany in July 1945, which was not graded with
any level of security.[91] Finally, on 15 March 1946, the Counter
Intelligence Bureau advised the JAG's office at the British War
Crimes Group that Kopkow was being held at Bad Nenndorf 'and
is likely to remain there for some time', which was an understatement. The letter also referred to the fact that the Americans
were interested in talking to Kopkow, and the Bureau promised to
tell the JAG's office when Kopkow was available for transfer.[92] As
this letter was written five months before Atkins made her request
to Haystack, it is clear that she had not been fully apprised of the
situation by her colleagues in the JAG's office. Whether this was by
accident or design, it is hard to tell. Once again, an attitude of
knowing cynicism seems attractive to adopt, and in this instance, it
is probably the correct one, as there was an enormous disparity in
attitudes held by British intelligence officers and British war crimes
investigators. The latter were still entrenched in the last war,
whereas the former were preparing for the next one. This is not to
state that the intelligence services were brilliantly far-sighted, or that

those on the war crimes teams were hopelessly backward looking, but there was certainly a difference in perspective. A sense of justice was common to all, but to an intelligence officer, a man such as Kopkow was far more valuable alive than at the end of a noose. When considering both the relatively ineffective efforts made to hunt down war criminals and operations such as Fleacomb in which so many were released, surely the odd Nazi mass murderer could be spared from justice in order to help fight the good fight against Communism? If that was the logic, then it was brutal but understandable.

Kopkow was held in Bad Nenndorf until 1947. According to his wife, Gerda, he was treated well, and the couple were even permitted to see each other in private. 'They were very kind to us,' Gerda remembered. 'One day they brought him to me and forgot to pick him up. We had a long time together.' During one of their earliest meetings in 1946, Kopkow convinced his wife that she had to abandon her belief in National Socialism. 'I was still a Nazi, even then,' she said. 'But he said no, no. It is not so important now.'[93] Gerda was surprised by the rapidity of Kopkow's conversion, but with the alternative being a death sentence, the former Gestapo officer had little choice. Although the meetings with his wife may have been pleasant, the encounters Kopkow had with war crimes investigators were less so. Kopkow was made available three times, twice to the British and once to the Norwegians. During one of his sessions with the British, he was asked about the fate of Major Chamier. When the name was mentioned, Kopkow is said to have nearly fainted and said, 'I don't know anything about that,' before asking for a glass of water. Kopkow did not deny that he had taken part in the interrogation of the MI6 agent, but he stuck to his story that Chamier had died in an air raid. The war crimes investigators did not believe him, but since he had the protection of MI6, there was little they could do. Vera Atkins also interrogated Kopkow, and was convinced of his guilt in the 'disappearance' of several of her agents. Despite being transferred to London in the middle of 1947, Kopkow was still pursued by the War Crimes Group, who understood that Kopkow would be prosecuted after his exploitation.[94]

By the end of the year, MI6 had clearly tired of the requests for

Kopkow to be brought to justice. It was time to bury him. In June 1948, a Lieutenant Colonel Paterson informed the War Crimes Group that there had been some bad news. Kopkow, he reported, had been sent to London for 'special interrogation', but when he arrived, 'he was found to be running a temperature and after two days he was sent to hospital, where we regret to say he died of Bronchopneumonia before any information was obtained from him'. Paterson included a copy of the death certificate, and added that Kopkow had been buried along with other German POWs in a military cemetery.[95]

Two years later, 'Peter Cordes' turned up at the home of Kopkow's widow in Gelsenkirchen in Germany. 'Uncle Peter', as the Kopkow children now had to call their father, started work at a textile factory in the British Zone of Occupation, although his real job was that of an MI6 agent. In order to maintain his cover, Kopkow and his wife even had to sleep in separate beds. Kopkow became a director of the factory, but he often made trips abroad on his own. It is unclear precisely what work he carried out for the British, but it is highly likely that he was organizing a network behind the Iron Curtain. It is also not known for how long 'Peter Cordes' acted as a British agent, but the fact that he changed his name to 'Horst Kopkow-Cordes' in 1956 suggests that his employment may have ended around that time. Until his actual death from, ironically enough, pneumonia in 1996, Kopkow lived largely un-molested by investigators or journalists. However, in 1986, he was discovered by the producer of a TV documentary called Robert Marshall. Kopkow would only speak to Marshall off the record, but Marshall recalled how 'he ranted and ranted and at one point said the British had scoured their prisons for low life and forced them to parachute into France and so killing them off was basically doing the British a service.'[96] Such a statement indicates that Kopkow was a man always in denial of the monstrosity of his crimes.

Judging the relative heinousness of war criminals is a difficult and perhaps unnecessary task, and the comparison of the numbers of those killed can too often reduce an assessment of criminals and their crimes to a kind of league table. Such a statistical approach to measuring moral turpitude would indicate that the murder of one hundred people is one hundred times worse than the killing of an individual, whereas morally mass murder is no greater a transgression than the murder of one man. The sin is the same, but repeated, and it is that repetition that courts of law rightly take into account. However, when comparing someone like Horst Kopkow to our next war criminal wooed by British intelligence, it is tempting to state that both the statistical magnitude and the level of immorality of Kopkow's crimes are insignificant when set against the actions of Viktors Arājs.

At four o'clock on the Sunday morning of 30 November 1941, German troops and Latvian policemen entered the Jewish ghetto in Riga. The Latvians were from the eponymous *Sonderkommando Arājs*, an SD unit which had taken part in numerous pogroms since the Nazis had invaded Latvia that summer. The three-hundred-strong unit was named after its leader, Viktors Arājs, a 31-year-old *SS-Sturmbannführer*, qualified lawyer and policeman, who had openly pandered to the Soviets during the Russian occupation. However, Arājs claimed that his adherence to Communism dwindled when he saw it in practice, and by the time the Germans entered Riga, he was conveniently ready to embrace the new political creed they had brought with them. On 1 July, Arājs presented himself to Franz Stahlecker, the commander of *Einsatzgruppe A*, and volunteered his services as well as those of a motley collection of students, policemen, fraternity members and soldiers that he claimed to lead.[97] Among them was a Latvian national hero, Herberts Cukurs, who had thrilled his fellow countrymen in the 1930s by his long-distance solo flights to Gambia and Tokyo. Although Reinhard Heydrich had not wished for the establishment of local killing units – he had advised that 'in their stead, it would be functional to unleash popular pogroms' – Arājs and his men soon proved to be willing helpers of the murderous *Einsatzgruppe*, which was tasked with eliminating Jews and other 'undesirables'.[98] At Bikernieki in southeastern Latvia, the Arājs Commando slaughtered four thousand Jews and a thousand communists between July and September 1941. The killings were carried out by groups of twenty men who would murder ten at a time, the victims simultaneously receiving a shot in the back and a shot in the head. Arājs himself was sometimes on hand to deliver 'mercy' shots to those who had not died immediately.[99] These, then, were the men who entered the ghetto in Riga that Sunday morning, battering on doors and crushing any signs of disobedience with the utmost brutality.

One of the leaders of the Arājs Commando was Herberts Cukurs, who many remembered as being horrifically brutal, beating and shooting those Jews who could not keep up with the march for an unknown destination. Isaak Kram, a Jewish engineering student, recalled how he had got close to the former pilot.

> An old Jewish woman screamed because her daughter was not allowed to climb with her on to the truck. Cukurs pulled out his gun and shot the old woman. I was an eyewitness to the shooting. I also saw with my own eyes how Cukurs aimed his gun at a baby who was crying because he could not find his mother. Cukurs killed that baby with a gunshot.[100]

Kram was not the only witness to Cukurs committing infanticide. Another was the twenty-year-old David Fiszkin: 'Many Jews could not keep pace, Cukurs who was always at the rear shot these people without explanation or reason. When a child cried, he took him from his mother and shot him on the spot. I have seen personally how he shot ten children.'[101]

By midday, the Arājs Commando and the Germans had cleared much of the ghetto, leaving behind a gruesome trail. 'Now the street was quiet,' remembered Frida Michelson, 'nothing moved. Corpses were scattered all over, rivulets of blood still oozing from the lifeless bodies. They were mostly old people, pregnant women, children, handicapped – all those who couldn't keep up with the inhuman tempo of the march.'[102]

The Jews were marched 6 miles south to a meadow near the railway station of Rumbula. There, they entered into a gauntlet formed by a mixture of Germans and Latvians, who included members of the Arājs Commando. As the Jews progressed down the gauntlet, they were forced to surrender their valuables and remove their clothes and shoes. The final stage of the Jews' journey was to lie down in one of three large pits, clutching their children and loved ones, and to receive a bullet in the back of the head. As the day wore on, subsequent victims were made to sprawl on top of the dead and those who were still struggling in their death throes; the pit reeked of excrement and brains. With the SS men fuelled by alcohol and hampered by the approaching darkness, their accuracy deteriorated, and many of the Jews died by being suffocated by the corpses that fell on top of them.[103] At the end of the day, some thirteen thousand had been killed. On 8 December, the process would be repeated, and a further twelve thousand lives were claimed. Incredibly, three Jews would survive the killings on that second day, and it is thanks to their testimonies that the involvement of the Arājs Commando is known.

After the massacres, the Arājs Commando would continue its barbaric work until mid-1944. It not only took part in anti-partisan operations, but it also crossed into Russia, where it carried out pogroms ordered by the Germans.[104] In Latvia alone, Arājs and his men killed some 26,000 people, which does not count its involvement manning the gauntlet at Rumbula, and neither does it include its operations in Russia. It has been estimated that the commando could have killed some fifty thousand during its operations in Minsk in 1942.[105] If this is correct, then it is feasible – but not proven – that the commando was responsible, either through murder or as an accessory to murder, for the deaths of some hundred thousand people. Towards the end of 1944, Arājs was sent to a German army training school in Bad Tölz and subsequently worked for the 19th Latvian SS Division. The following year, he shuttled between a variety of commands, for all of which he was found to be unsuitable. His final posting was to lead a battalion of five hundred Latvian convalescents, whom he referred to as 'half-cripples', and with whom he engaged the Russians at Güstrow, some 20 miles south of Rostock. Realizing that the war was lost, Arājs changed into civilian clothes and assumed the common Latvian name of Abols.[106]

Arājs did not enjoy his freedom for long, and he was captured by the British and interned in a POW camp for Latvians in Schleswig. There, the real identity of Arājs was betrayed to the British, and he was dispatched to an SS transit camp. At one point, it appears that Arājs escaped and made his way to Belgium under a false name to join a group of Latvian soldiers who were attempting to form a group to liberate their homeland. However, once again he was captured and sent to a British-run POW camp. On 31 December 1945, Arājs was betrayed 'for two bottles of beer' and subsequently interrogated, and, according to Arājs, abused by the British. For the next six months, Arājs was subjected to 'confrontation with witnesses and a thorough investigation', which would have revealed to the British that they had a major war criminal in their custody.[107] As investigating the 'Riga Ghetto' case was the responsibility of the British War Crimes Group, plenty of evidence was emerging from those who had survived the horrors. On 24 January 1948, Major Charles Kaiser listed at least twenty-seven Latvians and Germans who had been responsible for the crimes in Riga, which included both Arājs and Cukurs. 'All these people were mentioned again and again by every witness we have found up to now,' Kaiser wrote, 'and they are specially accused for their bestial behaviour and their crimes.' The officer recommended that the men should all be tried for 'mass murder, heavy ill-treatment and robbery'.[108] An appendix to Kaiser's letter showed that Arājs was being held at the Number 2 War Crimes Holding Centre, where he had been admitted on 13 November 1947.[109]

The whereabouts of Arājs between mid-1946 and November 1947 are something of a mystery. According to the criminal himself, at some point during the 1940s, Arājs was approached by British intelligence to work for them. He was asked – with a sweetener of five thousand dollars – if he would parachute into Latvia and undertake missions in that country and the Soviet Union. Arājs declined, not just because he feared arrest but also because he spoke no Russian.[110] If such an offer was made – and it has never been denied – then the British were knowingly trying to employ one of the worst criminals of the war. As we have seen, Arājs was no ordinary collaborator, but a man itching to participate in the slaughter of non-combatants and children. Although Kopkow's modus operandi as a desk murderer is no less reprehensible than any other form of illegal killing, it is easy to see how an MI6 officer could convince himself that Kopkow was in some way worthy of respect, and perhaps even feel that the Gestapo man's wartime actions were mitigated by the knowledge that the British and Americans also shot spies and enemy agents. But Arājs was a very different creature to Kopkow. His hands were literally splattered with the blood and brains of those he shot as acts of 'mercy'. Arājs burned down synagogues. Arājs guarded concentration camps. Arājs committed genocide. As well as being so bestial, Arājs lacked the qualities that would have made him a loyal and competent spy for the British. Had he been dropped into Latvia, he would have changed sides before his canopy had unfurled.

Arājs's unsuitability would suggest that his claim of a British approach was false, but, once again, it appears that the statements of a murderer hold more validity than the words spoken by those who had fought tyranny. The evidence for a deal lies in the fact that Arājs was released on 1 February 1949 by the British after several bail hearings. Although Arājs would later claim that he had been tried and acquitted, there is no record of such a trial.[111] It would be absurd to suspect that there was insufficient evidence to convict Arājs, let alone bring him to trial, because there was plenty. The name of Arājs was repeatedly mentioned in the testimonies of those who survived the Riga ghetto, and had he been brought to trial, he would have been hanged. Instead, under the name 'Viktors Zeibots', Arājs settled in Oldenburg with his wife and took a job as a driver for the British military government in Delmhorst. When a court in Hamburg tried to get him arrested, Zeibots disappeared, but he shortly reappeared in Frankfurt, where he lived and worked until his eventual arrest in 1975. He finally received justice in December 1979 when he was sentenced to life imprisonment. He died in captivity at the age of seventy-eight in 1988. Herberts Cukurs, one of Arājs's most loyal henchmen, would also be brought to justice long after the war, but, as we shall see, its dispensation was far more severe.

The *Einsatzgruppe* for which the Arājs Commando did its murderous bidding was *Einsatzgruppe A*, which carried out massacres from East Prussia across the Baltic States towards Leningrad. Further south, *Einsatzgruppe B* worked its horrific way from Warsaw via Minsk to the outskirts of Moscow. Although its structure remained fluid, *Einsatzgruppe B* was divided into six commandos, one of which was labelled *Vorkommando Moskau*, and it was tasked with operating in the Russian capital had it fallen. Initially led by SS-Brigadeführer Dr Franz Six – who would have led the *Einsatzgruppen* in an occupied Britain – the *Vorkommando Moskau* carried out most of its killing in and around Smolensk. After two more changes of leadership, an *SS-Sturmbannführer* called Dr Friedrich Buchardt was appointed its head in December 1941. Born in Latvia on 17 March 1909, Buchardt was a Baltic-German, and he studied at the German Gymnasium in Riga, before reading law at the universities in Berlin and Jena. In Germany, Buchardt found himself drawn to Nazism, and he joined the SA in October 1933. However, for the intellectual Buchardt, the SA was far too ple-beian, and he left the following year. While he remained in Germany, Buchardt remained intensely interested in Baltic affairs. His dissertation had been on 'The Rights of National Minorities in Latvia and its International Importance and Administration', which would prove to be a fateful choice. After he had completed his studies, he returned to Riga, where he tried to establish a national German–Baltic movement under the leadership of Dr Erhard Kroeger. Buchardt regularly contributed and helped to finance the *Rigaschen Rundschau* newspaper, which was closed down by the Latvian government in May 1934 for having too many Nazi connections.[112]

The closure of the paper resulted in huge financial losses for Buchardt, and so he returned to Germany, where he worked as a lawyer for a marketing company and subsequently as the economics head of the Baltic Institute. He also worked at Königsberg University, which is where he met Dr Franz Six, who recognized Buchardt as suitable material for the SD. The Nazis, who were look-ing to expand east in their now notorious quest for *Lebensraum*, were keen to engage the services of anybody who had specialized in Eastern European countries. Buchardt joined the SD in 1936, where he worked under Dr Six, studying the Soviet economy, its topo-graphy, and, more ominously, its distribution of Jews. By the late 1930s, Buchardt was to flourish at the Wannsee Institute, where numerous *Ostspezialisten* studied the Soviet Union. For the Nazis, it was a case of getting to know their enemy, and it was willing academics such as Buchardt who helped supply vital information to the occupying forces and civil servants.[113]

By the time Germany invaded Poland, Buchardt was an *Obersturmführer* (first lieutenant) and the head of a small unit of

German-Baltic SS officers deployed to the port of Gdynia to loot its archives, museums and libraries. The thirty-year-old clearly impressed his superiors, because by the following year, he was working at the 'Office for the Resettlement of Poles and Jews' in Poznań, in which he classified the level of 'Germanicness' of various sectors of the Polish population on a scale of 1 to 5. In 1940, Buchardt was made head of the SD in Lublin, where he worked under SS-Brigadeführer Odilo Globocnik.[114] It was here that Buchardt crossed a line from mere 'racial grading' to actual extermination. In the words of a 1950 CIC report, Buchardt was 'responsible for the deaths of many of the persons executed in the concentration camps in the area'.[115] In February 1941, Buchardt carried out similar work in Łódź, where he reported directly back to the RSHA. On the eve of the German invasion of Russia, Buchardt was withdrawn. By all accounts, he had been a great success, and had shown that he was willing to put academic theory concerning population control into horrific practice. His managerial and his legal background combined with his politically radical views made him the perfect Nazi bureaucrat, and he was soon recognized by Heydrich as someone destined to go far.

However, if Buchardt wanted to fulfil Heydrich's ambitions for him within the SD, then he needed 'blood experience'. Himmler demanded that his men were not just 'desk scholars', but those who blended ideology with practice.[116] Buchardt's move to the *Vorkommando Moskau* of *Einsatzgruppe B* was therefore a natural step for someone in Buchardt's position. For the first three months of the campaign in Russia, Buchardt acted as the liaison officer between his former mentor Dr Franz Six and the head of *Einsatzgruppe B*, SS-Gruppenführer (General) Arthur Nebe. As such, Buchardt helped to implement the 'collective measures' wrought upon the 'Jewish population as carriers of Communism'.[117] Despite such bureaucratic language, the job of the *Vorkommando Moskau* was no different to that of any other section within an *Einsatzgruppe* – it murdered people. When the offensive on Moscow was launched in October 1941, Buchardt played a crucial role in the *Vorkommando* as the Germans approached the city, and he was rewarded by promotion to *SS-Sturmbannführer* (Major) in November 1941. The following month, he was appointed head of the *Vorkommando*, but as the assault on the city failed, in January Buchardt was posted back to Łódź, where he continued his work as head of the SD. Once again, Buchardt impressed his superiors, for by September he had supervised the deportation of some eighty thousand Jews and Gypsies to Chelmno extermination camp.[118] In February 1943, Buchardt was rewarded with even more 'blood experience', as he was given the command of *Einsatzkommando 9* of *Einsatzgruppe B*. Based in Vitebsk, Buchardt conducted 'anti-partisan operations', as well as implementing the euphemistic 'collective action' against Jews and communists. Although it is impossible to be precise about how many deaths Buchardt's commando was responsible for, the figure is likely to be in the tens of thousands. The murders won him more distinctions, as Buchardt was awarded with a First Class Iron Cross, a First Class War Cross of Merit with Swords, a Silver Badge of Courage, and an Infantry Assault Badge in Silver. In June 1944, he would be promoted to *SS-Obersturmbannführer* (lieutenant colonel), which was the same rank as that of Adolf Eichmann.[119]

Having proved his 'blood experience', Buchardt was posted to Berlin, where he headed Amt III B 2 of the RSHA, specializing in racial and ethnic matters. In December 1944, Buchardt was also given the duty of heading *Sonderkommando Ost*, which gathered intelligence on Russian personnel residing in German territory, including members of General Andrei Vlasov's collaborationist Russian Liberation Army.[120] Buchardt's boss at the head of Amt III was SS-Gruppenführer Otto Ohlendorf, who had commanded *Einsatzgruppe D* and was responsible for the deaths of ninety thousand Jews.[121] In April 1945, Ohlendorf started making plans for the post-war world, and was instrumental in the establishment of an SD underground movement called *Bundschuh* (Tied Shoe), which was named after a series of peasant rebellions in sixteenth-century Germany. After the defeat, *Bundschuh* was to act as a Europe-wide information network of 'high-grade' agents that could be used by sabotage and terrorist organizations as they waged a guerrilla war against the Allies.[122] Ohlendorf chose Buchardt to head the south-eastern sector of the network, and Buchardt was dispatched from Berlin to Karlsbad. However, events moved too quickly for the plotters, and Buchardt's group retreated 200 miles southeast to Füssen on the Austrian–German border. As Füssen was also the centre of

Buchardt's *Sonderkommando Ost*, he doubtless had many contacts in the town. Towards the end of April, Buchardt was last seen near Innsbruck, where members of Vlasov's army were also reported to be in hiding.[123]

Buchardt was captured by the Americans shortly after the war, and he was handed over to the British, who held him at the vast POW camp in Rimini. It was during his internment that Buchardt was to produce a document that would save his life. Entitled 'The Handling of the Russian Problem during the Period of the Nazi Regime in Germany', Buchardt's paper was a complete run-down of his own espionage operations in Eastern Europe, and it emphasized the importance of native collaborators in SS operations. As a result, the document almost became a blueprint for MI6 operations in Eastern Europe, and it ensured that Buchardt was not only never brought to trial, but also employed by the British.[124] It is not known exactly what services Buchardt provided for MI6, but there can be little doubt that his knowledge of the Baltic States, Poland and Russia, as well as his enormous number of anti-communist Russian contacts, would have proved immensely useful. However, MI6 dropped Buchardt in 1947, and he offered his services to the Americans.[125] It is unclear whether they accepted, but it seems likely that they did. In March 1950, the CIC learned that the Bavarian Land Indemnity Office was gathering evidence against Buchardt for a possible trial, and it warned EUCOM, because it suspected that Buchardt 'may be presently employed by an American intelligence agency'.[126] The agency in question was presumably the CIA. In another report, the CIC indicated that 'this unit [i.e. the CIA] should be informed of such an investigation by a German organisation'.[127] If Buchardt was indeed employed by the CIA, then the warning was heeded, because the former *Einsatzkommando* leader escaped justice for his crimes. He lived out most of his days in Heidelberg, and he died in Nussbach on 20 December 1982.

At the time of writing, Buchardt can be regarded as the most murderous Nazi employed by the Allies after the war. Barbie, Kopkow and Arājs – although by no means petty criminals – were not in the same league as that of Buchardt, who not only supervised the killings, but also helped to construct the flawed academic easel upon which the Nazis mounted their picture of racial superiority, which in turn would lead to genocide.[128] Buchardt's criminality is therefore exceptional, and it is hard to believe that there were no misgivings expressed within the Allied intelligence agencies who hired him. Unfortunately, as no further documentation on the exploitation of Buchardt has been made available, it is easy for many to assume that MI6 and the CIA employed the man with a relish that was positively immoral. It is only by the release of such papers that the hiring of men like Buchardt can be seen within a moral context, and the level of their efficacy established and set against the horror of their crimes. Clearly, no operational brilliance manifested by Buchardt for MI6 can atone for working as a willing member of an *Einsatzgruppe*, but at least an examination of the decisions that led to his hiring would reveal the moral framework within which Allied intelligence functioned.

A glimpse of a seeming lack of any such framework can be found in a letter from February 1945, in which Lieutenant Colonel H. J. Baxter of MI5 explained to an MI6 officer that 'character' should not be regarded when considering potential agents.

> As you know in the past I have always discouraged officers from making any comment on the suitability of an alien for employment as an agent on grounds other than security grounds although I am well aware that from time to time examiners have expressed their opinion about a man's character. If OSS are anxious that in future we should express an opinion I am perfectly prepared to arrange that interrogators should do this provided that it is well understood that we are not experts in judgement of character nor would we be expressing an opinion within the ordinary scope of our duties.[129]

The Americans, British and French were not the only Allies to employ Nazi war criminals and former SS men. The Soviet Bloc, despite brazenly taking the West to task for such a policy in publications like the *Brown Book*, adopted a similar approach. The case of Heinz Felfe shows how the Soviets shared the seeming lack of moral queasiness in hiring their former enemies. Born in Dresden in 1918, Felfe had joined the SS at the age of seventeen, and earned his SS commission in 1943 when he joined the SD. He was assigned to the Swiss desk at Amt VI of the RSHA, before his talents next saw him sent to Holland, where he had an instrumental role in Operation North Pole. By the end of the war, he had reached the rank of *Obersturmführer* (first lieutenant), and was captured by Canadian troops in Holland. Felfe later recalled how he had been interrogated by the British and the Dutch in a very correct way. 'They even started to display a little sympathy,' Felfe wrote. 'It was obviously the chivalric behaviour of the British gentleman.' One of the British intelligence officers even offered to post a letter for Felfe when he reached Germany, as sending correspondence from Holland to Germany at that point was impossible.[130] The officer was presumably mounting a charm offensive, because in October 1946, Felfe was released in order to work for MI6 in their 6th Area Intelligence Office in Cologne, where he spied upon the Communist Party. Within two years, the British dropped him because they suspected – with some reason – that he was passing information on to the Soviets.[131]

By 1951, Felfe had started working for the Gehlen Organisation, the West German Intelligence Service commanded by the former German army general Reinhard Gehlen. Felfe would soon become as significant a figure in twentieth-century espionage as Kim Philby. In 1953, Felfe announced to his colleagues that he had established a network of agents in Moscow, which was headed by a colonel in the Red Army. Naturally, this network was nothing but a KGB dummy, which provided a mixture of information and disinformation to the West Germans. In the meantime, Felfe, who was codenamed 'Kurt', handed over an astonishing amount of material concerning the Gehlen Organisation, some of which was even concealed in tins of baby food.[132] In 1955, Felfe was put in charge of counter-intelligence against the Soviets, which meant that the man responsible for stymying Soviet espionage was himself working for the Soviets. It was the same trick that Philby had pulled off eleven years earlier, when he had been made head of the MI6's Section IX – the anti-Soviet section.[133] The Americans were suspicious of Felfe, noting how he enjoyed a relatively high standard of living compared to his colleagues. 'He has all the more material things in life,' commented a CIA report in July 1959, 'to wit: an unusually nice apartment in a better section of Munich, a home in the process of construction in Kufstein, a late model Taunus four-door sedan, good clothes, and a minimum of requests for FX items, which others of his co-workers so frequently request.'[134]

The Gehlen Organisation – which was transmogrified into the *Bundesnachrichtendienst* (BND or Federal Intelligence Service) in the mid-1950s – ignored the American warnings, but by 1961 the West Germans were all but convinced. On 27 October of that year, BND codebreakers deciphered a KGB signal that clearly referred to Felfe. On 6 November, Felfe was arrested.[135] The blow he had dealt the BND was immeasurably painful. 'The BND damage report must have run into tens of thousands of pages,' said one former CIA officer.[136] Ninety-four informers had been blown, together with their codes and courier channels, all of which had been captured by Felfe on 15,661 photographs he had passed on to the Soviets.[137] At his trial in 1963, Felfe acted the loyal Soviet, by 'revealing' that the British had been guilty of 'bestial conduct' with their POWs, and had beaten and tortured them. He also claimed a deep loathing of the United States, which his defence lawyer used to suggest that his client's judgement had been 'clouded'. Felfe was sentenced to fourteen years, but he was exchanged in 1969 for twenty-one political prisoners from East Germany.[138]

What the Felfe case revealed was not only the extraordinary penetration the Russians had made into a Western intelligence service, but also their willingness to employ former Nazis to do so. The Gehlen Organisation was crammed with SS and SD men who owed their new loyalty to Moscow rather than Bonn. At one point, Felfe claimed that the KGB had asked him to obtain a transfer from counter-intelligence because there was a surfeit of Soviet agents in that department.[139] Felfe could have been lying, but the CIA was minded to agree. Soviets who had defected to the Americans revealed that the Russians specifically targeted former SS men to use as spies. 'The thesis was simple,' stated a 1969 report. 'Some of these people might be susceptible to a Soviet approach because of their general sympathies. Others, such as [SS and SD] members, many of whom were now war criminals able to make their way only by hiding a past which had once put them among the elite, would be vulnerable to blackmail.'[140] Heinz Felfe, then, was yet another SS officer who found that the best means of escape was to stay at home. For those who had emigrated to South America and the Middle East, life was certainly nothing like as comfortable.

Chapter Eight

In Hiding

DURING THE middle of June 1949, Bishop Alois Hudal received a letter from a worried woman called Maria Fabris who lived in Trieste. 'In September 1948 I had news from Paul Stangl who told me of his immediate departure for Egypt,' she wrote, 'where he was to remain for a period of six months after which I would receive some more news. This period has elapsed and despite my prayers I am now concerned as to the uncertainty of his fate. My desire is to have news from the Pontifical Commission of Assistance to establish, albeit indirectly, whether he is still alive.'[1] Hudal replied to Fabris on 16 June, although it is not known what the priest told the woman concerning the fate of the former Commandant of Treblinka. He may have informed her that Stangl had in fact fled to Damascus, and although he was short of money, he was happy to have finally been reunited with his family in May that year. Who exactly Maria Fabris was – or perhaps *is*; she was born in March 1916 – is not known, although it is possible that she may have been a cousin of Stangl. She may have even been his lover when he was posted in the area during the war.

Shortly after his wife Theresa and daughters joined him, Stangl lost his job at the textile mill because the owner died. 'It was very hard,' Stangl's wife recalled. 'He looked desperately for some work but it took a long time before he found some.'[2] While her husband searched for work, Theresa worked as a masseuse, attending to the bodies of 'fat women'. Their living arrangements were also far from ideal, as they were housed in what was effectively a Nazi boarding house at 22 rue George Haddat. Theresa remembered how their fellow lodgers were mostly Germans, and they never seemed to use their real names. The family's luck changed in December, when Stangl found a job as an engineer at the Imperial Knitting Company. With an income of five hundred Syrian pounds per month, the family was able to move into a large flat in the old part of town, where they were visited by many of their German friends. For the best part of a year, all was well, but then a new problem arose. Their neighbour started fancying the Stangls' fourteen-year-old daughter, Renate. Unfortunately, as the neighbour also happened to be the chief of police, the Stangls knew there was little they could do if he wanted to add their daughter to his harem.[3]

Stangl decided that their only option was to leave, and he dispatched Theresa to Beirut in order to visit a selection of South American consulates. The Brazilians showed the most interest in Stangl's qualifications as an engineer, and within a month he had been issued with a visa. Two months later, the family travelled under their real names on a sea voyage that would take them via Genoa to Santos in Brazil. The trip was funded out of savings, and by the time they had settled in a boarding house in São Paulo, the Stangls were once more on the breadline. However, Stangl quickly found a job with a textile firm called Sutema, with which he stayed for two years until he found better-paid positions elsewhere. By the mid-1950s, the Stangls were able to live off his comfortable wage of eight thousand cruzeiros. Once again, everything was falling into place for the family, and Stangl was even single-handedly building a family home in the southern São Paulo suburb of São Bernardo do Campo.[4] The Stangls felt so comfortable and secure in Brazil that, in August 1954, they even registered at the Austrian consulate under their own names. Although registration was entirely voluntary, the Stangls felt that it was 'right and proper' to do so. Incredibly, the consulate did not make any inquiries concerning the Stangls. There are three potential reasons for this. The most likely explanation is that the diplomats may have never heard of Stangl, because at the time he was not a widely known criminal. Secondly, Stangl is a common name in Austria, and the name, even if it were associated with Treblinka, would not necessarily have alarmed a clerk. A third explanation is that the consulate was involved in sheltering war criminals, and although this is feasible, there is no evidence to support it.[5]

At the end of 1955, the family suffered another mishap: Stangl fell badly ill. 'It wasn't anything the doctors could put their finger on,' Theresa said, 'nothing we could really understand.'[6] For a long time, Stangl was severely weakened by this mysterious illness, and he was unable to walk or stand for any length of time. Theresa found some clerical work at Mercedes-Benz, and while he recuperated, Stangl built a small workshop from which he produced bandages that he sold to hospitals. During this period, the Stangl family did experience some lighter moments. Their daughter Renate married an Austrian in 1957, and their eldest daughter, Gitta, followed suit the year after. Throughout the second half of the decade, Stangl's health slowly improved and the new home was completed. Finally, in October 1959, Stangl was able to return to full-time employment, and through her contacts in the motor industry, Theresa found her husband a job at Volkswagen, where he worked under his real name. Stangl once more started at the bottom as a mechanic, but he would become head of preventive maintenance at the plant with a healthy salary of 25,000 cruzeiros. Their combined incomes enabled the Stangls to move to the upmarket Brooklin area of São Paulo, where over the next few years they built their second house. Stangl thought that the family would never be able to afford such a development, but Theresa was adamant, and it was her salary that paid for the majority of the building costs. The house was completed in 1965 and they moved in, and, although Renate had divorced, the Stangls felt once more at peace. 'Everybody had good jobs,' Theresa Stangl recalled, 'and was earning good money and I was looking after them and loving it.'[7]

Today, it seems astonishing that one of the greatest murderers of the last century could live so openly. Stangl had a fatalistic attitude towards being captured, and once told his wife that such a fate was

'unavoidable'. 'If it comes to it,' he said, 'I want to give myself up –
I don't want to run away.'[8] As a result, the Stangls did nothing to
hide their identity, and Theresa regularly corresponded with friends
in Austria to whom she gave their address in São Paulo. Stangl did
not even hide himself in February 1964 when the ex-husband of
Renate brandished a Viennese newspaper carrying a report that
Simon Wiesenthal was looking for Stangl. In March, the former son-
in-law threatened to tell Wiesenthal of Stangl's whereabouts. 'He
said that unless I got Renate to go back to him, he would destroy us
all,' Stangl recalled.[9] Although he did not know it, Stangl's name
even appeared on the official Austrian list of wanted criminals
which was sent to all Austrian embassies and consulates in the early
1960s.[10] His name was also very publicly aired at the Treblinka Trial
held in Düsseldorf from October 1964 to August 1965, in which
eight former officials from the extermination camp were found
guilty and sentenced to prison sentences ranging from four years to
life. The case was reported all over the world. Yet despite all this,
not one of Stangl's friends in Austria, nor one of his co-workers at
Volkswagen, nor even a diplomat or clerk at the Austrian consulate
revealed where he was. Neither is there any evidence to suggest that
Stangl's former son-in-law ever carried out his threat. It is little wonder that Stangl could afford to be so fatalistic. However, just as he
was on a high, the crest-and-trough pattern of Stangl's life was to
repeat itself once again, with devastating consequences.

Josef Mengele arrived in Buenos Aires on 26 August 1949. At the
Immigration Office he presented himself as 'Helmut Gregor', a 38-
year-old German mechanic who had come to Argentina in order to
work. He informed the official that he could both read and write,
that his health was good, and that he had no disabilities. The only
glitch he suffered was when a customs official inspected one of
Mengele's suitcases and came across his 'biological notes'. The port
doctor was summoned to examine them, but as he was unable to
read German, Mengele was nodded through to his new life on a
continent that would remain his home for the next three decades.[11]

   As soon as Mengele stepped out of the vast grey immigration hall,
he must have felt very alone. He was on the other side of the planet
in a city where he knew nobody. He had very little money, and the

little he had had not been changed into Argentine pesos, so he was unable to take a taxi. Instead, he hitched a ride with two Italians he had met on the *North King*, who deposited him at a seedy hotel called the Palermo. After a few days, Helmut Gregor found a job as a carpenter which enabled him to live in the superior district of Vicente López. Nevertheless, he had to share a room with an engineer, who at one point spotted medical instruments among Mengele's belongings and insisted that the doctor treat his feverish daughter. Mengele was reluctant, but he eventually tended to the girl on the proviso that her father was sworn to secrecy.[12] After several weeks, Mengele found new lodgings at Calle Arenales 2460, which was the home of a Nazi sympathizer called Gerard Malbranc.[13] The house, which still stands today in the upmarket suburb of Florida, would have suited Mengele's grand pretensions far more with its curved columned portico and leafy garden. Gregor was an ideal tenant, and soon Mengele was socializing with the great and the not-so-good of the German expatriate community.

Among them was the Luftwaffe ace Hans-Ulrich Rudel, who frequently travelled to Argentina and Paraguay on business, as well as running the help organization *Kameradenwerk,* which openly supplied money and assistance to former Nazis. It was Rudel who suggested to Mengele that he should create a market in Paraguay for the farm machinery produced by Mengele's family back in Günzburg, and throughout the early 1950s, Mengele effectively acted as a sales agent.[14] The trips to Paraguay were not only lucrative for Mengele, but they also enabled him to meet many influential figures who were to prove so helpful to him in later years. Although Mengele was to cut a well-liked figure in the capital Asunción, one of his acquaintances always suspected that he was holding something back, as he never mentioned the war. 'Mengele never brought it up,' recalled Werner Jung, a German expatriate businessman and fascist. 'Everyone knew that those Germans who had come to South America had started a new life and there was nothing else that we needed to know.'[15]

In early 1953, Mengele moved from Florida to downtown Buenos Aires, where he rented a flat on the first floor of Calle Tacuari 431. Like the house in Florida, number 431 still stands, and it is curious why the 42-year-old Mengele would have wanted to leave the gentility of Calle Arenales for the far shabbier Calle Tacuari. The building, although it features some grand architectural flourishes, is a far more modest affair, and the street is narrow and noisy. Perhaps Mengele wanted some independence, or maybe, as a de facto bachelor, the centre of the city offered a greater opportunity to meet members of the opposite sex. Within seven months, Mengele had moved back to the suburbs, where he rented one half of Calle Sarmiento 1875 in the Olivos district of Vicente López. The house is solid, unexceptional and nondescript – the perfect safe house for a fugitive. In 1954, Mengele's wife, Irene, was granted a divorce by a Düsseldorf court, which now left Mengele as an actual bachelor. Although his romantic life appeared to be unfulfilled, his professional life was going well, and around this time Mengele even established a woodwork business. The income from this and the family firm soon made Mengele comfortably off, and he was able to buy a car and eat out regularly.[16]

Back in Germany, Mengele's family was making plans to rectify the marital arrangements of their distant son. In December 1949, Mengele's brother Karl had died at the age of only thirty-seven, leaving a widow, Martha, and a five-year-old son, Karl Heinz. Mengele's father was concerned that if Martha remarried, her voting rights on the firm's board might be influenced by her new husband, a prospect that the head of the family found intolerable. The logical solution was to get Martha to marry Josef, and therefore keep the firm unsullied by outsiders. The only problem was to ensure that the two actually met each other, and for that to happen, Mengele would have to travel to Europe. In April 1955, Mengele applied for a passport in the name of Helmut Gregor, which was finally issued towards the end of the year.

One of the reasons for such bureaucratic slowness was the fact that Perón had been ousted by a coup in September. During his second term, which had started in June 1952, Perón had lost the support of the Church and the military, and, with a severely weakened economy, his grip on power steadily loosened. Perón's image had also been dented by the folly of the Huemul Project run by Ronald Richter, who had escaped to Argentina via the 'Nordic route' with Kurt Tank in 1947. Richter had met Perón in August 1948, and had convinced him that he could unlock the secret of nuclear fusion, which would solve all of Argentina's energy problems and make her the great power that the President had always envisaged.[17] Perón's trust in the German scientist would prove to be utterly misplaced. In short, Richter was all mouth and no reaction, as the British had established when they questioned him after the war. At first, like Perón, the British were excited by Richter's claims regarding the manufacture of catalysts, which they thought 'may be of very great importance in the field of atomic energy'.[18] However, after he was questioned in Berlin in August 1946, they found him to be little more than 'an enthusiastic optimist', although 'not a charlatan'. 'I was, however, not impressed by the practical value of his work,' reported Colonel B. K. Blount of the Chemical Research Branch. 'I scarcely think that the matter is worth pursuing further, indeed the original inquiry from Control Office has led to the waste of a good deal of my time to no purpose.'[19]

In Argentina, Richter was afforded a far more sympathetic reception, and by the beginning of 1949, the scientist, armed with a blank cheque from the President, had started to establish a series of vast laboratories on Huemul Island in the middle of Nahuel Huapi Lake four miles from the centre of Bariloche in Patagonia.[20] Flatbed lorries carrying building materials were transported across the often choppy waters of the lake by treacherously flimsy barges, and Richter acted the petty tyrant to ensure the construction was carried out quickly. On 8 April 1950, Perón and his wife, Eva, visited the complex, where they marvelled at the scale of the building that was to house the main 'reactor'. Twelve metres high and twelve metres in diameter, the edifice looked truly impressive. The following month, the reactor itself was constructed from concrete, for which Richter used some twenty thousand bags of cement. As no iron was involved in the construction, the reactor had to be built in a space of 72 hours without a break.[21] Towards the end of the year, he was able to start performing his atomic experiments. On one occasion, he was visited by Colonel Enrique González, the head of the Argentine atomic energy commission. The German scientist was only too happy to show him his work in progress, and performed an experiment that blew off the laboratory's door. After he had dusted himself down, Richter studied his instruments, and triumphantly announced, 'Atomic energy!'[22] Finally, on 16 February 1951,

Richter made his breakthrough, and in March he wrote to Perón advising him of his success. On 24 March, the President summoned the world's press, and together with Richter, he revealed that 'thermo-nuclear reactions under controlled conditions were performed on a technical scale'. This meant that Argentina would soon be able to deliver huge amounts of energy in containers the size of milk bottles. All that Richter needed to do was to step up the process to an an indust-rial scale, although the scientific community was extremely sceptical of Richter's ability to do so. By the following year, it was becoming apparent that whatever Richter had done, he had most certainly not produced nuclear fusion. Perón dispatched a technical committee to the island, who reported in September 1952 that the temperatures Richter had achieved were not high enough to produce a fusion reaction. It later transpired that all Richter had done was to explode hydrogen in an electric arc. As a result, the project was shut down and a sheepish Perón was left to count its cost, which was some $62 million or the equivalent of $484 million in 2007.[23] The buildings remain on Huemul as a testament to the folly of such an overly ambitious project. Although a handful of forlorn sailors from the Argentine Navy guard the island, the ruins are today largely ignored.[24]

Richter was not the only Nazi 'technician' in whom Perón placed too much faith. Hans-Ulrich Rudel was another who had charmed his way into the affection of Perón, who hired him as a test pilot and aircraft inspector and gave him a large salary. However, Rudel's daredevilry in the air quickly saw him lose three jets – a loss the cash-strapped air force could ill afford. Rudel was grounded, and without any new planes to test, he did nothing and yet continued to receive his income. As a result, he earned the resentment of the majority of Argentine air force personnel.[25] Another Nazi aviator employed by Perón was Werner Baumbach, a former Luftwaffe pilot who had headed the air force's *Kampfgeschwader 200*, which tested new aircraft during the war, as well as carrying out special operations. Baumbach, who remained a convinced Nazi, was hired as a test pilot and technical advisor, and he participated in the Argentine attempt to develop a guided missile. On 20 October 1953, when he was flying a Lancaster during a trial of the weapon, an engine caught fire and the plane crashed into the River Plate, killing Baumbach and several of the crew.[26]

One German technican who was more successful was Richter's friend Kurt Tank, who designed the Pulqui II jet fighter for the Argentine Air Force. However, the aircraft, although it showed promise, was unreliable and never progressed beyond the prototype stage, and as the economic crisis during Perón's second term worsened, the project had to be abandoned. Even if the Pulqui II had entered into production, the Argentines would not have used it effectively. In 1951, the Air Attaché at the British embassy in Buenos Aires produced a highly withering report on the state of the Argentine Air Force. Air Commodore W. E. Oulton identified one of the main reasons for the service's ineffectiveness as 'the inability of pilots to comprehend that their duties require anything more than to fly pleasantly from A to B for lunch and back again'. Oulton also highlighted that the annual training aim was 'nothing more than to put the maximum number of aircraft into the Presidential review on July 9th'. The Air Commodore ended his report with a cynical flourish. 'The Argentine Air Force continues satisfactorily to fulfill its primary function of providing a show for the edification of the public,' he wrote.[27] If Nazis such as Rudel and Baumbach had been brought into Argentina to improve its armed forces, then there can be little doubt that they failed. Another Luftwaffe ace drafted in was Adolf Galland, but he too did not appear to have achieved much during his time in Argentina, and in 1954 he returned to Germany to set up his own consultancy business.[28]

Towards the end of his second term, it was becoming clear that Perón was revising his attitude towards his Nazi immigrants. As he attempted to improve relations between Argentina and countries such as West Germany, the United States and the United Kingdom, the presence of so many Nazis started to become an embarrassment. In June 1954, Hans-Ulrich Rudel applied for an exit visa to leave the country to visit West Germany, but Perón refused to grant it, on the grounds that doing so would harm relations between the two countries. Perón's action earned him a letter from Sir Oswald Mosley, who begged the President to reconsider his decision. On 2 January 1955 Mosley wrote:

> Several of us have the impression that his [Rudel's] presence in Europe is of the greatest value for the maintenance of the position of

Germany and the whole of Europe against the dangers that now threaten. Confidence can always be had in him to sustain with ability and energy the true values of civilization, so much furthered by the work done by Your Excellency.'[29]

The British fascist's appeal did not change Perón's mind, but, in truth, many Western nations did not seem unduly concerned about the President's 'guests'. In October 1946, the United States and the United Kingdom bound themselves to a gentlemen's agreement that banned both countries from selling arms to Argentina until Perón's regime 'behaved itself' by liquidating Axis assets and refusing to play host to 'undesirables'. The agreement was swiftly broken by the British, who were desperate to acquire some of Argentina's sterling reserves. In early 1947, the British agreed a thirty-million-pound Vickers armaments contract, which Britain justified by stating that she needed the arms trade 'to feed itself'.[30] In February, the British informed the United States that as far as they were concerned, the Argentinians had done as much as was necessary to comply with their demands. The United States barely registered any disapproval and, later that month, the Argentine representative in Washington was told that the 'US government believed that every American nation should have complete freedom of action and independence to resolve the question of the refugees in the form it believed most appropriate to its interests'.[31] This was nothing less than a carte blanche, which was further confirmed in October 1947 when the British embassy in Washington reported that the United States was not minded to pressure Argentina into expelling any more 'undesirables'. 'The United States government will not risk an approach which seems almost sure to fail, and which may, into the bargain bring some odium upon themselves.'[32] Both countries therefore had little or no appetite for chasing war criminals in South America, on the grounds that it would yield little, and Argentina was a potentially valuable trading partner. This attitude was memorably crystallized by Air Commodore Oulton in his devastating 1951 report on the Argentine Air Force. 'From the British point of view, however, its capacity to absorb products of British aviation industry is of great importance. With a little care and attention, this capacity can be maintained.'[33]

If Perón's relationship with the United Kingdom and the United States was one of cold mutuality, then the one he enjoyed with West Germany was one of extreme cosiness. In July 1953, Perón signed a trade agreement with Bonn that was valued to run at some $136 million each way, and would include the importing of some fifty million dollars' worth of industrial machinery. However, much of the imports were on credit and, by October, the Argentinians owed $35 million to the West Germans, who were also beginning to find that there was little that they wanted to import from Argentina. Despite these anxieties, on 26 November the West Germans decorated Perón with the Grand Cross Extraordinary of the Order of Merit, which was the highest honour they could have given him. British diplomats in Buenos Aires watched these goings-on with wry interest, although what they found more disturbing was the news that the German embassy had ordered several hundred copies of a book called *Allied War Crimes and Crimes against Humanity*, which was published by the same firm that produced *Der Weg*. 'We hope to find out more about these people,' wrote British embassy official Richard Allen on 3 October 1953 to the Foreign Office, 'and the extent to which they represent the hard core Nazis who still flourish here on the admission of the German embassy.' Allen clarified his statement in November, when he emphasized that the phrase 'on the admission of the German embassy' in fact meant that the Germans had 'told us – with apparent disapproval – that there was a flourishing hard core of Nazis in Argentina'.[34]

In a sense, it is irrelevant whether the West German embassy admitted Nazis or admitted to them, because, as Josef Mengele was to find, his fatherland's diplomats had no interest in investigating the presence of men such as himself. Mengele's trip to Europe in the spring of 1956 went well, as did the meeting with Martha Mengele – exactly the way his father had wished it. Mengele also met his son, Rolf, who was then twelve, and who would recall the meeting with 'Uncle Fritz' with some fondness. 'He told us stories about the war,' Rolf said, 'and at that time no adults spoke about the war. I liked him – as an uncle.'[35] Upon his return to Buenos Aires, Mengele felt sufficiently emboldened to register with the West German embassy under his own name. The criminal needed to do so in order to take on a mortgage and to join the partnership of a pharmaceutical company. His 'Helmut Gregor' paperwork was insufficient, and Mengele was also keen to regularize his life. In the middle of 1956, Josef Mengele provided the West Germans with his name, address, date and place of birth, and the date of his divorce. On 11 September 1956, the embassy issued him with an identity certificate that stated that he was Josef Mengele and that he had been born in Günzburg. This certificate enabled him to be granted an Argentinian identity card and, with this, Mengele returned to the embassy to apply for a passport. A few weeks later, he was the proud holder of a West German Passport numbered 3415574.[36] Decades later, those who worked at the German embassy claimed never to have heard of Mengele. Even if this were true, it is astonishing that there was no list of war criminals against which Mengele's application could have been checked. Richard Allen's ambiguous phrase made three years previously was prophetic and appropriate. The complete lack of scrutiny by the West Germans was so negligent that it was tantamount to assistance.

In October, Martha and her son Karl Heinz came out to join Mengele, and although they were not to marry until July 1958, they lived as a family in the new home Mengele had bought at Virrey Vertiz 970 in the well-to-do Olivos suburb. Martha was even listed in the Buenos Aires phone book under the name 'Mengele'.[37]

For the next two years, Mengele lived the comfortable life of the European expatriate, and his investment in the pharmaceutical company earned him not only a return but also status. All seemed well, until one day in late 1958 when he was arrested by the Buenos Aires police. A young girl had died in a backstreet abortion clinic and Mengele was one of several doctors who were brought in for questioning. Although he denied the crime, Mengele realized that the quickest way to get himself freed was to 'prove his innocence' with five hundred dollars. After three days he was released without charge, but the experience certainly rattled him. The incident, however, was to provide the basis of countless stories that Mengele was responsible for many such abortions during his years on the run.[38] It is medically possible that Mengele could perform abortions, but it is unlikely that he had any need to do so, as he was not only financially comfortable, but also enjoying the respectability of his new position. The notion that Mengele continued to perform sadistic blood-soaked operations fits in with the popular image, but the circumstances in Buenos Aires in the late 1950s were very different to those in Poland in the early 1940s. Auschwitz provided the ultimate human laboratory, in which experimentation could take place outside a moral framework. In the concentration camp, death and savagery were ubiquitous, whereas Mengele was now living a bourgeois existence with a wife and a stepson. There was no need to risk all that for the supposed thrill of butchering a young girl, an act that would have earned him no medical knowledge. Auschwitz may have given him some fetishistic taste for taking life, but there is no evidence to support the notion that Mengele stalked the warm nocturnal alleys of Buenos Aires looking for fresh meat. Had Mengele really performed a backstreet abortion, then he would have prided himself on doing it well, and ironically, the young girl might not have been in better hands.

One of the first things that Ante Pavelić did upon disembarking in Buenos Aires on 6 November 1948 was to shave off his comically heavy beard and moustache.[39] Because of his status as former *Poglavnik*, the 59-year-old Pavelić was given VIP treatment when he arrived, and did not even have to produce a landing permit. It has been suggested that Pavelić was 'whisked off the ship' by agents of Perón, and the lack of suitable official documentation would support this.[40] Pavelić was formally welcomed by his former ambassador to Berlin, Branco Benzon, who greeted him in the name of the Argentine government, which, Benzon claimed, would extend its full help and cooperation. Over the next few days, Pavelić held many meetings with his Ustasha cronies, and he urged them to continue the fight for an 'Independent State of Croatia'. He then departed for the interior, with one CIA source believing him to have sought refuge in Tandil, a town some 200 miles south of Buenos Aires.[41] As well as bringing political leadership to his emigré Croatian community, Pavelić would bring wealth, although the majority of his treasure would not arrive until late 1951 or early 1952. That year, the CIA learned that Pavelić was trying to sell 200 kilos of gold on the Buenos Aires market.[42] With gold at $35 per fine ounce, Pavelić may have sold it for around $250,000, which was equivalent to 6.2 million pesos. This would have been an enormous amount in Argentina in the early 1950s. The hourly wage of Reinhard Kops as a factory worker was 1.6 pesos an hour, which approximates to 3,500 pesos per year. Had Kops stayed in that position, it would have taken him 1,771 years to earn the worth of Pavelić's gold.

During his stay in Argentina, Pavelić continued to plot his comeback. In October 1949, he held a meeting with forty former Ustasha government officials, during which he informed them that war in Europe was imminent. He insisted that all rivalries should be set aside, and that it was necessary to prepare for the forthcoming conflict. As well as consorting with his fellow countrymen, it was rumoured that he had met Adolf Galland, as well as Otto Skorzeny, who was reputed to have visited Buenos Aires around this time.[43] Despite his efforts, Pavelić's Ustashi continued to quarrel, and by the middle of 1950 they had Balkanized into two groups, one of which remained loyal to the *Poglavnik*, while the other allied itself with Dr Branimir Jelić, who lived in Britain.[44] Jelić, whose supporters included Father Draganović, was a doctor of medicine who had served as the Ustasha director of propaganda before the war. Between 1934 and 1939, he had enjoyed two protracted stays in the United States, where he acted as Pavelić's representative and spouted pro-fascist propaganda. This would eventually earn him his deportation, although he did not make it back to Yugoslavia before the war started, as he was arrested by the British in Gibraltar and interned on the Isle of Man until 1945.[45] However, backed by the pacifist Labour MP Rhys Davies and Countess Listowel, a Hungarian anti-communist and journalist who had been born Judith de Marffy-Mantuano, after the war Jelić was allowed to base himself in London, where he stayed at the Tocsowa Hotel on Dulwich Common.[46] From there, he raised money and painted himself as a more moderate Ustasha who did not approve of the violence wrought by Pavelić's regime. He also corresponded with Winston Churchill, pleading with him not to neglect the Croatian people. According to Jelić, Churchill replied that he regretted the conditions in Croatia and had welcomed some more information.[47]

By the middle of 1950, Pavelić had decided that the only way he could reunite the Ustashi was to threaten to kill those who were opposed to him. The appearance in Rome in July that year of

Vjekoslav 'Maks' Luburić would confirm the seriousness of Pavelić's intent.[48] Of all of the *Poglavnik*'s thugs, he was the worst. A former small-time crook, he was appointed an Ustasha general and the head of Jasenovac concentration camp, around which he would personally patrol two to three times per month committing random acts of murder. In October 1942, he held a banquet at the camp during which he congratulated his men for slaughtering more people in one year than the Ottoman Empire had managed during the height of its power in Europe. Luburić's reputed sadism was boundless. In December 1944, he and four others crucified a nineteen-year-old woman on a table and proceeded to burn her genitals with cigarettes. Although such stories may have been the product of post-war Yugoslav anti-Ustasha propaganda, Luburić arrived in the Italian capital with a fearsome reputation.[49] In August 1950, in order to assert his authority, he issued a proclamation in a Croatian newspaper in Chicago, warning that all Croatian subjects living in Europe were not permitted to join foreign armies.[50] Although it does not appear that Luburić went on a killing spree, his presence certainly reduced the volume of the anti-Pavelić faction. He returned to Spain, only to emerge the following year to travel to Hamburg, where he planned to establish a recruiting centre for Pavelić's forces. According to a CIA source in Buenos Aires, Luburić's plan even had the blessing of the British authorities.[51]

As well as having to deal with his unruly Ustashi, Pavelić's other concern was the health of his wife, Marija, who had been admitted to a hospital in Buenos Aires during the latter half of 1949.[52] However, Pavelić himself would be hospitalized with a far more serious condition a few years later. At ten past nine on the evening of Wednesday 10 April 1957, a gunman fired six shots at the former dictator near his home in the Buenos Aires suburb of Caseros. Four of the .32-calibre rounds missed, but one hit him next to the second vertebra above his pelvis, and the other hit him near his right collarbone. While the assassin fled, Pavelić managed to stagger back to his house, where he was given first aid by an Argentinian doctor. A Croatian doctor called Milivoj Marušić was summoned, and he sent Pavelić to hospital, where he underwent surgery to remove the bullets.[53] The following day, Pavelić had told a reporter exactly who he thought was behind the attempted killing. 'It is the Communist

Yugoslav delegation,' he said. 'Not directly, of course, but through some devious means.'[54] Such wounds were serious, especially for a 67-year-old man, but Pavelić was determined not to stay in hospital and discharged himself in the early hours after the shooting.

If the Yugoslavs were behind the attempt, then they were brazen enough to try to get Pavelić by more legal means. Later that month, Tito's government put in an extradition request for the war criminal, which the new, more democratic Argentine government did not seem averse to granting, while they kept Pavelić under surveillance at his home.[55] In all likelihood, Pavelić was tipped off about the request, and on 26 April the Argentine Ministry of the Interior reported that Pavelić had disappeared and was now considered a fugitive.[56] For the next three months, it is unclear where Pavelić hid, but according to 'the official Ustasha news' he crossed into Chile at Punto Arenas on 24 July. He stayed for four months in Santiago, and then travelled to Madrid, where he arrived on 29 November. For the next two years, Pavelić suffered from his wounds and, in November and December 1959, he was obliged to undergo a series of operations at the German Hospital in Madrid. The seventy-year-old did not make good progress and, on 18 December, Pavelić made what would be his last confession, and then took communion. On 27 December, he received a special blessing from Pope John XXIII, and at eight o'clock that evening he was given the last rites. He died in his sleep at three fifty-five the following morning, clutching a rosary that he had been given by Pope Pius XII in 1941.[57] Pavelić's funeral was held on New Year's Eve and he was buried in San Isidro cemetery in Madrid. Reverend Raphael Medić, who had been the *Poglavnik*'s private chaplain, said that Pavelić 'was a good Catholic' and 'a fighter all his life for freedom from tyranny for the Croatian people'.[58]

The Yugoslav organization most likely to have carried out the assassination was the State Security Directorate: the UDBA. Unlike Western intelligence services, the UDBA had a large appetite for hunting down and killing war criminals, as well as Croats who were not criminals but who were openly opposed to Tito's regime. Pavelić was of course a major scalp, and the organization was to carry out many such eliminations until 1989.

In the late 1960s, 'Maks' Luburić employed his godson Ilija

Stanić at his publishing firm near Valencia in Spain. Stanić's father, Vinko, had served with Luburić during the war, but, unlike his comrade, Vinko was imprisoned by the Yugoslavs and he died in 1951. Luburić presumably thought he was doing the right thing by employing the young Ilija, but what he did not know was that his godson's real sympathies lay with the Tito regime. At that time, Luburić was the head of the Croatian National Resistance, and as such represented a prime target for the UDBA. On or before 20 April 1969, Luburić met the type of violent fate that he had dealt out to so many, which was later related by his assailant in gruesome detail.

> In an instant I grab the hammer and hit him over the forehead. Whack! Maks falls down like a candle. I thought he would never get up again. To my astonishment he looks at me with an animal look in his eyes. I swing again with the hammer and he raises his arms to protect himself. I scream: 'Ustasha motherfucker! This is how you were killing children with a sledgehammer in Jasenovac! See what is coming to you!' The hammer strikes him between his fingers into the forehead. His skull breaks. I pull the hammer out of his head and turn around. I go to the door to check that I locked it well. When I get back into the kitchen Maks is on his feet and panting like an animal. He weighs a hundred kilos. I take the crowbar and hit him over the forehead. His head splits open like a water melon. Blood starts gushing all over the kitchen. Maks hit the ground as though he fell from a height of at least a hundred meters. I hit him yet again. He quietens down.

The assassin was of course Stanić, who successfully fled back to Yugoslavia after the murder, where he would be rewarded with a BMW, a job, and flats in Belgrade and Sarajevo.[59]

One fugitive who would have admired such cold-blooded acts of justice was Klaus Barbie, who arrived in Buenos Aires with his family on 10 April 1951. As they were in transit, the Barbies did not stay long in Argentina, and within two weeks they were stepping on to the railway platform at the Bolivian city of La Paz. For the first few days, the Barbies, like many other European visitors, were the victims of altitude sickness, a condition that was hardly ameliorated by the seediness of their lodgings at the Hotel Italia.[60] Like many of his fellow Nazi fugitives, Barbie had very little money, which is indicative of there hardly being an all-powerful escape network that provided for its clients. The former 'Butcher of Lyon' was reduced to begging for 'loans' off his fellow Germans in order to feed his family, and he earned a few more bolivianos by performing odd jobs. 'The first offer of work I got,' Barbie recalled, 'was to repair twelve Bunsen burners. I was really proud that I could do it.'[61] Eventually, Barbie found more remunerative work at a forestry and sawmill in the humid Yungas forest on the eastern slopes of the Andes. Although the owner was Jewish, Barbie worked for him conscientiously, and helped to manage the eighty Indian woodsmen on the estate. 'I had to decide whether I should shout at them Prussian-style,' he said, 'or say nothing because I couldn't speak Spanish.'[62] Barbie opted for the silent approach, and impressed the workers by toiling alongside them and cleaning their wounds.[63] In Barbie's words, this was simply the application of 'some of our good National Socialist ideals'.[64]

Barbie soon became a partner in the business, and in 1956, 'Klaus Altmann' moved back to La Paz, where he opened his own wood yard. As he began to prosper, Barbie, like Mengele, thought it best to regularize his situation; in October 1957, he was granted Bolivian citizenship in the name of 'Altmann'. Throughout the late 1950s and early 1960s, Barbie became a popular figure in the German community, although whenever he was inebriated, the former Gestapo officer would shock his fellow countrymen by singing Nazi songs.[65]

A huge turning point for Barbie came in November 1964 when General René Barrientos seized the presidency in a coup. A charismatic leader, Barrientos still required the apparatus of a dictatorship to maintain his hold on power, and Barbie volunteered his services as a type of 'counter subversion' consultant. He was soon installed in the Ministry of the Interior, and advised the army on how to deal with guerrillas and, more ominously, how to conduct interrogations.[66] Barbie's links with the new administration were to make him a rich man. In 1966, Barbie presented himself as a 'marine engineer', and persuaded the government to grant him and a consortium of investors a 49 per cent stake in 'Transmarítima Boliviana', which aimed to boost Bolivia's merchant-shipping industry. Barbie became the general manager, and with it came a diplomatic passport which allowed him to travel extensively throughout Europe and Latin America. In Madrid, he was said to have visited Otto Skorzeny.[67] At one point, the British wanted to do business with Barbie and sell him a few ships, but Barbie declined, stating that he 'hadn't spent the war trying to sink British ships in order to buy them now'.[68] As a legitimate shipping company, Transmarítima was a failure, and Barbie did little more than lease a few ships and paint them in the Bolivian colours. The more profitable aspect of the business was to smuggle arms, and until the business collapsed in 1972, Barbie had creamed off a personal fortune from illegal arms shipments. Like many arms dealers, he had few qualms about where the cargos went, and in March 1968 the anti-Semitic Barbie even arranged for a shipment to go to Israel.[69]

On 27 April 1969, General Barrientos was killed in a helicopter crash. Although the new regime was to remain militaristic and right-wing, Barbie knew that his position was less secure, and he started to spend an increasing amount of time in the Peruvian capital of Lima, where he eventually settled the following year. It was in Peru that Barbie 'went into business' with Friedrich Schwend, who had masterminded the Nazi wartime Operation Bernhard that forged millions of pounds' worth of British banknotes. Schwend was a highly sophisticated conman, who by the end of the war had adopted the rank of *SS-Sturmbannführer* (major) and was reputed to have hidden a large number of crates of valuables at Castle Rametz outside Merano. In the centre of the town, Schwend was also reported to have installed no fewer than two wives in a villa on the Winkelweg.[70] By late 1946, he and one of his wives had appeared in Venezuela, and in the early 1950s they were living openly in Lima. Schwend earned his living through arms dealing, extortion, fraud, blackmail and the peddling of state secrets.[71] In short, he was the perfect business partner for Barbie, and together the two men established a lucrative trade in arms, as well as selling stolen Bolivian government credentials. Barbie and Schwend also sold fake information to the Peruvian police about subversive activities, and even lured a young German journalist called Herbert John to Peru on the promise that they could arrange a meeting with Martin Bormann. After extracting several thousand dollars from John, Barbie and Schwend told the Peruvian police that the young man was a cocaine dealer, and John was forced to flee before he was arrested.[72] In 1970, Barbie profited from one swindle too many, the fallout from which would hit him over a decade later. In September, Bolivia's state mining company COMIBOL paid Transmarítima ten thousand dollars to ship some minerals, which Barbie failed to do. In all likelihood, he simply pocketed the money. What Barbie had bought with that money was the key to his destruction, although for the time being he continued to revel in the twilight Latin American world of corruption. However, his actions would make him many enemies, and their revenge would soon be served up.

On 14 July 1950, Adolf Eichmann stepped off the *Giovanna C* and entered his new life. 'From being a shadow, I was now a man again,' he wrote, 'leaving behind four ghosts. Eichmann I had left in Austria; Barth I had lost in Bavaria; Eckmann I had left in the Rhineland; and Henninger had stayed in Italy.'[73] Now as Riccardo Klement, Eichmann had just 485 pesos – some thirty dollars – to his name, half of which he had promised to share with a former SS man he had met on the boat. However, as soon as he left the customs building, he was offered work by a German who was looking for house painters. 'I thanked my countryman for his friendliness,' Eichmann recalled. 'But he was obviously just after green gringoes [*sic*] whom he could work to death. I left him there. I had other plans.'[74]

Eichmann's 'other plans' were in fact laid for him by Carlos Fuldner, who provided the fugitive not only with accommodation in the suburb of Florida, but also a valid identity card and a job with a hydro-electric company run by CAPRI, the Argentine–German company whose willingness to employ German immigrants was the subject of much local jocularity.[75] Fuldner also supplied Eichmann with what appeared to be a social life. 'I was invited to dine with many fine families in Buenos Aires,' Eichmann would later write. 'Soon I did not feel myself a stranger any longer.'[76] Whether such a claim is true is open to question, but the impression that Eichmann had suddenly emerged into high Porteño society is false. He may indeed have gone to the odd dinner, but it is unlikely that Eichmann's prickly gaucheness would have endeared him to the more sophisticated Argentines. As it was, he was not to stay long in the capital, as the job was near Tucumán, some 500 miles northwest of Buenos Aires. Eichmann's role was to lead a group of workers at the hydro-electric plant, and he appeared to perform his duties diligently and worked hard enough to gain a promotion. In his spare time, he was able to go riding and enjoy the mountainous scenery that reminded him so much of home. He learned Spanish, and he also learned how to relax. 'My days as a hunted animal seemed far away,' he recalled. 'I certainly could not think there were still dogs on the trail of Eichmann.'[77] In 1951, he rented a house in Graneros, a village 50 miles south of Tucumán, where he lived simply with few modern accoutrements.[78] Such a remote location meant that Eichmann could not have been better hidden.

By the following year, Eichmann had decided that it would be safe for his family to join him. He contacted his wife through what he called 'the organisation', and later that year arrangements were made by the 'Nazi headquarters' in Buenos Aires to provide his wife with the fare to South America.[79] Such clandestine bodies were almost certainly a blend of Fuldner's network and CAPRI. In Altaussee, Vera Eichmann made her own arrangements, and told her sons Klaus, Horst and Dieter that they would be going to Argentina to visit their 'Uncle Riccardo', who had a big white horse. Frau Eichmann then applied for and received a German passport in her maiden name, although the boys were to travel under the name of Eichmann. In Vienna, she obtained a visa from the Argentine consulate, and in June 1952, the family travelled by train through the Brenner Pass and down to Genoa, where they embarked on the SS *Salto*.[80] They arrived in Buenos Aires the following month, where, according to Klaus Eichmann, 'there were several gentlemen waiting at the dock', who 'were very kind to us'.[81] 'Joyful was the reunion,' Eichmann wrote. 'But even now I had to live an untrue life. I could not be my own sons' father. I had to be "Uncle Riccardo".'[82] Vera Eichmann was also to recall the moment she set eyes on her husband, whom she had not seen for five years. 'There was Adolf standing on his own,' she said. 'He looked aged. I was crying for joy.'[83] After a few days in Buenos Aires, Eichmann took his family back to Graneros, where life seemed to be relatively idyllic. The children explored the countryside and they learned how to ride, and Eichmann soon revealed that he was in fact their father. They found him to be just as strict as he had been on the day he had left them in Altaussee in May 1945. 'Our father was very correct,' Klaus Eichmann later said, 'everything had to be just so, everything had to be in exact order.' He taught his sons Spanish in the most rigorous fashion by insisting that they learned one hundred words a day, 'no more, no less'.[84]

Just as with Franz Stangl and Josef Mengele, the security of Adolf Eichmann's new life was not to last. In early 1953, the hydro-electric company went bust along with so many other businesses in Argentina. In April, Eichmann moved his family to Buenos Aires, where they rented a bungalow at 4261 Chacabuco Street in the Olivos district. The property, which the family would live in for the next six years, was modest and the area was scruffy. Although Josef Mengele was to live only a few blocks away, his part of Olivos was a great deal more salubrious. In social terms, the separation between the two men was even greater: the sophisticated Mengele inhabited a world that stopped just short of café society, whereas Eichmann, with his far more humble origins, would always be regarded as the lower-middle-class 'administrator'. However, the two men did actually meet on occasions at the ABC German restaurant at Calle Lavalle 545 in the centre of Buenos Aires. By all accounts, they were not close, and Mengele found that Eichmann exuded an aura of fear and sensed that he was a broken man.[85] For his part, Eichmann would later admit that he had met Mengele 'once or twice', but he claimed that he had 'no desire to mix with that type of person, because it was not good for me'.[86] The ABC restaurant is still in business, and it is extraordinary to imagine that these two most notorious war criminals could have been found innocently enjoying a coffee in its traditional German interior. To have chanced upon such a meeting would have been a great coup for any Nazi hunter, but as we shall learn, there were no Nazi hunters in Argentina throughout most of the 1950s. It is tempting – but perhaps glib – to observe that all a Nazi hunter had to do was to sit in the ABC for a few days and he would have rounded up the best part of the 'Fourth

Reich'. Naturally, even Martin Bormann was rumoured to have broken *brot* at the ABC.[87] Had the ABC been an Italian trattoria that favoured hanging up black-and-white photographs of its most illustrious customers, the interior would have been reminiscent of a Nazi rogues' gallery.

Throughout the remainder of the 1950s, Eichmann found it hard to find regular work. He opened a laundry business, but that failed, as did a fabric shop, which left him with no capital. Once again, he turned to leporids, and for a few years he ran a farm which bred angora rabbits, until that too went bust. In March 1959, he started work at his last ever job, which was as a mechanic at a Mercedes-Benz plant in the very north of Buenos Aires.[88] One of the few highlights of Eichmann's existence was the birth of his fourth son, Ricardo, in 1953. 'To me this meant more than the mere joy of proud fatherhood,' Eichmann gushed. 'It was a symbol of freedom, of life triumphant over the forces that were seeking to destroy me.' However, Eichmann's symbol was tainted by the fact that young Ricardo had to be registered under his mother's maiden name of Liebl. 'It pained me to do that,' Eichmann wrote, 'but one cannot let sentiment interfere with caution and efficiency.'[89] One other highlight was Eichmann's move in early 1960 to a house that would soon become famous: 14 Garibaldi Street. Little more than an ugly and forlorn unrendered one-storey block, which lacked both water and electricity, the house was built by Eichmann with the help of his sons on a plot that had cost him 65,000 pesos ($800) in 1958.[90] Situated near the busy Route 202 in the northern district of San Fernando, Garibaldi Street was little more than a dirt track in the middle of some marshy land, but for Eichmann, it represented a new beginning.

With his own property and a job at Mercedes, the 53-year-old Eichmann would have once again begun to feel secure. Along with so many other low-wage earners, the 'Architect of the Holocaust' commuted on the number 203 bus. One indication of his sense of security was the fact that he kept a routine. He would return home every evening at seven forty, having alighted from the bus near a little kiosk on Route 202 and walked the 100 metres back home.[91] Before he went inside, he would inspect his vegetable garden, for which he would often use a torch when the light was fading. He would then walk once round the house, and then join his family for supper.[92]

Initially, the evening of Wednesday 11 May 1960 was not an unusual one for Eichmann. He had taken a slightly later bus, but that was not exceptional. After he got off the 203, Eichmann and the cigarette vendor in the kiosk exchanged their customary friendly nods, and then he strolled up Route 202 towards the junction with Garibaldi Street. Although it was not bitterly cold, Eichmann could feel the approach of winter, and a full moon illuminated his way back home. As he turned left into his street, and was just 30 metres from inspecting his garden, Eichmann noticed a Buick parked some 20 metres from his house. The bonnet was open, and a few men appeared to be tinkering with it. As Eichmann approached, the men seemed to have had some success, as the engine suddenly coughed into life. He drew level with the car, but although he was curious, he was not suspicious. One of the men turned to him, and in somewhat poor Spanish said, '*Un momentito, señor.*' Eichmann stood still, transfixed, unwittingly giving the little moment he had been asked for. After a fraction of a second, the man grabbed him by the arms. Eichmann instinctively stepped back, which caused the two men to roll into a ditch. As he struggled, Eichmann's first thought was that he was being assaulted by bandits. His glasses came off, and although he wanted to shout out, it was impossible because his false teeth had dislodged into the back of his throat. He soon felt more arms grabbing him, and a heavy sack was placed over his head. Eichmann was then stuffed into the back of the Buick and the car roared off. A few seconds later, he received the first order he had ever been given by a Jew: 'Do not move and no one will hurt you. If you resist, you will be shot!' As he lay in the car and identified the man's German-Jewish accent, Eichmann realized that his kidnappers were not run-of-the-mill bandits. The man continued to ask him questions, but he was too shocked to reply. 'Can you hear me?' the voice was asking, first in German and then in Spanish. 'Do you understand me?' Eventually, Eichmann replied from under his hood. He spoke in German: '*Ich habe bereits mein Schicksal angenommen*' – 'I have already accepted my fate.'[93]

Chapter Nine

Eichmann

THE STORY of how Adolf Eichmann came to be bundled by Mossad agents into the back of a car in the middle of some dreary Argentine wasteland has been told many times, but not often with accuracy. The cliché of success having many fathers certainly applies, and the story of the Eichmann kidnap is laden with such paternal figures. The greatest of these was Simon Wiesenthal, but, as we shall see, Wiesenthal's role was extremely minor, and he played no direct part either in successfully locating Eichmann, or indeed in his capture. Wiesenthal's greatest role was unduly claiming credit, which he did with obscene chutzpah. As was his custom, the story told by Wiesenthal contains so many distortions, exaggerations and lies that the truth has almost been buried under the weight of his deception. Wiesenthal's version is certainly a thrilling one, but no more so than the real story. It will be helpful to examine both, because the tale of the capture of Adolf Eichmann was fundamental to the construction of the Wiesenthal legend, a legend that was self-built and then significantly enhanced by a media hungry for the heroic tale of the lone Jew against the Nazis. Wiesenthal's brief role as a stand-up comic while he was a student in Prague would have taught him to give the audience what it wanted, and when dealing with the press in years to come, he would adopt the same approach.

The true story of Eichmann's capture begins with a young couple in their early twenties called Klaus and Sylvia, who had started dating in Buenos Aires in mid-1956. By all accounts, Sylvia was attractive, and although the relationship did not appear to be serious, Klaus visited Sylvia's home on several occasions. Like Klaus, Sylvia was German, and she had lived with her parents in Argentina since 1938. Her father, Lothar Hermann, had been locked up in Dachau from 1935 to 1936 as a political prisoner, and after his release and the events of Kristallnacht, the half-Jewish Hermann decided that Nazi Germany was no place to raise his family.[1] In Buenos Aires, they had settled, like so many other Germans, in the suburb of Olivos, and in order to fit in, the family made no mention of their Jewish ancestry. During his visits to the Hermanns, Sylvia's boyfriend grew increasingly relaxed, and he soon began to express an array of alarming opinions. 'Once, when the conversation turned to the fate of the Jews in the Second World War,' Hermann recalled, 'he said it would have been better if the Germans had finished their job of extermination.' Klaus also spoke proudly of his father having been an officer during the war, and having done his 'duty for the fatherland'. On one occasion, Hermann's wife enquired as to why Klaus's German accent seemed to be an amalgam of so many different dialects. Klaus explained that because his father's war service had seen the family move around so often, his voice reflected this itinerancy.[2] The relationship ended either because of the un-palatability of Klaus's opinions, or because the Hermanns moved to the town of Coronel Suárez, some 300 miles southwest of Buenos Aires. The following year, Hermann heard a report about a trial in Frankfurt of a Nazi war criminal, during which the name of Adolf Eichmann was mentioned as being instrumental in the destruction of the Jews. The surname gave Hermann a jolt, as it was the same as that of Sylvia's former boyfriend, the anti-Semitic young Klaus who had boasted about his father's patriotic duty for the fatherland. 'Without any hesitation,' Hermann recalled, 'I wrote to the Public Prosecutor in Frankfurt, raising my suspicions.'[3]

Hermann's letter appeared on the desk of Frankfurt's

Attorney-General, Dr Fritz Bauer. Luckily for Hermann, it could not have gone to a better man. Appointed to the office the previous year, Bauer had been arrested and imprisoned by the Gestapo in 1933 for his active socialism. In 1936, he fled to Copenhagen, and when Denmark was invaded, the Jewish Bauer successfully sought refuge in Sweden, where together with Willy Brandt he founded the *Sozialistische Tribüne* newspaper. After the war, Bauer returned to Denmark, where he worked in the editorial offices of a news magazine for German refugees. Bauer was not to return to Germany until 1949, when he was appointed as a district court director and then as Attorney-General in Brunswick.[4] In 1956, at the age of fifty-three, he accepted the post in Frankfurt, where his uncompromising attitude towards Nazi war criminals earned him many detractors. Untainted by Nazism, the pugnacious Bauer sought to 'clean the nest', and saw through the 'superior-order defence' pleaded by many a low-ranking Nazi: 'There is no question, at least not for myself or for the prosecutors in the Federal Republic, that there was a long list of people who didn't act only on orders, but who acted as they did out of real conviction that what they were doing was right.'[5] Bauer's physical presence backed up the solidity of his opinions. Thickset and broad of face, his eyes staring through a pair of thick black-rimmed spectacles, Bauer had the features of a once-great pugilist.

Bauer wrote back to Hermann demanding more information, especially the address of the man who might be Eichmann. What the lawyer might not have known was that Hermann was not the most qualified person in Argentina to start making inquiries. He was not a poor man, but what he did lack was a pair of eyes: the beatings he had received at Dachau in the mid-1930s had rendered him blind. However, Hermann was determined, and he returned to Buenos Aires, accompanied by Sylvia. As Klaus had never told her exactly where he lived, Sylvia had to make some enquiries around Olivos, and eventually she was given the address of 4261 Chacabuco Street. One Sunday afternoon, she went round to the bungalow and knocked on the door. A man briefly appeared at the window and peered at her and then went away. A minute or so later, the door was opened by a large middle-aged woman who was holding a young boy at her hip. Sylvia introduced herself by saying that she was a colleague of Klaus and she was wondering whether he was at home.

The woman was Vera, Eichmann's wife, and she said that Klaus was out, but wouldn't Fräulein Hermann wish to have a coffee and a slice of cake? Sylvia accepted, and soon the two women were joined by Eichmann himself. He nodded slightly at her, and Sylvia got up and offered him her hand, which he took and said, 'I am pleased to meet you, young lady.'[6]

Instinctively, Sylvia asked the man whether he was Klaus's father. The question was of course a perfectly natural one in the circumstances, but Eichmann was on the defensive. He paused, and then said, 'No, I am his uncle.' For a few minutes the three made small talk, until they were joined by Klaus, who was surprised to find Sylvia. 'Who gave you my address?' he demanded. 'And gave you permission to visit me without an invitation?' Sylvia apologized, and told Klaus that she had been given the address by a friend and she simply wanted to see how he was. 'Did I do something wrong?' she asked. Klaus's father quickly informed her that she most certainly had not, and told his wife to make the promised cup of coffee. However, the uncomfortable Klaus motioned to Sylvia that she should go, and Eichmann accompanied her and Klaus to the front door. Klaus then told his 'uncle' that he would see Sylvia to the bus, but Eichmann said that it would be even more gentlemanly if Klaus escorted Sylvia back home. Klaus's reply would seal Eichmann's fate. 'Thank you, Father,' he said. 'I will take care of Sylvia and see to it that she gets home.'[7]

Shortly afterwards, Hermann wrote to Bauer telling him that Adolf Eichmann lived at 4261 Chacabuco Street. When the lawyer received this information, he knew that he could not simply disseminate it through the West German criminal justice system, as it was riddled with too many former Nazis. Instead, on Thursday 19 September 1957, Bauer met Dr Felix Shinar, the head of the Israeli Reparations Mission in West Germany, in an inn on the main road between Cologne and Frankfurt. 'Eichmann has been traced,' said Bauer, without offering any chit-chat. An excited Shinar wondered what Bauer would do, and the German told him that he was giving the information to the Israelis to act on since he could not trust his fellow countrymen. Shinar thanked Bauer fulsomely, and after the meeting he immediately informed the Israeli Foreign Ministry, which in turn gave the information to Isser Harel, the head of the Israeli secret service.[8]

Born as Isser Halperin in Vitebsk in Russia in 1912, Harel had emigrated with his family to Latvia in 1922 after the Soviets had confiscated their vinegar factory. A passionate Zionist, Harel decided that his future lay in the Jewish Settlement in Palestine, and so in 1930 he travelled down to Genoa, where he boarded a ship with a pistol hidden in a loaf of bread. After serving with distinction in the paramilitary *Haganah*, Harel was appointed as head of both the Mossad, which carried out foreign espionage, and the Shabak, which was the internal security service.[9] Initially, Harel knew little about Eichmann except for the fact that his 'principal function was the extermination of Jews'. He was also wary of such sightings, as the Israelis had received many tips concerning Eichmann's where-abouts, all of which had led to nought. However, after a night reading through the Mossad's file on Eichmann, Harel resolved to catch Eichmann 'come hell or high water'. It is unclear what made Harel act on Bauer's information, although he would later speculate that it was perhaps because he had caught some of the excitement off the Director-General of the Foreign Ministry who had told Harel the news. As Harel did not send an agent out to Buenos Aires until January 1958 – some four months after Bauer's meeting with Shinar – it is more likely that Harel did not treat the information with the reverence he would later claim.[10]

Harel's agent was Yoel Goren, who had only a limited knowledge of Spanish. To make up for this shortcoming, Goren was accompanied by Efraim Ilani, an academic who was studying the Jewish community in Argentina. Together, the two men reconnoitred Chacabuco Street and even managed to photograph Eichmann's bungalow. When Goren returned, Harel was immediately sceptical. 'The poverty-stricken suburb of Olivos, the unpaved street, and the wretched little house could in no way be reconciled with our picture of the life of an SS officer of Eichmann's rank,' Harel wrote.[11] The intelligence chief let the matter drop, but informed Bauer that little could be done unless Bauer revealed his source. Keen to protect Hermann, the Frankfurt Attorney-General only yielded his name and address with great reluctance.[12] Once again, it is a measure of Harel's scepticism that he did not arrange for Hermann and his daughter to be interviewed until he learned that a high-ranking police officer called Efraim Hofstätter was travelling to South

America for an Interpol conference in March. Harel told the policeman that he should present himself as a representative of Fritz Bauer,
as he had no wish to advertise the involvement of Mossad in
following up the lead.[13]

Harel's seeming insouciance looks alarming in hindsight, and his
own retrospective gloss claiming great excitement is unconvincing.
In fact, Harel's doubts were not unreasonable, as not only did the
information look suspect, but such rumours were commonplace.
Had the Mossad followed up every lead on, say, Martin Bormann
that had appeared in the newspapers, then it would have had few
resources left to deal with what was felt to be a more present threat
than fugitive Nazis: the Arab states. For this reason, the Israelis had
given little or no priority to hunting down Nazis. Tuviah Friedman
was once told by Israel's first consul in Vienna that his country 'was
not interested in the search for Nazi criminals and that he would not
support this work in Austria'.[14] In addition, the Mossad was not
particularly well funded, and like any other responsible civil servant
in democracies the world over, Harel would have had to ensure that
his department ran within budget. Sending men to South America
following up leads from blind old men was an expensive and time-
consuming business, and hardly looked worth the investment. In
addition, Harel has been censured for not initially realizing the full
value of Eichmann's scalp, but this may be unfair criticism.[15]
Although today Adolf Eichmann's name has a global notoriety, in
the late 1950s it was known by only relatively few. The Holocaust
too, despite being seen on newsreels in the wake of Germany's
defeat, was not well studied and its gruesome mechanisms and personalities were not fully examined. The roles of the RSHA, the SD,
the *Einsatzgruppen*, the Gestapo, and the *Totenkopfverbände* were
still opaque, and even today the roles of these institutions can cause
confusion to the layman and the academic alike. Harel also had to
consider legal questions. The decision to kidnap a foreign national
in a foreign country was hardly one that could be taken lightly,
especially by a young democracy such as Israel. In addition, there
was a general agreement between Jewish leaders and hunters such as
Wiesenthal and Friedman that the guilty should be brought back to
Germany to face justice, and not to be sent to Israel.[16] The structure
of due process for dealing with Nazi war criminals had been

established in the Federal Republic – it most certainly had not in Israel. If Eichmann were indeed brought back to the Jewish state, there was no guarantee that a legally sound conviction against him could be secured. It is too easy to dismiss Harel's hesitancy as sloppiness or lack of will, but this is to place the hunt for Eichmann in an elemental context of good versus bad, and ignores the wider political, legal, practical and budgetary issues.

However, unknown to both the Mossad and Fritz Bauer, there were others in 1958 who suspected that Eichmann was living in Argentina. While Efraim Hofstätter was making his plans to travel to the southern hemisphere, a CIA officer based in Munich met a counterpart from the West German intelligence agency the BND. Over the course of their conversation, the American managed to wheedle out of the German some 'generalisations' regarding the BND's activities in the Near and Middle East. One of these pieces of information was a report that Eichmann had been living 'in Argentina under the alias CLEMENS since 1952'. Eichmann's cover name was of course Klement, which was similar enough to Clemens to indicate – in retrospect – that the report had some validity. However, the BND man also said that there was a rumour that Eichmann was living in Jerusalem. After the meeting, the CIA officer gave the information to his chief of station, who in turn passed it back to CIA headquarters on 19 March.[17] Much to the surprise of many, the CIA did not act upon the information and neither is it known to have disseminated it.

When this was revealed in June 2006, it was often observed that the CIA was either negligent, or once again displaying the kind of moral ambiguity that saw American intelligence agencies employing the likes of Klaus Barbie. Some even suggested that the agency was hiding Eichmann, which was demonstrably untrue.[18] All these accusations are groundless, for the simple reason that the CIA emphatically did not know where Eichmann was hiding. Not only had it been given two potential locations – although one was clearly more likely than the other – but the revelation had been made on an informal basis, and was hardly an official communiqué from the BND to the CIA. The inference that the CIA knew Eichmann's location just because it is now known that one half of what it had been told was correct is the worst kind of misapplied *a posteriori* thinking and borders on casuistry. Similarly, the charge that the CIA could 'have done something about it' is also groundless. In the late 1950s, it was not the job of the CIA to hunt Nazi war criminals. If that policy is to be considered a failure – which is reasonable – then the blame must be laid at the feet of the CIA's masters in the government. The truth is, no government had a policy of hunting Nazis at that time, so the CIA's lack of action is hardly its fault. The CIA has also been accused of not giving the Israelis the information, but once again, such a charge is naive. As we have seen, the Israelis were not known to be hunting Eichmann, and the CIA had no knowledge that the Mossad were up to anything in 1958. Most crucially, the fact that the BND had leads as to Eichmann's whereabouts would have been reason in itself for the CIA to have done nothing, as it was widely seen as the job of the West Germans to bring such men to justice. If the blame for a lack of action must go anywhere, then it should be attached to the West Germans, but, as the likes of Fritz Bauer well knew, in Germany there was little or no hunger for Nazi hunting.

Had the Israelis known about 'Clemens', then it is feasible that Eichmann may have been brought to justice in 1958. Unfortunately, after Hofstätter had visited the Hermanns in Coronel Suárez that March, he shared Harel's scepticism. He pointed out to the family that it was feasible that Vera Eichmann had married again, and that the children were continuing to call themselves Eichmann. What Hermann lacked was definitive proof, and what he had given Bauer – and unbeknown to him, the Israelis – was nothing more than a strong suspicion. Much to Hermann's frustration, Hofstätter told him that if he supplied some actual evidence, then he would be very interested. Hermann complained that the whole business was costing him a considerable amount of money, and Hofstätter promised that he would be refunded. Before he left, he gave Hermann a contact address, which therefore shut Bauer out of the information loop.[19] Before he left Buenos Aires, Hofstätter also reconnoitred the house on Chacabuco Street, and he too felt that it was highly unlikely that a Nazi of Eichmann's status could be living there. When Hofstätter returned to Israel, he shared his doubts with Harel, who then effectively stalled the investigation by leaving matters with Hermann. As one member of the Eichmann kidnap team was to put it, 'the great Isser Harel and his secret service, supposedly one of the best in the world, left the task to a blind pensioner living more than 250 miles away'.[20] Such cynicism is understandable in retrospect, but, for the reasons outlined above, there were perfectly valid reasons for not following Hermann's lead.

Hermann refused to let the matter drop, and throughout April and May 1958, he conducted a series of researches into the house on Chacabuco Street, which revealed that it was owned by one Francisco Schmidt, although the electricity was supplied to a man called 'Clements'. However, because the name 'Clements' meant nothing to Hermann, he assumed that Eichmann was in fact masquerading as Schmidt and had had extensive plastic surgery. Harel found this fanciful, but what startled him more was Hermann's insistence that he needed to undertake costly researches into the Argentine interior to investigate Schmidt's past. 'It all sounded most peculiar to me,' Harel observed, who could see no reason as to why Hermann needed to trace Eichmann's footsteps when he in fact could place him at number 4261.[21] The back of Harel's camel was finally broken by more information that had come in from Efraim Ilani, which indicated that Schmidt did not even live in the house, and nothing about Schmidt matched what the Israelis knew about Eichmann. Hermann was intransigent, but Harel had heard enough; by August 1958, he had gently let the matter drop. For the time being Adolf Eichmann was safe from the Israelis.[22]

What may have spurred Hermann's eagerness to find Eichmann was not just a sense of justice, but also the prospect of a ten-thousand-dollar reward posted by the World Jewish Congress at the behest of Tuviah Friedman.[23] However, it would be unfair to label Hermann as being driven purely by money, as his motives for wishing revenge on the Nazis were clear enough.

Another potential clue came in February 1959, when Adolf Eichmann's stepmother died. Shortly afterwards, a death notice placed in the *Oberösterreichische Nachrichten* was spotted by Simon Wiesenthal. In the notice, he saw that named among the grieving family members was Eichmann's wife as well as his sons. Wiesenthal decided to make some enquiries, and he sent some 'private persons' to establish from the Eichmann family the

whereabouts of Vera Eichmann. Unfortunately, the family remained
tight-lipped, and divulged nothing to those acting on Wiesenthal's
behalf. As far as Wiesenthal was concerned, this strongly indicated
that Eichmann was living in Austria. Later that year, he shared his
thoughts with the Israeli ambassador in Vienna.

> The strong discretion of the family members in respect to the present
> whereabouts of Vera Eichmann may point to the eventuality that the
> searched for Adolf Eichmann may be found in their vicinity, if he is
> not in fact living with them. Otherwise, such rather embarrassing
> social discretion on the part of the family in this respect is rather
> incomprehensible.[24]

Wiesenthal was convinced that Eichmann was still in Europe. In
September 1959, he wrote a lengthy letter to the ambassador concerning the investigations being made by the police into the
whereabouts of Eichmann. One of the leads was the gossip
emanating from Eichmann's children's schoolfriends, who said that
the boys had told them 'that they will go to a property with vast
lands, where one can also do horseriding'. Furthermore, Wiesenthal
wrote that 'due to still other ways of expressing themselves, the
impression was, that they might be talking about Northern
Germany'.[25]

On 10 November, the ambassador wrote to Wiesenthal thanking
him for his help. He told Wiesenthal that he had discussed
Eichmann with 'our people' – by whom he presumably meant the
Mossad – and they were appreciative of Wiesenthal's efforts. Then,
in an extraordinary lapse of security, the diplomat told Wiesenthal
where they believed the criminal to be: 'According to the latest information in their possession, the Eichmann family is in Argentina.
His wife acts as if Eichmann would [sic] not be alive anymore. She
even remarried a German citizen. However, all the indications point
to it that this marriage is a fictitious one, in order to "confuse the
enemy".'[26]

Wiesenthal wrote back to the ambassador on 1 December, in
which letter he made no mention of the information he had been
given, and expounded on an obscure lead concerning Eichmann's
brother and a lawyer who had acted for another war criminal.[27] In

none of his correspondence with the Israelis did Wiesenthal mention the likelihood that Eichmann was in Argentina. He also had no inkling about Eichmann's alias of 'Klement'. All the information that Wiesenthal gave – and it was scanty – suggested that the fugitive was in either Germany or Austria. His lack of reaction to the ambassador's revelation suggests that Wiesenthal did not give it much credence.

Wiesenthal's memoirs paint a very different picture of these meetings and his actions. In fact, they are so mendacious that it is astonishing to consider that they remained unchallenged during his lifetime. In his 1967 memoir, *The Murderers Among Us*, Wiesenthal wrote: '. . . I sent one of my men to see Frau Eichmann's mother. Frau Maria Liebl was not very friendly to the visitor, but admitted that her daughter had in fact married a man named "Klems" or "Klemt" in South America . . . I sent what little information I had to Israel.'[28] In his 1989 account, *Justice Not Vengeance*, Wiesenthal presents a similar story: 'I sent one of my people to Frau Eichmann's mother, who seemed to regard a half-truth as the best form of concealment. She stated that her daughter had married a man called "Klems" or "Klemt" in South America. I sent this piece of information to Israel, and the Israelis were able to verify it.'[29]

These were complete falsehoods, because as we have seen Wiesenthal admitted to the Israelis that the conversations with the Eichmann family had born no fruit, and they had certainly never told him about 'Klems' or 'Klemt', or the fact that Vera Eichmann lived in South America. In fact, Wiesenthal had only discovered that 'piece of information' from the Israelis in the person of their ambassador to Austria. Wiesenthal's fabrications may appear minor when taken individually, but when they are combined in his memoirs, their multiplicity gives the misleading impression that Wiesenthal was positioned right in the centre of the hunt.

It took the bloody-mindedness of Fritz Bauer – and not Simon Wiesenthal – to resurrect the Israeli investigation. That December, he visited Israel on official business, and during his stay he told the Israelis that they couldn't let the opportunity go. Besides, he had valuable new information that he wished to share, information that had been found either by the BND, or perhaps by the police in

Austria. Wherever it had come from, the intelligence was good. Not only did Bauer provide an accurate account of Eichmann's flight from Europe and his time in Argentina, but he also said that Eichmann was now called Riccardo Klement. Although Bauer refused to reveal the source of his information, he confirmed, much to Harel's relief, that it had not come from Hermann. 'My mind was now at rest,' Harel later wrote. 'I had no means of assessing the reliability of the new source, but one item leapt to the eye and seemed to provide the key to the whole mystery: the name Riccardo Klement.'[30] It was obvious that Hermann's understandable mistake was to assume that the owner of the house – Francisco Schmidt – necessarily lived in the property, and was therefore Adolf Eichmann.

Harel's next step was to meet the Israeli Prime Minister, David Ben-Gurion, who decided that requesting Eichmann's extradition from Argentina would be pointless, and only give the fugitive a chance to go into hiding. He ordered Harel to kidnap Eichmann and smuggle him back to Israel for a trial. 'If it turns out that he is there,' Ben-Gurion wrote in his diary on 6 December, 'we will catch him and bring him here. Isser will take care of it.'[31] The Prime Minister's confidence was not misplaced, as Harel immediately set to work planning what would be a complicated operation. 'To me Argentina was an unknown country,' Harel recalled, 'and it was nine and a half thousand miles from Israel.' His largest problem was working out how Eichmann was going to be taken out of the country. There were no Israeli flights to South America, and chartering a special transatlantic plane to Buenos Aires would look suspicious. He consulted El Al, who informed him that the airline could mount an 'experimental' flight with a Britannia aircraft, which satisfied Harel for the time being.[32] Meanwhile, Harel needed to get a trustworthy man on the ground in Argentina, and for this he chose Zvi Aharoni, who had fought in the War of Independence and had worked in Israeli intelligence since 1948. During the war, Aharoni had served in the British army, where he had acquired an expertise at interrogating German POWs. Although he was not a fieldwork expert, Harel judged Aharoni to be a tenacious man, 'who never let go once he got his teeth into an assignment'.[33] After several weeks of preparation, Aharoni left Israel on 26 February 1960, travelling on a diplomatic passport. His cover story was that he was a Foreign

Ministry official who was investigating incidents of anti-Semitism in South America, although his real mission was to establish whether the man who lived at 4261 Chacabuco Street was definitely Eichmann. If Aharoni cabled back to Tel Aviv that 'the driver was black', then the kidnap mission was on.[34]

While the Israelis made their plans, a frustrated Lothar Hermann had made contact with Tuviah Friedman, who was now the Director of the Israeli Institute for the Documentation of Nazi War Crimes in Haifa. On 17 October 1959, Hermann wrote to Friedman informing him that recent news reports that Eichmann was living in Kuwait were false, and that he was in fact living 'near Buenos Aires'. 'I am willing to provide your institute accurate dates and material for a foolproof case,' Hermann confidently stated.[35] Friedman wrote back requesting that Hermann furnish him with some sort of evidence, as well as a photograph of Eichmann's 'present residence'. Reading between the lines of his reply, it is clear that Friedman regarded Hermann as little more than a speculative bounty chaser.[36] However, on 5 November, Hermann stated in a letter that he had numerous items of proofs including 'residence, street and house number, family status, name and exact details from the Argentinian identity papers, sales contract and official registration of the property, details on the arrival of Eichmann and members of his family between 1945 and 1948, and his distinguishing feature – a speech defect'.[37] Unfortunately, Hermann's material was the same misleading evidence that he had given Harel, as Hermann was still adamant that Eichmann was 'Francisco Schmidt'. Hermann added that he could not manage on his own, and asked if Friedman or a representative could visit him. There was also a tenor of anxiety in his letter: 'I happen to know for certain that Adolf Eichmann has helpers and spies everywhere, who can warn and protect him.'[38] Friedman took the letter to Professor Tartakower of the World Jewish Congress in Jerusalem, who said that he would find someone appropriate to investigate the matter. On 28 November, Friedman wrote to Hermann telling him that 'in the course of time, a man in Argentina will call on you'.[39] A frustrated Hermann had to wait until 26 December until such a 'man' came, who was in fact the leader of the DAIA, Argentina's most prominent Jewish organization.[40] Once again, Hermann told his story;

once again, he would be left in the dark to grow increasingly bitter.

Another Eichmann hunter who felt equally frustrated at the beginning of 1960 was Simon Wiesenthal. On 11 January, Wiesenthal was visited in his office in Linz by two Mossad operatives, who wished to know how an Austrian investigation into Eichmann was proceeding. Wiesenthal's relationship with the Mossad is unclear, but it is extremely likely that he was an agent for the organization throughout the 1950s. The CIC report of 16 January 1950 that had revealed Wiesenthal having recruited Höttl as a source had also mentioned that Wiesenthal was 'chief Austrian Agent of the Israeli Intelligence Bureau'.[41] Wiesenthal also appeared to be running an agent in the Austrian security service, who told him how investigations into Nazis such as Eichmann were proceeding.[42] Wiesenthal was thus able to tell the Mossad agents that the Austrian inquiries were somewhat inadequate, but they had unearthed the affidavit made by Vera Eichmann in the mid-1940s to have her husband declared dead. Wiesenthal was later to claim that it was thanks to him that the application had been thwarted, in a move that he described as his 'most important contribution in the search for Eichmann'.[43] However, during that meeting in January 1960, Wiesenthal made no mention of this fact, and neither could he tell the Israelis the name of Vera Eichmann's brother-in-law in Prague who was supposed to have witnessed Eichmann's death in 1945 and supported Vera's claim.[44] This is curious, as in his memoir *The Murderers Among Us*, he claims to have discovered the brother-in-law's name – Karl Lukas – in 1947. In fact, Wiesenthal even admitted in writing on 13 January 1960 that he had had nothing to do with stymying Vera Eichmann's claim, and it was only in that same month that he first learned of Lukas. The reason why Eichmann was never declared dead was not because of Simon Wiesenthal, but because 'of the instigation of the authorities'.[45] This is a direct contradiction – in his own words – of what Wiesenthal would write in his memoirs. Thus, what Wiesenthal would claim to be his 'most important contribution' is nothing less than a piece of fiction.

During that same meeting, the Mossad agents asked Wiesenthal whether he still had his file on Eichmann. Wiesenthal said he did not have it, as it was actually in Jerusalem: 'Wiesenthal told us that he himself had given Yad Vashem the entire dossier on Eichmann containing papers in his handwriting, photographs and also fingerprints, in addition to a great deal of other material, inter alia, his handwritten curriculum vitae and signature.'[46]

There can be no doubt that Wiesenthal had sent the Eichmann material to the Yad Vashem archive, because not only did he admit as much in his 1961 memoir, *Ich Jagte Eichmann*, but he also said the same to the Vienna correspondent of *The Times* of London in May 1960.[47] In fact, it was Tuviah Friedman who helped Wiesenthal make the arrangements: 'In 1955 [Wiesenthal] asked me to help him sell his Documentation to Yad Vashem. Thanks to my endeavours with the head of the Yad Vashem archives Dr Kermisch, Wiesenthal sent some cratefuls of documents to Jerusalem and received several thousand dollars for them.'[48]

However, in his 1967 memoir, *The Murderers Among Us*, and in *Justice Not Vengeance* in 1989, Wiesenthal was to make another claim that placed him at the heart of the hunt for Eichmann. In the 1967 version, he wrote that he sent almost half a ton of boxes to Yad Vashem, but 'I kept only one for myself: the Eichmann file.'[49] In 1989, Wiesenthal claimed: 'The only file I kept was the Eichmann file. I honestly don't know why, because I had in truth given up.'[50] As we have seen, the actual truth was very different from Wiesenthal's 'truth'.

On 18 February 1960, the Mossad agents met Wiesenthal once again. Wiesenthal reported that Eichmann's father had died on 5 February and his funeral had been held in Linz four days later. A Mossad report of the meeting shows how Wiesenthal acted upon the news:

> Wiesenthal asked the local security service to photograph those attending the funeral; but in his opinion, the photographs revealed nothing. He promised to let us have a series of photographs, with identifying particulars. He claimed the photography had cost him 600 schillings, but when we offered to cover the cost he refused as in similar instances in the past.[51]

As is now becoming sadly familiar, Wiesenthal's memoirs tell a different story. In *The Murderers Among Us*, Wiesenthal recounted how the two Mossad agents – whom he called Michael and Meir – urgently required pictures of Eichmann. Wiesenthal then claimed he hit upon the idea of photographing the family members at the funeral, in the hope that the faces of Eichmann's brothers would help to identify their fugitive sibling. He then briefed two press photographers to photograph the event surreptitiously, and when he received the pictures, he cut out the faces of Eichmann's four brothers and placed them next to a picture of Eichmann. 'If "Ricardo Klement" in Buenos Aires was identical with Adolf Eichmann, his face must have gone through the same evolution as the face of his four brothers. [. . .] I shuffled the faces like playing cards and threw them on the table. Somehow a composite face emerged: perhaps Adolf Eichmann.'[52]

Wiesenthal claims he next showed his 'Eichmann card trick' to Michael and Meir. 'Michael shook his head,' Wiesenthal wrote, 'staring at the pictures. "Fantastic!" he said.' Such a story of 'a composite face' was clearly preposterous, and by the time he wrote *Justice Not Vengeance* in the late 1980s, Wiesenthal had deleted the 'card trick' and instead claimed that Israelis were excited by the potential similarity that might have existed between Otto Eichmann and Adolf. 'Anyone with Otto Eichmann's photograph in his hands,' Wiesenthal wrote, 'would be able to identify Adolf Eichmann – even if he now called himself Ricardo Klement.'[53] As the narrative in both accounts then immediately cuts to the news that Eichmann had been successfully kidnapped, Wiesenthal gives the impression that the photographs were somehow crucial to the success of the mission. Curiously, they are not mentioned by any of those who took part in the operation in Argentina.

Ironically, despite claiming to be what one biographer described as 'an indispensable protagonist' in the hunt for Eichmann, at the end of February 1960 Wiesenthal nearly put the whole operation in jeopardy.[54] During that month, Wiesenthal's contact in the Austrian security service managed to befriend the 22-year-old secretary of Eichmann's brother Robert. In order to win her complicity, the Austrian informed the woman that Israel was looking for Eichmann, and if she cooperated, she would earn her rightful share of the large reward being offered. The secretary then revealed that she believed that Eichmann's wife lived in Germany. On 29 February, Wiesenthal met the Israeli ambassador, and told him this piece of news. On 2 March, the ambassador passed the information on to the Mossad agents, who understandably reacted sourly when they heard that Wiesenthal had told the Austrian about Israel's hunt for Eichmann. One of the agents reported that 'Wiesenthal had received explicit and repeated instructions from me never to mention to anyone that the State of Israel was searching for Eichmann.' The next day, the Mossad agents visited the ambassador and found him and Wiesenthal already in conversation. The ambassador said that the error was all his, and all that the secretary had been told about was the reward. The agents were unconvinced, and got the impression that 'the secretary was in fact explicitly told that the reward was from the State of Israel'. The agents also asked if Wiesenthal could amplify the secretary's claim that Vera Eichmann was in Germany, but Wiesenthal refused. It was at this point that the Mossad appeared to break off its relationship with Wiesenthal.

> We again found Wiesenthal to be avoiding full and sincere co-operation, although he is prepared from time to time to feed the Ambassador crumbs of general information. At the same time, however, he refuses to give details. As decided, we did not assign him any mission. We merely elicited from him the information that none of Adolf Eichmann's brothers or sisters had any married children.

The Mossad report ends with the words: 'We parted from Wiesenthal very coldly.'[55]

What is fundamentally clear from all the documentation concerning Wiesenthal's role in the Eichmann hunt is that in the late 1950s, Wiesenthal believed that Eichmann was in either Germany or Austria. In none of the correspondence with the Israeli ambassador or in his meetings with the two Mossad agents does Wiesenthal express any inkling that the criminal might have been in the southern hemisphere, let alone that he was called 'Klement'. The greatest tragedy for Wiesenthal is that in the early 1950s he had indeed been told that Wiesenthal was in Argentina, but he did not do enough to act on the information. In his memoirs, Wiesenthal used this knowledge to suggest that he was directly responsible for informing the Israelis of Eichmann's whereabouts, but as we shall now see, this claim is without merit.

In autumn 1953, Wiesenthal met a Baron Heinrich 'Harry' Mast, who lived in the Tyrol near Innsbruck. Mast was aware of Wiesenthal's interest in Eichmann, and he produced a letter sent from Argentina by a former German army officer. The letter, which was dated May 1953, contained a great scoop. The writer described how he had met Eichmann recently in Buenos Aires, and that the fugitive was working at a power station some 100 kilometres from the capital. This piece of information was immensely useful, and Wiesenthal knew it. In July, he had it confirmed by an Austrian cabinet minister, Dr Pammer, who told him that Eichmann had not been in Austria for 'quite some time', and that he was presently living in Argentina.[56] In his memoirs, Wiesenthal does not name Baron Mast, and instead refers to him merely by his title, and explains that the meeting came about because of a mutual love of philately, and not because of any interest in Eichmann. Wiesenthal also wrote that the baron produced the letter simply because the men happened to be discussing how so many Nazis were still in positions of power, and the baron wanted to show how one of the worst criminals had managed to escape.[57]

It was not unreasonable for Wiesenthal to have been coy about the baron, or the circumstances of their meeting, as Baron Mast was no mere stamp-collecting chum. Born in southern Germany on 26 December 1897, Mast had been an Abwehr agent in Austria before the *Anschluss*, and had been arrested for espionage. When the Germans occupied Austria in March 1939, he was released, and during the war he continued to serve in the Abwehr, although his doubts about Nazism caused him to be suspected of being a 'subversive influence against the will to defend the Hitler Fatherland'.[58] In 1947, Mast was employed by the Gehlen Organisation in Austria under Dr Emmerich Offczarek, for whom he worked until he was dismissed in March 1952.[59] The organization suspected him not only of fabricating intelligence material but also of working for the Americans. Furthermore, they did not care for the fact that Mast was on 'friendly terms' with none other than Wilhelm Höttl.[60] Mast certainly was in cahoots with Höttl, because as soon as he had been sacked, Höttl employed him as his chief assistant at his publishing house in Linz.[61] Mast's job was little more than a cover for his role of gathering together reports from Höttl's sources, to which his boss would then add his 'high level touch' before sending them off to the office of German CDU politician Theodor Blank, who had founded his own secret service – the *Amt Blank* – in Bonn with the approval of Chancellor Konrad Adenauer.[62] Höttl paid Mast the comparatively low salary of five thousand Austrian schillings per month, as well as providing him with a housing allowance. It seems that Höttl employed Mast out of some sort of obligation, presumably because Mast had been loyally supplying him with intelligence when he worked for the Gehlen Organisation. Höttl would also claim that he found it hard to raise the money to pay Mast.[63]

However, there were tensions within Höttl's loose network of agents and former agents, not all of whom approved of the former SD man's activities. One of those disaffected was Erich Kernmayer, who had worked with Károly Ney in Höttl's CIC-backed Montgomery network, and had taken over as its operational head when Ney was fired.[64] A former Austrian Nazi propagandist, an *SS-Sturmbannführer* (major) and an assistant to Otto Skorzeny when he was in Budapest, Kernmayer continued to be a convinced Nazi after the war. He evidently found Höttl's opportunism and lack of loyalty to his former Nazi masters repellent, because by March 1952, he had fallen out with Höttl, and unwittingly revealed his reasons to a CIA source that month.

KERNMAYR excitedly accused HÖTTL
a – that he had perfidiously betrayed some of his former comrades (f.i. Adolf EICHMANN, now a fugitive, who had sworn to kill HÖTTL) when acting as a witness at the Nuremberg war crime trials;
b – to have willfully invented the number of 6 million Nazi-killed Jews, and thereby having brought World Jewry protection;
c – to be closely connected with leading Jews in America and to work for Jewish intelligence.[65]

Some of Kernmayer's points were valid. Höttl had indeed betrayed Eichmann in his testimony at Nuremberg, during the course of which he had recounted his conversation with Eichmann in Budapest in which he had drunkenly revealed the figure of six million.[66] Neither was Kernmayer wrong when he accused Höttl of working for 'Jewish intelligence', because, as we have seen, Höttl worked for Simon Wiesenthal, who according to the CIC report of 16 January 1950 was the chief of Israeli intelligence in Austria, a position that is confirmed by the records of his meetings with 'Michael' and 'Meir' from the Mossad.[67]

The links between Wiesenthal, Mast and Höttl suggest that Wiesenthal's meeting with Mast in the autumn of 1953 could not have been happenstance. As Mast was Höttl's chief assistant – and indeed was indebted to him for his salary and accommodation – it is not unlikely that Mast passed on the information concerning Eichmann's whereabouts on the orders of his employer. This likelihood is strengthened by the fact that Höttl had passed information to Wiesenthal in the past, and, so long as there was money in it, Höttl would sell information to anybody. Höttl had another motive for wishing Eichmann's capture, which is contained within the first of Kernmayer's accusations. Although there is no record of Eichmann making such a threat, and even if he had, he evidently lacked the opportunity to realize it, it is possible that Höttl simply wanted Eichmann out of the way by being brought to justice to face an inevitable capital punishment. As Wiesenthal's meeting in July 1953 with Pammer reveals, Eichmann's location was known by some, and it is hard to envisage that the ubiquitous Wilhelm Höttl was not one of them.

If Wiesenthal was excited by the information he received from Mast and Pammer, then it appeared that he did very little about it. As he admitted in 1967 in *The Murderers Among Us*, 'What could I do, a private citizen half the world away?'[68] This was a fair point, as Wiesenthal lacked the resources and contacts to mount an expensive detective operation on a distant continent. However, Wiesenthal did not share his information with anybody until the end of March 1954, some six months after his meeting with Mast in autumn 1953. Although it is obvious why he may not have wished to have spoken with the Nazi-infested German and Austrian authorities, it is puzzling that Wiesenthal did not immediately turn to the Israelis, for whom, after all, he acted as an agent. It took a visit from the Israeli consul in Vienna, Arie Eschel, to make

Wiesenthal put pen to paper on 30 March 1954. Eschel told him that there was some chance 'to get hold of Adolf Eichmann' if the Israelis were furnished with precise intelligence. The consul told Wiesenthal to present a complete report on everything he knew about Eichmann, and to furnish copies to both him and the World Jewish Congress (WJC) in New York.[69]

Wiesenthal wrote to Dr Nahum Goldmann of the WJC that day, and for the first three pages of his letter, he presented lots of background information concerning Eichmann, including his family, his career, and the likelihood that he had access to vast piles of Nazi gold, which he used to finance Nazi underground networks such as *Edelweiss*, *Sechsgestirn* and *Die Spinne*. According to Wiesenthal, Eichmann had also had plastic surgery, and had lived in Austria until the spring of 1950. He dismissed claims that Eichmann was in Egypt, and wrote that his family had left Austria for South America in 1952. Wiesenthal then described his meetings with Mast and Pammer, as well as the contents of the letter sent to Mast by the former army officer, and on his final page he concluded: 'Based on the material described, I can of course not guarantee 100 per cent, that Eichmann is, or was, in fact in the year 1953 in Argentina. However, all the above indications have caused me to be convinced the possibility of Eichmann's stay in Argentina is most probable.'[70]

Along with the letter, Wiesenthal included Eichmann's curriculum vitae in his own handwriting and photographs of Eichmann and his wife. In short, if anybody wanted to find the 'Architect of the Holocaust', then Wiesenthal's dossier would have provided an excellent start. Its inaccuracies were forgivable – probably because they were the products of Höttl's imagination – but the mention of Buenos Aires and the power station were excellent clues.

For six weeks, Wiesenthal heard nothing. No doubt frustrated, he wrote to Arie Eschel on 13 May 1954 enquiring as to the fate of his Eichmann dossier. The consul wrote back the following day, informing Wiesenthal that 'the information about Eichmann has been passed on by us', presumably to the Israeli intelligence service. Eschel also told Wiesenthal that Dr Goldmann had indeed received the material. 'I did not want to deck myself out in borrowed plumes,' Eschel wrote, 'and I have at this opportunity drawn his attention to your especially fruitful activity.'[71] Although Wiesenthal would soon hear back from the WJC, he did not hear back from the Israelis. 'The Israelis no longer had any interest in Eichmann,' Wiesenthal later observed; 'they had to fight for their lives against Nasser.'[72] This was fair comment by Wiesenthal, as Israel did indeed have more pressing problems. It had to build itself as a state, deal with immense immigration and counter Arab hostility, which would only increase with the appointment of Nasser as Egyptian Prime Minister in February 1954.[73]

Wiesenthal eventually heard back from the WJC in a letter from Rabbi Abraham Kalmanowitz, who had also wanted to find Eichmann. Kalmanowitz, an escapee from the Nazi-occupied Soviet Union, was a leading figure in the North American-based Va'ad Hahatzvala, which aimed to assist the beleaguered European Jews. In September 1944, he had pleaded with the Allies to bomb the railway lines to Auschwitz, but to no avail.[74] During the war, he founded the Mirrer Yeshiva, a centre of Jewish learning that was based in Brooklyn. In 1953, Kalmanowitz and Adolf A. Berle Jr, a senior State Department official, had asked the CIA director Allen Dulles to mount a search for Eichmann, but Dulles had refused, saying that such activity was outside the remit of the Agency. Berle and Kalmanowitz persisted, and Dulles eventually yielded and authorized an extensive search for Eichmann in the Arab states, which is where Kalmanowitz believed Eichmann to be hiding. As Eichmann was in Argentina, the search was of course fruitless.[75]

Wiesenthal's letter would have arrived with Kalmanowitz a few weeks before he was to ask the CIA to look for Eichmann. The rabbi was so certain that Eichmann was in the Middle East that he completely ignored Wiesenthal's assertion that the fugitive was in Buenos Aires. He told Wiesenthal he was only interested 'in definite proof of Adolf Eichmann's whereabouts, as that is the only information upon which our government will act', and further hinted that Eichmann was probably in the Middle East, where he was committing 'diabolical acts against the free world'.[76] 'I fell down from the clouds,' Wiesenthal later wrote. 'I had waited for this letter for two months with such high hopes!'[77] Wiesenthal wrote back to Kalmanowitz, and said that he would be willing to send an agent to South America if the WJC could provide some five hundred dollars for travel expenses. Kalmanowitz claimed that they had no money, and there the correspondence effectively ended. 'It was time to give up,' Wiesenthal ruefully acknowledged. 'Obviously, no one cared about Eichmann.'[78]

What Wiesenthal could not have realized – and what he was never told – was that Kalmanowitz had passed his letter to the CIA. On 6 May 1954, the rabbi sent Wiesenthal's letter and enclosures to Allen Dulles, but in his covering letter, Kalmanowitz was to mislead the CIA director. 'You will readily agree that all the facts and reports previously forwarded you concerning Eichmann have been sub-stantiated,' he wrote. In effect, Kalmanowitz did not advertise Wiesenthal's claim concerning Argentina, and it appears Dulles did not have either the time or inclination to wade through the fifty-six pages of Wiesenthal's German-language dossier, not least because at this stage he had not agreed to hunt Eichmann. Had he read it, then it would have been apparent that what Wiesenthal had written was quite different to what Kalmanowitz had said he had written. A few days later, Dulles forwarded the material to the Department of State, and informed Kalmanowitz that the matter 'does not fall in the jurisdiction of this Agency'. There is no indication that anybody in that department read Wiesenthal's dossier, and it would remain buried there.[79]

This episode is a prima facie example of the cock-up theory of history. It would appear that either Kalmanowitz had not read the whole of Wiesenthal's dossier, or he was minded to ignore Wiesenthal's conclusions because they did not fit in with his own. Even if the CIA had been informed of Wiesenthal's tip, it is just as likely that Dulles would have passed on the file to the State Department, where it would have met the same subterranean fate. It is perhaps unwise to hazard whether a proper reading of Wiesenthal's dossier would have altered the location of the eventual CIA search, although Kalmanowitz's insistence that Eichmann was in the Middle East would have no doubt proved more compelling to Dulles than a rambling dossier sent from an unknown in the depths of *Mitteleuropa*. Throughout the rest of his life, Wiesenthal would present his letter to Goldmann as proof that he had 'got there first', which in a sense, he had. Unfortunately, his lead was buried and, as we have seen, by the time the hunt had started again in earnest, Wiesenthal was of the opinion that Eichmann was in Europe. In none of his dealings with the Mossad in the late 1950s and early 1960 did Wiesenthal mention his conversation with Harry Mast, and neither did he readvance the possibility that Eichmann was in Argentina. It is understandable why Wiesenthal would subsequently present his 1954 finding as being instrumental in the hunt for Eichmann, but sadly for him – and for an earlier dispensation of justice – that is simply not the case, as neither Isser Harel nor any of his Mossad colleagues ever saw Wiesenthal's 1954 letter, and would only do so in the mid-1970s.[80]

In short, the whole sorry episode can be summarized thus: in 1954, Wiesenthal correctly claimed that Eichmann was in Argentina and he was ignored. In 1959, Wiesenthal incorrectly claimed that Eichmann was in Europe, and he was ignored once more, as the Israelis knew he was in Argentina. In 1961, with the publication of *Ich Jagte Eichmann*, Wiesenthal made sure he was never ignored again by claiming that he always suspected Eichmann was in Argentina. Had Wiesenthal simply been honest about his knowledge and activities in 1959, he would have appeared no less praiseworthy. Wiesenthal's arrogance was so immense that he could never bear to admit fault, and besides, he loved giving the public what they wanted. He would continue to play the role for the rest of his life.

Zvi Aharoni first set foot on Chacabuco Street on 3 March 1960. 'Chacabuco was a nice, although untarred, street,' he recalled. 'There were trees and broad pavements. Within only a few hundred metres, the buildings changed from pretty, elegant villas to run-down two-story apartments.'[81] Eichmann's bungalow was on the poor end of the street, but when Aharoni and his helper 'Roberto' made discreet inquiries about its inhabitants, they found that they had moved, and the only people to be found at number 4261 were some decorators. Later that day, Aharoni requisitioned the services of another helper, 'Juan', to deliver a birthday present to the house, which was addressed to Eichmann's son, Klaus, and purported to be from a female admirer. The hope was that the decorators would supply the family's new address, but unfortunately all they knew was that they had moved to the north of the city. However, what they did reveal was that one of the sons was working as a garage mechanic nearby, and Juan was taken there. He was introduced to a young man who he thought was called 'Dito', who said that his family had indeed moved, but no, he would not tell Juan the address, but he would however take the packet. Before he left, Juan made a mental note of Dito's Siambretta 500 Sport moped. When Aharoni later spoke to Juan, he realized that Dito had to be Eichmann's son Dieter. The following day, the Mossad agent sent another helper around to number 4261, who posed as an insurance salesman and asked the decorators whether 'Riccardo Klement' was around. Once again, the workman said that the family had moved, but they confirmed that Klement was the name of the man who had lived in the house. This was an important breakthrough for Aharoni as it virtually comfirmed that 'Klement' was indeed Eichmann.[82] That evening, he sent a coded message back to the Mossad headquarters in Tel Aviv, in which he stated that he was almost certain that Klement and Eichmann were the same man. Isser Harel was delighted. 'Without further delay,' he wrote, 'I intensified the planning of the operational steps we'd have to take immediately upon verification of our assumption that Riccardo Klement was Adolf Eichmann.'[83]

Obtaining that verification and finding Eichmann's new address would prove to be difficult. Aharoni decided that the best way to do so would be to follow Dieter's moped when he left work, but tailing him was not a simple task, as the moped could easily – albeit un-wittingly – lose Aharoni in his rental car. On one occasion, Aharoni was held up by a funeral procession, and on another, his rental car broke down. As a result, Aharoni tried a different tack, and sent Juan back to number 4261 on 11 March armed with a story that the female admirer was complaining that the present had never arrived. This time, one of the decorators appeared to be more amenable, and he gave precise directions as to how to get to the house on Garibaldi Street. 'I asked him whether he was absolutely certain,' Juan informed Aharoni. 'He said he was, because he had done some work in the new house and the German still owed him some money.'[84] The following afternoon, Aharoni followed the directions given to Juan. He drove down Route 202, and soon found the house on Garibaldi Street. 'The house, like the whole area, looked poor and run-down,' Aharoni noticed. As he drove past, Aharoni spotted a thickset woman in her fifties standing on the terrace with a small blond boy. He correctly assumed this to be Eichmann's wife and his fourth son.[85]

For the next week, Aharoni continued to observe the house, and he made inquiries through a local Jewish architect about who owned the building. The local authorities in San Fernando were unable to help, as the area in which the house lay was a kind of no man's land subject to no official regulations. The architect then suggested they should try the GEOFINK company, which had bought up much of the area – perhaps they had sold the plot to the family. On 18 March, the architect reported back to Aharoni at the embassy. 'I have hit the jackpot!' he announced, before passing a piece of paper to the Mossad agent. The note revealed that the owner of number 14 was one 'Veronica Catarina Liebl de Fichmann' who had lived at 4251 Chacabuco. 'I was hard pressed not to show my excitement,' Aharoni recalled. It is easy to see why. Not only did the owner have the same maiden name as Eichmann's wife, but the name 'Fichmann' was certainly a misspelling of Eichmann. Furthermore, the difference in the number of the house on Chacabuco Street could also be explained as a clerical error.[86]

On Saturday 19 March, just sixteen days after he had arrived, Aharoni was rewarded with his first sight of Eichmann. As he drove down Route 202 that afternoon, he saw a man taking down some washing outside the house. The man was of a medium build, had a high forehead and was somewhat bald. Aharoni guessed that he must have been in his fifties. He was sure that the man was Eichmann, but he knew that he had to photograph him. After two weeks of following up other leads and maintaining his cover job as an official investigating anti-Semitism in Argentina, Aharoni drove to Garibaldi Street in a pickup truck on Sunday 3 April. With him were two more helpers – 'Rendi' and 'Roberto'. Fearful that he might be recognized after his numerous sweeps of the area, Aharoni instructed Rendi how to use a briefcase camera to photograph Eichmann. The three men parked the pickup at ten thirty that morning some 250 yards from the house, and while Aharoni lay in the back observing the property through binoculars, Rendi and Robert worked on the engine. Fifteen minutes later, Aharoni saw Eichmann go out into his garden, and he instructed Rendi to walk up to the house and start making conversation. For the next several minutes, Aharoni and Roberto watched as Rendi chatted to Eichmann, his wife and Dieter. The Mossad agent watched Eichmann break off the conversation after a while, and in order not to look suspiciously interested in his father, Rendi carried on talking to Dieter. Eventually, he left and, as instructed, made his own way back to San Fernando Station, where he was picked up by Aharoni.[87]

It is a measure of just how ill equipped Aharoni was that he did not have the facilities within the Israeli embassy to develop the film. As a result, he took it to a large photography shop in downtown Buenos Aires, where he explained that he only required the negatives as he was due to leave the city shortly. The shop assistant promised him they would be ready the following morning, but when Aharoni returned, he was told that the prints were not ready. 'What prints?' Aharoni demanded. 'Who asked for prints? I want my negatives and I want them now!' Understandably paranoid, the secret agent started to suspect that 'Eichmann's friends' had somehow intercepted the film, but after half an hour, both the negatives – and some prints – arrived. 'When I saw the pictures, my fears evaporated,' Aharoni recalled, because Rendi had taken four superb shots of Eichmann standing in his garden. On 8 April, Aharoni flew back to Tel Aviv via Paris. On the flight from Paris to Israel he chanced upon Harel, and after a few seconds of small talk, Harel asked, 'Are you certain he's the man we want?' Aharoni took one of the prints out of his pocket. 'There's not an iota of doubt,' he replied.[88]

Two weeks later, Aharoni was flying back to Buenos Aires disguised as a German businessman. Accompanying him were three other Mossad agents, and together they formed the advance party. After a few days, the remainder of the force joined them, and on 1 May, Harel himself arrived. Although as chief of the Mossad, Harel would be the most senior officer involved in the operation, the actual head of the task force was Rafi Eitan, a 33-year-old veteran of the *Haganah* and its operational arm, the *Palmach*. He had not only taken part in a mission that had destroyed the British radar installation on Mount Carmel, but also served in the War of Independence, during which he had been wounded and had continued to fight. Harel regarded him as a man with 'outstanding operational ability' and the group needed such a figure.[89] The agents were thousands of miles from home, operating in a land that was foreign to most of them. If they were caught, they could all expect lengthy prison sentences.

During the last week of April and the first week of May, the group maintained its surveillance of Eichmann and established his routine. For nine days in a row, the watchers saw Eichmann alighting from the number 203 bus at seven forty every evening, except at the weekends, when he would work in his garden. Meanwhile, more cars were hired and safe houses were rented. The details of the actual abduction were also worked out. Two cars would be taken, one of which would be parked near Eichmann's house on the evening of Tuesday 10 May. In the car would be Aharoni, Eitan, Zeev Keren and Peter Malkin, who would be the man who would initially grab Eichmann. After the criminal was bundled into the car, the four men would drive to the safe house, where Eichmann would be held for three days. On 13 May, Eichmann would be taken to Buenos Aires airport, where he would be flown in an El Al plane to Israel. The presence of the plane was a piece of good fortune. Due to arrive on 12 May, the plane would be carrying a group of Israeli dignitaries who were visiting Buenos Aires to help celebrate the 150th anniversary of the May Revolution that saw Argentina gain her independence from Spain. Although the dignitaries would be in the country for several days, the plane was due to return to Israel after a twenty-four-hour stopover to allow the crew to rest. For Harel, this represented a fantastic opportunity to get Eichmann and the entire task force out of the country.

However, on 3 May, Harel received some bad news. Unfortunately the Argentinians were not able to receive the Israeli dignitaries until the afternoon of 19 May, which meant that the special flight would be delayed for a week. Harel now faced a dilemma. If he asked the Israeli embassy to try to get the Argentinians to change their timetable, it would only draw attention to the special flight. However, the prospect of making his men wait for another week did not appeal. 'Our men were nearing the limits of their physical and mental potential,' he noted, 'and I knew it would be hard on them to be burdened with another week of such severe strain.'[90] Harel was also worried that Eichmann's seemingly immutable routine might not stay that way, and he therefore decided to proceed with the original date. However, on the morning of 9 May, Harel met Rafi, Aharoni and another member of the team to discuss last-minute preparations. It was clear that all three wanted a short postponement as a few elements were not in place. Harel was reluctant, and felt that any delay would now jeopardize the mission. The team nevertheless convinced Harel that they needed the hiatus, not least because the men needed a short rest. The Mossad chief reluctantly agreed to a twenty-four-hour delay.

At seven fifteen on the evening of 11 May, the kidnap team set off from the safe house and headed towards San Fernando. 'We drove in silence,' recalled Peter Malkin, 'first through the ever more desolate outskirts of the city, then on to the rush of the highway.'[91] The weather was starting to worsen; in the distance, the team could see thunder and lightning. If it rained, the kidnap would almost certainly have to be postponed, but for the time being, it stayed dry. Just after seven thirty, the team arrived and parked the Buick several yards short of Eichmann's house. The back-up car was parked further back, partially hidden by a railway bridge. The men now took their positions. Malkin and Keren got out of the car and started tinkering under its bonnet. Aharoni stayed at the wheel, while Eitan lay in the back.[92]

The men waited nervously. A few minutes after their arrival, a teenage boy cycled past and asked if he could help. Aharoni politely shooed him away. Just after seven forty, Eichmann's normal bus approached the small kiosk. The men watched in frustration as the vehicle carried on without stopping. Either Eichmann was late, or he was not coming back home that night. If he did not appear by eight o'clock, then the kidnap team planned to leave, reckoning to stay any longer would look suspicious. When the deadline had passed, Aharoni turned to Eitan and asked him what they should do. 'We wait,' Eitan ordered curtly. Unbeknown to the rest of the snatch team, Eitan had decided that they would stay until eight thirty.[93]

At five past eight, another bus drew up at the kiosk. Aharoni watched a man get off, but he couldn't tell who it was. Suddenly, the back-up car switched on its lights – the signal that the passenger was Eichmann. Aharoni warned the other members of the snatch squad, all the time keeping an eye on the man walking towards them. Then he spotted Eichmann putting his left hand in his pocket. 'Watch his hands!' he hissed at Malkin. 'I think he has a gun!' The news that Eichmann might be armed forced Malkin to rapidly change the way he would grab him. Instead of using the 'sentry tackle' manoeuvre in which the victim is seized from behind and dragged backwards,

Malkin decided that he would simply have to attack Eichmann from the front.[94]

Soon, Eichmann was no more than 15 yards away. 'I could hear his footfalls,' Malkin recalled, 'regular as ticks on a clock.'[95] After a few more seconds, Malkin now addressed his prey in the few words of Spanish that he knew: '*Un momentito, señor.*' Eichmann stopped. He stared at Malkin through his black-rimmed glasses and then took a step backward. The Israeli pounced, and the two men fell to the ground and rolled into a ditch. Now on his back in 2 inches of mud, Malkin wrestled with Eichmann, who was starting to make gurgling noises caused by the dislodging of his false teeth. When Malkin tried to pull him up, he had to relax his grip on Eichmann's throat, and the 54-year-old let out a hideous scream. While Aharoni gunned the engine to mask the noise, Eitan leaped out of the car and he and Keren helped Malkin manhandle Eichmann into the back. 'The whole thing seemed to be taking forever,' Aharoni later wrote, although the whole abduction could not have taken much longer than a minute.[96]

Eichmann was driven to a safe house where he was held for eight days. Forced to wear a pair of goggles taped to his face even during mealtimes and when he visited the lavatory, Eichmann spent much of his time shackled to a bed. Nevertheless, he was to admit that he was correctly treated by his captors, and at one point he was even brought a bottle of red wine 'by the huge muscular man who had originally knocked me over'.[97] This would have been Peter Malkin, who later claimed to have had numerous soul-searching conversations with Eichmann, despite the fact that they had no common language.[98] As well as giving Eichmann wine, Malkin even gave him a packet of cigarettes and played some records, all of which earned Malkin the opprobrium of his fellow agents. 'What the hell are you doing?' asked one of them when he entered the room, 'throwing a party for this murderer? Have you taken leave of your senses?'[99] Despite being blindfolded, Eichmann was well aware of the tensions between his captors, who soon found the long wait in the safe house torturous. 'I could not understand why I was being kept there for so long,' Eichmann wrote, 'but it seemed there was a hitch in my kidnappers' plans and during this period they appeared to be more fearful than I was.'[100] Even if Eichmann's bravado was a retrospective sham, he was certainly right about the uneasy atmosphere in the safe house. As Isser Harel noted, the building became a prison for the guards as well, and having to attend to the most intimate needs of a man who had masterminded the destruction of some of their families became increasingly distasteful.[101]

While their husband and father was held captive, Eichmann's family mounted a desperate search. On the morning of 12 May, Dieter rushed round to a building where Klaus was working on an elevator control panel. 'The old man is gone!' Dieter announced breathlessly. Klaus's first thoughts were that the Israelis had him. He dropped his screwdriver and the brothers rushed back home. On the way, they alerted a former SS officer, who told them to calm down and to think rationally. The officer, whom Klaus described as their father's 'best friend', was almost certainly Carlos Fuldner, and he ran through a list of possibilities of what might have happened. Eichmann was either in the clink because he had had some run-in with the police, or in hospital or the morgue because of an accident. If neither of those were the case, then the brothers could consider that the disappearance was the doing of the Israelis. For the next two days, the brothers and some volunteers from a Peronist youth movement fruitlessly searched every police station, morgue and hospital. 'Our feeling of bitterness grew,' Klaus said. 'The wildest plans were discussed.' One of the group suggested that they should kidnap and torture the Israeli ambassador, and another mooted bombing the embassy. Both plans were rejected.[102] At one point, Klaus claimed that some three hundred men on motorcycles were scouring the city, and every harbour, railway station, airport, and major road junction had 'one of our men stationed there'. The one thing the Eichmann brothers appeared not to do was to call the police.[103]

As the Eichmanns searched and the Israelis waited, Isser Harel examined the possibility that the team could kidnap another Nazi: Josef Mengele. 'The thought that Mengele might be hiding not far from us wouldn't let me rest,' Harel wrote. However, other members of the team thought that mounting such an undertaking was far too risky. Among them was Rafi Eitan, who argued vociferously with his boss, and quoted an old Hebrew proverb: 'Try to catch a lot – and you will catch nothing.'[104] Harel did not back down, and he ordered Aharoni to question Eichmann about Mengele's whereabouts. Eichmann would later recall Aharoni's interrogation.

He repeated that if I made any trouble I would be shot immediately. He asked me a lot of questions about other Germans living in South America. Suddenly he said, 'Where is Dr Josef Mengele?' At once I retorted, 'I don't know. And if I did, I would not tell you, for it would be betraying a member of the last German Reich.'[105]

Despite such a show of defiance, Aharoni gradually wore Eichmann down, and he eventually admitted that he had heard that Mengele was staying at a boarding house in Vicente López run by a Mrs Jurmann.[106]

Harel was determined to bring two scalps back to Israel, although his problem was a lack of manpower. Over the next twenty-four hours he assembled a scratch team of Spanish-speaking contacts who kept a watch on the boarding house, but all they saw were children leaving the property on their way to school. In desperation, one of the agents walked around the streets for two hours until he found a postman, whom he asked whether a 'Dr Menelle' lived in the neighbourhood. The postman said that a man of that name had indeed lived in the boarding house until a month ago, and no, he hadn't left a forwarding address. 'I presumed that the postman was telling the truth,' Harel noted, 'and I attached great importance to the discovery of fresh tracks of the killer-doctor.'[107] The next day, Harel sent the same agent back to the post office, where he enquired as to the whereabouts of 'Dr Mengele'. The clerk confirmed what the postman had said: Mengele had left about a month ago, and any post that arrived for him had to be returned to the sender.[108] Despite this setback, Harel persisted. On 20 May, the final day of Operation Eichmann, one of the agents simply phoned the house to enquire about previous tenants, but the woman who answered the phone was obviously new to the place and knew nothing. Later, a second agent appeared at the door posing as a boiler repairman, but the woman told him he wasn't needed, and that perhaps the previous tenant had had a problem, but there wasn't one now. 'Their findings came as a bitter disappointment,' Harel reflected. 'It was hard to reconcile myself to the fact that we had missed the opportunity of capturing the murderous doctor by as little as a couple of weeks.'[109]

Was Harel right? Had the Mossad narrowly missed capturing Mengele? As we shall see, while Eichmann was being held, Mengele was not even in Argentina, let alone Buenos Aires. However, Martha Mengele was in the city, and had Harel wanted to find her, then all he needed to have done was to look in the phone book.

During that day, Eichmann was prepared for his long trip to Israel. At 17.52 the previous afternoon, an El Al Bristol Britannia airliner had landed at Buenos Aires airport, and while the Israeli air-crew were spending much of the day of the 20th resting, their fellow countrymen in the Mossad were busier than ever. Eichmann was washed, shaved and dressed in the light blue uniform of an El Al cabin attendant. He was then made to lie down on a table. 'A splint was tied to one of my arms,' he dimly remembered, 'and a hypo-dermic syringe was inserted. I lost consciousness.'[110] At nine o'clock that evening, he was pulled to his feet, and in his drugged condition he gave the desired impression that he was an aircrew member who had overdone it at the Buenos Aires nightspots. Eichmann remem-bered coming round in the car; when he did so, the agent next to him topped up his sedation. At half past ten, the car – which was driven by Aharoni – pulled up at the airport, and because it had diplomatic number plates, it was waved through the gate. A few minutes later, Aharoni paused next to the bus of the El Al flight crew, and together the two vehicles drove up to the plane. The plane's captain and two other crew members boarded the aircraft and, after a minute, they signalled for the rest of the crew to come on board.[111] Eichmann was gingerly manhandled out of the car, and it was at this point that he once more came out of his stupor.

> The next thing I knew we were on an airfield. I was being led with a man on either side of me and another behind me up the steps into the aircraft. I had a sudden impulse to yell for help. *Himmel!* This was my last chance. But no sound came from my throat. It was as if I had been struck dumb.[112]

Eichmann was then placed in an aisle seat in the first-class cabin. Although he was aware of what was going on, he could not speak. For the next hour, there was an uneasy wait for the emigration officer to enter the plane to check their passports. Eichmann was now the proud holder of an Israeli passport in the name of 'George Doron', although the Argentine official, keen no doubt to get home, stamped all the crew's passports with barely a glance. Finally, at four minutes past midnight, the captain pushed forward, and Adolf Eichmann was finally on his way to the homeland of the people he had tried to eradicate.[113] At seven thirty-five on the morning of 22 May, he arrived at Lydda airport. 'It was a beautiful spring day when I arrived in Israel,' Eichmann commented later, as if he had been a tourist.[114]

At four o'clock the following afternoon, the Israeli Prime Minister, David Ben-Gurion, addressed the Israeli parliament. 'I have to inform the Knesset that some time ago Israeli security forces found one of the greatest Nazi war criminals, Adolf Eichmann.' The Prime Minister then astounded the world with the news that 'Adolf Eichmann is already in this country under arrest, and he will shortly be brought to trial in Israel under the Nazis and Nazi Collaborators (Punishment) Law of 1950.'[115]

Unsurprisingly, the news made headlines all over the globe, but other than Ben-Gurion's bald statement, the Israelis revealed little about how Eichmann had been captured. On the 24th, Harel gave a press conference in which he declared that the criminal had been traced through the efforts of his agents alone. Although this statement would appear to show a lack of gratitude for Fritz Bauer, he had already been thanked privately.[116] The world's press started to frantically hunt for a hero, and on 25 May, the Vienna correspondent of *The Times* of London asked Simon Wiesenthal if he was involved. Wiesenthal quite correctly 'denied a suggestion that he personally had something to do with Eichmann's arrest'. After telling the reporter that all his Eichmann material was at Yad Vashem, he then indicated that a friend who had emigrated to Israel six years before knew all about the material, although it was unclear whether this friend had contributed 'anything decisive to the arrest'.[117] Wiesenthal's admission that he had nothing to do with the capture of Eichmann would be the last time he would tell the truth about his role. With the lack of details coming from the Mossad, Wiesenthal soon realized that there was an information gap to close up and, as we have seen, he was more than happy to fill it with the most spurious claims.

The 'friend' in question was Tuviah Friedman, and for the next few weeks, the press were convinced that he was its hero. The day before Wiesenthal was interviewed by *The Times*, Friedman was named as the 'captor of Eichmann' by Benjamin Epstein, the national director of the Anti-Defamation League of the B'nai B'rith. Epstein claimed that Friedman had tracked Eichmann down to Kuwait, where he was working for a British oil company. Eichmann had then hidden in Israel, where, Epstein said, it had taken only days for the Israeli police to locate and catch him.[118] Other reports were a little more accurate. On 30 May, the *Washington Post* identified Asher Ben-Nathan as the man who had set Friedman on the initial hunt for Eichmann in 1946, but it was unable to provide any more information.[119] Friedman found himself deluged by the press. 'Reporters from every part of Israel descended on me,' he recalled. 'Then the photographers came, with cabled orders from abroad. They took my photo in my office, and then at home. Their cameras did not stop clicking.' When one photographer took a picture of Friedman's son on his potty, he admitted that he understandably became 'a little hysterical'.[120] Despite the intrusions, Freidman started giving the press what they wanted. In New York in June, he told a reporter that it was he who had finally tracked Eichmann down to Argentina, which, as we have seen, is untrue – it was a combination of Lothar Hermann and Fritz Bauer. The same reporter also began to ascribe heroic qualities to his interviewee. 'Friedman . . . is a quiet-spoken, intense Polish Jew who reminds you of a young edition of Premier David Ben-Gurion,' wrote Drew Pearson. 'His determined eyes flash as do those of the Prime Minister who has led the beleaguered little country through so many crises.'[121]

While Friedman was being lionized, his former correspondent Lothar Hermann wrote to him asking for what he felt to be his rightful ten-thousand-dollar reward. Hermann scrupulously listed all the information he had given both to Friedman and to Bauer, although much of it still concerned 'Francisco Schmidt', which Harel had found to be incorrect.[122] Nevertheless, without Hermann's initial approach to Bauer, Eichmann might not have been found and, despite his errors, there was a strong moral case to be made for giving Hermann the reward. Friedman approached the World Jewish Congress and asked them to pay, but they refused, citing the fact that Harel had said that only his agents were involved in locating Eichmann. When the Mossad was subsequently approached to give Hermann a reward, it too refused, for the simple reason that it had never promised one. Hermann was tenacious, and demanded that Friedman should pay the reward as he was the one who had announced it.[123] Friedman tried to ignore Hermann's letters, but the blind old man would persist for over a decade. On 10 November 1971, he wrote to Golda Meir, the Israeli Prime Minister, demanding that he be paid, not least because Isser Harel had mentioned Hermann's name in a series of articles he had written that April. He also sent a copy of his letter to Friedman, who in turn wrote to Meir indicating that Hermann should be rewarded.[124] Eventually, following yet more appeals, the Israeli government paid Hermann ten thousand dollars in April 1972.[125] It had taken him twelve years to get his reward, a period that could have been considerably shortened had Harel stepped in.

Although Friedman was quicker at claiming the credit for the capture of Eichmann, it was Wiesenthal who would end up keeping it. Wiesenthal had more charm, more chutzpah, and he was a better manipulator of the media and the lecture hall. Friedman would later recall that his former colleague made some of the most outrageous claims about his role: 'Wiesenthal claimed in his book and speeches that he was present at the capture of Eichmann in Argentina and actually fell into the ditch with him during the struggle.'[126] Although Wiesenthal never wrote that he took part in the kidnapping, Friedman was insistent that Wiesenthal would often say that he had. He once asked him why he did so, to which Wiesenthal was supposed to have replied: 'Journalists want sensations, so I told them and then repeated it in my speeches when I was questioned about the Eichmann operation. For the sake of my livelihood and prestige I am ready to do anything.'[127]

Throughout the 1960s, an increasingly bitter Friedman would glower at the ascent of his old friend. He once attended a talk Wiesenthal gave in Toronto, during which he watched Wiesenthal give his account of the struggle in the ditch. 'The audience applauded Wiesenthal enthusiastically,' Friedman remembered, 'and like a seasoned actor, he bowed again and again.' An enraged Friedman approached Wiesenthal at the end of the talk, demanding how he could tell such a story. Wiesenthal's reply – according to Friedman – was nothing less than brazen:

> These nitwits want a hero for their money, somebody who caught Eichmann with his own hands. The Shin Bet [the Israeli Security Service] agents didn't go hungry like we did in 1945 to 1955, with Isser Harel they stayed in the best hotels at the expense of the State of Israel. Now I've got to earn a few thousand dollars for my wife and child, and if for the sake of publicity and my fee I've got to fall into a ditch with Eichmann, so be it. If I won't I'll be like that blind old Lothar Hermann who passed Eichmann's address to you. And you yourself all you get is people in Israel laughing at you. Now you understand why I never wanted to emigrate to Israel. I heard about the people laughing at you for years and how the Shin Bet still bothers you if you mention your part in Eichmann's capture. I want to ask you to do me a favour, Tadek, don't come to my speeches. You might get angry and start shouting that I am telling a pack of lies. That would force me to grab my suitcase and never give another speech about the Nazi times and Eichmann. People want heroes and leading actors, not extras.[128]

Freidmann's recollection must of course be treated with extreme caution. Even if every word he claimed Wiesenthal said is untrue, then it is a measure of the level of resentment that existed between the two men. In the year after the Eichmann capture, both men had published books about their experiences on the trail of the criminal, but Wiesenthal's account, *Ich Jagte Eichmann*, gave the impression that he was in the centre of the pack. Friedman's *The Hunter* – although not without plenty of embellishments – presents a figure more at the margins. Friedman also comes across as a less attractive figure to the reader: brooding, resentful and constantly carping about his lot, whereas Wiesenthal is charming and seemingly modest about his achievements, which would appear to be considerable.

Wiesenthal and Friedman were not the only characters who saw the capture of Eichmann as an opportunity to promote themselves. In August 1960, two Israeli journalists, Zvi Aldouby and Ephraim Katz, wrote two articles for *Look* magazine concerning Eichmann and his kidnap. Although the pair were paid $5,500 for the pieces –

some $35,000 at the time of writing – Aldouby correctly surmised that Eichmann was a story that could be milked for a lot more. Soon afterwards, the pair signed a book deal with Viking Press that earned them five thousand dollars each, and ten thousand for the veteran journalist Quentin Reynolds, who was to write the book.[129] The resulting work, *Minister of Death*, was published on 29 September, and was written by Reynolds on a 'special twenty-four-hour-a-day schedule'.[130] A great portion of the material was obtained by Aldouby in an underhand fashion from the German magazine *Stern*, which had been considering the publication of Eichmann's self-exculpatory memoirs that he had dictated to a Dutch former SS officer called Willem Sassen while he was in Buenos Aires.[131] Much of the book was woefully inaccurate, and even placed its subject drilling for oil east of the Euphrates in 1958.[132] In his preface, Reynolds paid his respects to his two co-authors, who he described as having served as 'foreign correspondents throughout Europe' and having been commandos in the *Haganah* and officers in the Israeli Defence Force.[133]

Such a tribute made the men sound like seasoned veterans of both the pen and the sword. However, at the time of the kidnap, the 28-year-old Aldouby was in fact a journalism student at Columbia University in New York, and knew no more about Eichmann than the average newspaper reader.[134] Born of Romanian Jews who had emigrated to Palestine at the end of the war, Aldouby was far too young to have served in the *Haganah*, although he had been a sixteen-year-old scout in a cavalry unit of the 8th Battalion of the Negev Brigade during the War of Independence. After leaving school, Aldouby was reputed to have worked for one of the Israeli intelligence services, but he was dismissed after four years. Reduced to being a cotton picker while his young wife worked for the council in Petah Tikva a few miles northeast of Tel Aviv, Aldouby continued to have big ideas. At one point he was the great impresario, and he sold tickets for a show given by Danny Kaye, whom Aldouby had sensationally lured to Petah Tikva. Unfortunately, Aldouby never managed to inform Kaye of his plans, and he had to return the money after the ensuing scandal. Aldouby then joined the General Zionist Party; he became a youth organizer for them, and his town's correspondent for the party's newspaper. During the Sinai

Campaign, Aldouby filled the publication with highly fictitious accounts of his own derring-do ahead of the troops, and how he had even infiltrated himself undercover into Gaza. After divorcing his wife, Aldouby swiftly married a nineteen-year-old folk dancer, with whom he left Israel for the United States. Somehow, Aldouby had managed to wangle himself accreditation from an Israeli army journal, and sent back dispatches that were no more than rewrites of stories in US army publications.[135]

Aldouby, then, was the perfect blend of dynamism and hucksterism that was needed to exploit the exciting new activity of Nazi hunting inspired by the Eichmann kidnap. A fortnight before the publication of *Minister of Death*, Aldouby convinced Thomas H. Guinzburg, the president of Viking, that he knew where Martin Bormann was, and furthermore that he wanted to capture him in an operation he dubbed 'Cream-Puff'. Guinzburg found Aldouby completely plausible, not least because he had maps and details of Bormann's escape routes, and even knew the name of the U-Boat in which the *Reichsleiter* had fled to South America. Aldouby even told Guinzburg that he was aware of Bormann's day-to-day activities, and he backed up his own authenticity by telling the publishing executive that he personally knew many of the Mossad agents who had taken part in the Eichmann mission. On 12 September 1960, Viking advanced Aldouby $2,500, and a further thousand to cover his research costs. Guinzburg also promised the young Israeli four thousand more if they accepted a manuscript on Martin Bormann.[136] Aldouby then went back to *Look* magazine, from which he managed to extract a two-thousand-dollar advance for an article on Bormann, for which he would be paid another six thousand on delivery.[137]

In October or November 1960, Aldouby departed for Europe on the first stage of his great hunt for Martin Bormann, promising that he would get in touch with Guinzburg within four to six weeks. Aldouby headed back to Israel, where he started to spend his way through the eleven thousand dollars he had earned since the first articles had appeared in *Look*. He hired a secretary, a stenographer and a whole team of journalists, whom he employed to research stories on his quarry. Meanwhile, without his wife, Aldouby lived it up, and spent most of his nights in chi-chi bars and expensive restaurants, wooing women with promises of marriage. On 8 January 1960, he sent a letter to Guinzburg, in which he complained that despite the relatively meagre amount of funds he had been supplied, Operation Cream-Puff was steaming forward. In fact, he claimed to enjoy the most remarkable access to the world's secret intelligence agencies:

> With the aid of files that we managed to take out from The British War Office (MI-5), the British Foreign office, the Special Political International Branch of the Scotland Yard, the Interpol, the 2eme bureau, the Italian and Yugoslav Intelligence Agencies, the German War Crimes Office and reports of the volunteer groups, we have the most complete story of his escape and the pursuit after him. This material [. . .] includes for the first time (black on white) proof that the man is alive.[138]

Had Guinzburg had any suspicions about Aldouby, it would have required little effort to have had them confirmed. Notwithstanding the sheer unfeasibility of obtaining files from any of those organizations, Aldouby clearly had little knowledge of the intelligence world. The British War Office and MI5 (the Security Service) were never equivalent, and neither was there ever a 'Special Political International Branch' of the Metropolitan Police.

As well as 'working' on Bormann, Aldouby manufactured pieces for the Israeli press. His most ambitious project was a fifty-thousand-word illustrated article on Israeli beatniks. However, as he could not find any such free spirits in the Israel of early 1961, Aldouby simply invented some, and he paid a photographer to take pictures of a couple pretending to have sex in a bath. By the spring, it was becoming apparent that Aldouby could not sustain his lifestyle. Not only had he exceeded his credit on Diners' Club, but his cheques issued on a New York bank were starting to bounce. If Martin Bormann really had been alive, he would not have been overly worried about his pursuer.[139]

By the spring, Aldouby desperately needed to kickstart his 'hunt'. Without any evidence on Martin Bormann – there was, after all, none that could be found – and with a lack of cash, Aldouby decided to hunt for a more realistic target. He returned to New York and informed Guinzburg that he was now going to kidnap Léon Degrelle, as he was an 'integral part of the Bormann story'. A nonplussed Guinzburg admitted that he had never heard of Degrelle, who had been the leader of the Belgian pro-Axis Rexist Party. Described by Pierre Daye as a man with '*mystérieuses irradiations*', the charismatic Degrelle served on the Eastern Front with the *Légion Wallonie*, and he was to become the most decorated of all foreign members of the Waffen-SS by winning the Oak Leaves to his Knight's Cross. Hitler was famously to say that if he had a son, he would wish him to be like SS-Sturmbannführer Degrelle.[140] Sentenced to death on 29 December 1944 by a Belgian War Council, the Belgian managed to fly from Oslo to San Sebastián in Spain in the early morning of 7 May 1945, although his Heinkel III crashlanded on arrival, leaving him with numerous broken bones.[141] Degrelle would recuperate in a military hospital until August 1946, during which time the Spanish denied his presence on their soil.[142] Degrelle eventually lived openly in Spain, and became a leading figure in the European Far Right, whose friends included Otto Skorzeny and Hans-Ulrich Rudel, and he was even related by marriage to Werner Naumann's mistress.[143] Aldouby told Guinzburg that Degrelle was the administrator of a secret fascist organization called 'Capri', and Martin Bormann was its head. Once again, had Guinzburg wanted to check up on Aldouby, it would not have taken him a considerable amount of effort to ascertain that the real Capri was of course the Argentine company CAPRI, for which Adolf Eichmann had worked.

Aldouby was now so desperate to get his hands on some more Viking dollars that he told Guinzburg an enormous lie. Degrelle, he said, was already his captive, and he was being held on an estate in France. The story of his abduction was suitably sensational, involving Swiss bankers flying at hedge-top height into Madrid, glamorous women enticing Nazis on board yachts off the Riviera and interrogations by a leading British psychiatrist. Although Guinzburg expressed some concern that this wasn't quite the story about Martin Bormann that he had paid for, Aldouby managed to extract another $2,500 from the publisher. Aldouby also fed *Look* the same story, although they were not as easily gulled as Guinzburg, and told him that they only wanted a story on Bormann. Aldouby did manage to find another victim in the form of Harvey Breit, a literary journalist and Broadway producer, who funded Aldouby with three thousand dollars.[144]

His coffers once more replete, Aldouby sailed for Le Havre, France, on the SS *Liberté* from New York on 27 May 1961. While on board, Aldouby indulged in a mid-Atlantic romance with a 22-year-old from the Upper West Side of Manhattan called Carol Klein who was on her way to England to study drama. When the boat arrived in Le Havre, a lovestruck Klein decided to abandon her studies and accompanied Aldouby to Paris, where the Israeli was hatching his plans to kidnap Degrelle. Aldouby spent much of his time discussing the operation with three fellow conspirators, although he also continued his affair with Klein, whom he promised to marry in New York in August. Aldouby still seemed short of funds: he even borrowed fifty dollars from Klein in order to wine and dine her. Klein would later recall how Aldouby always carried a pocket-sized pistol, and claimed that the French secret police were following him. At one point, he bought a switchblade knife in a flea market, a purchase which Klein felt was made more to impress her than to deal with any assailant.[145]

On 1 June, Aldouby kissed Klein *adieu* and drove down to Spain with Jacques Feinsohn, a decorator and aspirant journalist. In the back of the car they brought eight revolvers, ammunition, and plans and sketches of Degrelle's house in Constantina, some 50 miles north of Seville. The plan was simple. Aldouby and Feinsohn would lure Degrelle out with a French-Moroccan girl called 'Barbara', and then kidnap him, drug him, and drive 400 miles east to the port of Calpe near Benidorm, where the fascist would be put on a yacht and dispatched to France.[146] On 3 July, the two men approached the French–Spanish border crossing just north of La Jonquera.[147] At the frontier post, a guard took their passports and went into the office. After a short wait, a policeman emerged and asked Feinsohn to pull the car over to one side in order to allow other vehicles to pass. After he had done so, the two Nazi hunters found themselves surrounded by armed policemen. They were ordered out of the car with their hands in the air, placed under arrest and taken 100 miles south for questioning in Barcelona. 'The Spanish police slapped our faces and knocked us about,' Feinsohn recalled later. 'They kept shooting questions at us. Who sent you? How do you know that Degrelle is in Spain?'[148]

The following day, Carol Klein arrived at the Palace Hotel in Madrid, where she was due to meet Aldouby. After two days, she received a cable from her parents, asking her to come back to New York. Upon her return, Klein's parents told her that Aldouby was already married to his folk dancer; on 14 July, Klein flew back to Spain in order to have it out with her lover. In Madrid, she soon heard of Aldouby's arrest, and she was advised by the American embassy to leave Spain immediately in case she was arrested as one of Aldouby's conspirators. She flew to London, where she claimed she was followed by a strange man, and fled back to New York City on 17 July. When she was questioned by the FBI about the affair ten days later, Klein said that Aldouby was a 'psychopathic liar', an assessment that appears accurate.[149] The young woman was lucky that she was not arrested and convicted, as her former lover would receive a nine-year prison sentence. Aldouby was released after three years. While his pursuer languished in gaol, Degrelle attended his daughter's wedding in August 1962 wearing his SS uniform, complete with his Knight's Cross.[150] Despite being such a charlatan, it seems a shame that Aldouby was not successful, as Degrelle was to die an unrepentant Nazi at the age of eighty-seven in Málaga.

One event that Aldouby missed while he was in prison was the trial of Adolf Eichmann, which opened on 11 April 1961 and ended on 15 December when the accused was sentenced to death. For many observers of the proceedings, Eichmann cut a surprisingly pathetic figure. 'I saw a frail, nondescript, shabby fellow in a glass cell, flanked by two Israeli policemen,' Simon Wiesenthal observed. 'They looked more colourful and interesting than he.'[151] The journalist Martha Gellhorn noticed how Eichmann would lean back in his chair impassively, 'and listens to the testimony of men and women he tormented'. Gellhorn thought that Eichmann only came awake when papers were presented to him or notes had to be made. Such activity, Gellhorn supposed, was 'the organisation man at his chosen task'.[152] Eichmann's demeanour made it easy for those such as Hannah Arendt to identify Eichmann as the embodiment of 'totalitarian man', the banal functionary who could organize ship-

ments of human beings to gas chambers with the same uncon-
scionable conscientiousness that he sent paperclips from A to B. This
is a fundamental misreading of Eichmann's nature. Although he was
a good organizer, he was far from banal. He was a braggart. His
Nazism was virulent. He had numerous affairs. He drank too much.
He wanted to see active service. He was hardly the deliberately
bland figure who appeared in the dock in Jerusalem.[153]

On the evening of 31 May 1962, Eichmann was served his last
meal. He had asked for and received a bottle of wine, and by the
time a priest arrived at around eleven thirty, he was a little drunk.
The priest asked him whether he wanted to repent, but Eichmann
did not. Instead, he just gave the priest some letters to give to his
family, and told the clergyman not to look so glum. 'Why are you so
sad?' he asked. 'I am not sad.' Just before midnight Eichmann was
shackled and taken from his cell. On the way to the execution chamber, he asked one of the guards to wipe his dripping nose. After a
pause, Eichmann was then led to the gallows and a rope was placed
in two loops around his neck. Before the button was pressed, he was
asked whether he had any last words. 'Long live Germany,' he said.
'Long live Argentina. Long live Austria. These are the three
countries with which I am most connected and which I will not forget. I greet my wife, my family and my friends. I am ready. We'll
meet again soon, so is the fate of all men. I die believing in God.'[154]
With a click, the trapdoor opened, and Eichmann dropped 10 feet
to his death. By one o'clock on the morning of 1 June, his body had
been burned, and at four o'clock a bucket of his ashes was on a
launch in international waters. After the ashes were thrown into the
Mediterreanean, the bucket was rinsed out and the launch
returned.[155]

Chapter Ten

Rough Justice

WHILE THE likes of Zvi Aldouby were conducting their own amateur sleuthing, and Wiesenthal and Friedman were fighting for ownership of the Eichmann capture, quieter and more modest individuals were working hard to bring Nazi war criminals to justice. In December 1958, in Ludwigsburg, 10 miles north of Stuttgart, the West Germans established the Central Office of the Land Judicial Authorities for the Investigation of National-Socialist Crimes. The Central Office – or ZS – was formed because there was a growing perception within the Federal Republic that too many Nazi criminals were – sometimes literally – getting away with murder. In addition, when the alleged criminals were brought to trial, they were often treated as accessories to crimes rather than as perpetrators. The judicial process had enshrined this unwillingness to regard the murderers for what they were, and too often it seemed that the only criminals responsible for the slaughters were Hitler, Himmler and Heydrich.[1] Under the leadership of Dr Erwin Schüle, the ZS was tasked with investigating Nazi crimes, collecting information and identifying potential criminals. Once a case had been built, it would then be passed to the appropriate prosecutor. Much of the information initially came from documents that had been collected for the Nuremberg trials, although as the public became increasingly aware of the ZS, new evidence and fresh testimony would soon come to swamp the office. In 1959, the ZS started no fewer than four hundred investigations into crimes committed by members of the *Einsatzgruppen* and the guards of concentration camps.[2] Along with its vast workload, one of the biggest problems the ZS faced was finding suitable staff. Dr Schüle soon discovered that some of the policemen he was being provided with were 'skeletons in the cupboards' from other police forces, and they were often unsuitable and inefficient.[3] In addition, able policemen were reluctant to join Schüle's team. Frederick Forsyth dealt with the ZS when he was researching his thriller *The Odessa File*; he recalled:

> I was made aware by the German police that it was the end of your career if you worked there. You could never get back to your old force, and you could never get promotion. If you wanted to be accepted into, say, the Bavarian Police after being in Ludwigsburg, you didn't have a hope. That gave me an indication of just how pro-Nazi the establishment still was.[4]

One of those who provided information to the ZS was Hermann Langbein, the secretary-general of the International Auschwitz Committee, which had been formed in 1952. Born in Austria in 1912, Langbein was a communist and a veteran of the International Brigade that had fought against Franco during the Spanish Civil War. Interned in France after that conflict, Langbein was soon incarcerated by the Nazis for his politics, and in August 1942, he was sent from Dachau to Auschwitz, where he became secretary to the garrison doctor, Dr Eduard Wirths. Because of his position in the camp, Langbein acquired an extensive knowledge of the barbarism that had taken place in the name of medical science. His office even overlooked the entrance to Crematorium 1, and he was able to watch prisoners being taken into the gas chambers alive, and then brought out as corpses by the *Sonderkommando*.[5]

By early 1961, the ZS had conducted more than 750 investigations, and it was clear that one case stood out: that of Auschwitz. The ZS had identified some nine hundred alleged criminals who had served at the camp, but of these, only twenty-eight had been caught and were able to stand trial.[6] Through the efforts of Fritz Bauer, preparations were made to try these men in a single series of trials at the Frankfurt Regional Court. In the summer of 1961, Heinz Düx was appointed by Bauer as the pre-trial judge, and it was Düx's role to evaluate the fifty volumes of prosecution files and to launch a preliminary inquiry which involved interrogating the accused and questioning witnesses. Shortly after Düx began his work in August, he found that two judges of the Frankfurt court were keen to thwart his progress.

> They thought it would ease my workload if I were to reject the jurisdiction of the Frankfurt Regional Court for at least some of the accused, given that there were so many. Should I follow this advice, I could count on the court administration to cover my back. It was easy to see through their proposal, which was not directed at my workload, but instead was aimed at preventing proceedings that would at long last record the structures of a German extermination camp, over 15 years after the end of the Second World War.[7]

Düx was to encounter other attempts to stymie his work. At one point, he needed to send an important letter to the Soviet embassy in Bonn, but the Hessian Ministry of Justice refused to send it because the letter used the term GDR and not SBZ (Soviet Zone), which Düx and the disingenuous Hessian officials knew full well the Russians disliked and would only see his letter being ignored. Unfortunately, Düx's enemies would get their way when Düx was to act as pre-trial judge in subsequent trials of Auschwitz personnel. During one inquiry, a defence lawyer for one of the accused requested that Düx be disqualified on the grounds of 'impartiality'. 'Ten lines were all it took to dismiss me from my post,' Düx recalled. 'Looking back at my professional experience up to my retirement in 1989, in particular the field of reparations for fascist injustice, the final balance is not particularly gratifying.'[8]

The Frankfurt Auschwitz Trials opened in December 1963, and within a few weeks the German public was slowly goaded into a sense of moral outrage. In January, the British consul in Frankfurt reported that the proceedings were 'making a certain impact on the thinking public'. Although many would not bring up the subject, they would readily express their horror when it was raised. Furthermore, the comments made by the accused that they knew nothing about the gas chambers were 'registered with disgust'.[9] By the time the trials had ended in August 1965, the world had been presented with a more detailed picture of Auschwitz than it had seen before, and the German public was reluctantly able to evaluate the horrors that had been committed in its name. Six of the defendants were given life sentences, five were released, and the remaining eleven received prison terms ranging from three years to fourteen.

One name that was often mentioned during the trials was that of Josef Mengele. The person who had done the most to attempt to track him down was Hermann Langbein, who had been compiling a dossier on Mengele for a few years. Langbein's biggest coup was to have discovered that during his divorce proceedings in 1954, Mengele had given the power of attorney to a Buenos Aires lawyer to engage the services of Fritz Steinacker, who would go on to defend many Nazi criminals. In September 1958, Langbein presented his dossier to the state prosecutor's office in Bonn in order to force them to issue an arrest warrant, but he was to encounter the same brand of suspiciously pro-Nazi bureaucracy met by Heinz Düx. The official told Langbein that he could not issue such a warrant, and that it had to be done by one of the eleven West German *Länder*. Which one, the official asked, had Mengele lived in? Langbein did not know. 'In that case,' the official replied, 'I can do nothing until you find out.'[10] An incensed Langbein slammed the file on the table and informed the official that pursuing Mengele was the responsibility of the German government. Had Bonn the will to act immediately, all it had to do was to cable the West German embassy to check whether Mengele had ever registered with them. As the criminal had done so in September 1956, it would have proved an easy matter to trace him and then apply for his arrest and extradition. But there was no such will, and as it was, by March 1959, Mengele had moved to Paraguay.

It is not clear what caused the recently married Mengele to move to one of the world's poorest countries. It has been suggested that someone in West Germany had tipped him off about Langbein's inquiries, although it is equally probable that Mengele was rattled by his wrongful arrest for the death of the young girl during the backstreet abortion. Before he left, he did tell one of the employees at the pharmaceutical company that he was leaving 'because of political reasons', and informed her that he would never see her again.[11] Whatever the reason, Mengele's move would prove to be extremely timely.

Mengele's home for the next fifteen months was in a farmhouse outside Hohenau in the Alto Paraná region of southeast Paraguay. Of all the places where criminals such as Mengele hid, nowhere comes as close to the popular image of the Nazi South American lair as this small Germanic town with its dusty streets of orange earth set in the middle of nondescript Paraguayan prairie, founded in August 1900. The town's inhabitants were mostly farmers who cultivated cassava, rice, maize, cane sugar, beans and coffee. Although life was tough, the townsfolk were proud of their community, and its ambition was even celebrated in a hymn written in 1938 that praised its place in the 'new Acropolis of Paraguay'.[12] Although the community was never rich, it did better than subsist, although to an outsider from Buenos Aires Hohenau looked like the rural backwater it was. Even though Mengele stayed with the relatively wealthy family of Alban Krug, he regarded his hosts as little more than hicks, whose habit of rising at five o'clock he soon found infuriating. 'For their health and productivity it would naturally be a lot better if they would sleep one or two hours longer,' Mengele caustically noted, 'rather than wasting their time with useless and mentally low-level chattering.'[13] For Mengele, Hohenau was more of a base than a home, and he spent much of his time extensively travelling around Paraguay selling his family's agricultural machinery.

Back in Germany, Hermann Langbein's efforts were starting to be recognized. On 5 June 1959, a court in Freiburg drew up an indictment against Mengele, in which it noted how, among other crimes, he had once killed a fourteen-year-old girl 'by splitting her head with a dagger'. The warrant was sent to Bonn in order to start proceedings to extradite Mengele from Argentina. According to Rolf Mengele, the police in Günzburg tipped off the family about the moves, although by this time Mengele was of course living in Hohenau, and furthermore was about to gain the prize of

Paraguayan citizenship, which would make him immune from
extradition. On 27 November that year, Mengele received his
naturalization certificate in the name of 'José Mengele'.[14] For the
next few months, he would feel secure, but his sense of calm would
be irreversibly shattered when he heard about the kidnap of Adolf
Eichmann. Despite Martha pleading for him to return to Buenos
Aires, Mengele knew that he would never again be safe. 'It seems to
me that things are coming to a head and might bring a drastic solution,' he wrote in his diary. '[. . .] what is nevertheless depressing is
how the entire situation has become unmanageable.'[15] Although he
claimed to be in a 'good frame of mind and optimistic', it would not
last.

On 7 June, the West German embassy in Buenos Aires received
a cable from Bonn requesting information on Mengele, but the
diplomats appeared to do little. The ambassador, a former
plenipotentiary of von Ribbentrop in wartime Yugoslavia, would
claim in an interview twenty-six years later that he either did not
know or could not remember anything to do with Mengele.[16]
Astonishingly – or perhaps predictably – it would take over a year
for the extradition proceedings to actually start in Argentina on 30
June 1960; three days later, a judge formally ordered Mengele's
arrest.[17] The police would of course search in vain, although the
addresses supplied to them by the West German embassy – who had
apparently been given them by Simon Wiesenthal – were woefully
inaccurate.[18] There was also a lack of will in the upper echelons of
the police to actually look for Mengele, and the chief of the federal
police told the judge that he didn't want to waste his men's time
chasing after a foreigner who had committed no crimes in
Argentina.[19] While the Argentinians mounted their half-hearted
hunt, Mengele would react with sham disbelief to the press reports
of his wartime cruelties. 'It is unbelievable what is allowed to be
slanderously written in German magazines,' he complained in his
diary. 'The magazines are illustrated proof of the lack of character
and lack of proper attitude of the current German government, that
tolerates such self-defilement.'[20]

Later that year, fearing capture, Mengele decided to leave
Hohenau and made his way across the border into Brazil. Now
more than ever his life was that of the fugitive, as he was to spend

Christmas on his own, away from Martha and Karl-Heinz. 'It was one of the most unenjoyable I have ever spent in my life,' Mengele wrote. 'The details are so sad that I don't even want to talk about it.'[21]

Mengele's helper in Brazil was Wolfgang Gerhard, a former Hitler Youth leader in Austria. He had emigrated to South America in 1948, and edited a far-right publication called *Der Reichsbrief*. So fanatical a Nazi was Gerhard that he was reputed to have decorated his Christmas tree with swastikas, and had christened his son 'Adolf'.[22] Introduced to Mengele by Hans-Ulrich Rudel, Gerhard was honoured to protect Mengele, and in 1961, he found Mengele a position and accommodation on a farm owned by a Hungarian couple called Geza and Gitta Stammer. The farm was in Nova Europa, 200 miles northwest of São Paulo, and Gerhard told the Stammers that Mengele was one 'Peter Hochbichler', a Swiss cattle breeder who wanted to invest in a Brazilian farm.[23] For the Stammers, Mengele was a godsend, as they needed the extra pair of hands and the capital. What was more, Mengele declined a salary and only asked for food and lodging in return.

Although the Stammers would later claim that they noticed nothing strange about 'Peter', some of the farmhands found his love of philosophy and history and Mozart somewhat out of character for a farmworker in deepest Brazil. He was also once able to operate successfully on a calf's hernia, which almost confirmed that he was not who he claimed to be. Despite the anonymity, Mengele was desperate not to be discovered. Almost comically, he wore a hat and a raincoat even in the height of summer. 'I never saw anyone on a farm dress like that,' a maid recalled.[24] Mengele hated working on the farm, and regarded it as being beneath his dignity. However, in 1962, the Stammers and Mengele moved to a new property at Serra Negra, some 90 miles north of São Paulo, which he found more to his liking. 'I now feel comfortable in this spot,' he wrote in his journal.[25] It was just as well, as the farm would be his home until the end of the decade.

If the Argentinians and Germans were looking for Mengele in the wrong country, then at least they were on the right continent. In April 1961, Wiesenthal claimed that he was approached by a former Nazi called 'Johann T' who told him that Mengele was in Cairo.

Wiesenthal was initially sceptical, but Johann told him that Mengele had fled to Egypt in the wake of the Eichmann kidnap. However, Nasser was worried about the adverse publicity that might ensue if the 'Angel of Death' was found in his country, and so Mengele had been found temporary sanctuary on the Greek island of Kythnos by some sympathetic Nazis based in Alexandria. 'The Germans promised to have him and his wife taken off the island as soon as it could be arranged,' Johann warned. 'You haven't got much time, Wiesenthal. If you move fast, you might get him on Kythnos.'[26]

Suspecting that approaching the Greek authorities would only slow matters down, Wiesenthal contacted a Dr Cuenca in Athens, a 'noted scientist' who during the war had been forced to work as one of Mengele's medical attendants.[27] Wiesenthal told Cuenca that he would be sending a reporter out to Kythnos, and if he found Mengele, then he would ask Cuenca to come and confirm the identification and then inform the police. Two days later, the reporter arrived on the island and found that there were only two large buildings in Kythnos, as well as a monastery and a small inn near the harbour. The reporter asked the innkeeper whether he had had any visitors recently. 'A German and his wife,' came the reply. 'They left yesterday.' The innkeeper told the reporter that a white yacht had entered the harbour and taken the couple away, and had headed west. The journalist then showed the islander some photographs of various men, and the innkeeper identified a portrait of Mengele as being his guest. Two monks who happened to enter the inn also selected the same photograph as being of the man who had left the day before. 'We had lost another round,' Wiesenthal ruefully recalled.[28]

Although the story is certainly dramatic, it is yet another Wiesenthal fabrication. The journalist who the Nazi hunter had dispatched to the island was Ottmar Katz, to whom Wiesenthal had written at great length in 1952 about Nazi gold and escape networks. According to Katz, none of what Wiesenthal wrote was true.

> I spent four or five days on Kythnos. Mengele was certainly not there. There was no monastery. I spent two days with the local justice of the peace, who was strongly anti-Nazi, and we inspected the register of the only hotel, and the only name we thought that was worth

checking we discovered belonged to a Munich schoolteacher. I did explain to Wiesenthal that it was all wrong and then seven years later I read his book and he said we'd missed Mengele by a few hours.[29]

Katz was also to deny the existence of the monks, who Wiesenthal's imagination had inserted as a charming piece of convincing local colour. 'I found no monk on Kythnos,' said Katz. 'There was no monk on Kythnos.'[30] Needless to say, neither was there a Mengele. If there is any truth to the story whatsoever, it is more likely that 'Johann T' was a Nazi sympathizer who was feeding Wiesenthal disinformation.

Over the next few years, such 'sightings' of Mengele would multiply. As they did so, Mengele's reputation as some kind of dastardly superman would increase by the same factor, and whenever there was some unexplained death, Mengele would somehow be behind it. On 23 March 1961, the police arrested their umpteenth 'Mengele', but this time they really did have the wrong man, as the suspect was none other than Lothar Hermann: the elderly blind German Jew who had written to Fritz Bauer about Eichmann's whereabouts. Released after a couple of days, a livid Hermann laid into the 'yellow press' that had been harassing him for no less than two months.[31]

The organization that came the closest to capturing Mengele was in fact the Mossad. Buoyed by the success of Operation Eichmann, in early 1961 Harel established a Nazi-hunting unit in Paris headed by Zvi Aharoni. 'Suddenly this business was quite in vogue,' Aharoni drily commented.[32] Harel identified that the best way to track down Mengele was to spy on his family, as well as following Hans-Ulrich Rudel. Aharoni himself spent much of the year in Paraguay, and although he appeared to have established that Mengele was living – or had lived – at the Krugs' farmhouse outside Hohenau, he admitted that 'we got nothing, not a thing from Paraguay'.[33] In 1962, Aharoni recruited the former Dutch SS officer Willem Sassen to help them find Mengele. Since listening to Eichmann record his memoirs, Sassen claimed to now realize that the stories of the Holocaust were more than just Allied propaganda, and for five thousand dollars per month he agreed to help the Mossad. Sassen was soon able to tell the Israelis that Mengele was living near São Paulo, and that his protector was Wolfgang Gerhard.[34]

Aharoni mounted a watch on Gerhard, and one day he followed the Austrian as he drove southwest out of São Paulo. After 25 miles, Gerhard turned up a dirt track that led to a small cluster of farmhouses, and for the next few weeks Aharoni did his best to keep them under surveillance. 'You couldn't sit there all day long with binoculars,' Aharoni recalled, 'so we had to think of something else, but our options were rather limited.'[35] The agent decided that a picnic would be the best form of cover, so one Sunday afternoon Aharoni and two others found themselves eating sandwiches and looking down at the farmhouses. As they ate, out of one of the buildings emerged three men: two Brazilians and one European. Before Aharoni had a chance to take a surreptitious photograph, the men approached and engaged the picnickers in conversation. Aharoni studied the face of the European carefully, and he soon became sure that the man was Mengele. 'He had a moustache,' he said later, 'he was the right height. There was a striking similarity with the photographs we had.'[36] Aharoni was so certain that the man was Mengele that he returned to Europe in order to plan a kidnap. When he got back to his office in Paris, he found Isser Harel was already there and he told Aharoni to drop the Mengele investigation in order to work on something else. 'Isser was in no mind to argue,' said Aharoni.[37]

By April 1963, Harel had fallen out with Ben-Gurion and he was forced to resign, regretting that he had never restarted Operation Mengele. Under the new leadership, the Mossad was never to invest much time or money in Nazi hunting. Just as in the mid-1950s, Israel had to deal with immediate and neighbouring enemies rather than trotting the globe on the hunt for enemies from decades past. It is unclear whether the man whom Aharoni had seen was indeed Mengele, although the agent was sure of it. Even if he were not, the fact that Aharoni was on to Wolfgang Gerhard meant that he was extremely close to his quarry. Unfortunately, it was as close as any of Mengele's hunters would ever get.

In the wake of the Eichmann kidnap, minor neo-Nazi outbursts were seen all over the globe. In London, the monument above Karl

Marx's grave in Highgate Cemetery was daubed with two yellow swastikas and slogans that indicated that the vandal loved Adolf Eichmann.[38] In Washington, DC, eight men led by the founder of the American Nazi party, George Lincoln Rockwell, picketed the White House while wearing khaki uniforms and swastika armbands. One of their placards read: 'Ike – Help Free Eichmann', a demand that was more catchy than it was realistic.[39] But members of the Far Right were not the only ones who were protesting. On 27 July 1960, the New York Yiddish newspaper *Der Tog Morgen* published a letter from Moshe Beilinson, a survivor of the Riga Ghetto. 'The blood of the innocent Jews from Riga is screaming and demanding to put on trial the SS Hauptmann Herberts Cukurs, the Eichmann of Latvia,' Beilinson wrote. 'He must be apprehended before he vanishes, and it doesn't matter where it happens, in Brazil, Israel, or any other place.'[40]

As it happened, the 'Hangman of Riga' and member of the Arājs Commando was living in Brazil. Cukurs had escaped there in 1946, after he had hidden both in a forest near Kassel in Germany and in Marseille, where he had even managed to start a boat-rental business. The former daredevil pilot and Latvian hero settled in Rio de Janeiro and, once again, tried his hand at renting out boats. However, he was recognized by some survivors from the Riga Ghetto, and from then on, Jewish groups in Brazil would constantly harass the authorities in order to see him brought to justice.

The efforts did not fall on entirely barren ground, because in September 1951, the Brazilians asked the US State Department for information on Cukurs. The State Department was quick to act, and cabled the US High Commission in Germany (HICOG) authorizing it to assist the Brazilians.[41] Although it is not clear what HICOG did, in February 1952, the Brazilian embassy in London approached the Foreign Office requesting whether various affidavits made against Cukurs by survivors of the ghetto were in fact authentic.[42] The British did not reply until July, and merely sent out a letter that tried to stall the Brazilians. That tactic worked until October 1953, when the Brazilians once more asked if the documents could be verified. On 20 October, the Foreign Office wrote to the Office of the Legal Adviser at the UK High Commission in Germany asking whether the Brazilian request could be met.[43] The short answer was

that it could not, as even if the witnesses could be traced, that would
not necessarily mean that what they had said about Cukurs was
true.[44] During that November, British Foreign Office officials
exchanged a series of memoranda, which included the opinion
espoused by one mandarin that 'the Brazilians are barking up the
wrong tree about this'. 'Cukurs has never been charged with war
crimes,' wrote H. W. Evans, 'and at this stage we cannot possibly
rake among the ashes to see whether he ought to have been.'[45] Never
was British officialdom's complete lack of will to see men like
Cukurs brought to justice so cynically crystallized. Had Evans
checked, he would have seen that Cukurs could not have been
charged, as he had never been in custody. Furthermore, the matter
of confirming the authenticity of the documents could have easily
been arranged by a perusal of the files of the War Crimes Group,
which, as we have seen, contained numerous pages of testimony
made against Cukurs and his boss Arājs. In the words of one of
Evans's colleagues, as far as the British were concerned, Cukurs was
'out of sight, out of mind'. Although one official suggested that
something could be done, the idea was smacked down by one
P. F. Hancock:

> I am not quite happy about this. The fact is that we are not prepared
> to pursue this business and we ought not to give the Brazilians the
> impression that we are so prepared [. . .] I am inclined to think that
> the right thing would be to do nothing at all and to hope that the
> Brazilians will forget about the affair. I expect the Brazilians are not
> unacquainted with such tactics.[46]

To their credit, the Brazilians persisted. Nearly three years later,
their ambassador once more asked the British about the Latvian. A
lack of action against Cukurs suggests that the Foreign Office
successfully tried the silent 'tactic' once again.[47]

While the diplomats and the mandarins obfuscated, some took
more direct action. One evening, a dozen Jews smashed up Cukurs's
boatyard, and forced Cukurs to leave Rio de Janeiro.[48] After an
itinerant few years, by 1960 the sixty-year-old Cukurs had a whole
string of failed businesses behind him, but his establishment of a seaplane joyride business on the shores of an artificial lake near São

Paulo seemed finally to bring some success. However, after the Eichmann kidnap, Cukurs feared for his life, and he successfully applied for police protection and a permit to carry a gun.

In November that year, Cukurs was interviewed by the celebrated Washington correspondent of *Parade* magazine, Jack Anderson. Guarded by two policemen and wearing a pistol on his hip, Cukurs told Anderson that he was innocent of all the charges made against him, and said that the only contact he had with Arājs was to repair some trucks. 'I was too busy for politics and Jew-killing,' he said, which raises the obvious question of how Cukurs might have spent his time had he had some to spare. 'Herbert Cukurs is a very frightened man,' Anderson noted.[49]

The murderer had more reason to feel afraid the following May, when his name was brought up during the trial of Adolf Eichmann in Jerusalem. The court was hearing testimony from one Eleazar Kashat, a survivor of the Riga Ghetto, who recounted how the Latvians collaborated with the *Einsatzgruppen*. 'One of them, Herbert Zuckus, is living in Argentina today,' he said. 'I saw him kill women and children myself. Of course today he claims, as many do, that he helped the Jews.'[50] Although Kashat had mistaken Cukurs's whereabouts, a mention in the highly publicized trial was not something Cukurs would have wanted to read in his morning newspaper. However, despite the mention, for the next few years Cukurs managed to grow his seaplane business unmolested.

Just after lunch on Saturday 19 September 1964, a portly and balding middle-aged man strolled down to the kiosk on the side of the reservoir where Cukurs kept his seaplane. The man, who purported to be an Austrian businessman called Anton Kuenzle, had just enjoyed a satisfying meal of a dozen oysters, and he told the young woman in the kiosk that he was looking for investment opportunities in the tourist trade. 'Do you see that tall man, with the white hair?' she asked. 'He's much more knowledgeable about such things than I.' Kuenzle approached the man in question and introduced himself, and noticed how he looked him up and down closely. The man seemed unimpressed, but his tone soon changed when Kuenzle asked if he could buy a ride in the seaplane. 'With pleasure,' he said. 'My name is Cukurs, please board the plane.' For the next twenty minutes, Cukurs flew around the skies over São

Paulo with the man who would murder him in five months' time.[51]

'Anton Kuenzle' was nothing less than an agent of the Mossad, who in Paris the previous August had been given his mission of contacting and befriending the Latvian. 'We are dealing here with a despicable sadist who actually enjoyed torturing his victims and murdering innocent people,' said the agent who had briefed him, who may have been Zvi Aharoni. 'And this Cukurs has the chutzpah to give interviews to Brazilian newspapers, and claim that he is innocent, that he has no idea what anyone would want from him.'[52] Kuenzle was the ideal man for the job. Born in Germany in 1919, the 45-year-old looked like any other anonymous northern European businessman. At the age of fifteen, he fled Nazi Germany for Palestine, and at the outbreak of war, he joined the British army. In 1948, he served as an artillery officer during the War of Independence, and after seven years in the Israeli Defence Force, he started to undertake secret missions for the Israeli intelligence services.[53] With his unremarkable looks and his fluency in many languages, Kuenzle was a model spy. For the next month, he worked swiftly to arrange his cover identity. He travelled to Rotterdam, where he opened a post office box and a bank account, applied for a visa to travel to Brazil, grew a moustache, acquired some stationery, ordered some suits and bought some thick-rimmed glasses. His next stop was Zurich, and while waiting for his flight, Kuenzle spotted one of his favourite entertainers, Danny Kaye, and asked him for his autograph.[54] In Switzerland, Kuenzle opened a bank account with Credit Suisse, into which he deposited six thousand dollars, and secured letters of credit that would enable him to withdraw money in Brazil, Uruguay and Argentina. The agent then returned to Rotterdam and collected his suits, stationery and visa, and on 11 September 1964, he boarded an Air France jet that took him to Rio de Janeiro.

After his ride in Cukurs's seaplane, Kuenzle was invited by the pilot for a brandy on his boat. The two men briefly discussed their experiences during the war, although both were reticent, with Kuenzle hinting that he had served in the German army on the Russian front. What Kuenzle really wanted to talk about were tourist business opportunities in the area, and this certainly got Cukurs's attention. His seaplane business was doing little more than stay afloat, and Kuenzle counted on the 64-year-old desperately wanting to finally make some decent money. When the 'Austrian' returned to Cukurs's house a week later, he noticed that the house was modest with very simple furniture, and that the family was existing just above the poverty line. As well as showing Kuenzle his formidable arsenal of weaponry and his military decorations, Cukurs took his guest on a guided tour of his workshop, which even featured a fine old Cadillac that Cukurs hoped to restore. Once again, the conversation turned to business, and Cukurs said that he would be very happy to help Kuenzle by driving him around and showing him areas of potential interest.[55]

On Tuesday 29 September, Cukurs took Kuenzle to what he described as his 'plantation' some 60 miles west of São Paulo near Piedade. Kuenzle was concerned that the ever-watchful Cukurs was trying to lure him into a trap, and the Jewish agent started to worry whether during one of their roadside breaks Cukurs would notice that he was circumcised. 'I was going to tell him that during the war I had contracted gonorrhoea on a visit to a military brothel on the Russian front,' Kuenzle recalled, 'and remind him that in the days before antibiotics the treatment of this sexually transmitted disease included, in some cases, the removal of the foreskin.'[56] Kuenzle's worry turned out to be groundless, as the 64-year-old Cukurs was more absorbed in his own genito-urinary condition during their frequent stops. When they arrived at the plantation, the unarmed Kuenzle was alarmed to see Cukurs producing a semi-automatic rifle.

'Let's have a shooting match,' said Cukurs, an invitation that the Mossad agent immediately suspected was some kind of test to establish whether 'Kuenzle' had served in the army. Aiming at a metal plate from a distance of some 50 metres, Cukurs shot swiftly and well, with the expertise that came from the experience of 'shooting naked and petrified Jews in the head', Kuenzle grimly reflected. Cukurs's shots ended up in a 5-centimetre grouping, which was a decent display. 'Your turn,' said Cukurs, handing Kuenzle the rifle. 'There was no fear in me, nor did I shake,' Kuenzle recalled. 'From the minute I had taken the mission upon myself, Anton Kuenzle had become an inseparable part of me.' Because of his military experience, he shot well, and even better than Cukurs – his rounds ended up in a 3-centimetre diameter. 'Way to go, Herr Anton!' Cukurs exclaimed, and from that moment on, Kuenzle noticed that the criminal was more relaxed.[57]

After a few weeks of wining and dining his prey, Kuenzle mooted the idea that the two of them should examine business opportunities in neighbouring Uruguay. In order to minimize any outbreaks of anti-Semitism, Kuenzle was keen to assassinate Cukurs outside Brazil with its large Jewish population, and he chose Montevideo as the most convenient location for the killing. Although Cukurs was advised against travelling out of the country by the Brazilian police, the Latvian was now so convinced that riches awaited him that he dropped his normal guard and joined Kuenzle in the Uruguayan capital on Friday 16 October. The two men scouted around for suitable properties for Kuenzle to rent as an office, although none were available. During the visit, the agent noticed that Cukurs seemed unusually tense, and it later transpired that the criminal thought he was being followed by a group of four Jews. 'In my view,' Kuenzle recalled, 'by that stage Cukurs was suffering from advanced paranoia, which only heightened his alertness.'[58]

Promising great things in the pipeline for Cukurs, Kuenzle returned to Paris to make plans with his fellow Mossad operatives. After considering poisoning or a distant sniper shot, the team opted to lead him into a trap and then to overpower and kill him. On New Year's Eve 1964, Kuenzle wrote to Cukurs advising him that he would shortly be returning to South America, and he asked if Cukurs could acquire visas in order to be able to accompany him to Chile and Uruguay. Cukurs replied three weeks later, and wrote that he had done as Kuenzle had asked, and that he was looking forward to 'our joint business trip'.[59]

When the Mossad agent walked off the aircraft at São Paulo airport on 28 January 1965, he was alarmed to see Cukurs waiting for him at the bottom of the steps. Worse still, Kuenzle noticed that Cukurs was actually filming him with an 8-mm camera. It was clear that the criminal was still wary of the 'businessman from Austria', a wariness that was later confirmed by his wife. 'My husband emphasised that if anything bad were to happen to him in the near future,' she said later, 'then it was this man, Kuenzle, seen here waving so jovially, who would bear direct and sole responsibility for

The POW camp in Rimini from where Erich Priebke escaped on New Year's Eve, 1946.

Left: Priebke as 'Otto Pape' on his Red Cross passport secured by Bishop Hudal.

Right: Ante Pavelić disguised as 'Pal Aranyos' around the time of his escape in October 1948.

Left: Eichmann's Red Cross passport, which stated that his profession was a 'tecnico'.

Above: 'Riccardo Klement' – also known as Adolf Eichmann (*centre*) – on the SS *Giovanni C* en route to Buenos Aires in June 1950.

Above: The ABC restaurant in the centre of Buenos Aires where Mengele and Eichmann would occasionally meet.

Above right: In the late 1950s, Eichmann ran a farm that bred Angora rabbits. The business failed.

Above: Mengele's Brazilian foreign resident's permit was adapted from that of a man fourteen years younger.

Left: A Mossad surveillance photograph of the Eichmanns' home on Garibaldi Street in the Buenos Aires suburb of San Fernando.

Above: Shortly after arriving in Buenos Aires, Mengele lodged at the home of a Nazi sympathizer at 2460 Calle Arenales.

Left: 62 Ufton Road in Hackney, east London, where Arnold Leese hid his two fugitive SS men.

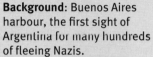

Background: Buenos Aires harbour, the first sight of Argentina for many hundreds of fleeing Nazis.

Left: Pavelić – now divested of his beard and spectacles – with his wife in Buenos Aires in 1957.

Above: Serge and Beate Klarsfeld in their Paris apartment in December 1969.

Right: Klarsfeld and Itta Halaunbrenner protesting in March 1972 at Barbie's presence in La Paz.

EN NOMBRE DE LOS MILLONES DE VICTIMAS DEL NAZISMO. QUE SE PERMITA LA EXTRADICION DE KLAUS BARBIE - ALTMANN!

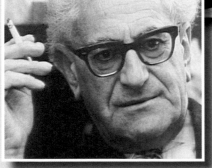

Above: Fritz Bauer, the Frankfurt Attorney-General, who revealed to the Israelis where Eichmann was hiding.

Above: Israeli journalist Zvi Aldouby saw Nazi hunting as a potentially lucrative business.

Right: Hermann Langbein, a former Auschwitz inmate, compiled an extensive dossier on Mengele.

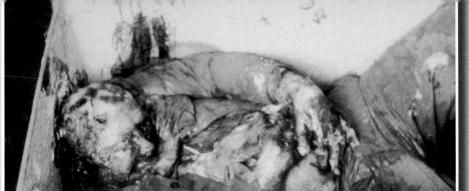

Above: The body of Herberts Cukurs, discovered by the Uruguayan police in March 1965.

Left: 'Anton Kuenzle', the Mossad agent who lured Cukurs to his doom.

Above right: The remains of the Klarsfelds' Renault after the car bomb, July 1979. A group calling itself ODESSA claimed responsibility for the attack (*below*).

Above: The envelope which contained the letter to the Klarsfelds from the supposed 'ODESSA'.

KLARSFELD,

ppelle O.D.E.S.S.A., nous sommes l'Organisation des Kameraden.
t, c'est nous.

aux disent que personne ne l'a revendiqué et cela nous étonne.
avant l'explosion, nous avons déposé sur le pare-brise de votre
s papillons portant les quelques mots dactylographiés suivants :
, cette bombe est un avertissement. Si tu continues tes activités
ine étape sera sanglante. ODESSA". Il semble que ces papillons
été retrouvés. Ils ont vraisemblablement été détruits par
on. Vous doutez peut-être de l'authenticité de la présente lettre.
sement pour vous, c'est sérieux. Voici d'ailleurs quelques
as pour confirmation :

iture était une R 5 L S de couleur rouge vif immatriculée
75.

t stationnée au premier sous-sol, près d'un pilier, à
ement numéro 55 (ça, on ne le trouve pas dans les journaux).
gariez toujours en marche avant.

-vous né le 17.9.35 à Bucarest.
-vous portez des lunettes en permanence.
-votre femme parle avec un fort accent Allemand.
-votre officine se trouve 142 R. de Rivoli (ça, c'est dans l'annuaire 79).
-vous avez une BP à la poste située rue Singer (BP n° 137).
-votre domicile : 230 Av de Versailles, tel 651.91.37 (liste rouge).
-pour commettre l'attentat, nous avons cassé la glace de la portière
  droite de votre R5 avec un marteau qui est resté sur place et qui a dû
  être retrouvé.
-pour pénétrer dans l'immeuble, nous avons utilisé la porte de l'escalier 3
  qui était restée ouverte. De toute façon, les portes ne constituent pas un
  problème pour nous. Nous sommes capables d'ouvrir n'importe quelle porte,
  quelque soit le système de verrouillage. Voilà, maintenant vous savez qui

Left: A drawing Wiesenthal made of a scene that supposedly took place in Mauthausen was in fact a copy of photographs of executed German soldiers featured in a post-war copy of *Life* magazine (*below*). Wiesenthal would always deny the plagiarism.

Isser Harel, the Mossad chief and mastermind of the Eichmann kidnap, disputed Wiesenthal's involvement in the operation.

Wiesenthal in London in 1975. Aged 66, he had become a darling of the media as the 'Man Who Never Forgets'.

Above: Barbie and his defence lawyer Jacques Vergès on the first day of his trial in Lyon in May 1987.

Below: Martin Bormann's skull. Despite overwhelming dental and DNA evidence, conspiracists remain convinced that Bormann survived the war.

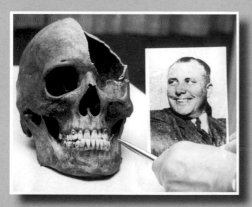

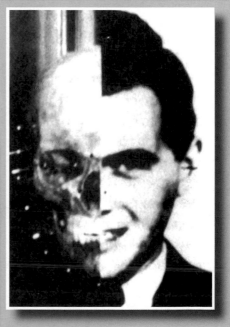

Above: A new process of 'electronic supraposition' merged photographs of Mengele with the skull unearthed in Embu in June 1985.

Left: Erich Priebke at his trial in Rome in July 1996.

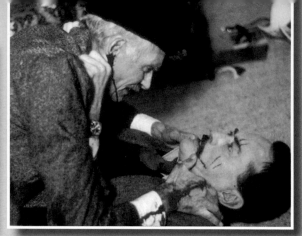

Above: Erna Wallisch, an SS guard at Ravensbrück and Majdanek, photographed by the author at her flat in Vienna in October 2007.

Right: Jon Voight as avenging journalist Peter Miller in the film of Frederick Forsyth's book *The Odessa File*.

Above: Nazi hunter Ezra Lieberman (Laurence Olivier) and Josef Mengele (Gregory Peck) fight tooth and nail in *The Boys from Brazil*.

Below: Is it safe? Laurence Olivier as the demonic Nazi dentist Christian Szell attends to Dustin Hoffman in *Marathon Man*.

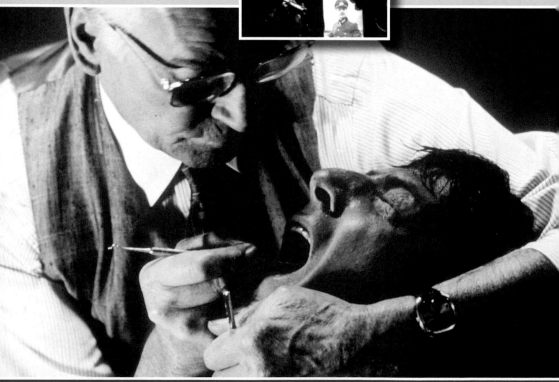

it.'[60] After a jovial greeting, Cukurs confessed that he still did not have all the documentation for their forthcoming trip, and Kuenzle scolded the Latvian as if he were a subordinate. As part of his cover, Kuenzle then flew on to Buenos Aires, where, on 5 February, he received a cable from Cukurs informing him that everything was finally in place. It was at this point that Kuenzle dispatched the following telegram to Paris: 'Negotiations have finished, and the transaction is about to take place. Request you send urgently the team of experts in order to complete this transaction successfully. Anton.'[61]

Over the next few days, four Mossad agents flew into Buenos Aires, all of whom were experienced field men and well trained in karate. Kuenzle warned the team that although Cukurs was nearly sixty-five, he was immensely strong and 'like a wild animal'. On 10 February, Kuenzle moved to Montevideo with one of the agents, 'Oswald', who was also posing as an Austrian. After several days' searching, the two men eventually found a suitable property in which the assassination could take place. Casa Cubertini was a small house on Cartagena Street, some 100 metres from the sea. Unfurnished and tatty, the house was also very exposed, and was in full view of some builders who were working nearby. Nevertheless, it was the best property that they could find, and so the agents put down two months' rent. Kuenzle cabled Cukurs to come on the 23rd, and within twenty-four hours Cukurs had wired back to say that he would be on Air France flight 083, which would arrive on the requested day at 9.30 a.m.[62] It would be the great aviator's last flight.

Cukurs's plane arrived on time that morning, and there at the airport to greet him was Kuenzle, who noticed that the Latvian was wearing a suit and tie and 'almost had the look of a respectable businessman'. The agent first drove Cukurs to his hotel, and allowed him a few minutes to settle in before they drove to the offices of Lufthansa to book flights to Santiago. Then Cukurs spent the morning with Kuenzle on a tour of properties that the 'businessman' was considering for his office. Kuenzle explained that the house he had rented was not really suitable, although he would like Cukurs to see it. As it neared twelve thirty, Kuenzle stopped his rented black VW Beetle outside Casa Cubertini. He turned off the engine and walked up to the front door of the house, hoping that Cukurs would follow him. The sound of a car door slamming shut indicated that he was doing so, and Kuenzle unlocked the door while Cukurs was a few metres behind him.[63]

Kuenzle entered the house, and he saw the members of the Mossad team standing against the walls. They were only wearing their underpants, as they did not wish to soil their clothes with Cukurs's blood. The Latvian approached the open door and then stepped into the room. Kuenzle shut the door behind him, and, as soon as he had done so, the agents leaped on Cukurs. Despite his age, Cukurs reacted swiftly and strongly, and he even managed to shake off his attackers. With one free hand, he desperately reached for the door handle, but the team held the door shut. Cukurs even managed to rip the handle off as he was dragged into the centre of the room. 'Let me speak!' Cukurs yelled, but his request was ignored and the violent struggle continued. At one point, he nearly managed to extricate his gun, but he was thwarted. Suddenly, a hammer connected with Cukurs's head, and blood gushed everywhere. The men stepped back, and one of them – it is not known who – produced a gun with a silencer and fired two rounds into Cukurs's skull, ending his life instantly. 'The voices of the builders filtered in through the windows,' Kuenzle recalled. 'They went on with their renovations of the building next door, completely unaware of the struggle that had taken place not thirty metres away from them.'[64]

The corpse was put in a large trunk, and placed on his chest was a piece of paper which read:

VERDICT
Considering the gravity of the crimes of which HERBERT CUKURS is accused, notably his personal responsibility in the murder of 30,000 men, women and children, and considering the terrible cruelty shown by HERBERT CUKURS in carrying out his crimes, we condemn the said CUKURS to death.
He was executed on 23 February 1965
   By 'Those Who Will Never Forget'[65]

After cursorily cleaning up the room, the team got dressed and left in two VW Beetles, before catching two separate flights back to

Buenos Aires. It was only there that they allowed themselves to celebrate over a bottle of champagne, but none of them could relax until they had reached the other side of the Atlantic.

At the beginning of March, the Mossad sent full details of the assassination to news agencies in Düsseldorf, Frankfurt and Bonn, although the packages came from 'Those Who Will Never Forget'. On 6 March, Inspector Juan José Braga of the Montevideo police broke into Casa Cubertini through a window and recoiled at the foul smell of decomposition. A trail of blood led him to the bedroom, where he found the trunk standing in a large pool of dried blood. He opened the lid to find the putrifying and bloated corpse of Cukurs, two bullet holes clearly visible on the right side of his head.[66] The discovery was widely reported and, predictably enough, a synagogue in Montevideo was bombed.[67] In São Paulo, the home of Jacob Rosemblat, a Jewish radio commentator, was defaced with a swastika and the words 'Viva Cukurs'.[68] For weeks, the identity of 'Those Who Will Never Forget' was discussed ad nauseam, although Cukurs's family had no doubt that 'Anton Kuenzle' was the man behind his death. Photographs of Kuenzle appeared in newspapers all over the world, and Cukurs's widow was photographed pointing to it with an accusatory index finger. 'This is the murderer!' she told reporters.[69] The press – or Interpol – was never to find Anton Kuenzle. He and the operation he had masterminded have today largely been forgotten, overshadowed by the kidnapping of Adolf Eichmann. Herberts Cukurs, on the other hand, is still a national hero in some quarters of Latvia, and in May 2005, a large exhibition entitled 'Herberts Cukurs: The Presumption of Innocence' opened in Liepāja. Ironically, those who support Cukurs use the manner of his extrajudicial execution as a means of defending him, which is hardly the outcome that the Mossad might have wished for.[70]

In the autumn of 1961, Wiesenthal moved with his wife Cyla and his fourteen-year-old daughter Paulinka from Linz to Vienna, where he set up his new Jewish Documentation Centre within the offices of the *Israelitische Kultusgemeinde*. The centre had three aims, which he outlined in his first newsletter, published on 2 April 1962. These were to represent Austria's Jews in combating anti-Semitism; to collaborate with the Austrian and German authorities and with

Jewish organizations to clear up the question of war criminals; and to carry out historical research.[71] Wiesenthal's first 'case' was that of Dr Erich Rajakowitsch, who had served as Adolf Eichmann's deputy in Czechoslovakia, Poland and Berlin, and had helped mastermind the deportation of Holland's Jews. Rajakowitsch was widely believed to have died on the Eastern Front, but during the Eichmann trial, a sharp-eared Wiesenthal had heard Eichmann relate how he had spoken to Rajakowitsch in 1955. Throughout the last few months of 1961, Wiesenthal investigated Rajakowitsch's post-war activities, and he discovered that after the customary Nazi sabbatical in South America, he had returned to Europe in the early 1950s and established himself as the successful owner of a Trieste-based import-export business. Many of Rajakowitsch's clients were in the Eastern Bloc, and he soon became a wealthy man trading with those he would have regarded as enemies during the war. By March 1962, Wiesenthal had presented a dossier of Rajakowitsch's activities to the Viennese prosecutor, and he even was able to supply an address: Villa Anita, Melide, near Lugano.[72]

What Wiesenthal did not know was that Rajakowitsch had been wooed by the Americans since the end of the war. In the January of 1945, the CIC were looking to arrest Rajakowitsch in order to 'send him to headquarters CIC Vienna for further exploitation', which suggests that he already had been exploited.[73] In December 1958, Rajakowitsch wrote a letter to a business contact in Shanghai which was intercepted by the CIA. As a result, the Agency considered that Rajakowitsch might make a suitable source of intelligence on Communist China. Despite the fact that Rajakowitsch was on the Austrian State Police's Wanted List,[74] a background check revealed nothing derogatory, and the CIA's chief of station in Italy was asked to make a 'direct approach'.[75] In June 1959, the approach was made in Milan, but although Rajakowitsch was willing to discuss a trip he had made to the Canton Fair in 1958, he was not willing to act on the CIA's behalf at that year's fair.[76] Indefinite plans were made to meet again, but nothing came of it – for the time being.

If Wiesenthal was hoping that the case of Rajakowitsch would lay the foundations for a productive working relationship between his Documentation Centre and the Austrian authorities, then he was to be disappointed. After presenting his case to the prosecutor, he heard nothing, and in March 1962 he went to Italy and discussed the case with the chief of police in Milan. Unfortunately, as the Italians had no grounds on which they could arrest Rajakowitsch, Wiesenthal returned to Vienna empty-handed. Once again, he entered the 'dark labyrinths of Austria's bureaucracy', only to discover that the investigation was 'still pending'. 'There was only one way out of this impasse,' Wiesenthal observed. 'To bring the case before the largest possible forum.'[77]

On the afternoon of 8 April, a reporter from Milan's *Corriere della Sera* appeared at Villa Anita and was received by Rajakowitsch's son. After asking the journalist to wait, the son went into the house and came back after a few minutes and said that his father would be happy to see the reporter in the morning. Naturally, Rajakowitsch did no such thing. The next day, with his face on the front of the paper, Rajakowitsch withdrew a hundred million lire from his bank and drove off in his red Fiat sports car. While he was making his escape, the CIA station in Vienna was watching the events warily. One of its sources was linked with Rajakowitsch, and as soon as the news broke, the Agency instructed him to 'disengage' from the fugitive. In addition, the source – who appeared to be a businessman – also returned thirty thousand Swiss francs that Rajakowitsch had given him for 'investment purposes'. The businessman was clearly concerned about his reputation, because he asked the CIA whether he should send Rajakowitsch a letter announcing their severance, should 'documentary proof' of the source's new attitude be required. The CIA station told him that there was no hurry, and that it 'would think about it'.[78] On 10 April, Rajakowitsch was rumoured to be in East Berlin, a story that the CIA tried to turn to its advantage. Despite having exploited the war criminal itself, the Vienna station informed headquarters that it was now going to 'push editorializing' in the newspapers concerning Rajakowitsch's links with the Soviet Bloc, and that it would encourage the 'angle that East Germans wittingly employ war criminals whereas West Germany takes court action when evidence available'.[79]

The CIA's hypocritical stance was pure Machiavellianism, but despite its efforts to influence the press, it was the East Germans who would win the propaganda battle over Erich Rajakowitsch. By the time Rajakowitsch had given himself up in Vienna on 23 April, it had emerged that one of his wartime superiors in Holland, SS-Gruppenführer Wilhelm Harster, was in fact a senior official in the Bavarian Ministry of the Interior in Munich. Foolishly, Harster had drawn attention to himself by publicly defending Rajakowitsch, and had stated that his former subordinate had nothing to do with the deportations of Jews from Holland, and that he was only responsible for the administration of Jewish property.[80] Although Harster had served a short prison sentence for his crimes, the German press found it abhorrent that such a man should hold a relatively senior post in the new Germany. He was immediately dismissed and in 1967 he would once again be tried and convicted.

Rajakowitsch's trial took place in Vienna in April 1965. In the courtroom, the war criminal was arrogant and appeared to offend not only his own defence lawyers and the judge, but also the jurors, when he told them he earned ten times more than they did.[81] Found guilty of 'having with malicious forethought created a situation which brought about danger of life for human beings and which resulted in their death', Rajakowitsch was slapped on the wrist with a mere two-and-a-half-year sentence, and released in October 1965 because of time served before the trial.[82] His conviction did little to suppress the CIA's appetite to exploit him, although because of his anti-Americanism, Rajakowitsch was recruited under a 'false flag', and did not know that the ultimate consumer of his intelligence was the CIA. In March 1966, Rajakowitsch promised to supply his handler with a full list of names of those with whom he did business behind the Iron Curtain. In addition, he promised to reveal 'numerous names of persons to this listing who are openly regarded as Communists and are, instead, pro-West'.[83] There can be little wonder, then, that the CIA was so keen to exploit Rajakowitsch. For the 'big boys' in the intelligence world, the activities of Simon Wiesenthal must have seemed little more than an annoyance.

It is not unreasonable to state that the case of Erich Rajakowitsch was Wiesenthal's first proven and successful Nazi hunt. The real Wiesenthal was finally starting to catch up with his own public image, and throughout the following decades, he was to have a few more successes, although not the 1,100 to 1,200 that are usually ascribed to him (without any substantiation). The true figure is in fact probably as low as a dozen. As we shall see, Wiesenthal's oft-used tactic was to throw around enough mud until some eventually stuck, which had the deleterious effect of wasting the time of many law-enforcement agencies and governments worldwide, as well as ruining the reputations of innocent elderly men. When it comes to identifying Wiesenthal's achievements, they are more likely to be found in his role as a figurehead and a symbol, rather than as a sleuth par excellence. Perhaps Wiesenthal's greatest success as a Nazi hunter was his role in the capture of Franz Stangl, but even here, the story is distinctly opaque.

Like so many other fugitive Nazi criminals, Stangl was understandably fascinated by the Eichmann trial. His wife, Theresa, recalled how he would sit in his armchair and avidly pore over the Brazilian and German newspaper accounts of the proceedings. Later, he would even read books about the trial, although he never spoke about it. 'It was taboo,' Theresa recalled.[84] Unlike Mengele, Stangl was bloodyminded enough to stay where he was. 'If that clever man Wiesenthal is looking for me,' he said, 'surely all he has to do is ask the police, or the Austrian consulate – he could find me at once – I am not budging.'[85] Stangl had a point. The family had been registered at the Austrian consulate in São Paulo since 1954, and numerous friends and relatives back in Austria had their address. Although Stangl did not advertise his presence, he certainly never hid himself, unlike Josef Mengele or Adolf Eichmann.

The first clue that Wiesenthal received concerning Stangl's whereabouts came on 21 February 1964. The day before, he had given a press conference in which he had spoken about the *Aktion T-4* 'euthanasia' programme, and its killing centres at places such as Schloss Hartheim. During the course of his talk, Wiesenthal mentioned the involvement of Stangl in *Aktion T-4*, and the following day he was visited by an 'excited' Austrian woman who claimed to be a cousin of Stangl's wife. 'Herr Wiesenthal, I had no idea that my cousin Theresia was married to such a terrible man,' she wept. 'A mass murderer! It's terrible. I couldn't sleep all night.' Wiesenthal immediately asked her where her cousin was now living. 'Why – in Brazil of course,' she replied, before snapping her mouth shut with the realization that she had said too much.[86] The next day, Wiesenthal was visited by a seedy-looking wino who claimed to have been a former member of the Gestapo. He told the Nazi hunter how he had seen the newspaper reports of Wiesenthal's conference, and that he would supply Stangl's location in return for $25,000. 'You might as well ask for two million,' Wiesenthal replied. 'I haven't got that kind of money.' Eventually, the price was haggled down to seven thousand dollars – one cent for each of Stangl's victims.[87] 'I wanted to throw him out,' Wiesenthal recalled, but he decided that such a price was worth paying if the man's information led to the arrest of one of the war's worst criminals. Wiesenthal promised the money, but the man wanted a guarantee. 'No one guarantees it,' said Wiesenthal. 'And if you don't like it, get out!' The man told Wiesenthal to calm down, and then told him his secret: 'Stangl works as a mechanic in the Volkswagen factory in São Paulo, Brazil.'[88]

When Wiesenthal wrote his second set of memoirs, *Justice Not Vengeance*, in the late 1980s, he omitted the story of Theresa Stangl's cousin. It is easy to see why, as the episode was no doubt a fabrication. Little about it rings true, especially the almost hammy detective-movie moment in which the cousin suddenly realizes she has said too much. If that was the case, then why would she be visiting Wiesenthal at all? Simply to get things off her chest? As the cousin has never been identified, not even by the Stangl family, she is surely a product of the imagination.[89] The incident with the dipsomaniac former Gestapo officer is also curious, because in *Justice Not Vengeance* Wiesenthal specifically writes that he gave the man both a written guarantee and a promise 'on his honour'. It is possible that Wiesenthal subsequently inserted the 'guarantee' in order to show future informants that he was a man of his word, but if this is the case, why not do so in 1967, when he wrote *The Murderers Among Us*? The most likely candidate for Stangl's betrayer is Stangl's former son-in-law, Herbert Havel, who had threatened to go to Wiesenthal in February 1964 after he had seen the reports of Wiesenthal's press conference.[90] Theresa Stangl even recalled Havel telling them that 'he had sent his Jewish uncle to see Wiesenthal', and in March 1964, Havel summoned Stangl to see him, and told him that he had no doubt that his former

father-in-law was the man Wiesenthal was hunting.[91] A few years
later, Wiesenthal would give the impression to the author Gitta
Sereny that Havel was indeed the informant, and numerous newspapers reported the same. In December 1970, the *Daily Express*
declared that Wiesenthal had paid Havel the reward money in 1967,
although threats of legal action from Havel forced Wiesenthal to
revert back to the story he had presented in 1967 in *The Murderers
Among Us*.[92]

Whoever it was who told Wiesenthal the whereabouts of Stangl
had to wait three years until the fugitive was brought to justice. On
the night of Tuesday 28 February 1967, Stangl met his daughter
Isolde for a beer in a bar, and then together they drove home for
supper. As soon as Stangl stopped the car outside the house, the
vehicle was surrounded by policemen. Theresa Stangl heard the
commotion and ran to the window, where she was shocked to watch
her husband being wrenched from the car, handcuffed and then put
into a police car. Isolde had fallen on the road and was shouting for
her parents, and by the time Theresa ran out of the house, the
convoy of police cars had sped off.[93] Bizarrely, the account of
the arrest given by Wiesenthal in *Justice Not Vengeance* some
twenty-two years later is totally at odds with that given by so many
others. According to Wiesenthal, Stangl was summoned to a
hospital in São Paulo with the fake news that his daughter had been
injured in a car crash. As soon as the worried father arrived outside
the hospital he was arrested.[94] It seems extraordinary that
Wiesenthal should have presented this version of events, which
serves no purpose other than to reinforce his reputation as a deeply
unreliable narrator. In the same book, Wiesenthal wrote that shortly
after the arrest he found himself in New York, where he personally
persuaded no less a figure than Robert Kennedy to telephone the
Brazilian ambassador to tell him that his country had to extradite
Stangl to West Germany.[95] Whether as a result of Kennedy's phone
call or not, Stangl was extradited on 22 June.

What Wiesenthal did not explain in *Justice Not Vengeance* was
why Stangl's arrest had taken three years to arrange. On 4 March
1967, while he was in Amsterdam en route to New York,
Wiesenthal told reporters that he had had to move with great
caution, because he did not want organizations such as the 'Odessa'

to know of his activities. 'There was a great danger that Stangl would escape once something leaked out,' Wiesenthal said. He also pointed out that if a formal extradition application were made, then some forty people would be involved in the process, one of whom was bound to warn Stangl. Wiesenthal claimed that he initially approached a trustworthy Brazilian official who he thought could help him, but unfortunately the man was voted out of office. It would not be until December 1966 that Wiesenthal was able to contact another Brazilian official who promised to handle the affair discreetly. On 12 January 1967, Wiesenthal was informed that the arrest could take place, but the Brazilians needed a formal request for it. Fearing that the Austrian diplomatic network was riddled with Nazis, Wiesenthal arranged with the Austrian Justice Ministry to have the papers secretly couriered to Brazil, where they reached the desk of the Austrian ambassador on the morning of Monday 27 February. Wiesenthal's Brazilian official visited the ambassador that day and, after taking the papers, he arranged for the arrest to be made.[96]

The capture of Stangl put Nazi hunting back on the front pages and, once again, Wiesenthal was to benefit. Just four weeks after the arrest, Wiesenthal's first English-language memoirs, *The Murderers Among Us*, were published. It is clear that Wiesenthal must have known that Stangl was going to be captured when he was preparing the book, as in its pages he reveals that he not only knows where Stangl is working, but also his address. 'If this man is ever brought to justice,' he wrote, 'I won't mind paying seven thousand dollars to a former Gestapo member.'[97] If Wiesenthal did not know that Stangl was going to be arrested, then his sense of caution would have caused him to withhold what he knew for fear of alerting his quarry. It is perhaps too cynical to speculate that Wiesenthal only contacted the Brazilians about Stangl in December 1966 in order to pull off a spectacular publicity stunt. Whatever the case, Wiesenthal's publishers were delighted, and they took out full-page advertisements in the press that played heavily upon Wiesenthal's recent coup.[98] Some advertisements even claimed that Wiesenthal had already 'tracked down' some 800–850 Nazis, which was an extraordinary claim and without any foundation.[99] Some of the book reviews were as gushing as the advertisements. Robert Kirsch of the

New York Times claimed that Wiesenthal had helped to secure the conviction of some nine hundred Nazi criminals, and wrote that Wiesenthal's 'story is almost biblical in its quality; the story of his quest is unique in the annals of human experience'.[100] The elevation of Wiesenthal to messianic status was no accident, as the idea that Wiesenthal had been saved by some higher power permeates the whole book. For the reporters, he was a much-needed hero, the tenacious little man fighting the big secret Nazi machine. Wiesenthal was shrewd enough to know this made good copy, and he did not disappoint. Throughout the following years, he would be labelled as the 'Sleuth with 6 million Clients', the 'Private Nemesis of Nazi Evildoers', the 'Man Who Never Forgets', and the 'Expert Nazi-Hunter'.[101] Although Wiesenthal cannot be held accountable for the eagerness of journalists to make him into such a figure, the persona certainly suited him.

While Wiesenthal was receiving his laurels, Franz Stangl was brought to trial in May 1970. On 22 December, the court in Düsseldorf found him guilty, and he was sentenced to life imprisonment. 'The Stangl case provided West Germany with their most significant criminal case of the century,' Wiesenthal commented. 'If I had done nothing else in my life but get this evil man, I would not have lived in vain.'[102] Stangl was to spend only a year and a half in prison, because just after midday on 28 June 1971 he died. Only a few hours before, he had had the last of his interviews with Gitta Sereny, during which he finally came close to acknowledging his responsibility for what he had done at Treblinka. 'In reality I share the guilt,' he had admitted in faltering tones. 'Because my guilt . . . my guilt . . . only now in these talks . . . now that I have talked about it all for the first time . . .' Eventually, Stangl was to tell Sereny that his guilt was that he was still alive. 'I should have died,' he said. 'That was my guilt.' Despite a suspicion of suicide, the post-mortem revealed heart failure. He was only sixty-three. As Sereny was to write, Stangl's death was brought on by the 'monumental effort to reach that fleeting moment when he became the man he should have been'.[103]

Chapter Eleven

'This whole
Nazi-hunting thing'

AT THE end of November 1972, readers of the British tabloid news-paper the *Daily Express* were thrilled to discover the 'true' story of Martin Bormann. In a series of articles written by the Hungarian-born American author Ladislas Farago, the newspaper revealed that Martin Bormann had successfully escaped from the *Führerbunker* in 1945, and had spent most of the past 27 years living as a rich recluse in South America.[1] The articles, which came complete with photo-graphs taken of 'Bormann' the previous October, were presented as 'incontrovertible evidence' that Bormann was still alive. The series was syndicated to both the *New York Daily News* and the *Chicago Tribune*, and it boasted how 'all speculation concerning his fate can be swept aside following a dramatic and sometimes dangerous nine-month search through six South American countries for Bormann, the world's most wanted and most elusive man'.[2] Farago's story seemed extremely plausible, not least because he served up plenty of authentic-sounding detail. Bormann was accompanied at all times by a bodyguard-chauffeur called 'Jorge O'Higgins', and the former *Reichsleiter* always wore plastic gloves so that he never left any fingerprints. The material also seemed fresh. Farago was able to report that just a few weeks earlier, Bormann had been staying on the Argentine *estancia* of Arndt von Bohlen und Halbach, a scion of the famous Krupp family. Unfortunately for Farago, much of his story had been rubbished within a fortnight, but nevertheless the author stuck to it. As we have seen, in 1974 he published *Aftermath*, in which he claimed to have solved the 'great Bormann mystery', but his assertions were soon ridiculed when it was revealed he had been duped by corrupt Argentinian spies and policemen.

Farago was not the only figure who believed that Bormann had survived the war, and it would be unfair to single him out as the only exponent of the 'Martin's Alive' school, whose members were very motley indeed. In February 1961, Horst Eichmann claimed to have had 'numerous conversations' with Bormann in Buenos Aires and Bariloche, and five years later, his brother Dieter even wrote an open letter to Bormann in the pages of the Munich-based *Quick* magazine. 'I am waiting for you to give yourself up,' he wrote. 'I am waiting for you to come forward for that part of the guilt for which you are responsible and for which my father stood in your place during the trial in Israel.'[3] These claims had seemingly been confirmed by their father's defence counsel at the trial in Jerusalem, during the course of which Robert Servatius told the court that his client believed that Bormann was alive.[4]

Fritz Bauer was also a believer. In April 1961, he admitted that he was convinced that Bormann was far from dead, and that the Nazi had been smuggled to South America by a 'secret international organisation'.[5] By July, Bauer had instigated a legal process called *Fahndung*, which was a type of search warrant, and in 1962, he got permission to excavate the site where Axmann said that Bormann had died. As no bones were found, the myth of Bormann lived on.[6] In July 1964, Bauer announced that he had heard that Bormann was living in Paraguay, and that he could often be seen in Asunción dining with none other than Josef Mengele.[7] Such sightings and the lack of a corpse resulted in the West German government posting a $25,000 reward for the capture of Bormann, which only served to encourage speculation. In July 1965, the back yard of a shipping company based in Berlin was dug over, but once more, no bones were found.[8] Until the day he died in June 1968, Bauer would continue to look for Bormann. Nevertheless, the prosecutor did not allow the 'Brown Eminence' to overshadow his mission to prosecute other Nazis. 'We still have a tremendous job ahead of us,' he said just seven weeks before his death. 'With every trial we can say "from the snowball grows a landslide".'[9] Naturally, there were those who suspected that Bauer's demise was more than a chain-smoking 64-year-old's heart attack in a bathtub. According to one conspiracist, Bauer had been killed with a cyanide spray on the orders of the dastardly Heinrich Müller, the former head of the Gestapo, who was another senior Nazi who would never seem to die.[10]

Simon Wiesenthal was also firmly of the opinion that Bormann was lurking in Latin America, and rare was the month when Wiesenthal did not make some dramatic announcement in which he revealed just how tantalizingly close he was to finding the *Reichsleiter*. In March 1964, Wiesenthal said that he had 'proof' that Bormann had escaped from a West German POW camp after the war, and it was Wiesenthal who told Bauer that Bormann was in Paraguay.[11] The following year, Wiesenthal dispatched a private detective to the Brazilian town of Marechal Cândido Rondon near the Paraguayan border, who did little more than spend three days in the area and report that the town's mainly Germanic population was without doubt the renascent Fourth Reich. This would later create problems for a local doctor called Friedrich Seyboth, who bore a remarkable resemblance to Bormann. Despite a twenty-year age gap between him and the supposed fugitive, Seyboth had to escape from a kidnap team in June 1975. Furthermore, it appeared that the doctor was not the only lookalike in the town. His rival was called Hans Joachim Gaza, who told a reporter he had been the 'offical "Bormann" of the city' before he was usurped by the young Seyboth.[12]

After the Stangl capture, Wiesenthal used his author tour of the United States in the spring of 1967 to promote not only *The Murderers Among Us* but also his theories about Bormann. The fugitive, he claimed, 'uses five or six names . . . he has many friends, money. I get reports on him simultaneously from two places too far apart to let there be just one man.'[13] Wiesenthal's implication was that Bormann used a double, which seemed to him far more plausible than the possibility that he was either a victim of dis-information or that his informants were merely seeing lookalikes.

The Nazi hunter seemed perfectly willing to share the details of some of the often comic sightings with credulous journalists. Wiesenthal recounted how one woman had bumped into Bormann on a bus in São Paulo: 'I spotted him among the passengers and called out in German, "Hello Herr Bormann, how nice seeing you again." Bormann stared at me, then turned around and jumped off the bus.'[14] Even if the man had not been the former Nazi bigwig, his reaction to the woman was perhaps understandable. Wiesenthal told another journalist that he even had a picture of Bormann walking his dog on the streets of Asunción, but unfortunately 'we can do nothing at this time,' Wiesenthal said.[15] With each interview, Wiesenthal made increasingly sensational claims, which would often contradict what he had told journalists not so long before. When he had reached France that October, he revealed to a radio station that he knew Bormann's doctor and even some of the false names that Bormann employed. 'When there is some danger,' Wiesenthal reported, 'Bormann crosses the Paraná River into Paraguay, where there are many German colonies.'[16] By the early 1970s, the trail had started to go cold, and Wiesenthal was to tell a journalist that the last 'credible' information he had received was in 1969, which had placed Bormann in the Brazilian town of Ibirubá, which was once again near the Paraguayan border.[17]

Ironically, it was Wiesenthal who did the most to try to destroy the claims made by Ladislas Farago. Clearly piqued by someone muscling in on 'his' territory, Wiesenthal claimed that the story was nothing more than an attempt to discredit Juan Perón. 'Either it's that, or the whole story is a lie from A to Z,' he declared. 'It may be a lie in both cases. I'm very sceptical.' Wiesenthal said that he had challenged Farago to provide strong evidence. 'If you have contacts with the Argentine secret service, you must also have been given Bormann's fingerprints. I have Bormann's fingerprints, and so do the West German authorities. We could establish within 48 hours whether your man is Bormann.'[18] Wiesenthal even had the gall to dismiss Farago's story as being just another in a long line of unproven sightings. 'I'm very, very sceptical as there have been about 25 to 30 false Bormanns since the war,' he said, conveniently ignoring the fact that many were of his own creation. 'There have been so many false reports because the man has such a common face . . . In Munich or Frankfurt you'll find 10 people on the streets with his face.'[19] A few days later, Wiesenthal's position had hardened. 'This is a bluff story,' he said. 'Time and time again the Nazi underground organization . . . has supplied a lot of journalists with false information.'[20] Wiesenthal would never reveal how he, unlike the journalists, was able to ensure that he never fell victim to such tactics, or how he could determine what was a sighting of Bormann rather than a mere ringer.

While the self-styled Bormann experts bickered, it was left to Frankfurt State Attorney Joachim Richter to provide a voice of reason. When asked to comment on the Farago story, Richter would sigh, 'What, again?' before he informed his latest interviewer that the Bormann file already ran to thirty-five volumes. 'Every story we have checked turned out not to be true,' he said, 'or remained simply a story – unconfirmed.' Although Richter was keeping the case on Bormann open, he strongly suspected that the man once called the 'Devil's Beelzebub' had been lying under the streets of Berlin since 1945.[21] Richter's suspicion would be proved right sooner than he suspected, because on 7 December 1972, workmen in Berlin unearthed two skeletons near the Lehrter Station, which were soon suspected as being those of Bormann and Hitler's physician, Ludwig Stumpfegger. On 9 February 1973, Dr Heinz Spengler, the director of the West Berlin Institute for Forensic Medicine, announced that the shorter of the two skeletons was definitely that of Bormann. 'We have proved it beyond a shadow of a doubt,' he said. Spengler explained that the teeth matched those in a sketch made by Bormann's dentist Hugo Blaschke in 1946,[22] and evidence of a broken collarbone caused by a riding accident in 1939 was also discernible.[23]

Richter formally announced Bormann's death at a press conference in Frankfurt on 11 April. However, the day before, *Stern* magazine had run a story leaking the announcement, which caused much bad blood during the official announcement. Simon Wiesenthal suggested that Richter had been behind the leak, and censured him for colluding with the magazine. The Frankfurt prosecutor stood up and, in front of the room crowded with journalists from all over the world, vented his spleen at the Nazi hunter:

You have given us only vague information without any specific names, addresses, and dates – tips, in fact, which proved useless in our investigation. On the other hand, Herr Jochen von Lang of *Stern* magazine cooperated with us closely and was instrumental in aiding our determination of the case with invaluable factual data.[24]

Naturally, this outburst was not reported, because the story that day was the death of Bormann and not the death of Wiesenthal's reputation. It also appeared that none of the journalists who questioned the Nazi hunter asked him about the numerous sightings that Wiesenthal had reported, and they continued to accept him as some sort of authority, despite the fact that his reports over the past few years had clearly now been shown to be bunkum. Instead, what Wiesenthal offered was a kind of condescending magnanimity, and he expressed his opinion as though it had more weight than the entire West German legal system. He praised the 'great earnestness' of the investigation, and said that he must 'accept the proof which has been assembled with German thoroughness, but I have my doubts on purely personal feelings'.[25]

Although Bormann was clearly dead – and DNA testing in 1998 would remove even Wiesenthal's doubts – he enjoyed an afterlife as a literary sub-genre. Even before his bones were unearthed, Bormann provided the meat in many a potboiler. In 1954, in Basil Heatter's *Act of Violence*, the 'Brown Eminence' lurks in the background as the man about whom the hero – an Austrian concentration-camp inmate turned New England ski instructor – 'knows too much'. Although Bormann does not appear, there is a satisfying fight with a giant ape. In 1965, the author of *The Blue Max*, Jack D. Hunter, published *The Expendable Spy*, a wartime thriller that features an American agent trying to penetrate a ring of Nazis and ends up on the hunt for Martin Bormann's treasure. If Hunter's novel had a stamp of authenticity, that was because the author had served in the CIC and had run a ten-month penetration operation from 1945 to 1946 called 'Nursery', in which some one thousand Nazis were rounded up as they conspired to re-establish some form of Nazism. In 1966, Bormann had a more central role to play in Geoff Taylor's *Court of Honour*, in which the dastardly *Reichsleiter* hatches a plot that tries to get the Russians and the

Americans to start World World III. Also somehow involved is an ageing German general and his nymphomaniac wife, who jumps out of a top-floor window to avoid being raped by one of Bormann's sadistic aides. Eliot Fremont-Smith for the *New York Times* was acerbic, and noted how 'Bormann's plan is recapitulated for the forgetful reader, the mistaken assumption being that the latter is still around.'[26] In 1977, somewhat late in the day, Harry Patterson – better known as Jack Higgins – joined the Bormann bandwagon and produced *The Valhalla Exchange*, in which the ever-cunning Bormann tries to barter his escape for five VIP Allied prisoners, including a general and an elderly female pianist. Patterson added nearly every ingredient required for a mid-1970s wartime thriller to produce what the *New York Times* called a 'vintage bouquet': a beautiful female spy; a German ace and his American rival; the Free French; some Finnish ski troops; an endless supply of German guards; and a battle at the end which turns the inside of a sinister Austrian castle into a 'charnel house'.[27]

If such fiction was ridiculously absurd, it was no more so than the books about Bormann that purported to be historical. The most sensational of these was William Stevenson's *The Bormann Brotherhood*, published by Bantam in 1973 with a paperback print run of 1.5 million copies. The book told of a tightly organized Fourth Reich controlled by Bormann, and according to its full-page advertisements it was both 'carefully researched and accurately documented'. 'Staggering in its implications,' ran the copy, '*The Bormann Brotherhood* may remind you of *The Odessa File*, except that it is chilling fact – not fiction.'[28]

Ultimately, it is Frederick Forsyth's thriller that alone survives the glut of early 1970s fugitive Nazi fiction. *The Odessa File*, which was also turned into a film starring Jon Voight, concerns the hunt mounted by a journalist called Peter Miller for the 'Butcher of Riga', Eduard Roschmann, who was second in command of the Riga Ghetto and, in Simon Wiesenthal's words, 'had some 35,000 human beings on his conscience'.[29] The idea for the book had come to Forsyth after he had successfully submitted the manuscript of *The Day of the Jackal* to Hutchinson in the summer of 1970. The firm was so thrilled with the book that they wanted to sign Forsyth up to a three-book deal, and they asked whether he had any more ideas.

'Well, of course one doesn't say, "No I don't,"' Forsyth recalled. 'So I said, "Oh yeah."' Forsyth was asked to write each idea on a single sheet of A4 and return them a week later. 'I stepped out on to Great Portland Street thinking, "What the fuck am I going to do?"' Forsyth thought back to his days as a journalist in Germany, and recalled stories about the 'Odessa', although he initially thought they were just communist propaganda. (Judging by the experiences of Stanley Moss in Paris in 1951, they were probably just that.)[30] Forsyth described the genesis of the book thus:

> So let's analyse *Day of the Jackal*, well, it's a manhunt story; actually it's a double manhunt story, I have a killer hunting the President and I have all the security forces hunting the killer. It's a manhunt . . . let's think manhunt . . . Nazis . . . manhunt . . . Eichmann . . . been done, done to death, can't make a novel on Eichmann, ten years ago, let's try something different. So anyway, I wrote down on this sheet of A4 a story about a notorious and savagely brutal Nazi camp commandant who has disappeared after 1945 but a hunt for him is being carried out, not by the Jews or the West German authorities, but by one single reporter, an investigative reporter, who being a Gentile German will not be so suspected, but he's just so utterly horrified by what his forefathers did that he decides to hunt the man down himself.[31]

Along with a second piece of A4 outlining the plot of a story about mercenaries in Africa, Forsyth took the idea to Hutchinson. His editor glanced at them and said, 'Nazis first, mercenaries second': a statement which perfectly encapsulated the 1970s publishing industry's love for the Third Reich.[32]

To help with his research, Forsyth visited Lord Russell of Liverpool, who had been one of the chief prosecutors in the office of the Judge Advocate General, and had served in numerous military courts from 1946 to 1950. In 1954, he published *The Scourage of the Swastika*, a detailed exposé of Nazi war crimes which sold some 250,000 copies. Liverpool recommended that Forsyth should meet Wiesenthal, and he wrote him a letter of introduction. Shortly afterwards, the author found himself in Vienna in the little alleyway where Wiesenthal's office was located.

I knocked on the door and noticed there was a spy hole. I said, 'My name is Mr Forsyth, I have a letter of introduction here from Lord Russell of Liverpool for Mr Wiesenthal, could you take it to him?' So through the letterbox it went, still no opening of the door, a bit clandestine but the guy could be threatened – there were all sorts of people who wanted him dead. Anyway, two, three minutes went by and the spy hole opened again and the voice said, 'Herr Wiesenthal can give you twenty minutes.' Anyway, the door opened, in I went, the door closed behind me, and I was shown into this incredibly small, cluttered little office, with Simon sitting behind the desk. He said, 'Please sit down and how is my friend Russell?' I said, 'Fine when I saw him.' And he said, 'What can I do for you?' So I said, 'I know you would prefer me to bring you information but I'm afraid I'm the reverse, I'm trying to write a book. It's novelistic, therefore it's fictional but I think nevertheless it may be useful in raising the profile of this whole Nazi-hunting thing. On that basis I hope you won't think this is a completely wasted twenty minutes.' So he said, 'Just tell me roughly what you want to do.' I told him it was about a fictional concentration camp commander, or Kommandant, who was savagely cruel, a brute, a monster and who after the Second World War 'disappeared'. He then asked, 'Why are you inventing one?' I said, 'Well, because I don't know one!' So that was his first hint of merriment, he was quite a jolly old soul actually, considering, and he turned and he said, 'Here, take your pick!'[33]

Wiesenthal suggested Roschmann would make the perfect Nazi for Forsyth, and he produced a copy of his SS file. 'I thought it a great breakthrough,' Forsyth said, 'because here was a man who wouldn't dream of suing me for libel in the High Court.' Indeed he would not have done, because Roschmann was hiding in Argentina like so many of his fellow SS officers. For Wiesenthal, collaborating with Forsyth was an opportunity to actually publicize one of his cases, and he told Wiesenthal that although some might accuse him of debasing himself 'to the level of a thriller', he did not care if the result was that the real Roschmann was captured. Wiesenthal provided Forsyth with a vast amount of material for *The Odessa File*, and he appears throughout the book, telling Peter Miller all about the Odessa and the former Nazis still in positions of power in West Germany. During the course of the book, Peter Miller finds himself up against many such figures, and some of the encounters were based directly on Forsyth's own experiences. One of the most notable is Miller's attempt to interview an official in the Hamburg Attorney-General's office about Roschmann, during which the bureaucrat proves to be highly unhelpful and immensely evasive.

> 'All I can say is that all matters concerning the area of responsibility of my department are under constant enquiry. I repeat, constant enquiry. And now I think, Herr Miller, there is nothing more I can do to help you.'
> He rose, and Miller followed suit.
> 'Don't bust a gut,' he said as he walked out.[34]

'That's exactly the reception I got,' Forsyth recalled. 'Like Miller, I wandered my way down through Germany back to Vienna where I met a very amused Simon Wiesenthal, who said, "What did you find?" I said, "Frightening, absolutely weird." Wiesenthal replied, "Yes, that's what I have to fight all day, every day." '[35]

Like *The Day of the Jackal*, *The Odessa File* was extremely successful, and it, more than any other work, is responsible for the promulgation of the notion of an organization called 'Odessa'. In his foreword, Forsyth confidently asserted that Odessa existed, and was specifically formed to help Nazi criminals to escape to 'more hospitable climes'. It was managed, he wrote, by a 'few very top men' who 'remained abroad to manipulate the organisation from the safety of a comfortable exile'.[36] Ultimately thanks to Wiesenthal, this has been the prevailing view ever since, but recently Forsyth has been a little more circumspect. 'There was undoubtedly what they would have called a *Netzwerk*, a net, a *réseau*,' he said, 'but it's like the Old Boy network, the old school tie. To say it doesn't exist isn't true. It's a case of helping out old so-and-so, he's fallen on hard times.'[37]

Simon Wiesenthal was not the only Nazi hunter to whom Forsyth could have turned for advice. His researches – or those of Peter Miller – might have taken him to Paris, where he could have met a couple in their mid-thirties called Serge and Beate Klarsfeld. Born in

1935, Serge Klarsfeld was raised in France by his Romanian-Jewish parents, Arno and Raissa, who had moved to Paris when they were students. In 1939, Arno enlisted in the Foreign Legion, and although he was captured in the wake of the French defeat, he managed to escape and in June 1940 took his young family to live in Nice, which lay in Vichy France. Until September 1943, the city was occupied by the Italians and the Jews were protected, but when they withdrew, the Germans moved in. Just after midnight on the night of the 20th–21st, Raissa Klarsfeld heard a lorry pull up outside the house. 'This was it,' she recalled. 'I quickly woke my husband, and we grabbed the children and put them in the hiding-place.'[38] Together with the eight-year-old Serge and his eleven-year-old sister Tanya, Arno and Raissa listened to the Gestapo abusing the Jewish family next door. After a while, Arno could no longer stand it and crawled out from the hiding-place. 'I'm leaving to save you,' he said. 'I can stand a concentration camp. I'm strong.' When he answered the door, he told the Gestapo that his family was in the countryside as the apartment was being disinfected. The Nazis conducted a search anyway, and although they came within inches of the hiding-place behind a wardrobe, Arno's family was not found.[39] Shortly afterwards, their husband and father was entrained to Auschwitz where he was gassed.[40] After the arrest, Serge was hidden in a children's home, while his mother and sister were sheltered by the Resistance. All three survived the war, and Serge would eventually study history at the Sorbonne and become a lawyer.

One lunchtime in May 1960, Serge spotted an attractive young woman at the Porte de Saint-Cloud Métro station. He walked up to her and asked her whether she was English. 'No,' she replied, 'I'm German.' By the time Serge had got off at the Sèvres-Babylone station, he had the telephone number of one Beate Kunzel, a 21-year-old German au pair from Berlin, whose father had served in an infantry regiment that was sent to France in the summer of 1940.[41] The two started dating, and Beate recalled how they never stopped talking. 'He brought history, art, the whole world of ideas into my life. When he realized how ignorant I was of my own country's history, Serge [. . .] undertook to teach me. That was how I came into contact with the terrifying reality of Nazism.' In 1963, the couple married, and Serge started working for the French national broadcaster RTF, while Beate joined the French–German Alliance for Youth, which was a friendship organization established by de Gaulle and Adenauer.

In 1966, the year after her son Arno was born, Beate wrote a piece for *Combat*, in which she alleged that Kurt Kiesinger, the new Chancellor of West Germany, had been a senior Nazi, a fact that had been ignored by the Federal Republic's political establishment. By 1968, she had mounted a full public campaign against the politician, which came to a climax in November at the Christian Democratic Union's annual party conference. Posing as a reporter, Klarsfeld drew near to the platform where Kiesinger was sitting with various other party leaders. After sweet-talking a guard to let her pass behind the platform, Beate was now ready to carry out one of the greatest pieces of political activism of the decade. 'I slipped behind the dignitaries. As I got behind Kiesinger, he sensed my presence and half turned around. My nerves tensed agonisingly. I had won. Shouting, "Nazi! Nazi!" at the top of my lungs, I slapped him. I never even saw the expression on his face.'[42]

The 'Kiesinger Slap' saw Klarsfeld being sentenced that very evening to a year in prison, but the sentence was suspended, and she would continue her protests against Kiesinger until he was voted out of office in 1969.

As well as fighting anti-Semitism throughout Europe, the Klarsfelds were to turn their attention to Nazi criminals who were living openly in Germany without fearing punishment for their wartime activities. In early 1971, the couple investigated Kurt Lischka, a former *SS-Obersturmbannführer* who was the wartime Gestapo chief for Jewish affairs in France, and one of those responsible for the deportations to Auschwitz. After the war, Lischka was held by the Czechs, although the French made no effort to have him extradited to face trial. On 22 August 1950, Lischka was allowed to return to Germany, where he settled in Cologne. Just a month later, the French sentenced him *in absentia* to life imprisonment, and when they finally asked the Czechs to hand him over, it was too late. As Beate Klarsfeld was to write, 'fortune smiled more on the executioner than on his countless victims.'[43]

Rather than spending months – or years – lobbying recalcitrant officials, the Klarsfelds decided to adopt a more extreme approach.

They planned to kidnap Lischka from his home and smuggle him back to France where he could be put on trial. The couple swiftly recruited a snatch squad, which consisted of a university friend of Serge called Marco, a doctor called David and a photographer called Eli. At 12.45 p.m. on Monday 22 March 1971, the four men drew up at the Maria Himmelfahrt Strasse streetcar stop, where they knew Lischka would alight just before one thirty. They waited nervously, standing around the Mercedes with its engine still turning over. 'People in the neighbourhood were peeking through their window curtains at us,' Marco recalled, 'and children were running back and forth.'[44] Eventually, Lischka appeared and, in view of the whole street, Marco and Serge Klarsfeld ran up to him, took him by the arms, and shouted, 'Come with us! Come with us!' At first, Lischka did as he was told, but he soon refused to move his tall and heavy frame. David and Eli quickly came to help, but moving the former Gestapo officer was harder than they had expected. Eli then snatched Lischka's hat and hit him over the head with a cosh, but it appeared to make little impression. 'Help! Help!' Lischka shouted in terror, his face turning purple. Eli hit him again, and the German collapsed to the ground, although he was still conscious.[45]

By now, a crowd had surrounded them and emerging from it was a small man brandishing a police badge. 'Fortunately, he was not armed,' said Marco. 'We told him in French to go away.' Realizing that all was lost, Serge yelled at the team to get to the car, and the four men bolted, with Eli still clutching Lischka's hat. The policeman gave chase, all the time shouting, 'Give back the hat, please! The hat!' As Eli did not speak German, he did not understand what the policeman wanted, and he even stopped and looked quizzically at their pursuer. The policeman pointed to the hat and Eli twigged and gave it to him. 'Thank you,' said the policeman, before Eli turned and ran. The four men got into the car, and within a few minutes they arrived at a wood, where they changed vehicles. As they headed towards the main road, they jettisoned the syringes and chloroform that they were to have used on Lischka. 'We were to meet Beate at the entrance to the highway,' Marco recalled, 'but since we could hear police sirens, we did not wait for her.' Despite accidentally heading back towards Cologne, the team eventually made it to the frontier, which they crossed without any problem.[46]

A few weeks later, Beate Klarsfeld returned to Cologne, where she continued the campaign against Lischka, and also Herbert Hagen, who had been Lischka's superior and an associate of Adolf Eichmann. However, when Klarsfeld tried to deliver her dossier to a German magistrate, she was rewarded with an arrest warrant made out not in the name of the two Nazis, but in her own.[47] Taken to Ossendorf Prison, Beate was charged with her part in the attempted Lischka kidnapping and faced a considerable jail sentence. However, thanks to a 'lively campaign' mounted by Serge, she was freed after three weeks. When she was released, a middle-aged prison warder approached her and said, 'I was worried that you would not be set free. You did well, very well indeed. I hope to see Lischka in your cell someday.'[48] The guard had probably retired by the time Lischka and Hagen were imprisoned, which would not be until February 1980.[49] Both men would be released after serving just five years of their sentences. Lischka would die in 1987, although Hagen lived until 1999.

In the summer of 1971, the Klarsfelds started working on bringing to justice a man with whom their names will forever be linked: Klaus Barbie. On 25 July, Beate was studying photocopies of the decision made by the Munich public prosecutor the previous June, in which the investigation against Barbie had been formally closed. 'I became aware of the shocking consequences of closing the case,' Klarsfeld wrote. 'Those ten pages, written in a dry, pedantic style, served to rehabilitate – through Barbie – all the Nazi criminals who had operated in France.'[50] As soon as Beate had read the documents, she and Serge compiled a dossier on Barbie's crimes, which they presented to the press a few days later. Outrage ensued, and in September, Beate took the campaign to Munich, where she was joined by a Madame Benguigui, who had had three boys at the orphanage in Izieu that Barbie had cleared in April 1944.[51] Benguigui had been incarcerated in Auschwitz since May 1943, and had hoped that her sons were safe in Izieu, but one day she recognized a sweater belonging to her thirteen-year-old son Jacques in a pile of clothing that had belonged to a group of recently gassed prisoners.[52] The two women stood outside the Munich courthouse all day. Above Benguigui's head was a sign that read, 'I am on hunger strike for as long as the investigation of Klaus Barbie, who murdered my children, remains closed.' Eventually, at around six o'clock that evening, the prosecutor, Manfred Ludolph, came down to see them, and was persuaded by Beate to reopen the case if she could produce the witness who had once heard Barbie talk of the Jews' fate by saying, 'shot or deported, there's no difference'. Within days, Serge had found the witness in the telephone book; he was now a Paris-based lawyer. He immediately dictated an affidavit to his secretary, and on 1 October, Ludolph reopened the case.[53] He also gave the Klarsfelds two mugshots of Barbie, as well as a picture of a group of businessmen sitting around a table, one of whom looked like the former Gestapo officer. 'The picture of the group was taken in La Paz, Bolivia, in 1968,' the prosecutor said. 'That is all I can say at this time. Since you have demonstrated how efficient you are, why don't you help me identify that man?'[54]

The Klarsfelds sent the photograph to *France-Soir*, but the newspaper refused to publish it, fearing legal repercussions in case the man was not Barbie. Beate then took the picture to the French government's 'anthropometric department' which was headed by a former member of the Resistance. For half an hour, the man scrutinized the picture, and told Beate that there was 'every likelihood' that the man was Barbie. The earlobes were turned outward, the folds at the corners of the man's mouth were identical and the shape of the frontal bone was similar. For the newspaper *L'Aurore*, that was good enough and on 2 November 1971, they ran the picture with the caption 'The Murderer of Jean Moulin'.[55] Eventually, word reached Herbert John, the journalist who had been swindled by Barbie and Schwend while he was on the hunt for Martin Bormann.[56] At last, John had the chance to take his revenge. Through an intermediary, he told the Klarsfelds that the man in the picture was not Barbie, but what he could provide was not only Barbie's address in Lima and cover name – Klaus Altmann – but also his address and a recent photograph.

On the early morning of Thursday 27 January, Beate boarded a flight at London's Heathrow airport bound for Lima. With her was a dossier that she and Ludolph had jointly prepared in Germany the day before, which was intended to show the Peruvian government that Altmann and Barbie were one and the same. In addition, Beate carried documents concerning the two extradition treaties signed by

Peru and France in 1888 and 1924. However, there was also a sense of urgency to her mission. At four o'clock that morning, Serge had woken her to say that the radio had announced that Barbie was making for Bolivia. 'We figured that he could not reach the border before Friday,' Beate recalled, 'by which time I would be in Lima, and, if necessary, could follow him to La Paz.'[57] She arrived at ten o'clock that night feeling exhausted and disorientated. 'It was hot and humid,' she recalled, 'and I was wearing a winter coat. There were no reporters, for I had made a mistake in my cables by giving Greenwich instead of Lima time.'[58] By the time she had checked into her hotel, the reporters had arrived, and she briefed them until 2 a.m. She was relieved to hear that Barbie could not have crossed the border, so there was still a chance that the Peruvians could arrest him.

At noon the following day, Herbert John took Beate to the headquarters of the military police where she outlined the Barbie case to a general and requested that he stop Barbie before he crossed the border. The general did little more than state that he would get the material to the relevant minister. Throughout that afternoon, Beate would see numerous 'relevant' officials, but not one of them did what she asked, which was to stop Barbie getting away. Later, she visited the French ambassador, and during their meeting he received a phone call reporting that Barbie had crossed the frontier at midday, and that he had been accompanied by two Peruvian police who had handed him over to their Bolivian counterparts.[59] Beate left immediately for La Paz, and as soon as she arrived, the press were on to her. Despite being afflicted by a violent headache brought on by the altitude, Beate spoke to dozens of journalists. 'The reporters reappeared and came into my room one by one while the others waited in the corridor,' Beate later wrote. 'I might as well have had a red light outside my door.'[60]

Klarsfeld was to find that Barbie was well protected in La Paz. Many of the officials she had met were put out by the stories that had already started appearing in the Bolivian press, and after two days on a bureaucratic merry-go-round, Beate was threatened with expulsion. Although the French ambassador did not wish to annoy the Bolivians by receiving Beate, one of the embassy staff saw her in secret and photocopied her documents. That same afternoon, the

French formally announced their request for extradition, which instantly earned Beate her oft-promised expulsion. While she waited overnight for her flight, the Bolivians insisted that she had a police escort. 'We are here to see you to your safety,' they informed her. 'You risk being killed by Nazi organisations in Lima that are furious over the campaign you have launched against them in South America.'

The policemen were not wrong. Herbert John informed her over the telephone that Friedrich Schwend had declared that if Klarsfeld returned to Peru, 'she would be taken care of'. Despite such a threat, Beate wanted to refuse the protection. 'Give me a revolver,' she told her guards, 'if you're so scared something will happen to me. I can take care of myself.' The police insisted on looking after her, and she had to spend the night in their office before she left the following morning.[61] Ironically, while Klarsfeld was being protected by the Bolivians, so was her quarry. As soon as Barbie had arrived in La Paz, he was also given police protection. Fearing an Eichmann-style kidnap, the former Gestapo officer was made to stay in a hotel under a false name. It was explained to him that the authorities regarded him as 'an honourable Bolivian citizen with all the rights that implied'.[62]

When she arrived back home, Beate found that neither Serge nor the six-year-old Arno had any clean clothes to wear. '[I] began buzzing around the apartment like a bee,' Beate recalled, 'for the problem of keeping my men's clothes clean was in the back of my mind during my trips, as they were sloppy by nature ... Now I could catch up with all those things, and I was overjoyed.'[63] Yet Beate did not allow domesticity to distract her from the hunt for Barbie; on 20 February, she returned to La Paz, accompanied by the 68-year-old Itta Halaunbrenner, whose husband, son and two daughters had all been killed on Barbie's orders. Once again, Beate's trip was a hectic succession of press interviews and fruitless encounters with officials. However, on the morning of Monday 6 March, she and Halaunbrenner chained themselves to some railings outside the offices of Barbie's company, Transmarítima Boliviana. They carried two signs written in Spanish. Itta Halaunbrenner's featured a photograph of her family and the words, 'Listen, Bolivians! As a mother I only claim justice. I want

Barbie-Altmann, who murdered my husband and three of my children, brought to trial.'[64] For hours the two women sat there, even when it rained, and a huge crowd gathered. 'What you are doing won't accomplish anything,' said one French embassy official, but Beate was adamant that even if the man were right, it was still worth protesting. One Bolivian woman was more supportive, although she advised the protestors, 'There is no such thing as justice in Bolivia. Kidnap him or kill him.' After six hours, Beate and Halaunbrenner released themselves and flew back to France. 'We did not have Barbie in our luggage,' she recalled ruefully, 'but for a while we had represented the eternal quest for justice.'[65]

For the time being, there was little the Klarsfelds could do but hope that the machinations of the French and Bolivian legal and bureaucratic systems would work in their favour. However, even such a seemingly passive position was not without risk. On 10 May, a parcel was brought up to the family's apartment by the concierge. As Beate and young Arno were in Cannes, where Beate was due to give a talk to the International League against Racism and Anti-Semitism (LICRA), the parcel was received by Serge's mother. Placing it on a table, Raissa Klarsfeld was struck by the fact that the postmark and the sender's address did not match, but what made her more suspicious was the fact that the family's cat showed no interest in the parcel's wrapping paper. When Serge returned home from work at six thirty that evening, he started opening the package, and removed the wrapping paper to reveal a cardboard box. Inside that, well padded by tissue paper, was a red box, which bore the name of a confectioner's. While he was removing the tissue paper, Serge had noticed some black sugar-like grains. 'He took some of these and held a match to them, and there was a little flame,' Beate recalled. 'He then got a shopping bag and put all the elements of the parcel into it and took it down to the police station. On the way he met a friend, who asked him what he was doing, and Serge replied, "I have a bomb in my shopping bag," and he was laughing about it.' At the police station such jocularity turned to shock after the parcel had been examined by the bomb-disposal team. The box of 'sweets' was found to contain 500 grams of dynamite and 300 grams of nails. 'We never knew who sent us the bomb,' said Beate, 'and neither did the police.'[66] Further threats were to follow, often in the form of poison-pen letters or abusive phone calls, some of which threatened the life of Arno.

Although there is no evidence whatsoever to link Barbie to the bomb and the threats, there can be no doubt that it was the type of action that the murderer would have approved of. Throughout the 1970s, Barbie was to find his skills as a torturer much in demand by the Bolivian dictatorship. 'The Bolivians used simply to beat people up,' one Interior Ministry official would recall. 'Under Barbie, they learned the use of techniques of electricity and the use of medical supervision to keep the suspect alive until they had finished with him. Barbie used to tour the camps, giving lectures.'[67] For Barbie, living and working under the Banzer regime was as fulfilling as being a member of the Third Reich. Very few pies in Bolivia throughout that decade lacked Barbie's fingerholes, and he could even be found working in the immigration service at La Paz airport.[68] Barbie also acted as a 'security consultant' to the drug baron Robert Suárez, and in 1978 procured for him a bunch of neo-Nazi mercenaries called the 'Fiancés of Death' led by a West German pimp, murderer, drugs dealer and all-round thug called Joachim Fiebelkorn, who almost idolized Barbie. 'He always said that he wished he had had the chance to do what Barbie did,' recalled a former drug trafficker. 'He would telephone Barbie or Barbie telephoned him almost every day.'[69]

Barbie's apotheosis would come in July 1980, when Luis García Meza Tejada took power in the infamous 'Cocaine Coup' supported both by Barbie and the Italian neo-Fascist terrorist Stefano Delle Chiaie. Now an honorary colonel in the Bolivian army, Barbie's new role was to work in the Ministry of the Interior helping to supervise internal intelligence. It is hard to envisage an organization more suited to Barbie's repellent 'talents': once again, he was a de facto Gestapo officer, and with Fiebelkorn he had his own team of thugs to carry out his wishes.[70] Now christened the 'Special Commando Group', Fiebelkorn's group not only helped carry out 'disappearances', but also aided the government to wrestle the drugs trade away from the barons and into government hands. Barbie acted as the linkman between Fiebelkorn and the brutal Minister of the Interior, Colonel Luis Arce Gómez. 'Whenever Arce Gómez gave an order, Fiebelkorn would call Barbie to discuss it with him and to ask for advice,' said the drug trafficker. 'Barbie always knew everything that was going on and Joachim always followed his advice.'[71]

Like many Bolivian dictatorships, the rule of García Meza would only last for a matter of months. Throughout the middle of 1981, armed protests against the regime were mounted, which soon coalesced into a rebellion in the Santa Cruz region. García Meza announced his resignation on live television on the night of 3 August, although Barbie was to continue to serve the new interim junta, albeit in a reduced capacity. Nevertheless, his glory days were over, and the installation of a new civilian government on 10 October 1982 would see the demand for his 'special services' dry up. Two weeks later, Barbie turned sixty-nine, and as he approached his eighth decade, he was looking forward to some peace. He was not going to get it, because in Barbie's unsettled life, the next five years would prove to be the most turbulent of all.

Throughout the 1970s, Simon Wiesenthal would enjoy a few successes. One of the most notable was the extradition from the United States of Hermine Braunsteiner, an Austrian female concentration-camp guard who had personally killed women and children. Nicknamed the 'Mare' because of her propensity to kick people to death, Braunsteiner also participated in the selections for the gas chambers at Majdanek, which she conducted with the utmost ferocity. 'The mothers wanted to hang on to their children,' one survivor told Wiesenthal, 'but she wouldn't let them. She tore them apart. Then the women had to climb up on the lorries by themselves, and Hermine flung up their children after them, like pieces of luggage.' At one point, Braunsteiner discovered a child hiding in a man's rucksack. When she ordered it to be opened, the child climbed out and ran away. Braunsteiner ran after it, and when she caught it, she shot the child through the face.[72] For her crimes, an Austrian court in Graz sentenced her to just three years in prison, which she served from 1948 to 1950. In the late 1950s, she met an American construction worker called Russell Ryan who was holidaying in Austria, and they fell in love and emigrated to Novia Scotia. After marrying in October 1958, the couple moved to the Maspeth area of Queens in New York City in 1959, and in 1963, she was granted US citizenship. To her neighbours, Mrs Ryan was 'one of the nicest

women we know', and her husband, who later claimed to be
ignorant of her past, regarded her as the 'best woman in the world',
who 'wouldn't hurt a fly!'[73]

Wiesenthal first learned of Braunsteiner on a visit to Israel in
January 1964, and by using a helper called 'Richard' who posed as
a potential relative of Braunsteiner's family in Carinthia, he was
soon able to learn the address of the former guard in Queens. 'That,
one might have thought, would have concluded the Braunsteiner
case,' Wiesenthal later wrote. 'In reality it was only the beginning.'[74]
Suspecting that an approach to the American government would
only see him mired in bureaucracy, Wiesenthal tipped off the *New
York Times* about the woman who lived at 5211 72nd Street. In
early June 1964, the paper's Joseph Lelyveld knocked on the door
and found the 44-year-old 'Mrs Ryan' painting her small sitting
room in mauve and yellow.[75] Wearing pink and white shorts and a
short-sleeved top, Braunsteiner was, as Lelyveld almost diplomatically put it, 'a large-boned woman with a stern mouth and blonde
hair turning grey', who spoke with a heavy German accent.[76] When
Lelyveld told her why he was there, she responded by saying, 'I've
suffered enough. You keep talking on the radio about peace, I have
a claim to be left in peace too. Is this never going to end?'[77]
Braunsteiner did not deny her past as a guard, and then broke down
into tears and said, 'This is the end, the end of everything for me'.[78]

The end was a lot further away than anyone might have
suspected. As Braunsteiner had lied on her immigration papers by
not disclosing her conviction in Austria, it should have been a
relatively straightforward procedure to get her deported. However,
for the next four years, the case would be shuttled between the
Immigration and Naturalization Service (the INS), the Department
of Justice and the Austrian authorities – who took a whole year to
check if Braunsteiner had a conviction.[79] Attempting to speed things
along was Simon Wiesenthal, but despite writing letters in his
broken English to American senators, little seemed to happen.
Finally, on 22 August 1968, the US government filed a complaint
charging that she had fraudulently obtained her citizenship, and
after another three years Braunsteiner consented to surrendering her
naturalization papers. However, her denaturalization did not mean
that she would instantly be expelled from the United States, and it

was not until 1973 that the German government asked for her extradition. Ryan's lawyers then tried a new tactic, and sought to overturn the consent that Ryan had given for her denaturalization. If this worked, then Ryan would once more become a US citizen, which would mean that she could not be extradited under the terms of the American–German extradition treaty. However, the attempt failed, and finally, after more legal toing-and-froing and just over nine years after Wiesenthal had given his tip to the *New York Times*, Braunsteiner was extradited to Germany on 7 August 1973. Tried as part of the *Majdanek-Prozess* held from 1975 to 1981, Braunsteiner was eventually sentenced to life imprisonment, although she was released owing to poor health in 1996. She died three years later.[80]

If the absurd length of time it took to deal with a proven criminal such as Braunsteiner cast some light on the weaknesses in the American system, those weaknesses would be further exposed by the full glare that radiated from the case of one of Simon Wiesenthal's biggest failures. Unsurprisingly, the name of Frank Walus appears neither in *Justice Not Vengeance,* nor in either of the two sympathetic biographies of Wiesenthal.[81] This is unfortunate, as the case tells us much about the irresponsible way in which the Nazi hunter would accuse individuals of being war criminals.

In 1974, Wiesenthal received word that one Frank Walus, a 52-year-old Polish immigrant and a retired factory worker living on Chicago's Southwest side, had collaborated with the Gestapo during the war in murdering Jews in Poland. Walus, claimed Wiesenthal in his January 1975 newsletter, 'performed his duties with the Gestapo in the ghettos of Częstochowa and Kielce and handed over a number of Jews to the Gestapo.' Furthermore, Wiesenthal claimed that after the ghettos had been cleared, Walus 'was transferred to a labour camp for Poles in Germany where he acted as a Gestapo secret police agent.'[82] These were clearly serious accusations, and the INS, respecting Wiesenthal's position and determined to look tough on war criminals, asked the Israeli police if it could find survivors of the two ghettos who would testify in support of Wiesenthal's claims. The INS supplied the Israelis with a hugely enlarged portrait taken from Walus's entry visa to the United States as well as the allegations made by Wiesenthal. The Israelis placed advertisements requesting survivors to come forward, and a total of forty-four did so. The survivors were each shown a selection of eight photographs – one of which was of Walus – and seven identified the indistinct image of Walus as being not just a collaborator but an actual Gestapo officer.[83]

In January 1977, the INS served Walus with a notice that denaturalization proceedings were to start against him, on the grounds that he had concealed his war crimes when he applied for admission to the United States in 1959. Walus denied all the charges contained within the INS's paperwork, for the simple reason that none of them were true. Walus was indeed from Kielce, but during the war he had been a labourer on farms in southern Germany. His lawyer, Bob Korenkiewicz, travelled to the Berlin Document Centre and found German national health insurance records from 1940 to 1945 showing that Walus was indeed a farm worker; but what he did not find was a single document that supported the claim that Walus had been in the Gestapo. Korenkiewicz also discovered witnesses who had worked with Walus, and even the parish priest at Kielce swore that Walus had never been a member of the Gestapo.[84] Furthermore, Walus could not have been a Gestapo officer because firstly, at 5 feet 4 inches he was too short; secondly, in 1939 he was aged seventeen and therefore too young; and thirdly, he was too Polish. It is worth considering that the material that Korenkiewicz had collected could have easily been gathered by Simon Wiesenthal before he made his accusation.

The lawyer's travails mattered little, because by now the INS, the newspapers and Wiesenthal all believed him to be guilty. For Walus, life quickly became a 'nightmare'. 'My neighbours treated me dread-fully,' he recalled. 'They called me Nazi, Gestapo. They threw rocks at me.'[85] The trial started in March 1978, and Walus had the mis-fortune of having the highly eccentric Julius Hoffmann sitting in judgement. Hoffmann had gained notoriety at the beginning of the decade for his partisan handling of the 'Chicago Seven' case, in which he had openly manifested his dislike for the defendants, who had been charged with various offences in connection with their protests at the 1968 Democratic National Convention. As far as the 81-year-old Hoffmann was concerned, Walus was guilty, and he even told the court as much before Korenkiewicz had made his case for the defence. 'The evidence is clear and convincing and unequivocal,' Hoffmann said on 4 April, 'and does not leave any of the issues in doubt, in the opinion of this court, that the defendant did commit war crimes and was a member of the SS and concealed his membership in the Gestapo and the SS.'[86]

The case for Walus was not helped by the presence in Chicago of Wiesenthal himself, who had arrived to gleefully take credit for his latest 'scalp'. He told the *Chicago Sun-Times* that he had 'never had a case of mistaken identity'. 'I know there are thousands of people who wait for my mistake,' he added. Wiesenthal was lionized in the Windy City. On the evening of Sunday 16 April, he was the guest of honour at a dinner hosted by the Decalogue Society, a Jewish attorneys' group. Wiesenthal was presented with the group's annual Merit Award, and during his acceptance speech, he urged the Jewish community to stand up against a Nazi march that was planned to take place in the suburb of Niles that June. Wiesenthal told the gathering that resistance to the march was 'your right and your duty . . . and your obligation to generations to come.'[87]

While Wiesenthal accepted his award and delivered his fine words, the man he had accused of being a Nazi on the flimsiest of evidence was suffering appalling harassment. 'We are feeling very bad,' confessed Walus in his poor English. 'We get really hurt. There's a bad reputation you know, and that's not all. When the whole thing started, people were throwing rotten eggs on the wall – they painted lots of swastikas on the sidewalks – and you can still see the swastika on the garage.'[88] He was having no less of an abusive time in court, where the testimony of the witnesses seemed to be utterly damning. One witness, Sarah Leichter, was sure that she had seen Walus shoot a group of young children in Kielce in May 1943. However, not all were so certain, and some remembered 'Frank' as being taller and heavier.[89] As well as these doubts, the judge dismissed any of Korenkiewicz's evidence, and explained away the physical difference by the fact that men often look bigger in uniform.[90] Hoffmann found Walus guilty, and he was stripped of his citizenship. Korenkiewicz tried to appeal, and even when new witnesses and documents came to light supporting Walus's innocence, Hoffmann dismissed them, as did Simon Wiesenthal, who in one of his newsletters would later accuse the witnesses – who included former POWs and forced labourers – of lying.[91]

Walus would eventually be cleared in November 1980, and the truth about how Wiesenthal had 'traced' Walus eventually emerged, although nobody seemed very interested. The source of the Nazi hunter's information was a Polish Jew in his mid-thirties called Michael Alper, who had lived with the Walus family for several months in 1971 and 1972. However, Alper and Walus had had a bust-up, with Walus accusing Alper of 'cheating another man'. To get his revenge, Alper then started spreading rumours about how Walus used to regale him with stories about killing Jews in Poland. It is unclear exactly how Wiesenthal received the tip-off, but unsurprisingly, a bitter Walus suspected that Alper had sold the information to the Nazi hunter.[92] Another possibility is that Wiesenthal heard the story from a Jewish refugee agency in Chicago, which is perhaps more likely.[93] Whatever the case, it mattered little to Walus, who died in 1996 having never fully recovered his reputation. He received a cheque for $34,000 and an apology from the US government, but he was to get neither a cent nor a word from the 'Man Who Never Forgets'.

As well as exposing the reckless and irresponsible methods of Simon Wiesenthal, the Walus case proved to certain members of the United States government that a new organization was needed to deal effectively with Nazi war criminals living on Main Street. One of those who lobbied the hardest for such a body was New York Congresswoman Elizabeth Holtzman, who had been elected to the House of Representatives in November 1972 at the age of thirty-one. The granddaughter of Russian and Ukrainian immigrants, a graduate of Harvard Law School and a passionate champion of civil liberties, the Jewish Holtzman had shocked the New York Democratic establishment in the primary by defeating Emanuel Celler, who had been elected to the House eighteen years before Holtzman had even been born. As the youngest woman ever to go up to Capitol Hill, Holtzman found that she was made to feel somewhat unwelcome. 'At the time women comprised about 2 percent of the membership,' she recalled, 'and did not have all the benefits that men did. The gym . . . for example, excluded women. I thought it unimportant until I realized that deal making and workouts seemed to go together.'[94] Holtzman was also to encounter anti-Semitism, which she found more prevalent, but, despite her 'handicaps' of being female, Jewish and young, she managed to secure a place on the House Judiciary Committee, which in 1974 would hold the Nixon impeachment hearings. 'When my turn to vote came, to my surprise a feeling of deep sadness washed over me,' Holtzman later wrote. 'I had to judge; I couldn't turn away from it. Richard Nixon was contemptible, but I still found it painful to vote in favour of the impeachment resolution.' Ultimately, Holtzman was to vote for all five resolutions.[95]

Holtzman also served on the Immigration Subcommittee, and in 1973, just a few months after she had been elected, she was visited by a middle-ranking official from the INS. 'There is a matter that is troubling me greatly,' the official said. 'The Immigration Service has a list of Nazi war criminals living in America, and it is doing nothing about them.'[96] At first, Holtzman was almost sceptical, and reflected that it 'made no sense for our government to allow Nazi war criminals to live here'. However, several months later, while taking part in a routine subcommittee hearing with the INS commissioner, Holtzman enquired as to whether the service kept a list of Nazi war criminals living in the United States.

> The commissioner, a former marine colonel, answered crisply, without hesitation. 'Yes,' he said.
> I had not expected that. Trying to suppress my surprise, I continued. 'How many names are on the list?'
> 'Fifty-three,' he said.
> I knew right then that I had to get as much information as possible. 'What is the Immigration Service doing about the fifty-three alleged Nazi war criminals on the list?'[97]

It was at this point that the commissioner started to obfuscate, but he eventually agreed to Holtzman's request that she be allowed to see the files. A few days later, the young congresswoman found herself at a metal table in an office in Manhattan studying the documents, each of which showed that its subject had committed atrocities and yet had never been investigated. 'As I pushed away the stack of files, I felt nauseous,' Holtzman recalled. 'Hadn't atrocities of the Holocaust occurred because so many people stood by idly and did nothing? Would I be like them?'[98]

Knowing that the INS would do little about the criminals, Holtzman decided to go public by holding a press conference in which she outlined a proposal to deal with them. She remembered:

> I said there had to be a special unit devoted to this task and that you couldn't just leave all this to chance. There needed to be a development of expertise and professionalism to track down the Nazi war criminals and to bring the cases against them. I also said that the US Government had to conduct a search for documents and witnesses more widely than it already had.[99]

For the next few years, Holtzman dedicated much of her time to 'fighting Nazis', and in 1978, with the backing of Senator Ted Kennedy, she succeeded in getting new legislation passed that enabled the United States not only to deport Nazis and those who collaborated with them, but also to refuse their admission to the country. Known as the 'Holtzman Amendment', the statute is familiar to anyone who has answered question C on the reverse of an I-95 Visa Waiver Form when entering the United States. Although the question, which enquires as to whether the foreign national has ever been involved in Nazi persecutions, often causes jocularity, a number of people do tick the box marked 'Yes' and find themselves on the first flight out of the country.

However, it was in 1979, when Holtzman became chair of the Immigration Subcommittee, that she was finally able to force the government to create a dedicated 'Nazi-fighting unit'. Although there had been some resistance from Attorney-General Griffin Bell, on 28 March Holtzman was able to announce the formation of the Office of Special Investigations (OSI), which would be part of the Criminal Division of the Department of Justice and have a budget of $2.3 million. 'There should be absolutely no question,' said Holtzman, 'that the Department of Justice and the US government will act unequivocally and vigorously to deny sanctuary in the United States to persons who committed the worst crimes in the history of humanity.'[100] It would be up to those employed by OSI to ensure that Holtzman's words were more than just political flannel. As we shall see, despite an enormous amount of scepticism, the office would more than live up to Holtzman's expectations.

*

After Martin Bormann, the most wanted Nazi during the 1970s was Josef Mengele. As each year passed, the image of Mengele grew increasingly fiendish, with the predictable result that his dark glamour soon became the stuff of the pulp thriller and the picture house. In 1974, *Marathon Man* by William Goldman featured Dr Christian Szell, an evil SS dentist who was clearly modelled on Mengele. Played in the 1976 film adaptation by Laurence Olivier, Szell became one of the most iconic movie villains of the 1970s, complete with his own catchphrase, 'Is it safe?', which he asks as he drills into the hero's teeth and gums. However, the most enduring of these fictional Mengeles was the 'Joseph Mengele' who appeared in Ira Levin's 1976 novel *The Boys from Brazil*, which was made into a film in 1978. Levin's Mengele was a smooth, white-suited, slick-haired, handsome and austere doctor who radiated an almost supernatural sense of menace. Played in a wonderfully hammy fashion by Gregory Peck, Mengele is shown to enjoy all the accoutrements of the diehard Nazi in exile: he has a massive plantation house in the middle of the South American jungle, a laboratory in which he concocts his diabolical plan to clone ninety-four Hitlers, the requisite bust of the Führer, topless native girls, horses, flunkeys and Wagner in the background. The effect is that of a queeny Tyrolean Mistah Kurtz. The Fourth Reich of popular myth is also portrayed, in which sinister Germans with their blonde wives attend formal dances in ballrooms bedecked with swastika banners. When Mengele comes to tell his fellow Nazis of his plan, he tells them that nothing less than the 'hope and destiny of the Aryan race' is at stake – 'a holy mission, gentlemen'. Also starring in the story is Simon Wiesenthal, although Levin calls him Yakov Liebermann, and in the film he is played by no less a figure than Laurence Olivier. Once again, the character is a caricature of the popularly held image, as Liebermann is presented as a charmingly scatty figure, somewhat cantankerous and doddering, and with an office that is overloaded with documents and water pouring in from the ceiling. At one point in the film, when Liebermann hears exactly what Mengele is up to, he delivers a line that is rich in – surely intentional – irony: 'Who would believe such a preposterous story?' he asks. Mengele also enjoys a similar moment of

Verfremdungseffekt, when he says that 'people are fascinated by Nazis.'[101]

'Josef Mengele' would star in another movie which is so execrable that it is unwatchable, but 1987's *Commando Mengele* (otherwise known as *Angel of Death*) helps to reinforce the stereotype of the Auschwitz doctor. In this film, Mengele is even more powerful than he is in *The Boys from Brazil*, and has a castle in Paraguay, a helicopter with a logo that features '4R' for Fourth Reich, an army of tight-trousered bodyguards with 4R red-and-white armbands, and a largely unexplained plan which involves crossbreeding humans with apes. 'My experiments aim at creating a new race,' cackles this Mengele, played by schlock actor Howard Vernon. 'A master race the Führer had hoped would one day rule the *world*!' Mengele's experiments involve injecting women with the foetuses of chimpanzees, which appears to result in little more than the women growing unfeasibly large eyebrows, but as this is obviously all very evil, it must be stopped. Once again, a Wiesenthal figure is dragged in, this time called 'Ohmei Felsberg' and played by the Luis Buñuel veteran Fernando Rey. Far from having a leaking office, this Wiesenthal has a talking computer, although like Wiesenthal he believes that Mengele should be brought to justice and not merely 'bumped off'. Much cheap nonsense ensues, until the viewer is rewarded with a line that appears to sum up the whole hunt for the real Mengele in the 1970s and the 1980s. 'You stupid Jew!' shouts one of the evil doctor's sidekicks. 'Mengele can't die! He's a myth! He lives forever!' After a final scene of badly directed violence, the last line of the film goes to Felsberg: 'Why? O Lord. Will this never end?'

Thankfully, it does, although the myth of Mengele the Mad Doctor in the Jungle lives on. In early 2009, an Argentinian writer called Jorge Camarasa published a book called *Mengele: The Angel of Death in South America*, which claimed that the doctor was responsible for the unusually high birthrate of twins in the Brazilian town of Cândido Godói.[102] 'I think Cândido Godói may have been Mengele's laboratory,' said Camarasa, 'where he finally managed to fulfil his dreams of creating a master race of blond-haired, blue-eyed Aryans.' According to Camarasa, Mengele posed as a kindly itinerant doctor called Weiss, and after attending to many of the town's pregnant women in the 1960s, established a birthrate in which one in five pregnancies now produces twins. Camarasa's theory appeared in thousands of newspaper articles in January 2009, although it was swiftly debunked by the science and history communities.[103]

Life for the real Mengele in the 1960s and 1970s was significantly unlike the existence portrayed in such books and films. Far from being the smoothly evil doctor with plans to create a new race, Mengele was turning into a bitter and anxious man. The Stammers, the couple who owned the farm where he lived, found their guest and business partner becoming increasingly irritable. He had violent mood swings and treated the workers badly. Whenever friends and acquaintances visited, Mengele would be overly suspicious and wary, and his behaviour deteriorated in the aftermath of the Eichmann kidnap and trial.[104] Eventually, the Stammers identified Mengele after they saw a photograph of him as a young man in a newspaper. The couple wanted to rid themselves of the criminal in their midst, but the provision of two thousand dollars from Hans Sedlmeier bought their complicity.[105] Now that he had been identified, Mengele's mood became increasingly sour. He started writing his biography, a monumental work of narcissism that featured forty pages alone on his birth, and one-and-a-half pages on his placenta.[106]

Mengele grew increasingly security obsessed, and even supervised the construction of an 18-foot watchtower from where he would look out over the countryside for hours. Whenever he went for a walk, he would take along a large pack of stray dogs for protection.[107] Mengele need not have worried unduly – most of the world believed him to be in Paraguay, and once in a while the West Germans would pressure President Stroessner to hand over the former 'Angel of Death'. Despite their stormy relationship, Mengele lived with the Stammers all the way through the 1960s. While his homeland was embracing the liberalism of that decade, Mengele did his own bit for free love by indulging in brief affairs with almost every female farmhand hired by the Stammers. When Mengele was once jokingly accused of having a fling with a black woman, he flew into a rage and insisted that he, as a 'race scientist', would never have an affair with a 'coloured woman'.[108] Clearly, the old Nazi attitudes remained.

In the early 1970s, Mengele's capacity for endless worry developed into the most extraordinary ailment. Over the course of several years, he had acquired a habit of chewing the ends of his moustache and swallowing the hair. By July 1972, the resulting hairball lodged in his intestines was causing him so much pain that he had to have an operation to remove it. Unlike cats, humans are not adept at vomiting hairballs, or trichobezoars as a medic like Mengele would have labelled them. Mengele was nervous about the operation not so much because of the physical intervention, but more because the doctors treating him would have to see his identity card, which was adapted from that owned by his protector, Wolfgang Gerhard, who was fourteen years younger. Indeed, the doctor did notice the discrepancy between his 61-year-old patient and the ID card, but he was told there had been a bureaucratic mix-up.[109]

In 1974, Mengele eventually split up from the Stammers, who had had enough of the vexatious old man. He moved to a run-down bungalow at 5555 Alvarenga Road in the poor Eldorado suburb of São Paulo, where his mood grew even darker. 'It has a wearing effect on me,' he wrote, 'to be left so very much isolated and excluded and all alone.'[110] Mengele yearned for his family in Germany, although in the occasional correspondence he had with his son Rolf, he would often chastise him for supposed transgressions, and was frustrated that his son was not achieving the level of academic success that he demanded. 'In September and December you passed your lawyer's exams and you received the mark "satisfactory",' he wrote. Mengele claimed that he was proud, but then noted that Hans Sedlmeier's son:

> . . . who was in the top quarter and still did not do well enough by 10 percent to obtain his doctorate. Your exam results, upon examination, obviously won't stand in the way of completing your doctorate [. . .] I hope that in a short time I will hear from you that it has been mastered.[111]

In 1977, Rolf made a secret visit to Brazil to see his father, whom he found to be an embittered man. The last time the two had met was in Switzerland twenty-one years before, and over the past two decades he had learned about his father's activities in Auschwitz. Rolf, naturally, had some big questions to ask. 'I told my father I was interested in hearing about his time in Auschwitz,' Rolf said. 'What was Auschwitz according to his version of events? What did he do there? Did he have a role in the things he was charged with?'[112] Mengele was never to give his son proper answers, and would often erect a barrage of pseudo-science and cod history. When he was no longer able to hide behind such displays of phoney erudition, Mengele simply presented his son with the time-stained excuse of all Nazis: he was simply doing his duty.

> He said everybody had to do so in order to survive, the basic instinct of self-preservation. He said he wasn't able to think about it. From his point of view he was not personally responsible for the incidents at the camp. He said he didn't 'invent' Auschwitz. It already existed.[113]

Mengele also told Rolf that his role at the railhead selections, far from being murderous, was akin to that of a surgeon in a field hospital who has to choose which of the wounded are worth operating on. In this way, Mengele tried to persuade Rolf that he had actually saved many lives. Rolf was not convinced, and tried to tell his father that he had had a choice whether to be a part of the whole genocidal apparatus, a charge that only made Mengele angry. 'Don't tell me you, my only son, believe what they write about me?' he shouted. 'On my mother's life I have never hurt anyone.'[114] Rolf realized that there was no point in continuing such discussion, and towards the end of his two-week stay, the atmosphere improved. Mengele even bought a five-hundred-dollar engagement ring for Rolf's fiancée, and when the two men parted at São Paulo airport, Mengele promised that they should try to meet again. A few weeks after he had returned to Germany, Rolf received a letter from his father congratulating him on his wedding, and thanking him for making the trip over to Brazil. 'Now I can die in peace,' Mengele wrote.[115]

While Mengele lived out his days in bitter isolation, the Nazi hunters continued to look for him, although at times their claims were almost as fantastical as the product of Ira Levin's imagination.

In 1967, after he had reported the 'near miss' on the Greek island of Kythnos in *The Murderers Among Us*, Simon Wiesenthal confidently stated that Mengele lived in 'a small white shed' in a jungle clearing in a 'restricted military zone between Puerto San Vicente . . . and the border fortress of Carlos Antonio López, on the Paraná River'. Mengele was also protected by a squad of Paraguayan soldiers who had orders to stop all vehicles and shoot all trespassers, and in addition the security-conscious doctor had paid for his own team of four heavily armed bodyguards.[116] By February 1971, Wiesenthal was claiming that Mengele was still near Puerto San Vicente, but he was now 'running two factories in an inaccessible jungle region near the Brazil and Argentina frontier'. Quite why anybody would build factories in an inaccessible location was not made clear, although the implication was perhaps that Mengele was now a drugs baron.[117] However, according to Wiesenthal, Mengele was quite the globetrotter; in March 1971, the Nazi hunter received 'reliable information' that Mengele had been seen driving a car in the resort town of Torremolinos in Spain. 'Unfortunately no action against Mengele could be attempted,' Wiesenthal wrote in his annual bulletin the following January, 'since he had already left when we received the information.'[118] In 1977, Wiesenthal placed Mengele firmly back in Paraguay, and reported that he was driven around in a black Mercedes 280SL, and would often frequent the German club in Asunción, where he would always wear a pair of dark glasses to conceal his identity.[119]

With so many sightings, it was inevitable that there were some who regarded Wiesenthal's reports with scepticism. One of them was Benno Wieser Varon, who had been the Israeli ambassador to Paraguay from 1968 to 1972. 'Sometime in the seventies,' Varon recalled, 'Wiesenthal confided to me in Boston that it was not at all easy to keep his outfit in Vienna going.' Varon suspected that Wiesenthal 'makes periodic statements that he is about to catch him, perhaps since Wiesenthal must raise funds for his activities and the name Mengele is always good for a plug'. In Varon's view, Wiesenthal was 'always a Nazi hunter, but never a Nazi catcher'.[120]

While Wiesenthal made his 'plugs', in 1977 a Vienna-born former policeman called Erich Erdstein claimed that he too had been on the hunt for Mengele, but unlike his competitors he had not only located the doctor near the Brazilian town of Marechal Cândido Rondon, but also shot and killed the war criminal in September 1968 while he was trying to flee. Claiming to be an 'invaluable undercover operative' for the British and the Americans, Erdstein was apparently nothing less than a 'real life James Bond', who had managed to penetrate the Fourth Reich with his almost superhuman cunning, and had only narrowly missed capturing Martin Bormann.[121] Mengele's demise is suitably violent, and occurs when a launch full of Paraguayan soldiers tries to attack Erdstein's barge.

> I raised my gun and fired four bullets at Mengele. They struck him in the chest and side. He turned toward me, started at me with a surprised expression, and I shot again. This time it was a direct hit in the throat. His body jerked violently, and he fell over the side of the barge headfirst into the water. His feet caught in some ropes that were laying on the deck; they held him face down in the water.[122]

As is traditional for such a memoir, Erstein ended the book with some junk philosophy, which – like the lines in *Commando Mengele* – would encapsulate the nature of the search for the 'Angel of Death': 'One Nazi dead. But what did it matter? A Nazi never dies.'[123]

In January 1981, Wiesenthal was able to use his bulletin to keep his followers informed of Mengele's latest movements. 'For a short time, we thought we had located Mengele in the Colonia Dignidad, an isolated German settlement in Chile,' he reported. 'But then it seemed we had been misled by people who wanted to give the Colonia Dignidad a bad name.'[124] The suggestion that Colonia Dignidad did not deserve a bad name was curious, as the colony was founded by a former Luftwaffe corporal called Paul Schäfer, who had absconded from Germany after being charged with sexually abusing two children. In 1966, an eighteen-year-old man had fled the colony saying that Schäfer had molested him, and in 1979, it was widely reported that Amnesty International had investigated human rights abuses there: it was suspected that the Chilean secret police used it as an interrogation centre.[125] Assured by the Chilean government that Mengele was not at the colony, Wiesenthal then 'managed to localise' Mengele in Santa Cruz in Bolivia, where he was living with a doctor friend. 'Unfortunately, he was gone again before we could act,' Wiesenthal wrote. However, there was still hope, as he had received 'serious information' that the fugitive was in Río Negro in Uruguay in October 1980. 'As we are told, his state of health is not at all good.'[126]

This was a somewhat dramatic understatement, as at the time when Wiesenthal was writing, Josef Mengele had in fact been dead for nearly two years. On 5 February 1979, Mengele had taken a two-hour bus ride down to Bertioga beach, where he stayed with his latest protectors, Wolfram and Liselotte Bossert, at their two-bed-room beach house. Over the next two days, an irritable Mengele remained mostly inside, although at around 3 p.m. on Wednesday 7 February, he was finally persuaded to get some air. As he walked down the beach with Wolfram Bossert, the 67-year-old Mengele voiced his homesickness for Germany. 'Over there is my country,' he said, looking out to sea. 'I would like to spend the last days of my life in my native town of Günzburg, somewhere at the top of a mountain, in a little house, and to write the history of my native town.'[127] At four thirty, Mengele decided to cool off in the ocean, but within ten minutes he appeared to be in trouble. Wolfram's son shouted at Mengele to come back in, but he didn't reply. Bossert swam out as quickly as he could, and as he approached, he realized that Mengele was paralysed. Holding Mengele with one arm and trying to swim with the other, Bossert battled against the strong tide. 'I got to a stage where I felt I couldn't hold on any longer,' Bossert said. 'But then, somewhere in my subconscious I had a thought that I should use the force of the waves.'[128] As they neared the shoreline, Mengele suddenly started trying to swim, and it appeared that the seizure had passed. However, a few seconds later, his arms stopped moving and Bossert found himself holding on to a dead weight. Completely exhausted, he eventually made it back to the beach, where a passing doctor attempted to revive Mengele with heart massage and mouth-to-mouth resuscitation. The efforts were of no use: the 'Angel of Death' was himself dead, dispatched by a massive stroke.

Chapter Twelve

What Remains

AT AROUND midnight on the evening of 5–6 July 1979, a red Renault 5 with the licence plate 564 AKX 75 exploded in an underground car park below a block of flats at 230 Avenue de Versailles in southeast Paris. The bomb was so powerful that it not only transformed the car into an unrecognizable pile of metal, but also destroyed a further twenty vehicles and started a fire. Three days later, on 9 July, the owners of the car received a letter which was emblazoned with twelve 10-centime stamps arranged in the shape of a swastika. Addressed to Serge Klarsfeld, the typed letter purported to come from an organization called 'O.D.E.S.S.A.' which claimed responsibility for the bomb, and indicated that it was a warning.

> WHAT WE NOW DESIRE: that the jews cease persecuting our comrades. If it becomes necessary, if the circumstances require it, we anticipate a more extreme solution. And the prospect of retaliation by the MOSSAD does not prevent us from acting. You should know that we fanatics mock death. We hope that this warning makes you think.[1]

Describing the bomb as a 'warning' was disingenuous. In fact, the device had been designed to explode the following morning, when Serge would have been taking their five-year-old daughter Lida to school.[2]

Although the letter did not make it explicit, the 'persecution' to which the letter referred was Serge's presence at the forthcoming trial in October in Cologne of Kurt Lischka, Herbert Hagen and Lischka's deputy Ernst Heinrichson. On 1 September, the self-styled 'ODESSA' sent Serge another letter, which claimed that the members of the organization had sworn a blood-oath to kill him if he gave evidence in the Cologne courtroom. The letter concluded with a paragraph that helpfully explained what the ODESSA of 1979 consisted of:

> At the beginning, the ODESSA was created to organize the escape of Nazis overseas at the moment of liberation. Since then, the organization has acquired another task: to reintroduce into German society former Nazi leaders to take up important positions and functions. At present, the organization is still working, although it is running idle. A former Nazi of high standing is pulling the strings. We were granted by this man the right to speak and act in the name of the organization ODESSA. However, our identification with ODESSA is not purely ideological. We are the true fighters of ODESSA. But between ourselves, we never use the word ODESSA when we talk of the organization. We simply say 'the friends' or the 'comrades'.[3]

Here then, was an example of the myth of the ODESSA becoming a reality. The organization responsible for the attempted murder was any one of a plethora of vile neo-Nazi groups active in Europe in the 1970s, and it suited their self-important desire to claim membership of some larger fascist grouping, no matter how spurious. But Nazi Walter Mittys or not, such men were clearly dangerous, and the Klarsfelds found themselves immediately issued with police protection.

Nevertheless, the letters still managed to come through, and later in the year it was Beate Klarsfeld's turn to receive some hate mail. This time it came not from the supposed ODESSA, but from a group calling itself the *Groupe Joachim Peiper*, which took its name from a highly decorated *SS-Standartenführer* whose battle group had carried out the Malmédy Massacre in Belgium in December 1944 in which around ninety American POWs had been slaughtered. After serving a sentence of eleven years and seven months, Peiper started working for Porsche in Stuttgart in 1957, although he was never to shake off his bipolar reputation as both a war hero and a war criminal. In April 1972, Peiper settled in the small village of Traves in the Haute-Saône *département* of eastern France and he worked as a freelance translator and attended to a small plot of land. However, on 21 June 1976, the peace of the 61-year-old Peiper was disturbed by an article in the communist newspaper *L'Humanité*, which featured photographs of Peiper's meadow and roadside mailbox. 'The criminal, guiltier than any criminal ever guillotined in France, guiltier than any criminal currently in prison, has been pardoned and set free,' the report stated.[4] Over the next few days, Peiper found himself surrounded by reporters and accused of further war crimes. He received death threats, and finally, in the early hours of 14 July, his house was petrol-bombed. At daybreak, the police discovered his carbonized corpse, which had a hole in its chest. Underneath the remains lay a Colt .38 Special revolver, and on the balcony upstairs a Remington shotgun was found, which suggested that Peiper may have put up a fight.[5] The result of his death – probably at the hands of communists or *résistants* or a combination of both – quickly saw Peiper's status as a neo-Nazi poster boy enshrined. Even today, the immensely good-looking Peiper continues to be championed by neo-Nazi inadequates who haven't yet admitted to themselves the real reason for their admiration. Within days of Peiper's death, the *Groupe Joachim Peiper* claimed responsibility for a hand-grenade attack on a Jewish social club in Marseille, and were highly likely to have been responsible for planting a timebomb at a synagogue in the same city.[6] In its letter to Beate Klarsfeld, the group accused her and LICRA of killing Peiper, and demanded that she cease her 'persecutions' against Kurt Lischka, who, it claimed, had a 'right to life'. The group also told Beate that she should never set foot in Germany again, and that she should also donate three hundred thousand Deutschmarks ($550,000) to Peiper's family. If the group's orders were not carried out, it said, it would assume her complicity in the 'affair at Traves' and would 'bump her off' in her home. Ominously, it added that the group also knew her regular points-of-call, although this was probably bluff.[7]

Although the Klarsfelds were not to be the victims of any further attempts on their lives, other Nazi hunters would be. On 11 June 1982, a large bomb was detonated at the entrance to the building that housed Simon Wiesenthal's office.[8] The explosion caused considerable damage, and it was fortunate that the gas main was not ruptured. The attack was one of a number of similar bombings carried out against Jewish-owned properties in Salzburg and Vienna that summer, and on 5 August 1982, a 33-year-old West German hospital orderly called Ekkehard Weil was arrested. In October 1983, he and eight fellow neo-Nazis were put on trial for the attacks, and in April 1984 Weil and three others were sentenced to terms of between twenty months and five years in prison. Although Weil was found not guilty of the attack on Wiesenthal's building,[9] Wiesenthal later recalled how Weil publicly manifested his hatred for the Nazi hunter: 'His aggression was still so unbridled in the courtroom that he tried to hurl himself at me and had to be restrained by a police officer.'[10] It is hardly surprising that Wiesenthal believed that Weil had in fact carried out the bombing.

In Bolivia, Klaus Barbie was trying to enjoy a more settled existence after the collapse of the García Meza dictatorship. However, the installation of the democratically elected Hernán Siles Zuazo in October 1982 represented a threat to the fugitive's status in his adopted country. The new President told *Newsweek* magazine that he was determined to 'solve the Barbie problem', and an extradition request made by the West Germans the previous May presented Siles Zuazo with an opportunity to show the world that Bolivia would no longer be a haven for criminality.[11] Barbie's personal life was also far from happy. In May 1981, he had watched his son Klaus kill himself in a hang-gliding accident; and in December 1982, his wife Regine died of cancer. Such tragedies seemed to affect Barbie's own health, and he developed a hernia as well as some mysterious leg pains.[12] At the end of the month, Barbie received another piece of bad news, although at first it seemed deceptively trifling. On 30 December, the sub-comptroller of Bolivia issued an order for Barbie to repay the ten thousand dollars Transmarítima Boliviana had effectively stolen from COMIBOL in September 1970.[13] If the debt was not repaid in five days, then a warrant was to be issued for Barbie's arrest.

At first, Barbie took no action, but eventually, on 25 January 1983, he visited the comptroller's office to repay the amount. Believing that the law enabled him to pay the debt in pesos, Barbie began to haggle with the officials about the rate of exchange. He maintained that he should be allowed to pay at the black-market rate, whereas the officials insisted that the official rate had to apply. Barbie's arrogant attempt to save himself some money would prove to be very expensive, as suddenly two figures appeared alongside him, placed him under arrest and took him to San Pedro Prison, where he was charged with fraud.[14] The day after Barbie's arrest, the Bolivian cabinet voted unanimously to expel Barbie, but there was one problem. Should he go to France or West Germany? For the next nine days, the diplomats of the two European countries consulted each other on an informal and yet frantic basis. Unlike the French, the Germans had an extradition request in place, although there was great reluctance in Bonn to actually accept Barbie. German officials knew that a trial might prove to be a public embarrassment, especially if Barbie were to receive a comparatively light sentence for his crimes. After a few days of prevarication, West Germany refused to take Barbie. Although this now left the French as the likely recipients, with no extradition request in place there was no guarantee that the wheels of bureaucracy would rotate quickly enough to outwit those on the right of Bolivian politics who were trying to free the former Gestapo officer.[15] A further complication was precisely how and to where Barbie should be expelled. The nearest French territory was Guyana, but the Bolivians were reluctant (for reasons of national prestige) to allow a French aircraft to land in La Paz. The expulsion, which was due to take place on 4 February, would have to be carried out by a Bolivian aircraft, but at the time Bolivian pilots were on an indefinite strike. 'We suddenly realised that we might lose Barbie,' said one French negotiator, 'because the situation in Bolivia suddenly became very tense.'[16]

While in prison, Barbie insisted that he was innocent of all the allegations that were now being made against him concerning his relationship with the previous regime. Speaking to a TV crew in his cell, he protested that his treatment was 'barbaric'. 'I have no ties whatsoever, neither physically nor politically, with the paramilitary groups,' he lied. 'In the thirty years that I have lived here, I have always vowed not to get involved in Bolivian politics.'[17] On 3 February, Barbie finally settled his debt with COMIBOL, arranging for a friend to pay the ten thousand dollars in pesos at the official exchange rate. Once the debt was settled, Barbie was confident that he would be freed. The amount came to just under 1.5 million pesos, which represented a whole suitcase of fifty-peso notes. 'They made me sit there and count it out,' recalled Álvaro de Castro, one of Barbie's associates, 'then they made me count it again. Finally it was paid, but then they said it wasn't enough, they wanted the interest.'[18] This was unusual, as normally interest on such debts was paid at a later date; it was clear that the authorities were trying to stall Barbie's attempt to free himself. Later that evening, de Castro was further alarmed to receive a phone call in which he was advised that a TV crew would be accompanying Barbie on his flight the next day. It increasingly appeared that, debt or no debt, Barbie was about to be expelled. The following morning, de Castro visited Barbie and found him calmly playing a board game. Even though de Castro told the prisoner about the flight and the TV company, Barbie was unperturbed and told de Castro simply to pay back the interest on the debt and then that would be the end of the matter.[19] De Castro returned to the comptroller's office, but was unable to find anybody who could tell him how much interest was owed. He would not obtain the figure until nearly four thirty that afternoon, by which time the banks had shut. 'I was desperate,' de Castro recalled. 'I even rang a friend, a money changer, and asked if he could get the bank to open.'[20] Eventually, de Castro found a friend who was able to pay back the money and the debt was cleared.

On the afternoon of Friday 4 February 1983, Klaus Barbie was taken from prison with a blanket over his head. Accompanied by Gustavo Sánchez, the sub-secretary of the Ministry of the Interior who had lobbied hard for the expulsion, Barbie was driven up a long and twisting road.

'What do you think of death?' Sánchez asked.

'Death is cruel,' Barbie replied.

'It is just as cruel for those who you sent to die in Lyon,' said Sánchez.[21]

The car soon arrived at La Paz military airport, where Barbie was told he was being sent to Germany. He seemed cheerful about the news. 'He only complained that he was cold because he had not been allowed to take any belongings,' one official remembered. 'I ordered a nearby policeman to hand over his parka.'[22] Ushered on to a Bolivian C130 cargo plane along with a Bolivian TV crew, Barbie did his best to look sanguine, and even jocularly enquired as to the cost of razor blades in Germany, because he had not been allowed to bring any of his belongings.[23]

After a seven-hour flight, the plane arrived at its destination. As soon as it had taxied to a halt, the pilots turned off all the lights, leaving Barbie and the TV crew in complete darkness. There was then a delay of several minutes, during which the Bolivian pilots demanded – and successfully received – some money. The plane's doors were eventually opened, and Barbie and the TV crew gingerly stepped out on to the dark airstrip. Voices could be heard, but they were most certainly not German. They were French. The plane had landed not in Barbie's homeland but in Cayenne, the capital of French Guyana. Barbie was taken to a hangar in the airport, where a judge read the charges against him. The man who had arrested and killed so many was now in shock; he even had tears in his eyes. Far from being his normal swaggering and arrogant self, he was crumpled, demoralized. He was soon put on a plane to France, and during the flight, he was interviewed by Carlos Soria, a member of the Bolivian TV crew.

'Do you think France, Europe and the rest of the world should forget these crimes?' Soria asked.

'Absolutely,' Barbie replied. 'There have been so many crimes lately. There have been more than a hundred wars since the Second World War. All these recent crimes are known to the general public.'

'But you know that European countries and, in particular, France, haven't forgotten?'

'Well, I've forgotten. If they haven't, that's another issue.'[24]

On the evening of Saturday 5 February, Barbie landed at Orange military airport and was driven 125 miles to Lyon in a blue prison van. He was incarcerated at Fort Montluc, the same prison where he had tortured and killed so many four decades before.[25]

*

That same evening in Grosse Pointe, Michigan, Erhard Dabringhaus sat down to watch the weekend edition of NBC's *Nightly News*. During the course of the afternoon, Dabringhaus had given an interview to the station in which he revealed that Barbie had worked for the CIC in the late 1940s.[26] At first, the reporters suspected that Dabringhaus was a crank, but when he showed them proof that he, Dabringhaus, had indeed served in the CIC, they took him very seriously. On the Sunday morning after the programme had aired, Dabringhaus awoke to find a long line of reporters outside his house, and for the next few weeks, the 65-year-old's claims made the front pages and the lead items around the world. 'They just couldn't believe what they had heard,' Dabringhaus observed.[27]

The United States reacted quickly, and on 11 February, the Assistant Attorney-General, D. Lowell Jensen, instructed Allan A. Ryan, the director of the Office of Special Investigations (OSI), to conduct a preliminary inquiry to establish whether Dabringhaus's allegations were true. It was Ryan who had initiated the investigation, because he knew that the matter could not be ignored, 'or expected to go away'. Ryan also had to field countless questions from the media, many of which concerned what he knew about Barbie's past. 'I didn't know a damn thing,' Ryan recalled, 'and I said so. The OSI had been investigating Nazis in America for three years, but Nazis in Bolivia – or in France, for that matter – were out of our jurisdiction.'[28] As soon as he received his instructions from Jensen, Ryan visited the Pentagon, where he was handed a 3-inch-thick red file marked 'Secret'. Within minutes of opening it, he knew that the charges made by Dabringhaus were true. After nearly a fortnight of investigating, he resolved that a full inquiry had to take place. 'If we did not put together the story, every network, newspaper, and self-styled Nazi hunter would do it for us,' Ryan later wrote. 'There was no telling what patchwork version of history would come out of that.'[29] After some vacillation by the Attorney-General, William French Smith, Ryan eventually received the authorization to carry out a full inquiry on 14 March.

After just four and a half months, Ryan presented his report to Smith. In his preamble, Ryan summarized his findings and suggested a course of action that the United States government should take. Noting that the CIC officers involved had been 'acting within the scope of their official duties', Ryan argued that the government therefore could not 'disclaim responsibility for their actions'. By covering up its involvement with Barbie, Ryan wrote that the United States had 'delayed justice in Lyon'.

> I therefore believe it appropriate, and I so recommend, that the United States government express to the government of France its regret for its responsibility in delaying the due process of law in the case of Klaus Barbie. We should also pledge to cooperate in any appropriate manner in the further investigation of the crimes for which Barbie will be tried in France. This is a matter of decency, and of honorable conduct. It should be, I believe, the final chapter by the United States in this case.[30]

In the main, the 'Ryan Report' was well received when it was published on 15 August. As suggested by Ryan, the French received a formal expression of regret, and the French Justice Minister wrote that the report 'reveals a concern for the investigation of the truth that honors your country'. The *New York Times* observed 'how rare it is for a proud and powerful nation to admit shabby behavior', and in Germany the *Stuttgarter Zeitung* wrote that the United States 'showed a powerful and impressive capacity for democratic self-purging'.[31] Others were more cynical. In *The Times* of London, the author Tom Bower commented that the blame laid by the report was too narrow, especially since it absolved the American High Commission in Germany (HICOG) of any responsibility: 'Ryan has resorted to extraordinary interpretations of the existing evidence to place the blame on individuals who bore little overall responsibility then and are unimportant now.' Bower claimed that Ryan's reluctance to ascribe blame to HICOG officials was rooted in a reluctance to avoid 'a bitter confrontation with many powerful political personalities still alive today'.[32] Even if Bower were right, unfortunately he lacked the proof to substantiate his accusation. Bower was suspicious of Ryan's inability to find documents which suggested that HICOG had acted badly, and he suggested that the appropriate documents had been 'lost'. However, as Ryan was also unable to find any HICOG-incriminating documents in the French archives, then the possibility of some sort of cover-up is unlikely.

'The French were indeed mystified by HICOG's lack of knowledge [concerning Barbie],' Ryan wrote, 'but nothing in the file suggested that HICOG was not acting in good faith.'[33] Until alternative evidence comes to light, the Ryan Report must stand as the most reliable and authoritative interpretation of the United States's association with Klaus Barbie. All other theories must be seen as conjecture, no matter how tempting and fashionable it is to regard with deep cynicism the actions of US officials.

For Ryan, the report on Barbie represented the culmination of three successful years as the director of OSI. During his time, steps were taken to expel well over twenty war criminals who were hiding in the United States, and scores more would follow. When Ryan first came to OSI in January 1980, he was asked for how long he thought the office would exist. 'Four or five years, maybe,' was his reply.[34] Ryan's prediction was somewhat inaccurate, as in 2009, OSI celebrated its thirtieth birthday. During those three decades, the office has won cases against 107 individuals, 86 of whom have been denaturalized and 66 removed from the United States. In addition, 178 individuals have been stopped from entering the country. In total, over 1,500 investigations have been opened, and in 2009, 53 persons were under investigation.[35] Among the defendants were Andrija Artuković, Pavelić's Justice and Interior Minister; Conrad Schellong, an SS guard supervisor at Dachau; Arthur Rudolph, who as the operations director of the V2 missile factory at Dora-Nordhausen was responsible for working slave labourers in inhumane conditions; Jakob Reimer, who had participated in a mass shooting of Jews near Trawniki in Poland; and Otto Albrecht von Bolschwing, a colleague of Adolf Eichmann who had been rewarded with citizenship for his services to American intelligence.[36] As the United States has no jurisdiction over crimes committed overseas, the cases against all such defendants have had to be brought in the civil courts, and it is the job of OSI to show with 'clear, unequivocal and convincing evidence that does not leave the issue in doubt' that those being deported are in fact guilty of war crimes.[37] Clearly finding such evidence is not the job of traditional detective work, and OSI has a team of full-time historians who collate and analyse historical documents from all over the world.

The Office is also proactive, and its prosecutors actively search for those who should be denaturalized, which has led some to regard it with distaste. Among the Office's harshest critics is the conservative commentator Pat Buchanan, who in the mid-1980s expressed his resentment of the public funds spent on '65- and 75-year-old Central European immigrants who permitted or perpetrated atrocities in a war that ended 40 years ago'.[38] For Buchanan, one of OSI's gravest errors was obtaining information from the Soviet Union, which he saw as meriting a congressional investigation.[39] However, unless OSI actively hunts what Ryan described as the 'quiet neighbours', it is hard to establish how it could fulfil its mandate. Tips received from Nazi hunters and the general public alike have all been found to be either unreliable or unproceedable. In fact, only one tip made to OSI has ever resulted in a successful prosecution, when a former Görlitz concentration-camp inmate recognized a man in Brooklyn as being a brutal *kapo* – a Jewish prisoner who supervised other prisoners for the Nazis.[40] 'Tip' letters would come in every week at OSI, and Ryan soon referred to them as 'my neighbour is a Nazi' letters, in which the possession of a crew cut and a German shepherd was supposedly enough to warrant a full investigation.[41] Information that came from Simon Wiesenthal was often found to be equally useless. Although the public position of the Office was to praise Wiesenthal, in private its members were far more circumspect. In April 1990, Ryan's successor at OSI, Neal Sher, wrote to Wiesenthal admonishing him for the quality of his leads.

> In general, I can tell you that a few of your allegations have resulted in active, ongoing investigations. The vast majority, however, were of little value: many 'suspects' had long been dead; in many instances you did not furnish basic identifying data, thus rendering the allegations virtually useless; as to others, there is no record of entry into the United States; in some cases you have identified the wrong person; in other cases, you have not even provided what could fairly be termed an 'allegation'; and, in many instances, we could uncover no incriminating evidence. In this regard it is important to note that you have not provided OSI with any concrete *evidence* against the individuals named in your correspondence. Moreover, several specific

requests to you seeking such evidence have gone unanswered. [. . .] The 'bottom line' is that, to my knowledge, for at least the time that I have served as Director, no allegation which has originated from your office has resulted in a court filing by OSI.[42]

Neal Sher was not the only member of OSI to have lambasted Simon Wiesenthal. In fact, one of the Nazi hunter's fiercest critics is no less than OSI's director, Eli M. Rosenbaum, who in 1993 published an account of the Kurt Waldheim affair in which he savaged Wiesenthal's role in protecting the Austrian President. Waldheim, who had been Secretary-General of the United Nations from 1972 to 1982, was campaigning for the presidency in early 1986 when it was revealed that he had been extremely opaque about his wartime service in the German army. In his 1977 autobiography, Waldheim claimed that he had ceased active military service after being wounded in December 1941, and had spent the rest of the war as a law student. However, in March 1986, the World Jewish Congress (WJC) revealed that Waldheim was lying, and further- more, it would emerge that Waldheim had been complicit in war crimes. As the then WJC's General Counsel, it was Rosenbaum who had been responsible for collating much of the evidence against the former UN Secretary-General, a task for which he was well qualified. A graduate of Harvard Law School, Rosenbaum had worked for OSI from 1980 to 1984 as a trial attorney, and had joined the WJC after a short spell as a corporate litigator in Manhattan. During his time at OSI, Rosenbaum had jointly inter- rogated Arthur Rudolph with Neal Sher, and had trapped the former Nazi into making 'a series of damning admissions'.[43] It was Rosenbaum who obtained the now famous photograph of Waldheim taken in Yugoslavia in May 1943 dressed in the uniform of an army *Oberleutnant* and standing next to SS-Gruppenführer Artur Phleps of the notorious Prinz Eugen Division. Far from studying law, Waldheim had in fact returned to active service in April 1942, and had helped to ruthlessly suppress partisans in Bosnia, for which he received the King Zvonimir medal with Oak Leaves 'for bravery under fire' from the Ustasha regime. In the spring of 1943, Waldheim had served as an operations officer in Salonika, during which time nearly all of the city's 54,000 Sephardic Jews

were deported and exterminated, and in 1944, Waldheim's Army
Group E intelligence branch was also responsible for the murder of
seven British members of the Special Boat Service who had been captured in April 1944.[44] In short, far from being a conscientious
student, Waldheim was, in the words of one historian, 'an efficient
and effective cog in the machinery of genocide'.[45] When the news of
Waldheim's lies broke, many in Austria saw the story as a Jewish
smear campaign and were resentful of an apparent attempt by outsiders to meddle in an Austrian election. 'We Austrians Will Elect
Whom We Want!' announced one poster which supported
Waldheim.[46] On 8 June 1986, the Austrians did indeed
elect Waldheim, although in 1987 the new Austrian President found
that he had been placed on the OSI watchlist of those not allowed
to enter the United States under the terms of the Holtzman
Amendment.

One person who could have halted Waldheim's bid to become
head of state was Simon Wiesenthal. It soon emerged that in 1979
Wiesenthal had been asked by the Israelis to investigate Waldheim's
past because the then UN Secretary-General was showing a marked
partiality towards the Arab states.[47] Although Wiesenthal was to tell
one biographer that the request was made informally, and was in no
way an Israeli government move, he gave the impression in the *New
York Times* that the approach was made by the government.[48]
Wiesenthal claimed that he then enlisted the help of a friend to
search through the archives, which revealed that although Waldheim
had been lying about his years of 'study', he was not – on the surface – a war criminal.[49] For Rosenbaum, this explained why
Wiesenthal had not been willing to damn Waldheim during his
election. Not only did the Nazi hunter have no desire to ruin
Waldheim's chances and therefore allow the Socialists to gain the
presidency, but to have told his fellow Austrians in 1986 that he had
investigated Waldheim and not found any evidence of his complicity
in war crimes would have irreparably ruined Wiesenthal's reputation as the great Nazi hunter.[50] Even sympathetic biographers
suggest that Wiesenthal should have displayed more curiosity in
1979.[51] However, Wiesenthal remained unapologetic, and said that
as Waldheim's Army Group E was a vast force, it would have been
'impossible to investigate every one of the 3,000 officers in that

group'.[52] However, nobody was asking Wiesenthal to investigate thousands; they were only asking him to look at one. In fact, Wiesenthal had seen the very same reports later unearthed by Rosenbaum and the WJC, and it is surprising that where the Americans found evidence of criminality, Wiesenthal found none.[53] As far as Rosenbaum was concerned, Wiesenthal had acted both politically and incompetently, whereas Wiesenthal saw Rosenbaum's subsequent account of the Waldheim affair as being 'dictated by hatred and larded with assumptions and suspicions'.[54]

Rosenbaum maintains his animus towards Wiesenthal two decades after the Waldheim affair, and regards the Nazi hunter as someone who was more of a hindrance towards bringing war criminals to justice than a help. In addition, Rosenbaum takes great exception to Wiesenthal's method by which he accused people of criminality before checking whether he was right. 'Defending a Nazi war criminal like Waldheim is terrible,' Rosenbaum said. 'Making Keystone Cops mistakes in the Mengele case, in the Eichmann case and the Bormann case – that's bad. But accusing innocent people, that is inexcusable.'[55] Rosenbaum, who returned to work at OSI in May 1988, cites the example of a Ukrainian immigrant in Philadelphia whom Wiesenthal had accused of being a Nazi collaborator after receiving information from a reporter on the *Philadelphia Enquirer*. The reporter had visited the Ukraine to research his family history; while he was there, he had obtained a list of those who had served in the Ukrainian police in his mother's town during the war. When he returned to the United States, the reporter checked the names against the Philadelphia phone book and found a match. By coincidence, Wiesenthal happened to be in the Philadelphia area, and the reporter approached Wiesenthal after a speech and gave him the name. As well as informing OSI, Wiesenthal duly put the man's name and location in his next annual report, along with the allegation that the man had been a murderer. Rosenbaum recalled:

> It took a lot of investigation, but we determined with near certainty that it was the wrong person. But Wiesenthal kept pressing, and even pressed the Attorney-General for us to work on this case. I ended up going to interview the guy, and I felt really bad about it, and I thought it was very unlikely that he was the right person, but we were

required to do it because of Wiesenthal's interest. The Ukrainian knew that Wiesenthal had included him in his annual report, and the guy was *terrified*. He wasn't surprised to see us, but he was an old man and he was terrified. We were persuaded by what he said, on top of all the other evidence, that it was the wrong person. But that still wasn't enough for Wiesenthal. So, when one of our staff historians was in the Ukraine doing some research, he found the police employment records from that little town, and none of the personal details such as birthdate and parents' names matched the man in Philadelphia. And if that wasn't enough, the records also showed that the Soviets had captured him and tried him. They had got the guy.[56]

Naturally, Wiesenthal would always pride himself that he never made accusations without proof. During the Waldheim affair he defended his actions by saying that he could not label the Austrian as a war criminal when he did not have any material to back up the charge. 'During more than four decades of work, I have accused none if I did not have proof against him,' Wiesenthal wrote in a letter to an American acquaintance. 'For this attitude, I have secured my reputation, not only with the Jews, but also with the historians, the judges, the public prosecutors of many countries and in the public opinion.'[57] Wiesenthal was misguided if he really thought that he enjoyed such universal respect. The only body in that list which held his reputation in such uncritically high regard was the public. Anybody who had had professional dealings with Wiesenthal realized that the man was little more than a showman acting out the role of a Nazi hunter. As we have seen, German prosecutors such as Joachim Richter and Fritz Bauer thought little of him, and those on the other side of the Atlantic such as Neal Sher and Eli Rosenbaum would come to a similar opinion. Nevertheless, Wiesenthal's reputation was to remain safe in the eyes of the public throughout his lifetime, and if anybody came out against him, they risked being accused of anti-Semitism or of demeaning in some way the perceived near-sacredness of Wiesenthal's mission. As a result, Wiesenthal's most vocal detractors have chiefly come from the lunatic fringe, but it is wrong that neo-Nazis, Revisionists, Holocaust-deniers and other cranks should have the monopoly on criticizing Simon Wiesenthal.

In the eyes of detractors such as Rosenbaum, it is Wiesenthal's 'hunt' for Josef Mengele and his reaction to the discovery of Mengele's bones that best reveal the almost ludicrous ineffectiveness of Wiesenthal's methods. Although the Nazi hunter cannot be blamed for not knowing that Mengele had died on Bertioga beach in February 1979, the confidence with which he made claims for Mengele's *post mortem* whereabouts are nevertheless extraordinary. In April 1979, Wiesenthal revealed that he knew Mengele's every move as he shuttled between Uruguay and Paraguay and 'from hacienda to hacienda'. 'He doesn't sleep two weeks in the same bed,' Wiesenthal claimed.[58] By December the following year, Wiesenthal had placed Mengele firmly in Uruguay, and stated that the fugitive was 'contemplating suicide, or has decided to give himself up to a West German embassy'.[59] In August 1982, Wiesenthal addressed a group of Jewish leaders in Newport Beach, California, during which he told them that Mengele was now moving between Bolivia, Paraguay and Uruguay, and furthermore, Wiesenthal had 'two South Americans following him' and that he was closer than ever to being caught.[60] He reiterated this claim in Bonn in August, and said that an increased reward of one hundred thousand dollars had resulted in a greater 'flow of information' about Mengele.[61] In early January 1983, Wiesenthal received the news that Mengele had recently been seen in the Paraguayan town of Philadelphia, and he asked his contacts in South America to contact the Paraguayan police. On 5 January, his two agents and a Paraguayan 'police agent' went to Philadelphia, but unfortunately they arrived just too late, because 'Mengele' had left on New Year's Eve.[62] For experienced Wiesenthal watchers, the pattern of near-misses and sightings was a familiar one, but it was a theme which would continue to be replicated. In January 1983, just a few days after he had narrowly missed Mengele in Paraguay, he told *Newsweek* that the fugitive was now living in 'a pacifist Christian community in South America'.[63] In June 1984, Wiesenthal reported that Mengele had been seen in Paraguay, and in January 1985 he said that he was 99 per cent sure that Mengele was still there.[64]

However, Simon Wiesenthal was not the only person who was convinced that Mengele was living in Paraguay. In June 1979, a group of fifty-seven US congressmen wrote to President Alfredo

Stroessner demanding that he extradite the Auschwitz doctor, and Senator Jesse Helms submitted a resolution calling on Paraguay to take legal action against Mengele.[65] As a potential sweetener, the House also dangled the possibility of four million dollars of economic aid in front of Stroessner, which was effectively the largest bounty yet issued for Mengele.[66] The Paraguayans soon grew exasperated with the repeated demands, and in a naive attempt to prove that Mengele had not been in their country for nearly two decades, they annulled his citizenship rights on the grounds that he had been out of the country for two years. 'I deny categorically that Mengele is in Paraguay,' said an official at the Ministry of the Interior. 'It's absolutely false and a slander against this country.'[67] Although the official was telling the truth, it was understandable why very few believed the Paraguayans, who had, after all, lied when Mengele was in the country.

Another who refused to take their word was Beate Klarsfeld, who travelled to Asunción in early 1984 to protest at what she believed to be Paraguay's continued sheltering of Mengele. Standing on the steps of the Supreme Court, Klarsfeld mounted the first un-authorized demonstration held in Paraguay for seventeen years when she produced a banner that read, 'President Stroessner, You Lie When You Say You Don't Know Where SS Mengele Is'. Chased back to her hotel by the police, Klarsfeld was told to leave the country because she had 'offended the Paraguayan people in the person of the president'. Her expulsion made Klarsfeld doubly convinced that Mengele was hiding in Paraguay. 'If you think logically, there is nowhere else he could be,' she said.[68] In November, Klarsfeld returned, but this time she was accompanied by Elizabeth Holtzman; Menachem Z. Rosensaft, a lawyer whose mother had been imprisoned in Auschwitz; and Bishop Rene Valero of the Brooklyn Archdiocese. For three days, the delegation held meetings with various Paraguayan officials, all of whom denied knowledge of Mengele's whereabouts, but they said they would consider running a newspaper advertisement offering a $25,000 reward for inform-ation that led to his capture.[69] Holtzman doubted the sincerity of such an offer, not least because she found Paraguay a 'very bad place'. 'We went to see some members of the Jewish community,' she recalled, 'and they were so terrified that it reminded me of what people were like when I visited the Soviet Union. Nobody wanted to talk to us.'[70]

For Klarsfeld, even though such trips did not bear immediate fruit, she felt that they achieved more than other methods of Nazi hunting. 'There's no other approach to do,' she said. 'We were different from Wiesenthal who just gave press conferences instead of going to the places where the criminals were.'[71] Certainly, the differences in the methods adopted by Wiesenthal and the Klarsfelds led to increasingly caustic comments being issued by both parties. Wiesenthal accused Beate of being a 'publicity hunter' and saw her methods as being counter-productive. The Klarsfelds regarded Wiesenthal as little more than an egomaniac who did not like others entering into 'his territory'.[72] During the Waldheim affair, the Klarsfelds claimed that 'the existence of Wiesenthal in Vienna is one of the reasons why nothing was done about Waldheim's past when he became UN Secretary-General.'[73] Wiesenthal's broadside would come five years later, when he seized upon a story published in *Der Spiegel* in July 1991 that accused the Klarsfelds of having allowed themselves to be used by the Stasi, an accusation that was not proved.[74]

By the beginning of 1985, a critical mass was starting to be reached in the search for Josef Mengele. At the end of January, a mock trial of Mengele was held in Auschwitz, which earned an enormous amount of publicity.[75] Around the same time, Israelis held protests in Mengele's home town of Günzburg, and on 6 February, the US Attorney-General instructed OSI to examine rumours that were starting to appear concerning the possible use of Mengele by the American army after the war.[76] At the same time, the US Marshals Service was tasked with actually hunting Mengele, a decision that was met with raised eyebrows at OSI, whose members regarded the Marshals as a somewhat unsophisticated instrument to deal with complexities of such a manhunt.[77] By March, other US agencies had become involved in the hunt, including the Drug Enforcement Agency, the FBI, the State Department, the army and, in the words of Stephen S. Trott, the assistant Attorney-General for the criminal division, 'the entire intelligence community'. Trott also defended the use of the Marshals, who, he said, had located and arrested seven thousand fugitives in the United States since 1980.[78]

It was unclear how many fugitives the Marshals had tracked down in Latin America, let alone Paraguay, but what was becoming apparent was that for the first time in forty years, the hunt for Mengele was finally getting the resources it required. In addition, the West Germans and the Israelis also launched their own investigations, and 'private' Nazi hunters such as the Klarsfelds, Tuviah Friedman and Simon Wiesenthal also continued with their efforts. Of these individuals, the Klarsfelds carried out the most dynamic investigations. In early 1985, Serge and Beate contacted a female friend in Berlin, who broke into Rolf Mengele's apartment and found the false passport which he had used to travel to Brazil in 1977.[79]

In May 1985, the Americans, West Germans and Israelis met in Frankfurt to coordinate their inquiries. During the meeting, the West Germans declared that they were in the process of obtaining a warrant to search the house of Hans Sedlmeier, who had loyally protected Mengele ever since he had fled Europe in 1949.[80] Among those who had always suspected that Sedlmeier was the key to finding Mengele was Simon Wiesenthal, who as early as 1964 had informed Fritz Bauer about the link that existed between the two men and Hans-Ulrich Rudel. 'That Hans Sedlmeier has met Josef Mengele several times in the past is known to us,' Bauer replied. 'That this happened six weeks ago is new to us. Herr Sedlmeier has been questioned by the prosecutor's office on this matter; perhaps we might try something or other again.'[81] Unfortunately, whenever an occasional search was mounted, Sedlmeier was always tipped off by an informant in the local police force, and was able to hide any evidence of his dealings with Mengele.[82] However, on 31 May 1985, when the police arrived at his house at Nordstrasse 3 in Günzburg, Sedlmeier was genuinely surprised. The Germans had taken the precaution of using police from outside the area, and after a thorough search they found addresses, telephone numbers, and even photocopies of letters to and from Mengele.[83]

The most promising addresses appeared to be those in São Paulo, and within hours of the search, the Brazilians were asked to help in the hunt. Personally led by the city's police chief, Romeu Tuma, the Brazilians kept watch on the houses owned by the Bosserts and the Stammers. After four days, both homes were raided, and at the home of the Bosserts at 7 Missouri Street a whole hoard of Mengele-related items was found, including writings, photographs and even a Christmas card sent by Rolf Mengele two years previously. As soon as the discovery was made, two members of the German federal criminal police flew to Brazil in order to interrogate the Bosserts. After two hours of questioning, the Bosserts broke, and admitted that Mengele was buried in the graveyard at Embu, about 15 miles to the west of the Bosserts' home. 'I didn't think you could find us so quickly,' said Wolfram Bossert.[84] The news soon leaked to the press, and to the Americans and the Israelis it appeared that the Germans were trying to hog the glory. 'The Germans went right to Brazil without telling us,' recalled David Marwell, a member of OSI's Mengele team. 'We learned about it on CNN.'[85] Neal Sher was equally unimpressed. 'If we were the ones who had made the break-through,' he said, 'we would have shared it with the other countries before going public.'[86]

On 6 June, a vast crowd consisting of hundreds of police and reporters gathered at the small cemetery in Embu to watch three gravediggers unearth the grave of 'Wolfgang Gerhard'. After digging down nearly 4 feet, they reached the coffin, which they were unable to dislodge. Instead, the gravediggers were ordered to smash the lid, and soon they started to extricate a grisly collection of bones and shreds of clothing, which were transferred to a large metal tray destined for a morgue in São Paulo. At one point, the morgue's director, José Antonio de Mello, picked up a skull and held it high for the photographers.[87] 'We should be able to identify the race, height, and colour without much difficulty,' he announced.[88]

For the next two weeks, the world waited and speculated. Many believed that the bones were not those of the 'Angel of Death'. 'This is Mengele's seventh death,' announced Simon Wiesenthal. 'Only in Paraguay has he been dead three times, always with witnesses who say it's him. On one of those occasions we found the body of a woman.'[89] Wiesenthal was adamant that Mengele's family was try-ing to pull off an incredible hoax. 'When the body is proven not to be Dr Mengele,' he said, 'this will show that Dr Mengele is alive and this is a family plot.' Wiesenthal also claimed that in 1964, the West German Chancellor, Konrad Adenauer, had offered sixteen million marks to President Stroessner to extradite Mengele, but the request had been turned down. Wiesenthal said that he remembered being told about the offer by Fritz Bauer. 'He asked me to be silent for the next few months about Mengele,' Wiesenthal recalled.[90] The West Germans instantly derided Wiesenthal's story. Not only did the West German ambassador to Paraguay at the time dismiss it as pure invention, but officials in Bonn were swift to point out that as Adenauer had retired in October 1963, the story could not be true. Wiesenthal sheepishly claimed that he had been mistaken about the date, and had meant 1963.[91] However, as there is no evidence to suggest that Wiesenthal had been discussing the Mengele case with Bauer in 1963, the claim is likely to be another of Wiesenthal's fabrications. At least his scepticism put him in good company, as many were unconvinced that the bones of 'Wolfgang Gerhard' were in fact those of Mengele. The Klarsfelds, the Israelis, OSI, Tuviah Friedman – all doubted that the man was dead. When Rolf Mengele announced on 11 June that his father had died, the suspicions were unallayed. 'Until the cask is handed to an international team of pathologists, including West Germans and Americans,' said Isser Harel, 'and they decide that it is Mengele, this story has no basis in truth.'[92] The Mengele family was equally dismissive of the sceptics. 'The only false trails were laid by Nazi hunters like Wiesenthal and Klarsfeld,' said Mengele's 34-year-old nephew, Dieter.[93] Despite the element of truth in the statement, members of the Mengele family, who had been lying about Josef Mengele's whereabouts for decades, were hardly in a position to take those such as Wiesenthal and Klarsfeld to task.

On 21 June 1985, the forensic team, which consisted of six American scientists, reported that the 'skeleton was that of Josef Mengele within a reasonable scientific certainty'. Like Mengele, the person unearthed at Embu was male and Caucasian, was similar in age and height, had a distinctively high brow, and in all likelihood had a large gap between his front teeth. Additional evidence was also supplied by Dr Richard Helmer from the University of Kiel, who carried out the relatively new process of 'electronic supra-position', which merged photographs of Mengele's face with that of the Embu skull. The resulting images were extremely eerie, and helped to convince many that the skull belonged to the Auschwitz doctor.[94] Despite the strength of evidence, however, there was certainly still room for doubt. David Marwell of OSI said:

> Reasonable scientific certainty is not a legal standard. In fact, it's not even a scientific standard. What does it mean, 'reasonable scientific certainty'? In an insurance case, that might be okay, but in this situation where there was a powerful motive to deceive the investigators, and you're dealing – in the popular imagination – with an evil genius who knows about medical stuff and could find a body that looks like his, you need more than 'reasonable scientific certainty'.[95]

Marwell was able to convince his boss, Neal Sher, that more evidence had to be found, and Sher agreed to let the investigation continue. Among those who also continued to have doubts about the results of the forensic examination was Eli Rosenbaum, who had joined the World Jewish Congress (WJC) in November 1986. Although Rosenbaum thought it highly probable that Mengele had died, one of his first acts as the organization's General Counsel was to persuade the WJC leaders to conduct a private investigation. A leaked WJC document raised the possibility that the Mengele family had indeed tried to fool the world: 'Mengele was in a position, from the standpoint of scientific, financial and logistical resources, to pull off a fairly sophisticated hoax.'[96]

The one person who did believe in Mengele's death was, at least for a while, Simon Wiesenthal, who wrote in his annual report at the end of January 1986 that 'for us, the case is thus concluded'.[97] In the meantime, the team from OSI was having some success in gathering new evidence. In Germany, it found Mengele's autobiographical writings, which confirmed much of the testimony that had been given by those such as the Stammers and the Bosserts. However, the real breakthrough came in March that year, when the US consul in São Paulo, Stephen Dachi, decided to carry out some investigations of his own. In a coincidence of the kind beloved of bad fiction writers, before Dachi had joined the diplomatic corps he had in fact been a dentist and oral pathologist. Fascinated by the English translations prepared by OSI of some of Mengele's autobiographical writings, Dachi had noted that Mengele had visited a 'Dr Gama in Sama' for root-canal treatment. The initial police investigation had been unable to locate Dr Gama, but Dachi hazarded that the town of 'Sama' in fact referred to Santo Amaro, a suburb of São Paulo. With his deputy, Fred Kaplan, Dachi went through the phone book and discovered a 'Dr Hercy Gonzaga Gama Angelo' in its pages. Dachi visited the doctor and found that not only did he specialize in root-canal treatment, but that he had also treated one 'Pedro Hochbichler' in 1978, who had given his address as 5555 Alvarenga Road. As the address matched that of Mengele's last hideout and the alias was one of those used by him, there was no doubt who it was that Dr Gama had treated. Gama told the Americans that the referring dentist had been a Dr Kasumasa Tutiya, and when Dachi visited him, he was delighted to find that Tutiya had kept his X-rays. 'When he dropped those X-rays on the table it was like winning the lottery,' said Dachi. 'In 40 years, no one has ever found a single X-ray of Mengele. We found a man who had eight.'[98] In November 1986, the forensic team issued a new report, which now declared with certainty that Mengele was dead.

Nevertheless, for some, the idea that Mengele had escaped justice was too much to bear. By the beginning of 1989, Simon Wiesenthal had once more become a sceptic, and expressed his 'grave doubts' that Mengele was in fact dead.[99] Even in April 1992, when a team of British scientists led by Dr Alec Jeffreys successfully matched the DNA found in the Embu skeleton with that of Rolf Mengele, Wiesenthal continued to entertain uncertainty.[100] As well as in Wiesenthal's imagination, the other place that Mengele survived was in the world of popular culture. Just a month after the Frankfurt public prosecutor had announced the findings of Dr Jeffreys, the American Jewish Theater in Manhattan staged Charlie Schulman's *Angel of Death*, a black comedy in which Josef Mengele has become a cabaret singer at the 'Club Führer' in Paraguay. Played by Daniel von Bargen, this Mengele could be found singing very Germanic versions of Sinatra's 'My Way' and Presley's 'In the Ghetto'. Blackly comic and absurd it may have been, but in some ways, Schulman's play was no less so than the real story of Mengele.

When Klaus Barbie entered the hall of Lyon's Palace of Justice on the afternoon of 11 May 1987, he appeared to smile.[101] Wearing a dark blue suit, a light blue shirt and a dark blue tie, the almost dapper effect was marred by the presence of a pair of handcuffs, which were removed when he sat down on a chair that had been specially swept for explosives. Over a thousand people were crammed into the magnificent hall, which had been requisitioned as a temporary courtroom to cope with the intense public interest. As the 'Butcher of Lyon' took his place, hundreds of heads craned to catch sight of the man who had terrorized their city over four decades before. After he had sat, Barbie was approached by his 62-year-old lawyer, Jacques Vergès, and the two shared an exchange that caused both men to grin. Of all the lawyers in France, Vergès was an inspired selection who would use the trial as a means of promoting his own political agenda. A Maoist, a de facto anarchist, a rumoured terrorist, a quondam associate of Pol Pot and numerous other diabolical figures such as Carlos the Jackal, Vergès had earned his notorious reputation by representing Algerian terrorists and using the platforms afforded by the law courts to attack what he saw as French colonial hypocrisy. Underpinning Vergès's approach was his philosophy that criminality and violence were legitimate political tools. 'Crime advances society,' he said. 'When I defended Algerians who committed crimes in the streets of Paris, they were considered to be murderers and arsonists. But today I can't help noticing that when representatives of the Algerian government come to France they get the red-carpet treatment.'[102] For Vergès, the courtroom in Lyon represented the most public stage in the world, and he was determined to make the most of the opportunity that such a large audience offered. It mattered little to Vergès whether Barbie was guilty or not, for the lawyer's tactics were not to mount a defence in the conventional sense, but rather to reveal to the world that every country had its Klaus Barbies, which made it hypocritical to prosecute just one Klaus Barbie. 'I told him, "I don't think you're innocent,"' Vergès recalled. '"Nor that you're the monster people say you are. You are a tragic figure of our times. You are no better or worse than an American officer in Vietnam, bombing civilians with napalm. You're no different from a Russian officer in Kabul, or certain French officers in Algeria."'[103]

Facing Vergès was a team of thirty-nine lawyers who represented the Gestapo's victims. Among them was Serge Klarsfeld, who during the trial produced Barbie's telex from April 1944 that showed his

personal involvement in deporting the Jewish children of Izieu.[104] At
one point, when Vergès was actually holding the fragile document,
Klarsfeld lost his cool and jumped up from his seat to tell the judges
that Barbie's lawyer should not be allowed to handle it for fear that
he might damage or alter the telex in some way.[105] Vergès simply dismissed the document as a fake, which was also how he regarded the
entire proceedings. 'This trial is an immense piece of trickery,' he
said. 'It is an immense mistake.'[106] Vergès also outraged most of
France by claiming that the deportation from Izieu was not the
product of a Nazi policy. 'Like any other French person living in
France,' he announced, 'we know that the fate of the Jewish children
was in fact a matter that interested the French political authorities.
Because, and you know this, members of the jury, the proposal to
deport Jewish children was a French proposal.' Despite holding such
low regard for the trial, Vergès was politic enough to allow the
witnesses to speak uninterrupted. One of the most moving
testimonies came from Simone Lagrange, who had been tortured by
Barbie and, along with her family, dispatched to Auschwitz and later
forced to watch her father being shot dead.[107] Her face wet with
tears, Lagrange told the court, 'Barbie didn't shoot him in the head,
but Barbie sent us there.' In the pre-trial hearing, Lagrange had
actually confronted Barbie face to face, and asked him if he recognized her. 'When you have been in prison for seven months,' Barbie
replied, 'it's always agreeable to see a desirable woman.' Lagrange
told her former torturer that the remark was insulting, but Barbie's
callousness ran deep. 'The trouble with you,' he said, 'is that you
can't take a joke.'[108] In his summation, Vergès dismissed such
accounts as 'an evolution of phantasms'. He also questioned the
very Holocaust itself. 'The idea that anti-Semitism, old as the world,
old as the Roman Empire, could have led to genocide is ridiculous.'
For Vergès the trial was nothing more than an attempt to 'expiate'
the sins of the West, and he begged the court to finish 'this
hypocritical pretension'.[109]

On the final day of the trial, Barbie was asked if he had anything
to say in his defence. Still wearing the same suit and tie, Barbie stood
up and announced that he did. Looking haggard, and once more
with an almost imperceptible grin, he told the court that he was not
responsible for the raid at Izieu. 'I never had the power to decide

who was sent to the camps,' he said, speaking in French. 'I fought
the Resistance, which I respect, harshly, but it was war and the war
is now over. Thank you.' Despite Vergès's defence, Barbie was
sentenced to life imprisonment, although the jury's decision
was based on a majority. When the verdict was announced, clapping
broke out, which the judge asked to cease for the sake of 'dignity'.
For Serge Klarsfeld, the moment had been a long time coming.
'There was an exceptional crime, and this was an exceptional trial,'
he told reporters. 'And because memory is related to justice, it
means that the children of Izieu will not die away in memory. They
will not be forgotten.'[110] For Jacques Vergès, the sentence was
another example of an equivalence between the French system of
justice and Nazism. Noting that senior Nazis such as Dönitz and
von Schirach had received lesser sentences at Nuremberg, he
reflected that by issuing Barbie with life imprisonment, the French
had managed to 'surpass our masters in this field'.[111] Under armed
guard, Barbie was driven off to Lyon Prison, where he would spend
the next four years until his death from leukaemia in September
1991 at the age of seventy-seven.

If justice had been dispensed just in time in France, in the United
Kingdom it would often arrive too late. On 22 October 1986, the
British consul in Los Angeles met Rabbis Marvin Hier and Abraham
Cooper from the Simon Wiesenthal Center. The centre, which had
been founded in November 1977, reputedly paid Wiesenthal around
$75,000 per year to use his name, although it acted largely
independently of the man himself.[112] Hier and Cooper presented the
diplomat with a list of seventeen suspected Nazi war criminals who
had emigrated to Britain after the war, eleven of whom were
Latvian, and six Lithuanian. The men came from a variety of backgrounds, but all were suspected of having participated in the
persecution and murder of civilians. The evidence came mostly from
Soviet sources, although some came from archives in the United
States, Israel and even Britain. As well as the list, the rabbis gave the
consul a letter addressed to Margaret Thatcher, the British Prime
Minister, in which they asked the British government to investigate
the charges, and 'if necessary create the required legal apparatus to
deal with them'.[113]

Within a few days of the list being presented, one of the names had been leaked to the press. Antanas Gecas, a 71-year-old retired mining engineer living in Edinburgh, had taken part in anti-partisan operations and civilian massacres while serving as a platoon commander in a Lithuanian police battalion. Although it was not credited by the Simon Wiesenthal Center's researchers, the source of the information about Gecas was in fact OSI, which had tipped off the British government about Gecas in 1981, and had even extracted a partial confession from him in front of the Scottish police in 1982.[114] Publicly, Gecas denied that he had taken part in any killings, citing his strict Catholicism as proof that he was somehow incapable of committing acts of murder.[115] Gecas claimed that the allegations were in fact part of a 'KGB plot', although a programme shown on British television featuring Eli Rosenbaum and Neal Sher the following January and February established that there was no doubt that Gecas was a criminal of the foulest stripe. One witness revealed how 'people doomed to death were stripped naked, driven to the pit, and on Gecas's command, shot'.[116]

Despite the revelations, the British government appeared to do little in response to the Wiesenthal Center's list. On 24 November 1986, the All-Party Parliamentary War Crimes Group was formed in order to pressurize the government into acting. It was chaired by the former Home Secretary Merlyn Rees, while the Group's secretary was Greville Janner MP, who as Lance Bombardier Janner had served in the British War Crimes Group in 1948.[117] As someone who was livid at the disbandment of the Group in the late 1940s, Janner saw an opportunity to deal with 'unfinished business'. 'I've always believed that it was monstrous of these people, not only to avoid prosecution,' Janner said, 'but also to come and live in Britain. They were brought in by the hundreds – perhaps by the thousands – to work in the pits and I couldn't do a thing about it until I got into Parliament.'[118] Although Janner's suggestion that British coal mines were stuffed with Nazi war criminals is somewhat of an exaggeration, there is no doubt that the substance of his words is correct. Thousands of Ukrainians and Balts were indeed brought into Britain after the war under the European Voluntary Workers Scheme (EVW), which was intended to fill a perceived 'manpower gap' in industries such as domestic labour, agriculture, textiles and indeed coal mining. As the screening of these immigrants was woefully inadequate, many war criminals such as those on the Wiesenthal Center's list successfully entered the country, despite being involved in some of the most bestial crimes committed during the war.[119]

One of the first meetings the Parliamentary Group had was with the Home Secretary Douglas Hurd. 'He was polite, but took no action,' Janner later wrote. 'He promised to look into our concerns but nothing happened for months and we suspected that his civil servants had buried this potentially explosive issue, which would unleash some citizens' disgraceful past.'[120] In March 1987, a delegation from the Wiesenthal Center led by Marvin Hier also met Hurd and found him to be similarly non-committal. One of those attending the meeting was Efraim Zuroff, who would later recall how the Home Secretary informed the delegation that the British government required more documentation and had no intention of mounting its own investigation. Rabbi Hier suggested that the government, with its vast resources, was far better placed to conduct such an inquiry, but Hurd refused. 'We found ourselves in the strange position of being asked by Her Majesty's government to do its work for her,' Zuroff observed.[121] Hurd outlined the government's position in a press conference, during which he indicated that the Wiesenthal Center's material was 'sketchy', and moreover that the British courts had no jurisdiction over crimes committed in foreign territories over forty years previously.[122] In legal terms, Zuroff was incorrect when he stated that the government had some sort of obligation to deal with the men on the list, but there was a growing call both from within and outside Parliament that something should be done. In order to press its case, the War Crimes Group enlisted the historian David Cesarani to produce a historical report that revealed how easily such criminals had entered into the country.[123]

For the next year, the Group and the Wiesenthal Center maintained its pressure on the government, and finally, on 8 February 1988, Douglas Hurd announced the establishment of an inquiry to be conducted by Sir Thomas Hetherington and William Chalmers. Although the news was broadly welcomed in the House of Commons, there were some loud voices raised against it. Ivor Stanbrook, the Conservative MP for Orpington, suggested that it was a 'bad decision', and enquired whether Hurd was 'not surrendering to a lobby whose main motivations are hatred and revenge?' Tony Marlow, the Conservative MP for Northampton North, was even more vitriolic. After wondering whether the government was attempting to enact retrospective legislation, Marlow asked, 'Would we, for example, find ourselves prosecuting the Israeli soldier who savagely beat to death a fifteen-year-old Palestinian boy if that soldier came to stay in this country?' Hurd swiftly rejected Marlow's points, but it was Greville Janner who lambasted Marlow for his 'odious question'.[124]

The War Crimes Parliamentary Group did not expect much of the Hetherington–Chalmers report, and for the first few weeks of its existence, its detractors were given much ammunition. In late March, a series of advertisements headlined 'War Criminals, Evidence Wanted' appeared in national newspapers, a move that seemed to suggest a much-feared witchhunt.[125] In April, it was discovered that Hetherington and Chalmers were still reading 'basic books' about the Holocaust, and that the inquiry was manned only by its two authors and a secretary.[126] However, much to the surprise of those such as Janner, when the report was published on 24 July 1989, the recommendation was made that the government should indeed introduce new legislation. 'The crimes committed are so monstrous that they cannot be condoned,' the report stated. 'To take no action would taint the United Kingdom with the slur of being a haven for war criminals.'[127] The report had also examined seven of the 301 cases that had been submitted to the government, and of these it suggested that in four, there was a 'realistic prospect of a conviction for murder on the evidence available were the jurisdiction of the British courts to be widened'. The report also indicated that another seventy-five cases should be further investigated.[128] 'Until that moment,' wrote Greville Janner, 'we had been stirring up the past, in the remote hope of action in the future. From that moment, our campaign lifted off into reality.'[129]

In November 1989, the Leader of the House, Geoffrey Howe, announced that the recommendations of the report would be debated the following month, first in the House of Lords and then in the Commons. In the Upper House, the majority of the peers spoke against Hetherington–Chalmers. Among them was Lord

Mayhew, who as an Under-Secretary of State in the Foreign Office in the late 1940s was partially instrumental in developing the policy that saw the abandonment of Nazi hunting and war crimes trials. On 6 July 1948, Mayhew had minuted his minister concerning the repatriation of Soviet citizens suspected of war crimes. 'We should also, I think, consider how to wind up the whole problem as soon as possible,' Mayhew wrote. '[And] inform the Russians that, after a certain date, we will cease searching for persons for whose extradition they have applied, and, if appropriate, issue a "short list" of persons whom we will hereafter consider handing over.' Mayhew advocated maintaining such shortlists in respect to other countries, but suspected that the idea of a 'comprehensive amnesty' for war criminals was not practicable, especially as the 'state of opinion in Western as well as Eastern Europe' would be against it. What Mayhew did not discuss was whether such an amnesty was undesirable.[130] During the Lords' debate in December 1989, Mayhew was in august company, and he was joined by weighty figures such as Lords Hailsham, Home and Callaghan in opposing any move to introduce a War Crimes Bill.[131] For Greville Janner, Mayhew's opposition to the report may not have been rooted only in defending his actions made forty years previously. 'Christopher Mayhew was regarded by the Jewish community as a man who was anti-Israel,' Janner later claimed. 'He was opposed to the formation of a Jewish state. I wouldn't say that he was a straightforward anti-Semite, but I believe that he was not a friend of the Jewish people.'[132]

Anti-Semitism was either implied or inferred during the debate in the House of Commons on 12 December. Robert Maclennan, the Social and Liberal Democrat MP, asked whether the jurisdiction of any new Act would cover the 'leaders of modern Israel, some of whom are responsible for the cold-blooded massacre of British subjects and are now received with warmth and hospitality when they come to Britain'.[133] To some, the fact that MPs such as Maclennan were specifically using Israel as an example of a re-habilitated enemy was nothing more than coded anti-Semitism. There can be little doubt that, in private, some MPs thought that the pressure for a War Crimes Act was nothing less than the work of some Jewish cabal, orchestrated by the likes of Janner and Rabbi Hier. However, the new British Home Secretary, David Waddington, was most emphatically in favour of the report, and stated that 'the terrible stories revealed in its pages and the evidence of foul deeds that is presented cannot be put aside or ignored'.[134] After three hours of debate, a vote was taken as to whether the House should support the need for legislation 'to permit the prosecution in this country for acts of murder or manslaughter or culpable homicide committed as war crimes in German or German Occupied Territory during the Second World War, of people who are now British citizens or resident here'.[135] The vote was passed by a majority that represented a proportion of almost three to one, a result that was broadly welcomed by the press. 'Hunt and Punish the Nazi War Criminals', urged *The Sun*, while the *The Economist* stated that 'Britain is set to become a less comfortable haven for Hitler's henchmen.'[136]

By 25 April 1990, the War Crimes Bill had passed through the House of Commons, and had enjoyed similar majorities. During the debate on 19 March 1990, Greville Janner had made the point that the Bill was not an attempted piece of 'retrospective legislation'.

> Retrospective legislation involves the creation of new crimes. The Bill provides, in effect, that an old crime, which has always been subject to the jurisdiction of the courts and which has always been a crime to humanity, will apply to those who were not previously subject to it. Even the most doughty opponents of the Bill have not suggested that anything but heinous offences have been committed. No one has suggested that we have thought up a new offence; murder goes back to pre-biblical days.[137]

All that stood in the way of the Bill being enacted was the House of Lords, but the Upper House was strongly opposed to the proposed legislation. That month, Lord Shawcross, the former Attorney-General and Chief British Prosecutor at Nuremberg, wrote to John Patten, the Minister of State at the Home Office, informing him that 'no lawyer of any distinction has supported the Government's present proposals'. He added that 'Winston Churchill must be turning in his grave at them'.[138] Patten disagreed, and told Shawcross that the 'circumstances of our times are very different from those of the immediate post-war years, and the obligation facing us today is to decide on a course of action which appears right now'.[139] When the Bill was debated in the Lords later that year, many impressive figures spoke against it. The 'antis' included one former Prime Minister, two former Lord Chancellors, one Master of the Rolls, one former Chief of the Defence Staff, two former Foreign Secretaries, as well as the historians Lord Blake and Lord Dacre. Unsurprisingly, the vote went against the Bill by a margin similar to that by which it had been voted for in the Lower House.[140] Mrs Thatcher was said to be furious and, determined not to be bullied by the House of Lords, she ensured that the Bill was reintroduced to the Commons in March 1991, where it once again passed through.[141] In April, it came back to the House of Lords, where it was rejected. The only way the Bill could now pass into law was for the government to invoke the Parliament Act of 1949, which allows for the democratically elected Commons to override the decisions made in the non-elected Lords. On 10 May 1991, the government did just that when the Queen gave the Bill her Royal Assent. 'We had won a great, unique and difficult battle,' Greville Janner recalled.[142]

One immediate result of the new Act was the establishment of war crimes units in the Crown Prosecution Service (CPS) and the Metropolitan Police. After investigating 376 cases, the police unit submitted 250,000 pages of evidence to the CPS, which decided that just ten cases were worth pursuing. In 1996, nearly a decade after the Simon Wiesenthal Center had presented its initial list, the Crown made its first charge under the new Act. The suspect was Szymon Serafinowicz, an 85-year-old retired carpenter who lived in Banstead in Surrey, who had been hunted by OSI since the early 1980s. In 1982, the Americans had found an emigré publication showing a meeting in England of Byelorussian activists; among them was Serafinowicz, who had been a wartime police chief in Belarus. Eli Rosenbaum cabled the British authorities, asking if they could check to see if Serafinowicz was resident in the United Kingdom. 'Scotland Yard cabled back and said, "No, there's no trace of him here,"' Rosenbaum recalled. 'It turned out they had misspelled the name when they ran the check.'[143] In the pre-trial hearings in 1995, it emerged that Serafinowicz had taken part in the eradication of the three-thousand-strong Jewish population around Minsk, and that he had personally shot at least three Jews himself.[144] Serafinowicz denied all the charges, but he never got the chance to prove his innocence in court as he was suffering from dementia, and, on 7 August 1997, he died. His family continued to protest his innocence. 'My grandfather completely refuted the allegations,' said Serafinowicz's grandson, the comedian Peter Serafinowicz, who claimed that the allegations were made in a book by a grudge-bearing friend. 'Unfortunately, due to a degenerative illness, he was denied the opportunity to demonstrate that there was no truth in the allegations by presenting his case.'[145]

The police and the CPS had more luck with the case of Antony Sawoniuk, who was arrested on 26 September 1997 at the age of seventy-six. Sawoniuk, a retired British Rail ticket inspector who lived in Bermondsey, south London, was charged with murdering three Jewish women and two Jewish men while he was serving in the Ukrainian Auxiliary Police in 1942.[146] Sawoniuk's past had been brought to the attention of the British police by the Soviet Union in the late 1980s, when it had presented a list of suspected war criminals drawn up by the KGB. Sawoniuk had unwittingly alerted the Russians to his presence in the United Kingdom when he had written to his half-brother in Poland in the early 1950s. Unbeknown to Sawoniuk, the letter, like all other mail from the West, had been vetted by the KGB.[147] During his trial, which started in early 1999, one witness, Alexander Baglay, recalled how Sawoniuk had once ordered three Jews to undress in front of an open grave.

> The Jewess did not want to take off her underpants. She was 28 or 29. When she refused, he threatened her with a truncheon. When she had undressed, they were lined up and shot. He shot them with his pistol in the back of the head. He was standing behind each of them and levered them into the pit by raising his knee.[148]

Another witness, Fedor Zan, testified that Sawoniuk had machine-gunned fifteen women as they stood naked by a pit near Domachevo on the border between Poland and Belarus.[149] In April, Sawoniuk was found guilty, and was sentenced to two life terms. An appeal failed, and he was to die while he was incarcerated in Norwich Prison in November 2005.

After Sawoniuk's conviction, the war crimes unit at Scotland Yard was disbanded. Since then, there have been no further trials brought under the 1991 Act, and to its detractors, the legislation is little more than an expensive gesture. Its defenders, such as Greville Janner, do not deny that it is a gesture, but they think it an important one. 'Whatever the prosecutions, at least some of these old Nazis who had so wrongly been given a refuge in our decent land may not have slept well in their beds,' Janner wrote. 'At least the land that had once stood alone against Hitler and his allies had made a gesture of intent, however late.'[150]

On the night of 20 September 2005, Simon Wiesenthal died in his sleep at his home at the age of ninety-six. Described as the 'conscience of the Holocaust' by Marvin Hier of the Simon Wiesenthal Center, the Rabbi also lauded Wiesenthal for becoming 'the permanent representative of the victims, determined to bring the perpetrators of history's greatest crime to justice.'[151] After a service held in Vienna's Central Cemetery, Wiesenthal's body was flown to Israel, where it was buried in the town of Herzliya, 10 miles north of Tel Aviv. The tributes and eulogies were many and fulsome, and at the time it would have been churlish to have detracted from the many positive aspects of the role played by Wiesenthal. It is partly thanks to Wiesenthal that the Holocaust has been remembered and properly recorded, and this is perhaps his greatest legacy. In addition, nothing should detract from the fact that Wiesenthal did bring some Nazis to justice, although in nothing like the quantity that is claimed, and Adolf Eichmann was certainly not among them. As has been observed, Wiesenthal was at heart a showman, and when he eventually found a role as the World's Head Nazi Hunter in the wake of the Eichmann kidnap, he played it well. It mattered little that he would eventually overplay it, because his audiences would continue to cheer and clap. As with so many popular performances, it was impossible for the critics to tell the public that the Great Wiesenthal Show was little more than an illusion. But it was a great illusion, and ultimately it was an illusion mounted for a good cause. Whatever his failings, Wiesenthal was at least on the side of the angels, and no matter what he really did during the war, he did more to atone for any transgressions than those he was trying to hunt.

Today, his work is professionally carried out by the organization that bears his name. Although the American OSI should be considered the most effective Nazi-hunting unit established since 1948, the Simon Wiesenthal Center does much to pressure governments all over the world into bringing the surviving Nazi war criminals to justice. The centre's current campaign is called Operation Last Chance, and it is headed by Efraim Zuroff, who occasionally displays some of the same idiosyncracies as Wiesenthal himself. In July 2008, Zuroff travelled to Argentina and Chile in the hope of catching Dr Aribert Heim, an SS doctor at Mauthausen who was at the head of the Wiesenthal Center's list of most wanted Nazis. Cast from the same mould as Mengele, Heim had carried out a series of horrific 'experiments' on human guinea pigs to see how much pain they could withstand. During one notorious 'operation' he castrated and decapitated a young athlete, before having his flesh boiled off his skull, which was then used as a display piece. 'In the last few days we've received information from two different sources, both relating to Chile, which we think have very good potential,' Zuroff told reporters.[152] He also told the media that the centre was 'putting in place certain initiatives which could reveal his hiding place within a couple of weeks'.[153] Although Zuroff was doing what Wiesenthal never did – travel to South America – his statements gave the impression that he was as tantalizingly close to finding his evil Nazi doctor as Wiesenthal had been to getting his. Furthermore, tracking down fugitives requires stealth and discretion, neither of which was in abundance as Zuroff toured towns such as Bariloche and Puerto Montt accompanied by a crowd of journalists whom Zuroff appeared to gladly embrace. Unsurprisingly, Zuroff flew back across the Atlantic empty-handed. Had Heim been in Patagonia as he believed to be the case, the Nazi hunter's noisy and triumphal entrance at the front door would have given Heim plenty of time to jump out of the back window. To some (more critical eyes) the whole trip looked suspiciously like a publicity exercise in order to promote the Wiesenthal Center, the main activities of which are fighting anti-Semitism and defending Israel. Nazi hunting is a minority activity for the centre, but it is a useful 'brand-builder'.

At the time of Zuroff's trip, Aribert Heim was in fact nowhere near South America, as he was actually lying in an unmarked grave in Cairo, where he had been buried in 1992. When convincing evidence of Heim's demise was presented by the *New York Times* in early February 2009, it was Zuroff alone who doubted whether Heim was really dead. 'We can't sign off on a story like this because of some semi-plausible explanation,' he said. 'Keep in mind these people have a vested interest in being declared dead – it's a perfectly crafted story; that's the problem, it's too perfect.' Zuroff was also suspicious of the lack of any evidence other than paperwork and oral testimony. 'There's no body, no corpse, no DNA, no grave,' he said, and maintained that the report of Heim's death raises 'more questions than it answers'.[154] What Zuroff failed to acknowledge – just like Simon Wiesenthal – was that he had a vested interest in keeping Heim alive. Unfortunately for Zuroff, dead Nazis can no longer be hunted, and without something to chase, Nazi hunters will soon be out of work.

However, Nazis are not the only war criminals worth hunting, a fact recognized by the American government when in December 2004 it gave OSI an enhanced brief to hunt war criminals from other conflicts hiding in its borders. Its investigators will find much that is familiar to the hunt for Nazis. Ironically, on the same day that Simon Wiesenthal died, Carla del Ponte, the chief prosecutor of the UN International Criminal Tribunal for the former Yugoslavia, accused the Catholic Church of hiding a suspected Croatian war criminal, General Ante Gotovina, who had been indicted for crimes carried out against Croatian Serbs. 'I have information he is hiding in a Franciscan monastery and so the Catholic Church is protecting him,' she claimed. 'I have taken this up with the Vatican and the Vatican refuses totally to cooperate with us.'[155] The crimes are the same – only the names change.

Epilogue

DURING THE course of my research, I met two Nazi war criminals. Although the circumstances of the two meetings were wildly different, they were both illustrative of the positions in which so many of their ilk found themselves after the war. My first encounter was with Erich Priebke, the *SS-Hauptsturmführer* who had participated in the Ardeatine Caves massacre. In 1996, Priebke had been deported from Argentina to Italy after he had given an interview in 1994 on the streets of Bariloche to Sam Donaldson of ABC News in which he had expressed a seeming lack of remorse for his participation in the murders. Tried in Rome in the summer of that year, Priebke was found guilty of murder by a three-judge military panel. However, because the judges found that he was following orders, his case was categorized as one that fell under a thirty-year statute of limitations and, at the beginning of August, Priebke was sensationally acquitted. The courthouse was besieged by demonstrators, and Priebke was quickly rearrested and once more put on trial the following April. In March 1997, after much legal toing-and-froing, Priebke was eventually sentenced to life imprisonment at the age of eighty-three. Because he was too old to be sent to gaol,

Priebke was instead sentenced to house arrest, and at the time of my visit in June 2007, he was living in a reasonably smart block of flats near the Via Aurelia in the undistinguished Boccea district of western Rome.

Graffiti on neighbouring blocks indicated that the presence of the former Gestapo officer in the area was most unwelcome, although as Priebke was only allowed out for two hours a week, such daubs might not have given him much cause for concern. After surrendering my passport to a policeman at the ground floor, I was escorted by another up several flights of stairs and a doorbell was rung. After a few seconds, a relatively spry nonagenarian opened the door and exchanged some banter in Italian with the policeman, who then left us. After shaking hands, Priebke escorted me into his apartment, which was spacious and well appointed. Heavy dark furniture and medieval weaponry on the walls gave an immediate, but not over-powering, Teutonic impression. Priebke ushered me into a small sitting room, and indicated that I should sit on a sofa. His manners were impeccable, his face was friendly, his English was good, and although it was only ten thirty in the morning, he suggested that we should share a bottle of red wine. I accepted, and reflected that if I were a 93-year-old under house arrest, I would probably start drinking at that hour as well. I thought about refusing, fearing that to accept such hospitality would in some way compromise me, but I felt that a show of relaxation would help engender a better interview.

We spoke for nearly two and a half hours, during which Priebke gave me a full and seemingly open account about his escape, as the preceding pages have shown. What we didn't cover were the events of the massacre itself, as I was certain that to have enquired would have either caused him to clam up or merely elicited a rehearsed response. Besides, as I had indicated to him, I was there to talk about his escape rather than his crimes, and to have changed subjects may have only angered him. It was only towards the end of the interview that Priebke started to muse about his present position. What he said revealed the mindset of a man, who, like Mengele and Eichmann before him, was desperate to maintain a world-view that he had held decades before. 'Many people wrote to the new Pope about me,' he said, referring to the then recently elected Benedict XVI. 'They didn't even get a note. Nothing. They are afraid of the Jews.' It is an indication of Priebke's naivety that he felt a German Pope should necessarily wish to help a convicted Nazi war criminal. That he ascribes Ratzinger's silence as being somehow the work of the Jews also indicates a complete lack of understanding and an inherent bigotry.

A little later in the interview, Priebke would once more talk about what some anti-Semites call 'the traditional enemy'. 'Wiesenthal turned against Pacelli,' he told me, talking about Pius XII, the wartime Pope. 'They say he didn't do enough for the Jews. But it was not true. All the Church – it was full of Jews. We did not act against them, for practical reasons. We needed the railway cars for other things.' Once again, Priebke had revealed the badly hidden Nazi under the kindly exterior. He seemed to be not only suggesting that the Catholic Church was somehow dominated by Jews, but he was also verging on Holocaust denial. What made his comments more disturbing was the implied claim that the only reason why the railway carriages were not used to transport Jews was one of practicality. This of course suggests that had the railway carriages not been needed elsewhere, then the actions against the Jews would have indeed intensified. It seemed pointless to have an argument with him, and so I merely drained my red wine, thanked him for his time, and left. At the time of writing, Erich Priebke is still alive.

Four months later, I found myself outside another block of flats in a European capital. Accompanied by a reporter, I had decided to try to interview the seventh most wanted Nazi war criminal on the Wiesenthal Center's list. Erna Wallisch, who at the time of my visit was eighty-five, had served as an SS guard at Ravensbrück and Majdanek, and had beaten women and children as they were forced towards the gas chambers. It had also been alleged that she beat a young boy to death, and yet, despite all these accusations, the Austrians allowed her to live peacefully in Vienna, citing the statute of limitations as her protection. Tracking down Wallisch involved almost no detective work whatsoever – I simply looked her up in the online Austrian telephone directory. Within a few days, I had flown to Vienna and at eight thirty on the morning of 17 October, the reporter and I stood outside her flat.

The array of buzzers clearly showed the name 'Wallisch', but we did not wish to ring it because we knew she would never let us in. Instead, we engaged some neighbours in conversation, who told us that they had no idea who Wallisch was, and that 'it was all in the past, and that people should just learn forgiveness'. After about half an hour, the postman arrived, and he unwittingly let us into the block. After sharing some small talk, he then left us in the hallway outside Wallisch's flat. The reporter handed me a large Nikon, and then rang her doorbell. I stood ready with the camera, feeling for all the world like a tabloid journalist. Finally, the door opened and out of the dim light shambled an almost translucent figure in a shabby blue dressing gown. The reporter started to tell her the reason for our visit, and the woman immediately started to close the door. I instantly pressed the shutter release and quickly fired off a couple of shots. Within less than a second the door was shut, and we knew that it was pointless to stay. As we walked out, we spoke to another neighbour. 'Forget it,' she told us. 'It's in the past. I don't have time to think about this now, I'm on my way to an aerobics class.'

After a brief flicker of interest in several newspapers, the world did largely forget Erna Wallisch. The Poles started to make some efforts to get her extradited, but it was all too little and too late. On 16 February 2008, four months after my visit, Wallisch died in a hospital bed. Like so many thousands of Nazi criminals before her, she had been able to leap free over the final fence.

Notes

Abbreviations
ASMA Archives of Santa Maria dell'Anima, Rome, Italy
GWDN Guy Walters's Document Number / Name
LHC Liddell Hart Centre for Military Archives, King's College, London, UK
NARA National Archives and Records Administration, College Park, MD, USA
UKNA National Archives, Kew, London, UK

Chapter One: 'The air became cleaner'
1   Richard Breitman, Norman J. W. Goda, Timothy Naftali, Robert
     Wolfe, *US Intelligence and the Nazis* (Cambridge University Press,
     2005), p. 266. Of course, Höttl's qualities also make him an
     unreliable witness and his statements must be treated with caution.
2   UKNA, WO 208/4478; GWDN: 09820
3   Breitman et al., *US Intelligence and the Nazis*, pp. 266–7
4   NARA, Wilhelm Höttl Name file, RG 263, Stack 230, Row C,
     Compartment 64, Shelf 04, Box 25; GWDN: 09620
5   Neal H. Petersen (ed.), *From Hitler's Doorstep: The Wartime
     Intelligence Reports of Allen Dulles, 1942–1945* (Pennsylvania
     State University Press, 1996), Document 5-107, quoted in Breitman
     et al., *US Intelligence and the Nazis*, p. 269
6   Breitman et al., *US Intelligence and the Nazis,* p. 269

7   NARA, Adolf Eichmann Name file, RG 263, Boxes 14–15, Directorate of Operations file – vol. 1, Document 6 (http://www.gwu.edu/~nsarchiv/NSAEBB/NSAEBB150/box14_do_file_vol1/doc06.pdf); GWDN: Hunted/Eichmann/doc06-1.pdf

8   David Cesarani, *Eichmann: His Life and Crimes* (London: William Heinemann, 2004), p. 163

9   Breitman et al., *US Intelligence and the Nazis*, p. 267

10 Höttl testimony to the Court of the First Instance, Bad Aussee, 19–21 June 1961, http://www.nizkor.org/ftp.cgi/people/e/eich-mann.adolf/transcripts/Testimony-Abroad/ftp.py?people/e/eichmann.adolf/transcripts/Testimony-Abroad//Wilhelm_Hoettl-07

11 Ibid.

12 For one example, see Hansi Brand's recollections in Cesarani, *Eichmann*, p. 187

13 NARA, Eichmann Name file, Document 6

14 Höttl interview with Ladislas Farago, *Aftermath* (New York: Simon & Schuster, 1974), p. 252

15 Cesarani, *Eichmann*, p. 201

16 *The People* (London, UK), 7 May 1961, pp. 2–4, 'How I Escaped by Eichmann'; GWDN: AE1. This four-week newspaper serialization of Eichmann's memoirs seems to be a forgotten source for Eichmann scholars. Its boastful and fanatical tone helps give the lie to Hannah Arendt's thesis that Eichmann was a dull cog in the Holocaust machine. In fact, Eichmann was very far from banal. For the best refutation of Arendt, see Cesarani, *Eichmann*, p. 201.

17 The accounts of Eichmann and his wife vary. She claims that Dieter had fallen into the lake, whereas Eichmann saw the measure as purely preventative. See *The People*, 'How I Escaped by Eichmann', and Cesarani, *Eichmann*, p. 201

18 Cesarani, *Eichmann*, p. 201

19 NARA, Eichmann Name file, Document 6, p. 3

20 The inn still exists and can be found at N 47.673999, E 13.745828 and http://www.blaa-alm.co.at/

21 N 47.692548, E 13.715572

22 Cesarani in *Eichmann* writes that Burger was the deputy commandant of Theresienstadt. However, he was in fact the commandant. See Karla Müller-Tupath, *Verschollen in Deutschland* (Hamburg: Konkret Literatur Verlag, 1994), p. 34. Anton Burger's career is digested at

http://forum.axishistory.com/viewtopic.php?f=38&t=22454.
Of the many websites and forums dedicated to the Third Reich,
this is the most reliable, and is not populated by the normal quota
of neo-Nazis, Revisionists and other nutcases. Whatever his precise
role, Burger was clearly no saint.

23   Cesarani, *Eichmann*, p. 202

24   Ibid., p. 202. According to Eichmann's account in *The People*, he
      travelled alone. It is unclear what identity Jänisch adopted.

25   *The People*, 'How I Escaped by Eichmann'

26   Louis L. Snyder, *Encyclopedia of the Third Reich* (London: Robert
      Hale, 1995), p. 286

27   Walter Schellenberg, *The Schellenberg Memoirs* (London: André
      Deutsch, 1956), p. 373

28   *The Last Days of Ernst Kaltenbrunner* (CIA Library's Center for
      the Study of Intelligence, 2007)
      (https://www.cia.gov/library/center-for-the-study-of-
      intelligence/kent-csi/vol4no2/html/v04i2a07p_0001.htm). Although
      the CIA coyly does not cite the author of this account, it is in fact
      by Robert E. Matteson. See http://www.mnhs.org/library/
      findaids/00379.html. Matteson's account states that von Westarp
      was just 22, although she was actually 24. See
      http://worldroots.com/foundation/royal/georg1anhaltdesc1390-
      6.htm and UKNA, WO 204/4478.

29   UKNA, WO 204/4478; GWDN: 09277

30   Arthur Scheidler RuSHA file at NARA, College Park, Maryland;
      UKNA, WO 208/4478. The latter comprises Scheidler's interroga-
      tion report in which he unsurprisingly omits his service at
      Sachsenburg. GWDN: 9275–9287

31   *The Last Days of Ernst Kaltenbrunner*

32   Ibid.

33   NARA, Höttl Name file, RG 263, Stack 230, Row C,
      Compartment 64, Shelf 04, Box 23; GWDN: 9342

34   Author interview with Hans Pucher, 25 June 2008, 148
      Fischendorf, Altaussee, Austria

35   Simon Wiesenthal, *The Murderers Among Us* (London: William
      Heinemann, 1967), p. 91; Ian Sayer and Douglas Botting, *Nazi
      Gold* (Edinburgh: Mainstream Publishing, 1998), p. 37. There
      have been numerous books about Nazi treasure, and this book is

not the place to explore the welter of crackpot conspiracy theories concerning its movements and present whereabouts.

36   Author interview with Hans Pucher

37   Christian Topf, *Auf den Spuren der Partisanen* (Grunbach: Buchverlag Franz Steinmassl, 2006), pp. 147–52. This is a great little book that features walks around the Salzkammergut that retrace the footsteps of both Austrian partisans and Nazis alike.

38   Wiesenthal, *The Murderers Among Us*, p. 90

39   *The Last Days of Ernst Kaltenbrunner*

40   Ibid.; Matteson received the Silver Star for his actions. For his post-war career and archive, visit http://www.mnhs.org/library/findaids/00379.html

41   Gerald L. Posner and John Ware, *Mengele: The Complete Story* (New York: Cooper Square Press, 2000), p. 66

42   Giles MacDonogh, *After the Reich* (London: John Murray, 2007), p. 339

43   *In the Matter of Josef Mengele: A Report to the Attorney General of the United States* (US Department of Justice, October 1992), p. 2; GWDN: crm12.pdf. The report can be downloaded from http://www.jewishvirtuallibrary.org/jsource/Holocaust/mengeleosi.html

44   UKNA, WO 309/1697; GWDN: 7193. Holocaust deniers would do well to study this file and WO 309/1698. Both contain exhaustive and horrifying testimonies of those who had survived the camps.

45   Gerald Astor, *The Last Nazi* (New York: Donald I. Fine, 1985), p. 59. Astor quotes Wachsberger's testimony from Robert Katz, *Black Sabbath* (London: Macmillan, 1969).

46   Robert J. Lifton, *The Nazi Doctors: Medical Killing and the Psychology of Genocide* (Basic Books, 1986); http://www.mazal.org/Lifton/LiftonT372.htm

47   Posner and Ware, *Mengele*, p. 27

48   UKNA, WO 309/1698; GWDN: 7229. Mengele was not the chief doctor at Auschwitz.

49   Wiener Library 978/2; GWDN: 09903

50   Posner and Ware, *Mengele*, p. 37

51   *New York Times*, 21 July 1985, p. 22, 'What Made This Man? Mengele' by Robert J. Lifton. See also Nyiszli's account of his time

in Auschwitz: *Auschwitz: A Doctor's Eyewitness Account* (New York: Arcade Publishing, 1993).

52   The town is today called Zatec and lies in the Czech Republic, N 50.317408, E 13.537903

53   Posner and Ware, *Mengele*, p. 57

54   There is some speculation that Mengele may have been in many places during this period, including Berlin, Ravensbrück and Mauthausen. See Sven Keller, *Günzburg und der Fall Josef Mengele* (Munich: R. Oldenbourg Verlag, 2003), p. 42

55   Poser and Ware, *Mengele*, p. 60; *In the Matter of Josef Mengele*, p. 26

56   Posner and Ware, *Mengele*, p. 60

57   *In the Matter of Josef Mengele*, p. 26

58   Posner and Ware, *Mengele*, p. 61

59   *In the Matter of Josef Mengele*, p. 28

60   Quoted on p. 62 of Posner and Ware, *Mengele*, from Mengele's autobiography in the possession of the Mengele family.

61   *In the Matter of Josef Mengele*, p. 30

62   Gitta Sereny, *Into that Darkness* (London: Pimlico, 1995), p. 264. Details of Stangl's post-war years are sketchy. Sereny found that Stangl was unwilling to discuss them, and most of what we know is learned from Stangl's wife who was also interviewed by Sereny.

63   Stangl is remembered as such by Stanislaw Szmajzner in *Hell in Sobibor: The Tragedy of a Jewish Adolescent* (Brazil: Edicion Bloch, 1968), which is quoted by Sereny in *Into that Darkness*, p. 125.

64   Sereny, *Into that Darkness*, p. 262

65   The figure for the number of those slaughtered at Treblinka has varied enormously from 1,400,000 to a minimum of 700,000. The most recent scholarship estimates some 780,863. See Jacek Andrzej Młynarczyk, 'Treblinka – ein Todeslager der "Aktion Reinhard"', in Bogdan Musial (ed.), *'Aktion Reinhard' – Die Vernichtung der Juden im Generalgouvernement*, (Osnabrück: Fibre Verlag, 2004), pp. 257–81. Stangl was also responsible for the deaths of some 100,000 in Sobibor.

66   N 52.626389, E 22.046944

67   Michael Burleigh, *The Third Reich* (London: Pan, 2001), pp. 384–5

68   http://www.britannica.com/EBchecked/topic/715711/Philipp-
      Bouhler
69   Burleigh, *The Third Reich*, p. 404; Schloss Hartheim is at
      N 48.281111, E 14.113889
70   Sereny, *Into that Darkness*, p. 51
71   Burleigh, *The Third Reich*, p. 404
72   Sereny, *Into that Darkness*, p. 55
73   Ibid., p. 58
74   Stangl's word, not the author's. Ibid., p. 201
75   Ibid., p. 201
76   Yankel Wiernik, *A Year in Treblinka* (New York: American
      Representation of the General Jewish Workers Union of Poland,
      1945), http://www.zchor.org/treblink/wiernik.htm#chapter2.
      Wiernik was to testify in the Eichmann trial in Israel in 1961.
77   Martin Gilbert, *The Holocaust* (London: Fontana Press, 1987),
      p. 399
78   Ibid., p. 458
79   Sereny, *Into that Darkness*, p. 202
80   Ibid., p. 265
81   N 47.765780, E 13.079297
82   Sereny, *Into that Darkness*, p. 265. It is hard to summon up any
      sympathy for Stangl's condition.
83   See, for example, the interrogation report of Albert Förster,
      Gauleiter of Danzig, UKNA, WO 208/5214; GWDN: 5996
84   Snyder, *Encyclopedia of the Third Reich*, p. 36
85   Schellenberg, *The Schellenberg Memoirs*, p. 359
86   Ibid., p. 359
87   Robert S. Wistrich, *Who's Who in Nazi Germany* (Routledge,
      2001), p. 18
88   Ibid., p. 19
89   Albert Speer, *Inside the Third Reich* (London: Phoenix, 1995),
      p. 138
90   Ibid., pp. 137-8
91   NARA, Otto Skorzeny Name file, RG 263, Stack 230, Row 86,
      Compartment 24, Shelf 04, Box 121; GWDN: 8772-8777
92   Ibid.
93   Schellenberg, *The Schellenberg Memoirs*, p. 360
94   NARA, Heinz Felfe Name file, RG 263; GWDN: 9258. For an

excellent demolition of claims of Bormann's supposed Soviet allegiance, see Hugh Trevor-Roper, *The Last Days of Hitler* (London: Papermac, 1995), pp. xi–xv. Trevor-Roper states that Gehlen thought Bormann was the source for the Lucy ring and not the *Rote Kapelle*.

95   See, for example, the fanciful *Untouchable: Who Protected Bormann and Gestapo Müller after 1945?* by Pierre de Villemarest (Slough, UK: Aquilion, 2005) and *Hitler's Traitor* by Louis Kilzer (California: Presidio Press, 2000).

96   NARA, Skorzeny Name file, Box 121; GWDN: 8772–8777

97   It still exists: http://www.maison-rouge.com/

98   Paul Manning, *Martin Bormann: Nazi in Exile* (New Jersey: Lyle Stuart, 1981), p. 27. An online facsimile version can be downloaded from http://www.animalfarm.org/mb/mb.shtml. There are many highly speculative accounts of what happened in Strasbourg that day, all of which feature numerous inaccuracies. Manning claims to have had access to the minutes of the meeting, although his version is highly coloured and also inaccurate. See also Martin A. Lee, *The Beast Reawakens* (London: Warner Books, 1997), p. 21; Simon Wiesenthal, *Justice Not Vengeance* (London: Weidenfeld & Nicolson, 1989), p. 50; William F. Wertz Jr, *The Nazi Rat-Lines, Time to Rid America of the 'Dulles Complex'* (www.larouchepub.com/eiw/public/2005/2005_30-39/2005_30-39/2005-31/ pdf/54-71_31_ratline.pdf). As with almost everything to do with Bormann, all must be treated with caution and much salt.

99   Manning, *Martin Bormann*, p. 27

100   Simon Wiesenthal, *The Murderers Among Us* (London: William Heinemann, 1967), p. 86

101   http://www.mi6.gov.uk/output/mis-in-wwii.html

102   UKNA, FO 371/49548, Documents 82–83; GWDN: 5199-5120

103   NARA, RG 263, Stack 2000, Compartment 8, Entry ZZ-20, Box 16; GWDN: _0055

104   UKNA, WO 208/4478; GWDN: 9287

105   *New York Times*, 22 May 1946, p. 4; GWDN: 88362184

106   Joachim Fest, *Inside Hitler's Bunker* (London: Pan, 2005), p. 83

107   Fest states that Hitler 'remained calm' and that two telegrams were sent by Göring; Hugh Trevor-Roper in *The Last Days of Hitler*,

p. 124, only mentions a single telegram, but suggests that Hitler
sent a reply forbidding any action.

108   Cross-examination of Albert Speer at the IMT at Nuremberg,
which can be found at
http://www.law.umkc.edu/faculty/projects/ftrials/nuremberg/Speer.
html; Speer spoke of only one telegram, the one sent from Göring
to Ribbentrop.

109   Trevor-Roper, *The Last Days of Hitler*, p. 124

110   Loringhoven, *In the Bunker with Hitler*, p. 158

111   Hugh Trevor-Roper (ed.), *The Bormann Letters* (London:
Weidenfeld & Nicolson, 1954), p. 198

112   *New York Times*, 22 July 1947, p. 11, 'Ex-Army Aide Tells of
Finding Frau Bormann Dying of Cancer'; GWDN: 87549370

113   Trevor-Roper, *The Last Days of Hitler*, p. 190

114   Fest, *Inside Hitler's Bunker*, p. 148

115   Trevor-Roper, *The Last Days of Hitler*, p. 192

116   Testimony of Erich Kempka taken at Berchtesgaden on 20 June
1945; see p. 579 of http://www.nizkor.org/ftp.cgi/imt/nca/
nca-06/nca-06-3735-ps

117   Ibid.

118   Trevor-Roper, *The Last Days of Hitler*, p. 193; and see WO
208/4428 for the ACABRIT files on Bormann's death.

119   *New York Times*, 4 May 1945, p. 1, 'Himmler Reported Hiding';
GWDN: 88220815

120   *Los Angeles Times*, 12 June 1945, p. 1, 'Hitler Deputy Held,
Prague Reports'; GWDN: 412465711

121   *New York Times*, 13 June 1945, p. 2

122   Farago, *Aftermath*, p. 161

123   *Washington Post*, 7 August 1945, p. 5, 'Belief Cited Deputy of
Hitler Still Alive'; GWDN: 214510752

124   UKNA, WO 311/584; GWDN: 9288

125   *New York Times*, 2 September 1945, p. 16, 'Bormann Not Held By
British'; GWDN: 94859761

126   *Chicago Daily Tribune*, 8 September 1945, p. 1, 'Hunt Yacht;
Hitler May Be Aboard'; GWDN: 478326972; *Los Angeles Times*,
8 September 1945, p. 8, 'Luxury Yacht Hunted in New Hitler
Rumor'; GWDN: 412644231

127   *New York Times*, 1 January 1946, p. 18, 'Bormann Report

Denied'; GWDN: 93008320; *Los Angeles Times*, 2 January 1946, p. 1, 'Nazi Bormann Believed Taken'; GWDN: 414799421

128 Schellenberg, *The Schellenberg Memoirs*, p. 360

129 NARA, *Interagency Working Group Analysis of the Name file of Heinrich Müller* by Naftali, Goda, Breitman and Wolfe (http://www.archives.gov/iwg/declassified-records/rg-263-cia-records/rg-263-mueller.html)

130 Schellenberg, *The Schellenberg Memoirs*, p. 360

131 *Interagency Working Group Analysis of the Name file of Heinrich Müller*

132 Ibid.

133 Ibid.

134 Junge, *Until the Final Hour*, p. 171

135 *Interagency Working Group Analysis of the Name file of Heinrich Müller*, and see also Villemarest, *Untouchable*, for theories that Müller worked for Eastern Bloc intelligence.

136 Serge Klarsfeld, *The Children of Izieu: A Human Tragedy* (New York: Harry N. Abrams, 1984), pp. 94–5

137 Ibid., pp. 35–6

138 Tom Bower, *Klaus Barbie: The Butcher of Lyons* (New York: Pantheon, 1984), p. 57; *Klaus Barbie and the United States Government, A Report to the Attorney General of the United States*, submitted by Allan A. Ryan Jr, August 1983; GWDN: crm15. It is unclear precisely when Barbie joined the Gestapo in Lyon.

139 Bower, *Klaus Barbie*, p. 61

140 Ibid., p. 63

141 Interview with Simone Lagrange in *Hotel Terminus* (1988) written and directed by Marcel Ophüls. This film, which is 4½ hours long, deservedly won the Academy Award for Best Documentary Feature in 1989.

142 *New York Times*, 23 May 1987, 'Torture Recounted at the Barbie Trial'

143 Magnus Linklater, Isabel Hilton, Neal Ascherson, *The Nazi Legacy: Klaus Barbie and the International Fascist Connection* (New York: Holt, Rinehart and Winston, 1984), pp. 128–9

144 Ibid., p. 129

145 Ibid., p. 130

146   Michèle and Jean-Paul Cointet (eds), *Dictionnaire historique de la France sous L'Occupation* (Paris: Tallandier, 2000), p. 506

147   Linklater et al., *The Nazi Legacy*, p. 87

148   Ibid., p. 88

149   Bower, *Klaus Barbie*, p. 73

150   Linklater et al., *The Nazi Legacy*, p. 91

151   Ibid., p. 92

152   In *Hotel Terminus*, Dr Dugoujon suggests that it was Aubry who broke.

153   Linklater et al., *The Nazi Legacy*, p. 130; Bower, *Klaus Barbie*, p. 106

154   Bower, *Klaus Barbie*, p. 106

155   Ibid., p. 110

156   Ibid., p. 111; Linklater et al. state that Barbie claimed that he was a French displaced person, *The Nazi Legacy*, p. 132

157   The suggestion is made in *Hotel Terminus*.

158   Raymond Aubrac interviewed in *Hotel Terminus*, at 13' approximately.

159   *New York Times*, 21 July 1985, section 6, p. 16, 'What Made This Man?' by Robert Jay Lifton

Chapter Two: 'To the uttermost ends of the earth'

1   Tom Bower, *Blind Eye to Murder* (London: Warner Books, 1997), p. 51

2   James Owen, *Nuremberg: Evil on Trial* (London: Headline Review, 2006), p. 2

3   Minutes of the Tripartite Dinner Meeting held at the Soviet Embassy in Tehran on 29 November 1943 are at http://images.library.wisc.edu/FRUS/EFacs/1943CairoTehran/reference/frus.frus1943cairotehran.i0012.pdf

4   Bower, *Blind Eye to Murder*, p. 50

5   Ibid., pp. 17–19; Owen, *Nuremberg*, pp. 1–2

6   http://www.un.org/aboutun/history.htm

7   Bower, *Blind Eye to Murder*, p. 40; Charles Ashman and Robert J. Wagman, *The Nazi Hunters* (New York: Warner Books, 1988), pp. 52–3

8   Ashman and Wagman, *The Nazi Hunters*, pp. 52–3

9   Bower, *Blind Eye to Murder*, pp. 41–2

10   UKNA, TS 26/66, United Nations War Crimes Commission Files:

General Correspondence, 1944–6; GWDN: 00011

11   Bower, *Blind Eye to Murder*, p. 48
12   UKNA, TS 26/66; GWDN: 09998
13   Bower, *Blind Eye to Murder*, p. 60
14   UKNA, TS 26/67; GWDN: 00019
15   UKNA, TS 26/67, 15th meeting of the UNWCC held on 25/4/44
16   UKNA, TS 26/67, 25th meeting of the UNWCC held on 25/7/44;
     GWDN: 00024-26
17   UKNA, TS 26/67, 26th meeting of the UNWCC held on 8/8/44;
     GWDN: 00027-28
18   Arieh J. Kochavi, *Prelude to Nuremberg* (University of North
     Carolina Press, 1998), p. 107
19   UKNA, TS 26/67, 28th meeting of the UNWCC held on 22/8/44
20   Bower, *Blind Eye to Murder*, p. 73
21   UKNA, TS 26/67, 33rd meeting of the UNWCC held on 26/9/44;
     GWDN: 00030
22   UKNA, TS 26/67, 38th meeting of the UNWCC held on 7/11/44
23   UKNA, TS 26/67, 45th meeting of the UNWCC held on 24/1/45
24   UKNA, TS 26/67, 40th meeting of the UNWCC held on 22/11/44
25   Bower, *Klaus Barbie*, p. 123
26   UKNA, TS 26/67, 44th meeting of the UNWCC held on 17/1/45
27   UKNA, TS 26/67, 37th meeting of the UNWCC held on 31/10/44
28   Gilbert, *The Holocaust*, p. 757
29   Bower, *Blind Eye to Murder*, p. 75
30   UKNA, TS 26/67, 47th meeting of the UNWCC held on 7/2/45;
     GWDN: 00034
31   UKNA, FO 371/46765; GWDN: 6208
32   UKNA, FO 371/46765; GWDN: 6209
33   UKNA, FO 371/46765; GWDN: 6218–6219
34   UKNA, FO 371/46765; GWDN: 6240–6241
35   Maynard M. Cohen, *A Stand Against Tyranny: Norway's
     Physicians and the Nazis* (Wayne State University Press, 2000), p.
     273
36   UKNA, WO 219/1559; GWDN: 03783
37   UKNA, WO 219/1559; GWDN: 03781
38   UKNA, WO 219/1559; GWDN: 03782
39   UKNA, WO 219/1559; GWDN: 03776–03777
40   UKNA, WO 219/1559; GWDN: 03784–03788

41 UKNA, WO 309/1895, Document 19; GWDN: 6180
42 Bower, *Blind Eye to Murder*, p. 119
43 UKNA, TS 26/68, 81st meeting of the UNWCC held on 16/10/45
44 UKNA, TS 26/67, 80th meeting of the UNWCC held on 3/10/45;
    GWDN: 00071
45 UKNA, WO 309/1895, Document 19; GWDN: 6180
46 Ibid.
47 UKNA, TS 26/68, 81st meeting of the UNWCC held on 16/10/45
48 Bower, *Blind Eye to Murder*, p. 120
49 Ibid.
50 UKNA, TS 26/69; GWDN: 0102
51 UKNA, FO 944/733, Document 34B; GWDN: 02239. $30,000 is
    worth approximately $500,000 in 2007.
52 UKNA, TS 26/67, 80th meeting of the UNWCC held on 3/10/45;
    GWDN: 00071
53 UKNA, FO 945/343, Document 2A; GWDN: 02266–02267
54 UKNA, TS 26/69; GWDN: 0099
55 UKNA, WO 309/1895, Document 19; GWDN: 6182
56 Ibid.
57 UKNA, FO 944/965
58 UKNA, WO 309/1895; GWDN: 06165
59 Ibid.; GWDN: 06174
60 Ibid.; GWDN: 06172
61 Ibid.; GWDN: 06202
62 Ibid.; GWDN: 06161
63 Gerald Draper in *The Liberation of the Nazi Concentration Camps
    1945* (Washington, DC: United States Holocaust Memorial
    Council, 1987), edited by Brewster Chamberlain and Marcia
    Feldman, p. 113; GWDN: 01914
64 Gilbert, *The Holocaust*, p. 795
65 Tom Pocock, *The Dawn Came up like Thunder* (Collins, 1983)
66 Alan Moorehead, *Eclipse* (Harper & Row, 1968), p. 266; James
    Owen and Guy Walters (eds), *The Voice of War* (Viking, 2004), p.
    564
67 UKNA, WO 309/1418; GWDN: 00199
68 UKNA, WO 309/1418; GWDN: 00200–00209
69 UKNA, WO 309/1418; GWDN: 00213
70 Guttman's account can be found in Chapter One.

71   UKNA, WO 309/1418; GWDN: 00211
72   UKNA, WO 309/1418; GWDN: 00219–00220
73   UKNA, WO 311/695; GWDN: 1135–1136
74   UKNA, WO 309/1464; GWDN: 7138–7142. It is not known what happened to Schneider.
75   UKNA, WO 309/1470; GWDN: 7165
76   UKNA, WO 309/1470; GWDN: 7177
77   UKNA, WO 309/1470; GWDN: 7178
78   UKNA, WO 309/1470; GWDN: 7165–7169
79   UKNA, WO 309/1470; GWDN: 7161
80   UKNA, WO 309/1470; GWDN: 7160
81   UKNA, WO 309/1470; GWDN: 7164
82   UKNA, WO 309/1470; GWDN: 7159
83   UKNA, WO 309/1664; GWDN: 2329
84   UKNA, WO 309/1664; GWDN: 2328
85   UKNA, WO 309/1664; GWDN: 2327
86   UKNA, WO 309/1664; GWDN: 2322
87   UKNA, WO 309/2034; GWDN: 2339–2341
88   UKNA, WO 311/625; GWDN: 1143–1145
89   UKNA, WO 311/625; GWDN: 1151
90   UKNA, WO 311/625; GWDN: 1150
91   Author interview with Ian Neilson, 29 April 2009, Marlborough, Wiltshire, UK
92   UKNA, WO 311/625; GWDN: 1156–1160
93   UKNA, WO 311/625; GWDN: 1155
94   UKNA, WO 311/695; GWDN: 1135–1136
95   *Counter Intelligence Corps History and Mission in World War II* (Counter Intelligence Corps School, Fort Holabird, Maryland), downloaded from http://www.fas.org/irp/agency/army/cic.pdf
96   *Robert Jan Verbelen and the United States Government: A Report to the Assistant Attorney General, Criminal Division, US Department of Justice* by Neal M. Sher et al. of the Office of Special Investigations, 16 June 1988, p. 12; GWDN: crm22.pdf
97   *Counter Intelligence Corps History and Mission in World War II*
98   Author interview with John Hodge, 5 April 2007, Chirton, Wiltshire, UK
99   Author interview with Ben Ferencz, 8 May 2007, conducted over the telephone

100   Author interview with Ben Ferencz

101   Author interview with John Hodge

102   Author interview with Brian Bone, 29 March 2007, Poole, Dorset, UK

103   Posner and Ware, *Mengele*, p. 63. Blood group tattooing was also a wartime practice – Mengele joined the SS before the war. See *In the Matter of Josef Mengele*, p. 43

104   Posner and Ware, *Mengele*, p. 62

105   *In the Matter of Josef Mengele*, p. 34. There is some speculation concerning whether Mengele was released under his real name (see Posner and Ware, *Mengele*, p. 62) although the OSI report reckons this is unlikely (see *In the Matter of Josef Mengele*, p. 47). The author sides with the latter – Mengele was not a reckless man.

106   Posner and Ware, *Mengele*, p. 63

107   *In the Matter of Josef Mengele*, pp. 40–1

108   UKNA, WO 311/10; MI14 was the intelligence section of the British War Office that dealt with German and German-occupied territory. See http://www.mi6.gov.uk/output/mis-in-wwii.html

109   UKNA, TS 26/72; GWDN: 0156

110   UKNA, WO 309/2239; GWDN: Mengele/WO 309/2239/1.pdf

111   UKNA, WO 309/2242; GWDN: 05921

112   Ibid.; GWDN: 5915 & 5918. One of Mengele's fellow 'medics' at Auschwitz was a Victor Capesius.

113   Keller, *Günzburg und der Fall Josef Mengele*, p. 46; Posner and Ware, *Mengele*, p. 64; *In the Matter of Josef Mengele*, p. 62. The last two sources state that Mengele's papers were in the name 'Ulmann', but Keller states that the modification took place in all likelihood at Helmbrechts.

114   Posner and Ware, *Mengele*, p. 65; *In the Matter of Josef Mengele*, pp. 66–7. The bicycle has never been found, and it was searched for even in 1985. See Posner and Ware, *Mengele*, p. 65 n.

115   Ibid., p. 65

116   Ibid., p. 66

117   *In the Matter of Josef Mengele*, p. 64

118   Posner and Ware, *Mengele*, p. 66

119   Keller, *Günzburg und der Fall Josef Mengele*, p. 47

120   Posner and Ware, *Mengele*, p. 67

121   Ibid.

122   Ibid., p. 68

123   Ibid., p. 71

124   Ibid., p. 73

125   *The People*, pp. 2–4, 'How I Escaped by Eichmann'; GWDN: AE1

126   Ibid.

127   Ibid., pp. 2–3; GWDN: AE1-AE2

128   Ibid., p. 3; GWDN: AE2. Cesarani in *Eichmann* states that
      Eichmann was picked up near Ulm along with Jänisch. Cesarani's
      source is another of Eichmann's memoirs, *Ich, Adolf Eichmann.
      Ein Historischer Zeugenbericht*, ed. Dr Rudolf Aschenauer
      (Germany: Augsburg, 1980).

129   Cesarani, *Eichmann*, pp. 202–3

130   *The People*, p. 3, 'How I Escaped by Eichmann'; GWDN: AE2

131   Ibid., p. 4; GWDN: AE3

132   Ibid.

133   Ibid.

134   Cesarani, *Eichmann*, p. 203

135   Höttl's post-war movements are examined in Chapters Five to
      Seven.

136   The website of the Yale Law School features the entire text of the
      International Military Tribunal at Nuremberg. The court's
      proceedings on 12 December 1945 can be found at
      http://avalon.law.yale.edu/imt/12-14-45.asp

137   Owen, *Nuremberg*, pp. 81–2; Dieter Wisliceny's affidavit to the
      International Military Tribunal can be found at
      http://www.ess.uwe.ac.uk/genocide/Wisliceny.htm

138   Owen, *Nuremberg*, p. 81

139   http://www.ess.uwe.ac.uk/genocide/Wisliceny.htm

140   Ibid.

141   Cesarani, *Eichmann*, p. 203

142   The nature of this network will be examined in Chapter Four.

143   *The People*, p. 4, 'How I Escaped by Eichmann'; GWDN: AE3

144   Ibid.

145   UKNA, WO 204/12394; GWDN: 09328

146   UKNA, WO 204/12394; GWDN: 09332

147   *The People*, p. 4, 'How I Escaped by Eichmann'; GWDN: AE3

148   Cesarani, *Eichmann*, p. 204

149   *The People* (London, UK), 14 May 1961, p. 2, 'Four Women Were

the Key to My Get-Away'; GWDN: AE4. At this point in their serialization, *The People* inserted the following: 'How easily the slate is wiped clean in this man's fiendish mind . . . a few months' "communion with nature" and the deaths of six million souls are forgotten.'

150   Ibid.
151   Owen, *Nuremberg*, p. 201
152   Ibid., p. 203
153   Rudolf Höss, *Commandant of Auschwitz* (London: Phoenix Press, 2000), pp. 184–5. The use of Zyklon B was pioneered by one of Höss's deputies and approved by Eichmann.
154   UKNA, FO 1078/54; GWDN: 6508–6514
155   CIC report downloaded from The National Security Archive, 'Uncovering the Architect of the Holocaust: The CIA Names File on Adolf Eichmann', edited by Tamara Feinstein. http://www.gwu.edu/~nsarchiv/NSAEBB/NSAEBB150/box14_do_file_vol1/doc14.pdf
156   Ibid., http://www.gwu.edu/~nsarchiv/NSAEBB/NSAEBB150/box14_do_file_vol1/doc12.pdf
157   NARA, RG 226, Stack 250, Row 64, Compartment 31, Shelf 01, Box 482; GWDN: 0059
158   'Uncovering the Architect of the Holocaust: The CIA Names File on Adolf Eichmann', http://www.gwu.edu/~nsarchiv/NSAEBB/NSAEBB150/box14_do_file_vol1/doc14.pdf
159   Ibid.; http://www.gwu.edu/~nsarchiv/NSAEBB/NSAEBB150/box14_do_file_vol1/doc06.pdf
160   Archives of the UNWCC, United Nations Archives, 304 East 45th Street, New York City
161   UKNA, WO 309/2199; GWDN: 2354

Chapter Three: 'The Man Who Never Forgets'

1   See Simon Wiesenthal, *Ich Jagte Eichmann* (Bertelsmann, 1961), pp. 35–7, for Wiesenthal's interest in the relationship between Eichmann and the Grand Mufti. It seems likely that the informant was Wiesenthal, but this is hard to establish.

NOTES TO PP. 74–81

2   Alan Levy, *Nazi Hunter: The Wiesenthal File* (London: Robinson, 2002), p. 4

3   Wiesenthal, *The Murderers Among Us*, p. 99; Wiesenthal, *Ich Jagte Eichmann*, p. 26

4   Wiesenthal, *The Murderers Among Us*, p. 99; a facsimile of the form can be found in Wiesenthal, *Ich Jagte Eichmann*, p. 29

5   Cesarani, *Eichmann*, pp. 48–9

6   Wiesenthal, *The Murderers Among Us*, p. 100

7   Wiesenthal, *Ich Jagte Eichmann*, pp. 32–33

8   Wiesenthal, *The Murderers Among Us*, p. 101

9   Wiesenthal, *Justice Not Vengeance*, p. 68

10   Wiesenthal, *The Murderers Among Us*, p. 113

11   Wiesenthal, *Justice Not Vengeance*, p. 68; Wiesenthal, *The Murderers Among Us*, p. 101

12   Ibid. In both accounts Wiesenthal incorrectly states that Burger was a Hauptsturmführer.

13   Ibid.; Ibid.

14   Ibid.; Ibid.

15   Wiesenthal, *The Murderers Among Us*, p. 102

16   Wiesenthal, *Justice Not Vengeance*, p. 69

17   Wiesenthal, *Ich Jagte Eichmann*, p. 37. Wiesenthal states that he started with the CIC in October 1945.

18   http://www.gwu.edu/~nsarchiv/NSAEBB/NSAEBB150/box14_do_file_vol1/doc12.pdf

19   Wiesenthal, *Ich Jagte Eichmann*, p. 33; Wiesenthal, *The Murderers Among Us*, p. 101

20   http://www.gwu.edu/~nsarchiv/NSAEBB/NSAEBB150/box14_do_file_vol1/doc17.pdf

21   Tuviah Friedman, *Isser Harel Attacks Simon Wiesenthal* (Museum of Tolerance Online, Special Collections), downloaded from http://motlc.specialcol.wiesenthal.com/instdoc/d09c07/index.html; GWDN: iss3.gif

22   Wiesenthal, *Justice Not Vengeance*, p. 21

23   Hella Pick, *Simon Wiesenthal: A Life in Search of Justice* (London: Weidenfeld & Nicolson, 1996), p. 53

24   N 49.063744, E 25.391464

25   Levy, *Nazi Hunter*, p. 17

26   Pick, *Simon Wiesenthal*, pp. 29–30

27   Ibid., p. 31
28   Levy, *Nazi Hunter*, p. 17
29   Pick, *Simon Wiesenthal*, p. 41
30   Levy states this event happened in 1918, when, he claims,
      Wiesenthal was 10. Wiesenthal was in fact 9 for all but half-an-
      hour of 1918. Pick states the event occurred in 1920, as does
      Wechsberg in his introduction to Wiesenthal's *The Murderers
      Among Us*, although Wechsberg incorrectly states that Wiesenthal
      was 12. Lingens makes the same mistake in Wiesenthal's *Justice
      Not Vengeance*, but also places the event in 1920. Petliura's forces
      occupied the region southeast of Lviv in the summer of 1920, so it
      is likely that the event happened then.
31   Pick, *Simon Wiesenthal*, p. 41. Wechsberg and Levy state the
      request was for 300 litres.
32   Levy, *Nazi Hunter*, p. 19; Wiesenthal, *Justice Not Vengeance*,
      p. 28. Pick states that Wiesenthal was fetching flour. See Pick,
      Simon Wiesenthal, p. 41.
33   Pick, *Simon Wiesenthal*, p. 41. This is a curious statement for
      Wiesenthal to have made. Unless he had a keloid scar, which is
      form of tumour, his scar tissue would not have grown.
34   Ibid. This author doubts very much whether the story is true.
      Firstly, it seems unlikely that a mother would risk her child in such
      a way. Secondly, why the urgent need for yeast? It is not an
      essential bread-making ingredient, as most Jews know. Thirdly,
      unless the street was very broad, how could the horseman have
      appeared without warning as Wiesenthal made his way across?
      Fourthly, would not Wiesenthal have waited and listened out for
      sounds such as the fall of horses' hoofs before he crossed the road?
      Fifthly, when approached by the horseman, why did Wiesenthal
      not run? In Pick, *Simon Wiesenthal*, p. 41, Wiesenthal says that he
      obligingly stood still 'on the pavement' while the horseman rode
      straight at him and attacked his front. Sixthly, if Wiesenthal was
      still on the pavement, why did he not go back inside? Seventhly, a
      stab to the upper thigh is an unlikely wound for an 11-year-old
      boy to have received from a man on top of a horse armed with a
      sabre. Wiesenthal would have been more likely to have suffered a
      wound across his head or his upper body. As Wiesenthal himself
      suggests in Pick – perhaps aware of the unlikeliness of the nature

of his wound – he was lucky that the sabre did not pierce his heart, a fortune that he ascribes to the possible insobriety of the horseman.

35 Levy, *Nazi Hunter*, p. 20
36 Pick, *Simon Wiesenthal*, p. 42
37 Ibid., p. 43
38 Ibid., p. 44
39 Levy, *Nazi Hunter*, p. 21
40 Author's correspondence with Mgr Magdalena Tayerlová at the Czech Technical University Archives, 4/7/08.
41 http://www.wiesenthal.com/simonwiesenthal
42 See, for example, Levy, *Nazi Hunter*, p. 27, Pick, *Simon Wiesenthal*, p. 48
43 Author's correspondence with Natalya Vovk at the Lviv Region State Archive, 7/11/08 & 27/11/08
44 Friedman, *Isser Harel Attacks Simon Wiesenthal*; GWDN: lss14.gif
45 Wiesenthal, *The Murderers Among Us*, p. 29
46 Levy, *Nazi Hunter*, p. 25; Pick, *Simon Wiesenthal*, p. 47
47 See *Romana Cielątkowska, Architektura i urbanistyka Lwowa II Rzeczpospolitej* (Okolice Kultury, tome 8), Art Styl, Zblewo 1998, pp. 379 and Index 6, p. 304 passim, *Katalog Architektów i Budowniczych* mainly based on *Lexicon of Architects and Builders*, by J. Nitsch, manuscript in the archives of the Association of Polish Architects, Warsaw.
48 GWDN: 033.jpg
49 Wiesenthal, *The Murderers Among Us*, p. 29
50 Pick, *Simon Wiesenthal*, p. 49
51 NARA, Record Group 238.4.4, M1019, Roll no. 79
52 Pick, *Simon Wiesenthal*, p. 49
53 Levy, *Nazi Hunter*, p. 25
54 Wiesenthal, *Ich Jagte Eichmann*, p. 229; Wiesenthal, *The Murderers Among Us*, p. 81
55 Pick, *Simon Wiesenthal*, p. 49
56 Wiesenthal, *The Murderers Among Us*, pp. 30–1; Levy, *Nazi Hunter*, pp. 3–5; Pick, *Simon Wiesenthal*, pp. 53–4
57 Wiesenthal, *Justice Not Vengeance*, p. 8
58 See Gilbert, *The Holocaust*, pp. 163–5
59 NARA, Record Group 549, Records of the HQ US Army Europe,

Folder 000-50-59

60   Gilbert, *The Holocaust*, p. 173

61   Sympathetic biographers are aware of the inconsistencies in Wiesenthal's stories, but they ascribe them to a natural distortion over a period of many years and frequent retelling. See Pick, *Simon Wiesenthal*, pp. 52–3. However, Wiesenthal's stories are distorted to such an extent they have to be considered fabrications. Pick even writes that the 'skeletal Wiesenthal who explained himself to his American liberators in 1945 still lacked the distance and detachment to call up, let alone evaluate, the seminal events of his wartime Odyssey. Wiesenthal soon grasped that some time must be allowed to lapse to give him a true perspective.' This is specious. Wiesenthal was in command of plenty of detail immediately after the war, and Pick's argument that time must be allowed to lapse in order to give a true perspective is in direct contrast to her suggestion that 'some aspects of the story had been distorted in the remembrance'. Time – or 'distance and detachment' – is no friend of accurate recall.

62   Wiesenthal, *The Murderers Among Us*, p. 31

63   Pick, *Simon Wiesenthal*, p. 60

64   Wiesenthal, *The Murderers Among Us*, p. 33

65   In *The Murderers Among Us*, Wiesenthal says that he counted 6 women and 38 men – including himself. However, in *Justice Not Vengeance*, published two decades later, Wiesenthal states that there were just 20 men. By 1993, in Alan Levy's *Nazi Hunter*, the number had swollen to 54, thereby matching Hitler's years. Hella Pick's 1996 biography states that the number was in fact 44, presumably basing her information on *The Murderers Among Us*.

66   Levy, *Nazi Hunter*, pp. 47–8

67   Wiesenthal, *The Murderers Among Us*, p. 34.

68   Wiesenthal, *The Murderers Among Us*, p. 35

69   Ibid.

70   Pick, *Simon Wiesenthal*, p. 63

71   Robert Drechsler, *Simon Wiesenthal: Dokumentation* (Vienna: Dokumente zur Zeitgeshichte, 1982), p. 133; GWDN: 047.jpg

72   NARA, Record Group 549, Records of the HQ US Army Europe, Folder 000-50-59

73   GWDN: 034.jpg

74　　Wiesenthal, *The Murderers Among Us*, p. 38

75　　See, for example,
http://www.ushmm.org/wlc/article.php?lang=en&ModuleId=
10005279

76　　Wiesenthal, *Justice Not Vengeance*, p. 11, which actually states
April 1943 twice, which has to be an error. It is puzzling that
Wiesenthal, with his supposedly accurate recall of dates, did not
have this corrected on the proof.

77　　Levy, *Nazi Hunter*, p. 55

78　　Wiesenthal, *The Murderers Among Us*, p. 39

79　　GWDN: 033.jpg

80　　NARA, Record Group 238.4.4, M1019, Roll no. 79; Levy, *Nazi
Hunter*, p. 52

81　　Pick, *Simon Wiesenthal*, p. 64

82　　Levy, *Nazi Hunter*, p. 54

83　　Ibid.

84　　Pick, *Simon Wiesenthal*, p. 64

85　　Eli M. Rosenbaum with William Hoffer, *Betrayal* (New York:
St Martin's Press, 1993), p. 47

86　　Wiesenthal, *The Murderers Among Us*, p. 40

87　　Ibid., p. 41

88　　Ibid.

89　　Pick, *Simon Wiesenthal*, p. 69

90　　Wiesenthal, *The Murderers Among Us*, p. 43

91　　Pick, *Simon Wiesenthal*, p. 70

92　　Ibid.

93　　Ibid.

94　　Ibid.

95　　Wiesenthal, *The Murderers Among Us*, pp. 43–4

96　　Pick, *Simon Wiesenthal*, p. 72

97　　Wiesenthal, *The Murderers Among Us*, p. 44. It is unclear when
Wiesenthal was in Poznan.

98　　Ibid.

99　　Pick, *Simon Wiesenthal*, p. 76

100　　Ibid.

101　　Ibid.

102　　Wiesenthal, *Justice Not Vengeance*, p. 13

103　　Wiesenthal, *The Murderers Among Us*, p. 49

104   Ibid., p. 50
105   Pick, *Simon Wiesenthal*, pp. 83–4
106   Ibid., pp. 85–6
107   Wiesenthal, *The Murderers Among Us*, p. 53
108   GWDN: 033.jpg
109   Friedman, *Isser Harel Attacks Simon Wiesenthal*; GWDN: lss7.gif
110   Pick, *Simon Wiesenthal*, p. 103
111   *The Yad Vashem Bulletin*, Jerusalem, April 1957, pp. 28–9
112   Levy, *Nazi Hunter*, p. 87
113   Pick, *Simon Wiesenthal*, p. 100
114   *The Yad Vashem Bulletin*, April 1957, pp. 28–9
115   Pick, *Simon Wiesenthal*, p. 118
116   Ibid., p. 119
117   Ibid.; Friedman, *Isser Harel Attacks Simon Wiesenthal*; GWDN:lss7.gif
118   Wiesenthal, *The Murderers Among Us*, p. 107
119   Pick, *Simon Wiesenthal*, p. 119
120   Ibid., p.109
121   Ibid.
122   Tuviah Friedman, *The Hunter* (New York: Doubleday, 1961), pp. 72–3
123   Ibid., p. 76
124   Ibid., p. 89
125   Ibid., p. 94
126   Friedman, *Isser Harel Attacks Simon Wiesenthal*; GWDN:lss7.gif
127   Friedman, *The Hunter*, p. 149
128   Ibid.
129   Author interview with Alfred Levy, 17 April 2007, Kenley, UK.
130   Author interview with Morris Harris, 24 April 2007, conducted over the telephone.
131   Author interview with Gideon Fiegel, 25 April 2007, conducted over the telephone.
132   Author interview with Cyril Pundick, 2 May 2007, Manchester, UK.
133   Michael Bar-Zohar, *The Avengers* (London: Arthur Barker, 1968), pp. 34–5
134   The group's full name was *Dam Yehudi Nakam* – Avenge Jewish Blood – but it is frequently just called *Nakam*.

135   Bar-Zohar, *The Avengers*, p. 56
136   Jim G. Tobias and Peter Zinke, *Nakam* (Berlin: Aufbau Taschenbuch Verlag, 2003), pp. 47–8
137   *New York Times*, 24 April 1946, 'Poison Plot Toll of Nazis at 2,238'
138   Tobias and Zinke, *Nakam*
139   Bar-Zohar, *The Avengers*, p. 57; and see Rich Cohen, *The Avengers: A Jewish War Story* (New York: Vintage Books, 2001), p. 212 and Michael Elkins, *Forged in Fury* (Piatkus, 1981)

Chapter Four: Helping the Rats

1   Ronald C. Newton, *The 'Nazi Menace' in Argentina, 1931–1947* (Stanford University Press, 1992), p. 352. Newton states that Hoppe was 54 at the time of his arrest. According to Hoppe's interrogation report, he was in fact born on 9 July 1891.
2   UKNA, KV 2/2636; GWDN: 06684
3   UKNA, KV 2/2636; GWDN: 06713
4   UKNA, KV 2/1722; GWDN: 01808
5   Uki Goñi, *The Real Odessa* (London: Granta Books, 2002), p. 20; Hugo Fernández Artucio, *The Nazi Underground in South America* (New York: Farrar & Rinehart, 1942)
6   UKNA, KV 2/1723; GWDN: 01818
7   Goñi, *The Real Odessa*, p. 20
8   UKNA, KV 2/1722; GWDN: 01810
9   Goñi, *The Real Odessa*, p. 17
10   Newton, *The 'Nazi Menace' in Argentina*, p. 350
11   UKNA, KV 3/90; GWDN: 06834
12   Newton, *The 'Nazi Menace' in Argentina*, p. 466, n. 35
13   D. F. Sarmiento quoted in Max Paul Friedman, *Nazis and Good Neighbors* (Cambridge University Press, 2003), p. 14
14   Ibid., p. 15
15   Newton, *The 'Nazi Menace' in Argentina*, p. 4
16   Friedman, *Nazis and Good Neighbors*, p. 16
17   Newton, *The 'Nazi Menace' in Argentina*, p. 37
18   Ibid., p. 46
19   Ibid., p. 67
20   Friedman, *Nazis and Good Neighbors*, p. 24; UKNA, KV 3/160; GWDN: 06823–06825

21   Newton, *The 'Nazi Menace' in Argentina*, p. 343

22   UKNA, FO 371/46765; GWDN: 06222

23   Goñi, *The Real Odessa*, p. 63. Goñi writes that Fuldner was 34. As he was born on 16 December 1910, he was 33 when he flew into Madrid.

24   Ibid., pp. 63–9

25   Ibid., p. 70

26   Ibid., p. 110

27   Newton, *The 'Nazi Menace' in Argentina*, p. 374

28   Goñi, *The Real Odessa*, pp. 78–92; Philip Rees, *Biographical Dictionary of the Extreme Right Since 1890* (New York: Simon & Schuster, 1990), pp. 80–1

29   Goñi, *The Real Odessa*, pp. 112–13; http://www.axishistory.com/index.php?id=9562

30   Ibid., p. 115

31   Ibid., p. 100

32   Ibid., p. 140

33   Ibid., p. 146

34   Ibid., p. 142

35   Ibid., p. 154

36   Ibid.

37   Because of the nature of politics in the former Yugoslavia, there will never be a definitive figure for the number killed at Jasenovac. This figure is taken from the memorial at the site.

38   Vladimir Dedijer, *The Yugoslav Auschwitz and the Vatican* (Amherst: Prometheus Books, 1992), p. 264

39   Ibid., p. 238

40   Curzio Malaparte, *Kaputt* (New York: E. P. Dutton & Co., 1946), p. 266. The story is quite likely to be fantasy, but the fact that many believed it is indicative of Pavelić's reputation.

41   Gerald Steinacher, *Nazis auf der Flucht* (Studio Verlag, 2008); unpublished English language edition downloaded from http://soc.world-journal.net/, p. 92

42   Ibid., p. 92

43   Goñi, *The Real Odessa*, p. 211

44   NARA, RG 263, Stack 230, Row 86, Compartment 22, Shelf 04, Box 28; GWDN: 08660

45   Ibid.; GWDN: 08680

46   Mark Aarons and John Loftus, *Unholy Trinity* (New York: St Martin's Press, 1991), p. 89

47   UKNA, FO 371/33431; GWDN: 04459

48   Ibid.; GWDN: 04456

49   Ibid.; GWDN: 04454

50   Ibid., GWDN: 04453

51   *Hrvatski Narod*, 5 September 1943, quoted in Dedijer, *The Yugoslav Auschwitz and the Vatican*, pp. 55–6

52   Linklater et al., *The Nazi Legacy*, p. 189; Aarons and Loftus, *Unholy Trinity*, pp. 89–90

53   Steinacher, *Nazis auf fer Flucht* (English language edition), p. 71; Goñi, *The Real Odessa*, p. 209

54   NARA, RG 263, Stack 230, Row 86, Compartment 22, Shelf 04, Box 28; GWDN: 08689

55   NARA, RG 263, Stack 230, Row 86, Compartment 26, Shelf 02, Box 63; GWDN: 09685

56   NARA, RG 263, Stack 230, Row 86, Compartment 22, Shelf 04, Box 28; GWDN: 08676

57   Ibid.; GWDN: 08677

58   Ibid.

59   UKNA, FO 371/67402; quoted in Stephen Dorril, *MI6* (New York: Touchstone, 2002), p. 346

60   Dorril, *MI6*, p. 347

61   Aarons and Loftus, *Unholy Trinity*, p. 90

62   Ibid., p. 113

63   Dorril, *MI6*, p. 336; Dinko Šakić, *S Poglavnikom U Alpama* (Split: Naklada Bošković, 2002); http://forum.axishistory.com/viewtopic.php?p=764867#764867. Dorril writes that Pavelić escaped on 4 May.

64   NARA, RG 263, Stack 230, Row 86, Compartment 22, Shelf 04, Box 28; GWDN: 08723

65   Šakić, *S Poglavnikom U Alpama*; http://forum.axishistory.com/viewtopic.php?p=764867#764867

66   *Globus* magazine, Croatia, 22 May 1992; quoted at http://www.jasenovac-info.com/cd/biblioteka/pavelicpapers/pavelic/ap0006.html

67   UKNA, FO 371/48890, cited in Aarons and Loftus, *Unholy Trinity*, p. 74

68   UKNA, FO 371/48892, cited in Aarons and Loftus, *Unholy Trinity*, p. 74

69   Aarons and Loftus, *Unholy Trinity*, p. 74

70   UKNA, WO 204/2194; GWDN: 06883

71   *New York Times*, 16 December 1945, p. 2; GWDN: 313731642

72   *Los Angeles Times*, 14 March 1946, p. 1; GWDN: 4149698111

73   Aarons and Loftus, *Unholy Trinity*, p. 75

74   NARA, RG 263, Stack 230, Row 86, Compartment 26, Shelf 02, Box 63; GWDN: 09683

75   Dorril, MI6, p. 338; Goñi, *The Real Odessa*, p. 208

76   Goñi, *The Real Odessa*, p. 210

77   Author interview with Richard West, 1 May 2007, Deal, Kent, UK

78   Richard West, *Tito and the Rise and Fall of Yugoslavia* (London: Sinclair-Stevenson, 1996), pp. 205–6

79   Author interview with Richard West

80   UKNA, FO 371/46653; GWDN: 06444

81   UKNA, FO 945/342; GWDN: 00989

82   UKNA, FO 945/342; GWDN: 00965

83   NARA, RG 263, Stack 230, Row 86, Compartment 22, Shelf 04, Box 28; GWDN: 08669

84   Goñi, *The Real Odessa*, p. 219; Aarons and Loftus, *Unholy Trinity*, p. 78

85   NARA, RG 263, Stack 230, Row 86, Compartment 22, Shelf 04, Box 28; GWDN: 08669; Goñi, *The Real Odessa*, p. 219; Aarons and Loftus, *Unholy Trinity*, p. 220; Aarons and Loftus, *Unholy Trinity*, p. 79

86   Aarons and Loftus, *Unholy Trinity*, p. 80

87   Breitman et al., *US Intelligence and the Nazis*, pp. 214–15, 'The Ustasha: Murder and Espionage' by Norman J. W. Goda

88   Steinacher, *Nazis auf der Flucht* (English language edition), pp. 102–3

89   Aarons and Loftus, *Unholy Trinity*, p. 81. The street is actually called Via Giacomo Venezian. Mikoiloff refers to Vancia Mihailov.

90   Breitman et al., *US Intelligence and the Nazis*, p. 215, 'The Ustasha: Murder and Espionage' by Norman J. W. Goda

91   Aarons and Loftus, *Unholy Trinity*, p. 81

92   Ibid., p. 85

93   Breitman et al., *US Intelligence and the Nazis*, p. 215, 'The Ustasha: Murder and Espionage' by Norman J. W. Goda

94   Ibid.

95   Aarons and Loftus, *Unholy Trinity*, p. 85
96   Goñi, *The Real Odessa*, p. 226
97   Ibid., p. 225
98   Ibid., Aarons and Loftus, *Unholy Trinity*, pp. 85–7
99   Goñi, *The Real Odessa*, p. 299
100   Ibid., p. 230
101   Alois Hudal, *Die Grundlagen des National Sozialismus: Eine ideengeschichtliche Untersuchung von katolischer Warte* (Leipzig and Vienna: Günther, 1937), p. 253, quoted in Johan Ickx, *The Roman 'non possumus' and the attitude of Bishop Alois Hudal towards the National Socialist ideological aberrations*, presented at the Workshop of the European Science Foundation in Ljubljana 6–8 June 2002. 'Non possumus' has its origins in the phrase 'Sine dominico non possumus' – 'We cannot live without Sunday' – which was used by the Abitene martyrs to refute Diocletian's prohibition of Christianity. As a result 'non possumus' indicates a refusal by Catholics to embrace those who do not embrace Catholicism.
102   Ibid. Dr Ickx is the archivist at the Anima, and regards Hudal as a more complex and ambiguous figure than the one that is often painted. 'People come to the archive expecting to find swastikas on every document,' he told the author. 'And they are often disappointed.' Nevertheless, the Hudal archive does contain plenty of 'swastikas', although not the plethora that many sensation-seekers wish for.
103   Goñi, *The Real Odessa*, p. 299; Goñi writes that this information comes from Aarons and Loftus, but he was unable to substantiate it.
104   Aarons and Loftus, *Unholy Trinity*, p. 33
105   Eckhard Schimpf, *Heilig: Die Flucht des Braunschweiger Naziführers auf der Vatikan-Route nach Südamerika* (Appelhans Verlag, 2005)
106   Bishop Dr Kostelecky to Markus Langer in Markus Langer, *Alois Hudal, Bischof zwischen Kirche und Hakenkreuz* (dissertation, University of Vienna, 1995) p. 11, quoted in Ickx, *The Roman 'non possumus'*, p. 3. Ickx writes that 'there is reason to be sceptical about this, not only because it is third-hand information, but also because of the good relationship Hudal enjoyed with

Cardinal Innitzer, even after he was appointed in Vienna.' However, Hudal's personal relationship with Innitzer cannot have any bearing on the depth of Hudal's nationalism.

107   Rauff's deposition to the Public Prosecutor at the West German Embassy in Chile on 28 June 1972. See http://www2.ca.nizkor.org/ftp.cgi/people/r/rauff.walter/Rauff-deposition-translation

108   Aarons and Loftus, *Unholy Trinity*, p. 34; Jarschel's account is published as Werner Brockdorff, *Flucht vor Nürnberg* (Munich-Wels: Verlag Welsermühl, 1969). See pp. 25–6.

109   Steinacher, *Nazis auf der Flucht* (English language edition), p. 56

110   Ibid.; Steinacher cites his source as NARA, Entry 210, Box 236, File 4, RG 226, location 250/64/26/01

111   Goñi, *The Real Odessa*, p. 230

112   Aarons and Loftus, *Unholy Trinity*, p. 34

113   Alois Hudal, *Romische Tagebücher: Lebenberichte eines alten Bischofs* (Graz-Stuttgart: Leopold Stocker, 1976), p. 21; quoted in Aarons and Loftus, *Unholy Trinity*, p. 37

114   Steinacher, *Nazis auf der Flucht* (English language edition), p. 57; Steinacher cites his source as NARA, RG 226, Entry 210, Box 236, location 250/64/26/01

115   Goñi, *The Real Odessa*, pp. 232–5; Steinacher, *Nazis auf der Flucht* (English language edition), p. 60

116   Ibid.

117   NARA, RG 263, Stack 230, Row 86, Compartment 22, Shelf 04, Box 28; GWDN: 08698

118   Ernst Klee, *Persilscheine und falsche Pässe* (Frankfurt am Main: Fischer Taschenbuch, 2005), p. 39

119   Ibid., p. 33

120   ASMA, K40, document 626; GWDN: SM15. The original letter is in Italian.

121   ASMA, K40, document 625; GWDN: SM13

122   ASMA, K40, document 593; GWDN: SM14

123   Steinacher in *Nazis Auf Der Flucht* states that Perón's 5,000 visas were issued around the time of this letter, yet the 5,000 visas were reported by a Monsignor O'Grady to have been issued around the time of O'Grady's visit in mid-1947.

124   Goñi, *The Real Odessa*, p. 155

125   Ibid., p. 238

126 ASMA, K40, Document 171; GWDN: SM16
127 ASMA, K41, Document 635; GWDN: SM11

Chapter Five: The Odessa Myth

1   Steinacher, *Nazis auf der Flucht* (English language edition), pp. 12–13
2   *Daily Express*, 1 March 1948, 'I Get Inside the Madrid HQ of the SS Escape Route' by Sefton Delmer; GWDN: 07042
3   UKNA, FO 371/46765; GWDN: 6240–6241
4   Newton, *The 'Nazi Menace' in Argentina*, p. 355
5   Ibid., p. 356
6   *The Times* (London, UK), 23 February 1938, p. 5, Issue 47926, Column F; GWDN: TT12; See also E. John B. Allen, *The Culture and Sport of Skiing: From Antiquity to World War II* (University of Massachusetts Press, 2007), p. 172
7   José Maria Irujo, *La Lista Negra: Los Espías Nazis Protegidos por Franco y la Iglesia* (Madrid: Aguilar, 2003), p. 82
8   Clarita Stauffer, *Sección Femenina de Falange Española Tradicionalista y de las JONS* (Madrid, 1940); by Wayne H. Bowen, *Spaniards and Nazi Germany: Collaboration in the New Order* (University of Missouri Press, 2000), p. 46
9   *The Historian*, 2005, vol. 67, 'Pilar Primo de Rivera and the Axis Temptation', Wayne H. Bowen; GWDN: pilaraxis.pdf
10 Curt Reiss, *The Nazis Go Underground* (New York: Doubleday, Doran and Co., 1944), p. 151; GWDN: undergrnd.pdf
11 UKNA; FO 371/49550; GWDN: 5229–5233
12 Paul Preston, *Doves of War* (Dartmouth, USA: University Press of New England, 2003), p. 240
13 NARA, RG 226, Stack 250, Row 64, Compartment 21, Shelf 06, Box 35; GWDN: 0023. Delmer writes that von Schiller was the widow of the Air Attaché in Madrid, but see Irujo, *La Lista Negra*, p. 34
14 Irujo, *La Lista Negra*, p. 83
15 UKNA, FO 371/70898; GWDN: 6749–6787
16 UKNA, FO 371/67902B; GWDN: 4174–4187; Carlos Collado Seidel, *Angst vor dem 'Vierten Reich': Die Alliierten und die Ausschaltung deutschen Einflusses in Spanien 1944–1958* (Paderborn: Ferdinand Schöningh, 2001), p. 126

17   Ibid.; GWDN: 4184. The numerals 88 have been used by several neo-Nazi groups since the war: Column 88 in the UK, Unit 88 in New Zealand, Légion 88 in France, White Legion 88 in Russia, ad nauseam.

18   NARA, RG 226, Stack 250, Row 64, Compartment 21, Shelf 02, Box 9; GWDN: 9856–9859

19   Ibid.; GWDN: 09866

20   NARA, RG 226, Stack 250, Row 64, Compartment 21, Shelf 06, Box 35; GWDN: 09972

21   Ibid.; GWDN: 09977

22   UKNA, FO 371/67902B; GWDN: 4178

23   Irujo, *La Lista Negra*, p. 83

24   NARA, RG 226, Stack 250, Row 64, Compartment 21, Shelf 06, Box 35; GWDN: 00039 & 0045

25   Ibid.; GWDN: 00012–00017, 00028, 00019, 09980

26   Holger M. Meding, *Flucht vor Nürnberg? Deutsche und Österreichische Einwanderung in Argentinien, 1945–1955* (Cologne: Böhlau Verlag, 1992), p. 110

27   NARA, RG 226, Stack 250, Row 64, Compartment 21, Shelf 06, Box 35; GWDN: 09976

28   NARA, Skorzeny Name file, RG 263, Stack 230, Row 86, Compartment 24, Shelf 04, Box 121; GWDN: 8908–8909. The journalist may have been Ferenc Vajta, but the report mentions that the source had sub-sources in Yugoslavia, which makes it unlikely. The report also gives the impression that the source was in Yugoslavia at the time, and to the author's knowledge, Vajta was in Bogotá in the early 1950s. (See Vajta's CIA Name file released under the IWG at NARA, 230/86/24/05 and GWDN: 9079–9119 for Vajta's movements.) Furthermore, as this report does not feature in Vajta's CIA Name file, it strengthens the possibility that the source was not Vajta.

29   The author can find no record of an SS officer called Pabbara. It is assumed that the name was a pseudonym.

30   Goñi, *The Real Odessa*, p. 353, n. 381 & 384

31   *New York Times*, 22 May 1946, p. 4; GWDN: 88362184. Although the report is of course ambiguous, it is assumed that the recent arrest does not refer to Martin Bormann.

32   Wiesenthal, *The Murderers Among Us*, pp. 80–4. In this account,

Wiesenthal omits the '*ehemaligen*' in Odessa.

33   Frederick Forsyth, *The Odessa File* (London: Hutchinson, 1972), p. ix

34   Glenn B. Infield, *Skorzeny: Hitler's Commando* (New York: Military Heritage Press, 1981), p. 180; Kurt P. Tauber, *Beyond Eagle and Swastika: German Nationalism since 1945* (Middletown, CN: Wesleyan University Press, 1967), p. 1109, n. 164

35   See the Internet. http://www.jimmarrs.com/ will do.

36   E.g. Nicholas Goodrick-Clarke, *Hitler's Priestess: Savitri Devi, the Hindu-Aryan Myth, and Neo-Nazism* (NYU Press, 2000), pp. 182–6; http://huss.exeter.ac.uk/research/exeseso/staff.php

37   Interestingly, the analogy of the 'old-boy network' is one to which Frederick Forsyth subscribes. Author interview with Frederick Forsyth, 23 May 2007, Hertingfordbury, Hertfordshire, UK

38   T. H. Tetens, *Germany Plots with the Kremlin* (New York: Henry Schuman, 1953), p. 73

39   UKNA, WO 204/12394; GWDN: 09326

40   Perry Biddiscombe, *The Denazification of Germany* (Stroud: Tempus, 2007), p. 201

41   UKNA, FO 371/46967; GWDN: 06295

42   Heinz Schneppen, *Odessa und das Vierte Reich: Mythen der Zeitgeschichte* (Berlin: Metropol Verlag, 2007), p. 17

43   NARA, RG 319, Box 64, File No. ZF015116, 'Odessa organisation'; GWDN: Scan10219

44   Lee, *The Beast Reawakens*, p. 21

45   Schneppen, *Odessa und das Vierte Reich*, p. 18

46   NARA, RG 319, Box 64, File No. ZF015116, 'Odessa organisation'; GWDN: Scan10223

47   Ibid.; GWDN: Scan10221

48   Ibid.; GWDN: Scan10223

49   Skorzeny's wartime missions are colourfully described in his memoirs, *Skorzeny's Special Missions* (London and Mechanicsburg: Greenhill Books, 1997)

50   Perry Biddiscombe, *Werwolf! The History of the National Socialist Guerrilla Movement, 1944–1946* (University of Toronto Press, 1998), p. 36

51   Skorzeny, Skorzeny's *Special Missions*, p. 196

NOTES TO PP. 142–52

52   UKNA, KV 3/195; GWDN: 9728

53   NARA, RG 263, Stack 230, Row 86, Compartment 24, Shelf 04, Box 121; GWDN: 8841

54   Ibid.; GWDN: 8850

55   Ibid.; GWDN: 8830

56   Ibid.; GWDN: 8810

57   UKNA, KV 2/403; GWDN: 7320 & 7322

58   See, among others, Infield, *Skorzeny: Hitler's Commando*; Charles Whiting, *Skorzeny* (London: Leo Cooper, 1998); Charles Foley, *Commando Extraordinary: Otto Skorzeny* (London: Weidenfeld & Nicolson, 1998)

59   Author interview with Jere Whittington, February 2008, conducted over the telephone. The ambassador may have been Baron Edmund von Thermann.

60   UKNA, FO 371/81233; GWDN: 4314–4315; *Reynolds News* (London, UK), 15 October 1950, 'Menace of the Spider'

61   ASMA, K44, Documents 585 & 591; GWDN: SM8

62   ASMA, K44, Document 603; GWDN: SM8i

63   ASMA, K44, Document 602; GWDN: SM7

64   *The Listener* (London, UK), 'The Quest for Skorzeny' by W. Stanley Moss contained within NARA, RG 263, Stack 230, Row 86, Compartment 24, Shelf 04, Box 121; GWDN: 8833–8834. The kidnapping of General Kreipe is recounted brilliantly in W. Stanley Moss, *Ill Met By Moonlight* (London: Harrap, 1952).

65   Goñi, *The Real Odessa*, pp. 300–1

66   The Kaminski in Moss's article may be the same as Jacques Kaminski, who was a founder of the MOI (*Main-d'œuvre Immigrée*), a union of migrant workers in France which carried out Resistance attacks during the Occupation. See Angelo Tasca, Denis Peschanski, Fondazione Giangiacomo Feltrinelli, *Vichy 1940–1944* (Feltrinelli Editore, 1985), p. 128. Kaminski may also be the 'Jacques Kaminski' who fought in the International Brigade during the Spanish Civil War. See http://www.jewishvirtuallibrary.org/jsource/History/spanjews.pdf

67   *Brown Book: War and Nazi Criminals in West Germany* (National Council of the National Front of Democratic Germany, Documentation Centre of the State Archives Administration of the German Democratic Republic, 1966), p. 86

68   Wistrich, *Who's Who in Nazi Germany*, p. 235; Meding, *Flucht vor Nürnberg?*, p. 113

69   NARA, RG 263, Stack 230, Row 86, Compartment 24, Shelf 04, Box 121; GWDN: 8920–8924

70   Ibid.; GWDN: 8925–8931

71   Ibid.; GWDN: 8923

72   NARA, RG 319, Box 64, File No. ZF015116, 'Odessa organisation'; GWDN: Scan10227–Scan10229

73   Ibid.; GWDN: Scan10232–10233

74   N 47.843226, E 12.162775

75   Ibid.; GWDN: Scan10242–10244

76   See, for example, UKNA, WO 208/5211; GWDN: 5935–5992, which shows the devastating extent to which former Abwehr agents such as Richard Gerken were able to penetrate Nazi groups on behalf of the British and the BND.

77   UKNA, FO 371/103898; GWDN: 5358–5360

78   Ibid.; GWDN: 5364

79   Documents concerning the Naumann Circle can be found in the UKNA in the series FO 371/103898 and onwards.

80   UKNA; FO 371/103914; GWDN: 4391

81   NARA, RG 263, Stack 230, Row 86, Compartment 24, Shelf 04, Box 121; GWDN: 8826

82   Ibid.; GWDN: 8901

83   Ibid.; GWDN: 8916

84   Perhaps the most reliable account of Skorzeny's dealings can be found in Lee, *The Beast Reawakens*, although Lee makes too much of Odessa.

85   Kenneth A. Alford and Theodore P. Savas, *Nazi Millionaires: The Allied Search for Hidden SS Gold* (Havertown: Casemate, 2002), p. 251

86   Ibid., pp. 25–3; NARA, Höttl Name file, RG 263, Stack 230, Row C, Compartment 64, Shelf 04, Boxes 23, 24, 25; GWDN: 9589

87   Alford and Savas, *Nazi Millionaires*, p. 278

88   NARA, Höttl Name file, RG 263, Stack 230, Row C, Compartment 64, Shelf 04, Boxes 23, 24, 25; GWDN: 9584

89   Ibid.; GWDN: 9585 (and see Breitman et al., *US Intelligence and the Nazis*, p. 273)

90   Ibid.; GWDN: 9530–9552

91 Ibid.; GWDN: 9585

92 Ibid.; GWDN: 9581 onwards

93 Ibid.; GWDN: 9397–9415

94 Wiesenthal, *The Murderers Among Us*, pp. 80–4

95 Breitman et al., *US Intelligence and the Nazis*, p. 278

96 Ibid., pp. 277–8

97 NARA, Höttl Name file, RG 263, Stack 230, Row C, Compartment 64, Shelf 04, Boxes 23, 24, 25; GWDN: 9597

98 Isser Harel, *Simon Wiesenthal and the Capture of Eichmann* (unpublished manuscript), p. 41

99 Author interview with Andrea Hofer, June 2008, Bad Aussee, Austria

100 NARA, Skorzeny Name file, RG 263, Stack 230, Row 86, Compartment 24, Shelf 04, Box 121; GWDN: 08875

101 NARA, Höttl Name file, RG 263, Stack 230, Row C, Compartment 64, Shelf 04, Box 23; GWDN: 9467

102 Ibid.; GWDN: 9383

103 Goñi, *The Real Odessa*, p. 239

104 Brockdorff, *Flucht vor Nürnberg*, p. 161

105 *Sunday Times* (London, UK), 23 July 1967, 'The Secret Lifeline for ex-Nazis on the Run' by Antony Terry

Chapter Six: 'Peculiar travel matters'

1 Owen, *Nuremberg*, p. 358

2 UKNA, FO 371/55115; GWDN: 6466

3 *Chicago Daily Tribune*, 4 February 1952, p. 20, 'Bormann Clew?'; GWDN: PQ499323012

4 UKNA, WO 208/4428; GWDN: 5771

5 Ibid.; GWDN: 5788

6 *Chicago Daily Tribune*, 7 February 1946, p. 1, 'Report Submarine Landed Bormann in South Patagonia'; GWDN: PQ462903822

7 *New York Times*, 4 April 1946, p. 4; GWDN: PQ93070140

8 *Chicago Daily Tribune*, 28 April 1947, p. 10, 'Egyptian Police Launch Hunt for Martin Bormann'; GWDN: PQ472863672

9 Mladin Zarubica, *The Year of the Rat* (London: Collins, 1965)

10 *Chicago Daily Tribune*, 19 October 1947, p. A2, 'Believes Chief of Nazis after Hitler is Alive'; GWDN: PQ495829252

11 Manning, *Martin Bormann*, p. 208

12 Wiesenthal, *The Murderers Among Us*, p. 282

13 Ibid., p. 283

14 *Chicago Tribune*, 31 December 1966, p. 4, 'Priest Looks Like Bormann – Says He Isn't'; GWDN: PQ609276542

15 http://news.bbc.co.uk/1/hi/world/europe/87651.stm

16 Wiesenthal, *The Murderers Among Us*, pp. 284–6

17 Michael Bar-Zohar, *The Avengers*, pp. 124–7

18 Author's visit to Nauders, May 2007. There is no 'Rudolf Blass' in the cemetery.

19 Farago, *Aftermath*, pp. 164–6

20 Ibid., pp. 216–17

21 Matteo Sanfilippo, *Ratlines and Unholy Trinities: A Review-essay on (Recent) Literature Concerning Nazi and Collaborators Smuggling Operations out of Italy* (http://www.vaticanfiles.net/ sanfilippo_ratlines.htm, 2003)

22 History has treated Farago somewhat unkindly, and it is often suggested that he was some form of hoaxer or wilful fraudster. Like many on the 'Nazi-hunting trail', Farago was a victim of both his own gullibility and the temptation of the riches that awaited him if his story stood up. Nevertheless, it would be an error to dismiss the entire content of *Aftermath*, much of which is accurate and well researched.

23 Farago, *Aftermath*, pp. 210–11

24 UKNA, WO 208/4428; GWDN: 5790

25 Ibid., GWDN: 5795

26 Ibid., GWDN: 5791–5792. Curiously, in the 1995 preface to the 7th edition of his book, *The Last Days of Hitler*, Trevor-Roper writes that the question of Bormann's death 'was left open'.

27 UKNA, WO 208/4428; GWDN: 5793

28 Trevor-Roper, *The Last Days of Hitler*, p. xv

29 UKNA, FO 371/46766; GWDN: 6261

30 UKNA; GWDN: 6372

31 NARA, RG 226, Stack 250, 64, Compartment 31, Shelf 06, Box 521; GWDN: 9921

32 Farago, *Aftermath*, p. 50

33 Ibid., p. 50

34 Ibid., p. 53

35 Ibid.

36   Ibid., p. 54
37   The film can be purchased at http://www.
      dvdsentertainmentonline.com/product/0/1948-Rogues-Regiment-
      DVD-Dick-Powell-HARD-TO-FIND-NEW_218179.html.
38   *Los Angeles Times*, 4 October 1948, p. A8, 'Bormann, Hitler's
      Missing Deputy, Alive in Hiding, Author Believes'; GWDN:
      PQ416912601
39   *New York Times*, 20 December 1948, p. 31, 'The Screen In
      Review'; GWDN: PQ96608875
40   *Washington Post*, 23 February 1949, p. B9, 'Reality Shames
      Mellerdrammer' by Richard L. Coe; GWDN: PQ215820922
41   Sereny, *Into that Darkness*, p. 266
42   Wiesenthal, *The Murderers Among Us*, p. 263
43   Sereny, *Into that Darkness*, p. 271
44   Ibid., p. 272
45   Ibid., p. 274 (footnote)
46   Ibid., p. 273
47   Ibid., p. 275
48   Ibid., p. 274. It is unclear which Alpine pass Stangl and his
      companions used.
49   Ibid., p. 275
50   Ibid., p. 290
51   Ibid., p. 289
52   ASMA, K27, Documents 611 & 612; GWDN: SM5 & SM6
53   Sereny, *Into that Darkness*, p. 290
54   Ibid., p. 289
55   ASMA, K40, Document 230; GWDN: SM34
56   Sereny, *Into that Darkness*, p. 290
57   Ibid., p. 340
58   Ibid.
59   Ibid., pp. 273-4
60   Wiesenthal, *The Murderers Among Us*, p. 263
61   Wiesenthal, *Justice Not Vengeance*, p. 80
62   ASMA, K23, Document 10; GWDN: SM 23/10
63   James Holland, *Italy's Sorrow: A Year of War, 1944-1945*
      (London: HarperPress, 2008), p. xliii
64   Ibid., p. xliv
65   UKNA, WO 310/137; GWDN: 00186

66 Ibid.
67 UKNA, WO 310/137; GWDN: 00167
68 Ibid.; GWDN: 00177
69 Ibid.; GWDN: 00186
70 Ibid.; GWDN: 00167
71 Ibid.; GWDN: 00180
72 Author interview with Erich Priebke, 5 June 2007, Via Cardinale Sanfelice 5, Rome, Italy
73 UKNA, WO 310/137; GWDN: 00186
74 Author interview with Erich Priebke
75 UKNA, WO 310/137; GWDN: 00191
76 Author interview with Erich Priebke. Simon Wiesenthal claims that it was Hudal who arranged for Rauff's escape, but it seems more likely that he was a beneficiary of his own ingenuity rather than the charity of the priest. See Wiesenthal, *Justice Not Vengeance*, p. 61.
77 Author interview with Erich Priebke
78 UKNA, WO 309/1893; GWDN: 06159
79 UKNA, WO 310/137; GWDN: 00184
80 Erich Priebke and Paolo Giachini, *Autobiografia: 'Vae Victis'* (Rome: Associazione Uomo e Libertà, 2003), p. 169
81 ASMA, K23, Document 9; GWDN: AH 23/9
82 Author interview with Erich Priebke; Goñi, *The Real Odessa*, p. 260
83 Priebke's baptism record appears in the parish register. See http://markus-lobis.blog.de/?tag=alois-hudal; GWDN: ep1.jpeg
84 Author interview with Erich Priebke; Priebke and Giachini, *Autobiografia*, p. 170
85 Goñi, *The Real Odessa*, p. 261
86 Author interview with Erich Priebke
87 Ibid.
88 Priebke and Giachini, *Autobiografia*, pp. 174–5
89 Goñi, *The Real Odessa*, p. 260
90 Posner and Ware, *Mengele*, p. 74
91 *In the Matter of Josef Mengele*, p. 66; GWDN: crm12.pdf.
92 Posner and Ware, *Mengele*, p. 74
93 Ibid., p. 75
94 Ibid.
95 Keller, *Günzburg und der Fall Josef Mengele*, pp. 48–9

96   Ibid., p. 49; Posner and Ware, *Mengele*, p. 76

97   Goñi, *The Real Odessa*, p. 284

98   Ibid., p. 285

99   Posner and Ware, *Mengele*, p. 87

100   *In the Matter of Josef Mengele*, pp. 68–9; GWDN: crm12.pdf; Posner and Ware, *Mengele*, p. 87

101   *In the Matter of Josef Mengele*, p. 122

102   Author's personal experience. As Mengele found, the walk is a pleasant one.

103   Posner and Ware, *Mengele*, p. 89

104   Ibid., p. 90

105   Goñi, *The Real Odessa*, p. 286

106   Posner and Ware, *Mengele*, p. 93

107   Ibid.

108   Author interview with Erich Priebke

109   Wiesenthal, *The Murderers Among Us*, pp. 154–5

110   Wiesenthal, *The Murderers Among Us*, pp. 113–18; Wiesenthal, *Justice Not Vengeance*, pp. 70–4

111   *The People*, 'Four Women Were the Key to my Get-Away'; GWDN: AE4-AE6

112   Cesarani, *Eichmann*, p. 204

113   *The People*, 'Four Women Were the Key to my Get-Away'; GWDN: AE4

114   Ibid.

115   The best online resource for such calculations is the superb http://www.measuringworth.com/

116   *The People*, 'Four Women Were the Key to my Get-Away'; GWDN: AE5; It is this author's contention that Eichmann became 'Riccardo Klement' only when he had reached Italy.

117   Cesarani, *Eichmann*, pp. 208–9

118   *The People*, 'Four Women Were the Key to my Get-Away'; GWDN: AE5

119   Ibid.

120   Ibid.

121   Fritz Liebreich, *Britain's Naval and Political Reaction to the Illegal Immigration of Jews to Palestine, 1945–1948* (Routledge, 2005), p. 86

122   In his memoir, Eichmann writes that 'Klement' was born in

Merano, whereas his Red Cross passport states Bolzano.

123 Goñi, *The Real Odessa*, p. 299; Cesarani, *Eichmann*, p. 208

124 British readers of a certain age will find the picture reminiscent of the late actor Michael Sheard in his role as the terrifying Mr Bronson in *Grange Hill*. See http://news.bbc.co.uk/1/hi/entertainment/tv_and_radio/4200884.stm

125 Goñi, *The Real Odessa*, pp. 298–9

126 *The People*, 'Four Women Were the Key to my Get-Away'; GWDN: AE6

127 Ibid.

1128 NARA, RG 263, Stack 230, Row 86, Compartment 25, Shelf 06, Box 44; GWDN: 9710

129 Goñi, *The Real Odessa*, pp. 128–9

130 UKNA, FO 371/70898; GWDN: 6749

131 Goñi, *The Real Odessa*, pp. 131–2

132 *Washington Post*, 1 July 1947, p. 20, 'Sweden Clamps Full Secrecy About Nazi Escape Ring Trial'; GWDN: PQ292849082

133 Goñi, *The Real Odessa*, pp. 130–1

134 Ibid., p. 302

135 UKNA, FO 371/70898; GWDN: 6749

136 The complete police report of the affair can be found in UKNA, KV 3/62; GWDN: 4875-4949. Much of the following is drawn from this source.

137 Readers familiar with Arabic can read about this charming parasite at http://www.ardalan.id.ir/large_animal_medicine/p2_articleid/14

138 A. S. Leese, *A Treatise on the One-Humped Camel in Health and in Disease* (Haynes & Son, 1928)

139 UKNA, KV 2/1367; GWDN: 4568-4569

140 Ibid.; GWDN: 4566

141 Arnold Leese, *The Jewish War of Survival* (London: The IFL Printing & Publishing Co., 1945), available online at http://www.jrbooksonline.com/leese.htm

142 Fellows Street no longer exists. According to http://www.census1891.com/streets-f.htm it was in the parish of St Mary in Haggerston, Shoreditch, which places it just south of Dalston.

143 Arnold Leese, *Out of Step: Events in the Two Lives of an Anti-Jewish Camel Doctor* (1951), available online at http://www.jrbooksonline.com/DOCs/Out_of_Step.doc

144   UKNA, KV 3/61; GWDN: 4865
145   UKNA, KV 3/60; GWDN: 4764
146   Ibid.; GWDN: 4765
147   UKNA, KV 2/1367; GWDN: 4551 & 4558
148   Graham Macklin, *Very Deeply Dyed in Black: Sir Oswald Mosley and the Resurrection of British Fascism after 1945* (London: I.B. Tauris, 2007), p. 87
149   Ibid.; GWDN: 4546
150   Ibid.; GWDN: 4542
151   Ibid.; GWDN: 4553
152   UKNA, KV 3/61; GWDN: 4869
153   Leese, *Out of Step*
154   Macklin, *Very Deeply Dyed in Black*, p. 86
155   Ibid.
156   Ibid., p. 87
157   UKNA, KV 2/892; GWDN: 9724
158   UKNA, KV 3/63; GWDN: 5038
159   Matthew Barry Sullivan, *Thresholds of Peace: Four Hundred Thousand German Prisoners and the People of Britain 1944–48* (London: Hamish Hamilton, 1979), p. 338
160   *News Chronicle* (London, UK), 12 February 1947, 'Woman Enticed PoW to Her Caravan'.
161   Macklin, *Very Deeply Dyed in Black*, p. 87
162   UKNA, KV 2/892; GWDN: 9715
163   Ibid.: GWDN: 9719
164   Ibid.; GWDN: 9720
165   UKNA, KV 2/895; GWDN: 9692
166   ASMA, K41, Document 177; GWDN: 08542
167   Macklin, *Very Deeply Dyed in Black*, p. 93
168   A particularly impressive analysis of Mosley's post-war activities can be found in Macklin, *Very Deeply Dyed in Black*.
169   UKNA, FO 371/89606; GWDN: 9299-9300
170   UKNA, KV 2/897; GWDN: 9683-9687; Macklin, *Very Deeply Dyed in Black*, pp. 104–5
171   UKNA, FO 371/103904; GWDN: 5463; Macklin, *Very Deeply Dyed in Black*, pp. 112–13
172   UKNA, FO 371/103908l; GWDN: 5508
173   UKNA, FO 371/103900; GWDN: 5397

174   UKNA, FO 371/103913; GWDN: 5535

175   Ibid.; GWDN: 5536–5537

176   Ibid., GWDN: 5552

177   Goñi, *The Real Odessa*, pp. 112–13 & 175

178   NARA, Skorzeny Name file, RG 263, Stack 230, Row 86, Compartment 24, Shelf 04, Box 121; GWDN: 8783

179   UKNA, FO 371/79720; GWDN: 8177–8183

180   UKNA, WO 309/1826; GWDN: 7285–7286

181   UKNA, FO 945/342; GWDN: 00985–00987

182   UKNA, WO 309/460; GWDN: 9756–9757

183   UKNA, WO309/1673; GWDN: 0116

184   UKNA, WO309/1673; GWDN: 0115

185   LHC, Mayhew 10/7, Lord Shawcross to Rt Hon. John Patten MP, 18 April 1990; GWDN: MAYHEW1

186   UKNA, WO309/1672; GWDN: 00093

187   UKNA, WO309/1672; GWDN: 00095

188   UKNA, WO 309/1674; GWDN: 0124; WO 310/6; GWDN: 1122

189   UKNA, WO 310/6; GWDN: 1118–1121

190   UKNA, WO 309/1651; GWDN: 6146–6147

191   UKNA, WO 309/1826; GWDN: 7269 & 7275

192   Brian Bone, Unpublished memoir; GWDN: BB21

193   Author interview with John Hodge

194   Greville Janner, *To Life!* (Stroud: Sutton Publishing, 2006), p. 32

195   Author interview with John Hodge; *Daily Mail*, 28 May 1946; *Daily Herald*, 28 May 1946; *Daily Telegraph*, 28 May 1946; GWDN: 01579–01580

196   http://forum.axishistory.com/viewtopic.php?f=6&t=104202

197   UKNA, WO 309/476; GWDN: 0179–0180

198   UKNA, WO 309/476; GWDN: 0187

199   UKNA, WO 267/601; GWDN: 5824

200   UKNA, WO 267/301; GWDN: 5830; WO 267/602; GWDN: 5834

201   Bower, *Blind Eye to Murder*, pp. 250–1

202   UKNA, WO309/1673; GWDN: 0119–0122

203   Author interview with Lord Janner, 10 May 2007, House of Lords, London, UK

204   Bower, *Blind Eye to Murder*, p. 251

Chapter Seven: Extremely Sensitive Individuals

1   Linklater et al., *The Nazi Legacy*, p. 137
2   UKNA, WO 208/5246; GWDN: 5656
3   Ibid., p. 139
4   Bower, *Klaus Barbie*, p. 123; UKNA, WO 208/5246; GWDN: 5656
5   *Hotel Terminus*
6   UKNA, FO945/831; GWDN: 1000–1006; WO 208/5246; GWDN: 5620
7   *Klaus Barbie and the United States Government, A Report to the Attorney General of the United States*, p. 28
8   UKNA, WO 208/5246; GWDN: 5654
9   UKNA, WO 208/5246; GWDN: 5655
10 UKNA, FO945/831; GWDN: 1002
11 Erhard Dabringhaus, *Klaus Barbie* (Washington, DC: Acropolis Books, 1984), p. 131
12 Bower, *Klaus Barbie*, p. 125
13 Bower, *Klaus Barbie*, pp. 126–7; Linklater et al., *The Nazi Legacy*, pp. 141–2
14 UKNA, FO 945/831; GWDN: 1032
15 Linklater et al., *The Nazi Legacy*, p. 144
16 UKNA, WO 208/5246; GWDN: 5620
17 UKNA, WO 208/5246; GWDN: 5645–5646
18 NARA, Hans-Ulrich Rudel Name file, RG 263, Stack 230, Row 86, Compartment 24, Shelf 02, Box 109; GWDN: 9645
19 UKNA, FO945/831; GWDN: 1002
20 Linklater et al., *The Nazi Legacy*, p. 142
21 UKNA, WO 208/5246; GWDN: 5646
22 UKNA, WO 208/5246; GWDN: 5644
23 UKNA, WO 208/5246; GWDN: 5648
24 Bower, *Klaus Barbie*, p. 136
25 *Klaus Barbie and the United States Government, A Report to the Attorney General of the United States*, p. 38
26 Ibid., p. 39
27 Ibid., pp. 39–40
28 *Robert Jan Verbelen and the United States Government: A Report to the Assistant Attorney General, Criminal Division*, p. 18
29 Ibid., p. 30

30   Dabringhaus, *Klaus Barbie*, p. 54

31   *Klaus Barbie and the United States Government, A Report to the Attorney General of the United States*, pp. 67–73

32   Linklater et al., *The Nazi Legacy*, p. 161

33   *Chicago Tribune*, 12 February 1983, p. 3, 'U.S. Agent Tells of Protecting "Arrogant" Nazi from French'; GWDN: PQ636756812

34   Linklater et al., *The Nazi Legacy*, p. 161

35   Dabringhaus, *Klaus Barbie*, p. 71

36   Ibid., p. 84

37   Ibid., p. 85

38   Ibid., p. 97

39   Bower, *Klaus Barbie*, p. 147

40   *Klaus Barbie and the United States Government, A Report to the Attorney General of the United States*, pp. 64–5

41   Ibid., p. 71

42   Ibid., p. 72

43   Ibid., pp. 73–4

44   Ibid., p. 87; Linklater et al., *The Nazi Legacy*, p. 176

45   *Klaus Barbie and the United States Government, A Report to the Attorney General of the United States*, p. 91

46   Ibid., pp. 91–3

47   Linklater et al., *The Nazi Legacy*, p. 177

48   *Klaus Barbie and the United States Government, A Report to the Attorney General of the United States*, p. 101

49   Ibid., p. 112

50   Linklater et al., *The Nazi Legacy*, p. 183

51   NARA; GWDN

52   Bower, *Klaus Barbie*, p. 175

53   James V. Milano and Patrick Brogan, *Soldiers, Spies, and the Rat Line: America's Undeclared War Against the Soviets* (Washington, DC: Brassey's, 2000), pp. 46–7

54   *Klaus Barbie and the United States Government, A Report to the Attorney General of the United States*, p. 150

55   Ibid., pp. 153–4

56   Linklater et al., *The Nazi Legacy*, p. 193

57   Ibid.

58   Goñi, *The Real Odessa*, p. 246

59   *Klaus Barbie and the United States Government, A Report to the*

Attorney General of the United States, pp. 155–6

60   Dorril, *MI6*, p. 250

61   NARA, RG 226, Entry 215, Stack 250, Row 64, Compartment 33, Shelf 07, Box 2; GWDN: 0093–0094

62   Ibid.; GWDN: 0095–0096

63   Ibid.; GWDN: 0078

64   Ibid.; GWDN: 0074 & 0082

65   NARA, Höttl Name file, RG 263, Stack 230, Row C, Compartment 64, Shelf 04; GWDN: 9601

66   Ibid.; GWDN 9532

67   Breitman et al., *US Intelligence and the Nazis*, pp. 273–4

68   NARA, Höttl Name file, RG 263, Stack 230, Row C, Compartment 64, Shelf 04; GWDN: 9601

69   Ibid.; GWDN: 9528

70   Ibid.; GWDN: 9508

71   Breitman et al., *US Intelligence and the Nazis*, p. 275

72   http://www.axishistory.com/index.php?id=9014

73   NARA, Skorzeny Name file, RG 263, Stack 230, Row 86, Compartment 24, Shelf 04, Box 121; GWDN: 8790–8791

74   NARA, Höttl Name file, RG 263, Stack 230, Row C, Compartment 64, Shelf 04; GWDN: 9368

75   Ibid.; GWDN: 9368

76   Breitman et al., *US Intelligence and the Nazis*, p. 276

77   NARA, Höttl Name file, RG 263, Stack 230, Row C, Compartment 64, Shelf 04; GWDN: 9370

78   Ibid.; GWDN: 9534

79   Ibid.; GWDN: 9374

80   NARA, RG 226, Stack 250, Row 64, Compartment 33, Shelf 07, Box 1, Folder 5; GWDN: 00062

81   *Robert Jan Verbelen and the United States Government: A Report to the Assistant Attorney General, Criminal Division*

82   *History Today*, September 2004, vol. 54, 'British Intelligence and the Nazi recruit' by Stephen Tyas

83   *Time* magazine, 10 August 1953, 'Operation North Pole', review of *Operation North Pole* by H. J. Giskes; http://www.time.com/time/magazine/article/0,9171,818692-1,00.html

84   Breitman et al., *US Intelligence and the Nazis*, p. 276

85   UKNA, KV 2/1500; GWDN: 11.pdf
86   UKNA, KV 2/1500; GWDN: 14.pdf
87   UKNA, KV 2/1500; GWDN: 6.pdf
88   http://www.bbc.co.uk/radio4/today/print/misc/kopkow_20040521.shtml
89   *Sunday Times* (London, UK), 7 August 2005, 'The Gestapo Killer Who Lived Twice' by Sarah Helm; http://www.timesonline.co.uk/tol/life_and_style/article551009.ece
90   UKNA, WO 208/4421; GWDN: 5758–5763
91   UKNA, WO 208/5209; GWDN: 5897
92   UKNA, WO 309/1898; GWDN: 6529
93   *Sunday Times*, 'The Gestapo Killer Who Lived Twice'
94   Ibid.
95   Ibid.
96   http://www.bbc.co.uk/radio4/today/print/misc/kopkow_20040521.shtml
97   Andrew Ezergailis, *The Holocaust in Latvia 1941–1944: The Missing Center* (Riga: The Historical Institute of Latvia in association with the United States Holocaust Memorial Museum, 1996), pp. 175–8
98   Ibid., p. 183
99   Ibid., p. 190
100 Anton Kuenzle and Gad Shimron, *The Execution of the Hangman of Riga* (London: Vallentine Mitchell, 2004), p. 42
101 UKNA, FO 371/104151; GWDN: 05068
102 Frida Michelson, *I Survived Rumbuli* (New York: Holocaust Library, 1979), p. 78
103 Ezergailis, *The Holocaust in Latvia 1941–1944*, pp. 253–5
104 NARA, RG 263, Stack 230, Row C, Compartment 64, Shelf 2, Box 1; GWDN: 9323
105 Ezergailis, *The Holocaust in Latvia 1941–1944*, p. 188
106 NARA, RG 263, Stack 230, Row C, Compartment 64, Shelf 2, Box 1; GWDN: 9323
107 Ezergailis, *The Holocaust in Latvia 1941–1944*, p. 179
108 UKNA, WO 309/1816; GWDN: 7213–7215
109 UKNA, WO 309/1819; GWDN: 7237
110 Ezergailis, *The Holocaust in Latvia 1941–1944*, p. 179; Interview with Professor Andrew Ezergailis on 'Four Corners' broadcast on

the Australian Broadcasting Corporation, 13 October 1997 (transcript: http://www.abc.net.au/4corners/stories/s72502.htm)

111   Ezcrgailis, *The Holocaust in Latvia 1941–1944*, p. 179

112   Matthias Schröder, *Deutschbaltische SS-Führer und Andrej Vlasov 1942–1945* (Paderborn: Ferdinand Schöningh, 2001), pp. 80–4

113   Ibid., pp. 84–7

114   Ibid., p. 94

115   Ibid., p. 94; GWDN: 09427

116   Ibid., p. 96

117   Ibid., p. 99

118   Ibid., p. 103

119   Ibid., p. 109

120   UKNA, WO 204/12395; GWDN: 9370

121   Snyder, *Encyclopedia of the Third Reich*, p. 260

122   UKNA, WO 204/12395; GWDN: 9360–9361

123   UKNA, WO 204/12395; GWDN: 9371–9372

124   Dorril, *MI6*, p. 218; GWDN: 09427

125   GWDN: 09427

126   GWDN: 09426

127   GWDN: 09427

128   For an exemplary study of *Ostforschung*, see Michael Burleigh, *Germany Turns Eastwards* (London: Pan, 2002)

129   UKNA, KV 4/150; GWDN: 7296

130   Heinz Felfe, *Im Dienst des Gegners* (Berlin: Verlag der Nation, 1988), p. 129

131   NARA, Heinz Felfe CIA Name file, RG 263, Second Release, Boxes 22–23; GWDN: 9187; Norman J. W. Goda, *CIA Name Files Relating to Heinz Felfe, SS Officer and KGB Spy* (http://www.fas.org/sgp/eprint/goda.pdf, June 2006). Goda states that Felfe worked for the British from 1947 to 1950, whereas the CIA chronology states 1946 to 1948.

132   Christopher Andrew and Vasili Mitrokhin, *The Mitrokhin Archive: The KGB in Europe and the West* (London: Allen Lane, 1999), pp. 571–2

133   Ibid., p. 572; Goda, *CIA Name Files Relating to Heinz Felfe*

134   NARA, Felfe CIA Name file, RG 263, Second Release, Boxes 22–23; GWDN: 9228

135   Heinz Höhne and Hermann Zolling, *Network: The Truth About*

General Gehlen and His Spy Ring (London: Secker & Warburg, 1972), pp. 235–6

136 Andrew and Mitrokhin, The Mitrokhin Archive, p. 572

137 Höhne and Zolling, Network, p. 236

138 Mary Ellen Reese, General Reinhard Gehlen: The CIA Connection (Fairfax, VA: George Mason University Press, 1990), pp. 167–9

139 Ibid., p. 168

140 Goda, CIA Name Files Relating to Heinz Felfe, p. 3

Chapter Eight: In Hiding

1 ASMA, K 24/230; GWDN: SM34

2 Sereny, Into that Darkness, p. 340

3 Ibid., p. 341

4 Ibid., p. 344

5 Ibid., pp. 353–4

6 Ibid., pp. 344–5

7 Ibid., p. 348

8 Ibid., p. 352

9 Ibid., p. 351

10 Ibid., p. 354

11 Posner and Ware, Mengele, p. 94; Mengele's landing card; GWDN: jmlc.jpg

12 Ibid., p. 95

13 Ibid., p. 101

14 Ibid., pp. 103–5

15 Ibid., p. 106

16 Ibid., p. 108

17 Mario A. J. Mariscotti, El Secreto Atómico de Huemul (Buenos Aires: Estudio Sigma, 2004), p. 96

18 UKNA, FO 943/296; GWDN: 5093

19 UKNA, FO 943/296; GWDN: 5099

20 S 41.106389, W 71.395000

21 Mariscotti, El Secreto Atómico de Huemul, p. 111

22 Newton, The 'Nazi Menace' in Argentina, p. 379

23 Mariscotti, El Secreto Atómico de Huemul; and see Physics Today, March 2004, p. 14 at http://scitation.aip.org/journals/doc/PHTOAD-ft/vol_57/iss_3/14_1.shtml

24 Huemul Island can be visited by anyone, although there is no

formal guided tour. In order to get to the island, a local boatman should be hired. As the tourist office in Bariloche is useless, the author takes the liberty of recommending Victor Katz, who can be contacted at victor_katz@yahoo.com.ar and +54 2944 1560 0794. He serves up a mean cup of maté.

25 NARA, Rudel CIA Name file, RG 263, Stack 230, Row 86, Compartment 24, Shelf 02, Box 109; GWDN: 9647
26 UKNA, FO 371/108816; GWDN: 5061
27 UKNA, FO 317/97415; GWDN: 5057–5060
28 Klee, *Persilscheine und falsche Pässe*, p. 25
29 NARA, Rudel CIA Name file, RG 263, Stack 230, Row 86, Compartment 24, Shelf 02, Box 109; GWDN: 9629
30 Newton, *The 'Nazi Menace' in Argentina*, pp. 363–4
31 Ibid., pp. 376–7
32 UKNA, FO 371/61123; GWDN: 4073–4074
33 UKNA, FO 371/108816; GWDN: 5059
34 UKNA, FO 371/104028, Commercial relations between FRG and Argentina; German influence in Argentina and other Latin American countries 1953; GWDN 4359–4377
35 Posner and Ware, *Mengele*, p. 111
36 Ibid., p. 113
37 Ibid., p. 114
38 See, for example, http://www.thesun.co.uk/sol/homepage/woman/real_life/article2162918.ece
39 NARA, Krunoslav Draganović CIA Name file, RG 263, Stack 230, Row 86, Compartment 22, Shelf 04, Box 28; GWDN: 8681
40 Goñi, *The Real Odessa*, p. 226
41 NARA, Draganović CIA Name file, RG 263, Stack 230, Row 86, Compartment 22, Shelf 04, Box 28; GWDN: 8682
42 Goñi, *The Real Odessa*, p. 228
43 NARA, Skorzeny CIA Name file, RG 263, Stack 230, Row 86, Compartment 24, Shelf 04, Box 121; GWDN: 8793
44 NARA, Ante Pavelić Name file, RG 263, Stack 230, Row 86, Compartment 26, Shelf 02, Box 63; GWDN: 9693
45 http://www.mi5.gov.uk/output/branimir-jelic.html
46 NARA, Pavelić Name file, RG 263, Stack 230, Row 86, Compartment 26, Shelf 02, Box 63; GWDN: 9697. See http://www.timesonline.co.uk/tol/comment/obituaries/

article852684.ece for an account of the life of Lady Listowel.

47   Ibid.; GWDN: 9700

48   Ibid.; GWDN: 9692

49   *Crimes in the Jasenovac Camp* (Zagreb: The State Commission of Croatia for the Investigation of the Crimes of the Occupation Forces and their Collaborators, 1946), available from http://www.jasenovac-info.com/cd/biblioteka/jasenovac1946/jasenovac1946.pdf

50   http://www.jasenovac-info.com/cd/biblioteka/pavelicpapers/luburic/ml0002.html

51   NARA, Pavelić Name file, RG 263, Stack 230, Row 86, Compartment 26, Shelf 02, Box 63; GWDN: 9703

52   NARA, Skorzeny CIA Name file, RG 263, Stack 230, Row 86, Compartment 24, Shelf 04, Box 121; GWDN: 8793

53   See http://forum.axishistory.com/viewtopic.php?f=104&t=30925&start=15 which quotes an edition of the Croatian newspaper *Hrvatska* from the time of the shooting.

54   *New York Times*, 12 April 1957, p. 12, 'Yugoslav Exile Shot'; GWDN: PQ84957942

55   *Washington Post and Times Herald*, 27 April 1957, p. A2, 'Ex-Croat Premier May Face Court'; GWDN: PQ160361092

56   *New York Times*, 27 April 1957, p. 2, 'Pro-Nazi is Hunted'; GWDN: PQ87262809

57   Dedijer, *The Yugoslav Auschwitz and the Vatican*, p. 416

58   *New York Times*, 1 January 1960, p. 19, 'Rites for Ante Pavelic'; GWDN: PQ105171637

59   Francesc Bayarri, *Cita a Sarajevo* (Valencia: L'Eixam, Col. El Tàvec, 2006). And see http://www.bayarri.info/. Serbian readers may wish to read the full account of the death of Luburić at http://www.suc.org/culture/library/Lopusina2/ubij/ubij7.html. The extract reproduced here was translated by Dan Mutadich.

60   Linklater et al., *The Nazi Legacy*, p. 216; Bower, *Klaus Barbie*, p. 181

61   Bower, *Klaus Barbie*, p. 183

62   Linklater et al., *The Nazi Legacy*, p. 220

63   Bower, *Klaus Barbie*, p. 183

64   Linklater et al., *The Nazi Legacy*, p. 220

65   Ibid., p. 223; Bower, *Klaus Barbie*, p. 185

66 Linklater et al., *The Nazi Legacy*, p. 225
67 Ibid., p. 227
68 UKNA, FCO 33/1773: GWDN: 5614–5615
69 Linklater et al., *The Nazi Legacy*, p. 229
70 UKNA, WO 204/298; GWDN: 6891
71 Linklater et al., *The Nazi Legacy*, p. 237
72 Ibid., p. 241
73 *The People* (London, UK), 21 May 1961, 'I Make Friends With Another Dictator'; GWDN: AE8
74 Ibid.
75 Goñi, *The Real Odessa*, p. 300
76 *The People*, 'I Make Friends With Another Dictator'; GWDN: AE8
77 Ibid.
78 Cesarani, *Eichmann*, p. 215
79 *The People*, 'I Make Friends With Another Dictator'; GWDN: AE9
80 Cesarani, *Eichmann*, p. 215; *The People*, 'I Make Friends With Another Dictator'; GWDN: AE9
81 Goñi, *The Real Odessa*, pp. 302–3
82 *The People*, 'I Make Friends with Another Dictator'; GWDN: AE9
83 Cesarani, *Eichmann*, p. 215
84 Ibid., p. 216
85 Posner and Ware, *Mengele*, p. 102
86 *The People* (London, UK), 28 May 1961, 'I Salute My Kidnappers'; GWDN: AE11
87 Manning, *Martin Bormann*, p. 206
88 Cesarani, *Eichmann*, p. 216
89 *The People*, 'I Make Friends with Another Dictator'; GWDN: AE9. At the time of writing, Ricardo Eichmann is a professor at the German Archaeological Institute in Berlin.
90 Cesarani, *Eichmann*, p. 220
91 Isser Harel, *The House on Garibaldi Street* (Abingdon, UK: Frank Cass, 1997), p. 142
92 Zvi Aharoni and Wilhem Dietl, *Operation Eichmann* (London: Cassell, 1996), p. 128
93 Aharoni and Dietl, *Operation Eichmann*, pp. 136–8; *The People*, 'I Salute My Kidnappers'; GWDN: AE10–AE11

Chapter Nine: Eichmann

1   Goñi, *The Real Odessa*, p. 312
2   Harel, *The House on Garibaldi Street*, p. 17
3   Ibid., p. 18
4   Biography from http://www.fritz-bauer-institut.de/texte/essay/
     07-98_wojak.htm
5   Rebecca Wittmann, *Beyond Justice: The Auschwitz Trial*
     (Cambridge, MA: Harvard University Press, 2005), p. 66
6   Unpublished manuscript by Tuviah Friedman from
     http://motlc.specialcol.wiesenthal.com/; GWDN: bli21.gif
7   Ibid.; bli22.gif & bli23.gif. Friedman sets this encounter in May
     1958, but this is out of kilter with other accounts, especially that
     by Harel in *The House on Garibaldi Street*. Friedman's memory is
     often no more reliable than that of Simon Wiesenthal.
8   Harel, *The House on Garibaldi Street*, pp. 3–4
9   Cesarani, *Eichmann*, p. 223
10   Harel, *The House on Garibaldi Street*, pp. 2 & 10
11   Ibid., p. 11
12   Aharoni and Dietl, *Operation Eichmann*, p. 80
13   Harel, *The House on Garibaldi Street*, p. 13
14   Eli M. Rosenbaum, *An Appraisal of 'Volume 4' of the CIA's
     Records on Adolf Eichmann* (Washington, DC: Unpublished
     manuscript, 24/3/2007), p. 2; GWDN: OSI/A
15   Cesarani, *Eichmann*, p. 223
16   Rosenbaum, *An Appraisal of 'Volume 4' of the CIA's Records on
     Adolf Eichmann*, p. 3; GWDN: OSI/A
17   Timothy Naftali, *New Information on Cold War CIA Stay-Behind
     Operations in Germany and on the Adolf Eichmann Case*
     (http://www.fas.org/sgp/eprint/naftali.pdf); GWDN: naftali.pdf
18   *Der Spiegel Online* (Germany), 7 June 2006, 'CIA Helped
     Eichmann Hide'; *New York Times*, 7 June 2006, 'CIA Knew
     Where Eichmann Was Hiding, Documents Show' by Scott Shane
     (http://www.nytimes.com/2006/06/07/world/americas/
     07nazi.html?_r=1).
19   Harel, *The House on Garibaldi Street*, pp. 20–2
20   Aharoni, *Operation Eichmann*, p. 83
21   Harel, *The House on Garibaldi Street*, pp. 25–6
22   Ibid., p. 27

23   Friedman, Unpublished manuscript; GWDN: rol23.gif
24   Isser Harel, *Simon Wiesenthal and the Capture of Eichmann*, p. 62
25   Ibid., p. 43
26   Ibid., p. 53
27   Ibid., p. 69
28   Wiesenthal, *The Murderers Among Us*, p. 123
29   Wiesenthal, *Justice Not Vengeance*, p. 77
30   Harel, *The House on Garibaldi Street*, p. 33
31   Cesarani, *Eichmann*, p. 225
32   Harel, *The House on Garibaldi Street*, p. 39
33   Ibid., p. 35
34   Aharoni and Dietl, *Operation Eichmann*, p. 88
35   Friedman, Unpublished manuscript in the Simon Wiesenthal
      Center's Museum of Tolerance digital collection at http://motlc.
      specialcol.wiesenthal.com/instdoc/d08c07/rol15z3.html; GWDN:
      rol15.gif
36   Friedman, *The Hunter*, pp. 244–5
37   Friedman, Unpublished manuscript in the Simon Wiesenthal
      Center's Museum of Tolerance digital collection at http://motlc.
      specialcol.wiesenthal.com/instdoc/d08c07/rol16z3.html; GWDN:
      rol16.gif
38   Friedman, *The Hunter*, p. 245
39   Ibid., p. 247. In the collection of Friedman's letters held at
      http://motlc.specialcol.wiesenthal.com/, Friedman claims that a
      member of the Israeli intelligence services visited Hermann on
      26/12/59. This is unlikely, as Harel does not mention it, and there
      is no evidence to suggest that the DAIA representative, G.
      Schurman, was acting on behalf of Harel. It is not unfeasible that
      the information would have made it back to Harel's team, who
      would have quickly dismissed it, as they had already given up on
      Hermann.
40   Goñi, *The Real Odessa*, p. 314
41   See page 154.
42   Harel, *Simon Wiesenthal and the Capture of Eichmann*, p. 110
43   See page 100.
44   Harel, *Simon Wiesenthal and the Capture of Eichmann*, p. 107
45   Ibid., p. 76
46   Ibid., p. 108

47 Wiesenthal, *Ich Jagte Eichmann*, p. 294; *The Times* (London, UK), 26 May 1960, 'Brother's Surprise': GWDN: article-2
48 Friedman, *Isser Harel Attacks Simon Wiesenthal*; GWDN: iss17.gif
49 Wiesenthal, *The Murderers Among Us*, p. 122
50 Wiesenthal, *Justice Not Vengeance*, p. 77
51 Harel, *Simon Wiesenthal and the Capture of Eichmann*, pp. 110
52 Wiesenthal, *The Murderers Among Us*, p. 125
53 Wiesenthal, *Justice Not Vengeance*, p. 78
54 Pick, *Simon Wiesenthal*, p. 147
55 Harel, *Simon Wiesenthal and the Capture of Eichmann*, p. 114–15
56 Simon Wiesenthal to Nahum Goldman, 30 March 1954, reproduced in Harel, *Simon Wiesenthal and the Capture of Eichmann*, pp. 125–6
57 Wiesenthal, *The Murderers Among Us*, p. 121
58 NARA, Höttl Name file, RG 263, Stack 230, Row C, Compartment 64, Shelf 04; GWDN: 9445 & 9614
59 Ibid.; GWDN: 9557
60 Ibid.; GWDN: 9557 & 9598
61 Ibid.; GWDN: 9559
62 Ibid.; 9574 & 9599
63 Ibid.; 9598
64 Breitman et al., *US Intelligence and the Nazis*, p. 276
65 NARA, Höttl Name file, RG 263, Stack 230, Row C, Compartment 64, Shelf 04; GWDN: 9599
66 See page 3. Because of Höttl's unreliability as a witness, his testimony at Nuremberg is often attacked by Revisionists. See, for example, http://www.ihr.org/jhr/v20/v20n5p25_Weber.html
67 See page 280.
68 Wiesenthal, *The Murderers Among Us*, p. 121
69 Harel, *Simon Wiesenthal and the Capture of Eichmann*, p. 120
70 Ibid., p. 126
71 Ibid., p. 132
72 Wiesenthal, *Justice Not Vengeance*, p. 77
73 Ian Black and Benny Morris, *Israel's Secret Wars* (London: Futura, 1992), p. 188
74 http://www.jewishvirtuallibrary.org/jsource/Holocaust/auplea.html
75 Rosenbaum, *An Appraisal of 'Volume 4' of the CIA's Records on Adolf Eichmann*, p. 3; GWDN: OSI/A

76   Kalmanowitz to Wiesenthal, 25 June 1954: GWDN: ek1.jpg
77   Wiesenthal, *Ich Jagte Eichmann*, p. 289
78   Wiesenthal, *The Murderers Among Us*, p. 121
79   Rosenbaum, *An Appraisal of 'Volume 4' of the CIA's Records on Adolf Eichmann*, p. 4; GWDN: OSI/A
80   Harel, *Simon Wiesenthal and the Capture of Eichmann*, p. 162
81   Aharoni and Dietl, *Operation Eichmann*, p. 90
82   Ibid., pp. 94–7
83   Harel, *The House on Garibaldi Street*, p. 52
84   Aharoni and Dietl, *Operation Eichmann*, p. 103
85   Ibid., p. 106
86   Ibid., pp. 111–12
87   Ibid., pp. 122–3
88   Ibid., pp. 122–5; Harel, *The House on Garibaldi Street*, p. 76
89   Harel, *The House on Garibaldi Street*, p. 83
90   Ibid., pp. 130–1
91   Peter Z. Malkin and Harry Stein, *Eichmann In My Hands* (London: Muller, 1990), p. 184
92   Aharoni and Dietl, *Operation Eichmann*, p. 136
93   Harel, *The House on Garibaldi Street*, p. 163
94   Ibid., p. 164
95   Malkin and Stein, *Eichmann In My Hands*, p. 186
96   Aharoni and Dietl, *Operation Eichmann*, p. 138; Harel, *The House on Garibaldi Street*, p. 164; Malkin and Stein, *Eichmann In My Hands*, p. 187
97   *The People*, 'I Salute My Kidnappers'; GWDN: AE11
98   Aharoni and Dietl, *Operation Eichmann*, p. 142
99   Malkin and Stein, *Eichmann In My Hands*, p. 233
100   *The People*, 'I Salute My Kidnappers'; GWDN: AE11
101   Harel, *The House on Garibaldi Street*, pp. 182–3
102   Aharoni and Dietl, *Operation Eichmann*, p. 144
103   Harel, *The House on Garibaldi Street*, pp. 180–1
104   Aharoni and Dietl, *Operation Eichmann*, p. 150
105   *The People*, 'I Salute My Kidnappers'; GWDN: AE11
106   Harel, *The House on Garibaldi Street*, p. 212
107   Ibid., p. 215
108   Ibid., p. 216
109   Ibid., p. 245

110 *The People*, 'I Salute My Kidnappers'; GWDN: AE11

111 Aharoni and Dietl, *Operation Eichmann*, p. 150

112 *The People*, 'I Salute My Kidnappers'; GWDN: AE11

113 Aharoni and Dietl, *Operation Eichmann*, p. 165

114 *The People*, 'I Salute My Kidnappers'; GWDN: AE11

115 Aharoni and Dietl, *Operation Eichmann*, pp. 166–7; Cesarani, *Eichmann*, p. 201

116 *New York Times*, 25 May 1960, p. 1, 'Secret Agents Seized Killer Nazi Abroad and Took Him to Israel'; GWDN: PQ99740807; Harel, *The House on Garibaldi Street*, pp. 274–6

117 *The Times* (London, UK), 26 May 1960, 'Brother's Surprise'; GWDN: article-2

118 *The Times* (London, UK), 25 May 1960, p. 12, 'Police Given Clue by Woman'; GWDN: TT4

119 *Washington Post*, 30 May 1960, p. A1, 'Survivors of Nazi Horrors Describe Man Who Captured Killer of Jews'; GWDN: PQ177756302

120 Friedman, *The Hunter*, pp. 255–6

121 *Washington Post*, 15 June 1960, p. D13, 'Bonn Knew of Eichmann's Hideout'; GWDN: PQ209879242

122 Letters downloaded from http://motlc.specialcol.wiesenthal.com/; GWDN: erg20.gif & erg21.gif

123 Ibid.; GWDN: rol24.gif & rol25.gif

124 Ibid.; GWDN: rol21.gif & rol22.gif

125 Ibid.; GWDN: erg45.gif

126 Ibid.; GWDN: iss11.gif

127 Ibid.; iss12.gif

128 Ibid.; iss13.gif

129 NARA, Léon Degrelle CIA Name file, Record Group 263, Stack 230, Row 86, Compartment 22, Shelf 04, Box 23; GWDN: 8626

130 Quentin Reynolds, Ephraim Katz, Zwy Aldouby, *Minister of Death* (New York: Viking Press, 1960), quote taken from dustjacket

131 NARA, Degrelle, CIA Name file, Record Group 263, Stack 230, Row 86, Compartment 22, Shelf 04, Box 23; GWDN: 8631

132 Reynolds et al., *Minister of Death*, p. 202

133 Ibid., p. v.

134 NARA, Degrelle CIA Name file, Record Group 263, Stack 230, Row 86, Compartment 22, Shelf 04, Box 23; GWDN: 8568

135   Ibid.; GWDN: 8569–8572

136   Ibid.; GWDN: 8641–8642

137   Ibid.; GWDN: 8650

138   Ibid.; GWDN: 8647

139   Ibid.; GWDN: 8572–8575

140   Rees, *Biographical Dictionary of the Extreme Right Since 1890*, pp. 85–6

141   NARA, RG 226, Stack 250, Row 64, Compartment 21, Shelf 06, Box 34; GWDN: 9868

142   Ibid.; GWDN: 9861–9865

143   UKNA, FO 371/103906; GWDN: 5468–5475

144   NARA, Degrelle CIA Name file, Record Group 263, Stack 230, Row 86, Compartment 22, Shelf 04, Box 23; GWDN: 8644

145   Ibid.; GWDN: 8620–8623, 8617, 8635–8639

146   Ibid.; GWDN: 8617; Bar-Zohar, *The Avengers*, p. 196

147   N 42.4607, W 2.865715

148   Bar-Zohar, *The Avengers*, p. 197

149   NARA, Degrelle CIA Name file, Record Group 263, Stack 230, Row 86, Compartment 22, Shelf 04, Box 23; GWDN: 8635–8637

150   Bar-Zohar, *The Avengers*, pp. 198–9

151   Wiesenthal, *The Murderers Among Us*, p. 96

152   Cesarani, *Eichmann*, p. 257

153   Ibid., p. 258. Cesarani's account is part of a whole raft of contemporary scholarship that refutes Arendt's view. See also, for example, Yaacov Lozowick, *Hitler's Bureaucrats: The Nazi Security Police and the Banality of Evil* (New York: Continuum, 2005)

154   Cesarani, *Eichmann*, p. 321

155   Ibid., pp. 322–3

Chapter Ten: Rough Justice

1   See 'Perceptions and Suppression of Nazi Crimes by the Postwar German Judiciary' by Joachim Perels in Nathan Stoltzfus and Henry Friedlander (eds), *Nazi Crimes and the Law* (German Historical Institute and Cambridge University Press, 2008), pp. 87–99

2   Wittmann, *Beyond Justice*, pp. 30–1

3   UKNA, FO 1042/254; GWDN: 6616

4   Author interview with Frederick Forsyth

5 Wittmann, *Beyond Justice*, pp. 147–8
6 *New York Times*, 19 February 1961, p. 2, 'Central German Office Pushes Investigations of Nazi Crimes'; GWDN: PQ109560606
7 Heinz Düx, *The Auschwitz Trial at the Landgericht Frankfurt and Its Importance for the Prevention of Genocide*, presented at the The Genocide Convention, 4–6 December 2008, Haus Gallus, Frankfurt. The author is grateful to Eli M. Rosenbaum for obtaining this paper.
8 Ibid., p. 7
9 UKNA, FO 1042/254; GWDN: 6610
10 Posner and Ware, *Mengele*, pp. 118–19
11 Ibid., p. 122
12 Joaquín Krueger and Erna Graf de Krueger, *Hohenau: De la Selva a la Floreciente Colonia* (Obligado, Paraguay: 1993)
13 Posner and Ware, *Mengele*, p. 124
14 Ibid., *Mengele*, p. 131
15 Ibid., pp. 148–9
16 Ibid., p. 150
17 *New York Times*, 3 July 1960, p. 12, 'Nazi's Arrest Ordered'; GWDN: PQ99749498
18 Wiesenthal, *The Murderers Among Us*, p. 148
19 Ibid., pp. 156–7
20 Ibid., pp. 153–4
21 Ibid., p. 160
22 Ibid., pp. 159–61
23 Ibid., p. 162
24 Ibid., pp. 164–5
25 Ibid., p. 174
26 Wiesenthal, *The Murderers Among Us*, p. 151. The author has yet to find evidence of the presence of a 'Doctor Cuenca' in Auschwitz.
27 Ibid., p. 152
28 Ibid.,
29 Posner and Ware, *Mengele*, p. 207
30 *Nazi-Jäger Simon Wiesenthal – Das Ende Einer Legende*, broadcast on ARD-TV (Germany) on 8 February 1996.
31 *Chicago Daily Tribune*, 25 March 1961, p. B4, 'Guard Blind German Accused of Being Nazi'; GWDN: PQ575728962
32 Aharoni and Dietl, *Operation Eichmann*, p. 177

33   Posner and Ware, *Mengele*, p. 166

34   Ibid., pp. 182–4

35   Ibid., p. 184

36   Ibid.,

37   Ibid., p. 185

38   *New York Times*, 6 June 1960, p. 9, 'Swastikas at Karl Marx's Grave'; GWDN: 105440382

39   *New York Times*, 12 June 1960, p. 32, 'Pickets Back Eichmann'; GWDN: PQ99500138

40   Kuenzle and Shimron, *The Execution of the Hangman of Riga*, p. 47

41   NARA, Herberts Cukurs CIA Name file, RG 263, Stack 230, Row 86, Compartment 22, Shelf 3, Box 22; GWDN: 8554–8555

42   UKNA, FO 371/104151; GWDN: 5066

43   Ibid.; GWDN: 5087

44   Ibid.; GWDN: 5082

45   Ibid.; GWDN: 5082

46   Ibid.; GWDN: 5085

47   Ibid.; GWDN: 5086

48   Kuenzle and Shimron, *The Execution of the Hangman of Riga*, pp. 44–6

49   NARA, Cukurs CIA Name file, RG 263, Stack 230, Row 86, Compartment 22, Shelf 3, Box 22; GWDN: 8560-8565

50   *Evening Star*, 5 May 1961, p. A4, 'Eichmann Unit Linked to Death Commandos'; GWDN: 8566

51   Kuenzle and Shimron, *The Execution of the Hangman of Riga*, pp. 54–8

52   Ibid., p. 10

53   Ibid., pp. xv–xvi

54   Ibid., p. 22. The reference to Danny Kaye could well be a dig at Zvi Aldouby.

55   Ibid., pp. 71–3

56   Ibid., p. 77

57   Ibid., pp. 78–9

58   Ibid., p. 97

59   Ibid., p. 106

60   Ibid., p. 109

61   Ibid., p. 113

62   Ibid., pp. 114–18
63   Ibid., pp. 121–5
64   Ibid., pp. 125–7
65   Ibid., p. 127
66   Ibid., p. 134
67   *Chicago Tribune*, 8 March 1965, p. 18, 'Bomb Blast Rips Synagog in Montevideo'; GWDN: PQ580674202
68   *New York Times*, 1 April 1965, p. 3, 'Home of Jew is Defaced'; GWDN: PQ106987510
69   Kuenzle and Shimron, *The Execution of the Hangman of Riga*, p. 139
70   Simon Wiesenthal Center news release, 'Herberts Cukurs: Certainly Guilty', 7 June 2005, http://www.wiesenthal.com/site/apps/nlnet/content2.aspx?c=lsKWLbPJLnF&b=4442249&ct=5853335
71   Pick, *Simon Wiesenthal*, pp. 152–3
72   Wiesenthal, *The Murderers Among Us*, p. 190
73   NARA, Erich Rajakowitsch Name file, RG 263; GWDN: 9034
74   Ibid.; GWDN: 9036
75   Ibid.; GWDN: 9042
76   Ibid.; GWDN: 9066
77   Wiesenthal, *The Murderers Among Us*, pp. 190–1
78   NARA, Rajakowitsch Name file, RG 263; GWDN: 9063
79   Ibid.; GWDN: 9064
80   *The Times* (London, UK), 13 April 1963, p. 7, col. A, 'Munich Search for Ex-SS Officer; GWDN: TT19
81   Wiesenthal, *The Murderers Among Us*, p. 195
82   Breitman et al., *US Intelligence and the Nazis*, p. 362
83   Ibid., p. 363
84   Sereny, *Into that Darkness*, p. 352
85   Ibid.
86   Wiesenthal, *The Murderers Among Us*, p. 265
87   Current scholarship estimates some 780,863 died at Treblinka. See Chapter One, n. 65.
88   Ibid., p. 266
89   Levy, *Nazi Hunter*, p. 370
90   Sereny, *Into that Darkness*, p. 351
91   Ibid., p. 352
92   Ibid., p. 351; See also *The Times* (London, UK), 23 December

1970, p. 4, col. E, 'Former Death Camp Commandant Given Life Sentence for Part in Murder of 400,000 Jews'; GWDN: TT6

93 Ibid., p. 355

94 Wiesenthal, *Justice Not Vengeance*, p. 86

95 Ibid., pp. 86–7; Wiesenthal's meeting with Robert F. Kennedy is not recorded in Kennedy's Senate papers held at the John F. Kennedy Presidential Library. However, as those documents do not represent a complete record of Kennedy's movements, Wiesenthal's absence does not necessarily mean that the meeting never took place.

96 *New York Times*, 5 March 1967, p. 21, 'Caution Delayed Stangl Capture'; GWDN: PQ93861165; Levy, *Nazi Hunter*, pp. 373–5

97 Wiesenthal, *The Murderers Among Us*, p. 266

98 See, for example, *New York Times*, 2 April 1967, p. 383; GWDN: PQ83046550

99 *Los Angeles Times*, 9 April 1967, p. C27; GWDN: PQ521395782

100 *New York Times*, 3 April 1967, p. C27, 'Pursuit of Nazi Criminals in the Interest of Justice'; GWDN: 521365502

101 Mary Cate Kelleher, *The Life of Simon Wiesenthal as Told by the New York Times* (Salve Regina University, Pells Scholars Honors Thesis, 2006); GWDN: nytsw.pdf; http://escholar.salve.edu/ pell theses/6

102 Sereny, *Into that Darkness*, p. 21

103 Ibid., pp. 364–6

Chapter Eleven: 'This whole Nazi-hunting thing'

1 See page 136 for details of Bormann's escape as alleged by Farago.

2 *Time* magazine, 11 December 1972, 'The Bormann File: Volume 36'; http://www.time.com/time/printout/0,8816,878106,00.html

3 Farago, *Aftermath*, p. 309

4 Hugh Thomas, *Doppelgängers* (London: Fourth Estate, 1995), p. 215

5 *New York Times*, 15 April 1961, p. 10, 'German Thinks Nazi Is Alive'; GWDN: PQ118907220

6 Farago, *Aftermath*, p. 34; *Martin Bormann: In the Führer's Shadow* (Biography Productions, directed by Chanoch Zeevi), 34 minutes

7 Thomas, *Doppelgängers*, p. 216

8   *Los Angeles Times*, 21 July 1965, p. 13, 'W. Berlin Police Dig to Find Body of Bormann'; GWDN: PQ484859602

9   *Washington Post*, 11 April 1968, p. A26, 'Nazi Foe Conducts Relentless Search'; GWDN: PQ167017282

10 Manning, *Martin Bormann*, p. 289

11 *Washington Post*, 21 March 1964, p. A6, 'Bormann's Real Brother Claims Fraud'; GWDN: PQ164654132; Wiener Library, Document Collection 1500, Reports of the Dokumentationszentrum des Bundes Jüdischer Verfolgter des Nazisregimes, 1962–1998, May 1965; GWDN: 9970

12 *Washington Post*, 24 August 1976, p. B4, 'Martin Bormann's Here, There, Everywhere'; PQ304087112

13 *New York Times*, 28 March 1967, p. 38, 'Bormann is Alive, Nazi Seeker Says'; GWDN: PQ83039236

14 *Chicago Tribune*, 26 March 1967, p. A3, 'Jew Keeps up Hunt for Bormann'; GWDN: PQ596405722

15 *Washington Post*, 12 April 1967, p. A3, 'Relentless Viennese Hunt Nazi Killers'; GWDN: PQ150540662

16 *Washington Post*, 7 October 1967, p. A15, 'Bormann Said to Live in Brazil'; GWDN: PQ198560452

17 *New York Times*, 12 November 1971, p. 47, 'This Ghost Didn't Go East'; GWDN: PQ79164534

18 *Chicago Tribune*, 29 November 1972, p. 2, 'Link Peron Foes, Bormann Story'; GWDN: PQ605463692

19 *Chicago Tribune*, 26 November 1972, p. 3, 'Vatican May Have Given Unwitting Aid to Bormann'; GWDN: PQ605446372

20 *Washington Post*, 28 November 1972, p. A21, 'Bormann Story "Bluff", Nazi Hunter Claims'; GWDN: PQ99717332

21 *Time* magazine, 11 December 1972, 'The Bormann File: Volume 36'; http://www.time.com/time/printout/0,8816,878106,00.html; *Chicago Tribune*, 26 November 1972, p. 3, 'Vatican May Have Given Unwitting Aid to Bormann'; GWDN: PQ605446372

22 See page 160.

23 *Chicago Tribune*, 10 February 1973, p. A27, '"No Doubt" Skeleton is Martin Bormann's'; GWDN: PQ639789562

24 Farago, *Aftermath*, p. 31

25 *Los Angeles Times*, 12 April 1973, p. 16, 'West German Court Declares Bormann Dead'; GWDN: PQ604201542

26 *New York Times*, 30 March 1966, p. 43, 'Books of the Times';
    GWDN: PQ284426072
27 *New York Times*, 20 March 1977, p. 258, 'Bormann's Back';
    GWDN: PQ80279104
28 *New York Times*, 6 May 1973, p. 462; GWDN: PQ90943876
29 Wiesenthal, *Justice Not Vengeance*, p. 97
30 See page 145.
31 Author interview with Frederick Forsyth
32 The author is aware of the irony.
33 Author interview with Frederick Forsyth
34 Forsyth, *The Odessa File*, pp. 99–100, beginning of Chapter 6
35 Author interview with Frederick Forsyth
36 Forsyth, *The Odessa File*, p. viii
37 Author interview with Frederick Forsyth
38 Beate Klarsfeld, *Wherever They May Be!* (New York: Vanguard
    Press, 1975), p. 11
39 Ibid., pp. 12–13
40 http://www.klarsfeldfoundation.org/chrono/timeline2.htm
41 As this Métro journey would have involved a change at Michel-
    Ange Molitor, Serge was indeed lucky. The couple could not have
    met at Boulogne-Pont de Saint-Cloud, as this station had not been
    built by 1960.
42 Klarsfeld, *Wherever They May Be!*, p. 56
43 Ibid., p. 159
44 Ibid., p. 149
45 Ibid.
46 Ibid., p. 150
47 Ibid., p. 194
48 Ibid., p. 197
49 http://www.klarsfeldfoundation.org/chrono/timeline2.htm
50 Klarsfeld, *Wherever They May Be!*, p. 215
51 See page 28.
52 Klarsfeld, *Wherever They May Be!*, p. 235
53 Ibid., pp. 240–1
54 Ibid., p. 242
55 Ibid., p. 245
56 See page 262.
57 Klarsfeld, *Wherever They May Be!*, p. 250

58   Ibid.
59   Ibid., p. 252
60   Ibid., p. 253
61   Ibid., pp. 256–7
62   Linklater et al., *The Nazi Legacy*, p. 258
63   Klarsfeld, *Wherever They May Be!*, p. 257
64   Ibid., p. 271
65   Ibid., p. 272
66   Author interview with Beate Klarsfeld, 31 January 2008, Paris, France
67   Linklater et al., *The Nazi Legacy*, p. 267
68   NARA, Rudel CIA Name file, RG 263, Stack 230, Row 86, Compartment 24, Shelf 02, Box 109; GWDN: 9643
69   Linklater et al., *The Nazi Legacy*, p. 274
70   Ibid., pp. 287–8
71   Ibid., p. 293
72   Wiesenthal, *Justice Not Vengeance*, p. 140
73   Ibid., p. 150
74   Ibid., p. 149
75   Lelyveld, whom Wiesenthal refers to as 'Leyland', claimed that he was never given an address. As Wiesenthal writes that he did supply one, this can be regarded as one of the smaller of Wiesenthal's fabrications. See the *New York Times*, 2 December 2005, 'A Nazi Past, a Queen's Home Life, and Overlooked Death' by Douglas Martin.
76   Pick, *Simon Wiesenthal*, pp. 195–6
77   Wiesenthal, *Justice Not Vengeance*, p. 150
78   Pick, *Simon Wiesenthal*, p. 196
79   Ibid.
80   Henry Friedlander and Earlean M. McCarrick, *The Extradition of Nazi Criminals: Ryan, Artukovic and Demjanjuk* (http://motlc.wiesenthal.com/site/pp.asp?c=gvKVLcMVIuG&b=395075)
81   Pick, *Simon Wiesenthal*; Levy, *Nazi Hunter*
82   Wiener Library, Document Collection 1500, January 1971; GWDN: 00009; Ashman and Wagman, *The Nazi Hunters*, p. 193
83   Ibid.
84   Ibid., p. 194

85   *New York Times*, 1 May 1983, 'Nazi Accusations Turn Life into a Nightmare'; GWDN: nytwalus.docx

86   *New York Times*, 5 April 1978, 'Chicagoan Denies any War Crime although 11 Witnesses Accuse Him'; GWDN: 110825617

87   *Chicago Tribune*, 17 April 1978, p. 12, '2,000 at Skokie Service Recalling Victims of Nazis'

88   *Chicago Tribune*, 17 April 1978, p. 1, 'Frank Walus Opened Door and Life was Never Same'

89   Ibid.

90   Ashman and Wagman, *The Nazi Hunters*, p. 195

91   Author interview with Eli M. Rosenbaum, 20 April 2007, Washington, DC, USA

92   *Chicago Tribune*, 31 May 1973, p. 1, 'I Will Go Where There is Fairness, Walus Says after Court Decision'; GWDN: ctwalus.pdf; *Chicago Tribune*, 'Frank Walus Opened Door and Life was Never Same'; *New York Times*, 'Chicagoan Denies any War Crime although 11 Witnesses Accuse Him'; GWDN: 110825617

93   Ashman and Wagman, *The Nazi Hunters*, p. 196

94   Elizabeth Holtzman, *Who Said It Would Be Easy?* (New York: Arcade Publishing, 1996), p. 36

95   Ibid., p. 53

96   Ibid., p. 90

97   Ibid., p. 92

98   Ibid., p. 93

99   Author interview with Elizabeth Holtzman, 12 February 2008, New York City, USA

100   Allan A. Ryan Jr, *Quiet Neighbours: Prosecuting Nazi War Criminals in America* (New York: Harcourt Brace Jovanovich, 1984), p. 61

101   Indeed.

102   Jorge Camarasa, *Mengele: El Ángel De La Muerte en Sudamérica* (Norma, 2009)

103   See http://www.newscientist.com/article/dn16492-nazi-angel-of-death-not-responsible-for-town-of-twins.html and http://www.dailymail.co.uk/news/article-1126816/Are-twins-Angel-Deaths-secret-tribe-Not-likely-says-GUY-WALTERS.html

104   Posner and Ware, *Mengele*, pp. 174–5

105   Ibid., p. 176

106   Ibid., p. 177
107   Ibid., p. 179
108   Ibid., pp. 178–9
109   Ibid., pp. 231–2
110   Ibid., p. 243
111   Ibid., p. 236
112   Ibid., p. 278
113   Ibid., p. 279
114   Ibid.
115   Ibid., p. 283
116   Wiesenthal, *The Murderers Among Us*, p. 164
117   *The Times* (London, UK), 1 February 1971, p. 4, col. E, 'Death Camp Doctor "Now Living in Paraguay"'; GWDN: 6996
118   Wiener Library, Document Collection 1500, January 1972; GWDN: 9987
119   *Time* magazine, 26 September 1977, 'Wiesenthal's Last Hunt', http://www.time.com/time/printout/0,8816,879774,00.html
120   Levy, *Nazi Hunter*, p. 286
121   Erich Erdstein with Barbara Bean, *Inside the Fourth Reich* (New York: St Martin's Press, 1977), dustjacket.
122   Ibid., p. 217
123   Ibid., p. 218
124   Wiener Library, Document Collection 1500, January 1981; GWDN: 0016
125   *The Times* (London, UK), 12 March 2005, 'Nazi Child Abuser who Set Up Cult Held after Eight Years on the Run'; http://www.rickross.com/reference/schafer/schafer10.html; Peter Levenda, *Unholy Alliance* (New York: Continuum, 2002), p. 361
126   Wiener Library, Document Collection 1500, Reports of the Dokumentationszentrum des Bundes Jüdischer Verfolgter des Nazisregimes, 1962–1998, January 1981; GWDN: 0016
127   Posner and Ware, *Mengele*, p. 287
128   Ibid., p. 288

Chapter Twelve: What Remains
1   Klarsfeld Collection; GWDN: 08410
2   Author interview with Beate Klarsfeld
3   Klarsfeld Collection; GWDN: 08412

4   Patrick Agte, *Jochen Peiper: Commander Panzerregiment Leibstandarte* (Winnipeg: J. J. Fedorowicz Publishing Inc., 2000), p. 597

5   Ibid., p. 600

6   *Los Angeles Times*, 19 July 1976, p. A2, 'Bomb Defused at Synagogue'; GWDN: PQ654671582

7   Klarsfeld Collection; GWDN: 08420

8   *The Times* (London, UK), 12 June 1982, p. 1, col. A, 'Vienna Bomb'; GWDN: TT16. In *Justice Not Vengeance*, p. 344, Wiesenthal mistakenly writes that the bombing took place on 11 July.

9   *New York Times*, 4 April 1984, 'Around the World; 4 Sentenced in Vienna in Neo-Nazi case'

10 Wiesenthal, *Justice Not Vengeance*, p. 344.

11 Linklater et al., *The Nazi Legacy*, p. 311

12 Ibid., p. 312

13 See page 262.

14 Linklater et al., *The Nazi Legacy*, p. 314; Bower, *Klaus Barbie*, p. 221

15 Linklater et al., *The Nazi Legacy*, p. 315–16

16 Bower, *Klaus Barbie*, p. 222

17 *My Enemy's Enemy* (2007), documentary film written and directed by Kevin Macdonald, extract available at http://video.google.com/videoplay?docid=165973183348003396

18 Linklater et al., *The Nazi Legacy*, p. 317

19 Ibid., p. 318

20 Ibid.

21 Ibid., p. 319

22 Bower, *Klaus Barbie*, p. 224

23 *My Enemy's Enemy*

24 Ibid.

25 Bower, *Klaus Barbie*, p. 225

26 See page 215.

27 Dabringhaus, *Klaus Barbie*, p. 26

28 Ryan, *Quiet Neighbours*, p. 280

29 Ibid., p. 282

30 *Klaus Barbie and the United States Government, A Report to the Attorney General of the United States*, pp. 1–2

31 Ryan, *Quiet Neighbours*, pp. 322–3
32 *The Times* (London, UK), 21 September 1983, p. 8, col. D, 'Conscientious or Cynical?'; GWDN: TT3
33 Ryan, *Quiet Neighbours*, p. 314
34 Ibid., p. 246
35 Figures supplied to the author by OSI.
36 *United States Attorneys' USA Bulletin*, January 2006, vol. 54, no. 1, p. 1; 'Pursuing Human Rights Violators in America: The Office of Special Investigations at 25', speech given by Eli M. Rosenbaum at Case Law School, Cleveland, Ohio, 22 February 2006; GWDN: OSI/3. When it was suggested by a reporter that von Bolschwing may have been a double agent during the war, Allan Ryan wrote on the press clipping: 'If this guy was a double agent for OSS, I am going to engage in hara-kiri in the lobby of the CIA. On network television. You are welcome to join me.'
37 *United States Attorneys' USA Bulletin*, January 2006, vol. 54, no. 1, p. 3
38 *Pat Buchanan's Unrelenting Defense of John Demjanjuk* (Anti-Defamation League, 1993); http://www.adl.org/special_reports/pb_archive/pb_demjanjuk_1993.pdf
39 Ashman and Wagman, *The Nazi Hunters*, p. 230
40 *United States Attorneys' USA Bulletin*, January 2006, vol. 54, no. 1, p. 3
41 Ryan, *Quiet Neighbours*, p. 257
42 Rosenbaum, *Betrayal*, p. 450
43 Ibid., p. 9
44 A digest of Waldheim's wartime career can be found on pp. 476–83 of Rosenbaum, *Betrayal*.
45 *New York Times*, 15 June 2007, 'Kurt Waldheim, Former U.N. Chief, Is Dead at 88'; http://www.nytimes.com/2007/06/15/world/europe/15waldheim.html?_r=2&pagewanted=all
46 Rosenbaum, *Betrayal*, plate 3 pages after p. 266
47 Pick, *Simon Wiesenthal*, p. 294
48 Ibid.; *New York Times*, 8 May 1988, 'Waldheim: The Missing Years', in which Wiesenthal wrote: 'In 1979, Israel put a request to me. Because of Kurt Waldheim's unfriendly attitude toward them, the Israelis asked me to check into his past to find out whether he had had any affiliations with the Nazis.'

49   Pick, *Simon Wiesenthal*, p. 294

50   Rosenbaum, *Betrayal*, p. 461

51   Pick, *Simon Wiesenthal*, p. 294

52   Ibid.

53   Rosenbaum, *Betrayal*, pp. 461–2

54   Wiener Library, Document Collection 1500, January 1994; GWDN: 0031

55   Author interview with Eli M. Rosenbaum

56   Ibid.

57   Pick, *Simon Wiesenthal*, p. 304

58   *Washington Post*, 30 April 1979, p. B3, 'Simon Wiesenthal's Legacy'; GWDN: PQ135656212

59   *New York Times*, 28 December 1980, p. 27, 'Nazi Found in Uruguay, Wiesenthal Tells Israelis'; GWDN: PQ113960108

60   *The Times* (London, UK), 27 April 1982, p. 6, col. G, 'Mengele "Near to Capture"'; GWDN: 7007–7008

61   *Washington Post*, 20 August 1982, p. A30, 'Search for War Criminal Near End, Nazi Hunter Says'; PQ124938282

62   *New York Times*, 13 March 1984, p. A26, Letters to the Editor; GWDN: PQ118737699

63   *The Times* (London, UK), 31 January 1983, p. 1, col. A, 'Mengele "found"'; GWDN: 7009–7010

64   *The Times* (London, UK), 12 June 1984, p. 7, col. H, 'Mengele Sighting'; GWDN: 7011; *Chicago Tribune*, 29 January 1985, p. 4, 'Nazi-hunter Rejected Offers to Kill Mengele'; GWDN: PQ767334772

65   *New York Times*, 9 July 1979, p. A3, 'Paraguay Pressed to Give Up Mengele'; GWDN: PQ112114953

66   *Washington Post*, 28 June 1979, p. A22, 'Nazi Extradition Asked of Paraguayan President'; GWDN: PQ131853902

67   *Washington Post*, 10 August 1979, p. A20, 'Mengele Hunt Focuses on Paraguay'; GWDN: PQ131907842

68   Levy, *Nazi Hunter*, p. 299

69   *New York Times*, 27 November 1984, p. A11, 'Paraguay Pledges to Hunt For Nazi'; GWDN: PQ120501779

70   Author interview with Elizabeth Holtzman

71   Author interview with Beate Klarsfeld

72   Pick, *Simon Wiesenthal*, p. 192

73   Ibid., p. 303
74   Ibid., p. 192
75   Posner and Ware, *Mengele*, p. 306
76   http://motlc.specialcol.wiesenthal.com/instdoc/d04c10/
      meng2z3.html; Posner and Ware, *Mengele*, p. 306
77   Author interview with David Marwell, 19 April 2007, New York
      City, USA
78   *Washington Post*, 20 March 1985, p. A18, 'U.S. Search For
      Mengele Is Expanded'; GWDN: PQ123763432
79   Author interview with Beate Klarsfeld
80   Author interview with David Marwell
81   Wiesenthal, *Justice Not Vengeance*, p. 112
82   Posner and Ware, *Mengele*, p. 315
83   Ibid., pp. 314–15
84   Ibid., pp. 316–17
85   Author interview with David Marwell
86   Posner and Ware, *Mengele*, p. 317
87   *Los Angeles Times*, 6 June 1985, p. 1, 'U.S. Experts Fly to Brazil
      to Check Mengele Death Report'; GWDN: PQ675935162
88   Posner and Ware, *Mengele*, p. 319
89   Levy, *Nazi Hunter*, p. 303
90   *New York Times*, 10 June 1985, p. A3, 'Bonn Offer in '64 on
      Mengele Reported'; GWDN: PQ228815482
91   *New York Times*, 11 June 1985, p. A4, 'Mengele's Son To Break
      Silence on Father's Fate'; GWDN: 118865569
92   *New York Times*, 12 June 1985, p. A1, 'Body is Mengele's, His
      Son Declares'; GWDN: PQ118865890
93   *The Times* (London, UK), 14 June 1985, p. 8, col. 8, 'Pressure
      Mounts on Mengele family'; GWDN: TT13
94   *In the Matter of Josef Mengele*, p. 156; GWDN: crm12.pdf
95   Author interview with David Marwell
96   *Washington Post*, 29 January 1986, p. C12, 'Jewish Group
      Questions Mengele Probe'; GWDN: PQ126292852
97   Wiener Library, Document Collection 1500, January 1986;
      GWDN: 0027
98   *Washington Post*, 28 March 1986, p. A23, 'Dogged US
      Dentist-Envoy Finds X-Ray of Mengele';
      GWDN: PQ128809272

99   Wiener Library, Document Collection 1500, January 1989;
       GWDN: 0029
100   See Levy, *Nazi Hunter*, p. 308
101   *New York Times*, 12 May 1987, p. A3, 'France Opens Barbie's
       Trial on Role in Nazi Crimes'; GWDN: PQ114948068
102   Erna Paris, *Unhealed Wounds: France and the Klaus Barbie Affair*
       (New York: Grove Press, 1986), p. 186
103   *My Enemy's Enemy*
104   See page 37.
105   *New York Times*, 2 August 1987, p. SM27; 'Voices from the
       Barbie Trial'; GWDN: PQ115186369
106   *New York Times*, 4 July 1987, p. 3, 'Barbie Is Found Guilty and
       Sentenced to Life'; GWDN: PQ114974000
107   See page 38.
108   *New York Times*, 2 August 1987, p. SM23; 'Voices from the
       Barbie Trial'; GWDN: PQ115186369
109   *New York Times*, 4 July 1987, p. 3, 'Barbie Is Found Guilty And
       Sentenced To Life'; GWDN: PQ114974000
110   Ibid.
111   *My Enemy's Enemy*
112   Private information
113   Efraim Zuroff, *Occupation: Nazi Hunter, The Continuing Search
       for the Perpetrators of the Holocaust* (Hoboken, NJ: KTAV
       Publishing House, 1994), p. 265
114   Eli M. Rosenbaum, *Nazi War Crimes Investigations/Prosecutions
       Abroad: Canada, Australia, the United Kingdom* (unpublished
       paper, 2003); GWDN: OSI/5
115   David Cesarani, *Justice Delayed* (London: William Heinemann,
       1992), p. 197
116   Ashman and Wagman, *The Nazi Hunters*, p. 38
117   See page 204.
118   Author interview with Lord Janner
119   For an excellent and definitive account of how the EVW
       immigrants were able to enter the United Kingdom, see Cesarani,
       Justice Delayed.
120   Janner, *To Life!*, p. 136
121   Zuroff, *Occupation: Nazi Hunter*, p. 271
122   Cesarani, *Justice Delayed*, p. 203

123   The fruits of this research are contained within Cesarani, *Justice Delayed*.
124   Cesarani, *Justice Delayed*, pp. 211–12
125   *New York Times*, 3 April 1988, p. 18, 'British Board Presses Effort to Find Nazis'; GWDN: PQ115338835
126   Cesarani, *Justice Delayed*, p. 213
127   Janner, *To Life!*, p. 137
128   Zuroff, *Occupation: Nazi Hunter*, p. 293
129   Janner, *To Life!*, p. 138
130   LHC, Mayhew 10/7, C. P. Mayhew to Minister of State, 6 July 1948; GWDN: MAYHEW2
131   Cesarani, *Justice Delayed*, p. 229
132   Author interview with Lord Janner
133   Cesarani, *Justice Delayed*, p. 230
134   Janner, *To Life!*, p. 138
135   Ibid., p. 139
136   Cesarani, *Justice Delayed*, p. 231
137   *Hansard*; http://www.publications.parliament.uk/pa/cm198990/cmhansrd/1990-03-19/Debate-7.html
138   LHC, Mayhew 10/7, Lord Shawcross to Rt Hon. John Patten MP, April 1990; GWDN: MAYHEW1
139   LHC, Mayhew 10/7, Rt Hon. John Patten MP to Lord Shawcross, 5 April 1990; GWDN: MAYHEW3
140   Cesarani, *Justice Delayed*, p. 239
141   Janner, *To Life!*, p. 141
142   Ibid.
143   Author interview with Eli M. Rosenbaum
144   *Daily Mirror*, 23 October 2007, 'Peter Serafinowicz Exclusive TV Comic on Heartache, Fatherhood and Stardom'; *The Independent*, 16 April 1996, 'Refugee, 85, Sent for Britain's First War Crimes Trial'
145   Ibid.
146   Eli M. Rosenbaum, *Nazi War Crimes Investigations/Prosecutions Abroad: Canada, Australia, the United Kingdom*; GWDN: OSI/5
147   http://news.bbc.co.uk/1/uk/309937.stm
148   http://news.bbc.co.uk/1/hi/uk/309559.stm
149   Ibid.
150   Janner, *To Life!*, p. 142

151 http://news.bbc.co.uk/1/hi/world/europe/4262892.stm

152 Reuters, 8 July 2008, 'Nazi Hunters Seek to Smoke Out "Dr Death" in Chile', http://www.reuters.com/article/latestCrisis/idUSN08309280

153 http://news.bbc.co.uk/1/hi/world/americas/7497078.stm

154 *Guardian*, 6 February 2009, 'Nazi Hunters Sceptical of Reports', http://www.guardian.co.uk/world/2009/feb/06/egypt-heim-holocaust; *Daily Telegraph*, 5 February 2009, 'Son of "Dr Death" Aribert Heim to Escape Charges for Concealing Nazi Father's Existence', http://www.telegraph.co.uk/news/worldnews/europe/germany/4524580/Son-of-Dr-Death-Aribert-Heim-to-escape-charges-for-concealing-Nazi-fathers-existence.html

155 *Daily Telegraph*, 20 September 2005, 'Vatican Accused of Shielding "War Criminal"'

Bibliography

As many of my copies of primary sources exist in digital formats, I am happy to send – at my discretion – image and audio files to bona fide researchers. Most of the interviews below are recorded as mp3s, and the documents are photographed as jpegs. When requesting a document, please include my document reference number (GWDN) as indicated in the endnotes.

UNPUBLISHED SOURCES

(a) Interviewees

Bone, Brian, interviewed by author, Broadstone, UK, 29 March 2007

Draper, Gerald, interviewed at a war crimes conference in Geneva, April 1975

Draper, Julia, interviewed by author, London, UK, 11 April 2007

Ferencz, Benjamin B., interviewed telephonically by author, 8 May 2007

Fiegel, Gideon, interviewed telephonically by author, 25 April 2007

Forsyth, Frederick, interviewed by author, Hertingfordbury, UK, 23 May 2007

Harris, Morris, interviewed telephonically by author, 24 April 2007

Hodge, John, interviewed by author, Chirton, UK, 5 April, 2007

Hofer, Andrea, interviewed by author, Bad Aussee, June 2008

Holtzman, Elizabeth, interviewed by author, New York City, 12 February 2008

Howard, Harry, interviewed by author, Minehead, UK, 12 June 2007

Janner, Greville, interviewed by author, House of Lords, London, UK, 10 May 2007

Klarsfeld, Beate, interviewed by author, Paris, France, 31 January 2008

Lachmann, Benjamin, interviewed telephonically by author, 24 April 2007

Levy, Alfred, interviewed by author, Kenley, UK, 17 April 2007

Marwell, David, interviewed by author, New York City, USA, 19 April 2007

Miete, Augusto, interviewed by Tim Phillips and author, Hohenau, Paraguay, March 2008

Neilson, Ian, interviewed by author, Marlborough, UK, 29 April 2009

Priebke, Erich, interviewed by author, Rome, Italy, 5 June 2007

Pucher, Hans, interviewed by author, Altaussee, Austria, 25 June 2008

Pundick, Cyril, interviewed by author, Manchester, UK, 2 May 2007

Rosenbaum, Eli M., interviewed by author, Washington, DC, USA, 20 April 2007 and 20 February 2008

West, Richard, interviewed by author, Deal, UK, 1 May 2007

Whittington, Jere, interviewed telephonically by author, February 2008

(b) Archives and libraries

British Library Newspaper Archive, Colindale, London, UK

Liddell Hart Centre for Military Archives, King's College, London, UK (LHC)

London Library, UK

National Archives, Kew, London, UK (UKNA)

National Archives and Records Administration, College Park, MD,

USA (NARA)
Santa Maria dell'Anima, Rome, Italy (ASMA)
United Nations War Crimes Commission Archive, New York City, USA
Wiener Library, London, UK

(c) Papers, speeches and lectures

Draper, Gerald, *Reflections on Nazi Atrocities: The Holocaust* (Recording in collection of Julia Draper, *c.* early 1970s)

Düx, Heinz, *The Auschwitz Trial at the Landgericht Frankfurt and Its Importance for the Prevention of Genocide* (presented at the Genocide Convention, 4–6 December 2008, Haus Gallus, Frankfurt)

Ickx, Johan, *Bischof Alois Hudal als Fluchthelfer: ein Mythos?*

Ickx, Johan, *The Roman 'non possumus' and the attitude of Bishop Alois Hudal towards the National Socialist ideological aberrations* (Paper presented at the Workshop of the European Science Foundation in Ljubljana, Slovenia, 6–8 June 2002)

Kelleher, Mary Cate, *The Life of Simon Wiesenthal as Told by the* New York Times (Salve Regina University, Pells Scholars Honors Thesis, 2006)

Rosenbaum, Eli M., *An Appraisal of 'Volume 4' of the CIA's Records on Adolf Eichmann* (US Department of Justice, Criminal Division, Washington DC, 24 March 2007)

Rosenbaum, Eli M., *Nazi War Crimes Investigations/Prosecutions Abroad: Canada, Australia, the United Kingdom* (Presentation made to the Washington DC Bar's Third Annual Legal History Seminar, 20 December 1995)

Rosenbaum, Eli M., *Reflections on OSI's Quarter-Century of Operations: Achievements and Disappointments* (Remarks made at a panel discussion entitled 'Hunting Nazis' at the United States Holocaust Memorial Museum, Washington DC, 25 October 2004)

Rosenbaum, Eli M., *Pursuing Human Rights Violators in America: The Office of Special Investigations at 25* (Lecture given at the Klatsky Annual Seminar in Human Rights at the Frederick K. Cox International Law Center, Case Law School, Cleveland, Ohio, 22 February 2006)

Rosenbaum, Eli M., *Remarks Made at OSI 25th Reunion Luncheon Banquet* (Marriott Crystal Gateway Hotel, Arlington, Virginia, 24 October 2004)

(d) Diaries and letters

Brian Bone's memoirs (from the late Brian Bone)

(e) Books

Harel, Isser, *Simon Wiesenthal and the Capture of Eichmann*

PUBLISHED SOURCES

(a) Printed

(i) *Biographies and memoirs*
Agte, Patrick, *Jochen Peiper: Commander Panzerregiment Leibstandarte* (Winnipeg: J. J. Fedorowicz Publishing Inc., 2000)
Aharoni, Zvi and Dietl, Wilhelm, *Operation Eichmann* (London: Cassell, 1996)
Annan, Noel, *Changing Enemies: The Defeat and Regeneration of Germany* (Cornell University Press, 1997)
Astor, Gerald, *The Last Nazi* (New York: Donald I. Fine, 1985)
Baumbach, Werner, *Broken Swastika* (Maidstone: George Mann, 1974)
Bower, Tom, *Klaus Barbie: The Butcher of Lyons* (New York: Pantheon, 1984)
Camarasa, Jorge, *Mengele: El Ángel de la Muerte en Sudamérica* (Norma, 2009)
Cesarani, David, *Eichmann: His Life and Crimes* (London: William Heinemann, 2004)
Christie, Stuart, *Stefano della Chiaie: Portrait of a Black Terrorist* (London: Anarchy Magazine / Refract Publications, 1994)
Critchfield, James H., *Partners at the Creation: The Men Behind*

Postwar Germany's Defense and Intelligence Establishments (Annapolis, MD: Naval Institute Press, 2003)

Dabringhaus, Erhard, *Klaus Barbie* (Washington, DC: Acropolis Books, 1984)

Dorril, Stephen, *Black Shirt: Sir Oswald Mosley & British Fascism* (London: Penguin Books, 2007)

Epelbaum, Didier, *Alois Brunner* (Paris: Calmann-Lévy, 1990)

Felfe, Heinz, *Im Dienst des Gegners* (Berlin: Verlag der Nation, 1988)

Foley, Charles, *Commando Extraordinary: Otto Skorzeny* (London: Weidenfeld & Nicolson, 1998)

Friedman, Tuviah, *The Hunter* (New York: Doubleday, 1961)

Freytag von Loringhoven, Bernd, *In the Bunker with Hitler* (London: Weidenfeld & Nicolson, 2006)

Gehlen, Reinhard, *The Gehlen Memoirs* (London: Collins, 1972)

Gimlette, John, *At the Tomb of the Inflatable Pig* (London: Arrow, 2004)

Harel, Isser, *The House on Garibaldi Street* (Abingdon, UK: Frank Cass, 1997)

Holtzman, Elizabeth, *Who Said It Would Be Easy?* (New York: Arcade Publishing, 1996)

Höss, Rudolf, *Commandant of Auschwitz* (London: Phoenix Press, 2000)

Hudal, Alois, *Romische Tagebücher: Lebenberichte eines alten Bischofs* (Graz-Stuttgart: Leopold Stocker, 1976)

Infield, Glenn B., *Skorzeny: Hitler's Commando* (New York: Military Heritage Press, 1981)

Janner, Greville, *To Life!* (Stroud: Sutton Publishing, 2006)

Junge, Traudl, *Until the Final Hour* (London: Weidenfeld & Nicolson, 2003)

Keller, Sven, *Günzburg und der Fall Josef Mengele* (Munich: R. Oldenbourg Verlag, 2003)

Klarsfeld, Beate, *Wherever They May Be!* (New York: Vanguard Press, 1975)

Kuenzle, Anton and Shimron, Gad, *The Execution of the Hangman of Riga* (London: Vallentine Mitchell, 2004)

Leese, Arnold, *Out of Step: Events in the Two Lives of an Anti-Jewish Camel Doctor* (1951)

Levy, Alan, *Nazi Hunter: The Wiesenthal File* (London: Robinson, 2002)

Linklater, Magnus, Hilton, Isabel and Ascherson, Neal, *The Nazi Legacy: Klaus Barbie and the International Fascist Connection* (New York: Holt, Rinehart and Winston, 1984)

Malaparte, Curzio, *Kaputt* (New York: E. P. Dutton & Co., 1946)

Malkin, Peter Z. and Stein, Harry, *Eichmann in My Hands* (London: Muller, 1990)

Manning, Paul, *Martin Bormann: Nazi in Exile* (New Jersey: Lyle Stuart, 1981)

Michelson, Frida, *I Survived Rumbuli* (New York: Holocaust Library, 1979)

Müller-Tupath, Karla, *Verschollen in Deutschland* (Hamburg: Konkret Literatur Verlag, 1994)

Naumann, Werner, *Nau Nau: gefährdet das Empire?* (Göttingen: Plesse Verlag, 1953)

Nyiszli, Miklos, *Auschwitz: A Doctor's Eyewitness Account* (London: Little, Brown, 1993)

Pick, Hella, *Simon Wiesenthal: A Life in Search of Justice* (London: Weidenfeld & Nicolson, 1996)

Posner, Gerald L. and Ware, John, *Mengele: The Complete Story* (New York: Cooper Square Press, 2000)

Priebke, Erich and Giachini, Paolo, *Autobiografia: "Vae Victis"* (Rome: Associazione Uomo e Libertà, 2003)

Reynolds, Quentin, Katz, Ephraim and Aldouby, Zwy, *Minister of Death* (New York: Viking Press, 1960)

Schellenberg, Walter, *The Schellenberg Memoirs* (London: André Deutsch, 1956)

Skorzeny, Otto, *Skorzeny's Special Missions* (London & Mechanicsburg: Greenhill Books, 1997)

Speer, Albert, *Inside the Third Reich* (London: Phoenix, 1995)

Trevor-Roper, Hugh (ed.), *The Bormann Letters* (London: Weidenfeld & Nicolson, 1954)

Valmont, Frédéric, *Un criminal nommé Klaus Barbie* (Editions Justine, 1987)

Vergès, Jacques, *Que mes guerres étaient belles!* (Monaco: Editions du Rocher, 2007)

Whiting, Charles, *Skorzeny* (London: Leo Cooper, 1998)

Wiernik, Yankel, *A Year in Treblinka* (New York: American Representation of the General Jewish Workers Union of Poland, 1945)

Wiesenthal, Simon, *Ich Jagte Eichmann* (Bertelsmann, 1961)

Wiesenthal, Simon, *Justice Not Vengeance* (London: Weidenfeld & Nicolson, 1989)

Wiesenthal, Simon, *The Murderers Among Us* (London: William Heinemann, 1967)

Zuroff, Efraim, *Occupation: Nazi Hunter, The Continuing Search for the Perpetrators of the Holocaust* (Hoboken, NJ: KTAV Publishing House, 1994)

(ii) *Histories*

Aarons, Mark and Loftus, John, *Unholy Trinity* (New York: St Martin's Press, 1991)

Akademie der Künste, *Rifugio Precario: Artisti e Intelletuali Tedeschi in Italia 1933–1945* (Milan & Berlin: Mazzotta, 1995)

Alford, Kenneth D. and Savas, Theodore P., *Nazi Millionaires: The Allied Search for Hidden SS Gold* (Havertown: Casemate, 2002)

Allen, E. and John B., *The Culture and Sport of Skiing: From Antiquity to World War II* (University of Massachusetts Press, 2007)

Andrew, Christopher and Mitrokhin, Vasili, *The Mitrokhin Archive: The KGB in Europe and the West* (London: Allen Lane, 1999)

Arendt, Hannah, *Eichmann in Jerusalem: A Report on the Banality of Evil* (Penguin, 1994)

Art, David, *The Politics of the Nazi Past in Germany and Austria* (Cambridge University Press, 2006)

Artucio, Hugo Fernández, *The Nazi Underground in South America* (New York: Farrar & Rinehart, 1942)

Ashman, Charles and Wagman, Robert J., *The Nazi Hunters* (New York: Warner Books, 1988)

Bar-Zohar, Michael, *The Avengers* (London: Arthur Barker, 1968)

Bayarri, Francesc, *Cita a Sarajevo* (Valencia: L'Eixam, Col. El Tàvec, 2006)

Beckman, Morris, *The Jewish Brigade: An Army with Two Masters 1944–45* (Staplehurst, UK: Spellmount, 1998)

Biddiscombe, Perry, *The Denazification of Germany: A History 1945–1948* (NPI Media Group, 2007)

Biddiscombe, Perry, *Werwolf! The History of the National Socialist Guerrilla Movement, 1944–1946* (University of Toronto Press, 1998)

Black, Ian and Morris, Benny, *Israel's Secret Wars* (London: Futura, 1992)

Blum, Howard, *The Brigade: An Epic Story of Vengeance, Salvation and World War II* (New York: Perennial, 2002)

Blum, Howard, *Wanted! The Search for Nazis in America* (New York: Touchstone, 1977)

Botting, Douglas: *From the Ruins of the Reich: Germany 1945–1949* (New York: Crown, 1985)

Bowen, Wayne H., *Spaniards and Nazi Germany: Collaboration in the New Order* (University of Missouri Press, 2000)

Bower, Tom, *Blind Eye to Murder* (London: Warner Books, 1997)

Bower, Tom, *The Paperclip Conspiracy: The Battle for the Spoils and Secrets of Nazi Germany* (London: Grafton, 1988)

Breitman, Richard, Goda, Norman J. W., Naftali, Timothy and Wolfe, Robert, *US Intelligence and the Nazis* (Cambridge University Press, 2005)

Brockdorff, Werner, *Flucht vor Nürnberg* (Munich: Verlag Welsermühl, 1969)

Brown Book: War and Nazi Criminals in West Germany (National Council of the National Front of Democratic Germany, Documentation Centre of the State Archives Administration of the German Democratic Republic, 1966)

Burleigh, Michael, *Germany Turns Eastwards* (London: Pan, 2002)

Burleigh, Michael, *The Third Reich* (London: Pan, 2001)

Cesarani, David, *Justice Delayed* (London: William Heinemann, 1992)

Chamberlain, Brewster and Feldman, Marcia, *The Liberation of the Nazi Concentration Camps 1945* (Washington, DC: United States Holocaust Memorial Council, 1987)

Cohen, Maynard M., *A Stand Against Tyranny: Norway's Physicians and the Nazis* (Wayne State University Press, 2000)

Cohen, Rich, *The Avengers: A Jewish War Story* (New York: Vintage Books, 2001)

Dedijer, Vladimir, *The Yugoslav Auschwitz and the Vatican* (Amherst, NY: Prometheus Books, 1992)

Dorril, Stephen, *MI6* (New York: Touchstone, 2002)

Drechsler, Robert, *Simon Wiesenthal: Dokumentation* (Vienna: Dokumente zur Zeitgeshichte, 1982)

Eisterer, Klaus and Bischof, Günter (eds), *Transatlantic Relations: Austria and Latin America in the 19th and 20th Centuries* (Innsbruck: StudienVerlag, 2006)

Elkins, Michael, *Forged in Fury* (Piatkus, 1981)

Ezergailis, Andrew, *The Holocaust in Latvia 1941–1944: The Missing Center* (Riga: The Historical Institute of Latvia in association with the United States Holocaust Memorial Museum, 1996)

Farago, Ladislas, *Aftermath* (New York: Simon & Schuster, 1974)

Fest, Joachim, *Inside Hitler's Bunker* (London: Pan, 2005)

Frank, Michael, *Die letzte Bastion: Nazis in Argentinien* (Hamburg: Rütten & Loening, 1962)

Friedman, Max Paul, *Nazis and Good Neighbors* (Cambridge University Press, 2003)

Ganser, Daniel, *Nato's Secret Armies: Operation Gladio and Terrorism in Western Europe* (Abingdon, UK: Frank Cass, 2005)

Gilbert, Martin, *The Holocaust* (London: Fontana Press, 1987)

Goñi, Uki, *The Real Odessa* (London: Granta Books, 2002)

Goodrick-Clarke, Nicholas, *Hitler's Priestess: Savitri Devi, the Hindu-Aryan Myth, and Neo-Nazism* (NYU Press, 2000)

Hagen, Louis, *The Secret War for Europe: A Dossier of Espionage* (London: Macdonald, 1968)

Hagen, Walter, *Die Geheime Front* (Linz & Vienna: Nibelungen Verlag, 1950)

Herf, Jeffrey, *Divided Memory: The Nazi Past in the Two Germanys* (Harvard University Press, 1997)

Höhne, Heinz and Zolling, Hermann, *Network: The Truth About General Gehlen and His Spy Ring* (London: Secker & Warburg, 1972)

Holland, James, *Italy's Sorrow: A Year of War, 1944–1945* (London: HarperPress, 2008)

Irujo, José Maria, *La Lista Negra: Los Espías Nazis Protegidos por Franco y la Iglesia* (Madrid: Aguilar, 2003)

Kilzer, Louis, *Hitler's Traitor* (California: Presidio Press, 2000)

Klarsfeld, Serge, *The Children of Izieu: A Human Tragedy* (New York: Harry N. Abrams, 1984)

Klee, Ernst, *Auschwitz, die NS-Medizin und ihre Opfer* (Frankfurt am Main: S. Fischer, 1997)

Klee, Ernst, *Persilscheine und falsche Pässe* (Frankfurt am Main: Fischer Taschenbuch, 2005)

Kochavi, Arieh J., *Prelude to Nuremberg* (University of North Carolina Press, 1998)

Krueger, Joaquín and Krueger, Erna Graf de, *Hohenau: De la Selva a la Floreciente Colonia* (Obligado, Paraguay: 1993)

Lee, Martin A., *The Beast Reawakens* (London: Warner Books, 1997)

Leese, Arnold, *The Jewish War of Survival* (London: The IFL Printing & Publishing Co., 1945)

Levenda, Peter, *Unholy Alliance: A History of the Nazi Involvement with the Occult* (New York: Continuum, 2002)

Liebreich, Fritz, *Britain's Naval and Political Reaction to the Illegal Immigration of Jews to Palestine, 1945–1948* (Routledge, 2005)

Lifton, Robert J., *The Nazi Doctors: Medical Killing and the Psychology of Genocide* (Basic Books, 1986)

Littlejohn, David, *The Patriotic Traitors: A History of Collaboration in German Occupied Europe 1940–1945* (London: Heinemann, 1972)

Liverpool, Lord Russell of, *The Trial of Adolf Eichmann* (London: Pimlico, 2002)

Liverpool, Lord Russell of, *The Scourge of the Swastika: A Short History of Nazi War Crimes* (Greenhill Books, 2005)

Lozowick, Yaacov, *Hitler's Bureaucrats: The Nazi Security Police and the Banality of Evil* (New York: Continuum, 2005)

MacDonogh, Giles, *After the Reich* (London: John Murray, 2007)

Macklin, Graham, *Very Deeply Dyed in Black: Sir Oswald Mosley and the Resurrection of British Fascism after 1945* (London: I.B. Tauris, 2007)

Mariscotti, Mario A. J., *El Secreto Atómico de Huemul* (Buenos Aires: Estudio Sigma, 2004)

Meding, Holger M., *Flucht vor Nürnberg? Deutsche und*

Österreichische Einwanderung in Argentinien, 1945–1955 (Cologne: Böhlau Verlag, 1992)

Milano, James V. and Brogan, Patrick, *Soldiers, Spies, and the Rat Line: America's Undeclared War Against the Soviets* (Washington, DC: Brassey's, 2000)

Moorehead, Alan, *Eclipse* (Harper & Row, 1968)

Naimark, Norman M., *The Russians in Germany: A History of the Soviet Zone of Occupation, 1945–1949* (Cambridge, MA: Belknap Press / Harvard University Press, 1997)

Newton, Ronald C. *The 'Nazi Menace' in Argentina, 1931–1947* (Stanford University Press, 1992)

Owen, James, *Nuremberg: Evil on Trial* (London: Headline Review, 2006)

Paris, Erna, *Unhealed Wounds: France and the Klaus Barbie Affair* (New York: Grove Press, 1986)

Pocock, Tom, *The Dawn Came up like Thunder* (Collins, 1983)

Pomorin, Junge and Biemann, Bordien, *Blutige Spuren: Der zweite Aufstieg der SS* (Dortmund: Weltkreis-Verlag, 1980)

Preston, Paul, *Doves of War* (Dartmouth, NH: University Press of New England, 2003)

Reese, Mary Ellen, *General Reinhard Gehlen: The CIA Connection* (Fairfax, VA: George Mason University Press, 1990)

Reiss, Curt, *The Nazis Go Underground* (New York: Doubleday, Doran and Co., 1944)

Rosenbaum, Alan S., *Prosecuting Nazi War Criminals* (Boulder, CO: Westview Press, 1993)

Rosenbaum, Eli M. with Hoffer, William, *Betrayal* (New York: St Martin's Press, 1993)

Ryan Jr, Allan A., *Quiet Neighbors: Prosecuting Nazi War Criminals in America* (New York: Harcourt Brace Jovanovich, 1984)

Saidel, Rochelle G., *The Outraged Conscience: Seekers of Justice for Nazi War Criminals in America* (Albany: State University of New York Press, 1984)

Šakić, Dinko, *S Poglavnikom U Alpama* (Split: Naklada Bošković, 2002)

Sayer, Ian and Botting, Douglas, *Nazi Gold* (Edinburgh: Mainstream Publishing, 1998)

Schimpf, Eckhard, *Heilig: Die Flucht des Braunschweiger*

Naziführers auf der Vatikan-Route nach Südamerika (Appelhans Verlag, 2005)

Schneppen, Heinz, *Odessa und das Vierte Reich: Mythen der Zeitgeschichte* (Berlin: Metropol Verlag, 2007)

Schröder, Matthias, *Deutschbaltische SS-Führer und Andrej Vlasov 1942–1945* (Paderborn: Ferdinand Schöningh, 2001)

Schröm, Oliver and Röpke, Andrea, *Still Hilfe für braune Kameraden: Die geheime Netzwerk der Alt- und Neonazis* (Berlin: Aufbau Taschenbuch, 2006)

Scotland, A. P., *The London Cage* (London: Evans Brothers, 1957)

Seidel, Carlos Collado, *Angst vor dem 'Vierten Reich': Die Alliierten und die Ausschaltung deutschen Einflusses in Spanien 1944–1958* (Paderborn: Ferdinand Schöningh, 2001)

Sereny, Gitta, *Into that Darkness* (London: Pimlico, 1995)

Simpson, Christopher, *Blowback* (New York: Collier Books, 1988)

Stauffer, Clarita, *Sección Femenina de Falange Española Tradicionalista y de las JONS* (Madrid: 1940)

Steinacher, Gerald, *Nazis auf der Flucht* (Studio Verlag, 2008)

Stoltzfus, Nathan and Friedlander, Henry (eds), *Nazi Crimes and the Law* (German Historical Institute and Cambridge University Press, 2008)

Sullivan, Matthew Barry, *Thresholds of Peace: Four Hundred Thousand German Prisoners and the People of Britain 1944–1948* (London: Hamish Hamilton, 1979)

Tasca, Angelo, Peschanski, Denis and Fondazione Giangiacomo Feltrinelli, *Vichy 1940–1944* (Feltrinelli Editore, 1985)

Tauber, Kurt P., *Beyond Eagle and Swastika: German Nationalism since 1945* (Middletown, CN: Wesleyan University Press, 1967)

Tetens, T. H., *Germany Plots with the Kremlin* (New York: Henry Schuman, 1953)

Thomas, Hugh, *Doppelgängers* (London: Fourth Estate, 1995)

Tobias, Jim G. and Zinke, Peter, *Nakam* (Berlin: Aufbau Taschenbuch Verlag, 2003)

Trevor-Roper, Hugh, *The Last Days of Hitler* (London: Papermac, 1995)

Troper, Harold and Weinfeld, Morton, *Old Wounds: Jews, Ukrainians and the Hunt for Nazi War Criminals in Canada* (Markham, Ontario: Viking, 1988)

United Nations War Crimes Commission, *History of the United Nations War Crimes Commission and the Development of the Laws of War* (London: His Majesty's Stationery Office, 1948)

Villemarest, Pierre de, *Untouchable: Who Protected Bormann and Gestapo Müller after 1945?* (Slough, UK: Aquilion, 2005)

Watt, Donald Cameron, *Britain Looks to Germany* (London: Oswald Wolf, 1965)

West, Richard, *Tito and the Rise and Fall of Yugoslavia* (London: Sinclair-Stevenson, 1996)

Wittmann, Rebecca, *Beyond Justice: The Auschwitz Trial* (Cambridge, MA: Harvard University Press, 2005)

(iii) *Reference and guide books*

Basti, Abel, *Bariloche Nazi: Sitios Históricos Relacionados al Nacionalsocialismo* (Bariloche: 2007)

Cointet, Michèle and Jean-Paul (eds), *Dictionnaire historique de la France sous L'Occupation* (Paris: Tallandier, 2000)

Rees, Philip, *Biographical Dictionary of the Extreme Right Since 1890* (New York: Simon & Schuster, 1990)

Snyder, Louis L., *Encyclopedia of the Third Reich* (London: Robert Hale, 1995)

Taylor, James and Shaw, Warren, *Dictionary of the Third Reich* (Penguin, 1997)

Topf, Christian, *Auf den Spuren der Partisanen* (Grunbach: Buchverlag Franz Steinmassl, 2006)

Wistrich, Robert S., *Who's Who in Nazi Germany* (Routledge, 2001)

(iv) *Bulletins, journals, newspapers and magazines*
Chicago (Daily) Tribune
The Daily Express
The Daily Mail
The Daily Mirror
The Daily Telegraph
The Evening Star
The Guardian
The Historian
History Today

The Listener
The Los Angeles Times
New Scientist
The New York Times
The News Chronicle
The People
Physics Today
Reynolds News
Der Spiegel
The Sun
The Sunday Times
Time
The Times (London)
United States Attorney's USA Bulletin
The Washington Post
The Yad Vashem Bulletin

(v) *Reports*
NB: The following are listed chronologically.
The Central Registry of War Criminals and Security Suspects, *Consolidated Wanted Lists, March and September 1947* (Facsimile edition by The Naval and Military Press, 2005)
Newsletters of the Dokumentationszentrum des Bundes Jüdischer Verfolgter des Nazisregimes, 1962–1998 (The Wiener Library)
Klaus Barbie and the United States Government, A Report to the Attorney General of the United States, by Allan A. Ryan Jr, August 1983
Robert Jan Verbelen and the United States Government: A Report to the Assistant Attorney General, Criminal Division, US Department of Justice by Neal M. Sher et al. of the Office of Special Investigations, 16 June 1988
In the Matter of Josef Mengele: A Report to the Attorney General of the United States (US Department of Justice, October 1992)

(vi) *Novels*
NB: Although the first two titles claim to be a mixture of history and memoir, they should be regarded as fiction.
Baz, Danny, *Ni Oubli Ni Pardon* (Paris: Bernard Grasset, 2007)

Erdstein, Erich, with Bean, Barbara, *Inside the Fourth Reich* (New York: St Martin's Press, 1977)

Forsyth, Frederick, *The Odessa File* (London: Hutchinson, 1972)

Goldman, William, *Marathon Man* (London: Pan, 1976)

Hunter, Jack, *The Expendable Spy* (Replica Books, 2001)

Levin, Ira, *The Boys from Brazil* (London: Pan, 1976)

Patterson, Harry, *The Valhalla Exchange* (London: Hutchinson, 1977)

Taylor, Geoff, *Court of Honour* (London: Mayflower, 1966)

(b) TV and film

The Boys from Brazil (1978), directed by Franklin J. Schaffner

Commando Mengele / Angel of Death (1987), directed by Andrea Bianchi

Four Corners: Home Free (1997), presented by David Hardaker, ABC

The Hunter and the Hunted (1981), written by William Bemister, ABC

Hotel Terminus (1988), directed by Marcel Ophüls

Marathon Man (1976), directed by John Schlesinger

Martin Bormann: In the Führer's Shadow (1998), directed by Chanoch Zeevi, Biography Productions

My Enemy's Enemy (2007), directed by Kevin Macdonald

Nazi-Jager Simon Wiesenthal – Das Ende Einer Legende (1996), ARD-TV

Rogues' Regiment (1948), directed by Robert Florey

(c) Electronic

NB: Shortly before going to press, the major proportion of the Simon Wiesenthal Center's Museum of Tolerance Digital Collection went offline. It can only be hoped that this will be remedied by the time of publication. Researchers are advised to consult the endnotes for the URLs of the documents referred to, and then to enter the addresses into http://www.archive.org/index.php. Another alternative is to email the author requesting the documents required. A small part of the collection can be found at http://swcdap.

legalinformationmanagement.com/ but none of the documents that I have consulted – many of which are highly critical of Simon Wiesenthal – appear to be on that site.

(i) *Biographies and memoirs*
Friedman, Tuviah, *Isser Harel Attacks Simon Wiesenthal*, http://motlc.specialcol.wiesenthal.com/instdoc/d09c07/index.html
Friedman, Tuviah, Untitled manuscript, http://motlc.specialcol.wiesenthal.com
Leese, Arnold, *Out of Step: Events in the Two Lives of an Anti-Jewish Camel Doctor*, http://www.jrbooksonline.com/DOCs/Out_of_Step.doc
Manning, Paul, *Martin Bormann: Nazi in Exile*, http://www.animalfarm.org/mb/mb.shtml
Matteson, Robert E., *The Last Days of Ernst Kaltenbrunner*, https://www.cia.gov/library/center-for-the-study-of-intelligence/kent-csi/vol4no2/html/v04i2a07p_0001.htm
Wiernik, Yankel, *A Year in Treblinka*, http://www.zchor.org/treblink/wiernik.htm

(ii) *Histories*
Counter Intelligence Corps History and Mission in World War II (Counter Intelligence Corps School, Fort Holabird, Maryland), http://www.fas.org/irp/agency/army/cic.pdf
Lifton, Robert J., *The Nazi Doctors: Medical Killing and the Psychology of Genocide*, http://www.mazal.org/Lifton/LiftonA0.htm
Lopusina, Marko, *Ubij Bliznjeg Svog: Jugoslovenska tajna policija 1945–1995*, http://www.suc.org/culture/library/Lopusina2/
Steinacher, Gerald, *Nazis auf der Flucht* (English language edition), http://soc.world-journal.net/

(iii) *Essays and papers*
Anti-Defamation League, *Pat Buchanan's Unrelenting Defense of John Demjanjuk* (1993), http://www.adl.org/special_reports/pb_archive/pb_demjanjuk_1993.pdf

Feinstein, Tamara (ed.), *Uncovering the Architect of the Holocaust: The CIA Names File on Adolf Eichmann*, http://www.gwu.edu/~nsarchiv/NSAEBB/NSAEBB150/box14_do_file_vol1/doc14.pdf

Goda, Norman J. W., *CIA Name Files Relating to Heinz Felfe SS Officer and KGB Spy*, http://www.fas.org/sgp/eprint/goda.pdf

Naftali, Timothy, *New Information on Cold War CIA Stay-Behind Operations in Germany and on the Adolf Eichmann Case*, http://www.fas.org/sgp/eprint/naftali.pdf

Naftali, Goda, Breitman and Wolfe, *Interagency Working Group Analysis of the Name file of Heinrich Müller*, http://www.archives.gov/iwg/declassified-records/rg-263-cia-records/rg-263-mueller.html

Sanfilippo, Matteo, *Ratlines and Unholy Trinities: A Review-essay on (Recent) Literature Concerning Nazi and Collaborators Smuggling Operations out of Italy*, http://www.vaticanfiles.net/sanfilippo_ratlines.htm, 2003

Wertz Jr, William F., *The Nazi Rat-Lines, Time to Rid America of the 'Dulles Complex'* www.larouchepub.com/eiw/public/2005/2005_30-39/2005_30-39/2005-31/ pdf/54-71_31_ratline.pdf

(iv) *Minutes, testimonies, affidavits, legal proceedings*

Wilhelm Höttl testimony to the Court of the First Instance, Bad Aussee, http://www.nizkor.org/ftp.cgi/people/e/eichmann.adolf/transcripts/Testimony-Abroad/ftp.py?people/e/eichmann.adolf/transcripts/Testimony-Abroad//Wilhelm_Hoettl-07

Erich Kempka's testimony taken at Berchtesgaden, http://www.nizkor.org/ftp.cgi/imt/nca/nca-06/nca-06-3735-ps

Full proceedings of the International Military Tribunal for Germany, http://avalon.law.yale.edu/subject_menus/imt.asp

Walter Rauff's deposition to the Public Prosecutor at the West German Embassy in Chile, http://www2.ca.nizkor.org/ftp.cgi/people/r/rauff.walter/Rauff-deposition-translation

Albert Speer's cross-examination at the IMT at Nuremberg,
    http://www.law.umkc.edu/faculty/projects/ftrials/
    nuremberg/Speer.html
Minutes of the Tripartite Dinner Meeting held at the Soviet Embassy
    in Tehran on 29 November 1943,
    http://images.library.wisc.edu/FRUS/EFacs/1943CairoTehran/
    reference/frus.frus1943cairotehran.i0012.pdf
Dieter Wisliceny's affidavit to the International Military Tribunal,
    http://www.ess.uwe.ac.uk/genocide/Wisliceny.htm

(v) Reference and archives
Axis History Forum,
    http://forum.axishistory.com/
Hansard,
    http://www.publications.parliament.uk/pa/pahansard.htm
Jewish Virtual Library,
    http://www.jewishvirtuallibrary.org/
The Klarsfeld Foundation,
    http://www.klarsfeldfoundation.org/
Measuring Worth,
    http://www.measuringworth.com/
Documents relating to Ante Pavelić and Jasenovac,
    http://www.jerusalim.org//cd/index_en.html
Simon Wiesenthal Center's Museum of Tolerance Digital
    Collection
    http://motlc.specialcol.wiesenthal.com/

Picture
Acknowledgements

The photographs were kindly supplied by the author except for the following:

First Section

Franz Stangl on the day of his arrest, 28 February 1967: akg-images/ullstein bild; SS officers socialize in their retreat at Solahütte outside Auschwitz. From left to right are Richard Baer, Josef Mengele, Josef Kramer, Rudolf Hess and Anton Thumann: USHMM, courtesy of Anonymous Donor. The views or opinions expressed in this book, and the context in which the image is used, do not necessarily reflect the views or policy of, nor imply approval or endorsement by, the United States Holocaust Memorial Museum.

Ante Pavelić and Benito Mussolini, Rome, 18 May 1941; Klaus Barbie in Nazi uniform: both Associated Press; Ernst Kaltenbrunner, Nürnberg, 11 April 1946: ullstein bild.

Bishop Alois Hudal, from the frontispiece to his book, *Die Grundlagen des Nationalsozialismus*, 1936: photo DÖW; Juan Perón, Buenos Aires, 1946: Getty Images.

Sir Robert Vansittart and Sir John Simon: Press Association Images/Topham.

Second section

Rimini POW Camp courtesy of the Estate of Derek G. Cole.

Serge and Beate Klarsfeld, 31 December 1969: ullstein bild/Roger Viollet; Herberts Cukurs's body, Montevideo, 6 March 1965: Jack Simon/Associated Press.

Isser Harel: Time & Life Pictures/Getty Images; Hermann Langbein photo: Dokumentationsarchiv des Oesterreichischen Widerstandes (DOEW).

Klaus Barbie at his trial, in the foreground is his lawyer, Jacques Vergès, 11 May 1987: Getty Images; Martin Bormann's skull and photograph, 1972: Associated Press; Erich Priebke at his trial in Rome, 16 July 1996: ullstein/AP.

Jon Voigt in *The Odessa File*, 1974: © Photo 12/Alamy; Laurence Olivier and Gregory Peck in *The Boys From Brazil*, 1978: Archives du 7ème Art/Photo 12; Laurence Olivier and Dustin Hoffmann in *Marathon Man*, 1978: Paramount/The Kobal Collection.

Index

Abakumov, General Viktor 29
ACA *see* Allied Commission
Ackerfield, Bobby 102
Adam, General Sir Ronald 62
Adenauer, Konrad 285, 349, 392, 393
Aharoni, Zvi 278–9, 290–6, 297–8, 299, 319, 320, 324
AK *see Armija Krajowa*
Aktion T-4 23–4, 25, 167, 333
AL *see Armija Ludowa*
Aldouby, Zvi 303–9
Alexander, Captain H. H. 59–61
Alford, Ray 190, 191, 193
'Alfred' 183
'Alfredo' 145–6, 183
Allen, Richard 253, 254
Allied Commission (ACA) 199–200
Alper, Michael 362
Alt, General Erich 15
Altaussee, Austria 7, 10, 12, 13–14, 15–18, 22, 79–80, 182, 263
Altenburg, Gunther 15
American Nazi Party 321
American War Crimes Branch 86, 174
American war crimes investigations *see* American War Crimes Branch; Counterintelligence Corps

Amonn, SS-Untersturmführer Günter 171
Anderson, Jack 323
Angel of Death (film) 366
Annesley, Lady Claire 192
Antonescu, Ion 9
Antonio Delfino, SS 110
Arājs, Viktors 231, 233–5, 239, 322, 323
Arājs Commando 231–3, 321
Arce Gómez, Colonel Luis 356–7
Ardeatine Caves massacre (1944) 170–1, 172, 173–4, 409
Arendt, Hannah 309–10
Armija Krajowa (AK) 91, 92, 93
Armija Ludowa (AL) 90–1
Artucio, Hugo Fernández: *The Nazi Underground in South America* 107
Artuković, Andrija 382
Assistenza Austriaca 127, 128
Atkins, Vera 227–8, 229
Attlee, Clement 61–2
Aubrac, Raymond 42
Aubry, Henri 40
Aurore, L' 352
Auschwitz concentration camp 27, 37, 39, 74, 312–13, 349, 351

Auschwitz concentration camp (*cont.*)
  Frankfurt Trials (1963–5) 313–14
  and Mengele 18, 19–20, 21, 68, 255,
    369, 390
Autenried, Austria 18
Axmann, Artur 34–5, 134, 150, 339

Bad Ischl, Austria 22, 26
Bad Nenndorf, Germany: MI5 camp
    228, 229
Baglay, Alexander 405
BAOR (British Army of the Rhine) 62,
    200, 202, 228
Bar-Zohar, Michael: *The Avengers*
    158–9
Barbie, SS-Obersturmführer Klaus
    37–42, 207–21, 239, 259–62,
    351–7, 376–82, 395–8
Barbie, Klaus-Jörg 210, 376
Barbie, Regine (*née* Willms) 42, 212,
    376
Bargen, Daniel von 395
Barkhausen, Kurt 207–9
Barrientos, General René 260, 261
Batt, Captain 192–3
Bauer, Dr Fritz 268–9, 270, 271, 272,
    273, 274, 277–8, 301, 313, 319,
    339–40, 387, 391, 393
Baumbach, Werner 250
Baur, Hans 33, 36
Baxter, Lt Colonel H. J. 240
Beccherini, Alfredo 174–5, 183
Bechtold, Herbert 218
Becker, SS-Hauptsturmführer Siegfried
    108
Becker, Fridolin 208, 210, 211
Bedford, John Russell, 13th Duke of
    192
Beilinson, Moshe 321
Bell, Griffin 364
Bell, Major P. Ingress 18
Belsen concentration camp 54–5, 56
BenGurion, David 278, 300, 301, 320
BenNathan, Asher 98, 99, 101, 301
Benedict XVI, Pope 410–11
Benguigui, Jacques 351
Benguigui, Madame 351–2
Benzon, Branco 255

Berle, Adolf A., Jr 288
Berne: Argentine Emigration Centre
    112, 130
Bernhardt, Johannes 137
Bibes, Louis 215
Bieck, Robert 148
Bikernieki, Latvia: massacre (1941)
    231–2
Bindermichel displaced persons' camp
    98
Birkenau concentration camp 9, 48
Blake, Lord 404
Blandon, Mario 38
Blank, Theodor 285
Blaschke, SS-Oberführer Hugo 160,
    342
Blass, Rudolf 159
Blount, Colonel B. K. 249
Blunda, Lieutenant George F. 123
BND *see Bundesnachrichtendienst*
Bodnar (Ukrainian) 86
Bohlen und Halbach, Arndt von 339
Bolschwing, Otto Albrecht von 382
Bömelburg, Karl 40–1
'Bond of Brotherhood' 195–6
Bondet, Maurice 38
Bone, Captain Brian 65, 203
Bormann, Gerda (*née* Buch) 27, 32,
    159, 160
Bormann, Martin 27–30
  'escapes' from Berlin 32–5
  and Göring 31–2
  portrayal in films and books 163,
    343–4
  rumours and 'sightings' 35, 138,
    145, 153, 155,
    157–60, 188, 262, 265, 272, 338–42
  searches made for 160–2, 305–8
  skeleton discovered 342–3
  tried *in absentia* 157
Bossert, Liselotte 372, 391, 392, 394
Bossert, Wolfram 372, 391, 392, 394
Bouhler, Philipp 23
Bower, Tom 381
Boys from Brazil, The (film) 163, 365
Braga, Inspector Juan José 329
Brandau, Hans 137
Brandt, Dr Karl 23

Brandt, Willy 269
Braun, Eva 13, 161
Braunsteiner, Hermine see Ryan, Hermine
Breit, Harvey 308
Brichah (organization) 98
British League 194
British War Crimes Group 173–4,
    201–6, 228, 234, 322, 399, see
    also 'Haystack'
British War Crimes Investigation Teams
    (WCITs) 55–6, 59–62, 76
British War Crimes Investigation Unit
    (WCIU) 199, 200–1
'Broderick-Hartley, Peter' 158
Brogan, Professor D. W. 48
Brookhart, Lt Colonel Smith 72
Brown Book 146, 147, 240
Bruderschaft (organization) 197
Bruskin, Sydney 15
Buchanan, Pat 383
Buchardt, SS-Obersturmbannführer
    Dr Friedrich 236–40
Buchenwald concentration camp 94, 226
Buckner, Robert 163
Buczacz, Poland 81–3
Buenos Aires 105, 106, 109–10, 130,
    246–8
  Chacabuco Street 264, 269–70,
      274–5, 290
  German Welfare Society (DWG) 109
  Vereine 109
Buenos Aires (tanker) 107
Buhn, Gunther 147–8
Bundesnachrichtendienst (BND;
    Federal Intelligence Service) 242,
    273, 274, 277
Bundschuh (underground movement)
    238
Burgdorf, General Wilhelm 32
Burger, SS-Obersturmführer Anton 11,
    79, 80
Büro Petersen 216

Callaghan, Lord (James) 402
Camarasa, Jorge: Mengele: The Angel
    of Death in South America 366–7
Canadian War Crimes Investigation
    Unit 58–9

Canaris, Admiral Wilhelm 30
CAPRI (company) 197, 262, 263, 307
Cartmell, Major Harry 201
Castillo, Ramón 105
Castro, Álvaro 378
Celler, Emanuel 362
Central Intelligence Agency (CIA) 30,
    137, 138, 142–3, 148, 150–1, 212,
    239, 240, 241, 242, 255, 257,
    273–4, 288, 289, 331–2
Central Office . . . for the Investigation
    of National-Socialist Crimes (ZS),
    Ludwigsburg 311–13
Central Registry of War Criminals and
    Security Suspects (CROWCASS)
    51–4, 62, 63, 66, 214
Cesarani, David 400
Chalmers, William 400
  Hetherington–Chalmers report 401
Chamier, Major Frank 226, 227, 229
Chaves, Colonel 63
Chemnitz concentration camp 94
Chicago Sun-Times 361
Chicago Tribune 338
Choter-Ischai, Captain 78
Churchill, Winston 44, 118, 201, 256
CIA see Central Intelligence Agency
Colban, Eric 46
Colonia Dignidad, Chile 371
Combat (magazine) 349
COMIBOL (mining company) 262,
    376–7, 378
Commando Mengele (film) 366, 371
Comper, Major Denis 76
Cooper, Rabbi Abraham 398
Cooper, Alfred 190
Corradini, Johann 169, 174, 175
Corrientes (boat) 221
Corriere della Sera 331
Counter Intelligence Bureau (BAOR)
    228
Counterintelligence Corps, American
    (CIC) 63–4, 160, 219, 225, 239,
    330
  and Barbie 208, 210–11, 213–21,
      380–1
  and Draganović 116, 128, 219–20
  and Eichmann 75–6, 77, 79–80

Counterintelligence Corps (*cont.*)
  and Höttl 71, 76, 154–5, 222–4
  and ODESSA network 140, 148,
    149, 152–4
  and Pavelić 119, 121–3
  and Wiesenthal 85, 90, 154, 280,
    286
Cox, Evelyn 194–5
Cox, Norman 194–5
CPS *see* Crown Prosecution Service
Crosby, Francis E. 161, 162–3
CROWCASS *see* Central Registry of
    War Criminals and Security
    Suspects
Crown Prosecution Service (CPS) 404,
    405
Cuenca, Dr 318
Cukurs, Herberts 231, 232, 234, 235,
    321–9

Dabringhaus, Erhard 215–16, 221,
    380
Dachau
  American camp 205
  concentration camp 18, 269, 382
Dachi, Stephen 394–5
Dacre, Lord (Hugh Trevor-Roper) 161,
    404
DAIE *see* Delegation for Argentine
    Immigration in Europe
Daily Express 131–2, 335, 338
Davidson, Major William 59
Davies, Major Peter 200, 204–5
Davies, Rhys 256
Daye, Pierre 111, 112, 307
Degrelle, Léon 307, 308–9
Delegation for Argentine Immigration
    in Europe (DAIE) 112, 127, 128,
    178
Delestraint, General Charles 40
Delle Chiaie, Stefano 356
Delmer, Sefton 131–3, 134, 135, 136
del Ponte, Carla 408
Demjanjuk, John 3
Diamant, Manus 99
Dömöter, Edoardo 186
Donaldson, Sam 409
Dönitz, Admiral Karl 33, 398

Dow, Sergeant 203
Draeger Works concentration camp
    203
Draganović, Monsignor Krunoslav 2,
    112–14, 115–17, 119, 124, 131,
    134, 176, 219–20, 256
Drancy transit camp, France 37
Draper, Lt Colonel Gerald 202–3
Driberg, Tom 135
Drljević, Dr Sekula 120
Duarte, Juan 130
Dugoujon, Dr Frédéric 40
Dulles, Allen 8, 288, 289
Dunderdale, Commander Wilfred
    ('Biffy') 221–2
Durcansky, Ferdinand 196–7
Düx, Heinz 313, 314

Easterman, Alexander 47
Eastern Railway Repair Works (OAW)
    87–8
Ecer, Colonel Dr Bohuslav 46, 52
Economist, The 403
Edelweiss-88 (organization) 135–6,
    153, 287
Eden, Sir Anthony 44
Edmunds, Frederick 192, 193
Edmunds, Gwyn 192
Eichmann, Adolf 8–12, 42, 66, 69–76,
    105, 181–6, 262–6, 319, 330, 351
  capture 266, 267–75, 277–9,
    290–300, 316, 323
  trial and execution 309–10
  and Wiesenthal's hunt 1, 77–80, 98,
    99–100, 153, 155, 181–2, 267,
    275–7, 280–4, 286–90, 300,
    406
Eichmann, Dieter 10–11, 263, 264,
    275, 276, 290–1, 292, 297, 339
Eichmann, Friedrich 75
Eichmann, Horst 10, 263, 264, 275,
    276, 339
Eichmann, Klaus 10, 263, 264, 268,
    269–70, 275, 276, 290, 297
Eichmann, Robert 282
Eichmann, Vera 10, 18, 75, 79–80,
    100, 263, 269–70, 274, 275–6,
    277, 280, 291, 292

Einsatzgruppen 23, 235–6, 237–8, 272, 323
Eisenerz Death March (1945) 199–200
Eisenhower, Dwight D. 141
Eitan, Rafi 293, 294–5, 296, 297
El Al (airline) 278, 294, 299–300
Ellersieck, Major General Kurt 208
Epstein, Benjamin 301
Erdstein, Erich 370, 371
Eschel, Arie 286–7
European Command (EUCOM), nr Frankfurt 214, 217, 218, 220, 239
European Voluntary Workers Scheme (EVW) 399–400
Evans, H. W. 322

Fabris, Maria 243
Falange party, Spanish 132, 133
Farago, Ladislas 338–9
   Aftermath 159–60, 339, 341, 342
Farouk, King of Egypt 75
Farrell, Edelmiro Julián 105
Faupel, General Wilhelm von 134
Fehlis, SS-Oberführer Heinrich 49, 50
Feinsohn, Jacques 308–9
Felfe, Heinz 240–2
Ferencz, Ben 64–5
Fermor, Patrick Leigh 145
Fiebelkorn, Joachim 356–7
Fiegel, Gideon 102
Findlay, Colonel 116
Fischer, Alois 68, 178
Fischer, Georg 68, 69
Fischer, Maria 68, 69
Fiszkin, David 232
Foreign Office, British 49, 51, 132, 135
Förster, Albert 29
Forsyth, Frederick 312, 344–6
   The Day of the Jackal 344, 345
   The Odessa File 139, 156, 180, 312, 344–7
France-Soir 352
Franco, General Francisco 131, 134, 136, 196, 225, 312
Frankfurter Zeitung 60
Franks, Lt Colonel Brian 56, 63
French War Crimes Investigation Unit 56–7

Freude, Ludwig 159
Freude, Rodolfo 112
Friedman, Tuviah 80, 84, 100–1, 103, 272, 275, 279, 281, 300–3, 391, 393
Fritsch, Eberhard 196
Froster, Baroness von 208–9
Fuldner, SS-Hauptsturmführer Carlos 110–11, 112, 113, 130, 146, 175, 178, 188, 198, 262, 297

Galitzine, Captain Yurka 62–3
Galland, Adolf 146, 251, 256
Gama Angelo, Dr Hercy Gonzaga 394–5
García Meza Tejada, Luis 356, 357, 376
Garvey, Lt Colonel Dale 213, 214
Gaulle, Charles de 349
Gaza, Hans Joachim 340
Gecas, Antanas 399
Gehlen, Major General Reinhard 30, 241
Gehlen Organisation 241–2, 285
Gellhorn, Martha 309
Genn, Lt Colonel L. J. 55–6
Genoa: Delegation for Argentine Immigration in Europe (DAIE) 112, 127, 128, 178
Genovés García, Julio 163
Gerhard, Wolfgang 317, 320, 368
Giovanni C (ship) 159, 186
Gittens, Anthony 191, 193
Glasenbach POW camp 26, 164
Globocnik, SS-Brigadeführer Odilo 237
Goebbels, Joseph 33, 134
Goldman, William: *Marathon Man* 365
Goldmann, Dr Nahum 287, 289
González, Colonel Enrique 249
Goren, Yoel 271
Göring, Hermann 31–2
Göth, Amon 97
Gotovina, General Ante 408
Göttsch, Werner 15
Gowen, William 121, 123
Graham, Major General 62
Griffiths, John 161–2, 163

Grimms, Heinz 152, 208
Grimms, Willie 152, 208
Groede, Dr von *see* Lagrou, René
Gros, Professor André 46
Gross, SS-Hauptsturmführer Kurt 187
Gross Rosen concentration camp 21,
    93–4
Guim, Father Juan 136
Guinzburg, Thomas H. 305, 307
Guttmann, Ruth 19–20, 56
Gwardia Ludowa (GL) 91

Haage, Sixten 187–8
Hacke (organization) 29–30
Haganah 101, 293, 304
Hagen, Herbert 351, 374
Hailsham, Lord 402
Hajdu, Camille S. 214
Halaunbrenner, Itta 354–5
Halifax, Lord 108
Ham Common: Camp 020
    interrogation centre 106, 107
Hancock, P. F. 322
Hardy, René 215, 217, 218
Harel, Isser 270–3, 274–5, 278, 290,
    291, 293, 294–5, 297, 298–9,
    301–2, 303, 319, 320
Harris, Lt Colonel Arthur 53, 54
Harris, Major 56
Harris, Morris 102
Harster, SS-Gruppenführer Wilhelm
    332
Hartheim, Schloss ('euthanasia centre')
    24, 165, 333
Hatton, Brigadier G. S. 58
Havel, Herbert 334–5
'Haystack' (search team) 199, 203,
    227–8
Heatter, Basil: *Act of Violence* 343
Heim, Dr Aribert 407–8
Heinrichson, Ernst 374
Hellmuth, Osmar 106–8
Helmbrechts camp 65–6
Helmer, Dr Richard 393
Helms, Senator Jesse 389
Hermann, Lothar 268–9, 270, 271,
    274–5, 278, 279–80, 301, 302,
    303, 319

Hermann, Sylvia 268, 269–70
Hess, Rudolf 27–8, 45
Hetherington, Sir Thomas 400
Hetherington–Chalmers report 401
Heycock, Lt Colonel P. J. 202
Heydrich, Reinhard 13, 231, 237, 311
HIAG (organization) 149–50
HIASS (organization) 147
HICOG *see* High Commission(er) in
    Germany
Hier, Rabbi Marvin 398, 400, 402,
    406
Higgins, Jack: *The Valhalla Exchange*
    344
High Commission(er) in Germany, US
    (HICOG) 217–18, 321, 381–2
Himmler, Heinrich 10, 23, 28, 30, 31,
    72, 74, 142, 182, 237, 311
Hirt, Dr August 74, 75
Hitler, Adolf 21, 23, 27, 28, 29, 30,
    32, 33, 48, 72, 87, 124, 134, 141,
    161, 170, 307, 311, 342
Hobbins, Lieutenant John 218–19
Hodge, Captain John 64, 65, 204, 205
Hoffmann, Emil 208, 211, 212
Hoffmann, Heinrich 13
Hoffmann, Julius 360–1
Hofstätter, Efraim 271–2, 273, 274
Hohenau, Paraguay 315–16
Hollerith machines 51
Holtzman, Elizabeth 362–4, 389
Homan, Dr Bailent 15
Home, Lord 402
Hoover, J. Edgar 161, 163
Hoppe, Ernesto 106
Hornetz, Heinrich 204–5
Horthy, Admiral Miklós 141, 224
Horton, Philip 222
Höss, Rudolf 27, 74, 178
Höttl, Dr Wilhelm 7–8, 9–10, 11–12,
    14, 15, 71, 76, 152, 154, 155,
    222–5, 284–5, 286
Howe, Geoffrey 401
Huber, Frau 184
Hudal, Bishop Alois ('Luigi') 2,
    124–30, 131, 134, 144, 153, 165,
    166–8, 169, 172, 174, 175, 181,
    185, 186, 196, 243

The Foundations of National Socialism 124
Huemul Project 248–50
Humanité, L' 375
Hummel, Dr Helmuth von 31, 138
Hunter, Jack D. 343
　The Expendable Spy 343
Hurd, Douglas 400–1
Hurst, Sir Cecil 46–8
al-Husseini, Haj Muhammed Amin 75
Hutchinson (publishers) 344, 345

Ilani, Efraim 275
Immigration and Naturalization Service, US (INS) 358–60, 363–4
Imperial Fascist League 189
INS *see* Immigration and Naturalization Service
'Insap' (network) 138
International League against Racism and Anti Semitism (LICRA) 355, 375
Israeli Institute for the Documentation of Nazi War Crimes, Haifa 279
Israeli Reparations Mission, West Germany 270
ITALMAR (shipping company) 176

Jackson, Justice Robert H. 162, 163
Jänisch, SS-Obersturmführer Rudolf 11, 69
Janner, Lance Bombardier Greville 204, 206, 399, 400, 401, 402, 403, 404, 406
Janowska concentration camp 87–90, 92–3
Jarschel, Alfred (pseud. Werner Brockdorff): *Fleeing Nuremberg* 125, 155
Jasenovac concentration camp 113–14, 115, 257, 259
Jeffreys, Dr Alec 395
Jelić, Dr Branimir 256
Jensen, D. Lowell 380
Jewish Brigade 101–3
Jewish Central Committee 98
Jewish Historical Documentation Centre, Linz 98–9

Jewish Historical Documentation Centre, Vienna 101, 329–30
'Johann T' 317–18
John XXIII, Pope 258
John, Herbert 262, 352, 353, 354
Johnson, Lt Colonel 119
Jordan, Colin 193
Judenkommissionen 71
Jung, Werner 247

Kaczorowski, Major Tadieusz 57–8
Kadow, Walter 27
Kahler, Dr Otto Hans 21, 22, 65
Kaiser, Major Charles 200, 204, 234
Kalmanowitz, Rabbi Abraham 288, 289
Kaltenbrunner, SS-Obergruppenführer Ernst 8, 10, 12–14, 15–18, 29, 31, 36, 74, 94, 151, 153, 226
Kaminski, Captain Jaques 145, 146
Kaplan, Fred 395
Kappler, SS-Obersturmbannführer Herbert 170, 171, 173
Kashat, Eleazar 323
Kasztner, Rudolf 75
Katz, Ephraim 303–4
Katz, Ottmar 153, 154, 318–19
Katzmann, SS-Gruppenführer Fritz 97
Kauffmann, Kurt 74
Kaye, Danny 304
'Kehlsteinhaus', Austria 26–7
Keleti Arcvonal Bajtársi Szövetség (KABSz; Alliance of Eastern Front Veterans) 224
Keller, Peter 195
Kempka, Erich 34
Kempton Park POW camp 188
Kennedy, Senator Edward ('Ted') 364
Kennedy, Senator Robert 335
Keren, Zeev 294–5, 296
Kernmayer, Erich 285, 286
Khan, Noor Inayat 226
Kiesinger, Kurt 349
Kirsch, Robert 336–7
Klarsfeld, Arno 348
Klarsfeld, Arno (grandson) 349, 354, 355, 356

Klarsfeld, Beate (*née* Kunzel) 347, 348,
    349–50, 351–5, 374, 375–6,
    389–90, 391, 393
Klarsfeld, Lida 374
Klarsfeld, Raissa 348, 355
Klarsfeld, Serge 347–8, 349–50, 351,
    352–3, 354–5, 373–4, 390, 391,
    393, 396–7, 398
Klein, Carol 308, 309
Kleyenstueber, Ernst Abro 134
Knoedler, Hildegard 203
Knothe, William 15
Koenig, General Pierre 224
Kohlrautz, Adolf 87, 88, 89
Kolb, Captain Eugene 216–17, 221
Kopkow, Gerda 229, 230
Kopkow, Horst 226–31, 234, 239
Koplin, Frau 151–2
Kops, Captain Reinhard 127, 128,
    130, 131, 134, 150, 155, 196, 256
Korenkiewicz, Bob 360, 361
Kram, Isaak 232
Krawietz, Nelly 73
Krebs, General Hans 32
Kreisky, Bruno 92
Krug, Alban 315, 319
Krügher, Richard 187–8
Krupp family 339
Krupski, Colonel 57
Krzepicki, Abraham Jacob 26
'Kuenzle, Anton' 323–8, 329
'Kurt' 179–80, 181
Kythnos, island of 318

La Boos, José 131
Lagrange, Simone 38, 397
Lagrou, René 111–12, 198
Lang, Jochen von 343
Langbein, Hermann 312, 314, 315
Lauterbacher, Hartmann 143, 144, 150
Law, Richard 50
Lawson, Jack 61–2
Leese, Arnold 2, 188–90, 191, 192–3,
    194
The Jewish War of Survival 189
Leibrandt, SS-Oberscharführer Alfred
    160
Leicester-Warren, Lt Colonel J. 200–1

Leichter, Sarah 361
Lelyveld, Joseph 358
Leontić, Dr Ljubo 118
Leopold, Fritz 36
Leslie, Edgeworth Murray 8
Levin, Ira: *The Boys from Brazil* 365
Levy, Alfred 102
Liberté, SS 308
LICRA *see* International League
    against Racism and Anti-Semitism
Liebl, Maria 277
Liebl (Eichmann), Ricardo 10, 265,
    269, 291
Lienau, Heinrich 35
Life magazine 96
Lindbergh, Charles 189
Lischka, Kurt 349, 350, 351, 374, 375
Listener, The 145
Listowel, Countess (*née* Judith de
    Marffy-Mantuano) 256
Look magazine 303–4, 307–8
Luburić, Vjekoslav ('Maks') 256–7,
    258–9
Luck, Lt Colonel R. F. ('Freddie') 53–4
Lüders, Walter 36
Ludolph, Manfred 352
Lukas, Karl 100, 280
Luke, Captain Michael 145, 146
Lviv: Technical University 83, 84–6
Lyon 38
    Barbie trial 395–8
    Fort Montluc 37, 39, 379

Maas, Haim 80–1
McCarthy, Mr 190, 191, 192, 193
McCarthy, Mrs 190, 191, 193
Maclennan, Robert 402
McNally, Stephen 163
Mahou, Enrique 136
Majdanek concentration camp 357,
    411
Malaparte, Curzio 113
Malbranc, Gerard 247
Malkin, Peer 294–6
Malmédy Massacre (1944) 375
Mangolding, Bavaria 68–9, 176–7
Marathon Man (film) 163, 365
Marburg, Germany 208, 209–11

Markworth, Robert 148
Marlow, Tony 401
Marshall, Robert 230
Marušić, Milivoj 257
Marwell, David 392, 394
Mast, Baron Heinrich ('Harry') 284–5, 286, 287
Matteson, Captain Robert E. 15–18, 151
Matthews, Freeman 46
Mauthausen concentration camp 94–6, 407
Mayhew, Lord (Christopher) 135, 401–2
Medić, Reverend Raphael 258
Meijer, Herman 188–93
Meir, Golda 302
Mello, José Antonio de 392
Mengele, Dieter 393
Mengele, Irene 18, 177, 178, 248
Mengele, Dr Josef 42
  at Auschwitz 18–20, 21, 68
  captured and released by Americans 20–2, 65–7
  death and burial 372, 392
  and Eichmann 264, 297–8
  exhumation and DNA testing 392, 393–5
  as farmhand in Bavaria 68–9, 176–8
  flees to Argentina 105, 178–81, 246–8, 253–5
  and Mossad 297–9, 319–20
  in Paraguay and Brazil 314–17, 339, 367–71
  portrayals in film and book 365–7
  and rumours regarding whereabouts 388–92
  and Wiesenthal 181, 316, 317–19, 370, 371–2, 388, 391, 392–3, 394
Mengele, Karl, Jr 177, 248
Mengele, Karl Heinz 248, 254, 317
Mengele, Martha 248, 253, 254, 299, 316, 317
Mengele, Rolf 20, 177, 178, 253, 315, 368–9, 391, 392, 393, 395
Merk, Kurt 212–13, 214, 215–16
MI5 108, 161, 191, 192, 193, 228, 240, 306

MI6 1, 107, 123, 229–30, 234, 239, 240, 241
Michelson, Frida 232
Milano, Jim 220, 223
Miller, Dr Albert 67
Miller, Ottilie 67
Miranda de Ebro camp, Spain 136–7
Mirrer Yeshiva, Brooklyn 288
Mistelbach, Maria 99
Mitford, Unity 192
Monte Albertia, SS 106
Montgomery, Field Marshal Bernard 62
Montini, Giovanni 114
Moor, Dr J. M. de 47
Moorehead, Alan 54
Morgan, Lt General Sir W. D. 62
Moscow Declaration (1943) 43, 44, 202
Moser, Fritz 14
Mosley, Lady Diana 150, 194, 195–6
Mosley, Sir Oswald 150, 193–4, 195, 196–8, 251–2
Moss, Stanley 145, 146, 183, 345
Mossad
  Cukurs' capture 324–9
  Eichmann's capture 266, 267, 270–3, 274–5, 278–82, 286, 290–300
  and Mengele 319–20
  and Wiesenthal 280–4
Moulin, Jean 39–41, 215
Mudd, Robert Clayton 116
Müller, Heinrich 29, 35–7, 66, 159, 340
Mussolini, Benito 108, 141, 145

Nakam (organization) 103–4
Nasser, Gamal Abdel 151, 288
Natzweiler concentration camp 74
Naumann, Werner 33, 150–1, 197, 198, 207–9, 307
Nazi Farmers' Organization: The Healthy Hen and You 182
Neagoy, George 219, 220
Nebe, SS-Gruppenführer (General) Arthur 237
Nedić, Field Marshal Milan 118
Neiger, Katherine 18–19

Neilson, Lt Colonel Ian 62
New York Daily News 338
New York Times 34–5, 337, 344, 358,
    359, 381, 385, 407
News of the World 158
Newsweek magazine 376, 388
Ney, Károly 224–5, 285
Nightingale, Lt Colonel Alan 199, 200,
    205–6
Nixon, Richard 363
NKVD 29, 84
North King (ship) 180, 247
Nova Europa, Brazil 317, 367
Nurember-Langwasser internment
    camp 103–4
Nuremberg Tribunals 71, 74, 112,
    178, 285–6
Nyiszli, Miklós 20

OAW *see* Eastern Railway Repair
    Works
Oberdachstetten POW camp 71, 73,
    74, 181
ODESSA network 3, 131, 138–41,
    142, 143, 148, 149, 153–4, 155–6,
    169, 180, 181, 182, 373–4
    see also Forsyth, Frederick: *The
        Odessa File*
ODS *see Organisation für den
    Deutschen Sozialismus*
Offczarek, Dr Emmerich 284
Office of Special Investigations, US
    (OSI) 364, 382–4, 386, 390, 392,
    393, 394, 399, 406–7, 408
Office of Strategic Services (OSS),
    American 8, 78, 126–7, 221–2,
    225
'O'Higgins, Jorge' 338
Ohlendorf, SS-Gruppenführer Otto
    238
Olivier, Laurence 365
Operation Baker 160
Operation Fleacomb 205, 229
Operation North Pole 226
Operation Reinhard 23, 25, 167
Oprzondek, Franz 195
*Organisation für den Deutschen
    Sozialismus* (Organization for

German Socialism; ODS) 208–9,
    210, 214
Osborne, D'Arcy 114–15, 122
OSI *see* Office of Special Investigations
OSS *see* Office of Strategic Services
Osterkamp, Colonel Walther 50
Oulton, Air Commodore W. E. 251, 252

Pabbara (SS major) 138
Palfrey, Lt Colonel William 51–3
Palmach 293
Pammer, Dr 284, 286, 287
Pannwitz, Heinz 36
Pape, Alice 169, 171, 172, 173, 174,
    175
Pape, Georg 169, 172, 173, 174, 175
Pape, Ingo 169, 172, 173, 174, 175
Pape, Otto *see* Priebke, Erich
Parade magazine 323
Parliamentary War Crimes Group,
    All-Party 399, 400, 401
Paterson, Lt Colonel 230
Patten, John 403
Patterson, Harry *see* Higgins, Jack
Pavelić, Ante 113, 114–15, 117–24,
    137–8, 153, 255–8, 382
Payot, Max 39
Pearson, Drew 301
Pearson, Major Ralph 15
Peck, Gregory 365
Peiper, Joachim 374–5
Perón, Eva (Evita) 130, 151, 249
Perón, Juan Domingo 2, 107–8, 111,
    112, 128, 129–30, 159, 163, 187,
    198, 248–50, 251–3, 341
Perowne, J. V. 116
Pesnikar, Vilko 115, 116
Petheren, Corporal 56
Petliura, Simon 82
Petranović, Monsignor Karlo 176
Philadelphia Enquirer 386
Philby, Kim 241
Phleps, SS-Gruppenführer Artur 384
Pick, Hella 85
Picture Post 48
Pineau, Christian 40
Pius XII, Pope 3, 111, 114–15, 117,
    121, 125, 126, 248, 411

Pobitzer, Father 174, 175
Pocock, Tom 54
Polish War Crimes Liaison Office 57–8
Powell, Dick 163
Prague: Czech Technical University 83
Praxmarer, Dr Rudolf 13
Priebke, Erich 169–76, 180, 183,
    409–11
Primo de Rivera, José Antonio 133–4
Primo de Rivera, Pilar 133, 134
Project Newton 225
Pucher, Frau Maria 79
Pundick, Cyril 102–3

Quick magazine 339

Radl, SS-Sturmbannführer Karl 142
Radom, Poland 100
Radziwill, Prince 94–5
Rajakowitsch, Dr Erich 330–2
Ramírez, Pedro Pablo 105, 107–8
Raudaschl, Sebastian 14
Rauff, SS-Obersturmbannführer Walter
    125, 172
Ravensbrück concentration camp 226,
    411
Rawson, Colonel Arturo 105
Red Orchestra (spy network) 226
Rees, Merlyn 399
Reimer, Jakob 382
Rey, Fernando 366
Reynolds, Quentin: Minister of Death
    304, 305
Reynolds News 143, 144
Ribbentrop, Joachim von 32, 316
Richter, Joachim 342, 387
Richter, Ronald 187, 248–50
Riedel, Walter 15
Riga: Jewish ghetto 231–3, 234, 321,
    323
Rigaschen Rundschau (newspaper) 236
'Ringel, Herbert' 148–9
Robbins, Sergeant John 204, 205
Rockwell, George Lincoln 321
Rogues Regiment (film) 163
Rome
    San Girolamo monastery 115–16, 121
    Santa Maria dell'Anima 125, 126,

        144, 165, 166–8, 174, 175
    see also Vatican, the
Roosevelt, Franklin D. 44, 45
Roschmann, Eduard 344, 346, 347
Rose, Bertha 227
Rosemblat, Jacob 329
Rosenbaum, Eli M. 384, 385, 386,
    387, 388, 394, 399, 404
Rosensaft, Menachem Z. 389
Röstel, Franz 138, 139
Rothmund, Heinrich 112
RSHA (Office of Jewish Affairs) 9, 12,
    37, 226, 237, 238, 240–1, 272
Rudel, Hans-Ulrich 146, 150, 197,
    247, 250, 251, 307, 317, 319, 391
Rudolph, Arthur 382, 384
Ruffinengo, Franz 127, 134
Rusinek, Kazimierz 96–7
Russell of Liverpool, Lord 345, 346
    The Scourge of the Swastika 345
Ryan, Allan A. 380–3
Ryan, Hermine (née Braunsteiner)
    357–9
Ryan, Russell 357, 358

Saaz, Sudetenland 20–1
Sachsenburg concentration camp 13
St Raphael Community, Bavaria (St
    Raphaelverein) 183
Salonika: Sephardic Jews 384–5
Salto, SS 263
Salzburg 69–70
San Giorgio (ship) 176
San Girolamo monastery see Rome
Sánchez, Gustavo 378
Santa, Luigi, Bishop of Rimini 173
Santa Maria dell'Anima see Rome
Santos, Vicente 129
Sargent, Sir Orme 115
Sassen, Willem 304, 319
Savill, K. E. 52
Sawoniuk, Antony 405
Schacht, Hjalmar 143
Schäfer, Corporal Paul 371
Schauenstein POW camp 22, 65
Scheidler, SS-Obersturmbannführer
    Arthur 13–14, 16, 17, 18, 31, 138,
    139, 151, 152, 153

Scheidler, Iris 13–14, 15, 16, 18, 138, 139, 151–2, 153, 222
Scheiman, Arthur 89
Schellenberg, Walter 30, 35–6, 108
Schellong, Conrad 382
Schiller, Cissy von 134
Schilling, Dr Walter 129, 196, 197
Schindler's List (film) 93
Schirach, Baldur von 13, 134, 398
Schirach, Frau von 75, 80
Schlottmann, Friedrich 187
Schmidt, Francisco 275, 278, 301
Schmidt, Werner 89
Schneider, Lieutenant 57
Schuchert, Hans 149
Schüle, Dr Erwin 311–12
Schulman, Charlie: Angel of Death 395
Schulz, Carlos Werner Eduardo 187, 188
Schulz, Leo 144, 183
Schulze-Boysen, Harro 226
Schwend, Friedrich 261–2, 352, 354
Scott-Barrett, Brigadier H. 55
Sechsgestirn (organization) 153, 287
Sedlmeier, Hans 177, 178, 179, 367, 391
Sedlmeier (son) 368
Serafinowicz, Peter 405
Serafinowicz, Szymon 404–5
Sereny, Gitta 168–9, 335, 337
Serenyi, Istvan 152–3
Serrino, Juan 162–3
Servatius, Robert 339
Seyboth, Friedrich 340
SHAEF see Supreme Headquarters of the Allied Expeditionary Force
Shapcott, Brigadier Henry 202
Shawcross, Lord (Hartley) 201, 403
Sheen, Colonel H. G. 50
Sher, Neal 383–4, 387, 399
Shin Bet (Israeli Security Service) 303
Shinar, Dr Felix 270
Silberschein, Aaron 98
Siles Zuazo, Hernán 376
Simcock, Major 116
Simon, Gustav 60–1
Simon, John Simon, Viscount 44–5, 49, 50

Siri, Archbishop Giuseppe 128
Six, SS-Brigadeführer Dr Franz 235, 236, 237
Skorzeny, SS-Obersturmbannführer Otto 140–8, 149, 150–1, 183, 197, 198, 224, 256, 261, 285, 307
Smith, William French 380
Sobibor concentration camp 165
SOFINDUS (conglomerate) 137
Somerhough, Group Captain Tony 200, 201–2
Soria, Carlos 379
Sozialistische Tribüne 269
Speer, Albert 29, 32
Spengler, Dr Heinz 342
Spiegel, Der 390
Spinne, Die (The Spider; escape network) 139, 142–7, 148, 149, 150, 153, 154, 155, 287
Stahlecker, Franz 231
Stalin, Josef 30, 43–4, 45, 118, 121
Stammer, Geza 317, 367, 368, 391, 394
Stammer, Gitta 317, 367, 368, 391, 394
Stanbrook, Ivor 400
Stangl, Franz 22–3, 24–6, 42, 164–9, 243–6, 333–6, 337
Stangl, Gitta 243, 245
Stangl, Isolde 335
Stangl, Renate 243, 244, 245, 246
Stangl, Theresa 26, 164–5, 166, 168–9, 243, 244, 245, 246, 333, 334, 335
Stanić, Ilija 258–9
Stanić, Vinko 259
Staniszewski, Eduard 95
Stauffer, Clarita 131, 133–5, 136–8, 151
Steinacker, Fritz 314
Steiner, Hans 165–6
Stephens, Colonel Robin ('Tin Eye') 106, 107
Stern, Der 304, 342, 343
Stettinius, Edward 132
Steudmann, Major General Hans 50
Stevenson, William: The Bormann Brotherhood 344
Stotzel, Heinrich 136

Straight, Colonel Clio E. 205, 206
Stroessner, President Alfredo 367, 388–9, 393
Stumpfegger, Ludwig 34, 342
Sturm, Frau 78–9
Stuttgarter Zeitung 381
Suárez, Robert 356
Sun 403
Sunday Times 155
Supreme Headquarters of the Allied Expeditionary Force (SHAEF) 50, 52
  Counter Intelligence (SCI) 222
Szabo, Violette 226

Tank, Kurt 144, 146, 187, 248, 251
Tarracusio, Captain 98
Tartakower, Professor Arieh 279
Taylor, Geoff: *Court of Honour* 343–4
Taylor, Robert S. 213, 214
Tehran Conference (1943) 43–4
Terry, Antony 155–6
Thatcher, Margaret 398, 404
Theresienstadt concentration camp 11
Thompson, Mrs Oshe 195
Tiecken, Hendrich 188–93
Time magazine 107–8
Times, The 281, 300, 381
Timm, Captain Eric W. 222
Tito, President (Josip Broz) 118, 119, 121, 123, 258, 259
Toepke, Günther 187, 188
Tog Morgen, Der 321
Torr, Brigadier W. W. T. 31
Transmarítima Boliviana (shipping company) 262, 354
Treblinka concentration camp 23, 25–6, 101, 164
Treblinka Trial, Düsseldorf 246
Trevor-Ropert, Hugh *see* Dacre, Lord
Trott, Stephen S. 390
Truman, President Harry S. 161, 162
Tuma, Romeu 391
Tutiya, Dr Kasumasa 395

UDBA (Yugoslav organization) 258, 259
Ulmann, Colonel Fritz 21, 66, 177

UM *see* Union Movement
Union magazine 196
Union Movement (UM) 194, 196
United Nations War Crimes Commission (UNWCC) 44–6, 47–9, 52, 53, 54, 66, 76, 207
United States Marshals Service 390–1
USFET (US Forces European Theater) 160, 161
Ustasha/Ustashi (Croatian nationalist movement) 113, 114, 115–16, 117, 119, 121–2, 123, 172, 256–8, 384

Va'ad Hahatzvala (organization) 288
Vaernet, Dr Carl 187
Valero, Bishop Rene 389
Vansittart, Lord (Robert) 49–50, 51
Varon, Benno Wieser 370
Vatican, the 114, 116, 119, 121–2, 123, 131, 175, 408, *see also* Pius XII, Pope
Verbelen, Robert Jan 225–6
Vergès, Jacques 396–8
Vernon, Howard 366
Verschoyle, Wing Commander Derek 123
Viking Press 304, 305, 307
Vlasov, General Andrei 238, 239
Voight, Jon 344
Vorkommando Moskau 235–6, 237–8
Vost, Herr 133

Wachsberger, Arminio 19
Waddington, David 402–3
Wagner, Gustav 165–8
Wald, Hans 102
Waldheim, Kurt 384–6, 390
Wallisch, Erna 411–12
Wallner, Woodruff 218
Walsh, Major William 71
Walus, Frank 359–62
Waneck, Wilhelm 15
Wannsee Institute 236
War Crimes Act (1991) 401–4
War Crimes Investigation Teams (WCITs) 55–63, 76
Warzok, SS-Hauptsturmführer Friedrich 92–3, 97

Washington Post 301
Watts, Charlie 194
WCITs *see* War Crimes Investigation
    Teams
WCIU *see* British War Crimes
    Investigation Unit
Weg, Der (magazine) 130, 196, 253
Weiden POW camp 71
Weil, Ekkehard 376
Werner, Kriminalrath 24
West, Richard 119, 120
Westarp, Countess Gisela von 13, 15,
    16, 17
Wetjen, Hauptsturmführer 171
Whittington, Captain Jere 143
'Wieland', Dr 176–7, 178
Wiernik, Yankel 25
Wiesenthal, Asher 81
Wiesenthal, Cyla (*née* Müller) 82, 83,
    84, 87, 93, 329
Wiesenthal, Hillel 81, 82
Wiesenthal, Paulinka 329
Wiesenthal, Simon 1, 2, 81–98, 223,
    272, 332–3, 361, 365, 366, 406
  and Bormann 340–3
  criticized by OSI 383–4, 386–8
  and Eichmann 1, 77–80, 98, 99–100,
      153, 155, 181–2, 267, 275–7,
      280–4, 286–90, 300, 309, 406
  helps Forsyth 345–7
  and the Klarsfelds 390
  and Mengele 181, 316, 317–19, 370,
      371–2, 388, 391, 392–3, 394
  and Mossad 280–4
  and ODESSA 138, 139, 153–5, 169,
      181, 346
  sets up Jewish Historical
      Documentation Centres 98–9,
      329–30
  and Stangl 164, 246, 333–7

successful cases 330–2, 357–8, 406
  and the Waldheim affair 384–6, 387,
      390
  and Walus trial 259–62
  books:
    Ich Jagte Eichmann 85, 139, 281,
        290, 303
    Justice Not Vengeance 86, 90, 93,
        99, 169, 181, 277, 281, 282,
        334, 335, 359
    *KZ Mauthausen: Pictures and
        Words* 95–6
    The Murderers Among Us 79, 84,
        85, 89, 90, 93, 94–5, 96, 99,
        100, 139, 153, 158, 169, 181,
        277, 280, 281–2, 286, 334,
        335, 336, 340, 370
Wiesenthal Center 398, 399, 400, 404,
    407, 411
Wilberforce, Brigadier Richard 52
Wilkenning, Dr 212
Willms, John 215
Winterton, Major General 199–200
Wirths, Dr Eduard 312
Wisliceny, SS-Hauptsturmführer Dieter
    72, 75, 99
Witte, Marianne 137
World Jewish Congress (WJC) 46–7,
    275, 279, 287–8, 301–2, 384, 386,
    394

Yad Vashem archive 80–1, 92, 95,
    281

Zabecki, Franciszek 25–6
Zan, Fedor 405
ZS *see* Central Office . . . for the
    Investigation of National-Socialist
    Crimes
Zuroff, Efraim 400, 407–8